The Collected Letters
of
St. Teresa of Avila

VOLUME TWO

1578–1582

Translated by
Kieran Kavanaugh, O.C.D.

ICS Publications
Institute of Carmelite Studies
Washington, D.C.
2007

ICS Publications
2131 Lincoln Road, NE
Washington, DC 20002-1199
800-832-8489
www.icspublications.org

Library of Congress Cataloging-in-Publication Data

Teresa, of Avila, Saint, 1515-1582
  [Correspondence, English]
  The collected letters of St. Teresa of Avila / translated by Kieran Kavanaugh.
    p. cm.
  Includes bibliographical references and index.
  ISBN 0-935216-27-8
  1. Teresa, of Avila, Saint, 1515-1582--Correspondence. 2. Christian
saints--Spain--Avila--Correspondence. I. Kavanaugh, Kieran, 1928- II. Title.

BX4700.T4 A31 2001
282'.092--dc21
[B]

                                                                        2001039191

Contents

Abbreviations

References to St. Teresa's other writings are from *The Collected Works of St. Teresa of Avila*, trans. Kieran Kavanaugh, O.C.D., and Otilio Rodriguez, O.C.D., 3 vols. (Washington, D.C.: ICS Publications, 1976–85). The following abbreviations will be used in referring to her works:

F	*The Book of Her Foundations* (vol. 3)
IC	*The Interior Castle* (vol. 2)
L	*The Book of Her Life* (vol. 1)
M	*Meditation on the Song of Songs* (vol. 2)
SC	*A Satirical Critique* (vol. 3)
ST	*Spiritual Testimonies* (vol. 1)
W	*The Way of Perfection* (vol. 2)

Other abbreviations:

BMC	*Biblioteca Mistica Carmelitana*, ed., Silverio de Santa Teresa, 20 vols. (Burgos: El Monte Carmelo, 1915–35)
CN	Carmelite Nuns of the Observance
DCF	Discalced Carmelite Friars
DCN	Discalced Carmelite Nuns
MHCT	*Monumenta Historica Carmeli Teresiani*, Institutum Historicum Teresianum (Rome: Teresianum, 1973–)

The Letters

Letters 225–282
(1578)

225. To Padre Jerónimo Gracián
Avila, January 1578(?)

A fragment preserved because of the praise given to the Carmelite nuns.

❖❖❖❖

I love them tenderly, and so I rejoice when you praise them and express your gratitude to me as though I were the one who had done something.

226. To Don Teutonio de Braganza, Evora
Avila, 16 January 1578

Responding to two of his letters, Teresa gives Don Teutonio the news he sought about the persecutions her nuns and friars were undergoing. He had told her in secret of his appointment to the episcopal see of Evora in Portugal, spoken of his love for the Society of Jesus, and proposed a Teresian foundation in his diocese. He had also mentioned some difficulties in his spiritual life. Teresa rejoices in the news of his new appointment, but regretfully explains why she cannot make a foundation in Portugal.

❖❖❖❖

1.   Jesus. The grace of the Holy Spirit be with your most illustrious lordship, amen. I received your letter more than two

months ago and I wanted so much to answer immediately, but I was waiting for some calm to return in the midst of the great trials that the discalced friars and nuns[1] have been undergoing since August. I wanted to send you some news, as you requested in your letter, but was waiting before doing so. However, up to the present things have been getting worse by the day, as I will explain later.

2.   Now there is nothing more I want than to see you, for I can only poorly describe in writing the happiness your letter—which I received this week from Father Rector—[2] brought me. And this, even though I had received very clear news about you more than three weeks ago, and afterward the same news from another source. So I don't know how you could think that something of that sort would be kept secret. May it please the Divine Majesty that this redound to his greater honor and glory and help you grow very much in holiness, as I think it will. Believe that God will not fail to hear such fervent petitions made by souls who in their prayers desire nothing more than that he be served. And I, although miserable, pray continually for this, and so do all these servants of yours in all these monasteries. Each day I find in them souls that certainly put me to shame. It definitely seems that our Lord himself is choosing them, bringing them to these houses from places where I do not know how they could have heard of us.

3.   You must take heart and not even let the thought cross your mind that this was not ordained by God—I am certain it was. His Majesty is now giving you the chance to put into practice the desire you have had to serve him. You have been idle for a long time and our Lord is in great need of someone who will favor virtue. We poor and lowly people, however much we want only what is for his service, can do little if God does not awaken someone to defend us. And so he chooses one who he knows can help him. For malice has reached such a point, and ambition and the pursuit of honor have been so canonized by many of those who should have trampled them underfoot, that even the Lord himself seems to want the help

of his creatures, although he is powerful enough for virtue to win the victory without them. Since those he has selected to defend virtue disappoint him, he has chosen those he knows can help him.

4. Strive to spend yourself in this work, as I know you will. God will give you the strength and health—I hope for this from His Majesty—and grace to succeed in everything. Here we will serve you by begging him unceasingly. And may it please the Lord to give you helpers interested in the good of souls so that you can go on without worry. I am greatly consoled that you can count so much on the Society; they are a wonderful help in everything.[3]

5. The happy outcome for my lady the Marchioness of Elche[4] brought me much joy, for that affair caused me a good deal of distress and worry until I learned of how well things turned out. May God be praised. As often as the Lord gives such a multiplicity of trials together, he usually causes good results. Since he knows we are so weak and does everything for our good, he measures out suffering in conformity with our strength. I think these storms that are lasting so long have to happen to us. If I were not certain that these discalced friars and nuns are striving to keep their rule in uprightness and truth, I would sometimes fear that the calced friars might succeed—considering the devil's wiles—in achieving their goal, which is to put an end to this beginning that the Blessed Virgin has initiated. God has given the devil the leeway to work toward this end.

6. Great effort and many plans have gone into discrediting us, especially Padre Gracián and me, the ones at whom they strike. I tell you that they have spread so many calumnies against this man and sent so many accusations to the king, very serious ones (and about these monasteries of discalced nuns), that you would be shocked if you knew about them and that they could invent so much evil. To my mind we have gained a great deal through all of this. The nuns go about so joyful that the matter doesn't even seem to touch them. Padre Gracián

bears everything with such perfection that I am amazed. God has stored a great treasure in that soul, for he prays especially for his accusers and has borne their calumnies with the joy of a St. Jerome.

7.   Only the matters that involved the discalced nuns caused him distress. Since for two years he has been their visitator and knows them, he cannot bear what is said; he considers them angels, and this is what he calls them. God was pleased that the things said against us were retracted by those who said them.[5] As for the other things said about Padre Gracián, an inquiry was made by order of the council and the truth became known. Other things, too, were retracted, and the prejudice spreading through Madrid was recognized. Believe me, the devil was trying to get rid of the good that these houses are doing.

8.   Now, besides what was done against these poor nuns at the Incarnation who, to pay for their sins, elected me as prioress (that is, judicial proceedings were initiated), the whole city is shocked by what they have suffered and are suffering.[6] And I still do not know when it will all end. Padre Tostado's[7] severity toward them has been unusual. For more than fifty days he has refused to allow them to hear Mass, and for three months now they have not been allowed to see anyone. He has been saying daily, with great threats, that they are excommunicated, but all the theologians in Avila deny this. The excommunication warning was directed toward preventing them from electing anyone outside the house. With a statement like that, no mention had to be made of me. The nuns thought that since I was a professed nun from that house and had lived so many years in it, they did not need to consider me as someone outside the house. In fact, if I wanted to return to that house, I could, for my dowry is there and I do not belong to a different province. Another nun who had less than a majority of votes was confirmed in the office of prioress.[8] Those being punished have appealed their case to the royal council. I don't know how it will end.

9. It hurts me deeply to witness so much disturbance and scandal in the city on my account and so many anxious souls, for there were more than fifty-four nuns excommunicated. My only consolation was that I did all I could to prevent the nuns from electing me. And I guarantee you that one of the greatest trials that could come to me on this earth would be to see myself at the Incarnation. I didn't have an hour of good health all the time I was there.

10. I greatly pity those souls. Among them are nuns who have attained great perfection, and this is evident in the way they have borne their trials. Yet what has most distressed me is that the two discalced friars who were confessors there have been held captive more than a month by those of the cloth, under orders from Padre Tostado. The two are excellent religious and have edified the entire city during their five years there. Because of their presence the house has remained in the state it was when I left it. One of them, at least, whose name is Fray John of the Cross, is considered a saint by everyone, men and women alike, and I don't think they exaggerate.[9] In my opinion, he is a gem. Since they were appointed to that position by both the Dominican apostolic visitator and the previous nuncio[10] and were subject to the visitator Gracián, what was done is so absurd it is frightening. I don't know where it will end. What pains me is that they have been taken away and we don't know where. Moreover it is feared that they are being treated harshly, and I'm afraid something unfortunate will happen. A protest about this has also gone to the royal council.[11] May God provide a remedy.

11. Pardon me for going on at such length, but it is gratifying to me that if Padre Tostado goes there[12] you know the truth about what is happening. The nuncio favored him very much as soon as he arrived and told Padre Gracián to stop making visitations.[13] This does not take away Gracián's appointment as apostolic commissary, for the nuncio did not show his faculties nor, according to what Gracián says, take Gracián's away. Nonetheless, Gracián went immediately to Alcalá, and

lived in a cave there as he did in Pastrana, suffering, as I said, abominable calumnies. He no longer exercises his position as commissary, but he stays there and has suspended all activity. His great desire is to be free of having to make any more visitations. This is what we all want, for they are the cause of many troubles for us—unless God gives us the grace to form a separate province; otherwise I don't know where things will end. On arriving there he wrote to me that if Padre Tostado makes a visitation, he is determined to obey him and that all of us nuns should do so too.

12.   Padre Tostado did not go there, nor has he come here. I think the Lord prevented this, for with the bad will he later showed, I believe it would have been very harmful for us. Nonetheless, those of the cloth say that Padre Gracián is directing everything and preparing to make a visitation, which is what is killing us. Truly no other reason lies behind this than the one I have told you. In a certain way I have found rest in the thought that you know this whole story, although you may not find reading it so restful since you feel most obliged to favor this order. I also wanted you to be aware of the obstacles that stand in the way of your desire that we come to Portugal, and others exist as well that I'll now mention, which cause us another embroilment.

13.   Since I cannot but strive in every possible way to prevent the ruin of this good beginning,[14] nor has any learned confessor of mine counseled me otherwise, these calced Fathers are very displeased with me and have informed our Father General so that he convened a general chapter,[15] which has taken place. This chapter ordained, and our Father General gave the orders, that no discalced nun could leave her house, and especially that I should choose a house to my liking and remain there under pain of excommunication.

14.   Clearly the purpose is to prevent any more foundations of nuns. It is a pity to see how many are crying out to enter these monasteries, which are so few, and that no more requests

can be accepted. Although the previous nuncio,[16] after all that I mentioned, gave me orders not to stop making foundations, and I have ample patent letters from the visitators to make them, I am very determined not to do so unless either our Father General or the pope ordains otherwise. Since nothing of this comes through my fault, I see it as a favor from God, for I was already very tired out. Nevertheless, to be of service to you would mean nothing but rest for me—it's hard to think of not being able to see you again—and were I given the command to undertake such a service, it would bring me great consolation. But even if this decision of the general chapter had not been made, the patent letters I received from the general were valid only for the kingdoms of Castile. A new mandate would be necessary.

15.   I am certain that for now our Father General would not give it. Getting the approval of the pope would be easy, though, especially if he saw the document prepared by order of Padre Gracián about how life is lived in these monasteries, and the benefit that others receive in places where these are found. So great is the benefit that it is said, even by serious-minded people, that this alone would be enough to canonize the nuns. Because I fear it may say too many good things about me, I have not read it. But I would want authorization from Father General before making the foundation and that he be asked to approve of our continuing to make foundations in Spain, for there are nuns who could do this without my going out to do so. I mean that once the house is ready the nuns could be sent there, for souls are being deprived of much benefit. If you are acquainted with the protector of our order, who they say is the pope's nephew,[17] he could obtain the permission from our Father General. I think you would be rendering a great service to our Lord and doing this order a great favor if you obtained it.

16.   There is another drawback—I want you to be informed about everything—which is that Padre Tostado has already been accepted as vicar general for the kingdom of Portugal, and it would be most unpleasant, especially for me, to fall into his

hands. I think he would make every effort to block a foundation. In Castile, it now seems, he doesn't have such power. Since he exercised his office without first having shown his faculties (especially in regard to the problems at the Incarnation, which made a bad impression), he was ordered by royal decree to hand over his faculties to the royal council—he had received another notification last summer—and they have not returned them to him, nor do I think they will.[18]

17.   We also have letters from the apostolic visitators that in these monasteries the official visitator must receive the task from Father General and be a discalced friar.[19] With nothing like this happening there in Portugal, we would be subject to "those of the cloth," and perfection would soon go crashing to the ground. Here they were beginning to do us much harm, but the apostolic commissaries came along. You can consider what the remedy might be for all these obstacles, for there will be no lack of good nuns ready to serve you. Padre Julián de Avila,[20] who already seems set to start on the road, kisses your hands. He is very happy with the news about your appointment. He already knew about it since I had told him before. He is very confident that you will gain much in the sight of the Lord because of your care for this new foundation.

18.   María de San Jerónimo, who is the one who was subprioress in this house, also kisses your hands. She says she would be eager to go to serve you, if our Lord so ordains. May His Majesty guide everything for his glory and watch over you with a great increase of his love.

19.   It is no surprise that now in the midst of such news you cannot enjoy the recollection you desire. Our Lord will give you a double measure as he usually does when recollection is set aside for his service, although I do desire that you procure some time for yourself, for in this lies all our good.

From this house of St. Joseph's in Avila, 16 January.

I beg you, for the love of our Lord, not to torment me with those titles.[21]

Your most illustrious lordship's unworthy servant and subject,

Teresa of Jesus

---

1. The new nuncio, Felipe Sega, had arrived in Spain in August with an unfavorable view of Teresa and her reform. At the end of August, the accusations against Gracián were initiated.
2. Gonzalo Dávila, the rector of the Jesuits in Avila.
3. Don Teutonio had been a Jesuit from 1549–54 and had known St. Ignatius Loyola in Rome.
4. Doña Juana de Braganza. The happy outcome refers probably to the marriage of her daughter.
5. She is referring to the calumnies made by Miguel de la Columna and Baltasar Nieto (see Ltr. 208.1).
6. She is referring to what has been called the "hammering" or "pounding" election that took place at the Incarnation monastery on 7 October 1577 in which the nuns were forbidden to vote for Teresa as prioress under pain of excommunication. But many nuns thought they were being deprived of their right to vote for Teresa and voted for her anyway. As the presider read the ballots, he pounded with his large key on any ballot that was cast for Teresa and excommunicated the nun who voted for her.
7. The Portuguese Carmelite appointed as visitator for the Carmelites in Spain and Portugal.
8. Teresa had received 54 votes, Doña Ana de Toledo, 39. The other votes among the 98 cast were scattered.
9. The other discalced friar was Germán de San Matías.
10. The visitator was Pedro Fernández; the nuncio, Nicolás Ormaneto.
11. She is referring to her letter to the king (Ltr. 218).
12. To Portugal.
13. The nuncio is Felipe Sega.
14. The Carmels she founded.
15. The chapter at Piacenza in Italy in May and June 1575. The general was Giovanni Baptista Rossi, called Rubeo by the Spaniards.
16. Nicolás Ormaneto.
17. The Cardinal Protector of the Carmelites was Felipe Buoncompagni, a nephew of Gregory XIII's and a relative of Sega's.
18. The royal council had prevented Tostado from exercising the powers given him for Spain.

19. She is referring to the "acts" of the visitators, especially of Fernández (see MHCT, 1:115) and Gracián (MHCT, 1:316).
20. The chaplain at the monastery of St. Joseph's in Avila.
21. As in Ltr. 69.1, she objects to the pompous titles he uses to address her.
22. Teresa turns right around and uses for him the kind of title she dislikes for herself.

227. To Padre Jerónimo Gracián(?)
Avila, 30 January 1578 (?)

(Autograph fragment: DCN, Algezares [Murcia])

This is an autograph fragment from a letter that has been lost. It allows us a glimpse of a little scene in which Teresa watches as her niece Teresita, about eleven years old, makes some first attempts at writing.

❖❖❖❖

Teresa is writing a letter. If you could see the faces she's making while writing you would be delighted. However badly our fortunes go I don't allow them to tell her anything. Today is January 30.

228. To Padre Juan Suárez, Madrid
Avila, 10 February 1578

(Autograph and Original: DCN, Salamanca)

Teresa was shown a letter in which the Jesuit provincial claims she was urging Gaspar de Salazar to transfer from the Jesuits to her discalced Carmelite friars. Disturbed by the false accusations, Teresa defends herself and insists on the truth of the matter in her regard.

❖❖❖❖

1.   Jesus. The grace of the Holy Spirit be with your paternity always, amen. Father Rector gave me a letter of yours that was

certainly a great surprise to me.[1] In it you mention that I have been trying to get Padre Gaspar de Salazar to leave the Society of Jesus and transfer to our Carmelite order, that God wants this and has revealed it!

2.   As for the first, His Majesty knows—and the truth of this will come to light—that I have never wanted this, still less urged him to take such a step. When some of this news reached me, it did not come through any letter from him, and I became so disturbed and distressed that it did anything but benefit the poor condition of my health at the time. And my knowledge of this is so recent that you must have heard about it long before I did, I think.

3.   As for the revelation you mention, I could not have known whether he had a revelation about the matter, for he had not written to me, nor had I any knowledge of his decision.

4.   If I had received the "revelation" in his regard of which you speak, I would not have been so shallow as to think that for so slight a reason a great change like the one mentioned should be undertaken, nor would I have even told him about it. Thanks be to God, I have been instructed by many persons about the value of such things and the credence that should be given to them. I don't think Padre Salazar would pay any attention to them, unless there was another factor to be considered, for he's a very sensible man.

5.   As for what you say about your desire that the superiors investigate, you are right, and you can order them to do so.[2] Obviously, in my judgment, he wouldn't do anything without your permission or informing you about it. I will never deny the great friendship that exists between Padre Salazar and me or the favor he shows me. Yet I am certain that in what he has done for me he has been moved more by the service it renders our Lord and our Blessed Mother than by any friendship. Truly, I think it has even happened that as much as two years went by without a letter passing between us. If the friendship is an old one,[3] it is because in the past I was in greater need of help, for

this order had only two discalced Fathers. At that time I would have had a greater motive for wanting him to transfer than I do now. Thanks be to God we have more than two hundred, I think, and among them not a few who are especially suited for our poor manner of life. I have never thought that the hand of God would be more sparing toward his Mother's order than to the other orders.

6.   As for what you say about my having written so as to have it said that you were preventing him, may God omit my name from his book if such a thought even crossed my mind. Allow me to insist so that you may understand my point of view. It is that in my dealings with the Society I hold their concerns close to my heart and would lay down my life for them, as long as I understood that I would not by that be doing a disservice to God. His secrets are great, and since I have played no more part in this matter than that mentioned (and God is the witness), neither would I want any in the future. If I am blamed without being at fault, it would not be the first time. In my experience, when our Lord is satisfied, he makes all things smooth. I would never believe, except for very serious reasons, that His Majesty would permit that his Society go against his Mother's order, for he took the Society as a means to repair and renew it.[4] How much less would he permit this for such a light matter. And should he permit this, I fear that what would be gained on the one hand, would be lost on the other.

7.   We are all vassals of this King. May it please His Majesty that those belonging to his Son and his Mother[5] be such that like courageous soldiers we look only at the banner of our King to follow his will. If we Carmelites truly do this, obviously those who bear the name of Jesus cannot turn away from us, a threat that has often been made to me. May it please God to preserve you for many years.

8.   Now I know the favor you are always showing us, and so, miserable though I am, I pray to our Lord very much for you, and I beg you to do the same for me. For half a year there has

been no letup in the rain of trials and persecutions coming down on this poor old woman,[6] and now this business is for me no minor matter. Nonetheless, I give you my word not to say anything that would encourage him or tell someone else to do so, nor have I ever said anything to him.

Today is 10 February.

Your paternity's unworthy servant and subject,

Teresa of Jesus

---

1. Gonzalo Dávila was the rector of the Jesuit school in Avila, Juan Suárez was the provincial, and Gaspar de Salazar was the Jesuit who was the reason for this letter.
2. Padre Suárez wanted Teresa, or her superior, to write to all the discalced houses to caution them in regard to Padre Sálazar (cf. Ltr. 229).
3. The friendship began in 1561 in Avila (cf. L 33.7–10).
4. She is referring to the decisive help given her by the Jesuits in her work of reform.
5. Jesuits and Carmelites. The imagery reflects the *Spiritual Exercises* of St. Ignatius.
6. The troubles began in August 1577 with the arrival of the new nuncio, Felipe Sega.

229. To Padre Gonzalo Dávila, Avila

Avila, 14 February 1578

The Jesuit rector in Avila had sent Teresa a note from his provincial, Padre Juan Suárez, asking her to prevent her Jesuit friend, Gaspar de Salazar, from leaving the Jesuits and, according to the rumor, entering the discalced Carmelite friars. Teresa thinks the provincial has been misinformed and that she would be ill-advised to carry out his wishes.

1. Jesus. May the Holy Spirit be with your honor. I read Father Provincial's letter more than twice,[1] and I always find in

it such a lack of openness and so much certitude about what never entered my mind that you should not find the distress it caused me surprising. But that doesn't matter. If I were not so imperfect, I would be delighted to suffer this mortification from you. Since I am your subject, you can mortify me. And since Padre Salazar is also a subject, it occurs to me that his plan should be cut short by his superior. This would be a better solution than having me write to those who are not subject to me to do what you want. This would be the task of their own superior, and they would be right in not paying much attention to anything I might say.

2.   Certainly, I don't see any better thing to do. Nor do I understand your reasons for wanting me to write. Unless I could say I had a report from heaven[2] that he should not do such a thing, there is nothing for me to do. As I have told you, there is no reason to go into detail about everything, for this would be offensive to someone to whom I owe a solid friendship. This is especially so, since as you said it is certain that from what he says and I understand, he would not make this change without informing his provincial. And if he has not said or written anything to him, it is because he is not going to transfer. And if the provincial can prevent him by not giving him permission, I would be offending a man of dignity and a good servant of God by defaming him in all our monasteries (assuming they pay any attention to me), because it is a detestable accusation to say that he wants to do something that he cannot do without offending God.

3.   I have spoken to you in all truthfulness and, in my opinion, I have done what I was obliged to do as an honorable person and as a Christian (the Lord knows I am speaking the truth here). To do more than what I have done, I think, would go contrary to the honorable and Christian thing to do.

4.   I have told you that when I do something that I think I must, God gives me the courage to undergo with his help all the conflicts that arise. At least I will not complain that they

were not foretold to me[3] or that I failed to do all I could, as I said. You would have had more fault for giving such an order than I for not obeying it.

5. I am also sure that if things should not turn out the way you want, I would be blamed just as much as if I had done nothing. Just to have spoken about the matter suffices for the prophecies to begin to be fulfilled. Well and good if trials come to me. I have committed enough offenses against the Divine Majesty to deserve more than might come.

6. But I do not think I deserve to receive trials from the Society, even were I to have had a part in this matter. It has little importance as far as your concerns go. Your foundations are from a higher source. May it please the Lord that mine will consist in never deviating from his will and that he always give you light for the same resolve. It would be a great consolation for me if our Father Provincial were to come here. For a long while now the Lord has not desired to comfort me with a visit from him.

Your honor's unworthy servant and daughter,

Teresa of Jesus[4]

---

1. The provincial is Juan Suárez (cf. Ltr. 228).
2. Teresa is using irony here. She had been accused of claiming to have received a revelation that Salazar should transfer to the discalced Carmelites.
3. Again, Teresa is using irony. She was told that if she didn't do what was asked unfortunate consequences would follow.
4. Padre Dávila's note to Teresa reads as follows: "Jesus be with your honor. Yesterday I received a letter from Father Provincial. He mentions that what he said in his letter caused you distress. He begs you to read it again after your distress passes and says you will then see that you can understand it better and have a better feeling about it. You should write to Padre Salazar and to the superior or superiors of your order, those who can accept or refuse him, giving them sufficient reasons to prevent him from making the transfer. Father Provincial is satisfied with having carried out his duty by informing at once those involved. Having done so, he cannot be blamed for knowing about

this and then not doing anything. He asks you, for love of our Lord, to recommend him to His Majesty in your holy prayers. Soon, please God, he will be passing through and will discuss whether something else ought to be done. This is what Father Provincial says. He sent me especially this note I'm sending you. I beg you on my part, for the love of Our Lord, to sincerely make this effort and also in the same spirit to write to Padre Salazar and to the superiors of the discalced friars telling the one not to go through with this plan and the others not to receive him, unless he has the express permission of His Holiness or of his Father General. I am certain that in doing so you will not be displeasing our Lord but pleasing him very much. Return this note and let me know what you are thinking of doing, for I believe that it is important for you to do what we ask in charity. Your letters were given by hand to Brother Bartolomé de Sicilia."

The note from the provincial, Juan Suárez, reads as follows: "If today I were informed that a religious of another order wanted to enter the Society, in this province, where there are twenty-six houses and schools, and I judged that it would not be opportune to receive him, I would send out instructions, with the help of our Lord, within one day, to all the superiors of the houses and colleges, that no one accept him. In most of the places the instructions would be there within eight days, and in the rest within fifteen. If Madre Teresa of Jesus judged it inopportune to accept Padre Salazar in the order, she could with one earnest letter to the superior of her order, who would inform the others, or by writing to the superior of each house, reach them all within fifteen days. And it has been more than fifteen days that Madre Teresa and the prioress here have known about this. With God's help, the effort would have been efficacious. Suarez"

230. To Padre Jerónimo Gracián, Pastrana
Avila, 16 February 1578

(Autograph fragment: DCN, Santa Ana, Madrid)

Despite her broken arm Teresa writes at length. The central topic is Padre Salazar and his proposal to transfer from the Jesuits to Teresa's discalced friars. She is enclosing the Jesuit provincial's letter to her and her own response as well as Salazar's to her and her response. She tries to give Gracián all the pertinent information as objectively as she can, as well as her own opinion.

❖❖❖❖

1.   Jesus. The grace of the Holy Spirit be with your honor, *mi padre*, and may he give you health this Lent for the work I see that you have ahead of you. I am wondering if you will have to be moving from place to place. For the love of God watch out lest you have a fall along the way. For since my arm has been in the state it is, I am very careful in this regard. It is still swollen, as is also my hand, and covered with plaster, which looks like armor, and so I get little use out of it.[1]

2.   It's extremely cold here now, which it hasn't been except at the beginning of winter. In fact the weather has been so good that it was much colder, at least for me, in Toledo. This perhaps is due to the door you ordered us to have made for the little room next to the one you said should become the infirmary. After this was done, the little room is like a stove. Anyway, I have been getting along extremely well in this cold weather. You always meet with success in the orders you give. May it please the Lord that I meet with success in obeying you. I would love to know if Padre Fray Antonio de Jesús is continuing to improve and what has happened to Padre Mariano who has so forgotten me. Give my regards to Padre Fray Bartolomé.[2]

3.   I am sending along a letter that the provincial of the Society sent me about the Carillo matter, which displeased me so much that I wanted to send him a worse answer than I did.[3] For I know that they told him I had no part to play in this proposal, which is true.[4] When I heard about it, I got very upset, as I wrote you, and greatly desired that he not proceed any further. I wrote him a letter urging him as strongly as I could not to do so, as I swear in this response of mine to the provincial. Their attitude toward me is such that if I do not use strong words, they will not believe me. And it is most important that they believe me so that they don't keep thinking that I received the revelations they speak of and used them to persuade him, which is a big

lie.[5] But I tell you that I have so little fear of their threats that I am amazed at the freedom God gives me. So, I told the rector[6] that neither the entire Society nor the whole world could keep me from carrying out something I understand to be for the service of God, but that in this matter I neither did nor would intervene.

4.   The rector nonetheless asked me to write to Padre Salazar and say what I said in the enclosed letter, that he can not do what he proposes without incurring excommunication.

5.   I asked the rector if Carillo knew of these briefs.[7] He replied that he understood them better than I. I then answered that I was certain he would not do anything that would offend God. He replied that because of his great attraction he could be fooled and rush ahead with his desire. So I sent him a letter by the means which he used to send his.

6.   Well, *mi padre*, see their simplicity. From certain indications I understood clearly that my letter had been opened, but I didn't mention this to him. I told him in my letter (knowing that they would read it) not to trust his brothers, that Joseph, too, had brothers. In fact, his own friends must have revealed his plan, and I am not surprised, for his brothers are extremely disturbed. They must be afraid that this might set a precedent.

7.   I asked him whether there were not some in the Society who had become discalced friars. He answered yes, that some had become Franciscans, but that the Society had first dismissed them and that afterward they received the permission to enter the Franciscans. I said that the Society could do the same thing in this case. But they are not thinking of doing this, nor am I thinking of telling him not to pursue his plans but only of cautioning him, as I do in this letter and leaving the matter to God. If it is God's will, they will give their consent. Otherwise (as I say here in this letter), a transfer would certainly not be possible—I have inquired about this. Those who are advising him must be basing themselves on the common law, as did another canonist who tried to persuade me at the time of the

foundation in Pastrana that I could accept an Augustinian nun,[8] but he was mistaken. The pope could give his permission, but I don't think that will come about, for they will block the way. Would you inquire about this and advise him, for I would be extremely disturbed if some offense were committed against God. I am sure that he would not knowingly do so.

8.   I am very worried, for if he remains among them after they know of his desire to transfer, he will not have the credibility he is accustomed to. We couldn't allow him to join us save under the most favorable circumstances. And I am always aware of what we owe to the Society, and I don't think God would permit them to do us harm for a reason like this. But to refuse to receive Padre Salazar out of fear of the Society would be wrong and would be a poor recompense for his affection. May God direct everything; may he guide him. But I fear that Padre Salazar will let himself be prompted by some experiences in prayer that he mentions and to which he gives too much credit. I have very often mentioned this to him, but that's not enough.

9.   I am also sorry that the nuns in Beas must have said something to him about this, so great was Catalina de Jesús' desire for him to transfer.[9] The good thing in all this is that he is definitely a servant of God and if he is mistaken it is in thinking that this is what God wants, and His Majesty will look after him. But he has got us into trouble, and if I hadn't heard from Joseph[10] what I wrote to you, believe me that I would have done all I could to prevent it. But even though I do not believe as much in those things, it costs me a great deal to try to dissuade him. Who can say that I would not be hindering some great good from coming to that soul? You should realize that in my opinion he does not have the spirit of the Society. I have always thought so.

10.   Ardapilla[11] wrote me about this matter telling me to try to get the ravens to write to Joanes asking him to send someone here to inquire about it.[12] I would be delighted, as long as I didn't have to get involved, but so many difficulties came to mind that

I excused myself as best I could. I realize that he did it for our good, but you know that if we don't get to the root of a thing there is no other way to provide a remedy, unless Paul[13] lends a hand. May the Lord bring this about, for I desire it very much. I worry about being the obstacle causing everyone to suffer. I have at times said that it would perhaps be best for them to throw me into the sea, as was done with Jonah, that the storm might pass. Perhaps my sins have caused all this.

11.   The prioress of Seville[14] wrote to ask me to petition you to give permission for her to accept another sister of the Portuguese nun, Blanca,[15] who is not old enough to enter, in fact must be far from it. This would provide a great help for them to pay the rent on the house. I don't recall how much it comes to. It wouldn't be a bad thing if the parents in paying the dowry for Blanca would lend the community what they would plan on giving for her sister, or pay the interest instead of providing for her food. The nuns never finish speaking of how much they owe this Portuguese woman. You can consider this and do what you think best.

12.   I don't know when to stop when I write you. My brother[16] always tells me to give you his best wishes. Accept these now all together and along with them those of all the sisters. May our Lord watch over you and bring you here soon, for your presence is very necessary, both for my sake and for other reasons. I don't mean that there is any problem you do not know about. Doña Guiomar[17] is doing poorly. She rarely comes here, for that humor from which she suffers is completely destroying her.

13.   As quickly as you can send this letter for Padre Salazar by way of the prior of Granada,[18] and insist that the prior give it to him secretly. For I fear that through the Society he will write to me again or to some of our sisters, and his code language is easy to decipher. You could send it by way of Madrid, paying good postage, urgently entrusting it to Roque[19] and making use of this same muleteer; it will be safe. Be careful, *mi padre*, and don't forget, for it is important to send this letter to Padre Salazar

and that he not take any further steps—if he hasn't already.[20] And you should delay giving permission, in my opinion, for all of this is for his greater good. May God also give you, *padre mio*, all the blessings I desire for you, amen.

It is the First Sunday of Lent.

14.   This letter from Father Provincial[21] and the reply may be useful to us some day. Do not tear it up, if you so think.

Your paternity's unworthy servant and daughter,

Teresa of Jesus

1.   Teresa fell down the stairs on Christmas eve in 1977 and broke her left arm. It wasn't reset until May.
2.   Antonio de Jesús (Heredia) was sick in Seville; Ambrosio Mariano de San Benito was staying in Madrid; and Bartolomé de Jesús was Gracián's secretary.
3.   The Jesuit provincial was Juan Suárez. Carillo was a code name for Gaspar de Salazar, a Jesuit residing in Granada.
4.   Gaspar de Salazar's proposal was to leave the Jesuits and transfer to the discalced Carmelites.
5.   The provincial reproached Teresa for using her supposed revelations to persuade Salazar to transfer.
6.   Gonzalo Dávila was the Jesuit rector at San Gil in Avila who brought Suárez's letter to Teresa.
7.   Cf. the papal bull Licet Debitum of Paul III (1549).
8.   Catalina Machuca, a protégé of the Princess of Eboli. The latter wanted to impose her on the Carmel of Pastrana without obtaining Teresa's consent.
9.   Catalina de Jesús was one of the sponsors of the foundation in Beas and was also inclined toward the extraordinary. (See F. 22.4–24).
10.   Code name for Jesus Christ.
11.   Juan Calvo de Padilla, a priest who was very much involved in the reform of religious orders.
12.   Joanes could be a code name for Gracián. The ravens are the Jesuits.
13.   Code name for Gracián.
14.   María de San José (Salazar).
15.   Blanca de Jesús (Freire). Her sister María de San José made profession in the Carmel of Seville on 1 January 1583.

16. Lorenzo de Cepeda.
17. Guiomar de Ulloa, Teresa's friend and collaborator.
18. Francisco de Jesús.
19. Roque de Huerta, Teresa's connecting link in Madrid for the safe transport of her letters.
20. It seems that Gracián decided to hold on to Teresa's letter to Salazar (cf. Ltr. 247.2).
21. Juan Suarez.

231. To Padre Jerónimo Gracián
Avila, 2 March 1578

(Autograph: DCN, Seville)

Responding to two letters from Gracián, who is engaged in a Lenten apostolate of preaching, Teresa tells again of her worries about Gaspar de Salazar's wish to transfer from the Jesuits to the Carmelites. She finds Salazar completely unruffled by what he is planning.

1.   May the Holy Spirit be with your paternity, *mi padre*. I received two of your letters a short time ago, the one that you wrote on the last day of carnival, and the other which contained a letter for the sisters from their pastor. Please God we will clothe him as well as you describe, but I believe he will give us much more than we will give to him.[1] The little notebook is also very good.[2]

2.   I don't know how Paul[3] can say that he doesn't know anything about the prayer of union, for that luminous darkness and the loving impulses lead one to the opposite conclusion. But afterward, since the experience goes away and is different, he does not completely understand it. I greatly envy the souls who will make progress through his help and am sorry to see myself here without doing anything else but eat, sleep, and talk about these fathers, our brothers.[4] The occasion to do this is ever present as you will see from the enclosed page,

for I asked Sister Catalina[5] to write to you about what is happening so as not to tire myself, for it is late and we are going to have a sermon this evening by Maestro Daza[6] who is a very good preacher. The Dominicans are very charitable toward us; they preach two sermons a week for us, and those of the Society one.

3.   I often remember your sermons, and I don't know what it is that prompts you to go from place to place, for the latest calumnies against you really distressed me. May God watch over you, *mi padre*. The times have become so dangerous that it is temerarious to travel about from place to place, for there are souls everywhere. Please God that what appears to be much zeal may not turn out to be a temptation that will cost us dearly. In that place where you are, one cat[7] would be enough, besides the other Franciscans and Dominicans that I think are there, although I cannot imagine that blessed man as preaching well.[8] Give him my regards and let me know if they listen to him. But notice my curiosity! Don't tell me and tear this up lest because of my sins it fall into his hands. About your eating in the hospital and those miserable codfish pies, how you made us laugh! But the things they said about you make me hope you will be more careful in the future.

4.   Carillo,[9] in his response to my first letter to him in which I told him the devil was tempting him and many other things as well, is right in saying that I have little courage. He says my letter made him laugh and that it did neither little nor much to induce him to change his mind. He says I'm like a mouse afraid of the cats and that he made his promise while holding the Blessed Sacrament in his hands and that the whole world would not suffice to make him renounce it. I tell you this frightens me, for his brothers say that he and whoever clothes him in that habit[10] will be excommunicated. He says he already has the permission from his provincial and that you wrote him a letter and that although, like a man, you are afraid, you write like an angel. And he is right, for your letter is like that.

5.   His brothers are being difficult in asking that we not accept him. This must be because they don't think we can do so. Judging by their concern, I believe they may have already written you that you should inform the monasteries.[11] They have pressed me so much that I told them I had written to you about the matter.

6.   Really, if it must be done and it can be, as he says, it would be much better to have the deed done before informing the monasteries and all the resulting commotion. I don't know what you are going to do, but if the transfer is something possible, in conscience we would have to accept him. I truly believe from the way in which he describes his situation that no one will block him, and so it would be better to delay if nothing has been done yet. May the Lord direct matters, for the more that obstacles are placed before him, the more it seems to me that God will be served and that the devil wants to prevent this from happening. They must be afraid that he will not be the only one. But they are so numerous that the loss of some will not matter, even if it be of those you mention.

7.   In what you write about Paul's scruples,[12] whether or not he can use his power, it seems to me that he was the prey of a little melancholy when he wrote that letter and is so whenever he has scruples. The reasons he gives for using his power are clear, and so I do not want to inquire again about the matter. From what Ardapilla[13] says, these doubts will not last long, for the memorandum from the great angel has been sent by Gilbert[14] and is expected any day.

8.   I was pleased about Elias's fears over your absence.[15] There is everything to fear over one who takes these risks. May it please the Lord to free Paul[16] from them, for their blindness is so great that nothing they might do would surprise me. What worries me more is the one who does not fear and goes from place to place without necessity.

9.   Returning to what I was saying, I already wrote to Paul some time ago that a very learned Dominican whom I told

about all that happened with Methuselah,[17] informed me, I believe, that it had no binding force. He told me that Methuselah was obliged to show his authorization for doing what he did. For the present there is no need to be talking about it any further.

10.   I would like to send you a letter from the prioress of Valladolid in which she speaks of the commotion stirred up by the Carillo matter.[18] Well, she thinks the Jesuit Fathers are very content with me and the discalced nuns. I think that all the threats will come to naught. What worries me and makes me fear and what I wish you would examine carefully and clarify is whether he can do what he wants without offending God or incurring excommunication. For if what the Jesuits say is true, you can in no way accept him. If the Count of Tendilla[19] goes to Rome—and even if he doesn't go personally—I believe that the permission will certainly be granted, judging by the report he is writing.

11.   I was delighted with our good luck that he is going to Rome, for our friars can go along with him.[20] May the Lord direct it all and protect you for me. I don't know if I answered everything, for I don't have any more time. But see how brief I am when I don't have time!

12.   All the nuns ask for your prayers and have been delighted with the tasks you are giving them.[21] I have not seen Doña Guiomar;[22] only rarely does she come here, for she is very sick.

Today is the second of March.

> Your paternity's unworthy servant and true daughter— especially the latter, for I am hardly this with the other fathers.

> Teresa of Jesus

13.   I am very sorry that Padre Mariano[23] feels so weak. Make him eat well and don't let him think at all about going to Rome, for his health is more important. Oh, how long it is taking your sister[24] to come and how much she is desired!

My Isabelita[25] is doing very well, they tell me.

1. According to the custom a letter from their pastor (Gracián) would assign each sister the task of practicing a certain virtue which would be the equivalent of making a garment for the Lord. This custom was observed especially at the beginning of Lent and Advent and on the feast of the Triumph of the Cross.
2. She is probably referring to one of the instances in which Gracián gave her an account of all that was spiritually taking place within him.
3. Gracián.
4. The Carmelites of the observance.
5. Catalina del Espíritu Santo, a Carmelite nun at St. Joseph's in Avila.
6. Gaspar Daza.
7. Referring to Padre Antonio de la Madre de Dios, she had written his name, but then crossed it out and wrote "cat" (cf. Ltr. 130.2).
8. Cf. Ltr. 328.2, where she is actually very happy with his preaching.
9. The Jesuit Gaspar Salazar.
10. The habit of a Carmelite friar.
11. Juan Suárez, the Jesuit provincial, desired that all the Carmelite monasteries be informed that they could not accept Gaspar de Salazar into their order.
12. Gracián (Paul), was doubting whether, with Sega's presence, he still had the authority to be superior and visitator.
13. Juan Calvo de Padilla.
14. The great angel is the president of the royal council, Antonio Mauricio Pazos; Gilbert is the nuncio, Felipe Sega. The hope was that Pazos would clarify matters concerning Gracian's authority.
15. Elías de San Martín, rector of the discalced Carmelite friars in Alcalá.
16. Gracián.
17. The nuncio, Felipe Sega.
18. The prioress was María Bautista, and Carillo, Gaspar de Salazar.
19. Luis Hurtado de Mendoza.
20. The two discalced friars who were going to Rome to carry out the business of the Teresian reform.
21. Cf. no. 1, note 1.
22. Guiomar de Ulloa, Teresa's friend in Avila.
23. Ambrosio Mariano de San Benito, one of the discalced friars being proposed for going to Rome.

24. María Dantisco, who entered the Carmel in Valladolid on 5 May 1578, taking the name María de San José.
25. Gracián's sister who was living at the Carmel in Toledo.

232. To Roque de Huerta, Madrid
Avila, 8–12 March 1578

The nuns at the monastery of the Incarnation who voted for Teresa to be prioress, against the orders given them, were excommunicated. They appealed to the Royal Council against the provincial. Teresa here asks for help since the provincial was trying to force them to withdraw their appeal. She had received confidential notes about the whole matter.

To the very magnificent Señor Roque de Huerta, chief forest guard of the woods.

1.   Jesus be ever with your honor, amen. Tomorrow, Monday, marks the eighth day since I wrote by way of the carrier from here informing you about what took place as regards the provincial Magdaleno,[1] and I sent you the ordinance and notification given him.[2] I don't know whether you have received these. I would very much appreciate your letting me know, for I am worried. What happened afterward you will see through these notes. I feel very sorry for these nuns, so much so that I don't know what to say, except that God must love them very much because he gives them so many and such long-lasting trials.

2.   All these ten days since the provincial and Valdemoro[3] have been here, they have done nothing but busy themselves with schemes, threaten the nuns, and seek out persons who will tell them about the penalties reserved for them if they do not obey and cast a vote contrary to the previous one they signed in an appeal to the royal council. Now that he has accomplished all that he wanted, the provincial is in a great hurry to go to Madrid to present the nuns' signatures to the council. I beg your honor, for goodness' sake, to do what is required to

make the truth known and tell about how the signatures were obtained by force. This would be a great help to these poor nuns so that the council doesn't think the information presented by the Fathers is true, for all the things that were done added up to tyranny. If it is possible for Señor Padilla[4] to see these notes,[5] show them to him.

3.   Here Magdaleno has said that he definitely carries a royal ordinance to imprison Padilla if he should find him here, that he was two leagues distant from Madrid when they called him back to give it to him, that Tostado[6] has full powers over both the calced and the discalced Carmelites, and that Padre Fray John of the Cross[7] has already been sent to Rome. May God in his power deliver him, and grant grace to your honor.

8 March

   Your honor's unworthy servant,

Teresa of Jesus

4.   For the love of God I beg you to strive to make known briefly to the members of the council the force that was used with the nuns, for this is a very important point of the entire affair. It is a great wrong that they can get away with doing whatever they want,[8] carrying on without justice and without truth in everything they have done, and there is no one showing compassion for these martyrs.

5.   This was written three days ago, and that provincial is still tormenting the nuns.

---

1.   The provincial of the Carmelites in Castile, Juan Gutiérrez de la Magdalena. These were the days in which he was pressuring the nuns with threats to withdraw the accusations made against him to the royal council.

2.   On 1 March the royal secretary Juan Chacón notified the provincial of the royal provision, 19 November 1577, that he must absolve the nuns at the Incarnation from the censures and excommunications imposed on them by himself. Teresa was enclosing copies of the documents.

3. The provincial had feigned absence from Avila. Alonso Valdemoro was the former prior of the monastery of friars in Avila.

4. Juan Calvo de Padilla, who will be taken under arrest on the following 27 June.

5. Cf. no. 1.

6. Jerónimo Tostado, the Carmelite visitator.

7. John of the Cross had been seized during the first days of December 1577 and was at the time held in the monastery prison of the Carmelites of the observance in Toledo.

8. The provincial and Valdemoro.

233. To Padre Jerónimo Gracián, Alcalá
Avila, 10 & 11 March 1578

Teresa communicates her feelings and thoughts about the problems at the Incarnation and the imprisonment of John of the Cross. She takes up some other matters concerning her nuns and new postulants.

1.   Jesus be with *mi padre* and free him from this people of Egypt,[1] for I tell you they have frightened me by what they have done with these poor nuns.[2] I tried to get the nuns to obey because the scandal was already great. This seemed to be the best solution, especially to the Dominicans. From what I surmise these fathers are helping one another and have united against this reform. I am tired of all their clamoring. To tell the truth the nuns have been suffering for a long time. Nonetheless, if I hadn't told them that in my opinion they would not do harm to their cause by obeying, I don't think they would have obeyed.

2.   Since the discalced friars are no longer present,[3] little progress has been made on their cause. In fact, I wrote to Roque and to Padilla[4] that if what concerned the discalced friars were not resolved and the calced friars remained as visitators, the nuns' cause would make no headway. Even if the council did favor the nuns, it would be foolish for me to go there. Yet it would

look very bad if I did not go but abandoned them after they suffered so much. In addition, I don't think I can shirk my duty, especially since I don't see things going in the right direction and the Lord must find some way of helping these souls. I pity them so much, for they are in distress as you can see through those notes.

3.　　For goodness' sake send Padre Germán[5] to them that he might pray for them. He is now really out of prison. As for Fray John, I am very disturbed with the thought that they might find some other fault to accuse him of. God treats his friends terribly. Truly, he does them no wrong since that is the way he treated his Son.

4.　　Read this letter that a gentleman brought from Ciudad Rodrigo, for he came solely to speak about this nun.[6] He has many things to say about her. If they are true, she will be most suited for us. She is bringing 450 ducats and a good trousseau as well. Alba is asking me for a nun. This aspirant would like to go to Salamanca, but she would go to Alba as well. In Salamanca, though, they are in greater need because of the bad state the house is in. She will be able to go wherever you decide to send her. I promised to beg you to admit her. She seems agreeable to going to either of the two houses.

5.　　Here in this house the talk is of two aspirants[7] from Burgos with 1500 ducats. They say they are very good and the dowry is needed for some work projects including what needs to be done on the enclosure wall. With another nun, everything can be completed. Will you give permission for this.

6.　　Look at all the confusion stirred up by a member of the Society over a sister of the prioress of Beas.[8] I asked the prioress of Medina to inquire.[9] She will find out what is being said. They must know much more than we do. You should be careful about what she might do, for I tell you there are persons whose nature doesn't change. Well, even though Anne of Jesus saw her two or three times for a short moment, she must have been told about it. I answered as if I knew everything that I do now. In my hurry I saw that neither she nor her brother spoke of her. The brother belongs to the Society, and it seems good that they help each other.

7. I regret having had to go so long without confessing to you, for here I don't find confessors as I did in Toledo. This is a great trial for me. I wrote this yesterday, and now I am being told of so many things about the injustices being done to the nuns at the Incarnation that I feel great pity for them. I think some of the nuns in this house[10] are afraid of falling into their hands, and I am not surprised by their fear, for they have reason to fear.

8. May God provide a remedy and watch over you. The night is far advanced, and the messenger will be leaving in the morning.

Today is 11 March.

Your paternity's unworthy servant,

Teresa of Jesus

1. The Carmelites of the observance.
2. The Carmelite nuns at the Incarnation who were being threatened by Gutiérrez and Valdemoro.
3. The two confessors, Fray John of the Cross and Fray Germán de San Matías.
4. Roque de Huerta and Juan Calvo de Padilla.
5. Germán de San Matías.
6. She was probably Isabel de la Cruz from Ciudad Rodrigo. She made her profession in Alba de Tormes 22 August 1579.
7. They were the two daughters of Catalina de Tolosa, the future founding benefactor of Burgos: Catalina de la Asunción and Casilda de San Angelo. They made their profession in Valladolid on 28 August 1579.
8. Anne of Jesus, the prioress of Beas, did not have a sister. Perhaps the allusion is to a cousin of hers. The Jesuit seems to be her brother, Padre Cristóbal de Lobera.
9. The prioress in Medina was Inés de Jesús (Tapia). Anne of Jesus was from Medina.
10. St. Joseph's in Avila.

234. To Padre Jerónimo Gracián
Avila, March 1578

This fragment was copied by Gracián's sister, María de San José, from a letter now lost. The date is uncertain. In Teresa's code Joseph is Christ and Paul is Gracián.

1.   The concept that Paul has formed of Joseph's grandeur is most elevated. Nonetheless, there is a greater or less amount of good in the works we do for him, and we are not always aware of how upright our intention is. So it is necessary to proceed with caution as in all things and trust little in ourselves.

2.   How he will laugh, *mi padre*, over all this foolishness, he who thinks he keeps this very much in mind. But with his other cares this could be forgotten, and it is good that I remind him; at least nothing is lost by my doing so.

235. To Don Luis de Cepeda, Torrijos
Avila, March 1578

Still handicapped with her broken arm, Teresa is nonetheless able to write a message of sympathy and encouragement.

1.   Jesus. The grace of the Holy Spirit be with your honor. God was pleased that it wasn't my right arm that suffered the damage, and so I can write this.[1] I am better, glory to God, and I can keep the Lenten observance. The gifts you are always giving me will help me do so. May our Lord repay you. Although you do this for me, Sister Isabel de San Pablo is so tempted to love me that she is happier than I about it.[2] It is a great consolation for me to be in her company, which seems like that of an angel. It is a consolation as well to know that your health is good, as is also that of those ladies, whose hands I kiss many times. I often pray to our Lord for them and do the same for you.

2. I was most distressed to hear of the death of that lady.[3] Not long ago I wrote to Señor Don Teutonio, in response to one of his letters, to congratulate him on the happy occasion of the wedding, for I owe him much. These people undergo great trials.[4] It seems clear they are servants of God, since trials are the greatest gift God can give us in life. If this life that is so short serves for any good, it is to gain eternal life.

3. I praise our Lord that you are not careless about this truth. So I beg him that this may be always the case and also for those ladies. Lorenzo de Cepeda kisses their hands many times as well as yours.

> Your honor's unworthy servant,
>
> Teresa of Jesus

1. Teresa had broken her arm the previous December, and both the arm and her hand were still swollen.
2. Isabel de San Pablo, a Carmelite nun, was a sister of Luis de Cepeda.
3. It seems she was the daughter of Doña Juana de Braganza, a resident in Torrijos and recently married niece of Don Teutonio de Braganza (cf. Ltr. 226.5).
4. Don Teutonio's family, for Doña Juana had also been widowed while young.

236. To Doña María de Mendoza, Valladolid
Avila, 26 March 1578

(Autograph: DCN, Ecija[Seville])

A letter of sympathy to a friend and benefactor.

❖❖❖❖

To the most illustrious Señora Doña María de Mendoza, my lady. Valladolid.

1. Jesus. The grace of the Holy Spirit be always with your most illustrious ladyship and give you strength to suffer so many

trials, for certainly this has been a harsh blow. I have felt great pain over what yours must be. I trust in the favors our Lord grants you that he will not fail to console you in this affliction and remind you during this holy season of the sufferings His Majesty and his glorious Mother underwent. If we felt them as we should, we would suffer all the pains of this life with great ease.

2.   I would love to be there in your company and help you by sharing your pain, although I have been doing so here. I had no other consolation than to beg St. Joseph and our Lord to be with you. All of us in our prayers have been careful to make supplications for you and for that holy soul.[1] I hope the Lord has already called her to his side and that he wanted to take her out of the world before she knew more about the things that are in it. Everything comes to an end so quickly that if our minds were awake and enlightened, it would not be possible to feel sorry over those who die knowing God, but rejoice in their good.

3.   I also felt sorry for the count,[2] in judging only from what we see, but the judgments of God are great and his secrets we cannot understand. Perhaps his salvation lies in his being a widower. I think His Majesty takes special care over all your concerns, for he is a most trustworthy friend. We can be sure that he has considered what is most suitable for souls; compared to this nothing else merits much of our attention. Eternal good or evil is what matters, and so I beg you for love of our Lord not to be thinking of the reasons you have for being afflicted but in those you have for taking comfort. In doing so you will receive much benefit. Otherwise you will lose, and even do harm to your health, which you are obliged to look after, for we all prize it highly. May God give you many years, as we all beg of him.

4.   These sisters and Mother Prioress[3] kiss your hands many times; I kiss those of Señora Doña Beatriz.[4]

Today is Wednesday of Holy Week. I did not write before this, because I did not think you would feel like reading letters.

Your illustrious ladyship's unworthy servant and subject,

Teresa of Jesus

1. This is probably María Sarmiento de Mendoza, Doña María's niece who was married to the Count of Uceda, Diego Mexía de Ovando.
2. Diego Mexía.
3. María de Cristo, prioress of St. Joseph's in Avila.
4. Beatriz Sarmiento de Mendoza, Doña María's sister.

237. To Madre María de San José, Seville
Avila, 28 March 1578

Teresa responds to letters asking her opinion about the admission of postulants and keeping a journal on one's prayer. The delicate matters are written in her own hand, the rest by the secretary. Her arm, head, and heart are all in poor condition, but she bears it with good humor.

1. Jesus be with you, my daughter, and grant you and all your daughters as happy an Easter as I beg him. For me it has been a great comfort to know that you are in good health. My health remains as usual, with my arm in bad shape and my head too; I don't even understand what prayers they are saying.[1] Truly, this must be the best thing for me. It would be a consolation if my head were such that I could write a long letter, and send many greetings for everyone. Do so for me, and especially to Sister San Francisco[2] whose letters are a delight for us. Believe me, during the time she was prioress she grew wings. Oh, Jesus, how alone I feel when I see you all so far away. Please God, we will all be together in eternity. I find comfort in the thought that everything passes quickly.

2. What you say about the fault you find with Fray Bartolomé's sisters amused me. Even though you could finish paying

off the house with their dowries, it would not be permissible to accept them. Under no circumstances should you take anyone who does not have good judgment. That would go against the constitutions and bring incurable harm. Thirteen years old is very young—I'm speaking of the other one; at that age they tend to change their minds a thousand times. You will have to see for yourself what is best. As for me, I believe that I want everything that is good for you.

3.   Before I forget, I am not in favor of the sisters writing about prayer, for this has many drawbacks which I would like to tell you about. You should know that even though doing this amounts to nothing but a waste of time, it impedes freedom of soul and allows one to imagine all kinds of things. If I remember, I will mention this to our *padre*;[3] and if I don't, you tell him. Important graces are never forgotten; and if they are forgotten, there is no reason to mention them. When they see our *padre*, it will be enough for them to mention what they remember. In my opinion, they are on a safe path, and if something can do them harm, it would be for them to give importance to what they see and hear. If they experience some scruple, they can tell you, for I so esteem you that if they trust you, God will give you the light to guide them. I insist so much on this because I understand the trouble they will run into from thinking about what they should write and from what the devil can put into their heads. If it is something very serious, you could write it down, but without their knowing this. If I had paid attention to the experiences of San Jerónimo,[4] she would never have finished. And if some of them seemed true, I still was silent about them. Believe me, it is better to praise the Lord, who gives these graces, and when they have passed to get beyond them, for it is the soul that will experience the benefit.

4.   What you tell me about Elias is good. But since I don't have your erudition, I don't know who the Assyrians are. My best regards to her for I love her very much, also to Beatriz and her mother.[5] It makes me very happy when you tell me about yourself and the good news about everyone. God pardon those friars who harass us so much.

5. And don't believe everything they say down there; up here we are given more hope. And in this we rejoice, although in darkness, as Madre Isabel de San Francisco says. With this painful arm, my heart is very bad on some days. Send me a little orange-flower water, and pack it so that the container doesn't break. That is why I didn't ask you for it sooner. The angel water you sent was so exquisite that using it caused me scruples, so I gave it to the church for the celebration of the feast of the glorious St. Joseph.

6. Give the prior of Las Cuevas[6] my best wishes, for I love this saint very much, and Padre Garciálvarez[7] and my Gabriela[8]—certainly there is a reason why our *madre* calls her "her Gabriela"[9]—whose presence there I could easily envy if it were not for all the love we have for one another in the Lord and if I didn't understand that the affection she has for you and your daughters is so well deserved. And how Madre Isabel de San Francisco does so much to make us aware of this. Even if she had gone to your house for no other reason than to praise you and all your nuns to the skies, her journey there was worthwhile. But wherever you are, *mi madre*, you will be praised. Blessed be God who gave you so many gifts, which you use so well.

7. I ask *mi madre* San Francisco for prayers—I cannot say more—and for prayers from all the nuns, especially Sister San Jerónimo. Teresa[10] asks for your prayers. Señor Lorenzo Cepeda is well.

8. Please God, *mi madre*, you will be able to read this, written so poorly and in great haste. What else could be expected?

Today is Friday of the Cross.[11]

Send me only a little orange-flower water, until we see how it arrives.

Your reverence's

Teresa of Jesus

9.   The secretary is Isabel de San Pablo,[12] servant of your reverence and of all in your house. *Madre mia*, now I remember that I heard it said that in Seville there are some paintings that are large and well done, that Julián Dávila[13] was praising them. Our *madre* told me to ask you for one of St. Paul. Send me one that is very beautiful. And pardon me, but it must be one that I will enjoy looking at.

---

1. She makes this remark in a humorous vein.
2. Isabel de San Francisco had been prioress in Paterna for some months.
3. Jerónimo Gracián.
4. Isabel de San Jerónimo, a member of the community in Seville, though good-intentioned was somewhat unbalanced.
5. Beatriz de la Madre de Dios. Her mother was Juana de la Cruz.
6. Hernando de Pantoja.
7. Garciálvarez had been confessor to the nuns.
8. Leonor de San Gabriel.
9. An interpolation by Teresa's secretary.
10. Teresa (Teresita) de Jesús, Lorenzo's daughter and Teresa's niece.
11. Good Friday.
12. Isabel de San Pablo was a relative of Teresa's and one of the first nuns to make profession at St. Joseph's in Avila.
13. Julián de Avila, the chaplain at St. Joseph's in Avila.

238. To Padre Jerónimo Gracián, Alcalá
Avila, 15 April 1578

Gracián, on the basis of his powers as commissary and apostolic visitator, has decided to form a separate province for the discalced Carmelites. Such a separation had been prohibited by the general chapter of Piacenza the previous year. Those Teresa consulted advised strongly against Gracián's plan and she attempts to point out the trouble he would be getting himself into. Teresa also discusses other matters: members of Gracián's family, different Carmels, John of the Cross's imprisonment, and Luisa de la Cerda's loss.

❧❧❧❧

1.   Jesus be with your paternity, *mi padre.* After Father Prior from Mancera left, I spoke to Maestro Daza and Doctor Rueda[1] about the matter concerning the province.[2] I would not want you to do anything that could be considered wrong, for even if such a thing turned out well, it would grieve me more than all the things done to ruin our plans at no fault of ours.

2.   Both of them say that it is something difficult to admit if the commission given to you does not make specific mention of your power to do so.[3] Doctor Rueda especially is of this opinion, to which I adhere because I consider him wise in all matters. In short, he is a very learned man. He says that since one is dealing with a matter of jurisdiction it would be difficult to hold an election, for without the intervention of the general or the pope one has no power to do so and the votes would have no force. That is all they[4] would need so as to have recourse to the pope and protest vehemently about passing beyond the boundaries of obedience and naming superiors without power to do so. It sounds bad, and he thinks it would be more difficult to get confirmation from the pope of such elections than it would to get permission to form a separate province. A letter written by the king to his ambassador would suffice for him to gladly grant it. This would be easy to obtain since the pope would be told of how the others are treating the discalced friars. It is probable that if one were to discuss this with the king, he would be happy to do so. That would be a great help to the reform, for the others would have more respect for it and not insist on saying that the reformed houses should be done away with.

3.   Perhaps it would be good for you to speak of this with Padre Maestro Chaves[5] and bring him the letter I sent you through Father Prior.[6] He is very discreet and enjoys the favor of the king; perhaps he could obtain what we desire. The friars who

are designated to travel to Rome could then bring a letter from the king about this matter, for in no way would I want them to fail to go. As Doctor Rueda says, the direct way to proceed is to address the matter to the pope or the general.

4.   I tell you that if Padre Padilla[7] and all of us had thought of seeking the king's help in this matter, everything would have been taken care of by now. And even you could speak to the king and to the archbishop. If the elected provincial needs to be confirmed by the king and enjoy his favor, it's better to seek this favor now. And if you don't obtain it, there would be less of a stir and less damage done than if the refusal came after the election. Our reputation would be stained, and you would lose credibility for having acted without authority and without good judgment.[8]

5.   Doctor Rueda says that even if the dominican visitator[9] or another were to do the electing, that would be better than having the discalced friars elect their own superiors. In these matters of jurisdiction you have to insist, and it's important, that the head receive his powers from a legitimate source. In thinking that they will accuse you with good reason I become disheartened. I don't experience this when they accuse you unjustly; rather, I grow wings and take off. And so I couldn't wait to write this so that you will be very careful.

6.   Do you know what crossed my mind? Perhaps the gifts I sent to our Father General were used against us (for they were very nice) and given to some cardinals. And the thought comes to me not to send anything until this matter is over. So it would be good, if the occasion presents itself, to give something to the nuncio. I notice, *mi padre*, that when you are in Madrid you accomplish much in one day. If you speak with this one and that and with the friends you have in the palace and with Padre Fray Antonio,[10] whom you could get to speak with the duchess, much could be done toward getting the king to favor our cause. He wants the reform to continue. And let Padre Mariano speak with him and present our cause to him and beg

him and remind him of how long it is now that that little saint Fray John has been prisoner.[11] In their furor over the visitation, they do these foolish things, which they wouldn't be able to do if they had a superior. Well, the king listens to everyone. I don't know why we should neglect telling him about this and asking for his support, Padre Mariano especially.

7.   But how I chatter on and what silly things I tell you! And you put up with it all from me. I tell you that I am terribly upset that I do not have the freedom to do myself what I am telling others to do. Now that the king is about to go so far away, I wish something could be done first. May God do it, as he can.

8.   We are eagerly awaiting those ladies.[12] The sisters here are determined not to allow your sister to pass by without giving her the habit. You owe them a special debt of gratitude. I have a high regard for this attitude of theirs. They are so many and in such need, but they set nothing above having someone from your family. Well, that Teresita,[13] the things she says and does! I, too, would be delighted because I wouldn't be able to enjoy your sister's company in the place where she is going, and perhaps never because it is a very out-of-the-way place. Nonetheless, it depends on me, and I will oppose them, for she has already been accepted in Valladolid and will be fine there, and to keep her here would be a great disappointment for them, especially Casilda.[14] We will keep Juliana here—although for now I am not mentioning anything to the nuns about her—because I think it would be too great a hardship for Señora Doña Juana if she were sent to Seville, and perhaps Juliana herself would regret this when older.[15] Oh, how I am tempted to become disturbed about your sister, the one who is in the boarding school.[16] Through failure to understand, she is refusing help and a life more peaceful than the one she has there.

9.   My brother Lorenzo is bringing this letter, for he is going to Madrid and from there, I believe, to Seville. Would you kindly allow him to enter the monastery in Seville to see a little stove

the prioress[17] has made for cooking—for they are raving about it—and we can not make one like it here if he doesn't see it. And if it is all that I am told it is, it will prove a treasure for both friars and nuns. I am writing to the prioress to allow him to enter for this purpose. But if this doesn't seem to you to be a good enough reason, let me know, for he will be staying in Madrid for a few days. But if you saw what they are writing about it, you would not be surprised that here they want to have one. They say it is better than Soto's little mule, and what more could one say of it. The prioress,[18] I believe, is writing you, and so I have no more to say than ask God to watch over you for me.

10.   The prioress in Alba[19] is very sick. Pray for her; despite all they say about her, her loss would be a great one. She is very obedient, and where obedience is present, a simple word of advice is enough to take care of everything. Oh, what the nuns in Malagón are going through without Brianda.[20] But I've laughed at the thought of their desire that she return.

11.   Doña Luisa de la Cerda's youngest daughter[21] has died. I'm extremely distressed over the trials God gives this lady. The only daughter she has left is the widow.[22] I think it would be good for you to write and console her. We owe her much.

12.   Consider the possibility of your sister[23] remaining here. If you think this would be preferable, I will not interfere, especially if Doña Juana[24] would like to have her close by. Since she already has it in mind to go to Valladolid, I fear that she will come to regret remaining here. She will learn of the conveniences they have there that we don't have here, even if they amount to no more than the garden, for the ground here is wretched.

13.   May God watch over you, *mi padre*, and make you as holy as I beg of him, amen, amen. My arm[25] is getting better.

Today is April 15.

Your paternity's unworthy servant and daughter,

Teresa of Jesus

14. Doña Guiomar[26] is here and feeling better; she longs to see you. She weeps for her Fray John of the Cross as do all the nuns. This has really been a hard thing to take. The Incarnation is getting back to life as usual.

---

1. The prior was Juan de Jesús Roca, a classmate of Gracián's at Alcalá. Gaspar Daza and Fernando Rueda were priests in Avila.

2. This matter concerned Gracián's authority to erect a separate province for discalced Carmelites.

3. They were referring to Gracián's official appointment as visitator on 8 August 1575 and to the kinds of authority that had been granted to him.

4. The Carmelites of the observance.

5. Diego de Chaves, a Dominican friar whom Teresa came to know in Avila, and now confessor to the king.

6. Juan de Jesús Roca, prior of Mancera.

7. Juan Calvo de Padilla.

8. These forewarnings by Teresa became a bitter reality for Gracián (cf. Ltrs. 262, 272).

9. Pedro Fernández.

10. Gracián's father and brothers were secretaries to the king, and Antonio de Jesus (Heredia) was a close friend of the Duchess of Alba who had a great deal of influence at the court.

11. Ambrosio Mariano was much esteemed by the king as a brilliant engineer. John of the Cross at the time had been in prison for over four months.

12. Gracián's mother and sister María Dantisco, who received the Carmelite habit in Valladolid on 5 May 1578.

13. Teresa's niece, Lorenzo's daughter.

14. Casilda de la Concepción (de Padilla).

15. Juliana was another of Gracián's sisters. Born in 1574, she was only four years old at the time. She entered the Carmel in Seville in 1582, at age 8, and made her profession there on 25 December 1590, at age 16.

16. This was another of Gracián's sisters, Juana Dantisco, who since 1567 had been at a school founded by Siliceo in Toledo.

17. María de San José, the prioress in Seville.

18. María de Cristo, the prioress at St. Joseph's in Avila.

19. María del Sacramento.

20. Brianda de San José, the prioress of Malagón, who because of a chronic illness was living at the Carmel in Toledo.
21. Catalina Pardo de Tavera.
22. Guiomar Pardo de Tavera, Juan Zuñia's widow, and future Marchioness of Malagón.
23. María Dantisco.
24. Gracián's mother.
25. Her left arm which she broke in a fall on 24 December 1577.
26. Guiomar de Ulloa, one of John of the Cross's directees, and now left without his guidance.

239. To Padre Jerónimo Gracián, Alcalá
Avila, 17 April 1578

Gracián is planning to accompany his mother and sister on a journey from Madrid to Valladolid. Teresa is eagerly expecting them to stop for a visit in Avila, but letters from Gracián arrive that raise doubts. There are fears of his being taken prisoner and of further calumnies. He could travel incognito, skipping the visit in Avila, and taking another route. Teresa proposes different possibilities.

1.   Jesus be with your paternity, *mi padre*. Oh, how dreadful of you to write such a short letter when you had as good a messenger as Juan. I was delighted to see him and to hear especially about you. I've already answered, in the letter brought you by Father Prior of Mancera,[1] some of the things you asked me about. I feel mortified that you would pay any attention to me. Do what seems best to you; that would be the better course to follow.

2.   I am so fearful after seeing that from everything good the devil draws out evil. Until the hour of those fathers[2] passes, I would not want there to be any occasion for more calumnies and abuse. As I have said at other times, they come out on top in everything. Thus, I won't be surprised by anything they do. It doesn't seem to them they are doing anything against God,

for they have the superiors on their side. They don't care about the king, for they see that he remains silent despite all they do. And if they should dare do something against you, the results would be terrible. Apart from the great pain and affliction this would cause everyone, they would feel discouraged and lost. God deliver us, and I think he will; but he wants us to do what we can to help ourselves. This along with the other things I wrote you compels me not to beg you to come here no matter how much I desire this.

3.   The prioress of Alba[3] is very sick. It is there that you are most needed. I wish you could go there with more calm than is now possible, and I would not want you to leave Madrid until things become more stable, and Peralta[4] goes away. I know what they did when the king sent for Padre Mariano,[5] even though they are less bold in Madrid than here. Yet, it is hard for me not to be able to give joy to a mother, and such a mother.[6] So I don't know what to tell myself except that one can no longer live in this world.

4.   You ask if it would not be better for you to go by another way, since if you come here you will be going out of your way. I tell you I long to see those ladies,[7] but if you have to accompany them, you can remain more hidden if you go the other way, for no monasteries of those blessed creatures[8] exist along that route. If such were not the case, I would find it hard if to avoid going eight leagues out of your way you failed to grant me this favor and rest here some days, and provide us with this joy that all the sisters hope for, as I wrote to you through my brother[9] who left today for Madrid.

5.   Thirdly, you tell me that Señora Doña Juana is coming with her daughter. It seems to me this is a demanding trip (eighty leagues) that she is now planning, a trip she could avoid and thus not risk her health which we so prize.[10] I have made that trip and did so surrounded with much comfort and diversion, for I traveled with Señora María de Mendoza; still, it seemed long.

6.   You should know that I am determined not to let your mother go beyond Avila. It is really not necessary because Señora Doña María has her brother[11] and another woman accompanying her. Everything has been taken care of there, and it would be a big mistake for her to so tire herself out now that she has already seen her daughter. It would be better to wait until the time for the taking of the veil when, God willing, the situation will not be so dangerous and you could accompany her more easily than now. Her health is so important to us that otherwise I would not dare give such advice. At least, I will make every effort to keep her from continuing on her journey after she arrives here. The journey this far, if the weather is good, is not long. And now I recall that if she comes by carriage, it is better to come this way, for there are no mountain passes as there are along the other road.

7.   I have been wondering, if Señora Doña Juana does not come and only Señor Tomás de Gracián accompanies his sister, if it would not be good for Padre Fray Antonio to travel with them, for he is well now.[12] You will say that he too is a discalced friar. But his white hair will be a safeguard for him against all gossip. If you are not involved, no one will pay any attention, for everyone is now concentrating on you. I will be happy to see him again, now resurrected. This is the thought that entered my mind. If it isn't practical, consider it foolishness, for I know no more than what I have said.

8.   I tell you that I would be overjoyed to see Doña Juana,[13] but I think we are taking a risk, especially if she wants to travel any further than here. God deliver me from myself, for I pay so little attention to my rest. May it please the Lord to give my soul rest in a leisurely visit with you.

9.   In the letter sent you through my brother,[14] I wrote of how difficult it seems to Doctor Rueda and Maestro Daza[15] that you elect prioresses[16] without orders from the pope or the general, since it is a matter of their jurisdiction. Since I wrote at length about this, I'll say nothing but that you consider it, for the love of

the Lord. You have a great deal of work and must always be so careful about everything. God will give us better times. For now, *mi padre*, we must take the path along which God may protect you. The prioress and subprioress sent you letters through my brother.[17] If you need anything from the judge Covarrubias,[18] you must tell my brother for they are good friends.

The Lord be with you and keep you many years for me and with much holiness.

Today is April 17.

> Your paternity's unworthy daughter.

> Teresa of Jesus

10.   You should know, *mi padre*, that I am very sorry that I didn't know that Señora Doña Juana[19] was going to come so soon. We've got the choir all exposed and the turmoil of workmen coming and going and the grilles removed. I was very happy at the thought of being able to have her here: what a life! It became impossible to stay in the choir because of either the cold or the heat. That will now be taken care of. See if it is possible to authorize Doña María[20] to enter inside when here, for although everything is a mess, it will help her appreciate the house in Valladolid.

---

1. Juan de Jesús Roca. The identity of the preceding Juan is unknown.

2. The Carmelites of the observance.

3. María del Sacramento.

4. Code name for Jerónimo Tostado, the Carmelite visitator, who was prevented by the royal council from carrying out a visitation in Castile, has now reappeared on the scene.

5. Ambrosio Mariano de San Benito, who was esteemed by the king and had undergone some ill-treatment, but nothing like the imprisonment of St. John of the Cross.

6. Doña Juana Dantisco, Gracián's mother. Teresa regrets that under the circumstances Gracián cannot travel with her.

7. Doña Juana Dantisco and María Dantisco, Gracián's mother and sister, who are planning a trip from Madrid to Valladolid and toying with the idea of going by way of Avila.
8. The Carmelites of the observance.
9. Lorenzo de Cepeda; see Ltr. 238.
10. The round trip from Madrid to Valladolid was 80 leagues.
11. Maria Dantisco and her brother Tomás Gracián.
12. Antonio de Jesús Heredia had been seriously ill and close to death. Gracián could not make the trip without exposing himself to new calumnies.
13. Juana Dantisco.
14. Lorenzo de Cepeda.
15. Fernando de Rueda and Gaspar Daza; see Ltr. 238.
16. This may well be a code word for electing a provincial.
17. María de Cristo and María de San Jerónimo sent letters to him through Lorenzo de Cepeda.
18. Juan de Covarrubias, future bishop of Guadix and a friend of Lorenzo de Cepeda.
19. Juana Dantisco.
20. María Dantisco was going to enter the Carmel in Valladolid and pass through Avila on her way there.

240. To Gaspar de Villanueva in Malagón
Avila, 17 April 1578

Teresa had received a letter from the confessor of the nuns in Malagón seeking advice about certain matters. It appears from her reply that the complaining and discontent in the community were continuing, which provokes some sharp comments by Teresa.

To the very magnificent and reverend Señor Licentiate Gaspar de Villanueva, *mi señor* in Malagón.

1.   Jesus be with your honor, *mi padre*. I assure you that if the condition of my head matched my desire to write to you at length, this would not be so short. I was very happy to receive your letter.

2.   As for the matter concerning your sister, and my daughter,[1] I am glad that it doesn't depend on you or her. I don't know what all the fuss is about or on what grounds the Mother President[2] is basing herself. The Mother Prioress, Brianda,[3] wrote me about this; I am answering her. I suggest that you do what she says in a letter she will write you, if you are in agreement. And if you are not, whatever the decision, I don't want to speak any more about this matter.

3.   Concerning Sister Mariana,[4] my desire is that she make profession according to her rank. As long as she knows how to recite the psalms and is attentive to all the rest, nothing else is required, I'm sure. Other professions have been made under the same conditions with the approval of learned men. I will tell this to the Mother President, unless you disagree. And if you do I submit in advance to your orders.

4.   I beg you to give my regards to Sister Juan Bautista and to Beatriz.[5] Since the nuns have you there, they don't need to go to Mother about their interior life, because it seems they don't feel consoled with her. I want them to stop their complaining! This woman is not killing them, nor is she neglecting the house, nor does she fail to provide for their needs, for she is very charitable. I have come to understand the nuns in that house, but until Padre Visitator[6] goes there nothing can be done.

5.   Oh, *mi padre*, what a trial it is to see so much instability in the nuns in that house. And how many things they found insufferable in the one whom they now adore![7] They practice the perfection of obedience mixed with a great deal of self love. And so God punishes them in the very thing where they are at fault. May it please His Majesty to perfect us in everything, amen. These sisters proceed very much like beginners, and if they didn't have you there, I wouldn't be so surprised. May our Lord watch over you. Don't fail to write, for your letters are a comfort to me, and I have few consolations.

17 April.

6.   I thought of answering Sister Mariana, but my head is certainly in no condition to do so. I beg you to tell her that if she behaves as well as she writes, we will pardon her not being able to read so well. Her letter consoled me very much. I am sending her in response the permission to make profession. Even if she cannot make profession in the hands of our *padre*, in the event that he delays a great deal in coming, you needn't prevent her from making it, unless you think otherwise. Your hands are good for giving the veil,[8] and she should consider only that she is making her profession in the hands of God, as is true.

> Your honor's unworthy servant and daughter,

> Teresa of Jesus

---

1.   Gaspar de Villanueva's sister was Ana de los Angeles.
2.   Ana de la Madre de Dios was presiding over the community in Malagón.
3.   The prioress of Malagón, Brianda de San José, was sick and residing in Toledo.
4.   Mariana del Espíritu Santo was a sister of the prioress, Brianda. She was a choir sister and made her profession on 4 May 1578.
5.   Juana Bautista was a novice and Beatriz de Jesús (Cepeda y Ocampo), a former president of the community.
6.   Jerónimo Gracián.
7.   They had complained heavily about the prioress, who at this time was sick and trying to recuperate in Toledo, and now were dissatisfied with her substitute.
8.   He would also give her the veil at the time of her profession.

241. To Doña Juana Dantisco, Madrid
Avila, 17 April 1578

Juana Dantisco, Gracián's mother, is planning a trip from Madrid to Valladolid, to accompany her daughter María and perhaps also Gracián. For various reasons Teresa doubts the advisability of the journey.

❖ ❖ ❖ ❖

1.   Jesus. The grace of the Holy Spirit be always with your honor. God reward you for favoring me with your letter and the news of your plan to come here with Señora Doña María.[1] You will be most welcome.

2.   You are right to be happy, for I don't know what greater fortune God could give you than to call your daughter to a state where in serving His Majesty a person can live with more peace than anyone can imagine. I hope in the Lord that this will be for his great service.

3.   On the one hand, I long for you to come, like someone who for a long while has had no cause for any great joy. On the other hand, I don't like to think of you having to undertake such a long trip when you could be excused, for I desire your health more than my satisfaction. I am writing to our Father Visitator[2] about this and about his coming with you, for there are many drawbacks to it. What he decides will be the best thing to do.

4.   May it please the Lord to deliver us from these times in which we have to fear even what is very good, for eyes full of suspicion are watching. The letter you said you wrote me, I never got.

5.   All these sisters and the prioress[3] kiss your hands. They very much look forward to your coming and that of Señora Doña María. May the Lord direct everything according to what best serves him. In Valladolid they are already getting the material for her habit.

6.   May His Majesty watch over you and the Lord Secretary.[4] I kiss your hands and the hands of all those ladies, especially of Señora Doña Adriana,[5] although she has very much forgotten me.

Today is April 17.

Your honor's unworthy servant,

Teresa of Jesus

7.   My Isabel de Jesús[6] is already writing to me; there is no end to the nuns' happiness with her, and rightly so.

---

1.   María Dantisco, Doña Juana's daughter and thus Gracián's sister, who was planning to enter the Carmel of Valladolid.

2.   Jerónimo Gracián.

3.   Prioress at St. Joseph's in Avila, María de Cristo.

4.   Diego Gracián de Alderete, Doña Juana's husband, who was the king's secretary.

5.   Another daughter of Doña Juana's who belonged to the Franciscan Conceptionist nuns in Madrid.

6.   Doña Juana's daughter who entered the Carmel in Toledo when only eight years old.

242. To Padre Jerónimo Gracián, in Alcalá
Avila, 26 April 1578

(Autograph fragment: DCN, Alcalá de Henares)

In the end, Gracián decided not to dare make the trip with his mother and sister. His sister stayed with the community in Avila inside the cloister, and his mother at Teresa's brother's house. The travelers brought a letter from Gracián, which Teresa here answers.

꙳꙳꙳꙳

1.   Jesus be with your paternity, *mi padre*—and my superior, as you say, which delighted me and gave me a good laugh. Every time I think of this I am amused at how sincerely you seem to tell me not to judge my superior.

2.   Oh, *mi padre*, what little need there was for you to swear—neither as a saint nor much less like a teamster—for I am fully persuaded. God who has given you the zeal and desire for the good of souls would not take it away when you deal with the good of your subjects. Now to set this aside, I only want

to remind you that you gave me permission to judge you and think whatever I want about you.

3.   Doña Juana[1] arrived late yesterday, almost at nightfall, which was April 25, and she felt well, glory to God. I greatly enjoyed being with her, for every day I love her more, and find her better and wiser. As for our nun,[2] she is so happy that her joy can not be put into words. After she entered, it seemed she had been here all her life. I hope in God she will become a great nun. She has a fine intelligence and is very capable.

4.   I would so much like Doña Juana not to continue on, but you have inspired this angel[3] with so much love for Valladolid that no pleas were sufficient to keep her here.

5.   Oh, and Teresa,[4] what she didn't say and do! But Doña María took it well, as a prudent person, saying that she would do whatever I wanted, but it was clear that she didn't want to stay.

6.   I spoke to her privately about this house and told her many things about it and how it came into being almost miraculously and other things. She answered that it didn't matter to her whether she was here or there. We thought we had made progress with her, but I then saw her become sad. Well, she spoke privately with Doña Juana and asked her not to fail to bring her to Valladolid and that she not let this desire of hers be known.

7.   It seemed to Doña Juana and me that there was nothing else we could do, for it could become a source of discontent for her to receive the habit here and afterward go there.[5] Doña María told me clearly that she would find staying here painful, that she wouldn't be able to bear leaving the monastery she had entered. And so I believe Doña Juana will leave tomorrow afternoon with her daughter. I would very much have liked her to stay at least until Monday.[6] But since I see the expense that would involve, I did not insist very much.

8.   She is staying at my brother's house, and Aranda[7] is taking good care of her. May God go with her, for I am concerned,

although she arrived in good shape after the most difficult part of the journey. Please God the rest of the trip will not do her any harm, for she is healthy and has a strong constitution. I embraced her at the door—for I am very fond of her—when Señora Doña María entered. May God bring her back home safely, for she is precious.[8]

1. Juana Dantisco, Gracián's mother.
2. María Dantisco, Gracián's sister, who had been accepted by the Carmel in Valladolid.
3. María Dantisco.
4. Teresita de Cepeda, who was a novice at St. Joseph's in Avila.
5. The nuns at St. Joseph's were determined to give her the habit there; cf. Ltr. 238.8.
6. Only a day longer, Monday being April 28.
7. Lorenzo, in whose house she was staying, employed Jerónimo Aranda as his servant. Don Lorenzo had left for Seville via Madrid.
8. The conclusion is missing.

243. To Madre Ana de San Alberto, Caravaca
Avila, 30 April 1578

(Autograph: DCF, Venice)

A formal statement granting permission for three nuns to make profession.

❖❖❖❖

1.   By the power that I have from Father Apostolic Visitator, Maestro Fray Jerónimo Gracián de la Madre de Dios,[1] I give permission to Mother Prioress, Ana de San Alberto, to grant profession to Sisters Florencia de los Angeles and Inés de San Alberto and Francisca de la Madre de Dios;[2] and I give them permission to make it.

2.   May it please the Lord that this be for his glory and honor and that he give them all that is fitting for daughters of the Blessed Virgin, our Lady and Patroness, amen.

Dated in St. Joseph's in Avila on the 30th day of April in the year 1578.

Teresa of Jesus, Carmelite nun

1. On 7 July 1578, the nuncio Sega will withdraw all Gracián's powers as visitator.
2. They made their profession on 1 June 1578.

244. To Padre Jerónimo Gracián, Alcalá
Avila, 7 May 1578

Among the items that Teresa informs Gracián of is the effort to reset her arm. The woman from Medina, big and strong, with the help of another woman of similar size, pulled forcefully on Teresa's arm in an effort to reset it. The pain was agonizing.

❧❧❦❦

1.   Jesus be with your paternity, my good *padre*. The day before yesterday I learned that Señora Doña Juana arrived in Valladolid in good health. And on the vigil or feast of Saint Angelus, they gave the habit to Señora Doña María.[1] May it please God to direct this to his own honor and make her very holy. The prioress[2] in Medina also wrote me that they would have gladly given her the habit if she had so desired, but I don't think she would care for that. As I wrote to you, the nuns in Valladolid were very sorry that you did not go there. I already told them that you will go soon, with God's help, and certainly the need for you there is great. Once Tostado[3] leaves, there will be nothing to fear.

2.   I am writing to Padre Mariano[4] that if he comes with the Sicilian he should arrange to have you come with them. For if he wants to reach an agreement on what he says in his letter, your presence will be necessary. I assure you that if what this friar says is true and we take these means, the negotiations with our Father General[5] will most likely be successful. All the

other possibilities seem to entail endless delay, and if after we pursue this course we find that it didn't work out for us, we will still have time. May the Lord guide things well.

3.   If this *padre* doesn't come here, I wish you would arrange to see him. I think that in everything it is necessary that we speak together, even if what you do is right. A short while ago I wrote you at length and so today I am being brief, for today they brought me letters from Caravaca,[6] which I have to answer, and I am also writing to Madrid.

4.   Oh, *mi padre*, I almost forgot! The woman came to cure my arm, for the prioress in Medina did very well in sending her.[7] The cure involved a real struggle both for the woman and for me. I had lost the use of my wrist, for it has been a long time since I fell. So the pain and toil were terrible. Nonetheless, I rejoiced to feel some little part of what our Lord suffered. I think the effort was successful, although the tormenting pain is such that it is difficult to know if the cure is complete. I can move the hand well and lift the arm as far as my head, but it will still take time before everything is all right. Believe me, if this had been delayed just a bit more, I would have ended up crippled. In truth, I would not have been terribly distressed, if God so willed. There were so many people who came to see the woman in my brother's house that one didn't know how to manage them all.[8]

5.   I assure you, *mi padre*, that since your departure from here, sufferings of every kind have had their day. Sometimes it seems, when they come one upon the other, that the body grows tired and the soul fainthearted, although the will, in my opinion, fares well.

God be with you always. Pray for these daughters of yours. Today is the vigil of the Ascension. Doña Guiomar is doing better; she is here.[9]

Your paternity's unworthy daughter,

Teresa of Jesus

1.   Gracian's mother and sister, Juana Dantisco and María Dantisco. The feast of St. Angelus was celebrated by Carmelites on May 5.

2. Inés de Jesús (Tapia).

3. Jerónimo Tostado.

4. Mariano de San Benito. The Sicilian seems to be Padre Mariano di Leone, the general procurator of the Carmelites of the observance in Madrid.

5. Giovanni Baptista Rossi.

6. The Carmelite nuns in Caravaca were still involved in a litigation with the vicar general of the diocese (cf. Ltr. 181, 10).

7. The woman was a bonesetter from Medina sent by Inés de Jesús, the prioress there.

8. Lorenzo de Cepeda gave the woman lodging in his house.

9. Guiomar de Ulloa

245. To Padre Jerónimo Gracián, Alcalá
Avila, 8 May 1578

Teresa intended this letter to be torn up immediately once it was read. In fact, Teresa herself opened the envelope and crossed out a paragraph lest the letter go astray. It contained strong words against Padre Mariano. Gracián saved the letter but the copy of the lost autograph includes nothing of the crossed-out part. Teresa is concerned about the community in Malagón and Padre Antonio's visitation there, and upset over Padre Mariano.

1. Jesus be with your paternity. After having written the letter enclosed with this one,[1] I received today, the feast of the Ascension, your letters that came by way of Toledo. They caused me much distress. I tell you, *mi padre*, that what you mention is a reckless thing. Tear this up right after you read it.

2. You can well imagine the consequences with all his complaining about me of which I am getting mighty tired.[2] Although I love him much, very much so, and he is a holy man, I cannot fail to observe that God has not given him a talent for discernment. Don't you see how much trust he placed in the more unruly nuns?[3] And without further information he wants to do and undo. I am well aware that she doesn't have what it

takes to govern.[4] But her defects are not something that brings dishonor to the order, for it's an in-house affair. I had earlier written them that you would go there and resolve matters, and that they should speak about their temptations with their confessor and not with her.

3.   To want Isabel de Jesús[5] to rule over them and be their subprioress is sheer nonsense. During the few days that they did have her while Brianda was prioress there, these very same nuns were ever telling stories about her and laughing over it all. They will never respect her. She is good, but not suited for that charge. To take away the office from Ana de la Madre de Dios for only a couple of days is foolish and judging by his hurry to have her, Brianda will be back there shortly. It would be hard for me to see her brought back, for with the exception of her being brought there for the purpose of moving on as soon as possible to a new foundation, I greatly fear her being in that place because of *the one who is there*.[6]

4.   That she does nothing for the discalced friars only means that she is following your orders.[7] As for the rest of the gossip, I don't think it has merit. Neither do I regret the way she behaves toward me, for I know her and she is by no means reserved but very straightforward. They must be telling him the opposite of what she says. You already know that Brianda wrote asking me to give her orders not to give anything to any discalced friar. Another nun wrote that they had spent more on the discalced friars than on all their sick nuns, and many of them were sick that year. It seems to me, *mi padre*, that even if St. Clare went there, they would find much to complain about because of the one who is there[8] and their own stubbornness.

5.   As for her not caring for the sick, that is a calumny, for her charity is great.[9] I was very embarrassed, *mi padre*, by her predecessor,[10] for all those things matter little as long as the honor of the house is not involved, especially in Malagón where everybody is passing through.[11] What they are saying about honor is a pretext, for she went to Toledo for her health

on the advice of her doctors. I truly don't know what you can do about this.

6.   It pleases me to observe how Padre Fray Antonio took care to forbid any mention of Brianda, which was the best thing he could do. You should examine the situation carefully, for goodness' sake. The best thing to do would be to bring in someone like Isabel de Santo Domingo[12] along with a good subprioress and remove some of those who are there. You need to write briefly to Padre Fray Antonio not to make any changes until you have carefully considered everything. I will write to him that I cannot do anything until I see what orders you give, and I will disillusion him about certain things.

7.   In regard to the house, I felt sorry, for it is a pity that there has been no one to lament this. They could have built some part by now, and I just wish they would finish two suites of rooms and the enclosure wall. That would prevent all from being lost if the entire work can't be finished now. For they will be better off there, however little there is, than where they are now. Please write to them about this.

8.   I don't know how, *mi padre*, you assigned him to a task in Malagón without first briefing him thoroughly.[13] I admit I feel like a dunce; nonetheless, I think that to remove and replace the superior there and without rhyme or reason brings great discredit to the house. If I thought that N[14] could amend her ways, it would be better for her to resume her office as prioress and finish out her term. But I have lost hope in her ever making amends. And Padre Fray Bartolomé de Jesús, and Fray Francisco de la Concepción, and Antonio Ruiz[15] have so insisted that she not return there that I think it would be rash not to pay heed to them. Please look into this and do as the Lord enlightens you. That is what will be the best thing to do. I will beg him to give you light. But it's most necessary that you warn this father at once and see that Padre Fray Antonio does not make a martyr of that saint,[16] for she certainly is one.

May God be with you always.

Your paternity's unworthy servant,

Teresa of Jesus

9.   I don't think it would be a mortification for Isabel de Santo Domingo to go there. She would bring order back into the house, and Brianda could go to Segovia, or María de San Jerónimo.[17] May God take care of this. As for Isabel de Santo Domingo's health, that region is hot, and since she is so esteemed, the sisters will not dare say anything about her. I reopened this letter to cross out what I said about Mariano lest the letter get lost. I'm very much tried by him.

1.   Letter 244.
2.   It seems she is referring to Padre Antonio de Jesús, always resentful of her. Now he failed by being too credulous in his visitation of the community in Malagón.
3.   The nuns at the Carmel in Malagón.
4.   The president of the community in Malagón, Ana de la Madre de Dios, who was presiding during the absence of the sick prioress, Brianda de San José.
5.   Isabel de Jesús (Gutiérrez), from the Carmel in Malagón; and later novice mistress there.
6.   These words supply for what Teresa later crossed out. She is referring to the licentiate Gaspar de Villanueva, confessor and chaplain for the nuns. The others alluded to are Ana de la Madre de Dios, the interim president; Brianda, the absent prioress. The visitator, Padre Antonio, is in a hurry to bring Brianda back to Malagón.
7.   Gracián had given orders to the nuns' Carmels not to provide meals for the discalced friars.
8.   "The one who is there" is Gaspar de Villanueva.
9.   She is referring to the charity of Ana de la Madre de Dios.
10. Brianda de San José.
11. Malagón was a small town, but on an important main road leading from Castile into Andalusia.
12. The prioress of Segovia, who was formerly prioress in Pastrana and had to deal with the erratic Princess of Eboli.
13. Gracián had given Padre Antonio, without any forewarning, faculties to make the visitation.
14. The "N" was inserted by the copyist in place of the name written by Teresa. She seems to be alluding to Brianda de San José.

15. Bartolomé de Jesús had been Gracián's secretary. Francisco de la Concepción had transferred to the discalced Carmelites from the Carmelites of the observance. Antonio Ruiz was a merchant friend of Teresa's from Malagón.
16. Antonio de Jesús and Ana de la Madre de Dios.
17. María de San Jerónimo (Dávila) had been vicaress at St. Joseph's in Avila during Teresa's absence there.

246. To Padre Jerónimo Gracián, Alcalá
Avila, 14 May 1578

Teresa is worn out by reading and writing letters. The newly-arrived letters from Gracián revive her. Her fears about having to return to the Incarnation as prioress linger. She hopes for a foundation in Madrid.

1.   Jesus be with your paternity. I had already written this enclosed letter and wanted to send it when the discalced brothers arrived and gave me yours. I tell you your letters restored my health. For yesterday evening when I received letters from Malagón I so tired myself out in reading and answering them that my bad cold got much worse. And now yours brought me such delight that I feel much better. May God be blessed who gives you the health to serve him so well and benefit so many souls. This is a tremendous consolation to me. Nonetheless, I would like to see you come here, for since there has been no rainfall in that region, it must certainly be very unhealthy. I don't know what you can do down there that you cannot do here. But the Lord who foresees everything undoubtedly must have waited for this opportunity to benefit those souls. For your presence could not have failed but to bear much fruit.

2.   I forgot to mention in the enclosed letter how displeased I was to learn that Fray Hernando Medina gave the habit to our nun.[1] I don't know what obsesses that little prioress that she thinks she has to satisfy those friars.[2] From the enclosed letter by Fray Angel[3] you will see how they already knew that

you were to come along with your sister. I have been happy that you didn't do so. Now is a much more favorable time to come. I have already written to Ardapilla[4] asking him to urge you to come. In adding some foolish things, I said that you are obliged to come even if you don't want to, that there is no alternative.

3.   I have already thought of how my daughter María de San José could help me get some rest. With her handwriting, ability, and joy, she would be a relief for me.[5] God will be able to bring this about after she makes profession, even though it may not be so easy for young women to fare well with old women. I am even amazed that you do not get tired with me. But God provides for this so that I may bear with the life he gives me, one with so little health and satisfaction, save in this. I also believe that those who care for God's affairs and truly love him cannot but enjoy the company of anyone who desires to serve him.

4.   It would distress me if Ardapilla were to come with his refrain about the Incarnation.[6] I have written to ask you if he has the authority to give me the order to return there, and you do not answer. I want you to know that I will do what I can to refuse, for without the confessors there, and also without a change of obedience, it would be foolish for me to return.[7] But if he obliges me under pain of sin to go, you can see what my situation would be.

5.   For goodness' sake write to me clearly what I must and can do, for these are not things to write about so obscurely. And always pray for me very much for I am now very old and tired, but not in my desires. I will give the sisters your regards. I would like you to come with the prior of Mancera.[8] I tell you, it seems to me that from now on you are wasting your time down there, for this is no longer the season for sermons.

6.   What a stir those nuns are causing over a hundred *reales*.[9] See if I am not right by saying that in these visitations it is necessary to proceed with great care in everything. It is very important that when another superior comes he find nothing to complain

about. I felt disgusted, for the one who gave the *reales*, who was overseeing everything, could well have avoided that so much importance be attached to this. As for Fray Antonio,[10] it doesn't matter, but when he reproaches me for even some small thing that involves my Pablo,[11] I cannot bear it. As for myself, I don't mind.

7.   God watch over you, *mi padre*, for you do me a great favor in getting so fat, as those fathers tell me, despite all your work.

May he be always blessed. Doña Guiomar[12] will be delighted with your letter. She is doing well.

Today is May 14, and I am your paternity's true daughter,

Teresa of Jesus

8.   I hope that all of this I have now written will not do me as much harm as did the letter I wrote to Malagón, but rather good. With regard to founding a monastery in Villanueva,[13] it would in no way be fitting if the Franciscans have become involved. For them it is an appropriate site and they will know how to help the sisters beg. You are right; begging is a terrible thing in these little towns. The foundation in Madrid is the one that is important, and there is a good basis for our being able to make it at once. And believe in the importance of this, and also of giving something to Huerta.[14] We will give you orders about this when you come.

---

1.   Hernando de Medina, a Carmelite of the observance who had tried the life of the discalced friars at Los Remedios in Seville. The nun was María de San José (Dantisco), Gracián's sister.
2.   María Bautista, the prioress of Valladolid. The friars were the Carmelites of the observance.
3.   Angel de Salazar, provincial of the Carmelites of the observance.
4.   The Licentiate Juan Calvo de Padilla.
5.   Gracián's sister having a good handwriting could serve Teresa well as a secretary.

6. The provincial Fray Angel kept wanting Teresa to return to the Incarnation as prioress there.

7. John of the Cross and Fray Germán, the discalced confessors, had been carried off under force as prisoners by the Carmelites of the observance. She did not want to return to the Incarnation without it being first placed under the jurisdiction of the discalced friars.

8. Juan de Jesús (Roca).

9. She is referring to the tightfisted actions of a certain prioress who was asked by Gracián for a hundred *reales* to cover the expenses of his visitation. Although she gave them to him, she did so only as a loan and kept insisting on their repayment.

10. Antonio de Jesús (Heredia).

11. Gracián.

12. Guiomar de Ulloa.

13. Discussions about a foundation in Villanueva de la Jara were underway, but no foundation was made there until 1580.

14. Roque de Huerta, who was handling Teresa's mail and business affairs in Madrid.

247. To Padre Jerónimo Gracián, Alcalá
Avila, 22 May 1578

Teresa states her opinions very frankly on a number of matters: Salazar; John of the Cross's disappearance; Gracián's neglect to communicate with the general; and his burdening of the nuns with more obligations.

1. Jesus be with your paternity. The *padre* who will take this letter is about to leave, and so I can't be long. I very much regret that no one told me last evening that he was departing today. I am better and so is the arm.

2. As for what you had to endure because of the cat,[1] I am amazed that he spoke so unpleasantly of Esperanza.[2] God forgive him. If he were as bad as he says, they certainly wouldn't have tried so hard not to lose him. I am glad you didn't send the letter to Seville.[3] I think it's better to be completely humble in dealing with them, for we truly owe them much, and much

is due to many among them. Judging from what I have seen, I don't think this father is very prudent, so I wouldn't want you to prolong any of your dealings with him.

3.   They have also written me from Toledo where there are many complaints about me. The truth is that I did everything I could, and even more than I should have.[4] And so I have concluded that the reason for the complaining about you and me is our great care not to cause them any displeasure.[5] And I believe that if we had looked only at God and done for his service alone what so good a desire required things would now be more peaceful and everyone happier, for the Lord himself would have smoothed everything over. But when we proceed with human respect, the goal is never reached; in fact the opposite happens, as it now appears. It's as though what he wanted to do was heresy![6] As I told them, they are sorry that it has become known. Certainly, *mi padre*, they, and we too, have had many earthly concerns in this whole affair. Nonetheless, I am happy that things turned out this way. I would want our Lord to be satisfied.

4.   I have already written you about how much the fathers of the Society here are insisting that Padre Mariano come to look at a fountain.[7] They have been pressing him to come for a long time. Now he has written that he will come during the course of this month. I beg you to write and tell him not to fail to keep his promise no matter what, and don't forget.

5.   I am shocked by this imprisonment of Fray John of the Cross[8] and the slow pace of all our negotiations. May God provide a remedy. From Toledo they write me that Tostado[9] has at last gone, although I don't believe it. They say he is leaving Fray Angel[10] in his place.

6.   I don't know what to think about your not coming here. I now see that you are right. But time is passing without anyone being sent to Rome.[11] And we are all lost with hopes that will go on a thousand years. I don't understand what's going on or why Nicolao[12] doesn't go, for this would not impede the other

action. Now I see that you are more careful than anyone, but fulfilling one's obligations toward the general[13] can in no way cause harm, and now is a good time. And if this is not done, I don't think all the rest will be of any lasting help. Diligent efforts are never wrong just because they are many.

7.   It is an excellent idea to name this college St. Joseph.[14] God reward you. This project will be great for the order. With regard to Toledo, things are going very well. The nun is obstinate, and the prioress[15] is foolish in asking you if you want to initiate a lawsuit since the house and a large sum of money are involved. Doña Guiomar[16] was delighted with your letter and I was too. I am not surprised.

8.   That *padre* senses the difference that must be noted in Guadalajara between himself and Paul.[17] The difference between the two persons is very great and the feelings of human nature are strong. I deeply wish you would be strong by treating him graciously, for I find him somewhat high-spirited in his speech. To put up with the weaknesses of each one is very important. May God give us the strength necessary to please him, amen.

9.   I don't know how to answer you in regard to those nuns.[18] Four hundred ducats for twenty! I wouldn't even want six hundred. It's necessary to await the decision of Doña María de Mendoza, who will not fail to do everything well. I deeply regret having to see such things in matters of income.

10.   Antonia[19] told us here about the many ordinances you had made so that we were all scandalized, so I sent to ask you about this. Believe me, *mi padre*, that these houses are doing well, and there is no need to burden them with more observances, for they would find it hard to take on any additional obligations. And don't forget this, but always insist that they keep the constitutions and no more, for they will be doing a lot if they keep them well. In matters concerning the nuns you can trust me, for from what is happening here I see what is going on there. However small the ordinance may be, it becomes burdensome, as it would first of

all for me, unless you were to ordain it in the name of God.

May he preserve you for many years.

Today is May 22.

Your paternity's unworthy servant,

Teresa of Jesus

1. She is probably referring to some Jesuit.
2. Gaspar de Salazar.
3. She is probably alluding to her letter to Salazar (Ltr. 228). Cf. Ltr. 230, note 20.
4. To prevent Salazar from carrying out his desires.
5. The Jesuits.
6. Transfer from the Jesuits to the discalced Carmelites.
7. The Jesuit rector at San Gil was seeking the assistance of Padre Ambrosio Mariano, who was well known for his engineering talents.
8. Five and a half months have passed since John was taken prisoner and they still have no news of his whereabouts.
9. Jerónimo Tostado.
10. Angel de Salazar.
11. In the chapter for discalced friars in Almodovar del Campo, convoked by Gracián, it was decided to send two discalced friars to Rome.
12. The Italian Nicolás Doria seemed a most suitable one to send to Rome.
13. Giovanni Baptista Rossi.
14. The college of the discalced friars in Salamanca. In the end, it was called San Elías.
15. The prioress in Toledo, Ana de los Angeles.
16. Guiomar de Ulloa in Avila.
17. The discalced friar was not the equal of Gracián (Paul) when it came to preaching. Perhaps Teresa is referring to Antonio de Jesús.
18. It seems she is alluding to the lawsuit of the Carmel in Toledo.
19. Antonia del Espíritu Santo (Henao) had returned from the Carmel in Valladolid to Avila.

248. To Madre María de San José, Seville
Avila, 4 June 1578

(Autograph: DCN, Valladolid)

Letters and gifts have once more arrived from Seville and along with them news of community problems: a nun with a mental illness; two nuns who have embarked on suspect paths in their prayer life; and new aspirants. Teresa's health is better and her arm, after the resetting, has improved. But she still suffers from the noises in head. She is earnestly but secretly trying to obtain a collection of sermons for someone.

❧❧❦❦

1.   Jesus. The Holy Spirit be with you, my daughter. I have received your two letters, the one by way of Madrid, the other brought this week by the muleteer who lives here and who is so slow that I get annoyed. All that you sent me is very good and arrived in excellent condition, including the water.[1] It's excellent, but now there's no need for more; this is enough. I was pleased with the little jars you sent; now they suffice. Since I am better, I don't need to be pampered; some day I am going to have to be mortified.

2.   The arm[2] is getting better, although not so that I can dress myself. They say that with the warmer weather it will soon be all right. The box of gifts was well packed, and so too was all the rest. Don't think that I will eat all those preserves. In fact, I don't care for them, but never in my life will I stop wanting to give. Since there is no lack of business matters to be carried out, and the charity of others to lend us help is not as openly ardent as in *mi padre*, the prior of Las Cuevas,[3] or in Padre Garciálvarez,[4] everything is useful.

3.   The design for the little stove[5] was so clear that I don't think a mistake can be made. It is now being manufactured. All the nuns are amazed at your talent and they thank you very much, very much indeed, and I do too. Your love for me is obvious in the way you please me in everything. I really believe this, but I tell you that you even owe me more love, for I am astonished

at how much I love you. Don't think that anyone surpasses you in this respect, for not everyone is to my liking the way you are. The unfortunate thing is that there is little I can do for you, since I am so wretched, but I take great care to recommend you to God.

4. I was disturbed by this heart trouble that you say you have, for it is very painful; and I am not surprised, with all the terrible trials you have suffered and your being very much alone. Even though the Lord has favored us by giving you the virtue and courage necessary to bear them, the body suffers from it. Be glad about one thing: your soul is now much more advanced—and believe me I don't say this just to console you, but because I know it to be so—and this, my daughter, never happens without great cost. The trial you are now going through[6] is terribly distressing to me, for it is something disquieting for all the nuns. It's about time for some improvement. I hope in our Lord that she will be cured, for many afflicted with this illness get better, and it is very important that one allow oneself to be cured. God will provide, for perhaps he wants to give you this cross for a short while and will draw from it much good. I earnestly beg this of him.

5. Take note now of what I am going to say. Try to see her as little as possible, for with your kind of heart trouble it would be so harmful for you that you could end up in bad condition—and note that this is an order. Choose two of the more courageous nuns to attend to her, and the rest should hardly ever see her. They should go about joyfully and be no more disturbed than they would if caring for a sick nun. And in a way they should feel less pity for her, since those who are in this state are less sensitive to suffering than those enduring other illnesses.

6. These days we are reading here of a monastery of our order where St. Euphrasia[7] was a nun and in it was someone like this sister, and she was submissive only to this saint who in the end cured her. Perhaps there might be someone there whom she would fear. If in these monasteries there were no trials arising from poor health, we would have heaven on earth

and no way to gain merit. Perhaps a thrashing will get her to stop screaming. This wouldn't do her any harm. You do well to keep her in a safe place. I have wondered if she isn't too sanguine, for I believe she was suffering from back pains. May God cure her.

7.   Know that even though these are painful things to have to bear, they are nothing in comparison with the suffering I would go through if I observed there imperfections or restless souls, and since that is not the case, I don't get too disturbed over bodily illnesses. You already know that if you want to rejoice in the Crucified One you have to suffer the cross. It's not necessary that you ask for this—even though Padre Fray Gregorio[8] thinks it fitting—because His Majesty leads those whom he loves along the same path as he did his Son.

8.   The other day I wrote to Father Prior of Las Cuevas. Give him my best regards, and read this that I am writing to Padre Garciálvarez, and if you think it's all right give it to him. The condition of my head—still filled with noises, although a little better—keeps me from always writing to them, for I love them very much. Continue remembering me to them.

9.   I was delighted that our *padre* gave orders that the two nuns who are so deep into prayer eat meat.[9] You ought to know, my daughter, that it occurred to me that if I had them near they wouldn't cause so much commotion. The fact that the graces received by them are so plentiful makes me wary. Even though some favors may be true, I think the proper thing to do is pay little attention to them, and neither should you nor our *padre*[10] give them much importance; rather, make little of them. And even when they are true, nothing is lost by so behaving. When I say "make little of them" I mean tell the two nuns that God leads some souls in one way and others in another and that this is not the path that leads to the greatest holiness, and that is the truth.

10.   I was happy with what Acosta[11] said and that he has such a good opinion of her. I wouldn't want him to speak much with

her so that he not lose it if something does not come about, as happened to me in her regard. I do not say that she lost merit in my eyes, for I know well that even though the grace is often from God, sometimes her experience may be the fruit of her own imagination. I have forgotten when that which the other nun predicted is to come about. Let me know whether it turns out to be true or false, for with this carrier the letters are safe. Now it occurs to me that it would not be good for me to respond to Garciálvarez until you let me know whether he knows anything about these matters so that I might write him about them, but give him my best regards and tell him that I was happy to receive his letter and that I will answer him.

11. As for those two nuns who want to enter,[12] be very careful about what you do. It's good that Padre Nicolao[13] is satisfied with them. Our *padre*, please God, will be down there in September, and perhaps before since he has already received his orders—as you will surely know, being there; do whatever he tells you.[14] I truly regret having to see him among those people. How necessary prayer is. All the sisters send their warm regards.

12. Oh, Teresa,[15] how she jumped up and down at receiving what you sent her! It's extraordinary, the love she has for you. I believe she would leave her own father to follow you. The older she gets the more she grows in virtue, and she is a very discreet little one. She now receives communion, and with no little devotion. But my head is getting tired, so I'll say nothing more other than may God watch over you, as I beg of him.

13. My best regards to all the nuns and to the Portuguese sister and her mother.[16] Try to avoid stress and tell me how you are doing with your heart trouble. The orange-flower oil is very good. For several days my heart has been better, for after all the Lord does not want to give so many ills all at once.

Today is 4 June.

14. Look at what I beg of you in the enclosed note, or better, order you to do for the love of the Lord. You must act with great attentiveness, for it is something I was entrusted with by

a person to whom I am very much obliged. I told him that if you do not manage to carry out the task, no other person will, and that I consider you skillful and lucky in carrying through on what you undertake. Set about this task with the greatest care, and you will make me very happy. Perhaps Father Prior of Las Cuevas will be able to do something, although the one whom I trust most is Padre Garciálvarez. It seems difficult, but when God wills a thing all becomes easy. This would be a wonderful consolation for me; and I even believe it would be of great service to our Lord since it is for the benefit of souls and will bring harm to no one.

15.   What you need to get is a whole year of sermons preached by Padre Salucio[17] of the order of St. Dominic, the best that can be had. And if you can't get so many, get as many as possible, provided they are very good. A year of sermons includes those for Lent, Advent, feasts of our Lord and our Lady, the saints for the year, and Sundays from Epiphany to Advent, and Pentecost to Advent.

16.   I was asked to keep this mission a secret, so I wouldn't like you to speak about it save to those who can be of help to you. Please God you will have good luck in this, and if you send the sermons to me, do so with this man and pay a good portage, and always address your letters to San José while I am here, which is better than addressing them to my brother,[18] even though they be for him; this is the safest thing to do in case he is away. Well, since you can't send all the sermons, send as many as you can. The good things that Padre Garciálvarez and Padre Fray Gregorio say about you and your daughters is a great consolation for me—as though being your confessors they could say otherwise! Please God what they say is true.

Your reverence's servant,

Teresa of Jesus

1.   The orange-flower water, which she asked for in Ltr. 237.5.

2.   Her left arm, which had been broken or dislocated on 24 December 1577 and reset by a bonesetter the previous month.

3. Hernando Pantoja.
4. The community confessor.
5. The precise design was sent through Lorenzo de Cepeda (see Ltr. 238.9).
6. One of the nuns in the community is mentally ill.
7. In Surio's *Vitae Sanctorum* (Toledo, 1578), St. Euphrasia is reported to have cured a nun of mental illness. "When the nun was in a frenzy, the others only needed to say 'Look, Euphrasia will come and whip you,' and she would be as gentle as a lamb."
8. Gregorio Nacianceno.
9. The two were probably Isabel de San Jerónimo and Beatriz de la Madre de Dios (see Ltr. 188).
10. Jerónimo Gracián.
11. Diego de Acosta, a Jesuit in Seville whom Teresa admired.
12. Perhaps Inés de San Eliseo and María de San Pablo, both from Seville.
13. Nicolás Doria, then a novice in the discalced novitiate, Los Remedios, in Seville.
14. Despite the opposition of the new nuncio, Felipe Sega, Philip II intervened and Gracián received orders to take up once again his task as visitator.
15. Her niece Teresita, 11 years old at the time and living at St. Joseph's in Avila.
16. Blanca de Jesús; her mother, Leonor Valera.
17. Agustín de Salucio, an Andalusian, professor at Prime in the Major College of Santo Tomás in Seville and a renowned preacher.
18. Lorenzo de Cepeda.

249. To Padre Gonzalo Dávila, Avila

Avila, summer 1578

The rector of the College of San Gil was very busy but also sick. In an earlier conversation he had discussed with Teresa how one should handle exterior tasks so as not to harm one's interior life. Teresa's words gave rise to a humble letter from the rector asking for spiritual instructions, to which she here responds. The reference to the spring enables us to date this

*letter as being written sometime between mid-May (Ltr. 247.4)
and 19 August (Ltr. 258.7).*

❖ ❖ ❖ ❖

1.   Jesus be with your honor. It has been a long while since
I have been mortified as much as I was today with your letter.
For I am not so humble as to want to be considered so proud,
neither should you want to show your humility at such a cost
to me. I have never desired so eagerly to tear up a letter from
you. I tell you that you know well how to mortify me and make
me understand what I am, for it seems to you that I think that
by myself I am able to teach. God deliver me! I wouldn't even
want to think of such a thing. But I realize the fault is mine,
while not knowing whether the greater fault may be my desire
to see you in good health. My foolish remarks could arise from
this weakness and the love I have for you, a love that makes
me speak freely, without reflecting on my words, so much so
that I too felt scruples afterward about some of the things I
spoke of with you. Were it not for feeling scruples about being
disobedient, I would not respond to your request, for I feel very
disinclined to do this. May God accept what I say, amen.

2.   One of my great errors is to judge these matters of prayer
from my own experience, and so you don't have to pay any attention to what I say. God will give you other talents than what
he gives to a poor little woman like me. Although the Lord has
given me the grace of experiencing him actually present, I find
that I am loaded down with things needing my direct attention—and neither persecutions nor trials would be as much an
impediment. If these things are such that I can do them quickly,
it very often happens that I don't get to bed until 1 or 2 AM, or
even later. But afterward the soul is not obliged to attend to
any other cares but only to the One whose presence it enjoys.
This has done serious harm to my health, and so it must be a
temptation, although it seems to me the soul remains freer, as
when one has a very important and necessary business matter

and finishes up with other things quickly so that they will in no way hinder what one understands to be the more important thing. And so I am most happy to leave all that I can for the sisters to do, even if it could be done better by me. But since that is not my goal, His Majesty makes up for it. I find myself notably more advanced in the interior life the more I try to withdraw from things. Even though I see this clearly, I often neglect to do it, and I certainly feel the harm and see that I could do more and be more diligent in this regard and find myself improved.

3.   With this I am not speaking of serious things that one cannot avoid, and my error must also consist in this, for your duties are serious and it would be bad for you to leave them for someone else to do; of this I am convinced, although when I see you sick, I wish you had less work. Indeed it makes me praise our Lord to observe how diligently you attend to the affairs of your house. I am not so foolish as to fail to recognize God's great favor toward you in giving you this talent and the great merit you gain. It makes me very envious, for I wish my superior were like you. Now that God has given you to me as my superior, I would like you to take as much interest in my soul as you do in the spring,[1] something that really amused me. But it is something so necessary for the monastery, that everything you do in that regard is worth it.

4.   Nothing more remains to be said. Indeed, I speak to you in complete truthfulness as I do with God, and I understand that all one does to carry out well the office of superior is so pleasing to God that after a short time he gives the person so occupied as much as he gives to another after a long time. And I know this also through experience, as I mentioned before. But I always see you so busy that I suddenly got the idea to speak to you as I did. The more I think of it, the more I see, as I told you, how there is a difference between you and me. I will try to correct myself so as not to speak on impulse, for this costs me so dearly. As soon as I see you in good health, my temptation will cease. May God bring this about, as he can and as I desire.

Your honor's subject,

Teresa of Jesus

1. She is referring to a spring to provide water for the College of San
   Gil. The rector had asked for a helping hand from Padre Ambrosio
   Mariano de San Benito (Ltr. 247.4). Teresa had transferred the request
   to Gracián (Ltrs. 247 & 258).

250. To Padre Domingo Báñez, Salamanca
Avila, 28 July 1578

*Padre Báñez had been thinking of spending his vacation
in Avila, but Teresa advises against it. The times are difficult for
her discalced friars and nuns. Her arm, though better, is still a
problem for her.*

1. Jesus. May the Holy Spirit be with your honor, *mi padre*.
I received your letter and with it your kindness and charity as
always; of these you have shown me so much that I don't know
what to say other than beseech God to repay you for them and
for everything else.

2. As regards your visit here, I tell you that I felt so sorry to
see you in the company of someone who caused you so much
grief and to see the poor health you suffered while here. Save
for a great need I would not have begged you to take a vacation at such a cost to yourself so as to please me. Now I have
no need, glory to God, although business matters and troubles
are never lacking and prevent me from enjoying the rest that
I would like. So rather, I beg you not to come, but to consider
where you would be happiest and go there, for one who works
the entire year has need of such a thing. Besides if Father Visitator[1] should decide to come while you are here, I wouldn't have
much chance to enjoy your company.

3. Believe me, *mi padre*, I have understood that the Lord
doesn't want me to have anything in this life but crosses and

more crosses. And what is worse is that all those who desire to comfort me end up sharing in them, for I see that he wishes to torment me even in this way. May he be blessed for everything.

4.   I deeply regret Padre Padilla's[2] misfortune, for I hold him to be a servant of God. May it please the Lord to make the truth known. For anyone who has so many enemies undergoes much tribulation, and we all run this same risk.[3] But it is only a small thing to lose one's life and honor for love of so good a Lord. Always recommend us to him, for I tell you everything is in chaos.

5.   My health is fair. Although the arm is always crippled,[4] for I cannot dress myself, it is getting better, and I would like to be getting better in loving God.

May His Majesty watch over your honor and give you all the holiness that I beg of him, amen.

Today is July 28.

Your honor's unworthy servant and true daughter,

Teresa of Jesus

6.   All these servants of yours[5] entrust themselves very much to your prayers. Don't give your consent for the prioress[6] to stop eating meat, and tell her to take care of her health.

---

1. Jerónimo Gracián, although a few days before, on July 23, the nuncio Felipe Sega had taken away his powers and annulled all his decisions.
2. Juan Calvo de Padilla had been imprisoned by the Inquisition on 27 June 1578.
3. Teresa sensed that she herself could end up in the hands of the Inquisition.
4. Her arm had been impaired since Christmas eve 1577.
5. The discalced nuns at St. Joseph's in Avila.
6. The prioress in Salamanca, Ana de la Encarnación.

251. To Sister María de Jesús, Toledo
Avila, end of July 1578

This fragment comes from Madre María Evangelista's (Toledo) testimony for the cause of Blessed María de Jesús. The text is not certain, although its content is.

✣✣✣✣

I already know what is taking place there and that Christ our Lord and his most Blessed Mother have ordered you to subsidize two feasts, one in honor of the Blessed Sacrament and the other in honor of the Nativity of Our Lady. Do so, for this is pleasing to God and I take special pleasure in it.

252. To Padre Jerónimo Gracián, Peñaranda (?)
Avila, August 1578

These two fragments (1–2; 3–4) seem to belong to one letter. They reflect the situation brought on by the nuncio Sega's brief of 28 July 1578, which stripped Gracián of all his powers for having exercised them "arrogantly" and "scandalously." Counseled by his ecclesiastical friends, Gracián avoided an authoritative notification of the brief's contents.

✣✣✣✣

1.   May the Holy Spirit be with your paternity, *mi padre*, and give you strength to undergo this battle, for nowadays there are few whom the Lord allows the devils and the world to attack so furiously.

2.   May his name be blessed, for he has willed that you gain so many merits all together. I tell you that if our nature were not so sensitive, reason would make us well understand the great motive we have for rejoicing. I am relieved to know that you do not fear excommunication, although I never thought that you could be excommunicated …

3.   May God watch over you and allow me to see you one day at a calm moment, if only for us to encourage each other so as to return to suffering. All the nuns send their best regards.

4.   Please God you will respond to everything, for you have become very Biscayan.[1] I know that there are reasons, but since this brings me so much suffering none of them suffices.

1.   The Biscayans had the reputation of being reserved and taciturn.

253. To Doña Juana de Ahumada, Alba
   Avila, 8 August 1578

(Autograph: DCF, Alba de Tormes)

In this letter to her sister Juana, the trials "here and there" refer to both those in Juana's family (fear that Gonzalo will leave for America and worry over financial problems) and also those her discalced friars and nuns must bear under the new nuncio Sega.

❖·❖·❖·❖

1.   Jesus be with your honor. Whether here or there, God gives us all trials; may he be ever blessed. You ought not grieve over the departure of Don Gonzalo with Lorencico, for my brother will not give his consent nor does he think it opportune.[1] I did not write to him because the servant lad had left by the time they gave me the letter. Now I am praying for both boys.

2.   You should know that our trials of every kind at this time have reached a peak, for we have received a counter-brief and now must all remain subject to the nuncio.[2] It doesn't distress me very much, for it seems perhaps to be a better path toward our becoming a province; and we will not have to see Padre Gracián among those people.[3]

3.   I am in such a hurry that I don't even know how I am managing to write this, for I am sending some counsels to those houses there. I only ask that they pray for me. I am my usual self, for trials are health and medicine for me.

4.   Many greetings to Señor Juan de Ovalle and to Doña Beatriz; the nuns here send their greetings to you. My brothers are well. They still don't know that Pedro is going there.[4]

It is August 8, and I am yours,

Teresa of Jesus

1.   Gonzalo (Juana's son) and Lorencico (Lorenzo's son) were planning a trip to Peru. By royal certificate, 1 June 1578, the rights of Lorenzo to territories in the Indies passed to Lorencico, who was 16. According to the plan Gonzalo was going to accompany his cousin. Only two years later did Lorencico embark, and then without his cousin.

2.   The trials were those of the discalced friars and nuns. The nuncio Felipe Sega in a counter-brief withdrew the faculties granted to Gracián by Ormaneto, the previous nuncio on 8 August 1575.

3.   The Carmelites of the observance for whom Gracián had been appointed visitator.

4.   Her brothers are Lorenzo and Pedro residing in Avila. Pedro Ries was a faithful helper of hers.

254. To Padre Jerónimo Gracián, Peñaranda (?)

Avila, 9 August 1578

This letter changes at midpoint when a brief from Felipe Sega arrives at the monastery revoking Gracián's faculties. Roque de Huerta had already sent some confusing news about the brief. According to him, Gracián was to report at once to Madrid. Meanwhile, Sega's delegates were looking for Gracián so as to deliver the brief to him and demand under pain of excommunication that he hand over all documentation granting him powers as visitator. To avoid reception of the brief, Gracián was in hiding and had sent the documentation concerning his faculties as visitator to the royal council. Teresa is afraid he will be taken prisoner like St. John of the Cross. Although the brief was sent to the prioress, Teresa quickly learned of its contents, and then the tone of her letter changes. The letter is

*purposely vague at times, and the meaning of the code words
is not always certain.*

❖❖❖❖

1.　Jesus be with your paternity, *mi padre*. Yesterday I wrote
to you by way of Mancera and I sent the letter to the subprior[1]
asking him to inquire whether you are in Peñaranda, as you
wrote that you would be, and not to let anyone know, even if
he be a friar, but to keep the matter to himself. And I included
two letters from Roque[2] in which he insists very much that you
go immediately to Madrid. Even though he says he is writing
to you, I fear that his letters will be intercepted, and so I am
writing you myself about what is taking place. If by chance you
did not go where you told me you were going, I am sending
another messenger to Valladolid and informing Mother Prioress[3] about how she should respond. Roque is very insistent that
nothing different be said, for that would be our ruin. He sent
me in writing what was sent to her. I have informed the other
monasteries. Please God, there will be no need for this, for it
is sad to see these souls entrusted to someone who doesn't
understand them.[4]

2.　Nonetheless, the only thing that worries and distresses
me is what concerns my Pablo.[5] If only I could see him free.
Certainly, I don't know why, but even were I to want to feel
disturbed about the rest of things, I could not. The Lord will
provide. I would be happy if you stayed up here and didn't go
down there.[6] But I am very afraid, for even in your going back
and forth to say Mass you cannot avoid danger.

3.　I am afraid of how things are going and wish you were
gone from there and in a safe place. And let me know where
you are, for goodness' sake, so that I don't carry on like a dunce
on the day I have to inform you about something, as I am now
doing with your code words, which you changed without letting
me know the meaning. I deeply wish you would travel with a
companion, even if he be a lay brother.

4.   Yesterday the prior of Santo Tomás[7] was here. He doesn't think it a bad idea that before going to Madrid you wait for the answer from Joannes[8] to see how everything went, and the rector[9] agrees and so does my brother.[10] I told them that you had written to Joannes. Since the briefs are delivered to the president,[11] I don't see any reason to hurry. There are only two reasons that prompt me to want you to go: First, a great fear that they will take you captive here, and if that were the case (God deliver you!), it would be better for you to go. Second, it would be good to know what the nuncio intends to do with you before you go to see the king. Nonetheless, it would be fitting that your meeting with the nuncio take place in the presence of the president.

5.   I wrote this to you in a letter yesterday. There you will see that I believe the Lord will give you light for this since he gives you peace with which to bear it, as I saw from your talks with him. What is happening is that last Sunday, which was the third of this month, Padre Mariano[12] was notified by a brief, which, as I understand, was the same as the one they brought there, although Roque[13] didn't explain much. He only says that it is very wordy and revokes what the previous nuncio did.[14] It must be the same brief you mention, but they don't understand it. And he says it is from the pope, but it must be only from the nuncio because in his reply Padre Mariano says he will obey the orders of the nuncio. Roque says they told him in it not to consider you his superior and to obey no one but the nuncio.

6.   I'm delighted about this, and perhaps he[15] will not give as free a hand to these wolves[16] as they think and after all will want to please the king. I don't hesitate to believe what you say about their seeking to put an end to the reforms, and nothing would make me happier than to see you freed from the task, for after that everything will turn out well.

7.   Here they haven't notified us of anything, nor have they in Mancera[17] because the provincial[18] hasn't left Avila. They must have to wait for something. Roque says that all monasteries

must be notified of the brief and he doesn't say whether this includes those of the friars or not. I already wrote to the prioress in Alba[19] to accept that sister and to Teresa de Layz[20] to give her approval. I am so consoled that God favors you with moments of happiness in the midst of so many trials that I don't know how I could feel sad.

8.   I was at this point when the Reverend Padre Rioja[21] arrived at the door with a notary to give notification of the brief. They didn't call me but Mother Prioress.[22] From what I understand of the brief it is the same as the one they must have brought there,[23] for they say it is now under consideration by the royal council. God forgive me, for I am still unable to believe that the nuncio ordered such a thing, I mean in that style.[24] Had you not followed the counsel of so many learned men, I would not be surprised that you were very distressed. But since you proceeded so justly in everything and since you waited almost a year without making any visitations until you knew that the nuncio stated that the faculties had not been revoked,[25] I don't know how one can speak like this. In a certain way, although this distresses me very much, I am inspired with devotion since I know with what prudence you proceeded in the midst of so much wickedness. I tell you, *mi padre*, God loves you very much and that you are advancing well in imitation of him. I am very happy because God gives you what you ask for, which are trials, and God will come to your defense since he is just. May he be blessed for everything.

9.   All the learned men here say that even though the nuncio gives you orders you are not obliged to obey since he does not show the patent letters that support his authority. Oh, what precious treasures these trials are, *mi padre*! They cannot be bought for any price because through them such a great crown is won. When I recall that our Lord himself and all his saints walked this path, all I can do is envy you, for now I don't deserve suffering, unless it is to feel what one whom I truly love suffers, which is a much greater trial.

10.   Tomorrow we will work out an agreement on how Padre Julián de Avila[26] will go to Madrid to show the nuncio our recognition of him as superior and win his favor so as to beseech him not to place us under the jurisdiction of the calced friars. I in turn will write to some persons to get them to try to placate him in your regard and explain how you didn't make any moves until you learned what he said and that you would be ever eager to obey him if it were not for the certitude that Tostado is out to destroy us.[27] Certainly I can sincerely express satisfaction because in exchange for not being subject to the friars of the cloth,[28] everything seems acceptable to me.

11.   Julián will ask him for the permissions necessary for these monasteries, such as permission for workmen to enter inside, and things of that sort, for I've been told that as soon as obedience is rendered to him, he immediately becomes our superior.

12.   May the Lord grant us his favor, for they cannot oblige us to offend him. The saintly Paul[29] remains at home with me and no one can take away what I promised this saint.[30]

13.   The sisters[31] here have regretted the brief most of all because of what it says about you, and they send their best regards and are praying hard for you. There is nothing to fear, *mi padre*, but praise God that he leads us by the path he followed. May His Majesty keep you for me and be pleased to grant that I may see you free of these conflicts.

Today is the vigil of St. Lawrence.

Your unworthy servant and true daughter,

Teresa of Jesus

---

1.   The subprior of the discalced friars in Mancera, Francisco de la Concepción. The prior, Juan de Jesús Roca, was in Madrid.
2.   Roque de Huerta, her friend who acted as her agent for her business matters in Madrid.
3.   María Bautista, the prioress in Valladolid.
4.   Who doesn't understand the way of life she established for her Carmels.

5. Gracián.
6. From Peñaranda (near Avila) down to Madrid.
7. The Dominican monastery in Avila.
8. An uncertain code name. It probably refers to Juan de Jesús Roca secretly carrying out business for the discalced Carmelites.
9. The rector of the Jesuit college of San Gil in Avila, Gonzalo Dávila.
10. Lorenzo de Cepeda.
11. The briefs that gave Gracián faculties to be visitator. The president of the royal council was A. Mauricio Pazos.
12. Ambrosio Mariano de San Benito.
13. Roque de Huerta.
14. The powers given Gracián by the previous nuncio, Nicolás Ormaneto, were revoked.
15. Felipe Sega.
16. Code name for the Carmelites of the observance.
17. Neither the discalced nuns in Avila nor the discalced friars in Mancera were yet notified of Sega's brief.
18. Juan Gutiérrez de la Magdalena, provincial of the Carmelites of the observance in Castile.
19. Juana del Espíritu Santo.
20. The founding benefactress of the Carmel in Alba de Tormes.
21. A Carmelite friar of the observance in Castile.
22. María de Cristo, prioress of St. Joseph's in Avila.
23. The brief that revoked Gracian's faculties and which was sent to notify him probably to either Valladolid or Peñaranda.
24. Teresa was justifiably shocked by the tone of the document (see the brief in MHCT II, 20–25).
25. Felipe Sega had stated that he had not revoked Gracian's faculties as visitator (see Ltr. 262.4). In the brief he accused Gracián of presumption, arrogance, and insolence for using them.
26. The chaplain at St. Joseph's.
27. Jerónimo Tostado was the Carmelite general's vicar in Spain. Teresa figured that Sega was trying to get him to make visitations of the discalced Carmelites.
28. The Carmelites of the observance.
29. Gracián.
30. Allusion to her vow of obedience (see ST. 36).
31. The Carmelite nuns at St. Joseph's in Avila.

255. To Roque de Huerta, Madrid
Avila, 9 (?) August 1578

Stripping Gracián of his powers, the nuncio ordered him to appear before him "under pain of excommunication and suspension." Before doing so, Gracián passed through Avila and sought an audience with the king at the Escorial.

To the very magnificent Señor Roque de Huerta, chief forest guard of his majesty.

I think this is the day he[1] must speak to the king, for he arrived at the Escorial[2] yesterday. Watch carefully that if he is placed under the authority of the nuncio[3] his safety will be guaranteed. For I see that many things are being done that have no legal backing. It's necessary to insist on the matter of our becoming a province ...[4] brother, I beg you to place the enclosed in his very hands.

---

1. Padre Gracián.
2. The king arrived at the Escorial on 8 August.
3. Felipe Sega.
4. Teresa desired that the discalced friars and nuns become a separate province within the order. Something is missing here because of damage to the text.

256. To Padre Jerónimo Gracián, Madrid
Avila, 14 August 1578

(Autograph fragment: DCN , Cabrera [Salamanca])

Two days previous to this letter, Gracián passed through Avila incognito and depressed. But now a copy of the royal stipulation arrived, which withdrew the nuncio Sega's brief of 23 July 1578. This meant that the king and the royal council sided with Gracián. Yet, Teresa longs for him to be free of his charge as visitator.

❖❖❖❖

For our Father Visitator, Maestro Fray Jerónimo Gracián de la Madre de Dios; hand deliver.

1.   The grace of the Holy Spirit be with your paternity, *mi padre*. If you had not passed through here,[1] I would have merited little from these trials, because they caused me almost no suffering, but afterward I paid for everything at once. I tell you I was so moved to see you that all day yesterday, Wednesday, my heart was in anguish not knowing what to do at seeing you so afflicted, and rightly so, on being in such danger in everything and constrained to go about in hiding like a criminal. But my trust in a good outcome does not leave me for a moment. The fact is, *mi padre*, that God has found a good means for me to suffer in desiring that the blows strike where they hurt me most.

2.   Today, the vigil of our Lady, the good Roque[2] sent me a copy of the ordinance, which consoled us greatly. Since the king takes the position he does, you will be free of danger, which is what was tormenting all of us nuns. As for all the rest, I see much courage in these sisters. The Lord has willed that my pain not last long, and it was lucky that you left when you did and went by way of the Escorial.

3.   By means of this messenger, whose name is Pedro, you can tell me what happened and what is happening in every respect.[3] Let Valladolid know, for they are disturbed.[4] They sent a messenger once they learned what happened to Padre Fray Juan de Jesús.[5]

4.   Moreover, don't forget to see if you can do anything for Fray John of the Cross[6] and to let me know if it would be opportune for us to send someone to the nuncio[7] so that he witness a certain obedience on the part of the discalced Carmelites, since we have in fact given him our obedience. We will also look into these matters here and do what seems best in the

event that you are not there. After we have obeyed, doing this will not be harmful to the justice of our cause. Today I received letters from Valladolid and Medina. They have not received any notification.[8] These brothers of mine must have known what was happening here, for I don't believe they were just being lazy.

5.   *Mi padre*, I am very worried that in this ordinance[9] and in all this turmoil no visitator is named other than *mi padre* Gracián. I would not want anything to come from Rome against him. So it seems to me you ought to recall the light that Paul saw—for it seems it was confirmed by what Angela saw[10]—and withdraw as much as you can from this fire, as long as you don't anger the king, and no matter what Padre Mariano tells you.[11] Your conscience is not of the kind that can adapt to contrary opinions.[12] In fact even when there is nothing to fear you go about in torment, as has happened these past days; and everyone will approve of what you do. Let them manage their own battles.

6.   Once everything is very settled and secure, you will be doing a great deal by exposing yourself to danger without having scruples to add to it. I tell you certainly that the greatest distress I have felt in this turmoil is the fear, hidden I don't know where in me, that you will not be freed of your charge as visitator. If the Lord wills this, he will watch over you as he has up to now, but I will not be free of torment.

7.   For you to withdraw as I have mentioned, your sound judgment will be necessary so that you don't appear to be afraid of anything other than offending God, and that is true. And if you should speak with the nuncio, defend your position if he is willing to listen and explain that you will be always happy to obey him, and that you accepted that charge because you knew that Tostado[13] wanted to cut short the reform that has been started and that he could inquire about how we are living and things of that sort. Take advantage of every opportunity to speak about our becoming a separate province[14] and the required conditions. For everything depends on this, and the reform as well.

8.   You must speak with the king, the president, the archbishop[15] and all explaining to them the scandals and battles
that arise when this is not done, especially with these friars in
Castile.[16] Since they have no visitator or means for safeguarding
justice, they do whatever they want. You will know how to say
it better, for it's foolish of me to be putting this down here, but
all your other cares might cause you to forget. I don't know if
Pedro[17] will be the one bringing this, for he can't find a mule. In
any event the messenger will be a safe one. Keep me informed
about everything, for goodness' sake, even though you have
little time, and tell me how Padre Mariano is.

9.   The sisters here entrust themselves very much to your
prayers. Were you to know how concerned they are about
you in your sufferings, you would be pleased, and their praise
is all for you, *mi padre*. I regret that we sent a messenger[18] to
the sisters in Beas and Caravaca. They must be distressed,
and they will not be able to know anything further for a while,
even though our letters were filled with hope, except for what
referred to your suffering so that they would pray harder to God
for you. If there is someone in those parts who can inform them,
tell Roque,[19] for charity's sake. Yesterday I sent him 50 ducats
and today the remainder of the 1,000 *reales*. I am very sorry
you have to remain there in this heat and go hungry. Since it
will take a long time for these affairs to be settled, it might be
good if you came to Mancera. Consider this, out of charity, for
we would be closer.

10.   Let me know what has happened with those from Pastrana who were imprisoned.[20] Oh, if your visit to me could be
repeated so as to repair the torment caused by the previous
one. May God bring this to pass and grant me the favor of seeing you in a situation in which I don't have to go about with so
many fears, amen.

It is the feast of the vigil of our Lady of August. After all, on her
feast days trials and consolations come as her gifts.[21]

Your paternity's unworthy subject and daughter,

Teresa of Jesus

1. Gracián stayed in Avila on 11 and 12 August on his way to the Escorial, one of the king's palaces.
2. Roque de Huerta brought a copy of the Royal Council's order (8 August 1578) that Gracián continue his visitation. This contradicted the nuncio Sega's order (7 July 1578).
3. Pedro Ries, one of Teresa's messengers, could bring back news about Gracián's visit with the king.
4. The Carmelite nuns in Valladolid, among whom was Gracián's sister, María de San José.
5. The prior of Mancera. On account of difficulties with the diocesan curia of Valladolid, he had recourse to the nuncio Sega, who, without giving him a hearing, jailed him in the Carmelite monastery in Madrid.
6. He was still a prisoner in Toledo but would escape a few days afterward.
7. Felipe Sega.
8. They had not received notice of Sega's brief.
9. The ordinance of the royal council.
10. Paul is Gracián and Angela, Teresa. This may refer to what she recounts in ST. 33.
11. Ambrosio Mariano was always inclined to act more forcefully.
12. Sega forbade him to continue making visitations, and the king ordered him to do so.
13. Jerónimo Tostado, vicar general for the Carmelites in Spain.
14. She wanted a separate province for the discalced Carmelites.
15. The king, Philip II; the president of the royal council, Antonio Mauricio de Pazos; the Archbishop of Toledo, Gaspar de Quiroga.
16. The Carmelites of the observance.
17. Pedro Ries, one of Teresa's faithful helpers.
18. A messenger to notify them of the contents of the brief (see Ltr. 254).
19. Roque de Huerta.
20. Probably, discalced Carmelites who were being punished by the nuncio.
21. It was the vigil of the feast of the Assumption of the Blessed Virgin Mary. She is alluding to a dangerous situation Gracián encountered

in Seville on the feast of the Presentation of Our Lady in the Temple (21 November 1578).

257. To M. Anne of Jesus, Beas
Avila, August 1578 (?)

This fragment was passed on by Jerónimo de San José, St. John of the Cross's biographer. It probably corresponds with John's final days of imprisonment in Toledo before his escape during the octave of the Assumption in 1578. He was later to enter into a deep spiritual relationship with Anne of Jesus, which is revealed in his prologue to the Spiritual Canticle.

You will not believe, daughter, the pain I suffer because of the disappearance of *mi padre* Fray John of the Cross. We find no trace of him and have no light as to his whereabouts. These calced fathers are making every effort to put an end to this reform. For the love of God I beg you, since you and my daughter Catalina de Jesús[1] commune so familiarly with our good Jesus, to beg him to favor and help us. For this intention recite the litany in choir for fifteen days. And during these days, in addition to the hours of prayer you have, add another hour. And inform me, daughter, of how you are implementing this.

---

1. Catalina de Jesús (Sandoval) was one of the founding patrons of the Carmel in Beas and a future directee of St. John of the Cross.

258. To Padre Jerónimo Gracián, Madrid
Avila, 19 August 1578

At the time of this letter the situation of Gracián, safely hidden in Madrid, is better, yet Teresa has her worries about him and longs that the discalced Carmelites may have rule over themselves as a separate province. As for other matters, she doesn't know that John of the Cross has escaped from prison in Toledo. The Carmelite general who doesn't respond to

Teresa wrote a discouraging letter to a nun at the Incarnation, and she had to calm the Carmelite nuns in Medina who were frightened by the arrival of Valdemoro. Finally, she seeks the help of Mariano for the Jesuits in Avila.

❧ ❧ ❧ ❧

For *mi padre*, Maestro Fray Jerónimo Gracián de la Madre de Dios, hand deliver.

1.　　Jesus. The grace of the Holy spirit be with your paternity, *mi padre*. We greatly rejoiced over the letter that Pedro[1] brought filled with hopeful news of good things which, it seems, will not fail to be realized. May our Lord provide in the way by which he will be best served. Nonetheless, until I know that Paul[2] has spoken to Methuselah[3] and how the meeting went I will not be without worry. For goodness' sake when you get news of it, write to me.

2.　　I felt very sorry about the death of so Catholic a king as was the King of Portugal and angry with those who allowed him to get into such danger.[4] Everywhere we turn the world lets us know that we cannot be sure of any happiness unless we seek it in suffering.

3.　　In every possible way or, if you will, under whatever conditions strive that we be made a separate province. Even though other trials will not be lacking, it will mean a lot to have security. If, then, those of the cloth[5] also urge the nuncio in this regard—for I think they would willingly do so—it would be wonderful. I would not like it if you stopped trying, for if the nuncio sees that no one is opposed he will do so willingly.

4.　　We were very amused by his response to the calced friars on the action they were to undertake in Medina and on how they might persuade the nuns[6] to obey the provincial of those of the cloth. Valdemoro[7] is there as vicar, for he didn't have a sufficient number of votes to be prior. The provincial[8] left him there as vicar that he might find a solution for the problems in that house. After what happened some time ago, he is on bad terms with Alberta, the prioress.[9] The calced friars go about saying that the nuns owe them obedience and many other things. The nuns are dying from fear of him. I have reassured them.

5.   As soon as you think that it would be good on our part to manifest some courteous submission to the nuncio, let us know; and tell us quickly, for goodness' sake, how your meeting with him went. I will be worried until I know, although I have hope in the Lord that so many prayers will bear fruit and that all will go well. I am delighted that you have such good lodging.[10] You needed all this after having suffered such trials. I would like it if you went with the Count of Tendilla[11] the first time you went to see the nuncio. If the nuncio wishes to excuse you, you will be fully clear of blame for all you were accused of.

6.   I tell you I am certain that if some influential person were to ask the nuncio to have Fray John[12] set free, he would at once give orders that he be returned to his house. It would be enough to tell the nuncio about this father and how he is kept in prison unjustly. I don't know what is happening that no one ever remembers this saint. If Mariano were to speak to the Princess of Eboli,[13] she would intercede with the nuncio.

7.   The fathers of the Society are in a great hurry for Padre Mariano to come, for they are in serious need.[14] If he would not be greatly missed there, I beg you out of charity to arrange that he come. It is a long time that they have been asking for this. Now they are sending a letter to the nuncio so that he might give his authorization. Including the trip here and back, it will take Mariano only five or six days in all. He will only have to stay here for a day or half a day. Do not let all your other business cause you to forget this. Consider how opportune the time is to entrust you with this charge, for though it may seem to be of little importance, it is considered most important here.

8.   I don't know how we can repay Don Diego[15] for all we owe him. Payment for so much charity has to come from above.

Give him my best regards and tell him I beg him not to leave you until you are safe, for I am frightened by all these deaths that are happening to travelers on their journeys. May God in his divine goodness keep you from danger. I ask Señora Juana[16] for prayers; give my regards to the secretary[17] and those ladies. Great is my desire that we will no longer be the cause of so many trials for them.

9.   You should know that our Father General[18] wrote a letter to Doña Quiteria as you will see from the enclosed letter. May God forgive the one who informed him so badly. If His Majesty should grant us the favor of being made a separate province, we must then send someone to Rome at once, for I believe we will become his most cherished subjects. Let us be so for His Majesty, and let whatever happens happen. And may he watch over you, amen.

10.   They are ringing for Matins, so I'll say no more except that the prioress[19] and sisters are well and feel very calm and ask for your prayers, as does my brother.[20] All of them are most content with the way our affairs are going. My great joy is that the end of those miserable visitations is in sight and that you will not have to be involved in them, which costs me so dearly. Although I desire so much that you be free of having to make visitations, I fear that so great a blessing will not last long.

Today is August 19.

Your unworthy servant and daughter,

Teresa of Jesus

God reward you for the image you sent as a gift.

---

1. Pedro Ries.
2. Gracián.
3. The nuncio, Felipe Sega.
4. The King of Portugal, Don Sebastián, died on 4 August in the battle of Alcazarquivir.
5. The Carmelites of the observance.

6. The discalced Carmelite nuns in Medina.
7. Alonso Valdemoro had been formerly the prior of the Carmelite friars in Avila.
8. Juan Gutiérrez de la Magdalena.
9. Alberta Bautista was the prioress of the discalced Carmelite nuns in Medina. What happened some time ago alludes to the incident in 1571, in which the provincial, Angel de Salazar, imposed a nun from the Incarnation in Avila, Doña Teresa de Quesada, as prioress on the discalced Carmelite nuns in Medina.
10. He was staying in Don Diego de Peralta's house rather than with his family lest the friars of the observance find him and take him prisoner.
11. Luis Hurtado de Mendoza, a friend of the discalced Carmelites.
12. St. John of the Cross, who during the night of 17–18 August had escaped from his prison in Toledo where he had been held for 8 months. Teresa had not as yet heard this news.
13. Ana de Mendoza, the founding benefactor of the suppressed Carmel in Pastrana, from which the discalced nuns escaped in frustration over Doña Ana's behavior. But it seems that Padre Ambrosio Mariano had not lost his influence with her.
14. They needed a source of water for their College of San Gil (cf. Ltr. 247.4).
15. Diego de Peralta.
16. Gracian's mother, Juana Dantisco.
17. Gracián's father, Diego Gracián, secretary to the king.
18. Giovanni Battista Rossi, the Carmelite general, had written to Doña Quiteria Dávila, a nun at the Incarnation in Avila.
19. María de Cristo, the prioress at St. Joseph's in Avila.
20. Lorenzo de Cepeda.

259. To Roque de Huerta, Madrid

Avila, 19(?) August 1578

Teresa is anxiously concerned about Padre Gracián who is hidden in a friend's house in Madrid waiting for the right moment to approach the nuncio who is angry with him. Roque is acting as an intermediary between Teresa and Gracián. The first part of the letter is missing.

❧·❧·❦·❦

To the very magnificent Señor Roque de Huerta, chief forest guard of his majesty.

1.   ... Don't worry about anything; the Lord will provide when you least expect. My worry now, the greatest I've had, is whether our *padre* has fallen into the nuncio's hands.[1] I would much rather see him in the hands of God and amid the dangers of travel to Rome,[2] even if worse, and among those friars chosen to go. Perhaps I don't know what I am talking about.

2.   For goodness' sake let me know what is happening as soon as possible, for we are all troubled over this. And how is Padre Fray Antonio, for I have been very distressed in his regard. Those were heavy blows to take by one who was so ill and weak.[3] He is a saint, and God is treating him as one.

3.   Great was the consolation I derived from the count's letter,[4] for it seems to me God has chosen him as a means to help us. I am answering with the enclosed letter. It is a most important letter, and I wouldn't want any mishap to come to it. If his lordship is there, you can give it to him yourself. Otherwise, send it to him through a private messenger. And note how important it is, for it not to be lost.

    Your honor's unworthy servant,

Teresa of Jesus

---

1.   On 23 July Gracián had been summoned by the nuncio, Felipe Sega, but by remaining hidden he was avoiding the official notification.
2.   She reasoned that in Rome they could present their cause to the Holy See more effectively.
3.   Padre Antonio de Jesús (Heredia) was imprisoned for a short time in the Carmelite friars' monastery in Toledo by order of the nuncio.
4.   The Count of Tendilla, Luis Hurtado de Mendoza, who favored the discalced Carmelites, soon came into conflict with the nuncio.

260. To Padre Jerónimo Gracián, Madrid
Avila, 21–22 August 1578

These are two fragments from one letter. They reflect Teresa's first impressions on learning of St. John of the Cross's escape from his prison cell in Toledo and of what he suffered there.

❖❖❖❖

1.　... I tell you that ever present to me is what they did with Fray John of the Cross, for I don't know how God bears with things like that; even you don't know everything about it. For all these nine months[1] he was held in a little prison cell where small as he is he could hardly fit. In all that time he was given no change of tunic, even though he had come close to the point of death. Only three days before his escape the subprior gave him one of his shirts. He underwent harsh scourges, and no one was allowed to see him.

2.　I experience the greatest envy. Surely our Lord found in him the resources for such a martyrdom. And it is good that this be known so that everyone will be all the more on guard against these people. May God forgive them, amen.

3.　An investigation should be conducted to show the nuncio[2] what those friars did to this saint, Fray John, without any fault on his part, for it is a pitiful thing. Tell this to Fray Germán;[3] he will do it because he's quite mad about this ...

1. He was taken prisoner during the night of 3 December 1577 and escaped from his prison in the night of 17 August 1578.
2. Felipe Sega.
3. Fray Germán de San Matías was a confessor for the nuns at the Incarnation along with John of the Cross. He was taken prisoner at the same time as John, but very soon afterward broke free from his captors.

261. To Padre Jerónimo Gracián, Madrid
Avila, End of August 1578

Gracián in a downhearted moment has written Teresa, confiding to her his fears about whether or not he has incurred excommunication through the brief from the nuncio, Sega. Teresa tries to cheer and console him, and she adds also some good practical advice.

❖❖❖❖

For *mi padre*, Maestro Fray Padre Jerónimo Gracián.

1.   Jesus be with your paternity, *mi padre*. I had a strong desire to write you a long letter in response to the one you sent me so filled with pessimism and melancholy, but since I had these others to write, which I am enclosing, my head can no longer function. Please have the address put on the enclosed letter to the nuncio,[1] for I'm not doing so lest I make a mistake. One of the ladies there could do it, one whose handwriting may be more like mine.

2.   Regarding what I said in the beginning, my Paul[2] is very foolish to have so many scruples. You ought to tell him this. There is nothing to say regarding you. All the learned men say that until he receives notification of the brief[3] your conscience is clear. It would be folly to submit to the nuncio before the president has smoothed the way for you. And the first time you speak to the nuncio you should do so if possible in the presence of the president.[4]

3.   Don't go about prophesying, for goodness' sake, for God will do all things well. Now I understand all that Joseph[5] said to me during the absence of Ardapilla,[6] that this was more fitting for our business matters. I don't doubt it since he is so disliked. As for those other hermits, there's no need to pay any attention, for just as God wants evil to be discovered so does he reveal what is good. Mass is not obligatory for you. I inquired about this, but you know the answer yourself. Try to stay there, in great

secrecy however. This is what worries me. If while having so good a life you become this pessimistic, what would you have done had you had to suffer what Fray John did?[7]

4.   The money will be paid to Antonio Ruiz.[8] If he has not gone, tell him that I already have a hundred bushels and that it is necessary to send the money from Malagón at once; and that is where his bushels will be sent. I haven't the head for writing any more, my good *padre*. Remain with God, and since you serve as great a lady as is the Blessed Virgin, who prays for you, don't be troubled about anything, although I see you clearly have reason to be troubled.

Warm regards to Señora Juana.[9]

Teresa of Jesus

Tell the president that we are diligently praying to God for his health.

---

1.   Felipe Sega. She preferred to have Gracián take care of addressing the letter since she wasn't sure of the correct form.

2.   Gracián.

3.   Sega's brief, 23 July 1578, gave rise to most of Gracian's scruples and troubles. It was not to take effect until Gracián was notified of it in the presence of a notary. He was in hiding so as to avoid the official notification.

4.   Antonio Mauricio Pazos, president of the royal council who could try to pacify the nuncio.

5.   Jesus Christ.

6.   Juan Calvo de Padilla, who had been imprisoned by the Inquisition.

7.   Fray John of the Cross.

8.   Teresa's merchant friend from Malagón.

9.   Gracián's mother, Juana Dantisco.

262. Defense of Gracián Against Felipe Sega's Brief
Avila, end of August 1578

This draft of a defense of Padre Gracián against the accusations made against him in the nuncio Sega's brief of 23 July 1578 was written in haste. Teresa submitted it to one of her learned advisors in Avila. She wanted it copied in good handwriting and circulated among some influential people in Madrid. The autograph ended up in the hands of Gracián.

❧❧❧❧

1.   When the previous nuncio[1] died we thought for sure that the visitation had ended. The theologians and law scholars from Alcalá and Madrid, and some from Toledo, with whom we discussed this case said that it had not because the visitation had already been started. They said that although the nuncio died the visitation did not end but had to be completed. They held that if it hadn't commenced then it would have ended with the death of the one giving the faculties.[2] And the president, Covarrubias,[3] said again that because the visitation hadn't ended it should not be stopped. All were in agreement with this.

2.   Afterward, when this nuncio[4] arrived he told Gracián to bring him his faculties and the processes. Gracián was wanting to give the whole thing up, but he was advised that the king would be displeased, because he was also under the king's command. He went to the archbishop[5] and told him what was happening. The archbishop scolded him and told him he had the courage of a fly and that he should go and give an account of everything to the king. And when Padre Gracián explained, for love of the nuncio,[6] the disadvantages that could arise, the archbishop replied that anyone can have recourse to a higher authority, and he made him go to speak to the king. The king ordered him to go to his monastery and said that he would inquire into the matter.

3.   Some learned men and even the presentado Romero,[7] whom I asked about this here, said that since the nuncio had not shown his faculties for issuing orders in this case, Padre Gracián was not obliged to stop, and they gave many other reasons for this. He had not shown the faculties previously or up to now (unless he has done so within the past ten days). I know definitely that the king would require that he show them.[8]

4.   Despite all these opinions Padre Gracián remained nine months—more or less—without using his faculties,[9] not even for a signature, even though he knew what the nuncio said and swore that the nuncio had never forbade him to carry on the visitation. And there are many witnesses to this and also to the nuncio's answer to a friar who asked that he remove Gracián, which was that he had no authority to do so.[10]

5.   After these months the present president[11] sent for Padre Gracián to order him to resume the visitation. Gracián ardently begged him not to give him such a command. The president responded that this was impossible because it was the will of God and of the king, and that he himself didn't want the office that he held either. And he said other things of this sort. Padre Gracián asked whether he should go to see the nuncio. He said no but that if anything was needed he should have recourse to him. The council furnished him with many writs so that everywhere he could call for help from the secular arm.

6.   It had always been thought through what was heard from the nuncio that he did not have authority over religious orders. For since the king was displeased with what he had done so quickly in Gracián's regard without reporting to him, the nuncio didn't do anything.[12] Now we think he has received some superior order from the pope to act the way he does, not that he has shown it to the council or to anyone as far as is known.

7.   Padre Gracián became very troubled, for if he paid heed to the nuncio and did not do what the king ordered, we would be lost, without the king's favor, for it is the king who supports and intercedes for us with the pope.[13] This is especially so since it is definitely known that the nuncio was seeking to have Tostado[14] do the visitation, for he was the vicar sent by the general and one of those of the cloth.[15] And we know for certain that Tostado was determined to close down all our houses, in accord with the decision of the general chapter,[16] that only two or three be left of them all, that no more friars be accepted among them, and that they dress no differently from other Carmelites. Only

so as to support us did Padre Gracián accept the task of visitator, much to his own affliction.

8.   He also found it hard to have to present documentation relative to the faults of the friars of the cloth[17] in Andalusia, for much was told to him in secret. By doing so he would disturb everyone and defame many while not knowing whether the nuncio had the powers to carry out such reforms, for the nuncio had never shown proof of his authority.

9.   This is the whole truth, and there are other things as well, which anyone who knew them would see clearly how unjust is the treatment Gracián receives in that brief.[18] He has done nothing without the opinion of good men of learning, for even though he is a learned man himself, he never proceeds on his own.[19] Not showing one's faculties is something new in Spain, for nuncios always show them.

10.   See if it would not be good that this infomation copied in good handwriting be sent to Madrid and given to certain persons.

Teresa of Jesus

---

1.   Nicolás Ormaneto, who died 18 June 1577.
2.   Sega's brief of 7 July 1578 accused Gracián of arrogance and presumption for having continued the visitation after Ormaneto's death and claimed that the mandate to make the visitation terminated with the death of Ormaneto.
3.   Diego de Covarrubias y Leiva, president of the royal council.
4.   Felipe Sega, who arrived in Madrid in August 1577.
5.   Gaspar de Quiroga, the Archbishop of Toledo.
6.   Felipe Sega.
7.   Pedro Romero, a Dominican at Santo Tomás in Avila.
8.   The previous nuncio had received a pontifical commission to intervene in the reform of religious orders. The point in question is whether Sega received one.
9.   From August or September 1577 to May or June 1578.

10. Fernando Suárez and Diego de Coria, Andalusian Carmelites of the observancem petitioned Sega to remove Gracián (see MHCT 2:14–19).

11. Antonio Mauricio Pazos, president of the royal council since the beginning of 1578.

12. In the beginning Sega ordered Gracián to continue the visitation and give him an account. The king was thus led to inquire of the pope into the powers of the nuncio.

13. Gracián explains the situation thus: "The nuncio Ormaneto from whom I received the commission died.... The nuncio Sega came to Madrid and claimed to have ordinary jurisdiction over religious as he did over clerics. He called for me and told me with much largess to continue my visitation and keep him informed of what I was doing. I went to the king (for he had given me the brief from Ormaneto and the patent letters for the visitation) and told him what Sega said and asked what I should do. He told me to wait until he wrote to the pope on this matter.... I found myself placed between the king and the nuncio in so burdensome a matter of jurisdiction. The king was saying I should not obey the nuncio until the answer came from Rome. The nuncio was shouting because I was not paying heed to him, blaming me for impeding the apostolic jurisdiction. The response from the pope ordered the nuncio not to meddle in the friars' affairs except in cases where the king might ask him to intervene. The nuncio's feelings in this matter were such that he asserted that if they didn't deliver me over to be burned, for having impeded his jurisdiction, that he would have to return to Rome.... These two things so angered him that I considered any other death good, for I feared being burned to death" (MHCT 19:36–37).

14. Jerónimo Tostado.

15. Carmelites of the observance.

16. The chapter of Piacenza (May–June 1575). Teresa's information about the decisions of this chapter was distorted.

17. The Carmelites of the observance.

18. Sega's brief of 23 July 1578.

19. Gracián had degrees in the arts and in theology from the University of Alcalá.

263. To Sister María de Jesús, Toledo
Avila, August (?) 1578

This text is taken either from a note or a fragment from a letter. María de Jesús (Blessed Mary of Jesus) made her profession on 8 September 1578.

❖❖❖❖

This is the authorization for Sister María de Jesús to make her profession. I grant it with great pleasure. May the blessing of the Lord de rore coeli et de pinguedine terrae be granted her.[1]

---

1.   "Of the dew of heaven and the fatness of earth," words from a blessing given by Isaac to Jacob (Gn. 27:28).

264. To Madre María de San José, Toledo
Avila, September (?) 1578

Scrupulous, indiscreet, and of limited intelligence, Padre Garciálvarez continued to cause trouble for the nuns in Seville. But Teresa remains ever grateful to him for the help he gave the nuns in the beginning, as is obvious in this fragment from a letter of hers.

❖❖❖❖

For love of our Lord I beg you, daughter, to suffer and be silent and not try to send that *padre*[1] away from there, no matter how many trials and troubles he causes, unless something amounts to an offense against God. I cannot bear our seeming to be ungrateful to someone who has helped us. For I remember that when others wanted to deceive us about a house they were selling, he alerted us to their deceit.[2] I can never forget the good he did us in that instance and the trouble he saved us from. And he has always seemed to me to be a servant of God and well intentioned. I see clearly that this need in me to show gratitude is not a sign of perfection. It must be a natural trait, for I could be bribed with a sardine.

---

1.   Garciálvarez.
2.   See F. 25.4–5.

265. To Doña Inés y Doña Isabel Osorio, Madrid
Avila, middle of September 1578

(Autograph: DCN, Maluenda [Zaragoza})

The two sisters were hoping to enter one of Teresa's Carmels. She would have liked to receive them into the Carmel she was planning for Madrid. But the arrival of the nuncio Felipe Sega had placed in doubt the survival of even the Carmels that had already been founded.

❧❧❦❦

1.   Jesus be with your honors.[1] I received your letter. It always makes me very happy to have news from you and to see how our Lord keeps you faithful to your good resolves. That is no small thing with your being in that Babylon,[2] where you will always hear things more apt to distract the soul than to recollect it. It's true, though, that for those with good intelligence the sight of so much going on, and such a variety, will lead them to recognize the vanity and short duration of all things.

2.   The events that have been going on in our order for more than a year are of a kind that would cause much grief to anyone who does not understand our Lord's designs. But in seeing that everything is for the greater purification of souls and that in the end God will favor his servants, we have no reason to grieve, but should long for the trials to increase and praise God that he has granted us the favor of suffering for justice' sake. And you both should do the same and trust in him, for when you least expect it you will see your desires fulfilled.

May His Majesty shield you with the holiness I beg of him, amen....[3]

---

1.   Inés and Isabel are daughters of Antonio de León and Ana Osorio.
2.   Madrid.
3.   Teresa's signature is missing.

266. To Padre Jerónimo Gracián, Madrid
Avila, 29 September 1678

(Autograph fragment: DCN, Medina de Rioseco)

She wrote hastily, urging Gracián in view of Sega's hostility toward her reform to send discalced friars to Rome to carry on their business there. But the mail carrier got sick and returned the letter. Teresa is now sending it again after the delay. The text is damaged and the first two pages missing.

❧❧❧❧

For *mi padre*, Maestro Fray Jerónimo Gracián de la Madre de Dios.

1.   … all this would be most important, or at least to send one, but it would be better for two to go. Both are good friends of the Jesuits, which would be no small help in the negotiations.[1] In any case, for goodness' sake, write to us at once and don't keep us waiting any longer. Everyone is amazed that we don't have anyone in Rome to carry on our business for us, and so those others do whatever they want. The two chosen to go ought to bring a record of the request made by the discalced friars to have their own protector.[2]

2.   The moment has come for us to move quickly; there is little time, as you see. You can inform me from there if it is already too late, for however much we want to hurry, it seems a month will be needed. I laugh to think that I am speaking as though everything is ready, those who are to go and the means necessary for such a trip. But if we don't begin, nothing will get done. We should have started when we obeyed the brief.[3]

3.   Fray Antonio[4] is complaining terribly that we did not say anything to him, and he is right. I am surprised at Roque,[5] since there are so many messengers between Madrid and Granada. I told Fray Antonio that you should have informed him and that he had been able to use his powers without scruple as long as nothing was known. I don't know where the letter ended up.

If I find it I will send it to you. I tell you I felt sad that you have discalced friars like that with so little loyalty. I am referring to the one who went off with Fray Baltasar.[6] The calced jailers treated you better.[7] Please God he won't try anything else when he is free; as for the rest, it's better that he is out.[8]

4.   I'm afraid those of the cloth have taken Fray Juan de la Miseria prisoner, for ever since they say they last saw him, he has not been seen.[9] May the Lord provide a remedy for everything and guard you for us, as I and these daughters of yours beg of him, amen.

5.   My health is fair. The prioress of Salamanca[10] has written me that she wrote informing you she has already received the nun.

Today is the feast of St. Michael.

Your paternity's unworthy servant and daughter,

Teresa of Jesus

6.   Tell Padre Mariano what you think you should from this. Give my regards to him and to Fray Bartolomé.[11] And answer me soon about Rome. You ought to know that there is someone in Madrid from the Society who is a good friend of mine. They say that he is there by order of the president. It could be that they are from the same region. If it would be helpful, I will write to him. His name is Pablo Hernández.[12]

7.   This letter was entrusted to a carrier who got sick, and it was returned to me. I opened it to see what I said and it seems to me that you should see it, even if it might tire you.

---

1.   She is referring to the discalced friars appointed to go to Rome to take up the affairs of the Teresian reform with the general, who unbeknownst to her was already dead.

2.   They wanted a cardinal protector different from Filippo Buoncompagni, the one given to the Carmelite order, who they thought was opposed to the discalced friars and nuns.

3.   Felipe Sega's brief of 23 July 1578, which stripped Gracián of his powers.

4. Antonio de Jesús (Heredia), who was delegated by Gracián to carry on the visitation and not notified of the brief.
5. Roque de Huerta, who handled Teresa's correspondence for her in Madrid.
6. Baltasar Nieto and Miguel de la Columna authored a slanderous statement against Gracián.
7. Gracián must have spent some days in the prison of the Carmel in Madrid where he was treated courteously.
8. Miguel de la Columna returned to the Carmelites of the observance from whom he had transferred to the discalced friars.
9. The discalced Fray Juan de la Miseria had received letters of recommendation from the prior of the Carmelites of the observance in Madrid and from Doña Leonor Mascareñas, and set out for Rome to render obedience to the general.
10. Ana de la Encarnación.
11. Ambrosio Mariano de San Benito and Bartolomé de Jesús, both discalced Carmelites.
12. The president of the royal council was Antonio Mauricio de Pazos. He and Hernández were from Galicia.

267. To Padre Jerónimo Gracián, Madrid (?)
Avila, end of September 1578

A fragment. St. John of the Cross, in fragile condition after his months in prison, will be going to the chapter convoked with dubious authority by Padre Antonio de Jesús and scheduled to open on 9 October in Almodóvar del Campo.

It grieved me deeply to learn of what Fray John[1] had to suffer and that they are allowing him, as sick as he is, to go down there right away. Please God he doesn't die on us. Be sure, as a favor to me, that they take good care of him in Almodóvar[2] and that he doesn't go any further. Don't fail to give the necessary orders. And be careful not to forget. I tell you that you would have few like him left, if he were to die.

1. St. John of the Cross (cf. Ltrs. 260 & 261).
2. Almodóvar del Campo.

268. To Padre Jerónimo Gracián, Alcalá de Henares
Avila, October 1578

Perhaps Gracián himself confided to Teresa news about his being encouraged to transfer to another order. Her reaction is found only in these two fragments. The date is uncertain.

❖❖❖❖

1. ... May God give you fortitude so that you remain steadfast in righteousness, even if you find yourself surrounded by great danger. Blessed are trials when, however heavy, they do not make one turn aside in the least from righteousness. I am not surprised that anyone who loves you wants to see you free of those dangers and looks for means toward this, although it would not be a good thing to abandon the Blessed Virgin[1] in times of such great need. Certainly, Señora Juana would not give you such advice, nor would she consent to such a change. God deliver us. Nor by doing so would you be escaping trials but walking right into them. For these trials of ours with God's help will soon pass, but those of another order could perhaps go on for the rest of your life. You ought to consider this.

2. The more I think about your faculties as visitator being restored the worse it seems to me. Every day I would have to live with the shock of seeing you in a thousand battles of a thousand kinds. And, after all, I see that the honor of your being a visitator will not last any longer than a mouthful of bread, while our torment at seeing you in such danger could last always. For the love of God I beg you to refuse even if the nuncio himself orders it.

---

1. To abandon the Carmelite order would be equivalent in the minds of Teresa and others to abandoning our Lady. Padre Gracián wrote that when he was taken prisoner he was falsely accused of wanting to transfer to the Augustinian order and that his mother sent a message that if he did so she would refuse to have anything to do with him (see MHCT 3:611–612).

269. To Padre Pablo Hernández, Madrid
Avila, 4 October 1578

(Autograph in part: DCN, Monte Estoril [Portugal])

Pablo Hernández was an old friend of Teresa's and had known her from the time he was her confessor in 1562 when she was residing in Doña Luisa de la Cerda's house in Toledo. Now she had received word that he was living in Madrid and was a friend of the president of the Royal Council. Teresa turns to him for help so that someone might get to the nuncio with the truth about the discalced, and especially about Gracián, who had been calumniated.

✦ ✦ ✦ ✦

To the very magnificent and reverend *señor* and *padre mío* Doctor Pablo Hernández of the Society of Jesus, my lord, in Madrid; hand deliver.

1.   Jesus. The grace of the Holy Spirit be with your honor, *padre mío*. Eight days ago I received a letter from the prioress in Toledo, Ana de los Angeles, in which she tells me that you are in Madrid. It gave me great consolation since I think God brought you there to give me some relief from my trials. I tell you they are so many—having started a year ago last August—and of such variety that it would bring me much relief if I could see you and find rest in recounting some of them to you.[1] It would be impossible to tell you about all of them. To top everything off we are now in the situation that the one who delivers this letter will tell you about. He is a person who loves us much and shares in our distress and is someone we can trust.[2]

2.   The devil cannot bear the genuine way in which these discalced friars and nuns serve our Lord. I tell you, you would be consoled to witness the perfection of their life. There are now nine houses of discalced friars[3] and many good subjects in them. Since they have not been joined into a separate province, the disturbances and trials they undergo from those of the cloth[4] are so many as to be indescribable.

3.   Now all of our fortune or misfortune, after God, lies in the hands of the nuncio,[5] and, for our sins, those of the cloth have so informed him—and he gives them so much credit—that I don't know where it will end up. Of me they say that I am a restless vagabond[6] and that the monasteries I have founded were established without permission from the pope or general. Think of it, what could be more wicked or could there be any worse kind of Christian behavior.

4.   Many other things, unrepeatable, do those blessed friars say about me. And as for Padre Maestro Gracián,[7] who was their visitator, it is a pity, the shameful assertions they make against him. I can testify to you that he is one of the greatest servants of God with whom I have dealt and of surpassing honesty and purity of conscience. Believe me I am speaking the truth. After all, he was brought up by the Jesuits in Alcalá as you may know.

5.   All this comes from the fact that the nuncio is very mad at him for certain reasons for which, if the nuncio would listen to him, he would find that he deserves little or no blame.[8] And the nuncio is also mad at me, without my having done anything contrary to his service. Indeed, I have most willingly obeyed a brief he sent here and written him as humble a letter as I could.[9]

6.   I think it all comes from above, that the Lord wills that we suffer and that there be no one to side with the truth and put in a good word for me. Truly I tell you that I don't feel troubled or distressed over what concerns me personally, rather I feel a special joy. But it seems to me that if it were ascertained that what those fathers are saying about me is not true, then perhaps what they say about Padre Maestro Gracián will not be believed, which is what is most important to us. So I am sending you a copy of the patent letters that authorize our foundations because the nuncio says we are in bad standing for having founded houses without permission. I think the devil is making every effort to discredit these houses. And so I would

like there to be servants of God who would defend them. Oh, *mi padre*, how few are one's friends in time of need.

7.   They tell me that the president[10] regards you very highly, that you are in Madrid for his sake. I think he has been informed of all this, and more, by the nuncio. It would be most helpful to us if you could undeceive him, for as an eyewitness, knowing my soul, you can.[11] I believe you will be rendering our Lord a great service. And tell him how important it is to go forward with what was begun for this holy order, for you know how fallen it was.

8.   They say that it is a new order with many novelties. Let them read our first rule, for we are doing no more than observe it without mitigation, with the rigor at first given to it by the pope.[12] And let them believe only what they see, and learn about how we live and how the calced friars live and not listen to them. I don't know where they get so many things that are not so, and with these they wage war against us.

9.   And I also beg you to speak for me to the nuncio's confessor and give him my regards and inform him about the whole truth so as to oblige him in conscience not to publish things so injurious without first investigating,[13] and tell him that despite my being so wretched, I wouldn't dare do what they are saying. Do this if you think it would be appropriate, otherwise, no.

10.   If it seems right to you, you could show him the patent letters,[14] the authority on which I have founded monasteries. One of the letters includes a command that I not stop making foundations. And in one letter our Father General wrote me, after I asked him not to order me to make any more foundations, that he would like me to found as many monasteries as I have hairs on my head. It is not right that so many nuns who are servants of God be discredited through false declarations. Since I have been reared in and given being, as they say, by the Society, I think it would be right to make known the truth so that a person as important as the nuncio (since he comes to reform religious orders—and he is not from this country) be

enlightened about who needs reforming and who needs to be favored. And he should punish the one who goes to him with so many lies. You will see what must be done.

11. What I beg of you for love of our Lord and his precious Mother is that since you have favored us from the time you came to know us that you do so in our present need and defend the truth in the way you think most suitable. Our friars will repay you very well—and you owe it to my affection for you. And I beg you to keep me informed about everything and mainly about your health. Mine has been very poor, for the Lord has tried me in every way this year. But what regards myself wouldn't pain me much if it were not for the suffering I experience at seeing that on account of my sins these servants of God are suffering. May His Majesty be with you and watch over you. Let me know if you will be residing for long in Madrid, for I've been told you will.

Today is the feast of St. Francis.

Your honor's unworthy and true servant.

Teresa of Jesus, Carmelite

---

1. The nuncio had arrived in Madrid at the end of August 1577.
2. The carrier is Roque de Huerta.
3. Actually there were ten at the time: Mancera (Duruelo 1568–70), Pastrana (1569), Alcalá de Henares (1570), Altomira (1571), La Roda (1572), Granada (1573), La Penuela (1573), Seville (1575), Almodóvar del Campo (1575) and El Calvario (1576).
4. The Carmelite friars of the observance.
5. Felippo Sega.
6. She is alluding to a statement the nuncio made in his first meeting with Juan de Jesús María Roca: "She is a restless, vagabond of a woman, disobedient and contumacious, who under the guise of devotion was inventing bad doctrines, going about outside the enclosure against the prescriptions of the Council of Trent and her superiors, acting as a teacher, in contradicton to what St. Paul taught that women should not be teachers."
7. Jerónimo Gracián de la Madre de Dios.

8. On 23 July 1578, Sega issued an order that revoked all of Gracian's powers and discredited him in harsh terms (see MHCT 2:20).
9. The letter has been lost.
10. The president of the royal council, Antonio Mauricio de Pazos.
11. Hernández had been a confessor of Teresa's (see ST. 58.3).
12. Teresa erroneously thought that the Carmelite rule observed in her houses and approved by Pope Innocent IV in 1247 was the first to be approved. An earlier form of the rule was approved by Honorius III in 1226.
13. She is alluding to Sega's brief of 23 July 1578 which contained insulting words against Gracián.
14. She is alluding to the patent letter of 6 April 1571 (see MHCT 1:110–112).

270. To Roque de Huerta, Madrid
Avila, 4 October 1578

(Autograph: DCN, Amiens [France])

The worrisome situation had continued. The discalced friars had decided at a bad time to hold a chapter on their own in Almodóvar del Campo on 9 October. This action added to the nuncio's disapproval of them. Teresa wants to be sure the nuncio receives correct information. Through Roque de Huerta she sends letters and documentation to an influential Jesuit friend and to the nuncio's confessor. The first part of the letter is missing.

❧ ❧ ❧ ❧

To the very magnificent Señor Roque de Huerta, chief forest guard of His Majesty, Madrid

1. … with brevity, and send it to me through a trustworthy person, and pay a good portage. I hope in God the outcome will be good, for I don't see in our fathers there the capability of finding a better solution. May God help us with something from that inheritance[1]—for there will be need of a lot of money—and allow us to live in peace so that we can serve you in return for the many things for which we are always indebted to you, for

otherwise I don't know what would have come of us. Please urge our *padre*[2] to send me a brief summary of everything.

2.   For your assurance I am sending you copies of the authorized patent letters,[3] and I am writing to a father from the Society,[4] who is a good friend of mine and my confessor—I don't know what office he now holds. He is very good and a close acquaintance of the president's.[5] I ask you to inform him of what I am being silent about, and I am begging you to do so, and tell him of the scandals caused by these fathers and how they held that saint, Fray John of the Cross, for nine months.[6] For you still may not know of what he suffered and the accusations they are making. If the president should want to see the patent letters, give them to him, so that once he has seen them, you may show them to whomever you think should see them. Perhaps he will show them to the president or to the nuncio's confessor.[7] I am also sending the latter a message. Take him aside and speak to him privately.

3.   I would like it if some of the lies they tell were investigated so that what involves our *padre* would not be believed. Consider how beneficial this could prove; don't think it would be a waste of time. Tell him about the nuncio's attitude toward us and how those others have deceived him. Let us do our part, and God will then do what he wills. This is God's cause, and all will end well. My hope is in him; do not be distressed.

4.   Let me know where those fathers went. Since I do not think they are there I am not writing to them. If by chance our *padre* is in Almodóvar,[8] send him these letters by special courier if there is no other trustworthy way, but I don't think he will be there.

5.   God be with you. My head can do no more for now. I kiss the hands of those gentlemen many times.

6.   You should know that when our general tells me to found as many monasteries as I have hairs on my head, he does so not in a patent letter but in an ordinary letter.[9] The enclosed letters should be sufficient. May God be with you.

It is 4 October.

Your honor's unworthy servant,

Teresa of Jesus

7.   I was happy to learn of the arrival of Don Alonso[10] and the other news. Please God we will receive a full report.

Be careful not to speak of the matter concerning Rome except with our *padre*—even though the other be a friar—and do whatever could be of benefit. There is no basis to what was said about Fray Juan de Jesús[11] going there.

1.   An inheritance in Alcalá. See Ltr. 272.5.
2.   Jerónimo Gracián.
3.   She is referring to the patent letters authorizing her to be a foundress given by the general, Rossi, on 27 April 1567 and 16 July 1567.
4.   The Jesuit, Pablo Hernández. See Ltr. 269.
5.   President of the royal council, Mauricio de Pazos.
6.   He was in prison from the beginning of December 1577 until his escape in mid-August.
7.   The nuncio, Felippo Sega; his confessor is unknown.
8.   The discalced friars at the time were gathering for a chapter to be held in Almodóvar del Campo.
9.   See Ltr. 269.10.
10. Probably Alonso Velázquez, the Bishop of Osma, passing through Madrid.
11. Juan de Jesús Roca, who eventually went to Rome.

271. A Memorial for Father General Juan Bautista Rubeo
Avila, October 1578

(Autograph: DCN, Corpus Christi, Alcalá de Henares)

The Father General had died on 4 September 1578, but word of his death had not yet reached Teresa. For some time she had not been receiving answers to her letters. She knew that he had been misinformed about her and her work, as had also the new nuncio. For the sake of clarifying matters, two discalced friars were about to depart for Rome. This memorial was meant for them as a reminder of three particular points she wanted brought to the general's attention.

❧❧❧❧

1.   ... the truth of all the letters she writes to him, whereas at first he wrote to her quite frequently and treated her favorably. Nor does he write to or deal with the other monasteries, but acts as though he were not their superior. Obviously they must have said things to him that drove him to such an extreme.[1]

2.   What is requested from his most reverend paternity are three things very important for those monasteries. First, if possible, that he become persuaded not to accept as true what they have told him about Teresa of Jesus, for truly she has done nothing but be a very obedient daughter. This is the whole truth and nothing else can be said against her. And since he knows that she would not tell a lie for anything on earth[2] and he has seen for himself what prejudiced persons are likely to do and that they do not communicate with her, he must try to be correctly informed. And since he is the shepherd, he must not condemn unjustly without hearing all sides. If, nonetheless, only what they have said carries weight, may it lead him to apply the penalty and punish her and give her a penance so that she no longer remain in his disfavor. For any punishment would be easier for her than to see him angered. Parents are wont to forgive their children for even serious faults, all the more when there aren't any. But she has instead suffered many great trials in founding these monasteries, meaning to please him. For apart from his being her superior she has the greatest love for him. Let him not allow so many servants of God to remain in his disfavor since nobody places any blame on them. Let him consider them to be his daughters as he always has and recognize them as such, for their works deserve this.

3.   Second, since the office of apostolic visitator has now terminated and these monasteries of discalced nuns are immediately under his lordship's jurisdiction[3] that he assign superiors to whom they may have recourse whether for visitations or for

the other many things that surface; and that these superiors be from among the discalced friars of the primitive rule, and that he not order them to be governed by the friars of the mitigated rule, because their way of life in many respects is very different from that of these latter friars, and it is impossible for anyone not living as they do to be able to understand and offer a remedy for any faults that exist. He knows how poorly they did under these friars. And whenever he pleases, he may inquire about how badly the task has been carried out by the friar he has ultimately appointed and whom the nuns themselves chose as the best.[4] And this perhaps is not the fault of that friar but due to the fact that he has no experience of the life, as I said, which causes much harm. Furthermore, setting this aside, both apostolic visitators[5] have issued statutes prescribing that the discalced nuns be subject to his lordship and to the one appointed as his representative, who should be a friar living under the primitive rule—I mean a discalced friar—in view of the harm that resulted from the opposite procedure.

4.   If he does not agree to this, it should be explained to his most reverend paternity—not as something coming from the discalced nuns, but as a surmise—that, since his lordship is so far away, they would rather be subject to their bishop than agree to be governed and visited by the calced friars. These latter could cause much harm before any remedy comes, as he already knows has happened. And this in part has been the reason why our houses have not resisted the visitators, which as reformed they could have done; they did not want to find themselves subject to the calced friars, having learned their lesson.

5.   You must not even speak of this unless, after having insisted strongly on the preceding point, you find that his lordship still does not want to heed the nuns. For indeed it would be an indescribable torment for them to have to cease being subject to our Father General,[6] unless they would otherwise end up lost and without protection. Apart from the fact that they are highly esteemed both by the king and by people of high rank, there

are women of quality among them, and they are not lacking the money for their needs. All of these monasteries are now established and they are not in need, and some of them were founded by illustrious persons. May God not allow them to be drawn into a situation in which they would be required to withdraw from so good a shepherd. God forgive the one who has sown such a weed. This is a most important point, which, for love of our Lord, you must highly stress.

6. Once a province for the discalced friars is established,[7] the monasteries of nuns will always be entrusted to the provincial. Even though their conversation in these monasteries is with God alone, it would be opportune if, in matters pertaining to mortification and perfection, they were placed, if possible, under the authority of Padre Maestro Fray Jerónimo de la Madre de Dios Gracián. He has been a visitator these past years; and with his spirit and discretion and gentleness, so perfect and upright that it seems the Blessed Virgin has chosen him, these nuns will make great progress. In every visitation they say they experience a renewal of their desires and many benefits.[8]

7. If this could be done, it would be what is most fitting, and none of them would say anything else. But it seems to be impossible, for the most reverend general is very displeased with him also, as he is with Teresa of Jesus, and even much more so for reasons that will be mentioned when the rest of the facts are stated.[9] He is the one who has been apostolic visitator by order of the previous nuncio and the king.[10] And considering the calumnies they raise against him, it is no wonder that the general is so aloof.[11]

8. It would be of great service to God if this could be brought about, but it seems impossible. So it is necessary to name other friars, either Padre Presentado Fray Antonio de Jesús or Padre Fray John of the Cross, for these two fathers were the first discalced friars, and they are very great servants of God. And if he should not want either of them, let it be anyone his lordship might appoint, as long as he not be a calced friar or an

Andalusian. Do as much as possible, for as time passes, another course of action, with the help of the Lord, may present itself. It will be great at first just to be free from the calced friars.

9.   Any of these visitators, whoever he may be, in recognition of the most reverend general, must take care when making the visitation each year to send the ordinary taxes to the general; and if he does not do so—but he will because he is obliged to—the monasteries will send it. If the monasteries are given Padre Maestro Fray Jerónimo Gracián as visitator, they will double the amount, and if they even gave much more, they would gain because of how important this is to them. It goes without saying that what was just said should not be mentioned except to a companion of the most reverend general after finding out who is closest to him. And it would be well to speak first with him about all that was said. It would be most important to win by words and deeds the favor of those close to him so that the effort will bear fruit.

10.   The third request is that his lordship be pleased not to bind the superior who governs these monasteries more rigidly than are those of all the other religious orders. For if they are given a monastery or a house for the religious life or procure one themselves for nuns, they have the power to bring some nuns there so as to begin the foundation. Without this provision, the order could be poorly planted. And never has a general been opposed to this for his order; rather generals help and rejoice that new foundations are multiplying, as the most reverend general of the Carmelite order used to do before he was so badly informed. One does not understand what could have been said to him about people who are so religious, and give and have given such good example, and went with so much modesty and piety to live in the monasteries, that he should take from them a good that all religious orders enjoy, as was said.

11.   In the general chapter, the most reverend general gave orders that, under pain of excommunication, no nun should

leave her monastery and that prelates should not consent to her doing so, especially Teresa of Jesus.[12] The latter, when a house was ready, went with some nuns to establish the observance of the order there and take possession of the house in accordance with the patent letters that had been given her by the most reverend general with the greatest zeal. Those who saw these foundations were edified as will be seen if more information is necessary ...

1. The autograph is torn and the first part is missing. As for her letters receiving no answer, see Ltr. 102.14. As for her fear that the general was being badly informed see F. 28.2; Ltr. 258.9; and no.5 of this letter.
2. The same protestation of truthfulness may be found in Ltr. 102.2; see L. 28.4; IC. IV.2.7; F. prol. 3.
3. Since Gracián's powers as visitator had ceased, Teresa thought that her nuns were under the immediate jurisdiction of the general.
4. Angel de Salazar.
5. Pedro Fernández and Jerónimo Gracián.
6. Giovanni Battista Rossi.
7. On her keen desire for the establishment of a separate province see Ltrs. 124.9,16; 86.2.
8. For similar praise of Gracián, see F. 23.1,3; Ltrs. 86.3; 208.
9. See no.11 of this letter.
10. Ormaneto and Philip II.
11. These were two recent statements, one signed by the discalced friars Baltasar de Jesús (Nieto) and Miguel de la Columna, and one by the Carmelite provincial of Andalusia Diego de Cárdenas. See Ltrs. 208.1; 219.1; 226.6,11.
12. See Ltr. 102.11.

272. To Padre Jerónimo Gracián
Avila, 15 October 1578

(Autograph fragment: DCN, Corpus Christi, Alcalá)

Teresa had received two letters from Gracián, who had finally gone to see the nuncio. He was now without juridical powers. Presuming that he was in Madrid, Teresa hoped he would serve as an intermediary for her with the provincial chapter in session in Almodóvar del Campo since 9 August, a chapter she had not been in favor of convoking. She gives full expression to her grief over the death of their Father General and deeply regrets the trouble they caused him.

❖·❖·❖·❖

1.   Jesus. May the Holy Spirit be with your reverence, *mi padre*. Because I see you freed from that turmoil,[1] my distress has left me. As for the rest, let whatever comes come. I greatly grieved over the news written to me about our Father General.[2] I feel deep sorrow, and the first day cried and cried without being able to do otherwise. I so regret the trials we caused him, for certainly he didn't deserve them, and if we could have gone to see him, everything would have proceeded smoothly. May God forgive the one who always prevented this,[3] for with you I could have reached an agreement even though in this matter you did not trust my opinion very much. The Lord will bring everything to a good end. But I feel sorry about all this and about what you suffered, for certainly what you wrote to me about in your first letter—I received two after you spoke with the nuncio—[4] was like the drink of death.

2.   You should know, *mi padre*, that I was being consumed with anxiety because you were not handing over those documents[5] at once, but probably receiving counsel from someone who feels little grief over what you suffer. I am delighted that now through experience you know how to conduct the business matters along the right path and are not struggling against the current, as I was always pointing out. Indeed, there were certain things that created obstacles everywhere, and so there is no need to talk about this, for God ordains things so that his servants suffer.

3.   I wanted to write more at length, but they are coming to collect the letters tonight—and it is already almost night. I first wrote to the Bishop of Osma to get him to speak with the president and with Padre Mariano[6] about the matter of which

I wrote to you. I asked him to keep you informed. Just now I was with my brother,[7] and he sends you his best regards.

4.   We are all in agreement here that the friars should not go to Rome—[8] especially after the death of our Father General—for these reasons: First, because this plan is not secret, and before they depart, they might be taken captive by the calced friars, which would expose them to death. Second, they would lose their documents and money. Third, they don't have much experience with doing business in Rome. Fourth, on their arrival there, in the absence of Father General, they could be taken for fugitives, for they would end up wandering through the streets without any help, as I am insisting with Padre Mariano.[9] If here with all the favor we enjoy we could not rescue Fray John,[10] what will happen there? Everyone here thinks it would be bad to send friars, especially my brother who is very pained by the way our friars are being treated. It seems to us here that someone should be chosen as our representative to go and press our cause and carry on our business. My brother, especially, thinks this, for he knows the calced friars. He says that this is very important and that everything should be directed to the person about whom I wrote to you.[11] Doctor Rueda[12] has so much trust in him that he doesn't think it is necessary to send any religious.

5.   Consider all of this carefully, and if you and Padre Mariano agree with it, send a messenger to Almodóvar[13] and have them cancel the trip of the two friars to Rome, and inform me as soon as possible about what you decide. The one who would go from here is very experienced, although that means that it would cost us more. If for the moment we provide the cost, afterward each house would contribute to it. We could borrow from the Alcalá inheritance and then pay it back, for I certainly don't know how we could get a quick loan here. I am writing about this to Padre Mariano as you will see.

6.   Keep well, *mi padre*, for God will bring everything to a good end. May he be pleased that finally we will all be in

agreement and do nothing that would allow the friars to turn us into martyrs.

May God keep you, amen.

Your paternity's unworthy servant,

Teresa of Jesus

7.   It's terrible now the way everything is going, and the devil is helping them.[14] I tell you that he did a good deed for himself when he took the great angel away from us and gave us the dawdler who is in now.[15] I don't know how this blunder happened, but I believe that if Ardapilla[16] had been involved it could have been worse. Now I see, *mi padre*, what a martyrdom you suffered in finding yourself caught between contrary opinions.[17] Had you been given the freedom to proceed according to your own discernment, it would have been clearly seen that God was guiding you. All these daughters send their best regards.

8.   I am glad you told them not to discuss this with anybody. Let us go slowly and move ahead with the plan for Rome, for time smooths things over and there they will settle everything, as you say. I would only like to be nearby where we could see each other frequently, which would be a great consolation for my soul. I don't deserve this, but deserve only cross upon cross. On condition that you be spared, well and good if the cross comes.

9.   I am reasonably well, although this head of mine is in a sorry state. God be with you always. Don't tire of writing frequently, for goodness' sake. I am delighted they are not going to elect a provincial,[18] for according to what you say, doing this would be inappropriate. Even though Fray Antonio[19] told me they were obliged under pain of sin to elect a provincial, I did not contradict him. I thought that everything could be concluded here, but if they have to go to Rome for the confirmation, they will also have to go in order to become a separate province.[20] Keep me informed about all that needs to be done in the event that they accept what I proposed.[21]

Today is 15 October.

Your paternity's subject and daughter,

Teresa of Jesus

---

1. She is alluding to the termination of Gracián's office of visitator after he delivered his documentation to Sega, the nuncio.
2. Giovanni Battista Rossi died in Rome during the night of 4 September.
3. She is probably alluding to Ambrosio Mariano, who was too rough in his handling of delicate matters.
4. Gracián had been summoned by the nuncio in the brief of 23 July 1578. Before responding to the summons, he anguished for a long period over what he should do.
5. All the documents requested by Sega concerning Gracián's visitation in Andalusia.
6. The bishop was Alonso Velázquez; the president was Antonio Mauricio Pazos.
7. Lorenzo de Cepeda.
8. It had been proposed that two discalced friars go to Rome to present to the general and the pope the cause of the discalced Carmelites. See Ltr. 266.1–2.
9. Padre Ambrosio Mariano persisted in his idea that some discalced friars should be sent to Rome.
10. St. John of the Cross had been a prisoner in Toledo for eight months and during that time no one was able to get him released.
11. Teresa thought that someone else should be chosen to represent the discalced Carmelite cause in Rome instead of having the friars go there themselves, and that all paperwork should be sent to this representative. She perhaps had in mind Diego de Montoya, a canon from Avila living in Rome.
12. Fernando de Rueda, a jurist in Avila.
13. Teresa was hoping the chapter of the discalced friars that was in session in Almodóvar would decide against sending two discalced friars to Rome to represent their cause. Paying little heed to Teresa's wishes, the chapter appointed Padre Pedro de los Angeles and Fray Juan de San Diego. Charmed in Italy by the vicar general of the Carmelites, Giovanni Battista Cafardo, Padre Pedro revealed to him the entire plan of the Almodóvar chapter, handing over all the official letters and documents that he carried. This, of course, was detrimental to the designs of Teresa's friars and nuns. Once back in Spain, Padre

Pedro understandably returned to the Carmelites of the observance whom he had previously left to join the discalced friars.

14. The Carmelites of the observance.

15. The "great angel" was the president of the council, Diego de Covarrubias y Leyva; the "dawdler," his successor, Antonio Mauricio de Pazos, took his time about getting things done.

16. Juan Calvo de Padilla, who was in prison at the time.

17. The contradictory advice given to Gracián over whether to submit to the nuncio or to the president of the council.

18. On this very day the members of the chapter in Almodóvar had elected Padre Antonio de Jesús provincial. The following day, 16 October, the nuncio declared the election invalid and placed the discalced Carmelites under the jurisdiction of the Carmelites of the observance. See MHCT 2:33.

19. Antonio de Jesús (Heredia).

20. Given the weak juridical grounds for holding the chapter of Almodóvar, the proposal was made to seek confirmation of the chapter decisions directly from Rome and to request legal status for the discalced Carmelites as a separate province.

21. That is, if Gracián and the chapter members accept the services of an agent from Avila, as suggested in no. 5 of this letter.

273. To Roque de Huerta, Madrid
Avila, 24 October 1578

The discalced friars held an emergency chapter in Almodóvar del Campo on 9 October. Hardly had the meeting closed when the nuncio, Filippo Sega, annulled everything that had been done and place the discalced Carmelites under the jurisdiction of the provincials of the Carmelites of the observance in Andalusia and Castile (cf. MHCT 2:33–36). On 22 October Teresa received a copy of the acts of the unsuccessful chapter. She clearly disapproves of the chapter but focuses on the good will of the chapter members. She sent the acts to Roque with this cover letter. The present letter has come down to us only through a Latin translation.

※ ※ ※ ※

1.   Jesus be with you, my lord. I received the letter you wrote to me on the feast of St. Luke. But in it you do not tell whether you received the supplicatory letters that I sent you. As a result, I am a little worried. In fact, that letter of yours addressed to me to obtain permissions from our Father General as well as from our Father Visitator, the Dominican Padre Fray Pedro Fernández, and finally from Fray Angel,[1] was certainly sent from here. But indeed it seems it ended up in the hands of the Bishop of Osma.[2] It would be regrettable if it was lost along with my previous letter. I ask you then to inform me in this regard. Now, however, I am not as worried over the fact that you might think you have been responsible, as though in this entire affair you committed or caused the commission of some fault. If there is anyone who has little reason to torment himself in this matter, it is certainly you.

2.   The letters of convocation for the chapter held on 9 October were promulgated. I have read them. What the constitutions order to be observed is mentioned in them: let no one be guilty, neither in small matters nor in great, of a transgression or offense against God. Also promulgated is the injunction against going forward with the house of Santa Ana,[3] in effect until tranquility is restored to the province at the end of the visitation.

3.   Padre Fray Antonio de Jesús has consulted learned men who affirmed that he was bound in conscience,[4] and he wrote me about this. I answered that if this was really the case, God would in no way be offended; he could do as he wished ...[5] insofar as otherwise they would cast us headlong into tribulation.

4.   The Archbishop of Seville, whom it is right that we obey completely, is firm in these words, asserting that he did not do otherwise. Truly in this whole affair he has no reason for

moving against those whose only intention was to please and serve God. It seems prudent nonetheless, taking into account the testimonies that were given and the information received, and in consideration of the persons implicated, not to become involved in the promotion of the cause.[6] Rather one should remain silent until it is seen more clearly what the wiser thing to do might be.

5.   They[7] were convinced that so things should be if his submission[8] won them over. But in this regard they were mistaken, for from that moment the nuncio seized the occasion to show that he paid little attention to all their efforts. They tried everything, but he[9] was deprived of the power to do anything. Nonetheless, it could be that things will turn out better for him. I cannot convince myself that he[10] had wanted to propose a superior for them chosen from among their own discalced friars, since, as I also made known to you, I cannot rid myself of this suspicion that stays with me as if I were an accomplice in the whole affair. I beg you to try to find out from the Count of Tendilla if he[11] ever mentioned a desire to appoint one of the discalced friars, those observing the primitive rule. What he says corresponds to the truth, but could be interpreted as referring as well to the other Carmelites. Perhaps I alone am the cause of this misfortune in that I called the other one provincial, providing the Bishop of Osma, who was the first to write to Rome, a good occasion for doing so.

6.   O unfortunate friars, called by their superior to a chapter that became the sole reason for their imprisonment. Padre Antonio received much in writing against his convoking the chapter at this time. Now I am begging these unfortunate friars to be silent for the love of God and to wait and not do anything precipitously in this regard. There is no doubt that they have given the nuncio good reason for being angry. In the very beginning he was forewarned by the other Carmelites.

7.   Now believe me, I was never able to bring myself to approve this chapter; it displeased me very much. As a result, I

was not one of its promoters. However, others who weighed the matter better than I, made a judgment in its favor.

8.   I beseech you for the love of our Lord that, to the best of your ability, you do all you can to avoid arriving at any settlement before the matter has been brought to the attention of Rome. I would be greatly displeased if anything took place without permission from our *padre*[12] and the others[13] who are there. Please send me at once news about these things. Tell our *padre* and Padre Fray Antonio that in the meantime they should have patience until God provides a remedy.

9.   See how all of this is the work of God who wills that his servants be exercised in patience and put you to the test so that you do not grow fainthearted in those things that pertain to the service of His Majesty. There is hope that Padre Antonio will depart soon—he is old and sick and our *padre*[14] would find it difficult to do without his presence and help. If the nuncio bases his judgments on the information and testimony coming from Andalusia, Padre Antonio would be at a loss on how to defend against this and the situation would go from bad to worse. As you yourself will see, this is a question of great importance.

10.   Enclosed is a letter addressed to Padre Fray Diego de Chaves.[15] Also enclosed for you are the chapter acts transcribed by the one from whom I have received them. No one should read them except you and Padre Mariano, who would have an interest in them. Afterward let Padre Chaves present them to the king; or if he thinks it more prudent, give an account of all that took place while defending the whole affair and the persons involved and explaining that Padre Antonio used the greatest care in making known and energetically publishing the act of convocation and without any offense against God. The fact that he may not have acted entirely well in this matter does not mean he was purposely neglectful or had any bad intention; of this I am certain. Therefore I would like you to hold fast to this assertion and get the others to hold fast to it as well. If we are not united, or you with us, or we with the others, a great

trial will come upon us. And people will think badly of you and so will Padre Mariano. I don't have time now to write to Padre Mariano. It is best that, in seeing that others had not wanted to follow his advice, he be led by charity and not think he has any reason to become angry with them. Many such adversities occur in the life of men. I ...[16] Padre Fray Antonio, if you are informed about it, must be very dejected.

11.   By that time the deed was done, nor you ...[17] We are greatly indebted to the count. He impels me to praise God. Undoubtedly, our order owes him much; so we must pray always to the divine Majesty for him. May God protect him, and you as well. I beg you not to become discouraged. Few there are with a competence like yours. A good work will be done if you can obtain freedom for Padre Fray Antonio, Padre Mariano, and Padre Juan de Jesús. And may Jesus be always with you.

12.   Don't torment yourself any further. God knows how to draw good from evil. And the good is all the greater in the measure that we diligently strive that he not be offended in anything.

Today is 24 October.

Your unworthy servant,

Teresa of Jesus

13.   I kiss many times the hands of those ladies.[18] The rumor is going about in Avila that the pope has died. But there is no news about this here. It doesn't seem to be true. I am enclosing a letter to our *padre*, in which I inform him about everything that is taking place. Be very careful so that it reaches him safely.

14.   Take care also that you get back the enclosed letter to Padre Chaves so that you can read it. He will be able to inform you well and tell you about all the trials we are undergoing. Don't forget to write frankly to Padre Mariano about all the

other things that are going on. For lack of space I must close this letter.

1. Angel de Salazar, the provincial of Castile.
2. Alonso Velázquez.
3. We don't know what she is referring to here.
4. It is not clear what he is bound in conscience to do; it may be to reconvene the chapter.
5. The text is damaged here.
6. She may be referring to what was decided on in Almodóvar.
7. The chapter members.
8. Submission of either Padre Gracián or Antonio de Jesús to the nuncio.
9. This probably refers to Antonio de Jesús.
10. This could be either the nuncio or the provincial.
11. Either the nuncio or the provincial.
12. Jerónimo Gracián.
13. The discalced friars.
14. Jerónimo Gracián.
15. A Dominican friar who was at the time confessor to Philip II.
16. The text is damaged here.
17. Again the text is damaged.
18. Members of Roque's family household.

274. To Roque de Huerta, Madrid
Avila, end of October 1578

The nuncio, Filippo Sega, had given orders that the discalced friars and nuns submit to the jurisdiction of the provincials of Andalusia and Castile. The provincial of Castile, Juan Gutiérrez de la Magdalena, was the one who had taken action against the nuns at the Incarnation and St. John of the Cross. The provincial of Andalusia, Diego de Cárdenas, had plotted a slanderous process against Gracián in Seville. The Castilian provincial's emissaries rudely and obstreperously appeared at St. Joseph's in Avila, served notice of the nuncio's brief, and demanded submission from the nuns.

✦ ✦ ✦ ✦

1.   Jesus. The grace of the Holy Spirit be with your honor. I am enclosing a letter for Padre Maestro Chaves.[1] In it I tell him that you will inform him about the state of our affairs. Look for an occasion to give it to him and speak with him and tell him about how these blessed fathers[2] are treating us. I think the letter will be efficacious because I beg him with urgency to speak to the king and tell him about some of the harm that we nuns suffered when we were subject to them. May God forgive them, for they burden you with so much work that I don't know where you get the strength.

2.   I understand well that the cost for doing this must be great, and it bothers me that on account of the expenses I have here I cannot do as much as I would like. Even though I would like to help those fathers for their trip to Rome,[3] I don't see how I can, for these monasteries must pay their share for the project I am undertaking, which will not be small if everything is brought to a conclusion. But I consider all our effort worthwhile, for if we obtain peace, then we can do what I desire for the one to whom we are so obliged.

3.   By the enclosed information you will see what little effect the royal provision[4] has on these fathers. I don't know if they would have any respect even for the king himself, accustomed as they are to getting away with whatever they want, and things are going well for them here. I assure you that having to deal with them now is like struggling in the most dangerous quicksand that exists. Since you tell me they obeyed in Pastrana and Alcalá[5] and I don't know if they responded as we nuns did, let me know for goodness' sake, for our *padre*[6] doesn't write anything about this to me. He must not have gone.

4.   I received all the documents you sent. They came too late for these other houses. Let us know how they might be of benefit to us, unless the officials of justice are receiving

orders to send these fathers into exile or something like that. This morning was a time of judgment. All who were there (the justices, the learned men, and the gentlemen) were astonished by their irreverent behavior, and I was very distressed. I would have gladly refused to listen to them, but we did not dare say anything.[7]

5.   Believe me, they cannot truthfully say they saw us do anything blameworthy here. Pedro[8] was at the door and when he saw them he went to tell my brother.[9] I regretted that my brother brought the magistrate with him, for doing so was useless. What their imaginations dream up will perhaps be given more credit than the truths we assert. For goodness' sake tell our *padre* about everything that has happened—for I don't have time to write to him—and let me know how they all are.

6.   The letter from Valladolid that I told you to read and send on to our *padre* got mixed up with another, for though it was supposed to go, it was left here. It told of how things went with the friars and gave an account of everything, but I told them to write to you about it and also to Medina.[10]

7.   Tell me if you heard anything about Fray Baltasar, for he went to see the nuncio,[11] and if those calced friars can legitimately serve notice to our fathers. Here they say that according to the brief only the provincial can do so;[12] I don't know if they are right.

8.   You should know it is being said that they are going to bring me to another monastery. If it be one of their own, they would treat me worse than they did Fray John of the Cross! At one moment today I asked myself if they were sending me notice of some excommunication, for a small piece of paper was included with the large one. I don't merit to suffer as much as Fray John of the Cross did![13]

9.   I was extremely delighted that at such a favorable time ...

---

1.   A Dominican who at the time was confessor to the king.
2.   The Carmelites of the observance, perhaps those who had come to notify them of the nuncio's decree.

3. The chapter in Almodóvar (9 October) had decided to send friars to Rome to carry out the negotiations necessary so that the discalced friars could become a separate province.

4. The royal provision of 9 August 1578 ordered that any brief from the nuncio interfering with or annulling Gracian's faculties as visitator should be withdrawn. The provincial's agents notified the nuns in St. Joseph's of the nuncio's brief and decree (see MHCT 33:–36). The city official notified the agents of the royal provision. The nuns submitted to the nuncio's brief, but the friars of the observance did not submit to the royal provision.

5. Fathers Gracián, Antonio, and Mariano were confined to Pastrana, for they submitted to the nuncio's notification (see MHCT 3:602–605). In Alcalá the rector was Padre Elías de San Martín.

6. Jerónimo Gracián.

7. She is referring to those who came to notify them at St. Joseph's of the nuncio's decree.

8. Pedro de Ries, a messenger for the nuns at St. Joseph's.

9. Lorenzo de Cepeda, who was living at La Serna on the outskirts of Avila.

10. The Carmels of Valladolid and Medina del Campo, where notice of the nuncio's decree had also been served. The letter that got mixed up was from Madre María Bautista, who gave an account of how the Carmel in Valladolid was notified.

11. She is inquiring about the sinister Baltasar de Jesús, who went to see the nuncio, Felippo Sega.

12. In his brief of 16 October 1578, Felippo Sega decreed that the discalced friars and nuns submit to the provincials of Andalusia and Castile, Diego de Cárdenas and Juan Gutiérrez de la Magdalena.

13. St. John of the Cross had been imprisoned by order of the provincial Juan Gutiérrez de la Magdalena.

275. To Roque de Huerta, Madrid
Avila, Beginning of November 1578

Roque de Huerta and the Count of Tendilla (Luis Hurtado de Mendoza) were in favor of resisting the decisions of the nuncio

until he showed his pontifical faculties. Teresa had preferred
submission to him. The date of this fragment is uncertain.

❧❧❧❧

You needn't have paid so much attention to my words, for I
know little about litigations and would like to see peace come
about in everything. But I believe that permitting this would
heighten the war, but it's enough that the Count of Tendilla is
of this opinion.

276. To María de San José, Seville
Avila, November 1578

To support the establishment of a province for the discalced
friars and nuns, various bishops and other friends wrote letters
of recommendation and praise for Teresa and her work. The
idea for seeking this advocacy was Padre Nicolás Doria's.

❧❧❧❧

1. I am confounded and humbled to see what these lords
of ours have said. This has placed a great obligation on us to
be what they have painted us to be so that we don't turn them
into liars.

277. To Mother Anne of Jesus and the Community in Beas
November–December 1578

It is not certain whether these two fragments (nos. 1 & 2)
belong to the same letter. The text comes from the process for
the beatification of St. John of the Cross. At the end of October
the saint began his ministry in Andalusia as prior of the mon-
astery of El Calvario, not far from Beas.

❧❧❧❧

1. I was amused, daughter, at how groundless is your complaining, for you have in your very midst *mi padre* Fray John
of the Cross, a heavenly and divine man. I tell you, daughter,

from the time he left and went down there I have not found anyone in all Castile like him, or anyone who communicates so much fervor for walking along the way to heaven. You will not believe the feeling of loneliness that his absence causes me. Realize what a great treasure you have there in that saint. All the nuns in your house should speak and communicate with him on matters concerning their souls, and they will see how beneficial it is. They will find themselves making much progress in all that pertains to spirituality and perfection, for our Lord has given him a special grace in this regard.

2.   I declare to you that I would be most happy to have my father Fray John of the Cross here, who truly is the father of my soul and one from whom it benefited most in its conversations with him. Speak with him, my daughters, in total simplicity, for I assure you that you can do so as though you were speaking with me. This will bring you great satisfaction, for he is a very spiritual man with much experience and learning. Those here who were formed by his teaching miss him greatly. Give thanks to God who has ordained that you have him there so close. I am writing to tell him to look after you,[1] and I know from his great charity that he will do so, whatever be your need.

---

1.   Many persons in Avila had known and benefited from St. John of the Cross's ministry there. He had resided in Avila from 1572 to December 1577 when he was taken prisoner and brought to Toledo.

278. To Doña María Enríquez, Duchess of Alba
Avila, 2 December 1578

Teresa hoped that the Duke and Duchess of Alba would help the discalced Carmelites out of their difficulties with the nuncio. At the time, however, the duke and duchess were having their own problems on account of the secret marriage of their son Don Fadrique.

❖ ❖ ❖ ❖

1.   Jesus. The grace of the Holy Spirit be always with your excellency, amen. They have told me some news here that

made me rejoice, that the marriage between Señor Fadrique and Señora María de Toledo has taken place. Understanding what must be your happiness, I have found that all my trials have been thereby softened. Although I cannot be completely sure from the persons who have informed me, there are many indications of the marriage from the rumors going about.[1] I beg you to let me know that my joy may be complete. Please God, this will be for the Lord's great honor and glory, as I hope it will, for we have been praying a long time for this.

2.   Here they have informed me of the favor you are showing us all. I tell you that it is so great ...[2]

3.   If you favor us in this regard it would be like liberating us from the captivity of Egypt.[3] They have told me that you have given orders to Padre Maestro Fray Pedro Fernández[4] to attend to this affair. It is the best thing that could happen to us, for he knows those on each side. It seems like an idea from heaven. May our Lord be pleased to guard you as a help for the poor and the afflicted.

4.   I kiss your hands many times for so great a grace and gift and I beg you to do me the favor of urging with insistence and much ardor that Padre Fray Pedro Fernández go to the court. Consider this to be a matter that concerns the Blessed Virgin, our Lady, who now needs to be protected by persons like him in this war waged by the devil against her order, for many men and women will not enter if they think they will have to be subject to those persons now being imposed on us.

5.   We have been much more comforted ever since our fathers have been governing us, and so I hope in our Lord that everything will turn out well.

6.   May it please His Majesty to preserve you for us for many years with the holiness I beg of him, amen.

Written at St. Joseph's in Avila on 2 December.

Your excellency's servant,

Teresa of Jesus

1. The Duke of Alba's son, Don Fadrique de Toledo, who had a distinguished record of service in Flanders, secretly married his cousin against the express orders of the king. Don Fadrique was already pledged to marry a lady-in-waiting of the queen, a person of unequal status. When the king, rigid over questions of marriage among the aristocracy, learned that the duke had given his approval, he ordered Don Fadrique's arrest. Relationships among the higher aristocracy were always delicate, and nowhere more than in questions of marriage. Both father and son were placed under house arrest in Uceda.
2. The text is damaged here.
3. She is referring to the situation recently created by the nuncio Sega's decree placing the discalced friars and nuns under the jurisdiction of the order's provincials in Castile and Andalusia.
4. The former Dominican visitator appointed for the discalced friars and nuns in Castile.

279. To Padre Jerónimo Gracián, Madrid(?)
Avila, December 1578

This is a fragment probably from before the day (20 December 1578) the nuncio deprived Gracián of his freedom to carry on correspondence.

❧ ❧ ❧ ❧

Oh, my Paul, how well this name fits you! At one moment raised aloft, at another in the depths of the sea.[1] I tell you we can truly glory in the cross of our Lord Jesus Christ.

1. These are allusions to St. Paul: 2 Cor 11:26;12:2 and Gal 6:14.

280. To Roque de Huerta, Madrid
Avila, 28 December 1578

On 21 December Gracián was notified of the nuncio's sentence in which, among other things, he was forbidden to write to Teresa or receive letters from her. Teresa heard of this on

Christmas eve, a blow she would never forget (see Ltr. 317.4).
But a few days later she received more comforting news.

❧❧❧❧

1.   Jesus be with your honor and grant you a joyful ending
of the Christmas celebration and an entry into the new year as
happy as the one you procured for me with such good news.
For two days previous to the arrival of your letters I was greatly
afflicted because of the ones Pedro Ries[1] had delivered. On
the morning of the feast of St. John, that other message arrived
which consoled us to no end.[2] Blessed be God for such a great
favor. I tell you that compared to it, the rest is less painful; although it would console me very much to see the two fathers
free.[3] I hope in the Lord that since he granted us this favor he
will grant the rest.

2.   As for the establishment of a province,[4] may His Majesty
do what he sees is necessary. May God reward you for what
you did for me by informing the licentiate about the money and
all the rest.[5] And even though more was promised, it doesn't
matter to me. This will be enough until we receive an answer.
As soon as the amount is paid, let me know and I will reimburse
you without fail.

3.   I beg you to have the enclosed letters hand delivered, for
that would be fitting. And always inform me of the receipt of the
letters I send you, for otherwise I worry about them, and with
good reason. Consider it very important that all these letters
be delivered with caution. When I see our fathers free, these
other things will not trouble me much, for God will do things
better than we can; this is his work.

Give my regards to Señora Inés[6] and to those ladies.

Today is Sunday, feast of the Holy Innocents.

Your honor's unworthy servant,
Teresa of Jesus

---

1.   Her messenger at St. Joseph's in Avila.
2.   Perhaps this good news had something to do with the king's willing-
ness to intervene to free the discalced Carmelites from the jurisdiction
of the older Carmelites.

3. She is referring to the other two friars sentenced with Gracián: Antonio de Jesús (Heredia) and Ambrosio Mariano. When Mariano was questioned about the last time he had spoken with or written to the king, he answered that it was not since the last time. When the notary warned him lest he dare make fun of the nuncio, he answered that the question deserved no other response since it implied that it was a fault for a vassal to speak and write to so Catholic a king as King Philip. Noting that the king and the court had become suspicious of his anger against the discalced Carmelites, the nuncio decided to bring the matter to a conclusion by freeing Mariano so that he could direct a water project for the king in Jerez de la Frontera. Antonio also was freed with an odd penance, "a short prayer to be said once" (see MHCT 3:615).

4. She is referring to negotiations in Rome to procure the establishment of a separate province for discalced Carmelites.

5. Teresa was raising money to pay for the negotiations in Rome. The licentiate was probably Diego de Montoya, an Avilan living in Rome.

6. Inés Benevente, Roque de Huerta's wife.

281. To Roque de Huerta, Madrid

Avila, 28 December 1578

This is a second reply to Roque, which Teresa sent by a different route so as to be sure that he received it.

❖ ❖ ❖ ❖

To the very magnificent Señor Roque de Huerta, chief forest guard of His Majesty.

Jesus be always with your honor, amen. I received your letter and because I am sending you a reply by another route, I will not be long. I only beg you to let me know through this carrier if you have received my letters and how many. I wouldn't want them to get lost as they are very important. I worry until I know that they have been delivered into your hands. So, through the first messenger let me know and do me the favor of giving the enclosed from my brother to Captain Cepeda.[1] Entrust it into safe hands, and keep me informed about everything using the carrier who will give you the letters that I mentioned, for I believe that this will be the safest method.

May our Lord grant you his holy grace. Give my regards to Señora Inés[2] and those ladies.

Today is Sunday, 28 December.

Your honor's unworthy servant,

Teresa of Jesus

1. Hernan de Cepeda, Teresa's cousin.
2. Inés Benavente, Roque de Huerta's wife.

282. To Doña Juana Dantisco, Madrid
Avila, 28 December 1578

(Autograph: Iglesia de San Vicente Mártir, Huesca)

Confined to the monastery in Alcalá, Gracián was forbidden by the nuncio to carry on correspondence with the nuns (MHCT 2:81). Teresa continued communicating with him through his parents. This letter reflects the hopeful news Teresa had just received (Ltr. 280.1). Only a fragment of the autograph remains.

❖❖❖❖

1. My lady,[1] you should know that for a long time in all his prayer and with great desires he was asking for trials from our Lord. I saw in this that His Majesty was disposing him for those that he had to give him. And what trials they have been! Blessed be God's name. Now he must find that his soul has so benefited that he doesn't recognize himself. He has enabled us all to receive benefit greatly. I have had very much in mind the pain you both[2] have suffered; but you, too, will have drawn gain from this.

2. When I see that the ones still detained[3] have also been released—and we will certainly see them free because they will not have so many accusers—my happiness will be

complete. For I am sure, as I said, that our Lord will take care of the negotiations that matter most. There are so many good souls begging this of him, and he will do what contributes best to his glory and service.

3. May His Majesty guide and keep you and the lord secretary[4] as well, whose hands I kiss along with the hands of all those ladies. The sisters here kiss your hands. They are very happy with what has been done. I also am because of what I mentioned. Nonetheless, all of us have to do some penance, for the letters from our *padre*[5] were always good for our souls and we read them together as though they were sermons. Even this the devil wants to take from us. God is over all.

Today is the feast of the Holy Innocents.

Your honor's unworthy servant,

Teresa of Jesus

1. These initial words may not be authentic since the beginning of the letter is missing.
2. Gracián's parents.
3. Those still detained were Ambrosio Mariano, Antonio de Jesús Heredia, and Gabriel de la Asunción.
4. The king's secretary, Diego Gracián de Alderete, Doña Juana's husband.
5. Jerónimo Gracián.

Letters 283–321
(1579)

283. To Padre Hernando de Pantoja, Seville
Avila, 31 January 1579

(Autograph: DCN, Aguilar de la Frontera [Córdoba]; DCN, Seville)

The Andalusian provincial, Diego de Cárdenas, initiated an investigation in the Carmel of Seville during which some foul calumnies were asserted against Gracián, María de San José, and Teresa herself. The provincial appointed as vicaress a recently professed nun and sent all the documents, plus Teresa's letters written to the nuns, to the nuncio in Madrid. Deciding to penalize Gracián, the nuncio deposed him from all offices and confined him to the discalced Carmelite house in Alcalá de Henares. There he had to forego all correspondence except with his parents.

❖❖❖❖

To my illustrious and Very Reverend Señor Don Hernando, prior of Las Cuevasin Seville.

1. Jesus. The grace of the Holy Spirit be with your paternity, *mi padre*. What do you think of the way things are going in

153

that house of the glorious St. Joseph[1] and how they are treating and have treated those daughters of his? And this is happening over and beyond all the spiritual trials and grief that for a long time they have been suffering from one who should have been consoling them. I think it is apparent that they have been praying fervently to God for trials. May he be blessed forever.

2.   I certainly do not worry much about the nuns who went there earlier with me to make the foundation,[2] and I even feel joy in seeing all that they will gain in this war the devil wages against them. I do, however, feel bad for those who entered there afterward,[3] for when they should be learning about the order and how to remain quiet, they are very distracted by all the turmoil, which can do much harm to souls that are new. May the Lord provide a remedy. I tell you that for some time the devil has been trying to disturb them. I wrote to the prioress to talk to you about all her trials.[4] She must not have had the courage to do so. It would be great consolation for me to be able to speak openly with you, but I don't dare do so in writing. If this messenger were not so reliable, I wouldn't even mention this.

3.   This young man came to ask me if I knew anyone down there who would kindly vouch for him for some service job. Since the weather is cold up here and is very harmful for him, he cannot stay here, even though he is a native of this place. The one he has been serving, who is a canon here and friend of mine, assures me that he is virtuous and faithful. He has good handwriting and knows how to do sums. I beg you, for love of our Lord, if you see some opening that would be suitable for him, do me a favor that would be of service to His Majesty, by giving him a recommendation, if needed, for the things I mentioned. The one from whom I know these things would never tell me anything but the whole truth.

4.   I was happy when he spoke to me, for it gave me the chance to find comfort in communicating with you and asking you to tell the previous prioress[5] along with the other nuns

who came from up here to read this letter of mine. You will have learned how they deprived the prioress of office and replaced her with someone who entered there and how the nuns suffered many other persecutions and were even made to surrender the letters I had written them, which are already in the hands of the nuncio.[6] The poor nuns truly missed having someone to counsel them. The learned men here are astonished at the things they were made to do through fear of excommunication.

5.   My fear is that the interrogators have completely confused the nuns. This must have happened without it being realized, for in the process[7] things were deduced from the nuns' remarks that are totally false, for I was present there at the time the supposed events occurred, and nothing of the sort took place. But I am not surprised that they managed to confuse the nuns, for in one case the interrogation lasted six hours, and someone of little intelligence may have signed everything they asked her to sign. We benefitted from this here by being careful about what we were signing,[8] and so they had nothing to say against us.

6.   For a year and a half[9] our Lord has afflicted us in all kinds of ways. But I remain most confident that His Majesty will turn to the defense of his servants—friars and nuns and that the snares the devil has laid in that house will be discovered, and that the glorious St. Joseph will bring the truth to light and make known the caliber of those nuns that went to Seville from up here. I don't know the ones who entered down there, but I know they are given more credit by the one who deals with them,[10] which has been most harmful in many ways.

7.   I beg you for the love of our Lord not to abandon the nuns and to help them with your prayers in this tribulation, for they have only God and they have no one on earth to console them. But His Majesty who knows them will support them and give you the charity to do the same.

8.   The enclosed letter[11] I am sending unsealed so that if they have been given orders to hand over to the provincial[12] any

letters they receive from me, you can have someone read it to them, for it might afford them some relief to see my handwriting. It is thought that the provincial was wanting to expel them from the monastery; the novices were desiring to go with them.

9.   What I have come to realize is that the devil cannot bear that either the discalced friars or discalced nuns be in Seville, and so he wages war against them. But I trust in the Lord that this effort will be of little benefit to the devil. Consider all that you have done to sustain the nuns there. Now when they are in their greatest need, give a helping hand to the glorious St. Joseph.

10.   May it please the divine Majesty to preserve you very many years for the protection of the poor, for I know the favor you have shown those poor discalced fathers. May he give you the increase of holiness that I always beg of him for you, amen.

Today is the last day of January.

Your paternity's unworthy servant and subject,

Teresa of Jesus

If it doesn't tire you, you are welcome to read the enclosed letter that is for the sisters.

---

1.   The Carmel of discalced nuns in Seville.
2.   Six nuns accompanied Teresa from Beas to the foundation in Seville. They were Ana de San Alberto, María del Espíritu Santo, Leonor de San Gabriel, Isabel de San Jerónimo, Isabel de San Francisco, and María de San José, who reported their names in her *Libro de Recreaciones*, no. 8. See also F. 24.6.
3.   About 13 others entered the Carmel after it was founded.
4.   The letter was probably lost. Teresa often sent letters to María de San José through Pantoja so that he could read them to her and the nuns.
5.   María de San José, who had been deposed from the office of prioress.
6.   Felippo Sega.

7. The process was instituted by the Carmelite provincial in Andalusia, Diego de Cárdenas, in the Carmel in Seville (November–December 1578). Teresa is alluding to the calumnies against Gracián.

8. The Carmels in Castile were also being harassed in similar ways.

9. Since the time the previous nuncio, Ormaneto, died.

10. This person was the confessor Garciálvarez who took the side of the provincial, Cárdenas.

11. To the discalced Carmelite nuns in Seville, Ltr. 284.

12. Diego de Cárdenas, who sequestered Teresa's letters and sent them to Madrid. María de San José described her own situation thus: "They so guarded me that I could neither speak nor communicate with anyone, not even with my own sisters" (Recreaciones, 9).

284. To the Discalced Carmelite nuns, Seville

Avila, 31 January 1579

(Autograph: DCN, Seville)

The community in Seville was going through a crisis. Stripped of his powers as visitator, Gracián underwent a trial initiated against him by the provincial of Andalusia. The trial was seconded by the community's former confessor, Garciálvarez. The objective of the scheme was to discredit Gracián and depose the prioress, María de San José. Then the provincial appointed one of the most inept nuns in the community, Beatriz de la Madre de Dios, to take the prioress's place. Teresa knew all about what was happening. Lest her letter be confiscated, she sent it to her good friend, the prior of the Carthusians, so that he might read or give it to the interested nuns (see Ltr. 283).

1. The grace of the Holy Spirit be with your charities, my daughters and sisters. You should know that I have never loved you as much as I do now, nor have you ever been so obliged to serve the Lord, for he has given you the great favor of being able to taste something of his cross and share in the terrible abandonment that he endured on it. Happy the day you entered that house where such a fortunate event was reserved

for you! I envy you very much, and indeed when I learned of all those changes—for everything was carefully communicated to me[1]—and that they wanted to expel you from that house and about other details, I felt the greatest interior joy. I saw that, without your having crossed the sea, our Lord revealed to you mines containing eternal treasures.[2] Through these, I hope in the Lord, you will be left very rich and able to share with those of us who are here. For I believe that he will enable you to bear all without your offending him in any way. Don't be afflicted that you feel it very much, for the Lord would want you to understand that you are not capable of as much as you thought when you were once so desirous of suffering.

2.   Courage, courage, my daughters. Remember that God does not give anyone more trials than can be suffered and that His Majesty is with the afflicted.[3] For this is certain, there is no reason to fear but to hope in his mercy. He will reveal the whole truth; and some machinations, which the devil kept hidden so as to create a disturbance, will be made known. This was more painful for me than all that is happening now. Prayer, prayer, my sisters, and now let humility shine forth—and obedience in such a way that no one, especially the former prioress,[4] practices it more toward the appointed vicaress.[5]

3.   Oh, what a good time it is for gathering fruit from the resolutions you made to serve our Lord. Consider that often he desires to have proof that our works are in conformity with our resolutions and words. Bring honor to the daughters of the Blessed Virgin, your sisters, in this great persecution, for if you help one another, the good Jesus will help you. Even though he sleeps at sea, when the storm gathers strength he calms the winds.[6] He wants us to ask of him, and he loves us so much that he is always looking for ways to be of benefit to us. May his name be blessed forever, amen, amen, amen.

4.   In all these houses they are urgently praying to God for you, and so I hope in his goodness that he will soon provide the remedy for everything. So strive to be joyful and reflect that, if

carefully considered, all that is suffered for so good a God, who suffered so much for us, is small, for you have not reached the point of shedding your blood for him. You are among your sisters and not in Algiers.[7] Let your Spouse act and you will find that it won't be too long before the sea will swallow up those who wage war on us in the manner of King Pharaoh.[8] And he will set his people free, and everyone will be left with the desire to suffer again, so great will be the gain they feel from what they underwent.

5. I received your letter and I regret that you burned what you had written,[9] for it would have been useful. According to learned men here you could have refused to hand over my letters, but it doesn't matter. Would that the divine Majesty be pleased to let me bear the weight of all the blame, although the afflictions of those who have suffered without blame have weighed heavily upon me.

6. What distressed me very much was that in the investigative process[10] carried out by Father Provincial some things were asserted that I know to be completely false because I was there at the time. Out of love for our Lord consider carefully whether anyone said something out of fear or confusion, for when there is no offense against God, it all amounts to nothing. But lies, lies prejudicial to others, are what hurt me deeply; although I cannot bring myself to believe what was said, for everyone knows of the integrity and virtue with which our Padre Maestro Gracián[11] converses with us and how much he has benefitted us and helped us go forward in the service of our Lord. And since this is so, even if the accusations are insignificant, it is a serious fault to make them. Inform the sisters of this, for goodness' sake, and remain with the Holy Trinity, in God's safekeeping, amen.

7. All the sisters here send their best regards. They are waiting for these clouds to pass so as to receive an account about everything from Sister San Francisco.[12] My regards to good Gabriela,[13] and I ask her to be happy, for I have ever present in

my mind the affliction she must have suffered in seeing Madre San José treated the way she was. I do not feel sorry for San Jerónimo[14] if her desires are genuine, and if they are not I would feel more sorry for her than for all the nuns.

Tomorrow is the vigil of Our Lady of Candlemas.

8.   I would much rather speak to Señor Garciálvarez[15] than write. Since in a letter I cannot say what I would like to say, I am not writing to him. My regards to the other sisters to whom you dare make mention of this letter.

Your charities' unworthy servant,

Teresa of Jesus

1. She is alluding probably to news given by a messenger rather than by letter.
2. Her analogy refers to the fact that it was from Seville that boats set sail for the Americas and their treasures.
3. Allusion to 1 Cor. 10:13.
4. A euphemism for the "deposed prioress," María de San José.
5. Beatriz de la Madre de Dios, the nun appointed by the provincial, Cárdenas, to take over as superior.
6. Allusion to Mt. 8:25–26.
7. An allusion to the plays that were a custom in the community in which the nuns would act as Christians in a foreign land longing to suffer martyrdom (see no. 1 of this letter).
8. Allusion to Ex. 14:28.
9. Probably they had written a report documenting the events of the process to which they had been subjected by the provincial.
10. This process was carried out by Diego de Cárdenas in the Carmel of Seville in November–December 1578. An account of it is given in María de San Jose's *Libro de Recreaciones*.
11. Jerónimo Gracián, the main casualty of the process.
12. Isabel de San Francisco.
13. Leonor de San Gabriel, who was of a delicately sensitive nature and who had been Teresa's nurse.
14. Isabel de San Jerónimo, who used to make a show of her ardent desires to suffer.
15. Garciálvarez, the community's former confessor who, because he

had been dismissed as confessor by María de San José, joined ranks with the provincial.

285. To Doña Inés Nieto, Alba
Avila, 4 February 1579

(Autograph: DCN, Toro [Samora])

The Duke of Alba (Don Fernando), his son Don Fadrique, and his secretary, Juan de Albornoz, the husband of Doña Inés, were imprisoned by the king. Their offense was that Don Fadrique, who had a distinguished record of service in Flanders, secretly married his cousin, against the express orders of the king. Don Fadrique was already pledged to marry a lady-in-waiting of the queen, Magdalena de Guzmán. The duke and his secretary were considered accomplices in the act. Teresa wrote this letter of condolence to the secretary's wife.

1.   Jesus. The grace of the Holy Spirit be always with your honor and so favor you that you will gain through these trials. They have caused me grief, and so I am praying to our Lord for you, although I understand from another perspective that trials are favors His Majesty grants to those he loves deeply. He does this to awaken us so that we do not prize the things of this life—which are so changeable and unstable—but seek eternal life.

2.   This year we have undergone so many storms and calumnies that at first I became all the more distressed by the imprisonment of Señor Albornoz.[1] After learning that it happened over the matter of Don Fadrique,[2] I am left with hope in God that the ordeal will not last long. I kiss his honor's hands and trust that the time will come when he will not want to exchange one day of his being in iron chains for all the golden chains of earth. May God be pleased to give him health, for it enables one to suffer trials better.

3.   I don't feel so sorry in your regard, for I think our Lord has given you the resources to suffer even greater trials. May His Majesty increase his grace within you more and more and keep you for many years, amen.

Today is 4 February.

Your honor's unworthy servant,

Teresa of Jesus

<hr />

1.   Juan Albornoz, Doña Inés's husband.
2.   Fadrique de Toledo.

286. To Padre Nicolás Doria, Madrid
Avila, 10 February 1579

Gracián and other friars among the discalced were being confined as punishment by the nuncio, Sega, but Nicolás Doria had escaped condemnation. Teresa now discusses with Doria problems and possibilities about what to do. The autograph was tampered with by editors of the 18th century who found bothersome several of Teresa's assertions, such as the last two sentences.

❀❀❀❀

1.   In view of the desire we have to negotiate, I wouldn't want us to offer to do anything that we cannot easily carry out. It is also necessary to consider whether it would be wise to found a house in Rome, even though now the situation is favorable, or wait until we are stronger. For if those living there, being so near to the pope, become hostile toward the discalced friars—and they will, because goodness is offensive where faults exist—a war terrible for everyone would result. But if you should send the letter to the king's canon,[1] your reverences should let him know whom you intend to name as provincial. In the brief they singled out some who, allowing for a few exceptions, I believe, don't know anything. It would be a real trial if they should perhaps choose one of these.

2.   For the time being I would not want you to undertake this journey[2] so that those here who are being punished are not left without the help of anyone and it doesn't seem necessary since everything there seems to be in good order. If you should have to go, it would be more fitting to wait and go for the general chapter,[3] since it will be the duty of the provincial to go—that is, if God should want you to be elected. If those who go now are waiting for you, you could represent us as our delegates and free us from our embarrassment.[4]

May our Lord direct everything to his greater glory and guard you with an increase of holiness.

3.   I don't have time to tell you more. Thus you won't have to be suffering further annoyance over so many things that are true. I fear that they will let Padre Mariano go without a sentence, for God sees that he is weak.[5] May we be given the strength to die for His Majesty; certainly this brawl has come from his mercy.

Today is 10 February.

Your reverence's unworthy servant,

Teresa of Jesus

4.   But what a letter this is, so characteristic of an old woman with little humility and full of advice! May it please God that some of it be correct; if it isn't, that we still be friends.

---

1. Diego de la Montoya.
2. A journey to Rome.
3. The chapter was scheduled to take place in Rome in 1580.
4. The embarrassment was caused by the two discalced friars (Pedro de los Angeles and Juan de San Diego) previously sent to Rome, who had hardly arrived when they deserted the cause.
5. Teresa is speaking ironically. Ambrosio Mariano de San Benito had been sent on an engineering project by the king, and the nuncio had forgotten about punishing him.

287. To Roque de Huerta, Madrid
Avila, 12 March 1579

Roque was disturbed at being restricted from communicating with Gracián, Antonio de Heredia, and Mariano. In the meantime Sega and the appointed judges deliberated on the future of the discalced friars and nuns; and the discalced friars sent to Rome were negotiating there for the erection of a separate province. Teresa, with the assistance of Roque, was sending out many letters.

❖ ❖ ❖ ❖

1. Jesus. The grace of the Holy Spirit be with your honor. I am sorry about the distress our affairs cause you. You should know that they do not disturb me that much, for I understand that they are from God and that His Majesty looks after our affairs more than we do. So, with whatever happens I will be content, for many prayers have been offered for this intention, and by good souls. Thus, perhaps what seems to us most adverse is what is most fitting for his service. Thus you should not be disturbed about anything. The end of the world is not at hand.

2. Since I see that those fathers[1] are well and that justice is being observed, there is nothing to fear. Even if justice is not being observed, there is no better time than now for us to suffer without fault. Furthermore they tell me the nuncio is very much the servant of God, and so he will gather information about everything, and the same goes for the other judges.[2] Since it is forbidden to write or speak to those fathers,[3] there is no point in writing to them, but I would love to console them and tell them how I envy them.

3. I have already received the letter that came by way of Toledo and also this one that Pedro Ríes[4] brought, so filled with doubts that it made me laugh and praise our Lord for your charity and how much you take our affairs to heart. Some day we will be able to serve you.

4.   The judges are more than right in saying that they will not do anything as a favor. It wouldn't be real justice if anyone were moved by favoritism rather than the truth.

5.   Señora María de Montoya[5] is wrong to think that it has ever entered our minds that the letters brought to the canon[6] will be sufficient to bring our affairs to a close. His Majesty has to do this. But the letters usually help by recommending the petitioners as religious persons and considered to be so in Spain. The more this is said of them, the better.

6.   Doctor Rueda[7] sent me the enclosed letters to be delivered to his majesty, the king. Give them to him yourself and tell him I kiss his hand. I would like to have written to the count.[8] I kiss his lordship's hands many times. We were very happy to learn of his son's health.[9] Tell him this and that we are comforted to know that he is in Madrid.

7.   Would you send the letter addressed to the prior of St. Augustine's[10] to someone who will hand deliver it, and do not let on that it comes from me or from you. Believe me, that could do us harm. And the one addressed to the discalced Franciscan father[11] should also be sent through a reliable person, for this father is a very good friend of mine. The other one is from my brother.[12] I beg you to give it to the one to whom it is addressed and tell him to send the answer to you, and then send that to me, and pardon me. Except for this last one the letters are very important for the matter that concerns us.

8.   I always notice that these letter-carriers deliver the letters to you safely and to me also. There's no need for other round-about ways. Since these fathers[13] now have what they want, they won't be so diligent. Take care to seal the letter well.

9.   Be assured that if I could see our Padre Gracián freed from the task of visitator, I think the rest would be bearable. This is what always tormented me. And if they were to send someone from any other order, I would be truly content, as long as he would not be one of these fathers of ours.[14]

May God provide, as he can, and protect you and those ladies, for whose prayers I beg.

Today is the 12th.

Your unworthy servant,

Teresa of Jesus

1. She is referring to the three who were being punished by the nuncio, Felippo Sega: Jerónimo Gracián, Antonio de Heredia, and Ambrosio Mariano.
2. The other judges appointed were Luis Manrique, Pedro Fernández, Hernando del Castillo, and Lorenzo de Villavicencio. They were to judge the way Gracián had been carrying out his work as visitator.
3. In Sega's sentence against Gracián, the latter had been forbidden to receive business letters from anyone, especially nuns (see MHCT 2:81). Teresa seems to think that the punishment given to Gracián was meted out to the other two as well.
4. Teresa's messenger and mail carrier in Avila.
5. The sister of the canon lawyer, Diego de Montoya, who in Rome took an interest in the cause of the discalced Carmelites.
6. The letters they brought to Montoya were probably letters of recommendation from prelates and other persons in favor of the discalced Carmelites. For an example of this kind of letter, see the one to the king's secretary from Don Alvaro de Mendoza, Bishop of Palencia, of 22 October 1578 in MHCT 2:40.
7. Fernando Rueda, a canonist in Avila and advisor to Teresa.
8. Luis Hurtado de Mendoza, the Count of Tendilla.
9. López de Mendoza.
10. The prior of the Augustinians in Madrid, Lorenzo de Villavicencio, one of the judges appointed to deal with Gracián's case.
11. Probably, Antonio de Segura.
12. Lorenzo de Cepeda.
13. The Carmelites of the observance who were placated by the condemnation of Gracián.
14. A Carmelite of the observance.

288. To Padre Jerónimo Gracián, Alcalá
Avila, Beginning of April 1579

This passage from one of Teresa's letters was copied by Gracián in his book, Peregrinación de Anastasio *(dialogue 16). When Gracián was confined to the monastery in Alcalá, the rector there because of sickness asked him at times to conduct the chapter for the friars. Three of the friars wrote complaining to the nuncio that Gracián was back to governing and not complying with the orders given him. The nuncio was infuriated and sent a letter of reprimand to Gracián.*

I was astonished and very angered by the letters from Alcalá, especially by the one you wrote. Oh, good God, how true it is that we do not know ourselves! Well, I tell you, as I have written you before, that after what has been done I am so afraid that I wish you weren't there, and I think this will come about. Would to God you were back with the cats![1] The threat is a good one.

1. The Carmelites of the observance.

289. To Padre Jerónimo Gracián, Alcalá
Avila, April (?) 1579

Diego de Cárdenas, the provincial in Andalusia, supported by Garciálvarez, set up a malicious process in the Carmel of Seville toward the end of 1578, gathering calumnies against Gracián, Teresa, and María de San José. He deposed the latter from her office as prioress and appointed in her place a nun recently professed, Beatriz de la Madre de Dios (Chaves). For a complement to this fragment see Ltrs. 283 & 284.

1.   I am shocked and saddened by those two souls;[1] God help them. It only seems that all the furies of hell have joined together there to deceive and blind persons both within the community and outside.

2.   Your paternity should know that all the terrible distress I experienced when you wrote me about the process going on there resulted from my having foreseen what is now happening, that they would raise some calumny against Paul.[2] And this miserable vicaress[3] has always been known for spreading some serious calumnies. For days I have been living with this affliction. O Jesus, how it has weighed down on me! All the trials we have suffered were nothing in comparison.

3.   God is indeed teaching us what little attention we ought to pay to creatures, however good they may be, and how we need to be shrewd instead of so simple, and, please God, that will be enough for Paul and for me.

---

1.   Beatriz de la Madre de Dios and Margarita de la Concepción, members of the Carmel in Seville who were spreading calumnies.
2.   Jerónimo Gracián.
3.   Beatriz de la Madre de Dios, who was appointed vicaress of the Carmel in Seville.

290. To Padre Jerónimo Gracián, Alcalá
Avila, Mid-April 1579

(Autograph: DCN, Corpus Christi, Alcalá de Henares)

Gracián had been allowed his freedom again, and so Teresa eagerly awaits a visit from him. The nuncio, Sega, withrew his decree of 16 October 1578, in which he annulled the elections carried out by the discalced friars in the chapter of Almodóvar (9 October 1578) and placed them under the jurisdiction of the provincials of Andalusia and Castile. At this time he appointed Angel de Salazar, a Carmelite of the observance, as vicar general of all the discalced Carmelites. After commenting on these events, Teresa gives her thoughts about the way to present the discalced cause in Rome and about what should be done in the Carmel of Seville. Part of the letter is missing.

❖❖❖❖

1.   Jesus. The grace of the Holy Spirit be with your reverence, *mi padre*, and reward you for the consolation you have given me

through the hope I can have of seeing you, which will certainly be a great joy for me. And so I ask you for the love of our Lord to arrange for this to come about, for the loss of a joy is not as disturbing as it is when the lost joy is what one was hoping for. I think His Majesty will be served if you come.

2. This happiness has helped me receive well the election of a new superior.[1] May it please our Lord that he hold the office for only a short time. I don't mean that he die,[2] for after all he is the most talented one among them; and with us, he will be very restrained, especially because he has the good sense to understand where a thing will end up. In a way those fathers were dealt with as badly as we. For persons seeking perfection, we couldn't desire anyone more befitting than the Señor Nuncio, for he has made us all gain merit.[3]

3. I praise our Lord that Padre Fray Gregorio[4] has already arrived at his house. And I will do the same if you succeed in having the prioress of Seville reinstated,[5] for it is certainly the right thing to do. And if not her, then Isabel de San Francisco,[6] for the present one is a mockery and will end up destroying the house. May the Lord direct everything for his greater service, and reward you for the care you take in looking after those poor foreigners.[7] Since the provincial of the fathers of the cloth[8] is not in command over them, they will feel greatly relieved, for they will be able to write and receive letters. I wrote to them through the prior of Las Cuevas,[9] and I wouldn't mind if the letter fell into the provincial's hands, for I wrote it with this intention.

4. The traveler[10] has everything ready now, and the more I deal with him, the more hope I have that he will do everything very well. We had an argument here because I wanted a copy made of the letter to the king so as to send it with the first shipment of mail to the canonist Montoya[11] along with a parcel of letters that I am now sending his mother for delivery to him. And I am writing him that this letter will be brought to him now, or if not, that two fathers will bring it who are going to Rome to render obedience to our Father Vicar General.[12] And it seems

to me that in a matter so serious it is good to proceed along two different paths, for we are not certain of the successful outcome of a particular path. And it would be a troublesome thing in our present situation to have to wait for another trip to be made. Also, since the canonist has already taken up this cause, it is better not to turn aside from his help—as time goes on, he will prove a good friend, and this business is no easy matter—for that would do harm. And I hold that it is better for him to do the negotiating and that those fathers go directly to Father Vicar General. I have little trust that their mission will remain a secret, and if they go about negotiating with this one and that and the vicar general finds out, he will perhaps be displeased that they did not come to him first, something that would not be so with the canonist.

5.   Padre Fray Juan[13] says that if the canonist does the negotiating there is no reason for him to go, but there is so much to do that there will perhaps be need for both of them. Would to God that he would find that the negotiations were finished. It would still be no small matter if discalced friars got to be known there who had more religious spirit and substance than those seen before.[14] And these friars could explain everything to Father Vicar General. It also seems to him that he would be spending ...

1. Angel de Salazar was appointed vicar general for the discalced friars and nuns by the nuncio, Felippo Sega, (see MHCT 1:89).
2. Teresa was hoping that soon the discalced Carmelites would be allowed to become an autonomous province with a provincial of their own.
3. After having previously opposed the discalced Carmelites, Sega now with this brief of 1 April 1579 (see MHCT 1:86–90) challenged the Carmelites of the observance.
4. Gregorio Nacianceno, a discalced Carmelite sent by the nuncio to Andalusia.
5. María de San José, who was unjustly deposed by the provincial in Andalusia, Diego de Cárdenas.
6. A nun in the Carmel of Seville who had also been punished by Diego Cárdenas.

7. Allusion to the nuns who had come from Castile for the foundation in Seville.
8. Diego de Cárdenas.
9. The Carthusian prior, Hernando de Pantoja (cf. Ltrs. 283 & 284).
10. Juan de Jesús Roca was in Avila preparing for his secret trip to Rome to plead the cause of the discalced Carmelites.
11. Diego de Montoya from Avila, the king's canonist in Rome. His mother, residing in Avila, was María de Montoya.
12. The vicar general for the whole order was Giovanni Battista Caffardo.
13. Juan de Jesús Roca.
14. She is alluding to the two friars sent previously by the chapter of Almodóvar against her advice: Pedro de los Angeles and Juan de Santiago (cf. Ltr. 272, note 13).

291. To Padre Jerónimo Gracián, Alcalá
Avila, April 1579

(Autograph fragments: DCN, Terre Haute, Indiana [U.S.A.])

These two autograph fragments are from the same letter, but without a connection between them. The dating is approximate.

1.   … All the nuns in this house send you their best regards. I am not surprised by the holiness they attribute to your paternity, but I would be surprised by the contrary considering all the prayers that have been said by such good people, and I believe these daughters of yours are indeed so. But how many changes of superiors our Lord has delivered us up to,[1] and how many fears for me![2] I tell …

2.   … Blessed be God who is pleased that we so pass our lives! What you are going through adds greatly to my pain. God forgive you for the days you made me go through with your fevers and blood spitting. And they tell me you have been suffering like this for some time. I don't know why it is that you did not let me know. I tell you, *mi padre*, that I feel so provoked

that I don't know how I will manage to say a good word to you, for although I …

1. She is referring to the changes made in the three briefs from Sega in which the discalced Carmelites were placed under three different jurisdictions within less than a year.
2. Cf. Ltr. 289.2.

292. To Padre Jerónimo Gracián, Pastrana
Avila, 21 April 1579

Gracián had been granted his freedom, so Teresa held on to the hope of seeing him. She also had reason to hope for an improvement in the situation of the Carmel in Seville and for the possibility of establishing a separate province for her discalced Carmelites. Gracián's sister María de San José would be making profession in Valladolid.

❧❧❦❦

For *mi padre*, Paul, in Elijah's cave.[1]

1.   Jesus be with your paternity, *mi padre*. I had already written this letter when I received those you sent me. I hope our Lord has given you as happy an Easter as I desired and his daughters begged for him.

2.   God be blessed that our business affairs are so progressing that the separation will soon end and poor Angela[2] will be able to confer about her soul. For since your absence she has not been able to speak to anyone about anything that might bring her relief. Truly, our afflictions nonetheless have taken up all our attention. It seems to me that you have borne the greater part, since our Lord has so quickly repaid you by the fact that you have been of benefit to so many souls.[3]

3.   Señora Doña Juana[4] has now written me a letter concerning the matter of our sister, María de San José.[5] She never mentioned you. Although she said she was writing in haste, that was not enough to keep me from complaining about it. I

wrote to the prioress of Valladolid[6] that Sr. María should make her profession when she has completed her year.[7] The prioress answered that the thought of delaying the profession had never entered her mind until I told her to wait. Truly, it seemed to me that a delay would matter little if it meant that you would be able to attend. But it is better now not to delay, since we have such solid hope of becoming a province,[8] and I agree with you that all will go well.

4.   My brother kisses your hands, and little Teresa[9] is very content and as much a little child as ever.

5.   I feel some relief about matters in Seville, now that the calced friars have no authority over the nuns.[10] The archbishop wrote me that the discalced friars were very distressed until the nuncio's decisions arrived; now they are very happy.[11] They are confessors to the nuns, and Fr. Vicar, Fray Angel,[12] says that in a month Nicolao will return there, and María de San José's voice and standing will be restored and there will be an election.

6.   From the letters that Padre Nicolao[13] writes me, I gather that he is very prudent and will be of benefit to the order. Before leaving, he will come to see me. This is necessary so that he will better understand what has happened there and I can give him some advice to give to María de San José in the event that she is reelected. Garciálvarez[14] no longer goes there. He says the archbishop forbade him to. May God take care of everything and be pleased to allow me to speak at leisure with you about many things. I understand that all is going very well for you with Padre José.[15] That is what is important.

7.   I'm amused to learn that now you are again wanting trials. Leave us alone for a while, for the love of God, for you don't suffer them alone. Let's rest for a few days. I well understand that trials are the kind of food that when really tasted will make one understand that there can be no better sustenance for the soul. But since I do not know whether they will involve others besides myself, I cannot desire them. I mean to say that there must be a great difference between suffering ourselves and

seeing our neighbor suffering. This is a disagreement we have that needs clarifying when we meet.

8.   May it please our Lord that we succeed in serving him in whatever way he desires. And may he keep you many years in the holiness I beg him to grant you, amen.

9.   I wrote to Valladolid that there was no reason for them to write to Señora Doña Juana about covering the dowry since she doesn't have to give it until after the profession,[16] and even then not for certain. And I said that since her daughter was received without a dowry the nuns shouldn't even talk about the matter, for in other places the nuns would lift their hands to God in thanksgiving. I didn't want to speak of anything else, and I sent the prioress the letter you sent to Señora Doña Juana. So for now everything is settled. I wouldn't want her to say a word about this to Padre Angel,[17] for there is no reason to and it wouldn't be necessary, even though she is his good friend. You know how these friendships can come to a quick end; such is the world. I think you brought me to understand this in one of your letters; although you may not have done so with this in mind. Nonetheless, you might advise her about this, and remain with God.

10.   Do not forget to recommend me to His Majesty along with all the other souls you keep in mind, for you know that you have to render God an account for mine.

Today is the last day of the Easter feasts.

Your unworthy servant and daughter,

Teresa of Jesus

11.   Write to Señora Doña Juana about when the profession[18] will take place, for I don't have time to write her now. I am so afraid to write in this regard that I am not doing so, and will do so as little as possible. I have already answered my daughter María de San José. It would be a great comfort to have her with me. But our Lord is not disposed to give me any.[19]

---

1.   Paul is Gracián. He is in retreat in one of the caves on the property of the discalced friars in Pastrana.

2. Angela is Teresa. Gracián had been confined by the nuncio to Alcalá.
3. Gracián was called by the Duke of Alba to be his confessor when the Duke was confined to Uceda on account of the planned marriage of his son Don Fadrique without permission from the king.
4. Juana Dantisco, Gracián's mother.
5. Gracián's sister, María de San José, was a novice in the Carmel of Valladolid. The subject matter of the letter concerned María's profession.
6. María Bautista.
7. María de San José (Gracián) received the habit on 5 May 1578 and made her profession on 10 May 1579.
8. With Sega's latest brief, she grew in hope that the discalced Carmelites could become a separate province.
9. Teresa's niece, daughter of Lorenzo de Cepeda, living in the Carmel of Avila.
10. The painful situation in Seville in which the prioress was calumniated and deposed from office.
11. The Archbishop of Seville, Cristóbal de Rojas. The nuncio had withdrawn the jurisdiction over the discalced Carmelites that he had previously given to the provincial in Andalusia, Diego de Cárdenas (see MHCT 2:90–94).
12. Angel de Salazar, appointed vicar for the discalced Carmelites by the nuncio.
13. Nicolás Doria, who being in Madrid was ordered by Salazar to return to Seville.
14. A confessor at the Carmel in Seville who collaborated with Diego de Cárdenas.
15. Jesus Christ.
16. Gracian's mother, Juana Dantisco. Because Doña Juana's deceased husband had been in his service, the king did give 500 ducats as a dowry for María de San José (Dantisco).
17. Angel de Salazar.
18. The profession of her daughter, María de San José.
19. Teresa had wanted to keep her as her secretary (cf. Ltrs. 242.3 & 246.3).

293. To Pedro Juan de Casademonte, Madrid

Avila, 2 May 1579

Don Pedro Juan was a businessman in Madrid who had befriended the Carmelite nuns in Medina and had won the esteem of King Philip II. He was supportive in the preparations for the journey of the two discalced friars to Rome.

❧❧❧❧

1.   Jesus. The grace of the Holy Spirit be with your honor. I received your letter and those of José Bullón.[1] May our Lord watch over him, for it is hard to have to see him go so far, but since the need is great something has to be suffered. We all owe him much; he has the virtue and talents for this, and even more. May God bring him back safely. I beg you to let me know on what day and in what manner he left.

2.   I can't wait for him to leave our country, seeing that he is traveling in such a manner.[2] May no misfortune befall us; we would find ourselves in a terrible situation.

3.   May our Lord reward you for the good news you sent me. You should know that ever since those lords and those Dominican fathers of mine were appointed assessors to the nuncio,[3] all my worries about our affairs left me. For I know them and with persons like the four of them, I am certain that what they ordain will be for God's honor and glory, which is what we are all seeking.

4.   The ones whom I'm now very worried about are the fathers of the mitigation, for such ugly events cannot but deeply hurt those who wear this habit. May God provide a remedy, watch over you, and repay you for the goodwill you have shown toward this order and your good deeds, which certainly cause me to praise God. Where charity is present, His Majesty provides ways for exercising it.

5.   May it please him to watch over your honor and Señora Doña María. Although miserable, I do not neglect to beg him for this and that he make you both very holy.

Today is 2 May.

> Your honor's unworthy servant,

> Teresa of Jesus

---

1. A pseudonym for Juan de Jesús (Roca) during his trip to Rome.
2. Juan de Jesús and his companion, Fray Diego, traveled in disguise so as not to be recognized. His apparent motive for going to Rome was to obtain a dispensation for Francisco de Bracamonte, who wanted to marry his cousin. Don Francisco provided the disguises for the two friars, a mule, and 400 ducats for the journey.
3. The "lords" were Luis Manrique, the king's chaplain, and Lorenzo de Villavicencio, an Augustinian. The Dominicans were Hernando del Castillo and Pedro Fernández. They were appointed by the king to assist in the process against Gracián.

294. To Isabel de San Jerónimo and María de San José, Seville
Avila, 3 May 1579

This letter was written when the painful events that occurred in the community in Seville were being resolved. Diego de Cárdenas, the provincial of the Carmelites of the observance in Andalusia, had deposed the prioress and appointed in her place a somewhat unbalanced nun, Beatriz de la Madre de Dios. Garciálvarez, the confessor, and a recently professed nun, Margarita de la Concepción, had sided with Beatriz in their opposition to María de San José. Angel de Salazar, the vicar general, then began to set matters right by deposing Beatriz and appointing Isabel de San Jerónimo in her place. Teresa wrote this open letter to both Isabel, the acting superior, and María de San José, the former prioress, so that at their discretion they might read it to the community. This letter is best understood in conjunction with Letters 283 and 284.

❧❧❧❧

For Madre Isabel de San Jerónimo and Madre María de San José, discalced Carmelite nuns at St. Joseph's in Seville.

1.   Jesus. The grace of the Holy Spirit be with your reverence, my daughter. I received your letter and that of my sisters the

day before yesterday. O Jesus, and what a great consolation it would be for me to be present now in that house, just as it would have been for me before so as to share in the treasures our Lord has given you in such abundance! May he be blessed forever! Amen.

2.   The love I had for you has doubled to the extreme, even though it was great; and for you especially since you are the one who has suffered the most. But be assured that when I learned that they had deprived you[1] of your office, voice, and standing in the community, I felt a particular consolation. For even though I know that my daughter Josefa is very wretched, I am convinced that she fears God and would not have done anything against His Majesty that would deserve such punishment.

3.   I wrote you a letter[2] through *mi padre*, the prior of Las Cuevas, so that he may have it delivered to you. I would like to know if he received it, and another one that was for him, and to whom he gave it, even if I have to write again. When Padre Nicolao[3] learned of what happened with your brother's letter, he tore it up. You owe him very much. You have fooled him more than Padre Garciálvarez.[4]

4.   I am sorry that he may no longer say Mass[5] there, although it is the house that loses thereby; for him a great trial is being removed. Certainly we owe him a lot, but I don't know what can be done. If the most reverend archbishop has not listened to the prior of Las Cuevas or to Padre Mariano,[6] I don't know who will be able to do anything.

5.   In a way, these notes from Padre Mariano have irritated me—that it could even pass through his mind that such a thing be sought in that house, or even spoken of.[7] The fact is that the devil in the excess of his fury has wanted to afflict us in every way, especially in ...[8] Now it seems our Lord does not wish to give him so much license, and I hope His Majesty will so ordain that the truth will be discovered.

6.   In that house there has been little truth. It distressed me very much when I learned of the statements made in the process[9] and of some things that I knew were seriously false, since they had to do with the time when I was living there. Now that I have seen what is happening with those sisters,[10] I have given great thanks to our Lord for not having allowed them the opportunity to raise any more calumnies.

7.   These two souls have worn me out, and we all need to pray especially that God will give them light. Ever since Garciálvarez began acting in such a way,[11] I feared what I now see. If you recall I wrote twice that I believed that the trouble came from within the house, and I even named one person—Margarita never entered my mind—so that you would be on your guard. The truth is that I was never satisfied with her spirit, although sometimes I thought my dissatisfaction was a temptation and that I was a wretch. And I even spoke of the matter with Padre Maestro Gracián. Since he spoke with her so often,[12] I brought his attention to the matter, and so now I have not been very surprised. And it is not that I thought she was bad, but deluded through an unstable imagination, a ready prey for the wiles of the devil, the one behind this. He knows very well how to profit by one's natural condition and poor judgment. So, there is no reason to blame her so much but to have great pity on her. In this case you and all the other sisters must do me the favor of not turning aside from what I am now going to tell you, and believe that, in my opinion, it is the suitable thing to do. And you should praise the Lord that he did not permit the devil to tempt any of you so strongly. For as St. Augustine says, we should think that if he had, we would have done worse things. Do not desire, my daughters, to lose what you have gained at this time. Remember what St. Catherine of Siena did for the one who accused her of being a bad woman and let us fear, let us fear, my sisters. If God were to withdraw his hand from us, what evils might we not commit? Believe me, this sister has neither the mind nor the talent for inventing such things, and so the devil arranged to

give her this other companion, and she certainly must have been the one who taught her. God be with her.

8.   First, I say that you should heartily recommend her to His Majesty at all times in all your prayers, as we will here, that he might enlighten her and that the devil will let her awaken from this dream in which he holds her fast. I consider her to be a person partly deranged. You should know that I know some persons, although not in these houses, with unstable imaginations who think they truly see everything that comes into their minds; the devil must prompt them in this. And my grief is that he must have made this sister think that she sees what in his opinion is suited to bringing about the ruin of that house. And perhaps she is not as much to blame as we think, as is so with a madman who, if he really gets it into his head that he is God the Father, no one can convince him otherwise. Here you ought to manifest, my sisters, the love you have for God by showing her great compassion, just as you would if she were the daughter of your parents; for she is the daughter of this true Father to whom we owe so much and whom the poor little soul has desired to serve all her life. Pray, sisters, pray for her. Many saints have also fallen and have returned to being saints. Perhaps all this was necessary for her humility. If God should grant us the favor that she come to her senses about what she has done and retract it, we will have all gained through suffering, and it could be the same for her, for God knows how to draw good from evil.

9.   Second, don't let it enter your minds for now to have her leave your community.[13] That would be a great folly and by no means appropriate, for the more you think you are getting rid of hazards, the more you will encounter them. Let time pass, for this is not the moment for such a change. I could give many reasons for this, and I am surprised that you do not see them. Think about this, and God will show them to you, and trust in His Majesty and in those of us who are considering with more calm what is suitable for your community. For now be careful

not to speak about such a move and don't even let it enter your mind if possible.

10.   Do not manifest toward them any kind of dislike, and be even more gracious to the one who was superior, all the nuns showing her sisterly kindness, and they should do so toward the other nun also. Try to forget the things that took place and let each one consider what she would like done if this had happened to her.

Be certain that this soul must be undergoing a real torment even though she may not be aware of it. The devil will see to that, since he didn't succeed in doing anything worse. He could induce her to take some action that would cause her to lose both her soul and her mind. For the latter it would perhaps require little. This is what we all ought to consider and not what she did. Perhaps the devil led her to think that her soul was gaining and she was rendering great service to God. Don't say a word to her mother, for I feel very sorry for her.[14] How is it that no one says anything to me about how she bore all these things and what she said—I've wanted to know this—and whether she knew about her daughter's schemes?

11.   I fear that now again the devil will stir up in them other temptations—that you wish them harm and treat them badly— and it would make me very angry if you gave them any occasion for so thinking. I have already been informed that those in the Society do not think it right that she be treated badly. Be very careful.

12.   Fourth, that she not be allowed to speak to anyone without another nun present—someone very astute. Nor should she confess to anyone but a discalced friar. He may be one chosen by her since Father Vicar General[15] has ordered that they be your confessors without exception. Take care, without showing it, that the two not speak much to each other. Don't put any restrictions on them—for we women are weak—until the Lord begins to heal them. And it wouldn't be bad to keep her busy with some duty as long as it would in no way allow her

to have contact with outsiders, but only with those living inside the monastery. Her being alone and with only her thoughts can do her much harm, and so now and again let those who think they could be of help spend some time with her.

13.   I believe that before Padre Nicolao goes down there we will have a meeting together—I would like it to be soon—and talk more about everything. For now, out of charity, do what I tell you. At any rate, those who really desire to suffer do not bear any bitterness toward the ones who do them harm, but rather more love. From this you will see whether you have benefitted from the time in which you had to bear the cross. I hope in our Lord that he will soon provide a remedy and that the house will remain as it was before; and even better, for our Lord always gives back one hundred percent.

14.   Consider that I am again urgently asking that you in no way talk with one another about what happened, for no benefit can come from so doing, but much harm. In the future it will be necessary to proceed with great care. As I have said, I fear that the devil will lure poor Beatriz—the other one I'm not so worried about, for she's smarter—into some vile scheme, or tempt her to leave. Keep careful watch, especially at night. Since the devil is working to discredit these monasteries, he at times makes possible that which seems impossible.

15.   If the bond between these two sisters is broken and something happens that puts them at odds with each other, they will come closer to getting to the bottom of things, and the door will be opened for them to become disillusioned with each other. You will notice that the friendlier they are with each other, the more support they will find for their intrigue. Prayer can do much, and so I hope the Lord will enlighten them. They cause me much grief.

16.   If it's a solace for you to write down all that happened, it would not be bad for you to do so in order to learn from the experience, for on account of my sins I do not learn from that

of others. But if Sister San Francisco[16] is going to be the histo-
rian, she should not exaggerate but state very simply what has
taken place. A copy ought be made by my daughter Gabriela.[17]
I would like to write to all the nuns, but my head isn't up to it.
I have called down many blessings on you, the blessing of the
Blessed Virgin, our Lady and of the entire Most Holy Trinity.

17. You have rendered a service to the whole order; those
especially who have not made profession have proved well
that they are your daughters. And I pray that they may be so
more and more. And let those who have written me consider
this letter as meant for them. For even though it is addressed
particularly to Madre María de San José and the vicaress,[18] my
intention is that it be for all the nuns.

18. I would have liked to write to my sister Jerónima.[19] Tell
her that she has greater reason to regret the discredit that
Padre Garciálvarez's departure brings to the house than what
has happened to him; he is well known in Seville. The poor
foreigners[20] are the ones who have to carry the whole burden.
It was clear that once it was thought that he committed some
fault, the nuns could not be excused from any. But I am sure
that, as I say, his virtue is well known. As for the rest, he has
been relieved of a heavy load. Certainly we could never exaggerate all that he has endured here and all that we owe him,
nor could we repay him for it; only God can.

19. Give him my best regards. I would have written him at
great length had my head been up to it, and what I would like
to say is expressed poorly in a letter. I am not going to write
then, for I might get into some complaining. Since others know
about the great misdeeds those two blessed souls said were
committed in the house, you would not have been going to
extremes by keeping me informed at times—seeing that I was
the one who would find it most painful—and not wait for those
who have so little love for us,[21] as everyone knows, to find a
remedy. In the end, the truth suffers but does not perish, and
so I hope that the Lord will make it known more and more.

20.   Give my regards to good Serrano.[22] I look for the day in which we can repay him for all we owe him. To my holy prior of Las Cuevas send my best wishes. Oh, if I could spend an entire day with him! May God watch over you for me and make you as holy as I beg him to, amen. These sisters have wept more over your trials than I have, and they beg for your prayers. I will write again soon, and the matter concerning Madre San José[23] that you recommend to me will perhaps be settled by the time this arrives. You are doing well now; don't be in a hurry. There's no reason to hold the election until you receive directions to do so from here; there's no lack of diligence here in attending to this matter.

21.   If Padre Mariano is there, send this letter to him and have him return it. Since I don't think a letter from me will reach him there, I am not writing now. Give my regards to Padre Fray Gregorio.[24] I would like to have a letter from him. As for the Mass, I don't know what to tell you; don't be in a hurry. If you do not have anyone to say it for you, don't kill yourselves. Let the nuns be satisfied with Sunday Mass until the Lord provides. Thus they will not miss the opportunity for gaining merit. I am feeling fairly well.

22.   Padre Julián[25] has been distressed about your trials. I believe that if he thought he could do something to free you from them, he would willingly go down there. He begs you for your prayers. May God give you the strength to suffer more and more, for you have not yet shed your blood for him who shed all of his for you. I assure you that we have not been idle up here.

Today is the feast of The Finding of the Cross.

Teresa of Jesus

23.   Oh, how distressed my brother[26] was about your trials! It was necessary to console him. Pray for him, for you owe it to him.

To Madre Isabel de San Jerónimo, the vicaress, I say that all the counsels she gives in her letter seem very good to me and show more courage than Madre San José's. My regards to Sister Beatriz de la Madre de Dios and tell her I rejoiced that she is now without a trial, for in a letter I received from her, she told me what a great trial that office was for her. Give my best wishes to Sister Juana de la Cruz.

1. The former prioress, María de San José, whom she later calls Josefa (no.2) or Madre San José (no. 23).
2. Actually she wrote two letters, one for the community (Ltr. 284) while Beatriz was the vicaress, and another to the prior of the Carthusians, Hernando de Pantoja (Ltr. 283).
3. Nicolás Doria.
4. She is being ironical, contrasting the esteem Doria has for Madre María with the dislike shown her by the community's former confessor, Garciálvarez.
5. The Archbishop of Seville expressly forbade Garciálvarez to say Mass for the Carmelite nuns.
6. Padre Ambrosio Mariano de San Benito.
7. She was irritated because of the drastic measures Mariano must have suggested against the two nuns who were culpable (see no. 9).
8. The text is illegible because the paper in the autograph is worn.
9. She is alluding to the sham process conducted by Cárdenas, the provincial.
10. Beatriz de la Madre de Dios and Margarita de la Concepción.
11. Opposing the prioress, he favored two or three others in the community.
12. It was Padre Gracián who introduced her to Carmel (see F. 26. 11–12).
13. Transfer to another Carmel.
14. Beatriz's mother, Juana de la Cruz, was also a nun in the Carmel of Seville.
15. Angel de Salazar appointed discalced friars to be confessors for the community.
16. Isabel de San Francisco had the reputation of being a good chronicler.
17. Leonor de San Gabriel.
18. Isabel de San Jerónimo was the vicaress.
19. Jerónima de la Madre de Dios, a cousin of Garciálvarez.
20. She refers to the nuns who came from Castile as "foreigners."

21. These would include the provincial and some of the other friars of the observance in Seville.
22. Serrano was one of Teresa's messengers.
23. She is alluding to the desire that Madre María de San José be reinstated in her office as prioress.
24. Gregorio Nacianceno, a discalced friar living in Seville.
25. The chaplain at St. Joseph's in Avila who had accompanied Teresa to Seville for the foundation there.
26. Lorenzo de Cepeda, a close friend of the community in Seville.

295. To the prioress and community, Valladolid

Avila, 31 May 1579

The community in Valladolid would receive 500 ducats from the king as a dowry for Gracián's sister who had just made profession there. Teresa makes an urgent request that they help pay for the negotiations in Rome to establish a separate province for the discalced Carmelites. She also encourages them to be sensitive to the financial needs of Gracian's mother.

For Mother Prioress and my sisters and daughters of Mount Carmel in the monastery of Valladolid.

1.   Jesus. The grace of the Holy Spirit be with your reverence, my mother, and all those dear sisters of mine. I want you to keep in mind that from the time that house was founded I have never asked you, that I can remember, to accept a nun without a dowry or anything else of consequence, which has not been the case with other communities. In one community they have accepted eleven nuns without dowries. Not for this reason are they worse off; their situation is the best of all.[1] Now I want to ask you to do something that you are obligated to do for the good of the order and for various other reasons. And although it lies in your own interest to do this, I want to assume the debt myself, and I ask that you do me this favor. I am worried that

what is so important for the service of God and for our peace might fail for lack of money.

2.   The enclosed letters from a discalced father, the prior of El Calvario,[2] who has arrived in Rome, show what urgent need there is for two hundred ducats. Since the discalced friars have no one in charge,[3] they can't do anything. Fray Juan de Jesús and the prior of Pastrana —[4] who have also gone to Rome, although I don't know if they have arrived—could collect so little that without what I gave them, they brought only one hundred fifty ducats, which they got from Beas.[5] It is a great grace from our Lord that some of our houses can contribute to this need, for after all it arises but once in a lifetime.

3.   Padre Nicolao[6] writes me from Madrid that he has found a person who out of deference to him will advance two hundred ducats in view of Sister María de San José's dowry[7] on the condition that your house send him a promissory letter. He will be satisfied with this even if you delay reimbursing him. I consider this very fortunate, and so I ask you out of charity that as soon as this letter arrives you call for a notary so as to testify that sister has made her profession. Thus the action will be completely valid, for without this nothing can be done. Send it to me at once along with your promissory letter. The two statements should not be together, but kept on separate pages. Note how important it is that you act quickly.

4.   If the amount seems a lot to you and you are wondering why all the houses don't contribute, I tell you that each house does do what is possible, and any house that cannot give anything, like this one, doesn't give anything. This is why we all wear the same habit, that we might help one another, for what belongs to one belongs to all. And he who gives all that he can gives a great deal. How much more so because expenses are so high that it's frightening. Sister Catalina de Jesús[8] can affirm this. If the houses do not provide the money, I cannot earn it, for I am crippled.[9] Moreover, it pains me to have to go around raising money and begging. Certainly for me it is a torment, and only for God can I bear it.

5.   Apart from this I now have to raise two hundred ducats that I promised Montoya, the canonist,[10] for he has given us life; and please God that amount will be enough and bring all this to an end. It is a great mercy that money can play a role in the attainment of so much peace.

What I have said is a matter of obligation. What I am about to say now is up to you, although it seems reasonable to me and something that will be pleasing to both God and the world.

6.   You well know that you received Sister María de San José because of her brother, our Padre Gracián.[11] Her mother,[12] being in serious need, postponed her daughter's entry there—from what I've learned—until she could negotiate over those four hundred ducats. She thought the charity you extended to Padre Gracián would remain in effect and that with the promised ducats she could provide for her own needs, which as I say are many. Now I am not surprised that she is upset at having to give up her plan. But she is so good that despite everything she does not cease being grateful for the favor that has been shown her. With regard to the one hundred ducats, you already know from Padre Maestro Gracián's letter, which I sent you, that he requests that you deduct all that his mother spent on her daughter, which amounts to the one hundred ducats that he mentions there. So the promissory letter should be for three hundred ducats.[13]

7.   Don't pay much attention to whether she will inherit anything or not, for everything they have comes from the king's generosity; they have no income. And when the secretary[14] dies, they will receive nothing. As for whatever is left, there are so many brothers and sisters that it would be useless to bother about it, as she wrote me afterward. I don't know if I saved the letter, if I did I will send it to you. Anyway, the promissory letter should be for at least three hundred ducats.

8.   What I say is that it would be nice if you would promise the whole four hundred, for she would not fail to send you the other hundred when she has received the money.[15] And even

if she doesn't, she definitely deserves something for all the bitter afflictions—the present ones and others too—she has had to suffer on account of her son; they have been terrible ever since he was given the task of making visitations. All of this I say apart from what is owed to our Padre Gracián, for if so many nuns have been accepted into the order without a dowry, all the greater is the reason that something be done for him.

9.   For her sister who is in Toledo,[16] the nuns did not ask for either a bed or a trousseau or a habit or anything, nor was anything given for her. And they would very willingly have accepted another sister of hers under the same conditions if she had desired to enter there. For God has given them such qualities and talents that the nuns would desire this other one rather than someone else with a dowry. With regard to the one hundred ducats, do whatever you think best. As for the rest, nothing else can be done, for the need is urgent.

10.   What must be done when the negotiations in Rome are over is to consider what each house is entitled to and return money to those who have given more. And so this will include your house. For the present let us help one another as we can. I ask Mother Prioress[17] not to oppose what the sisters want to do, for I am very confident that they are no less daughters of the order than the sisters in our other houses who are doing what they can.

May God make you all as holy as I beg of him, amen.

      Your servant,

                 Teresa of Jesus

11.   In any case, let Sister Catalina de Jesús read this letter to everyone—I would be very much saddened if anything were omitted—and the other enclosed letters from Rome as well.

---

1.   She is probably referring to the house in Toledo.

2.   Pedro de los Angeles was sent to Rome to negotiate the affairs of the discalced Carmelites. But he betrayed the discalced and abandoned the reform.

3. Both Gracián and Antonio de Jesús Heredia had been deposed.

4. Juan de Jesús (Roca) and Diego de la Trinidad (prior of Pastrana) were commissioned to go to Rome to carry on with the negotiations in favor of the discalced Carmelites.

5. Cf. Ltr. 277.

6. Nicolás de Jesús María (Doria).

7. María de San José (Gracián's sister) was accepted without a dowry. She made her profession on 10 May 1579. Then the king decided to endow her with 500 ducats in gratitude for the services rendered to him by her father, his secretary. This money will serve to pay the 200 ducats that the friend in Madrid will advance for the negotiations in Rome.

8. A nun in Valladolid who later accompanied Teresa on the foundations she made in Palencia and Burgos.

9. Teresa had broken her arm, which was never set properly, in December 1577.

10. Diego de Montoya was carrying on business for Teresa in Rome.

11. Jerónimo Gracián.

12. Juana Dantisco.

13. Teresa, it seems, wanted them to promise 200 ducats for the friars in Rome and 100 ducats for Juana Dantisco, who had many expenses because of her large family and was in urgent need. This was to be advanced by Doria's friend in Madrid.

14. Diego Gracián.

15. The additional 100 ducats would cover Doña Juana's expenses for her daughter's entry. Teresa may be implying that they not require her to pay it back.

16. Isabel de Jesús (Gracián).

17. María Bautista. In Teresa's opinion this prioress's interest was to store up provisions for her own house. Nonetheless, the response was quick, and 400 ducats were promised.

296. To Madre María Bautista, Valladolid
Avila, 9 June 1579

(Autograph: DCN, Seville)

Teresa expresses her joy and gratitude to the community in Valladolid for their prompt and generous response to her request for a promissory letter. She is planning a long trip that will bring her to Valladolid, Salamanca, and Malagón among other places. Part of the letter is missing (cf. Ltrs. 295 & 297).

❖❖❖❖

1. Jesus. May the Holy Spirit be with your reverence and repay you and all the sisters there for the happy Pentecost you gave me by sending the promissory letter[1] with such good will. It came just in time, for the messenger had not yet left for Madrid. They had written urging me to hurry, so I was overjoyed.

2. I assure you that even had the money been given for my own use, I could not be more grateful. You have all shown your generosity and in a gracious way. May the Holy Spirit repay you. I am asking God to give you back much more than you have given. Read this part to the sisters. I recommend myself very much to their prayers. I wrote to Madrid about what you said so that they could see what they possess in all of you.

3. I have written so much today and it is so late that I will be able to say little here. The first thing, for goodness' sake, is that you take care of yourself so that if God brings me there, I will find you in good health. Father Vicar, Fray Angel,[2] has somewhat implied this possibility in a letter to me. There's some hope. But since I would be just passing through, I wouldn't want to come. It would mean traveling many leagues only to feel more pain for having to leave you so soon. He wrote that he has thought of making me gain merit by confirming an order that I go to Malagón, for by so doing I would gain more merit than if I made a foundation and that on the way I could go to console Lord and Lady de Mendoza,[3] for they are requesting this. And he is sending me the letter from the bishop,[4] saying that I should go at once to Salamanca and buy the house. And you ought to know, my daughter, that there is the greatest need of my going there, and they are as silent as the dead, which urges me all the more to provide for them. Look at this poor old woman! And then at once to Malagón.[5] I tell you that all this made me laugh, and I have the courage for more. May God direct it all.

4.   It may happen that before I finish in Salamanca, our document[6] will arrive and I can come to you more leisurely. Someone else can take care of the matter in Malagón. There is no lack of suspicion—and signs supporting it—that perhaps the calced friars are pleased that I will be so far away and that his paternity will not regret my being far from the Incarnation.[7] My attending to the needs of those monasteries will require time, and there won't be so much occasion for grumbling about my going out; I am not doing so for a mere trifle. May the Lord direct matters so that I may best serve him.

5.   He says in the letter that I should take what he is now telling me as a sketch for a painting, for he first has to discuss everything with Fray Pedro Fernández.[8] Until he does this no action can be taken. In the enclosed letter to the bishop he explains himself more clearly. He certainly desires to please him and indeed is so good he doesn't know how to say no.

6.   He has approved of a college for discalced friars,[9] but not the monastery for the nuns.[10] And that not for his own reasons, but Fray Antonio de Jesús and the prior of La Roda[11] thought that the foundation would not be opportune. I was delighted because I had refused many times on account of the eight beatas[12] who are there. I would rather found four monasteries.

7.   Padre Fray Pedro Fernández has insisted that we not found a monastery until we have our own province, even though he might give the license. And he gives good reasons—they have written them down for me. For since the nuncio[13] is so easily moved, and there are those who will talk about it to him, we could be harmed. Everything must be well thought out.

8.   As for the Casilda matter,[14] I am disappointed. It means that they won't give you anything. I tell you that all they had to do was give you the twenty-five hundred ducats they had mentioned, or at least two thousand. What use is all this uproar? Never has there been so much noise for so little ...

---

1.   In the letter of 31 May (Ltr. 295), Teresa had requested a promissory letter for 200 ducats. The response was positive and exceptionally quick.

2. Angel de Salazar.
3. Don Alvaro de Mendoza (the former bishop of Avila) and his sister María de Mendoza were grieving over the unexpected death of the Duke of Sessa (3 Dec. 1578) who had recently married Doña María's daughter (Nov. 1577).
4. Don Alvaro de Mendoza, who was currently the Bishop of Palencia.
5. She left Avila on 25 June, passed through Medina and arrived in Valladolid on 3 July. On 30 July she left for Alba, and by mid-August was in Salamanca. In November she set out for Malagón.
6. The permission from Rome to establish a separate province for the discalced friars and nuns.
7. Elections for prioress of the Incarnation were due in the following spring, and the superiors did not want a repeat of what had happened in the elections of 1577 (cf. Ltrs. 210–212;215;218–221).
8. It was expected that Pedro Fernández, the former apostolic visitator for the Carmelites in Castile, would have a role to play in the erection of a province for the discalced Carmelites.
9. The college for discalced Carmelite friars was actually founded on 1 January 1581.
10. She is referring to a foundation for Villanueva de la Jara, where one in fact was made in February 1580.
11. Gabriel de la Asunción (see F. 28.11).
12. Nine women were living a life of recollection together in a little house near a shrine to St. Anne (see F. 28.8).
13. Felippo Sega.
14. Despite their wealth the family reneged on paying the dowry (see Ltr. 164).

297. To Padre Jerónimo Gracián, Alcalá
Avila, 10 June 1579

(Autograph: DCF, Teresianum, Rome)

Teresa was going to be ordered to set out once more on some travels through Spain, and ultimately to Malagón. She was living in the presence of Christ and was willing to go to the ends of the earth for him. But she did not want to be prioress either at the Incarnation or in Malagón. She was being sent away partly to prevent the possible trouble of her receiving votes again at the coming election for prioress at

*the Incarnation. Her thoughts were turning to heaven (her
Pentecost which had not yet arrived).*

❧ ❧ ❧ ❧

1.   Jesus. The grace of the Holy Spirit be with your paternity,
mi padre. I hope that this Pentecost[1] has brought you so many
of his gifts and blessings that through them you may render His
Majesty the service you owe him for having willed to come to
the aid of his people, at so great a cost to yourself.[2] May he be
praised for everything. Certainly there is a great deal to reflect
on and write about regarding this whole story.

2.   Although I don't know all the details of how it was brought
to a conclusion, I understand that everything went very well.
At least, if the Lord allows us to become a province, nothing
will ever have been done in Spain with so much inquiry and
authorization. This must mean that the Lord wants the discalced
friars for more purposes than we imagine. May it please His
Majesty to keep Paul[3] for many years that he may place his effort
and find his joy in this work; I will be watching from heaven, if
I am worthy to go there.

3.   They have already brought the promissory letter[4] from
Valladolid. I am delighted to send this money. May the Lord so
ordain that the matter will be concluded quickly. Even though
the superior we have now is very good, something else is
needed for us to be properly established, and, after all, he is
only on loan to us.[5]

4.   In this letter of his, you will see what is being arranged
for this poor little old woman.[6] From certain indications one
can suspect that the desire my calced brothers have to see
me far away from here is greater than the need in Malagón.
This caused me a little distress. But the rest didn't stir any
emotions, not even in their first movements—I mean going
to Malagón—although going there to be prioress bothers me,
for I am not suited for that, and I fear failing in the service of
our Lord. Beseech him that I might be without flaw, and as for

the rest let whatever comes come, for the greater the trial, the greater the gain. In any case, tear up this letter at once.

5.   It is a great consolation for me that you are feeling so well, but I don't like seeing you there in that heat. Oh, how each day adds to the loneliness of my soul at seeing you so far away—although it seems to be always near Padre José.[7] In this way one passes through life well, without earthly consolation, yet continually consoled. It seems you are no longer of this earth, since the Lord has withdrawn the occasions of your becoming attached to it and filled your hands with what keeps you in heaven. Truly, the more I think about this storm and the means the Lord has taken, the more stupefied I become. And if he be pleased that those Andalusians[8] make some amends, I would consider it a special favor that he help them through the hands of someone else, since it was not in you to rule with the strong hand required for their good. And their good is what I have always desired. I was pleased with what Padre Nicolao[9] writes me in this regard, so I am sending his letter to you.

6.   All the sisters here ask for your prayers. They are distressed at the thought that I must go away. I will keep you informed. Pray hard for me to the Lord, out of charity. You will surely remember how they criticize my goings about,[10] and who is the source of their criticisms. What a life! But it doesn't matter.

7.   I have written to Father Vicar[11] about the drawbacks to my being prioress, my not being always able to follow the community acts and other reasons. The truth is that I would feel no pain even if I had to go to the ends of the earth as long as it were out of obedience. In fact, I believe that the greater the trial, the greater my joy would be in doing at least some little thing for this great God to whom I am so indebted. I especially believe that he is served more when something is done only out of obedience. With my Paul[12] it is enough to know that I am pleasing him for me to do something with joy. I could speak of many things that would bring me joy, but I fear putting them in letters, especially in matters of the soul.

8.   That you may have a few laughs, I am sending you these couplets from the Incarnation, although the situation of that house is rather something to cry over.[13] The poor sisters are trying to distract themselves. They will feel very sad over my going away, for they still have hope,[14] and I do too, that a way to help that house can be found.

9.   The nuns in Valladolid have very willingly given the two hundred ducats, and the prioress has also.[15] If she hadn't had it, she would have gone looking for it. And she is sending a promissory letter for the entire four hundred ducats. I have greatly appreciated this, for truly she stores up all she can for her own house. But what a letter I wrote to her![16]

10.   I was amused at how well Señora Juana[17] knows the prioress—I was amazed. She writes me that she is somewhat afraid of her, for she has given the money without telling her about it. And truly, as for what regards Sister María de San José,[18] I've always seen that the prioress is very nice to her. For, after all, this shows the goodwill she feels toward you.

11.   My regards to Father Rector,[19] and the same to the *padre* who wrote me the other day.

Yesterday was the last day of the Easter season. Mine has not yet arrived.

Your paternity's unworthy servant,

Teresa of Jesus

---

1.   It was on the vigil of this Pentecost Sunday (7 June 1579), while praying in the hermitage of Nazareth, that Teresa received the four counsels for the discalced friars (see ST 64).

2.   So as not to prolong the investigation into his actions as visitator and provincial and thereby hold up the establishment of a separate province for the discalced Carmelites, Gracián allowed himself to be sentenced without proven blame (see MHCT 19: 165–66).

3.   Gracián.

4.   The promise to pay the 200 ducats needed to finance the negotiations being carried on in Rome.

5. Angel de Salazar was appointed superior for the discalced Carmelites on 29 May 1579. Although he treated them well, he secretly opposed their becoming a separate province (see MHCT 2: 140–43).

6. In being transferred to Malagón, she was to go by way of Salamanca.

7. A code name for Jesus Christ.

8. The Carmelites of the observance in the province of Andalusia.

9. Nicolás Doria.

10. In fact, in Avila she was complying with the sentence imposed on her by the general chapter of Piacenza (1575), by which she was to withdraw definitively to a monastery in Castile and not go out to make any new foundations.

11. Angel de Salazar.

12. Gracián.

13. The nuns at the Incarnation had not yet recovered from the divisions created by the painful election for prioress in October 1577, at which they were forbidden to vote for Teresa.

14. Hope of having Teresa for their prioress.

15. Although María Bautista was prioress, the decision to promise the money was made by the community.

16. For that letter see Ltr. 295.

17. Juana Dantisco, Gracián's mother.

18. Gracián's sister.

19. Elías de San Martín, rector of the college for discalced friars in Alcalá.

298. To Madre Inés de Jesús (?), Medina

Avila, June 1579 (?)

This is a fragment from one of Teresa's letters recorded by the historian at the Incarnation, María Pinel. The addressee and date are uncertain.

❖❖❖❖

I don't know what this poor old woman is doing that they don't let me rest; they want me to go to Malagón.[1] At the Incarnation they are very unhappy that I am going away, for they still have hopes of having me there.[2]

1. See Ltrs. 296.3 and 297.4.
2. She is alluding to their failed attempt to get permission to vote for her as prioress in 1577.

299. To Madre Ana de la Encarnación, Salamanca

Avila, 18 June 1579

The letter carrier was waiting, so she wrote in a hurry, telling of the traveling orders just received and adding some other details.

✦✦✦✦

1.   Jesus. The grace of the Holy Spirit be with your reverence. Today, the feast of Corpus Christi, Padre Vicario, Fray Angel,[1] sent me the enclosed letter for your reverence and an order under precept of obedience that I go to your house. Please God it wasn't a scheme of yours, for I am told that Señor Luis Manrique[2] asked this of you. But if I can do something to help bring you rest, I will gladly do it, and would be willing to go at once. But he wants me to go to Valladolid first. He must not have been able to avoid it, for I certainly did not contribute to the idea. In fact (between you and me), I did what I reasonably could so as not to go, for I thought that at this time my going there could be avoided. But the one who stands in the place of God understands better than I what is suitable.

2.   He says that I should stay there just a short time, but however short, I will be there during the coming month, and hope that, please God, the time will be long enough. It doesn't seem to me that this delay will matter much as regards your concerns. You must keep this secret from Pedro de la Banda;[3] otherwise he will kill us with his contracts, while what most suits us is to have none. If some need arises, you can write to me in Valladolid.

3.   The letters did not arrive, but the student's father is going around looking for him. Don't be disturbed, for now I am setting out for a place close to where Padre Baltasar Alvarez[4] is. They tell me that the bishop in that place[5] is feeling well again, which made me happy.

4.   Tell Sister Isabel de Jesús[6] that I am very sorry about her illness. I wrote to the prioress in Segovia[7] to tell Señor Andrés de Jimena[8] that if he wants to talk with me he should come here quickly; I don't know what he will do. Father Vicar tells me that he is giving me permission to enter into contracts. My desire is that he not fail to come. We will not have disagreements, with the Lord's help, for I desire very much to please and serve him.

5.   Tell my Isabel de Jesús that I wouldn't want to find her in a weak state. Her bodily health is what I desire, for I am content with that of her soul. Tell her this. The messenger is waiting and so I cannot say more than may God watch over you, and regards to all the sisters.

Today is the feast of Corpus Christi.

Your reverence's servant,

Teresa of Jesus

1.   Angel de Salazar.
2.   Philip II's almoner, who was very interested in helping the discalced Carmelites.
3.   The irascible "gentleman" from whom Teresa bought the house for her foundation in Salamanca.
4.   Her former Jesuit confessor in Avila.
5.   The Bishop of Salamanca, Jerónimo Manrique.
6.   Isabel de Jesús (Jimena), who had returned from Segovia to the monastery in Salamanca where she had entered.
7.   Isabel de Santo Domingo.
8.   Isabel de Jesús' brother, a benefactor of the house in Segovia.

300. To Madre María Bautista, Valladolid
Avila, 21 June 1579

Teresa received orders from her new Father Vicar to set out once more on some business matters. She would be visiting a few Carmels along the way and doesn't want any grand receptions from any of them.

❖❖❖❖

1.   Jesus be with your reverence. However great my hurry to send this messenger on, it is late because today is Sunday. I was also delayed a little because Padre Nicolao[1] just arrived. I was delighted to see him.

2.   I am now going to send your letter to Father Vicar.[2] I am writing myself to his paternity listing the advantages or reasons there seem to be for him to give the permission; and I am telling him why Ana de Jesús[3] was not accepted there. Understand that I am always fearful of much money, although the things they tell me about this young woman make me think that God is drawing her.[4] Please God, this will be for his service, amen. Give her my best regards and tell her I am happy that I will be able to see her so soon. The illness of Doña María[5] has grieved me very much. May God give her health, which is what I am begging of him, for I certainly see how much I care for her now that I am without her.

3.   You must know that on the feast of Corpus Christi[6] our Father Vicar sent me a command to go to your house. There were many censures in the bishop's orders lest the vicar would resist carrying out well what the bishop[7] wanted him to do. So, I suppose I will be leaving here a day or two after the feast of St. John.[8]

4.   In your charity, forward to me in Medina a letter that our Father Vicar will send you, for it is necessary that I see it there. And tell them not to prepare for my arrival with any noisy reception, and I ask the same of you, for I tell you definitely that such receptions mortify me instead of making me happy. This

is really true, for within myself I become upset to see how little I deserve all the attention; and the bigger the fuss, the more upset I become. See that they don't do anything special if they don't want to greatly mortify me.

5.   Regarding the other things you wrote about, I am not going to say anything because, with God's favor, I will be seeing you soon. I'll stop off in Medina no more than three or four days, since I'll be returning there on my way to Salamanca. This is in accord with the orders of Father Vicar; and he does not want me to stay long in Valladolid.

6.   Inform Doña María and the Lord Bishop about what is happening. They are right to be glad that our Father Vicar has received this task, for naturally he desires to be at their service. And so he broke through all the obstacles to my making this trip—for he encountered many; and your desires, too, are being met. May God forgive you. Ask God that my journey will be for your benefit and that you not be so bent on having your own way. To me this sounds impossible, but God can do all things. May His Majesty make you as good as I beg of him, amen.

7.   I haven't given your regards to the sisters yet. As for the Casilda business,[9] don't do anything until I get there. And when we know what her mother[10] is going to do, we will give a report to Father Vicar. Since her tertian fevers are mild, do not be distressed. Give my regards to all the sisters.

Today is Sunday within the octave of the feast of the Blessed Sacrament.

This messenger arrived at 5 o'clock this morning; we are going to send him on his way around noon today.

     Your reverence's unworthy servant,

Teresa of Jesus

---

1.   Nicolás Doria.

2.   Angel de Salazar.

3.   Ana de Jesús (from Valencia) made her profession in Valladolid on 20 April 1579 and was now to be sent to another Carmel where there was a need.

4. She is speaking of another aspirant.
5. María de Mendoza.
6. 18 June 1579.
7. Alvaro de Mendoza, the Bishop of Palencia.
8. St. John the Baptist, celebrated on 24 June. Teresa left Avila on 25 June.
9. The business concerned the dowry of Casilda de Padilla.
10. María de Acuña.

301. To Madre María de San José, Seville
Avila, 24 June 1579

Teresa writes in haste, on the day before her departure, to urge Madre María not to refuse the office of prioress. She asks that a complete account of all that happened in the Seville Carmel be written up for her. At the time, she is trying to balance all she has to do with a visit from Padre Doria.

❧❧❧❧

For Madre María de San José, in the monastery of the discalced Carmelite nuns in Seville.

1.   Jesus. The grace of the Holy Spirit be with your reverence, my daughter. I don't know how you can be silent for so long a time when at every moment I am wanting to hear how you are doing. I tell you I am not being silent here in what regards your house.

2.   You should know that Padre Nicolao[1] is here, for he is prior of Pastrana and came to see me. His visit was a wonderful consolation and I praised our Lord for having given our order a person like this, who is so virtuous. It seems His Majesty chose him as the means to set things right in your house, judging from the effort he has made and the cost to him. Pray much to our Lord for him, because you all owe this to him.

3.   And, my daughter, set aside those foolish notions about perfection that lead you to refuse to be prioress again.[2] We

are all working and hoping to bring this about, and you come along with this childishness—and there is no other name for it. This is a matter that pertains not just to you but to the whole order. It is so fitting for the service of God that I wish it were already done—also for the honor of your house and that of our Padre Gracián. And even if you had no capacity for this office, no other solution would be suitable; even more so, since "for want of good men ..." as they say.[3]

4.   If God grants us this favor, just be silent and obey. Do not speak a word; think of how angry you will make me. What you have said is enough for letting us know that you do not want the office. And truly anyone who has such experience doesn't need to be told anything in order to understand that it is a heavy cross. God will help you; the storm has passed for now.

5.   I very much want to know whether those nuns[4] are aware of what they have done (or are they denying it in some way—for I am worried about the state of their souls), and how they are getting along. For goodness' sake give me a long report about everything. If you send the letters to Roque de Huerta through the archbishop,[5] they will be sent to where I am. Sister Isabel de San Pablo[6] will write now about what is happening here, for I don't have time.

6.   Give my regards to my daughter Blanca,[7] with whom I am very pleased; I feel obliged to her father and mother for all they have done for you. Thank them for me. I assure you that what happened in your house is a story that frightens me, and I desire that you write telling me everything about it clearly and truthfully. Tell me now especially about how those two sisters are behaving; as I have said, I am very worried about them.

7.   Give my regards to all the sisters and to Mother Vicaress.[8] She can read this letter as though addressed to her. And I also send best wishes to my Gabriela.[9] I haven't found out how Sister San Francisco[10] behaved in all this business.

8.   They are calling me now for Padre Nicolao,[11] and tomorrow I am leaving for Valladolid; our Father Vicar General[12]

has sent me orders that I go there at once, and from there to Salamanca. There was little need for me in Valladolid, but this was requested by Doña María and the bishop.[13] In Salamanca the need is great, for they are in that house which is very unhealthy, and they are undergoing much difficulty from the one who sold it to them. The trouble, the daily confrontations, and what they have undergone because of him is great, and this still goes on every day. Pray to our Lord that a good house can be bought at a low price. May His Majesty watch over you for me, my daughter, and allow me to see you before I die.

Today is 24 June.[14]

9.   I am leaving tomorrow. I am so busy that I cannot write to those daughters of mine. Let me know if they received a letter from me.

Your reverence's unworthy servant,

Teresa of Jesus

---

1. Nicolás Doria.
2. Four days after this, Angel de Salazar restored María de San José in the office of prioress for the Seville Carmel (see MHCT 2:97–98).
3. She is partially quoting from the Spanish saying: "For want of good men, my husband was made mayor."
4. Beatriz de la Madre de Dios and Margarita de la Concepción.
5. She probably means the Archbishop of Toledo, Gaspar de Quiroga.
6. From the time she broke her arm on 24 December 1577, Teresa was receiving secretarial help from Isabel de San Pablo.
7. Blanca de Jesús María. Her parents were Enrigue Freyre and Leonor Valera, benefactors of the community in Seville who continued to support María de San José.
8. Isabel de San Jerónimo.
9. Leonor de San Gabriel.
10. Isabel de San Francisco, the former prioress in Paterna.
11. What follows was dictated to her secretary.
12. Angel de Salazar.

13. María de Mendoza and her brother, Alvaro de Mendoza, Bishop of Palencia.

14. The rest is in Teresa's handwriting.

302. To Padre Jerónimo Gracián, Alcalá

Valladolid, 7 July 1579

In compliance with the orders of Angel de Salazar, Teresa had begun her travels. She was at this time in Valladolid and, contrary to her wishes, had received a huge welcome. She was tired from all the visiting. Recalling her talks with Doria in Avila, she begins to urge Gracián to be open to a good relationship with him. Her thoughts are also on Alba de Tormes and Salamanca, where she would be going soon.

❖❖❖❖

1.   Jesus. The grace of the Holy Spirit be with your paternity, *mi padre*. I arrived here in Valladolid four days ago and feeling well, glory to God, and without fatigue, for the weather was very cool. It is something that frightens me, the delight that these nuns, as well as Lord and Lady de Mendoza, found in my being among them; I don't know why. All the nuns ask for your prayers. And the prioress here says you shouldn't write to her, that because she is so loquacious, she cannot carry on a conversation with the dumb.[1] I found my María de San José[2] to be very well and happy, and everyone happy with her. I was delighted to see her; and to see how all these houses are doing, considering the poverty in which they were founded. May the Lord be praised forever.

2.   Now a postulant, very capable and talented, has received the habit here.[3] Her patrimony is valued at twenty thousand ducats. But we don't think she will leave much to the house in comparison with what she could, for she is very attached to her blood sisters. Nonetheless the amount will be reasonable, and with what the prioress adds, little

will be lacking for the nuns to have a sufficient income; and all want them to have one.

3.   As for Paul[4] going to Rome, it would be foolish, something that should not even be mentioned or allowed to pass through our minds. My greater fear is that if he is provincial, he will be required to go to the general chapter; for as far as the council goes, that father is very resolute, without giving any whys or wherefores. There is no need to speak of it, but to praise the Lord for having guided the negotiations in such a way that your going is not necessary. All we lack now is another trial to make up for those we've passed through! Not for even a moment would I want you to have this thought in your head.

4.   Padre Nicolao[5] was with me in Avila three or four days. I was very consoled that you now have someone with whom you can confer about matters in the Carmelite order and who can help you, for I am satisfied with him. I was very distressed to see you so alone in this order in all you had to do. Certainly, he has seemed to me to be wise and a good adviser, and a servant of God; although he doesn't have that charm and gentle manner that God has given Paul—few there are to whom God gives so much together. But certainly he is a man of substance and very humble and penitent and honest, and he knows how to win the favor of others. He will clearly recognize Paul's worth and is determined to follow him in everything. He made me very happy. If Paul gets on well with him, as I believe he will, even if for no other reason than to make me happy, this will prove most beneficial, for they will be of one mind.[6] And it will bring me the greatest relief. For every time I think of what you have suffered from those who should have helped you, I consider it to have been one of your greatest trials. So, *mi padre*, do not be distant with him; either I am very deceived or he will be most helpful to you in many areas. We spoke of a lot of things and projects. May it please the Lord that the time will come for carrying them out, and that this flock[7] of the Virgin, which has cost Paul so much, may have some order put into it.

5. I praise our Lord for your good health. For goodness' sake I beg you as a favor to me to stay as little as possible in Alcalá during this heat. I don't know how long I will remain here, because I am concerned about Salamanca,[8] although I enjoy being here. In all truth I cannot say that I am unhappy anywhere. I think I will try as hard as I can not to stay here longer than this month. I am afraid of some mishap in Salamanca, that a buyer might come along for the house offered to us. It is an excellent one, although expensive. But God will provide.

6. So as not to trouble you, I have never wanted to mention how difficult to bear is the licentiate Godoy's daughter in Alba.[9]

I have done as much as I can so that everything be tried, but nothing works. Since she lacks intelligence, she doesn't reason things through. She must be most unhappy, for she will burst out in loud cries. She claims this is due to a heart ailment; I don't think so.

7. I had written to the prioress[10] to write down some of the many things she says about her so that I may show it to the licentiate, and she wrote this, which I am enclosing. And afterward it seemed to me better that he not see it, but that he understand in a general way that she is not meant for us. This is painful for me because we owe him so much, but in no way would she be bearable.

8. Now I will be going there and will learn about everything, but I believe this will be of little benefit, for the things they have written me tell of someone who is without reason. Since she fears her father, she will be best off near him. I have not seen him yet. In a letter I received from him in Avila he asks that she remain in that house until he can find another way of helping her. And this we will allow. I always feared accepting her, surmising the pain he would feel if he saw she had to leave. Well, all that could be done has been done.

9. Best regards to Padre Fray Bartolomé.[11] I was delighted with his letter. May he never tire of rendering me this kindness.

I, instead, am so tired now from the visits of all the ladies who come to see me, that I am unable to write to him. Yesterday I had a visit with the countess of Osorno.[12] The Bishop of Palencia[13] is here. You owe him much, and so do we all.

10.   My regards to Father Rector.[14] May the Lord watch over you and keep you in the holiness that I beg of him.

Today is 7 July.

> Your paternity's true daughter,
>
> Teresa of Jesus

1.   María Bautista was known for her strong opinions and decisiveness. Teresa here jestingly alludes to Gracián's situation in which silence was imposed on him by the nuncio.
2.   Gracián's sister.
3.   Probably Isabel of the Blessed Sacrament.
4.   Gracián.
5.   Nicolás Doria.
6.   What actually happened was quite the opposite, and Teresa seemed to have an uncanny premonition of this.
7.   The discalced Carmelites, both friars and nuns.
8.   The definitive acquisition of the house was bogged down by fault of its seller, Pedro de la Banda (see Ltr. 299.2).
9.   Godoy was a lawyer in Valladolid and a good friend of Teresa's.
10.   The prioress in Alba de Tormes, Juana del Espíritu Santo.
11.   Bartolomé de Jesús, Gracián's secretary.
12.   María de Velasco y Aragón.
13.   Alvaro de Mendoza.
14.   Elías de San Martín, rector of the discalced Carmelites in Alcalá.

303. To Padre Jerónimo Gracián, Alcalá
Valladolid, 18 July 1579

Teresa has had visits from Godoy, the abbot, and a hermit prioress. The negotiations prompting these visits went well. She

is now eager to continue on to Salamanca to resolve an issue
there over the purchase of a house.

❖❖❖❖

1.   Jesus. The grace of the Holy Spirit be with your paternity,
mi padre. After I wrote you, the licentiate Godoy[1] came here,
which seemed to me most opportune. We talked at length
about his daughter, the nun. God has allowed that she be accepted in a Bernardine monastery—I believe in Valderas. And
so we agreed that when I go to Alba, I will investigate everything.
If I then still think she is not meant to stay with us, he will bring
her to this other monastery.

2.   This delighted me, for I was bothered by it. From the information given me I think it better that she leave, and indeed
necessary, lest by further delay the present opportunity be lost.
Her father is bearing all this like a good Christian. In addition,
the other day he had an attack of high tertian fevers. Although
they are not harmful, he is in agony. Pray for him.

3.   You should know that the abbot here[2] is a good friend of
the Bishop of Palencia.[3] I also spoke with him, and he was very
affable. There is as well a different vicar general. If God gives us
the means, we will certainly obtain the license for San Alejo.[4]
The prioress is not well.[5] She came here. She is very resolute.
Having been close to death, she appointed the licentiate Godoy
to be her executor and set up a solid basis for the negotiations.
May His Majesty bring this foundation about, as he can, for I
greatly desire it.

4.   Sister María de San José is fine,[6] and loved by everyone;
she is a little saint, and so is Casilda. All the nuns beg for your
prayers, as does Mother Prioress[7] very much so. I am doing fairly
well, and am happy to be here. I will do all I can to leave soon,
for I am worried about the need in Salamanca.[8] Nonetheless,
I will be staying beyond this month.[9]

5.   I want to tell you about a temptation I had yesterday, and
that is still going on, concerning Eliseo.[10] It seems to me that
he is sometimes careless in telling me the whole truth about

everything. I know well that the matters are of little importance, but I would rather that he be more careful about this. Out of charity, urge him on my part to do this, for I don't think there can be complete perfection where negligence like this is present. Look at what I get involved in as if I had no other worries.

6.   Take care to pray for me; I have much need of prayer. Remain with God, for I have written to a number of places and am tired.

Today is 18 July.

Your unworthy servant,

Teresa of Jesus

7.   My greetings to Father Rector[11] and to Padre Fray Bartolomé.[12] I ask you for the love of God to write me and let me know how your health is in this heat.

---

1. See Ltr. 302.6.
2. Alonso de Mendoza; he ruled the church in Valladolid, which was not an episcopal see, but dependent on the diocese of Palencia.
3. Alvaro de Mendoza.
4. The permission was for a foundation of discalced Carmelite friars at the shrine of San Alejo on the outskirts of Valladolid. The change in vicar generals made it easier to obtain the license.
5. The prioress was the hermit nun who took care of the shrine.
6. Gracián's sister.
7. María Bautista.
8. The purchase of a house for the discalced Carmelite nuns.
9. Actually, she left on 30 July.
10. Padre Gracián.
11. Elías de San Martín.
12. Bartolomé de Jesús.

304. To Madre María de San José, Seville
Valladolid, 22 July 1579

The painful problem in Seville has been settled and María de San José has been reinstated as prioress. Teresa is happy with the way all things have turned out. Recommending Padre Nicolao as an advisor, she also wants nuns to seek direction from their discalced friars. She advises them about the number of siblings acceptable in the same monastery and to try to pay back what they owe her brother.

❖❖❖❖

1.   Jesus. The Holy Spirit be with your reverence, my daughter. And how rightly I can call you this. Although my love for you was great, it has now increased so much that it amazes me. And so I experience desires to see you and embrace you warmly. May God be praised, from whom comes every good; he has drawn you victoriously out of so ruthless a battle. I do not attribute this to your virtue but to the many prayers that have been offered in these houses up here for that house. May it please His Majesty that we may be worthy to thank him for the favor he has granted us.

2.   Father Provincial[1] sent me the letter from the sisters; and Padre Nicolao,[2] yours. Thus I learned that you have been reinstated in your office, which for me was the greatest of consolations. Anything else would never have sufficed to put their souls at rest. Be patient. Since the Lord has given you so much desire to suffer, rejoice in its thus being satisfied. I well understand that it's no small trial. If we were to go around choosing the trials we want and setting aside others, we would not be imitating our Spouse, who after suffering so much in the garden from his Passion concluded: "Fiat voluntas tua."[3] We need to do God's will always; let him do what he wants with us.

3.   I asked Padre Nicolao to give you the advice that he thinks suitable, for he is very wise, and he knows you; so I submit to whatever he may write to you. I only ask you to have as little to do as possible with those who are not among our discalced friars (I mean you and the nuns in matters concerning your souls). Don't bother too much if at times the friars are not available. If communion is not received so frequently, you needn't be concerned. What is important is that we don't find ourselves

in a situation like the one in the past. If a nun at times should want to consult some other friars, do not oppose it. I have so little time that I didn't think I would even be able to write to you.

4.   My very best regards to all the nuns. On my part I thank them for the praiseworthy manner in which they conducted themselves. I also thank them for bringing me joy. May the Blessed Virgin reward them, bless them for me, and make them saints.

5.   I don't believe you can refuse to accept Enrique Freire's eldest daughter,[4] for much is owed to him. Do what Padre Nicolao tells you, to whom I submit. By no means would it be fitting to accept the youngest one now, both because of her age and because it isn't right that three sisters be together in one monastery—all the more so in our monasteries where there are so few nuns. You can delay by saying she's too young; don't discourage them.

6.   When you can begin repaying my brother,[5] know that he has his needs, for he has had many expenses all together. You know well how obligated you are to him. Oh, how much he has suffered from your trials. May God give you the calm that is best suited to your pleasing him. Write to me at length about everything, especially about those two poor souls,[6] for they have me very worried. Show them favor and strive if you can through means that seem right to you to get them to understand. I am leaving here on the day after the feast of St. Anne,[7] God willing. I will be staying in Salamanca for some days. Your letters can be addressed to Roque de Huerta. All these sisters send their best regards to you and to all the nuns. You owe them very much.

7.   These monasteries make one want to praise God on all counts. Pray to His Majesty for Malagón,[8] and for the business for which I am going to Salamanca,[9] and don't forget all those to whom we are indebted, especially those from recent times.

Today is the feast of the Magdalene.

8.　There are so many things to do here that I still don't know how I have written this; it was done at intervals. For this reason I am not writing to Padre Fray Gregorio,[10] for I thought of doing so. Write to him and give him my greetings and tell him I am happy that he played so important a role in this war, and that he will as a result share in the spoils. Tell me how our good father, the prior of Las Cuevas,[11] is doing so that I can tell how I should write to him about these affairs.

Your reverence's servant,

Teresa of Jesus

1.　Angel de Salazar, actually the vicar general.
2.　Nicolás Doria, who would be returning to Seville.
3.　"Your will be done."
4.　They already had one daughter in the Carmel (cf. Ltr. 301.6). Eventually the two others entered the Seville Carmel; but the youngest did so only after the first of them moved to the foundation in Lisbon, Portugal.
5.　Lorenzo de Cepeda, who had not yet been repaid the money he had lent for the foundation of the Carmel in Seville.
6.　The two responsible for so much of the trouble the community had suffered: Beatriz de la Madre de Dios and Margarita de la Concepción (see Ltr. 294).
7.　St. Anne's feast was on 26 July, but Teresa did not leave Valladolid until 30 July.
8.　For the building of a new monastery for the nuns.
9.　The complicated matter of buying the house.
10.　Gregorio Nacianceno, who was the vicar of Los Remedios, the monastery of discalced Carmelite friars in Seville.
11.　Hernando de Pantoja, the Carthusian prior.

305. To Don Teutonio de Braganza, Evora
Valladolid, 22 July 1579

Two reasons for this letter were the printing of The Way of Perfection *and the fear of a war between Spain and Portugal. Teresa begs Don Teutonio, uncle of one of the claimants, to*

*do all he can to prevent it. She would rather die than see war
break out.*

❧·❧·❦·❦

To the most illustrious and reverend Don Teutonio de Braganza, Archbishop of Evora, my lord.

1.   Jesus. May the grace of the Holy Spirit be always with
your most illustrious lordship, amen. Last week I wrote you
a long letter and sent you the little book,[1] and so I will not be
lengthy. I am only writing because I forgot to ask you to have
printed along with it the life of our Father St. Albert, which is in
a little notebook enclosed with the other book. This would be
a great consolation for all of our sisters since it now only exists
in Latin. This translation was done by a father from the order of
St. Dominic[2] out of love for me. He is one of the most learned
men around here and a real servant of God. He did not think
this was meant to be printed, for he doesn't have, nor did he
ask for, permission from his provincial. But if you are satisfied
with it and have it printed, the other doesn't matter much.

2.   In the letter I referred to, I give you an account of how
well our affairs[3] are coming along and how I received orders
to go to Salamanca from here, where I think I plan to stay for
a number of days. I will write to you from there.

3.   For the love of our Lord do not fail to let me know how
your health is, if for no other reason than as a remedy for the
loneliness I will feel in not finding you there in Salamanca. And
let me know if you have any news about peace in that place,
for I am very distressed over what I am hearing around here.
If, for my sins, this affair leads to war, I fear a terrible disaster
in that kingdom, and that great harm will necessarily come to
ours as well.[4]

4.   They tell me it is the Duke of Braganza who is fomenting it.
And that he is actually a relative of yours pains me to the depths
of my soul, apart from the many other reasons there are for
such pain. For love of our Lord—since in this regard you rightly

have an important part to play in his lordship's decision—strive to bring about an agreement. According to what I am told, our king is doing all he can, and this greatly justifies his cause. They must keep in mind the terrible harm that can result, as I said, and you should look to the honor of God without respect to any other thing, as I believe you will.

5.   May it please His Majesty to put his hand to this task as we are all beseeching him, for I tell you I suffer so deeply from what is happening that if God were to permit so great an evil, I would rather die than see it.

6.   May He keep you for many years in the holiness that I beg of him for you and for the good of the church, and give you so much grace that you will be able to work out a peaceful solution in his service.

7.   Here everyone is saying that our king is in the right and that he has made every effort he can to find out. May the Lord give the light needed to understand the truth without the many deaths there would be by taking a risk. And in a time when Christians are so few it would be a great misfortune were they to start killing one another.

8.   All these sisters, your servants whom you know, are well and in my opinion their souls are making good progress. All of them are being careful to pray for you. Although a wretched person, I do so always.

Today is the feast of the Magdalene.

From this house of the Conception of Our Lady of Mount Carmel in Valladolid.

Your illustrious lordship's unworthy servant and subject,

Teresa of Jesus

1. *The Way of Perfection*, which Don Teutonio will arrange to have printed in Evora. It wasn't actually published until 1583, a number of months after Teresa's death.

2. Diego de Yanguas. The 1583 edition of *The Way of Perfection* has as an appendix the text entitled *Vida y milagros del glorioso padre San*

Alberto (The Life and Miracles of our Glorious Father St. Albert). Diego de Yanguas dedicated this life to St. Teresa and at her insistence wrote: "many unhistorical things are added here for the greater glory of this glorious saint." St Albert, Patriarch of Jerusalem, gave the hermits on Mount Carmel their rule sometime between 1206 and 1214.

3. She is referring to the establishment of a separate province for the discalced Carmelites. On 15 July 1579, the nuncio Sega with his advisors proposed the erection of a separate province (see MHCT 2:99–107).

4. When the young king of Portugal was killed in battle, the nearest male heir was his great-uncle, Cardinal Enrique. The cardinal was Don Teutonio's uncle and had preceded him as Archbishop of Evora. The principal claimants to the throne were King Philip II and Don Juan, Duke of Braganza, Don Teutonio's nephew. Philip was threatening a possible military and naval intervention.

306. To Roque de Huerta, Madrid
Valladolid, 23 July 1579

On 15 July 1579, Felippo Sega and his counsel came to a favorable decision regarding the discalced Carmelites and allowed them to form a separate province (MHCT 2:99–107). Teresa now desires urgently to communicate with Padre Gracián.

1.   Jesus be with your honor. I received your letter; the favor you do me by writing gave me great joy. These letters that the messenger is carrying are addressed to my brother.[1] I told the messenger that if my brother is not there to turn to you. And so I ask you to open the packet that goes to my brother, take out a letter addressed to our Padre Maestro Gracián, and find out where he is, either in Toledo or Alcalá—I think he will be in Alcalá. And send this messenger to the place where he is, for the matter is important and is the reason I am sending this messenger.

2.   For love of God, hurry to send him on his way, for as I say the matter is important and he must be in either Toledo or Alcalá.

3.   Since I had no other purpose in writing, there is no more to say than may God be with your honor and watch over you.

Yesterday was the feast of the Magdalene.

Your unworthy servant,

Teresa of Jesus

---

1.   Lorenzo de Cepeda.

307. To Padre Jerónimo Gracián, Alcalá

Valladolid, 25 July 1579

The future for the discalced Carmelites is looking better, and Teresa is also happy with the community in Valladolid. She is worn out from the many business matters that occupied her, but will be leaving in a few days for Salamanca.

❧❧❧❧

1.   Jesus. The grace of the Holy Spirit be with your paternity. I have been so occupied since the arrival of the messenger who is bringing this letter that I feared being unable to write even these lines lest I leave my duties undone.

2.   Señora Doña Juana[1] tells me that you are not well and have a rash and that they were wanting to bleed you. This brother tells me[2] you are very well and portly looking, which took away my distress. You must be suffering from the heat. I have been afraid of it. For goodness' sake, try not to stay in Alcalá any more than necessary. I am doing fairly well. Next Thursday I will be leaving for Salamanca.[3] I am very happy to see how our Lord is guiding the affairs. May he be always praised, and go ahead and speak now that you can,[4] if for no other reason than that you find some relief among so many trials.

4.   I have written you twice from here. Sister María de San José[5] is in good health and is an angel. Everything is going very well here, and thanks to the novice who has just entered the

income is as usual sufficient. She is also an angel and very happy. May the Lord be with you, for my head is exhausted.

5.   I tell you that I laugh when I think that they made you rest for your penance and left us here to do battle unto the end. Please God we will soon see victory, and may he give you health which is what is important.

6.   Mother Prioress[6] sends her best regards. She says she doesn't want to write to you until you answer her. She's smarter than I am.

Today is the feast of Santiago.

Your paternity's servant and true daughter,

Teresa of Jesus

1.   Juana Dantisco, Gracian's mother.
2.   A discalced Carmelite from Alcalá, who it seems was going to bring the letter.
3.   She did in fact leave on the next Thursday, 30 July.
4.   She is alluding to the penalty of silence that was imposed on him by the nuncio.
5.   Gracián's sister, who was a member of the community there.
6.   María Bautista.

308. To Roque de Huerta, Madrid

Valladolid, 26 July 1579

Teresa expresses her joy in receiving the good news that Roque de Huerta sent her from Madrid as well as hope that the negotiations in Rome will turn out well.

1.   Jesus. The grace of the Holy Spirit be with your honor always, amen. I received your letter, and the good news you gave me about his majesty's favorable response was a great consolation.[1] May God preserve him for us many years, and all those counselors of his.[2]

2.   You should know that when your letter arrived in which you told me that Señora Doña María from Montoya[3] was here, she had already left for Madrid. I greatly regretted not having known this before, for I had very much wanted to see her.

3.   Let me know what you have done with the money you advanced,[4] for I am worried about this. May it please our Lord that everything turn out as well as you desire.

4.   The messenger consoled me with news of our travelers,[5] about whom I was very worried. Blessed be God who preserved them from so many dangers and brought them to safe harbor.

5.   Your honor should know that although Padre Fray Nicolao[6] keeps me informed about the negotiations, I am also happy that you do, for even though what gives so much joy is heard many times, one never tires of it. May it please our Lord that we soon see the desired end, and may he give you his holy grace.

It is 26 July.

Your honor's servant,

Teresa of Jesus

1.   She is alluding to the king's acceptance of the favorable decision rendered by the nuncio and his counsel concerning the discalced Carmelites.

2.   The four judges designated to assist the nuncio in judging the cause of the discalced Carmelites were two Dominicans, Hernando del Castillo and Pedro Fernández; one Augustinian, Lorenzo de Villavicencio; and the king's almoner, Luis Manrique.

3.   The mother of Diego de Montoya, the canonist in Rome who was looking after the discalced Carmelite cause.

4.   He had advanced the money needed for the negotiations in Rome (cf. Ltr. 280.2).

5.   The two discalced friars, Juan de Jesús (Roca) and Diego de la Trinidad, who went to Rome disguised to work toward the erection of a separate province for the discalced Carmelites.

6.   Nicolás de Jesús María (Doria).

309. To Don Lorenzo de Cepeda, Avila
Valladolid, 27 July 1579

Calm returned after a two–year storm of troubles over her reform. Now on the road again and about to leave for another of her houses, Teresa speaks of a silver chalice bought for her brother and gives him some advice on family matters. She sends news as well of other recent events.

❖❖❖❖

To Lord Lorenzo de Cepeda, my lord.

1.   Jesus. The grace of the Holy Spirit be with your honor. In a certain way the visit of that relative of ours here has tired me out. Such is life. And because we who by right ought to be so separated from the world have to pay all this respect to its proprieties, you shouldn't be surprised that although I have been here quite some time I have not spoken to my own sisters—I mean privately—even though some of them want very much to speak with me. There has not been time. And I am leaving, God willing, this coming Thursday. I will leave a letter for you, only a short one, so that the person who usually brings the money can bring the letter as well. He will also bring you three thousand *reales*, which they say are ready. This made me very happy. And he is bringing a beautiful chalice that couldn't be nicer. It's valued at twelve ducats and, I believe, one real. The workmanship is for forty *reales*. The entire amount comes to sixteen ducats minus three *reales*.[1] It's all silver. I think you will be happy with it.

2.   From those made of that metal you mention, they showed me one. Though not being very old and having been gilded, it already gives signs of what it is. It is turning black on the inside at the bottom, which is disgusting. I immediately resolved not to buy one like it. It seemed to me that for you to eat off silver and look for another metal for God would be intolerable.[2] I didn't think I would find one costing so little for such a good size, but this bargain-hunter prioress[3] through a friend arranged

the purchase for this house. She sends you her regards, and because I am writing, she will not write. Her talent and the way she cares for this house is something to praise God for.

3. My health is the same as it was in Avila and even a little better. As for those around you, it is better to pretend you don't notice anything. It is preferable that the melancholia—and it couldn't be anything else—manifest itself in this form rather than in some worse form.[4] I am happy that Avila has not died.[5] After all, since he is well-intentioned, God has granted him the grace to take sick in a place where he has been so carefully cared for.

4. I am not surprised by your trouble, but I am surprised that you have such desire to serve God and at the same time find so light a cross so heavy. You will at once say that it is for the purpose of serving God more that you do not want him living with you.[6] Oh, brother, how we fail to understand ourselves, for a little self-love lies in everything.

5. Don't be surprised by Francisco's[7] instability; that goes with his age. And you shouldn't think—although this is a different matter—that everyone must be as exact as you are in everything. Let us praise God that he doesn't have other vices.

6. I will stay in Medina three or four days at the most, and less than eight in Alba; it will take two days to go from Alba to Medina—and then to Salamanca.[8]

7. In this letter from Seville you will see that they reinstated the prioress in her office,[9] which made me very happy. If you want to write to her, send the letter to me in Salamanca. I have already told her to remember to continue paying back the money they owe you since you need it; I will take care that they do so.

8. Fray Juan de Jesús has arrived in Rome.[10] The negotiations here are going well. Montoya,[11] the canonist who was carrying on our business for us in Rome, passed by on his way with the cardinal's hat for the Archbishop of Toledo. He won't be needed any more.

9.   Go to see Señor Francisco de Salcedo, in your charity, and let him know how I am. I am delighted that he is better, to the point that he can say Mass. Please God he will recover completely. These sisters here are praying to His Majesty for him. May he be with you.

10.   You can speak about anything with María de San Jerónimo,[12] if you want. Sometimes I wish Teresa[13] were here, especially when we walk through the garden. May God make her a saint, and you as well. Give my regards to Pedro de Ahumada.

11.   Yesterday was the feast of St. Anne. I thought of you and how you are devoted to her and that you are going to build a chapel in her honor, or may have already done so, and I rejoiced.

Your honor's servant,

Teresa of Jesus

---

1.   A ducat was worth eleven reales.
2.   The chalice was destined for liturgical use.
3.   Lorenzo's cousin María Bautista.
4.   She is probably referring to Pedro de Ahumada.
5.   This could be Tomás de Avila, a friend of Lorenzo's.
6.   The two brothers did not get along well. Pedro, who was well-off financially, was residing with Lorenzo. Eventually they separated.
7.   Francisco, Lorenzo's oldest son, was 19 at the time. He lacked firmness of purpose, and after Lorenzo's death caused Teresa much displeasure.
8.   She meant to say from Medina to Alba. She traveled from Valladolid passing through Medina and Alba on her way to Salamanca.
9.   María de San José, a close friend of Lorenzo's, was reinstated as prioress, after having been deposed and calumniated, at the beginning of 1579.
10. Juan de Jesús Roca had been sent to Rome to negotiate the formation of a separate province for the Discalced Carmelites. He had left in May 1579.

11. Diego López de Montoya, a canonist from Avila, was an agent for Philip II in Rome, who had helped Teresa with her business matters there. He had now returned to Spain for the conferral of the cardinal's hat on Gaspar de Quiroga, the grand inquisitor.
12. She was taking Teresa's place as superior of St. Joseph's in Avila.
13. Lorenzo's daughter, Teresa de Cepeda, who resided in the same Carmel.

310. To Doña Inés Nieto, Alba
Salamanca, 17 September 1579

Doña Inés has been grieving over the imprisonment of her husband and now is suffering from the recent death of the holy Marchioness of Velada. Both these events were a sorrow for Teresa as well.

1.   Jesus. The grace of the Holy Spirit be with your honor. I received your letter; also, the chaplain who brought it came to speak with me. May the Lord reward you for the favor you always show me. I feel your trials so deeply that if by this I could provide a remedy, your trials would be over. But since I am so wretched, I merit little before our Lord. May he be praised for everything. For since he permits this, it will serve to bring you greater glory. Oh, my lady, how deep are the judgments of this great God of ours! The time will come when you will prize your troubles more than all the repose you have had in this life. Now the present trial is painful to us, but if we think of the path His Majesty took in this life, and all those who we know rejoice in his kingdom, there should be nothing that would give us greater joy than to suffer, nor could there be any safer assurance that we are proceeding well in God's service.

2.   This is what has consoled me now on learning of the death of this saintly lady, the Marchioness of Velada,[1] over which I have experienced deep sorrow. Most of her life was a cross, so I hope in God that she is delighting in that eternity that has

no end. Take courage, for when these trials are over—and this will be soon, with the help of God—you and Señor Albornoz[2] will rejoice in having suffered them and will experience the benefit in your souls. I kiss his hands. I greatly wish you were here; it would be for me a great grace. May our Lord grant you every blessing, as he can and as I beg of him.

It is 17 September.

> Your unworthy servant,
>
> Teresa of Jesus

---

1. Juana Enríquez de Toledo of the house of the Marquis of Velada died on 12 August 1579.
2. Juan de Albornoz, husband of Doña Inés.

311. To Padre Jerónimo Gracián, Alcalá
Salamanca, 4 October 1579

(Incomplete autograph: DCN, Jaén)

Teresa reports on the difficulties in Salamanca with Pedro de la Banda. She also seeks Gracián's assistance in her opposition to the prioress of Seville, who wants the community to move to a new house.

✤ ✤ ✤ ✤

1.   Jesus. The grace of the Holy Spirit be with your paternity. Angela[1] is still unable to put her suspicions entirely to rest. It is no wonder that she does not find relief in anything, nor does her will allow her any, and, from what she says, has many trials. Nature is weak, and so she feels disturbed when she sees she is being badly repaid. You should tell that gentleman,[2] for goodness' sake, that although he is by nature careless, he should not be so with her. Where love is present, it cannot be asleep for so long a time.

2.   This aside, I am sorry about the mental fatigue you are undergoing. For the love of God, cut down on your workload.[3]

If you do not attend to this in time, you will see later that you will not be able to find a remedy even though you may want to. Learn to be your own master, avoid extremes, and profit from the experience of others. This is how you serve God, and try to see the need we all have for you to be in good health. I greatly praise His Majesty at seeing the good results of our negotiations,[4] for by his mercy we can consider them concluded. We have so much authority supporting us that it truly seems that it is God who has thus arranged matters. Apart from the essential thing, I am happy that you will see the fruit of your labors. I tell you that through them you certainly paid dearly for it. Your joy will be great when everything has calmed down and those who come after us receive the great benefit.

3.   Oh, *mi padre*, how many trials this house costs me! And after everything was done, the devil so arranged things that we were left without it.[5] And it was the house that was most suited for us in all Salamanca, and the owner profited by our presence. You cannot trust these sons of Adam. He was the one who made us the offer, one of those gentlemen who they say here is most honest, and all agreed that his word is as good as when put in writing. Not only did he give his word, but he signed an agreement before witnesses and brought the notary himself. Later he nullified the contract. Everyone is amazed, except those other gentlemen who urged him to do this for their own or their relatives' profit. And they were able to influence him more than those who tried to reason with him. And a brother of his spoke with us in great charity, and he is very disturbed over the matter. We have recommended all this to our Lord. This must be what is best for us. My regret is that I find nothing else of worth for us in Salamanca.

4.   In fact, if these sisters had the house that the sisters in Seville have, they would think they were in heaven. I regret the foolishness of that prioress,[6] and she has lost much credit in my eyes. I fear that the devil has begun to meddle in that house and wants to destroy it completely. I tell you that if this lady, whose letter made me happy (I mean the one you sent me through

Señora Doña Juana[7]), meets with your satisfaction—they told me down there that she is admirable—I want to please her and receive her there when God wills that someone be there to do so. For I observe in that house a greed that I cannot bear. The prioress is shrewder than her state requires. So I fear that she is deceiving us; and, as I told her, she has never been open with me. She has a lot of the Andalusian in her.[8] I tell you, I had to suffer a lot from her when there. Since she has often written to me with great repentance, I thought she had made amends, which seemed evident. To put it into the poor nuns' heads that the house is unhealthy is sufficient for them to think they are getting sick. I have written terrible letters to her, but I might as well be trying to make a dent in iron. You can see for yourself from this letter that Padre Nicolao[9] has now written me.

5.   For the love of God if you think you can influence her, write to her through some other friar.[10] I think it would suit us well if we sent some other nuns there who would carry more weight and deal with such serious business matters in a befitting way. Tell Padre Nicolao to write to the prior[11] at once, so as not to allow her to speak any more of this, for he must bear much of the blame for what is happening. I certainly think it is wrong to allege that the house is the cause for one's being sick. But it will be unhealthy for the nuns to live where they have well-water, as they state, and not have the refreshing views of flowing water, as they do where they are now, the best views you can find in that area. The nuns here envy them. May God provide the remedy.

6.   Padre Nicolao gave me your regards,[12] but I would not want you to forget to recommend me to our Lord in your prayers; you have so much to do that you could forget. My health is fairly good. The prioress[13] and sisters here send their best regards. May God watch over you and allow me to see you. It is past three o'clock, and I haven't recited Prime.

Today is the feast of St. Francis.

Your unworthy servant and daughter,

Teresa of Jesus

1. She is referring to herself and probably to Gracián's excuses for not writing to her.
2. Gracián himself.
3. Although as a punishment Gracián was confined to Alcalá, he remained active, teaching courses in both Scripture and Pseudo-Dionysius' De mystica theologia, preaching in several churches, and at times governing the college of the discalced Carmelites in Alcalá.
4. The negotiations to set up the discalced friars and nuns into a separate province.
5. This house where the Carmelite nuns in Salamanca were living belonged to the irascible and unpredictable Pedro de la Banda.
6. María de San José. Her foolishness in Teresa's view consisted in wanting to move from the house Teresa had bought to another. In the end María de San José won out.
7. Juana Dantisco, Gracián's mother.
8. This text is crossed out in the autograph.
9. Nicolás Doria.
10. Gracián had still to comply with a prohibition against writing letters.
11. The prior of Los Remedios in Seville, Gaspar de los Reyes.
12. Gracián was not permitted to write to her.
13. The prioress of Salamanca, Ana de la Encarnación (Tapia).

312. To Don Pedro Juan de Casademonte, Medina
Salamanca, 10 October 1579

Teresa has been in Salamanca for about a month after traveling from Avila and stopping at Valladolid, Medina, and Alba de Tormes. She had wanted to purchase a new and more suitable house for the community, but when the time came for signing the contract the owner backed out. Such is the situation as she writes this letter. The negotiations in Rome are also on her mind and making financial demands of her.

To the Illustrious Señor Pedro Juan Casademonte, in Medina, my lord.

1.   Jesus. The grace of the Holy Spirit be with your honor. I had not written you because they told me you were in Valladolid. I was happy that you and Señora Doña María[1] arrived there in good health. I rejoice that you are going to Madrid because you will help me there in everything as always. Let me know where you will be staying, for I have many letters to send you there.

2.   You may have learned how well the negotiations within the order have gone. As for what you wrote to me about Rome,[2] it grieves me that they are so financially pressed. I have already written to them, and if Padre Nicolao has not sent the letters, do me the favor of sending them.[3]

3.   In regard to the dispensation, the one involved came here to speak with me.[4] He is very sorry that they failed him. Soon, with the help of God, it will be given.

4.   In respect to the fifty ducats about which you wrote,[5] I sent a message to Padre Nicolao to pay you, for he has my ducats.

5.   I am delighted that the good Padilla is well. If you write to him, please give him my regards.

6.   I kiss Señora Doña María's hands. Mother prioress kisses those of your honor. All of the nuns are concerned about your business affair. May the Lord work it out for his holy service and watch over you with an increase of his grace.

At St. Joseph's in Salamanca, 10 October.

Please pardon my having another person write this for me; my head is in a bad condition.[6]

Your honor's unworthy servant,

Teresa of Jesus

1.   Pedro Juan de Casademonte's wife.
2.   The negotiations were to obtain permission from the Holy See for the foundations made by Teresa. The two discalced Carmelites who had gone to Rome to carry out these negotiations were now in financial straits.

3. Nicolás Doria was one of the few discalced Carmelite leaders not being punished by the nuncio, Felippo Sega. He was then carrying on business for Teresa in Madrid.

4. The veiled way of speaking refers to all the dispensations and permissions needed to buy the property in Salamanca.

5. Casademonte had contributed money for the business in Rome. Teresa is raising funds to pay off this debt. Nicolás Doria is also helping with this project. In Seville he has deposited 600 ducats for the undertaking.

6. Only this final line is in Teresa's own hand.

313. To Doña Isabel Osorio, Madrid
Toledo, 19 November 1579

(Autograph: Palace of the Count of Berberena, Miranda de Ebro)

Isabel hoped to enter a Carmel. She was accepted in Salamanca, but Padre Doria and Teresa preferred that she wait to enter the foundation planned for Madrid (cf. Ltr. 265).

1.   Jesus. The grace of the Holy Spirit be with your honor. I did not think I would be able to write to you, and since Mother Prioress[1] has written, I will say no more here than that Padre Nicolao[2] is very set on your not entering anywhere else than in the monastery that with the Lord's favor will be founded in Madrid. We hope in His Majesty that this will come about soon.[3] If you have the patience to wait a little longer after having already waited so long, no one must know of your plan or that a foundation will be made there. This is very important.

2.   The nuns in the monastery of Salamanca have already agreed to accept you. I say this because if there is some doubt over the other new foundation, you can be certain of being received in Salamanca. But for some reason it seems to Padre Nicolao that it is more fitting for God's service that you help that foundation, and the aim of all of us is nothing else than the service of God. Padre Nicolao will soon be coming from

Seville; in the meantime consider what will be more satisfying to you. May His Majesty guide things to your desired goal and make use of your soul for what renders him the most honor and glory, amen.

3.   It consoled me very much to see the great happiness of your sister, and ours, Encarnación.[4] If you are as good, we will be happy. Certainly she is an angel. She has rejoiced to be with me.

Today is 19 November.

Your honor's unworthy servant,

Teresa of Jesus

---

1.   Ana de los Angeles, the prioress in Toledo.
2.   Nicolás Doria.
3.   A foundation in Madrid never came about until 1586, after Teresa was dead.
4.   Isabel Osorio's sister, Inés de la Encarnación, a novice in Toledo.

314. To Doña Isabel Osorio, Madrid
Malagón, 3–4 December 1579

(Autograph: DCN: Capuchin Nuns: Toledo)

Doña Isabel was eager to enter a Carmel without delay, but Teresa, without insisting, suggests a different course of action. Tired from all that has to be done, Teresa is writing at night because she would not have time to do so on the following day.

✤ ✤ ✤ ✤

1.   Jesus. The grace of the Holy Spirit be with your honor and make you as holy as I beseech of him each day. I received your two letters through Father Prior of La Roda.[1] One of them must have reached me when I was in Toledo.

2.   I praise our Lord to see the desire you have to leave the world, for such disillusionment with it cannot come but from

above. So I hope in God's divine mercy that you will render him truly genuine service responding to such good desires with the works of a true daughter of the Blessed Virgin, our Lady and Patroness. Certainly I would not want to impede for one day so great a call. I desire to explain to you in complete openness the intention I have in this matter, for you are already our sister and my lady.

3.   You should know that several years ago many persons implored me to found a monastery in Madrid. Because of the great weariness I experienced with some ladies there during my eight-day stay on my way to Pastrana, I refused. Now, since we have had so many trials and I see the benefit that could come to the other monasteries by our having a foundation there,[2] I am convinced this should be done. But there is a great obstacle, for they assure me that the archbishop[3] will not give the license unless the house is founded with an income. And although there are some persons who could give a good one and have been desiring to do this for years, they are not free to give anything before they enter. And since your honor is able to help very much in this matter, it seems to Padre Nicolao[4] and me that you should wait for some days. With God's help, I don't think the delay would be longer than you say.

4.   Pray about this, and if you think otherwise, feel free to let me know, and you can enter when your wish. But that would put in danger a foundation in Madrid, and if you might be the means through which such a great work could be accomplished, I would consider this something wonderful. May our Lord do what is for his greater glory.

5.   Father Prior came so late that I wasn't able to speak to him much about this matter. Tomorrow I will do so and tell you in this letter his opinion. Since I will be very busy with a matter that he will tell you about himself, I am writing tonight. I am fairly well, glory to God, although I arrived tired; and all that I found here was enough to tire me more. May His Majesty be served by this, and keep you for many years that you may employ them in the service of this our great God and Lord.

6.   I beseech you to give my best regards to Padre Valentín.[5] Each day I recommend him to His majesty and beg him to repay me. Even if he does so in a small way, I will be well rewarded, wretched as I am.

Today is 3 December.

Your honor's unworthy servant,

Teresa of Jesus

7.   Note that what I have said here is for you alone. I don't ever remember having said so much about it.

8.   Truly, we did speak a long time today concerning your situation, about which I have nothing else to add. I was very much consoled by his reverence's presence. He will tell you about everything, and inform me about what you and he agree on, which I am certain will be for the best.

---

1.   Gabriel de la Asunción.
2.   She is alluding to the convenience of having a foundation in Madrid so that the discalced Carmelites may carry on more easily whatever business matters they have at the royal court.
3.   The Archbishop of Toledo, Gaspar de Quiroga.
4.   Nicolás Doria (See Ltr. 313).
5.   Valentín López, a Jesuit in Madrid.

315. To Padre Jerónimo Gracián, Alcalá (?)

Malagón, November 1579(?)

The date and addressee of this fragment are uncertain.

✦✦✦✦

1.   I am displeased by how these nuns are placed in higher positions. I am speaking of that subprioress. She must be unaware. If she does well, do not dishearten her.

316. To Padre Jerónimo Gracián, Alcala
Malagón, 12 December 1579

(Autograph: 1ˢᵗ part: DCN, Alcalá; 2ⁿᵈ part: DCN, Zaragoza)

Teresa arrived in Malagón on 25 November after a long, difficult journey (Salamanca–Avila–Toledo–Malagón). Hardly had she arrived in Malagón when all her time was taken up with both final construction work on the new monastery and a reorganization of the community. She had brought along with her a new prioress and a new confessor. She would like to spend more time in Malagón but is being called upon for other tasks.

⁕⁕⁕⁕

For *mi padre* Maestro Fray Jerónimo Gracián de la Madre de Dios, Alcalá.

1.   Jesus. The grace of the Holy Spirit be with your paternity. You should know that I was already in Malagón when they gave me Paul's[1] letter. So, it wasn't possible for me to stay longer in Toledo as he ordered me in the letter. This worked out better, for on the feast of the Immaculate Conception these sisters moved to the new house. I had already been here for eight days, which were no less burdensome than those spent in travel, for there was much to be done so that the move could be made on that special day. I got very tired; nonetheless I am feeling better than usual.

2.   I am sorry about the trouble you had; there is nothing more I can do. The move took place with much rejoicing, for they came in procession with the Most Blessed Sacrament from the other house. The nuns were very happy; they seemed like little lizards that come out into the sun in summer. Certainly they suffered a lot there; and even though nothing is finished except eleven cells, they could go on living here for many years even if nothing more were done.

3.   Oh, *mi padre*, how necessary was my coming here, whether for this move—it doesn't seem they would have been

able to make it so quickly—or for the rest of the things. God could have done it, but I don't know now what other means could have been used there to break this spell. The nuns have come to understand how foolishly they were behaving. The more I learn about the way they were governed by the one who was presiding here, the more convinced I become of how reckless it would be to put her in any position of government.[2] This poor licentiate[3] seems to me to be a great servant of God, and I believe it is he who is less at fault. That other person deserves all the blame, for she kept him on the go constantly with her noisy restlessness. He is in complete accord with all that I tell you should be done here, and he is so humble and sorry for any fault he might have had for what happened that I was very edified.

4.   Paul and I are much to blame. Tell him to confess this, for I have already done so. We gave too much leeway in some matters and should not have trusted so much in young people, however holy, not at all.[4] Since they don't have experience, with good intentions, they cause great havoc. It is necessary, *mi padre*, that we keep this in mind for the future. I hope in our Lord that all will go well now. The prioress[5] we brought is very God-fearing and wise, and has so good a knack for governing that all have grown to love her greatly. She urgently asks for your prayers. She is very much your daughter. I don't think anyone else could have been chosen who is so apt for this house. Please God she will always be so, for it seemed the other one would do very well.

5.   It's a terrible thing, the harm that a prioress can cause in one of these houses. Even though the nuns see things that scandalize them—which they often did in this case—they think they should not judge badly, that it would be against obedience. I tell you, *mi padre*, the one who makes a visitation must proceed very carefully so that the devil doesn't use some small things to cause much harm.

6.   May God have Fray Germán[6] with him in heaven; he had good qualities, but he did not have the talent to understand

better the nature of perfection. Our Lord is acting in such a way that it seems he does not want some things to be concealed. Please God that I am not at fault for having insisted so much on bringing a confessor here with me—that is, Fray Felipe—or Fray Germán for having opposed me in this. Since Father Vicar[7] finally did what I wanted, Fray Germán was so displeased that he told someone who went to see him that he was sick in bed because of me. But in my opinion I would have been doing nothing had I arrived without a confessor, and there wasn't any other. Nonetheless, I have become fearful lest I committed some fault. Write to me what you think, for there is no one I ask who satisfies me.[8]

7.   Through Padre Fray Gabriel,[9] I wrote the other day to Father Rector[10] there so that you might receive some news about me. I did not dare write to you, although I truly believe I could have. This father came here, but I cannot understand his purpose for doing so, although he spoke about the project of a monastery in Villanueva.[11] Now that I have been well informed about it, I think it would be the most foolish thing in the world to agree to it. And Padre Fray Antonio de Jesús[12] has got it into his head that the foundation should be made. I made a strong appeal to their conscience. I don't know what they will do.

8.   He also was attending to the matter of Doña Isabel de Osorio, the sister of the one he placed in Toledo.[13] But Doña Isabel and I and Nicolao[14] had already dealt with this matter. He seemed better than usual, but he is so simple about some things that I was amazed.

9.   With regard to his being definitor, according to what Father Vicar writes to me, the purpose was to honor the discalced friars;[15] at least he gives that impression. I don't know what harm can come to them for doing this or if he can be blamed for their having elected him. They are keeping this election very secret. Don Luis Manrique[16] told him that the documents were already sent to Rome. I asked him if they were sending them to the chapter.[17] He answered that since the king was a

petitioner they would not do that. He didn't stay more than a day, for he had thought I was in Toledo; and since he didn't find me there, he came here.

10.   I am amused by Paul's[18] pride. It's about time! Have no fear that I am saddened by that or think that it causes him harm. That would be most foolish—which he is not—unless one recalls this waterwheel with its buckets that are as quickly filled as emptied. I well remember the journey from Toledo to Avila with him, how nice it was and without my suffering any illness.[19] Happiness is a great thing, and it seems his letter has now brought me relief from my work. Thank him[20] for me.

11.   I don't think I will be able to stay here all of January, even though this place is not a bad one for me, for there are not so many letters or so much to attend to. Father Vicar is so eager for a foundation in Arenas[21] and that we meet there that I believe he will give me orders to finish up quickly here, and truth to say most of the things are done. You wouldn't believe all that I owe him. He treats me with the utmost kindness. I tell you that I remain very much obliged to him, even though his office is coming to an end.

12.   Read the enclosed letter from the good Velasco.[22] Be careful about speaking of this if his sister does not have a genuine desire and is not suited (for I would be very sorry if something unpleasant happened, since I like him very much); nor should you say anything about where she might enter. I believe that to him, to Padre Maestro Fray Pedro Fernández,[23] and to Don Luis we owe all the favor now being shown to us.

13.   May God show you this favor, *mi padre*, as I beseech him and keep you for many years, amen, amen.

Today is 12 December.

May God grant you a blessed Christmas with the increase in holiness I desire for you.

Your paternity's true daughter and subject,

Teresa of Jesus

1. In her usual code, Paul is Gracián. She arrived in Malagón on 25 November 1579. On 8 December the community moved into their new house.

2. The presider had been Ana de la Madre de Dios (de la Palma).

3. Gaspar de Villanueva who had been chaplain and confessor to the community.

4. Here she humbly retracts her previous position, in which she favored Ana de la Madre de Dios (see Ltr. 245.3).

5. Jerónima del Espíritu Santo (Acevedo), who had made profession in Salamanca (16 Jan. 1576) and later made the first Italian foundation in Genoa (12 Dec. 1590).

6. Germán de San Matías, former confessor with St. John of the Cross at the Incarnation in Avila.

7. Angel de Salazar, the vicar general for the discalced friars and nuns.

8. Padre Germán, the prior in Mancera as of 14 June 1579, died in November of 1579. He had tenaciously opposed the idea that Teresa take P. Felipe de la Purificación (professed in Mancera on 2 Feb. 1576) with her to Malagón to be confessor there. He blamed Teresa for his illness from which he died, and she is now feeling some pangs of conscience.

9. Gabriel de la Asunción, prior in La Roda. He was in Malagón on 3–4 December.

10. Elías de San Martín, rector of the college in Alcalá.

11. She is referring to the efforts toward a foundation in Villanueva de la Jara. Later she agreed to make the foundation (cf. F. 28).

12. Antonio de Jesús (Heredia), founder with St. John of the Cross in Duruelo.

13. Isabel de Osorio had a sister who was a Carmelite nun in Toledo, Inés de la Encarnación. The matter concerned Isabel's entry into Carmel.

14. Nicolás Doria (see Ltr. 313).

15. The vicar general for the discalced Carmelites, Angel de Salazar, managed that in the provincial chapter of the Carmelites in Castile celebrated in La Moraleja in mid-November 1579, a discalced friar, Gabriel de la Asunción, be elected a provincial definitor.

16. Luis Manrique, the king's chaplain and chief almoner, had been one of the nuncio Sega's advisors in the investigation of Gracián, and at present he was negotiating for the separation of the discalced Carmelites into a separate province. This was the secret confided to P. Gabriel.

17. This general chapter of the Carmelite order took place in Rome in 1580. Giovanni Battista Caffardi (d. 1592) was elected prior general.

18. Gracián.

19. She is referring to her trip from Toledo to Avila (July 1577) in the company of Gracián and Antonio de Jesús.

20. Thank Paul, that is, Gracián himself.

21. The Carmel of Arenas de San Pablo was not founded until after Teresa's death.

22. Juan López de Velasco, who was Philip II's secretary, chronicler, and chief cosmographer for the Indies, had a sister wanting to enter Carmel. She did in fact enter in Segovia, taking the name Juana de la Madre de Dios (López de Velasco). The hesitation seemed to stem from concern over her limited intelligence.

23. The Dominican who had been the apostolic visitator of the Carmelites in Castile.

317. To Padre Jerónimo Gracián, Alcalá
Malagón, 18 December 1579

Teresa has presided over some final construction work on the new monastery in Malagón. Though it was still unfinished, the nuns were able to move in. She has also settled some of the problems that had arisen in the community and restored peace and a certain discipline. Her thoughts turn to the approaching feast of Christmas.

1.   Jesus. The grace of the Holy Spirit be with your paternity. I recently wrote you a long letter by way of Toledo, and so now I will be brief. Also they told me late that the one bringing this letter, who is the brother-in-law of Antonio Ruiz,[1] is leaving before dawn. I would really have wanted a letter from you, even though without one I was happy to receive the news of your health and of the good you are doing in that place through your preaching.[2] He told me of your sermon on the feast of San Eugenio. May God be praised from whom comes all good. He grants a great favor to anyone he selects as a means to bring benefit to souls.

2.   I forgot to mention how Ana de Jesús[3] is doing very well; and the other nuns, it appears, are content and at peace. I do not allow that person[4] to speak to or confess any of the nuns. As for the rest, I show him much kindness, which is necessary, and I often speak with him.

3.   Today he preached for us, and he is certainly a good man and he wouldn't maliciously do any harm to anyone. But I am convinced that it is better for the nuns in these monasteries to speak little with others, even if these others are holy, for God will teach the nuns. And unless the teaching is given from the pulpit, a great deal of conversation, even if it is with Paul,[5] is not beneficial; rather it is harmful, however good the topic. It causes such persons to lose some of the credibility that with good reason they should enjoy.

4.   Oh, *mi padre*, what grief I have undergone at times over this. And how I remember during these days what a letter from you made me suffer on Christmas night a year ago.[6] May God be praised who now gives us better times. Certainly it was a night that were I to live many years I would not forget.

5.   I am no worse than usual; rather I am feeling healthier these days. We are doing well in the new house. It will be a very good one if it gets finished. But even now, there is plenty of living space.[7] The prioress[8] and all the sisters recommend themselves much to your prayers, and I to those of Father Rector.[9] It is already night, so I'll say no more except that it would be a very blessed Christmas for me if I could hear the sermons you will be preaching for the occasion. May God give you a blessed Christmas and many others as I desire.

Today is the feast of Our Lady of the "O,"[10] and I am your paternity's daughter and subject,

Teresa of Jesus

1.   Antonio Ruiz was a businessman and friend of Teresa's in Malagón who dealt in livestock.

2.   Although confined to Alcalá as a penance imposed by the nuncio, Gracián was preaching and teaching classes in Alcalá.

3. Ana de Jesús (Contreras), because of her many unusual trials and strange behavior, was thought at one time to be possessed by the devil.

4. Gaspar de Villanueva, who had been confessor and chaplain for the community. For some strong words written to him by Teresa, see Ltr. 201.

5. Gracián.

6. She is probably alluding to a letter in which Gracián informed her of the penalties imposed on him by Sega, the nuncio (20 Dec. 1578; see MHCT 2: 80–82), and of some calumnies raised against him.

7. Eleven of the cells in the new house were finished. See Ltr. 316.2.

8. Jerónima del Espíritu Santo.

9. Rector at the college for discalced Carmelites in Alcalá, Elías de San Martín.

10. Our Lady of the Waiting (or of the Hope) was also called Our Lady of the "O" because of the "O" antiphons recited at Vespers during the days preceding Christmas.

318. To Padre Nicolás Doria, Seville

Malagón, 21 December 1579

(Autograph: DCN, Ubeda)

Padre Doria, who is the prior in Pastrana, has gone to help the nuns in Seville. The prioress had been deposed, but recently reinstalled, and now the time had come for another election. Teresa gives him some practical instructions. She also gives him an account of the firm measures she had to take in order to restore peace to the community in Malagón.

1.   Jesus. The grace of the Holy Spirit be with your reverence. Today, the feast of St. Thomas, Serrano[1] arrived. I welcomed your letter, for I wanted to know if you had a good trip. May God be blessed who grants us so much favor. May it please him to grant you the same on your return, which you will not undertake very willingly. A willing spirit helps to lessen the burden of it.

2.   I thought your reverence would have received two of my letters; at least one, for I wrote it as soon as I arrived here, which was the feast of St. Catherine.[2] I sent both to Señor Francisco Doria.[3]

3.   On the feast of the Immaculate Conception,[4] God was pleased that we move into the new house; although the move cost me a great deal of work, for much had to be done on it before we could move in. And so I remained here eight days before the nuns came, and got very tired. But I considered it all well worth it, for even though much still needs to be done, the sisters are settled in very well. The rest[5] the Lord has done in a way better than I deserve.

4.   I am amazed at the havoc the devil works through bad government and at the fear, or deception, he inculcated in these nuns, for, they are all good and desirous of perfection. And in what they saw was wrong, most or almost all of them felt an uneasiness, but didn't know how to correct it. Now they are truly freed from deception, and I firmly believe that there isn't one of them who would want anything else than what she has now, not even Brianda's sister,[6] for Brianda was delighted not to have to come here.

5.   I tell you, *mi padre*, it is necessary to be careful about who is given these offices, for the nuns are so submissive that their greatest disturbance came from the scruple they felt over judging their prioress[7] to be doing something bad, and in itself what she was doing was not good. They are most happy with their present prioress,[8] and they are right in being so. What two or three must have regretted was the removal of the confessor,[9] for the others—I think all the rest of them—were delighted. I immediately told them that we didn't bring the permission for him to be the confessor of any of us. All the others, to repeat, were delighted. I tried to do everything secretly but spoke with him very clearly. And I truly think he is a soul of God and that there wasn't any malice in him. Since we live far away from him and he has much to

do, what I did was done without attracting any notice. And I arranged to have him preach to us, and I see him sometimes. Everything has now been cleared up, glory to God.

6.   What I regret are the many debts they have. Everything is in ruin, since they have had such bad government for so long. They well understood what would happen, but she didn't give them an account of anything. Since she had been a nun for so short a time,[10] she couldn't have known more. This resolve to trust only in one's own opinion does great harm.

7.   Advise the one who is now going to begin again[11] so that she understand well her obligations according to the observance of the order's directives and the constitutions, for in such observance they cannot err. When they do otherwise, God wants their very closest friends to be their accusers. And they shouldn't think they can do and undo whatever they want as married people. And show her this letter. Sometimes I get angry with her and the rest of them that I brought from up here, since they never informed me of anything, although at first not much happened compared to what took place later.

8.   If a nun wants to confess with someone other than the ordinary confessor, designate someone to give this permission, as long as the confessor be a friar of your choice from Los Remedios.[12] Even in this respect they suffered great torment here. They are souls who have suffered many things hard to digest.

9.   I've been told that the nuns there wrote to the nuns here urging them to ask for Brianda,[13] for since they succeeded there in having the prioress they wanted, they thought the nuns here could as well. Give the prioress a good penance, for she should have known that I am not so bad a Christian as to insist so much on something without serious reasons and that I would not have gone to such expense in buying the house without it being necessary. I pardon them for the judgments they must have made in this regard. May God pardon them. May it please God that if I should see that this prioress would not be bad for them that I would try to bring her back as I did

for their prioress. I tell you that if she were to return, the peace of this house would be completely destroyed, aside from all the rest. In so serious a matter one ought not speak from afar against the deeds of someone who would give up her own rest for the good and tranquillity of another soul.

10. I learned some days ago that the friars in Pastrana[14] were sick. I haven't learned anything more. They must be well now. Don't be disturbed, nor for this fail to do what needs to be done down there, although whatever is not finished by the Feast of Epiphany will require much prudence. For the response from Rome,[15] if God gives it to us, will require that you be back here on time.

11. Before the feast of the Immaculate Conception, Fray Gabriel,[16] the prior of La Roda, came to see me. He indicated to me that he came for the matter concerning Doña Isabel Osorio.[17] I asked him to wait until we know whether what she brings would help the foundation in Madrid, for Doña Luisa[18] told me that the archbishop[19] would not give his permission unless the foundation were to have an income, and I don't know how it can have one even if she gives everything she has. Someone would have to advance us the amount knowing for certain what she will give. For she can't do anything before her entry. We will speak about it here.

12. The secret that was kept about sending a message to Rome pleased me. He told me that it was already gone and that Don Luis[20] was the one who had informed him. He's convinced that with the king asking for it, the permission will come quickly and that they will not wait for the chapter.[21] Please God this will be so. I let on that this was all news to me. He says he is delighted, and he has every reason to be. The rest must wait until we see each other.

13. The prioress in Beas[22] has sent me letters for Casademonte.[23] She is asking him to decide where he wants her to send the one hundred ducats that she has there. So you need not be concerned about this.

14.   What you tell me about the archbishop[24] is a great consolation. You are very wrong not to give him my best regards. Give them to him now. You can tell him that I pray to the Lord for him each day particularly at communion time.

15.   May His Majesty protect you and bring you here in good health, and do not fear that I will let you leave so quickly.

The prioress sends you her regards. Among the others, some are looking forward to your coming.

Your reverence's unworthy servant,

Teresa of Jesus

16.   Padre Fray Felipe[25] is doing well. Best regards to Padre Fray Gregorio from me and his sister;[26] she is very good and cannot contain her happiness. It would be appropriate for the prioress to be the mistress of novices,[27] lest their love be divided and not centered on the prioress, since there have been so many changes. She could have someone help her instruct them. And in regard to interior matters about their prayer and temptations, inform her that she should not ask for more than what they willingly tell her (as is stated in the document you had others sign);[28] this is important. I am delighted that Father Prior of Las Cuevas[29] is satisfied. Truth is a great thing. Give him my regards.

1.   One of Teresa's messengers.
2.   She arrived in Malagón on 25 November.
3.   A relative of Padre Doria's residing in Toledo.
4.   On 8 December.
5.   The settling of matters in the community (see Ltr. 316.3).
6.   Brianda de San José was the former prioress in Malagón and was residing in Toledo. Her sister, Mariana del Espíritu Santo, made profession on 4 May 1578.
7.   The previous prioress in Malagón, Ana de la Madre de Dios.
8.   Jerónima del Espíritu Santo, whom Teresa brought with her.
9.   Gaspar de Villanueva (see Ltr. 316).

10. Teresa has switched to another topic, the Carmel in Seville, where Doria was dealing with some problems of the community, and alludes to the vicaress, Beatriz de la Madre de Dios, installed by Diego Cárdenas when he deposed María de San José.

11. María de San José has been reinstalled as prioress.

12. The monastery of discalced Carmelite friars in Seville.

13. The previous prioress who because of sickness was residing in Toledo.

14. The discalced Carmelite friars in the novitiate in Pastrana where Doria was actually prior.

15. A response to the request for a separation of the discalced Carmelites into a separate province.

16. Gabriel de la Asunción.

17. The aspirant who was asked to wait to enter Carmel for a projected foundation in Madrid.

18. Luisa de la Cerda, Teresa's friend and benefactor in Toledo.

19. Gaspar de Quiroga, the Archbishop of Toledo.

20. Luis Manrique, chaplain for the king and advisor to the nuncio with regard to the discalced Carmelites.

21. The general chapter for the Carmelites that would be celebrated the following year (1580) in Rome.

22. Ana de Jesús (Lobera), who was sending money for the expenses in Rome.

23. Pedro Juan de Casademonte, a merchant in Medina.

24. The Archbishop of Seville, Cristóbal de Rojas.

25. Felipe de la Purificación, the confessor Teresa brought for the community.

26. Gregorio Nacianceno, discalced Carmelite friar in Seville. His sister was a Carmelite nun in Malagón, Catalina de San Cirilo.

27. Teresa is commenting on whether María de San José might be prioress and novice mistress at the same time (see Ltr. 319.9).

28. Perhaps this is the paper prepared by Gracián to stop the interference of Garciálvarez in the Carmel of Seville. It was signed by others through Doria's intervention (see Ltr. 173.7).

29. Hernando de Pantoja, prior of the Carthusians in Seville.

319. To Madre María de San José, Seville

Malagón, end of December 1579

(Autograph: DCN, Valladolid)

A "terrible letter" had been written by Teresa to Madre María, and the latter responded in a gentle and humble manner admitting her mistake. Teresa had arrived in Malagón to reorganize the community that suffered from bad government and unrest. The nuns in Seville had previously interfered in this community's affairs with ill-advised letters. Teresa now softens her tone and answers many of Maria de San José's questions, telling her also to read her letter to Doria of 21 December.

1.   Jesus. The grace of the Holy Spirit be with your reverence, my daughter. In Padre Fray Nicolao's[1] letter, I enlarged on some things that I will not mention here because you will be seeing them. Your recent letter is so kind and humble that it deserves a long response. But you want me to write to the good Rodrigo Alvarez,[2] and so I am doing that and don't have the head for much more. Serrano[3] says he will give these letters to the one who will deliver them to their destination. Please God this will be so. I was happy to see him and regret that he must leave. I am so grateful to him for what he has done in a time of such need that you didn't have to remind me. I will try to get him to return there, for it is very important for us to have someone we can trust in that region.

2.   Here my health is not as bad as it is in other places. I felt sorry over your poor health, about which Sister Gabriela[4] wrote me. The trials were so great that even if you had a heart of stone, they would have done you harm. I would not have wanted to contribute to them. Please pardon me, for with those I truly love I am unbearable, for I wouldn't want them to err in anything. The same happened with Madre Brianda[5] to whom I wrote terrible letters, but they did little good.

3.   Certainly, in a way, I consider that what the devil contrived in this house was worse[6] than what happened there in Seville. For one thing, it lasted longer, and for another the scandal was much more damaging to outsiders, and I don't know whether the community will be left as unharmed; although a remedy has been found for the disquiet inside. The Lord has smoothed things over. May he be blessed, for the nuns are not much to blame. The one with whom I am more annoyed has been Beatriz de Jesús,[7] for she has never said a word to me, not even now on seeing that all the nuns are telling me about it and that I am aware of everything. This has seemed to me to be a sign of very little virtue or discretion. She must think she is being loyal to a friendship; but in truth she is very attached to herself, for true friendship does not show itself by hiding what, if revealed, could have provided a remedy without so much harm.

4.   For the love of God be on guard against doing anything that if known could cause scandal. Let us free ourselves from these good intentions that cost us so dearly. And don't say anything to anyone about this father from the Society eating there, not even to our own discalced friars. For if they know, the devil, being what he is, will stir up a fuss about it. Don't think that it cost me little for the rector[8] to become gentler—and here they all have become so—for I tried hard even to the point of writing to Rome from where I believe the remedy has come.

5.   I am most grateful to that saintly Rodrigo Alvarez for what he does and to Padre Soto.[9] Give him my regards and tell him that I think he is more of a friend through deeds than through words, for he has never written to me or even sent greetings.

6.   I don't know why you say that Padre Fray Nicolao has turned me against you, for you have no greater defender on earth. He was telling me the truth so that by being informed of the damage done in that house I would not be deceived. Oh, my daughter, how useless it is to excuse yourself so much in what regards me! I tell you truly, I don't care whether they pay any attention to me or not if I know they are striving to do

what they are obliged to do. The mistake comes from the fact that since with so much care and love I think I am looking out for what concerns the nuns, it seems to me that they won't do what they ought if they don't pay attention to me and that I have tired myself in vain. And this is what got me annoyed, to the extent that I wanted to abandon the whole thing, thinking, as I say, I was doing no good, as is true. But my love is so great that as soon as I see some little fruit I am unable to give up, and so there is no more to say about this.

7.   Serrano has told me that a nun[10] has now been accepted and that according to the number of nuns he thinks there are in the house—he tells me twenty—the number is complete. If it is, no one can give permission for her to be accepted, for Father Vicar[11] can do nothing against the acts of the apostolic visitators.[12] Consider carefully, for the love of God, that you would be amazed at the harm that comes to these houses from there being many nuns, even though there may be an income and enough food. I don't know why you pay so much interest every year since you have the means of freeing yourself of this obligation. I was delighted over what is coming from the Indies.[13] May God be praised.

8.   As for what you say about the subprioress, since your health is so poor and you cannot keep up with the choir observance, you need someone who knows it very well. That Gabriela[14] seems so young matters little. She has been a nun for a long while, and her virtues are what matter. If in speaking with outsiders she is deficient, San Francisco[15] can accompany her. At least she is obedient and will not stray from what you wish. And she is healthy—since it is necessary that she not be missing from choir—and San Jerónimo[16] is not. In conscience, she is the one I think most suited. And since she was in charge of the choir during the time of that miserable vicaress,[17] they will have seen that she did well and more willingly give her their vote; and for a subprioress, you look more to one's ability than to one's age.

9.   I am writing to the prior of Pastrana about the mistress of novices[18] since what you say seems good to me. I would like the novices to be few in number, for a large number of nuns, as I said, is in every respect, a great drawback, and there is no other reason than this for houses to come to ruin.

10.   I would greatly desire—since down there you have the means to help the order in its needs—that from what is in Toledo you gradually reimburse my brother.[19] He is truly in need, in such a way that he has had to borrow in order to pay the five hundred ducats each year for the property[20] he bought; and now he has sold objects that in Seville would be worth a thousand ducats. He has mentioned this to me at times, and I see that he is right. Although you don't do so all at once, you can pay something; see what you can do.

11.   The alms of bread that the prior of Las Cuevas[21] gives is great. If this house here had as much they could get along well, for I don't know what they will do. They have done nothing but take in nuns without dowries. As for what you say about Portugal, the archbishop is in a hurry.[22] I am thinking of taking my time about going there. If I can, I will write to him now. Will you see that the letter leaves at once and in a safe manner.

12.   Regarding the repentance of Beatriz,[23] I would like her, for the good of her soul, to retract what she said to Garciálvarez.[24] But I have a great fear that she doesn't know herself; only God can bring this about.

13.   May he make you as holy as I beg of him and watch over you for me. However wretched you are, I would like to have some more like you, for I wouldn't know what to do if I had to make a foundation now. I don't find any prospective prioresses, although there might be some. Yet because these lack experience and I see what has gone on here,[25] I have become very fearful, knowing that the devil can make use of good intentions to carry out his own works. So it is necessary to walk always with fear clinging to God and with little trust in our own opinions. However good they may be, if this care is not present,

God will abandon us, and we will make a mistake in the very thing we were more sure of.

14.   You can learn from what happened in this house, since you have already heard about it. I tell you that certainly the devil was planning an assault and that I was frightened by some of the things you wrote and gave importance to.[26] Where was your good sense? And then San Francisco! Oh, God help me, the foolishness contained in that letter, and all so as to achieve your goal! May the Lord give us light, for without that light there is no virtue but only the ability to do wrong.

15.   I am happy that you are so disillusioned, for this will help you with many things. In order to succeed it is beneficial to have erred, for in that way you acquire experience.

May God watch over you, for I did not think I could go on at such length.

> Your reverence's servant,
>
> Teresa of Jesus

The prioress[27] and the sisters send their best regards.

---

1.   Nicolás Doria (see Ltr. 318).
2.   Rodrigo Alvarez (see ST 58 & 59).
3.   A messenger of Teresa's who came from Seville to Toledo.
4.   Leonor de San Gabriel.
5.   Brianda de San José, the former prioress in Malagón.
6.   She is alluding to the imprudent actions of the chaplain in Malagón, Gaspar de Villanueva (see Ltrs. 316 & 317).
7.   Beatriz de Jesús (Cepeda), the former vicaress in Malagón.
8.   The rector of the Jesuits in Seville, Diego de Acosta. She is probably alluding to the rumors about Gaspar de Salazar's efforts to transfer from the Jesuits to the discalced Carmelites.
9.   A priest friend of the discalced Carmelites in Seville.
10.   Probably María de la Cruz (Céspedes), who then made her profession on 15 January 1581.
11.   Angel de Salazar.
12.   Pedro Fernández, Francisco Vargas, and Jerónimo Gracián.

13. The community in Seville received an inheritance of 800 *pesos* from the Indies.

14. Leonor de San Gabriel. She was in fact elected subprioress.

15. Isabel de San Francisco, who had been sent as prioress for the reform of a community of Carmelite nuns in Paterna.

16. Isabel de San Jerónimo.

17. Beatriz de la Madre de Dios.

18. See Ltr. 318.16.

19. Lorenzo de Cepeda.

20. La Serna.

21. Hernando de Pantoja.

22. The Archbishop of Evora (Portugal), Teutonio de Braganza.

23. Beatriz de la Madre de Dios.

24. The former confessor of the discalced nuns in Seville.

25. See no.3 of this letter.

26. See Ltr. 318.9.

27. The prioress Teresa brought for Malagón, Jerónima del Espíritu Santo.

320. To Padre Jerónimo Gracián, Alcalá

Malagón, end of December 1579

A fragment with only an approximate date. Teresa was enjoying a restful time in the new monastery in Malagón.

I tell you that I find here a wonderful leisure that I have desired for many years. Although one's nature feels abandoned[1] without the one who usually provides it with solace, the soul is at rest. And the reason is that there is no more thought of Teresa of Jesus than if she were not in the world. And this will be the cause for my not making any attempt to leave here, unless I am ordered to do so.[2] I was disheartened at times to hear so much foolishness; for when they say there that someone is a saint, it's bound to be nonsense.[3] They laugh because I say they should declare someone else in that place to be one, for it doesn't cost them any more than words.

---

1. An allusion to the absence of Gracián, who is being confined in Alcalá as a punishment.

2. See Ltr. 316.11.
3. She has in mind the elaborate reception given her in Valladolid (see Ltrs. 300.4 and 302.1).

321. To Madre María Bautista, Valladolid
Uncertain Date (1579–1581?)

This fragment is found in the first biography of St. Teresa (1590) by the Jesuit Francisco de Ribera (bk. 4, chap 24).

You should know that I am not the same when it comes to governing. Everything is done with love. I don't know whether this is because I have no reason for acting otherwise, or because I have come to understand that things are better dealt with in this way.

Letters 322–364
(1580)

322. To Padre Jerónimo Gracián
Malagón, 10–11 January 1580

These four fragments are from different letters probably addressed to Padre Gracián.

❧❧❦❦

1. I tell you—and for the love of God always be attentive to this if you do not want to see your house lost—that the price of things is so increasing that a house needs close to 300,000 *maravedis* in income when it is not a house of poverty. With the amount actually being given, the nuns in this house—which will then acquire the reputation of receiving an income—will starve to death; no doubt about it.[1]

2. You should realize that if it depended on me I would not want to see any of the houses now founded in poverty to have an income. For I understand and see it now, and it will always be so: the communities that do not fail God will prosper most. If they fail him, it's better that they come to naught, for there are too many relaxed monasteries.

3.   May God pardon those who opposed the foundations, for these foundations were a means for setting things right. And since the foundations were not well established, this opposition did much harm. His Majesty will provide a remedy; nothing short of this is possible. But until then, you must proceed very cautiously when giving permission to receive nuns. This should be done only if there is great need and it would be beneficial for the house. The well-being of a house requires that there be no more nuns than can be maintained.[2] If careful attention is not paid to this, we will end up with unsolvable problems ...

4.   It would be better not to make a foundation than to bring in melancholic nuns who will ruin the house.

---

1.   If a house was endowed with a benefice, the people thought they did not need to worry about supporting it. The houses founded in poverty were dependent on divine providence for their needs, and the people then responded well. According to a note in an early edition of these letters (Antonio de San José, 1771–93), this fragment refers to the Carmel in Medina del Campo that was thinking of accepting a small income.

2.   This was also a norm imposed by the Council of Trent.

323. To Madre Ana de San Alberto, Caravaca
Malagón, January (?) 1580

A nun in Caravaca was undergoing a spiritual trial and the prioress wrote to Teresa about it. Teresa in turn asked St. John of the Cross to go to Caravaca to give spiritual direction to this sister and others in the community. This fragment comes from a declaration made by Madre Ana of some words Teresa wrote to her in a letter.

❖·❖·❖·❖

Daughter, Father John of the Cross is going there. Let the nuns in that monastery speak to him of matters concerning their souls with simplicity as though they were speaking with me, for he has the spirit of our Lord.

324. To Padre Jerónimo Gracián, Alcalá

Malagón, 11 January 1580

Teresa does some conjecturing about Gracián, who is being suggested as a future provincial for the discalced Carmelites. This possibility was under consideration in Madrid, and it seemed it could receive the approval of the general of the order in Rome. Gracián mentioned that the duke and duchess of Alba have a copy of Teresa's Life. *She wants to be sure of this and that the copy will be preserved.*

✤✤✦✦

1.   Jesus. The grace of the Holy Spirit be with your paternity. A short time ago I received a letter from Señora Doña Juana[1] who awaits daily an end to the silence[2] imposed on you. Please God that when this letter arrives the matters in Toledo and Medina will be taken care of.[3]

2.   Padre Fray Felipe[4] fits perfectly. He has gone to the other extreme, not engaging in talk outside of confession. He is a very good man.

3.   Oh, the rejoicing of the nuns in Medina when they were told you were no longer obliged to be silent. It's amazing, what you owe those nuns. A lay sister here has taken a hundred disciplines for you. It all should be of benefit to you in doing good for souls.

4.   Yesterday they gave me this letter from Padre Nicolao.[5] I was delighted that what he mentions can be done. At times I was worried about the Salamanca matter,[6] but I didn't see any better thing, and now he has a great deal to attend to. Certainly he has to attend more to his own affairs than to those of others. I told Padre Nicolao in Toledo something about the disadvantages but not everything I know. A great good came out of this. I believe the Most Reverend Vicar General[7] will do everything to improve our situation. Only one doubt remains, and it is that when the nuncio[8] died, as you know, the powers that he had given were no longer considered valid. It would be a great trial

to have to listen to different opinions in a matter so important.[9] Tell me what you think, for I don't see any other obstacle. On the contrary, it would seem to be a gift from heaven if among ourselves we could organize everything, as he says there.[10] May the Lord bring this about, as he can.

5.   If everything does not come about as we desire, I wonder what good it is for Padre Nicolao[11] to be waiting down there; our cause would be left abandoned. True, Velasco[12] will do much, but nothing will be lost by his having help. Don't speak of this, however, lest they accuse you, when they do what they say they will,[13] that you acted out of self-interest. It is necessary to proceed with caution in everything so as to remove any occasion for false accusations, especially while Methuselah[14] continues in office. He strongly opposes me as regards Paul having an office;[15] but one has to put up with that.

6.   Another drawback comes to mind now: I am wondering whether you could be provincial while remaining in that other office.[16] Although I don't think this is a question of great importance, it would amount to your having it all, and it would be good if Macario[17] could be appointed provincial. And we would put an end to his discontent so that he could die in peace, since the desire to be provincial is at the root of his melancholy; and this little clique will end. And this could be a reasonable thing to do since he had been appointed before. By his having a superior[18] he couldn't do any harm. Tell me, for goodness' sake, what you think about this, for it is a matter concerning the future; but even if it involved the present, there's no reason to be scrupulous about it.

7.   In the enclosed letter from Fray Gabriel[19] you will see the temptation he undergoes in my regard; yet I have not failed to write to him when I had a carrier. And notice what jealousy does, for he says there that from the letters of mine you have sent him he sees that I have not written him. I will be delighted when this letter arrives if that matter concerning you will have ended so that you can write to me at length.

8.   I forgot to mention the duke and duchess.[20] You should know that on New Year's Eve the duchess sent me a courier with the enclosed letter, and another one, only so as to have news of me. In what she says about you telling her that I cared more for the duke, I did not agree. I said that since you told me so many good things about him including the fact that he was a spiritual man, you must have misunderstood my response. But I added that only God did I love for himself and that I didn't see anything in her that would be a reason for my not loving her and that I owed her more love than I did the duke. I said it in a better way than this.

9.   I think that book of which you say Padre Medina[21] had a copy made is my long one. Tell me what you know about this. Don't forget for I would be very happy if it were not lost; there is no other copy but the one the angels[22] have. In my opinion the one I wrote afterward is superior,[23] even though Fray Domingo says it's not good; at least I had more experience at the time I wrote it.

10.   I have already written to the duke[24] twice and at greater length than you tell me to.

11.   May God preserve you, for if something now were to make me happy, it would be to see Paul.[25] If God doesn't will it, well and good; let him give me cross upon cross.

Beatriz[26] sends her best regards.

Your unworthy servant and true daughter,

Teresa of Jesus

---

1.   Juana Dantisco, Gracián's mother, during her son's confinement often acted as a messenger for him.

2.   The silence imposed by the nuncio (20 December 1578) limited Gracian's freedom to write and receive letters.

3.   See Ltr. 322.1.

4.   Felipe de la Purificación, a very reserved man, was brought from Mancera to be confessor at the Carmel of Malagón (see Ltr. 316.6). He was just the opposite of the former confessor, Gaspar de Villanueva.

5. Nicolás Doria, who was in Seville. She is probably referring to a letter of his dated 30 December 1579 (see Ltr. 325.1).

6. This statement is intentionally veiled. The probable meaning could be that the Salamanca matter referred to Pedro Fernández, who was prior of the Dominican house of San Esteban in Salamanca and had been considered a possible visitator of the discalced Carmelites. As prior he had many things to attend to and would naturally pay more attention to these than to Teresa's reform. Teresa had mentioned these disadvantages to Doria in Toledo. And he suggests a plan that would exclude Pedro Fernández (see Ltr. 325.7–9)

7. Giovanni Battista Caffardo, the vicar general of the Carmelite Order.

8. Nicolás Ormaneto died on 18 June 1577. Her doubt is that the solution now planned for the discalced Carmelites might lack a juridical basis.

9. That the discalced Carmelites have their own provincial.

10. As Doria says in the letter being forwarded to Gracián.

11. Nicolás Doria. Teresa would prefer that he come to Madrid to avoid any need that Gracián intervene in the naming of a provincial, for it was hoped that the office would be given to Gracián. Doria was prior of Pastrana at the time.

12. Juan López de Velasco, the king's secretary, who lobbied in favor of Teresa at the court.

13. They want to make Gracián the superior of the discalced Carmelites.

14. The nuncio, Felippo Sega.

15. Teresa foresees trouble with the nuncio if Gracián is named superior.

16. In the solution perhaps proposed in Doria's letter, Gracián would remain vicar general of the discalced Carmelites, an office, Teresa thinks, that would be incompatible with being provincial.

17. Antonio de Jesús (Heredia); though old and infirm, he aspired to the office of provincial, supported by a small band of discalced friars. He had already been elected to the office in the second chapter at Almodóvar (1578).

18. According to the plan, if Padre Antonio were to be provincial, he would still be under the authority of Gracián.

19. Gabriel de la Asunción, a discalced friar recently appointed provincial definitor at the chapter of La Moraleja (15 November 1579).

20. The duke and duchess of Alba.

21. The Dominican, Padre Bartolomé de Medina, a professor at the University of Salamanca. He had arranged that a copy be made of Teresa's *Life*.

22. The angels were the inquisitors, who had the manuscript of her *Life* in their possession.

23. She is referring to *The Interior Castle*, which she wrote in 1577.

24. The Duke of Alba, Fernando Alvarez de Toledo.

25. Gracián.

26. Beatriz de Jesús (Cepeda y Ocampo), a nun in the Malagón Carmel.

325. To Padre Nicolás Doria, Seville

Malagón, 13 January 1580

(Autograph: DCN, Consuegra [Toledo])

The paramount concern of the moment is the separation of the discalced Carmelites into a separate province. Teresa thought that Doria should be in Madrid collaborating with Velasco toward this goal. Doria had proposed a plan for the government of the separate province to which Teresa responds favorably.

To mi padre, Fray Nicolao de Jesús María, prior of Pastrana, Seville.

1. The grace of the Holy Spirit be with your reverence. Three or four days ago I received your letter dated 30 December, and previously I had received the ones Serrano[1] brought. I answered you at length[2] and also Mother Prioress,[3] and I also wrote to Padre Rodrigo Alvarez.[4] I gave these letters to Serrano and he attended to them, and afterward they told me that the letters were certainly given to the carrier. Apart from those, after I arrived here, I wrote you two other times and sent the letters to Señor Oria[5] to send to you. Truly, I was disappointed to see that they were all lost. Please God that won't happen to this one, for I am sending it through Velasco.[6]

2. You submit in everything to the Mother Prioress there, but she doesn't say a word to me. Since she is well, I believe that

she will establish good order in everything else, especially with such a steward. What doesn't loving God bring about, since that steward wants to favor those poor souls![7] I earnestly beg him for prayers. Why don't you tell me anything about our Lucrecia?[8] Give her my warmest greetings.

3.　　Before I forget, the prioress of Beas informed Casademonte in a message that she had the one hundred ducats[9] and asked where he wanted her to send them. He said Madrid. I have already written you about this.[10] So there's no need to worry about it.

4.　　You should realize that this place is so out of the way that you cannot count on my informing you of anything, as if I were in Seville, where I would be able to do much better; and even were I to send letters through Toledo, there are few messengers who go there; and these letters I also find get lost. I say this because you ask me to let you know when it will be necessary for you to come and about what is happening.

5.　　I informed Velasco not to count on me as long as I am here. And if you stay in Seville a long while, it could happen that you will not find me here, for I think the foundation of nuns in Villanueva—which is near La Roda—will be made and that it will be possible for me to go with the nuns. For if anywhere there is need of my presence, it's there. Padre Fray Antonio and the prior[11] have been making such a fuss about this and insisting that it is the least we can do, our Lord must want it. I still don't know for certain; but if it is to be, I will leave before Lent.[12] I regret not speaking with you, for I thought I would have that relief in Malagón.

6.　　My health is good, and, as for this house, everything is going so well that I cannot thank God enough for my having come. Spiritually, the community is doing very well and with much peace and contentment; in temporal matters it is improving, for it was a lost cause.[13] May God be blessed for everything.

7.　　What you say about the most Reverend vicar general[14] pleased me so much that I wanted to see it already done, and so I wrote about it to Velasco and to the caveman.[15] I have only pointed out that there should be no doubt concerning the validity of this substitution,[16] for when the nuncio died there were various opinions as to whether the commission he had given to Padre Gracián was still valid or not, and we are tired of conflicts.[17] And so, whether yes or no, it would be good—if God grants us the grace of a good outcome—to hurry to do what is fitting while the person this mainly concerns is still alive. All the reasons you give me seem to be very good, and go beyond what I understand. So, we must not delay in this.

8.   If you remain down there, we could be left in need of you if everything doesn't go according to our plan. I am writing this to Velasco and will submit to his opinion. In this regard, if it were not for the hardship it would cause you, since it is not easy to come up here so quickly, I would consider it preferable that you come, even though you would then have to go back down there. Although it is true that if Velasco is in Madrid, your presence might not be needed—and I wrote this to him—it is very important that the two of you be able to discuss things together. Something could happen in which your absence would result in serious harm, or at least in your being very sorry you weren't there, even though our friends love us very much. And even though our Padre Gracián is free, it would not be appropriate for him to become involved in these matters; if afterward our plan is realized, they will say that he was acting in his own interests.[18] And although this does not matter much, it is good to avoid being the occasion for such judgments.[19]

9.   I have thought that if the caveman[20] is not to be provincial and if he is given that other office, it would be good to elect Fray Antonio de Jesús. He has been chosen for the office before[21] and will certainly do well if he has a superior over him—he demonstrated this when the one from Salamanca[22] entrusted that task to him—and especially if he has a good companion. And we would be putting an end to this temptation and also to this little clique—if there is one—for that would be a much greater evil than any deficiency there might be

should he become provincial. I say this now because I don't know when I will be able to write you again, considering the ill-fortune these letters can run into. I have recommended the greatest care with this one.

10.   I would like to know how this discord that has now arisen began. Please God they will put an end to it down there. And may he watch over you. I am tired, for I have written much. Although my health is better here than it usually was when I was down there, my head never leaves me alone.

11.   If the prior of Almodóvar[23] is there, give him my best regards and tell him I am doing much for his friends. From each one I have accepted a nun, and please God he will be grateful to me. One was sent by Juan Vasquez; and the one who left Beas, by Cantalapiedra.[24] I am told his reverence has a very good opinion of her.

12.   The prioress[25] asks for your prayers. All the nuns, especially myself, recommend you to our Lord, for I never forget you. I don't fail to have some suspicion that you would be delighted with any opportunity there is for you to remain in Seville. If it is a rash judgment, may God forgive me. May His Majesty make you very holy and keep you for many years, amen.

Today is 13 January.

Your reverence's unworthy servant,

Teresa of Jesus

---

1.   Teresa's messenger.
2.   See Ltr. 318.1.
3.   See Ltr. 319.
4.   Rodrigo Alvarez, the Jesuit consultor to the Inquisition in Seville and spiritual director of Teresa's for whom she wrote two accounts of her spiritual life (see ST. 58 & 59).
5.   Francisco Doria, a relative of Nicolas Doria's residing in Toledo.
6.   Juan López de Velasco, the king's secretary, who supported Teresa's reform at the court.

7. "Those poor souls" were the Carmelite nuns in Seville who had undergone much adversity during the previous year. The "steward" was a benefactor.

8. Probably one of Doria's former housekeepers in Seville and perhaps the one whose Carmelite vocation he unsuccessfully sponsored.

9. The prioress in Beas was Anne of Jesus; she provided financial help for the negotiations in Rome and in Madrid (see Ltr. 318.13). Pedro Juan de Casademonte was a merchant friend of Teresa's.

10. See Ltr. 318.13.

11. Padre Antonio de Jesús (Heredia) and the prior of La Roda, Padre Gabriel de la Asunción (see F. 28.11).

12. She left Malagón on 13 February. Lent began that year on the 17th.

13. On the situation of the Carmel in Malagón, see Ltrs. 319.3 (to María de San José), 316 & 317 (to Gracián), and 201 & 240 (to Gaspar de Villanueva).

14. The vicar general of the Carmelite Order, Giovanni Battista Caffardo (see Ltr. 324.4).

15. Gracián, who after being exiled from Madrid by the nuncio spent some time living in the caves in Pastrana.

16. In Doria's plan Gracián would take Angel de Salazar's place as vicar general for the discalced friars and nuns (see Ltr. 324.4).

17. Nicolás Ormaneto died 18 June 1577. Troubles and disputes arose over whether or not the faculties he had given remained in force after his death.

18. Their plan is for Gracián to be vicar general of Teresa's discalced friars and nuns.

19. See Ltr. 324.5.

20. Gracián.

21. Antonio de Jesús (Heredia) had been elected provincial in the chapter of Almodóvar in October 1578. As provincial he would be subject to the authority of Gracián, if the latter were named vicar general of the discalced Carmelites.

22. The Dominican prior at San Esteban in Salamanca, Pedro Fernández, as visitator of the Carmelites in Castile, at times chose Padre Antonio to be his delegate.

23. Ambrosio de San Pedro.

24. Juan Vázquez was from Almodóvar; Cantalapiedra has not been identified.

25. The prioress of Malagón, Jerónima del Espíritu Santo.

326. To The Discalced Carmelite Nuns, Seville
Malagón, 13 January 1580

(Autograph: DCN, Santiago de Compostela)

A year has passed since the days of the slanderous process in the Carmel of Seville. Beatriz, the inept vicaress, has been removed. Most of the nuns had written to Teresa for Christmas, and two novices were recently professed. As a result Teresa has an occasion for writing this letter addressed to all the nuns in the community. Though peace and harmony had been restored, some unpleasant aftereffects could still be lurking, and Teresa wants to be sure of Beatriz's reintegration into the community.

✢✢✢✢

1.   Jesus. The grace of the Holy Spirit be with you, my sisters and daughters. I was greatly consoled by the lines you wrote and would like to respond to each one at length. But my duties prevent me from finding the time to do this. So may you pardon me and accept my good will. It would be a great consolation for me to know those who have made profession and those who have just entered.[1] Congratulations to you in being espoused to so great a King. May it please His Majesty to make you the kind of nuns I both desire and beg of him so that in that eternity that has no end you may rejoice with him.

2.   To Sister Jerónima,[2] who signed her name as "dungheap," I say, please God this humility will amount to more than words; and to Sister Gabriela,[3] that I received the St. Paul, which was very beautiful and in being so small resembled her and pleased me very much. I hope God will make her large in her obedience. In truth it seems His Majesty wants to make you all better than the nuns here—since he has given you such great trials—unless you lose out through your own fault. May he be praised for everything, especially for the good choice made in your elections. It has been a great consolation for me.

3.   Here we find through experience that the Lord seems to give the first superior he appoints for a foundation more help

and more love for the benefit of the house and of the sisters than to those who come afterward, and so they succeed in helping souls make progress. In my opinion, as long as there is nothing seriously wrong in the conduct of the one who is the first superior in these houses, she should not be changed, for there are more disadvantages in this than the nuns may suppose. May the Lord enlighten you that you may be certain of doing his will in everything, amen.

4.   I beg Sister Beatriz de la Madre de Dios[4] and Sister Margarita[5] to do what previously I asked of all the nuns, that they no longer speak of the things of the past except to our Lord, or with their confessor. If they were deceived in some way, giving out information without that simplicity and charity we are obliged to by God, they should make every effort to return to speaking clearly and truthfully. Where satisfaction is called for, they should render it; if they don't, they will go about disturbed; the devil will not stop tempting them.

5.   Let them just please the Lord; there is no reason to pay any more attention to the matter. The devil has gone about in a very angry way, seeking to prevent those holy beginnings from going forward. There is no basis for being surprised except by all the great harm that he has not caused everywhere. Often the Lord allows a fall so that the soul will be more humble, and when it returns to the right way of acting and grows in self-knowledge, it advances further in the service of our Lord, as we see among many saints. So, my daughters, you are all daughters and sisters of the Blessed Virgin and should try to love one another and take care to behave as though nothing happened. I am speaking to each one of you.

6.   I have taken particular care to pray to the Lord for those who think I am angry with them. Certainly, I was saddened, but I will be more so if they don't do what I am saying here, which I beg them to do for the love of our Lord. I always keep my dear Sister Juana de la Cruz[6] very much in mind. I imagine she is continually gaining merit. And since she has taken the

title "of the Cross," she has received a good share of it. May she pray to our Lord for me and believe that it was neither on account of her sins nor mine, which are much greater, that he imposed this penance on all the nuns.

7.   I ask the same of all of you, not to forget me in your prayers, for you owe me more than do the nuns here.

May our Lord make you as holy as I desire, amen.

        Your servant,

                                        Teresa of Jesus

---

1. Juana de San Bernardo (in December) and Archangela de San Miguel (in January) had just made profession. Those who had now entered were probably María de la Cruz (Céspedes), Jerónima de la Corona (Hervás), and Juana de la Concepción (Ortega).
2. Isabel de San Jerónimo.
3. Leonor de San Gabriel.
4. Beatriz de la Madre de Dios, appointed vicaress of the community by the provincial, was the one mainly responsible for the deplorable things that had occurred.
5. Margarita de la Concepción was Beatriz's confidante who prompted her in her misdeeds.
6. Juana de la Cruz was Beatriz's mother.

327. To Doña Juana de Ahumada, Alba
Malagón, the second half of January 1580

        (Autograph: D. Andrés Fuentes, Cascante [Navarra])

In Malagón they have finished the construction work on the new monastery, which was supervised by Teresa herself. The life there is now a tranquil one, but it is difficult to get mail to and from Malagón. Teresa is now planning a trip back to Medina and Avila.

                    ✥ ✥ ✥ ✥

1.   Jesus. May the Holy Spirit be with your honor, my sister. I tell you that if I were to go about looking for my own satisfaction, I

would consider it a trial that we are always so separated. Since, however, we are in a land of exile, we will have to endure it until our Lord brings us to the place that will last forever.

2.   In a letter I wrote to my brother a short time ago, I wrote to you that the fever is gone, glory to God. I sent the letter to Mother Prioress in Medina.[1] Certainly, since I have been in this region, I've found it painful not to know a messenger through whom I could send you a word from time to time. I was feeling very sorry about this when the Señor Licentiate,[2] who is sending this for me, told me that I could have done this often if I had given the letters to him. But I just got to know him now when I accepted a sister-in-law of his for one of our houses. In any case, answer me soon, for here they will forward the letter to me wherever I may be.

3.   I am leaving, God willing, on Ash Wednesday. I will be in Medina for eight days—for I cannot delay—nor do I even know if it will be that long; then another eight days in Avila. I'll be greatly consoled to see you there even if for only one day ...[3]

---

1. Inés de Jesús (Tapia). Her "brother" probably refers to Lorenzo de Cepeda even though she does at times refer to her brother-in-law, Juan de Ovalle (Juana's husband), as her brother.
2. This could be Juan Vázquez, who was from Almodóvar (see Ltr. 328.1).
3. These plans did not materialize. Ash Wednesday came that year on 17 February, but on 26 January Teresa received the license for a foundation in Villanueva de la Jara. On 13 February she set out from Malagón for this new foundation.

328. To Padre Jerónimo Gracián, Alcala

Malagón, 15 January 1580

(Autograph: Discalced Mercedarian Nuns, Toro [Zamora])

Teresa here completes the information she had given Gracián in her previous letter (Ltr. 324). The overall view is one of peace now in Malagón, but with three prospective foundations, she has to begin now to think of possible prioresses and subprioresses for them. She surmises that she can find suitable ones in Malagón, Avila, and Medina.

❧❧❧❧

1.   Jesus. May the Holy Spirit be with your paternity, *mi padre*. Seeing that I have a messenger as reliable as this brother, I did not want to miss a chance to write these lines even though I wrote you at length yesterday[1] through Juan Vázquez, the one from Almodóvar.

2.   Fray Antonio de la Madre de Dios[2] was here and he preached three sermons that pleased me greatly. He seems to be a fine man. It gives me great consolation when I see persons like this among our friars. And I grieved over the death of the good Fray Francisco.[3] May he be with God in heaven.

3.   Oh, *mi padre*, how worried I am, if this foundation in Villanueva[4] is made, that I won't find a prioress or nuns who will satisfy me![5] This San Angel[6] from here seems to have some good qualities, as I wrote you, but since she was formed amid the liberties taken in this house, I am very fearful. Tell me what you think. And her health is very poor. Beatriz[7] doesn't seem to me to have the qualities that I am looking for, although she has kept this house peaceful. Now that I have got over my worries about the house here,[8] I find myself weighed down with concerns about another one.

4.   As for Arenas,[9] I think the Flemish nun,[10] who is very calm after having provided for her daughters, will be good, and she has fine qualities. If God should will that the foundation in Madrid[11] become a reality, I have Inés de Jesús. Recommend all of this to His Majesty, for it is very important to start off right; and tell me what you think, for goodness' sake.

May our Lord preserve you with the holiness I beg of him, amen. Today is 15 January.

Your paternity's unworthy daughter and subject.

Teresa of Jesus

1. Ltr. 324. The carrier Juan Vázquez is a friend of Teresa's.
2. He was teaching moral theology in Almodóvar del Campo at the time; later he died on the first missionary expedition to the Congo.
3. Francisco de la Concepción had been confessor to the discalced Carmelite nuns in Malagón. He died in Baeza, when St. John of the Cross was rector there. He had founded the house with him the previous year, 1579.
4. Villanueva de la Jara, a projected foundation (see F.28.8–15).
5. For prioress, she took with her to the foundation María de los Mártires (Hurtado) from the Carmel in Toledo.
6. Elvira de San Angel went as subprioress to the foundation in Villanueva de la Jara.
7. Beatriz de Jesús (Cepeda y Ocampo) governed the house in Malagón during the absence of the sick prioress.
8. The serious problems of the house in Malagón had been only recently resolved.
9. Arenas de San Pedro, a foundation that never materialized during Teresa's lifetime.
10. Ana de San Pedro (Wasteels), a Belgian nun in St. Joseph's in Avila. Her daughters were María Dávila (married) and Ana Wasteels (a Carmelite nun at St. Joseph's in Avila).
11. Another foundation in the planning stage. Inés de Jesús (Tapia) was at the time prioress in Medina del Campo.

329. To Sister María de Jesús, Beas
Malagón, the first days in February 1580

(Autograph: DCN, Darlington [England])

The Sandoval sister, to whom this letter is addressed, and her sibling Catalina are the two protagonists in the story of the foundation in Beas (F. 22.4–24). They were also dear disciples of St. John of the Cross (see his three letters to Madre María de Jesús). Teresa was now about to resume her task of making new foundations. After a four-year interruption that had been imposed on her, Angel de Salazar, vicar general for the

*discalced friars and nuns, gave her orders to make personally
a foundation in Villanueva de la Jara.*

❖·❖·❖·❖

Malagón, the first days of February 1580.

For my sister, María de Jesús, Carmelite.

1.   Jesus. The grace of the Holy Spirit be with your charity,
my daughter. If you had my headache and so many business
matters to deal with, you would be excused for not having
written me in so long a time. But since you are without these,
I don't know why you leave me to complain about you and my
dear Sister Catalina de Jesús.[1] Well, certainly you ought not to
do this! If I could, I would be writing to you so frequently that
I wouldn't allow you to sleep in forgetting me so much. It is a
comfort to me to know that you are in good health and happy
and that, according to what they say, serving our Lord.

2.   May it please His Majesty that this be so, for I beg it of him.
In the thought of that house I would now like to find comfort
after the many tiresome problems and trials of such diverse
kinds that I have gone through in these past years. This desire
corresponds to my sensual nature. But when reason returns, I
see well that I do not deserve anything but the cross and more
of the cross and that God is doing me a great favor in not giving
me anything else.

3.   Your Mother Prioress[2] will have already told you how they
are ordering me to go to a place to make a foundation[3] there,
something I have been resisting for years. Well they have per-
severed so long—and it seems a good thing to our superior —[4]
that I am now going, very confident that it will be of service to
our Lord. Will you ask this of him and that he will always allow
me to do his will.

4.   Give my regards to Sisters Catalina de Jesús, Isabel de
Jesús,[5] and Leonor del Salvador.[6] I wish I had the time and
head to go on at greater length. Do not be brief in writing to me

or surprised if I do not answer at once. Be assured that I am delighted with your letters and that I do not forget to recommend you to our Lord.

May His Majesty make you as holy as I desire.

Your charity's unworthy servant,

Teresa of Jesus

1. Catalina de Jesús (Sandoval), Sister María's blood-sister.
2. The prioress in Beas, Anne of Jesus.
3. The foundation in Villanueva de la Jara.
4. The superior was Angel de Salazar (see F. 28.13–14).
5. Isabel de Jesús (Vozmediano y Salida), who also received the habit in the hands of Teresa and made her profession in 1576 along with the two Sandoval sisters.
6. She probably meant Luisa del Salvador (Godínez de Sandoval), niece of the founding benefactors. In Beas there was another sister named Leonor Bautista de Jesús (Pérez de Castillejo).

330. To Madre María de San José, Seville
Malagón, 1 February 1580

Everything had settled down. The troubles in Seville passed with the election of María de San José and the disorder in Malagón was corrected through Teresa's presence and charm. Now she is planning the new foundation in Villanueva de la Jara. This long letter also has three postscripts added on in different places.

For Mother Prioress of San José in Seville, Carmelite.

1.   Jesus. The grace of the Holy Spirit be with your reverence, my daughter. Today, on the vigil of Our Lady of the Transfiguration,[1] I received your letter and the ones from those sisters of mine. I was most delighted. I don't know why it is that despite all the displeasure you cause me I cannot help but love you much. I soon get over it all. And now since your house has

gained through the suffering of those conflicts, I love you more. Praise God, for everything turned out so well, and you must be somewhat better, for the nuns no longer shed tears over you as they usually do.

2.   To wear the tunic in summer is foolish.[2] If you want to please me, take if off when this letter arrives however great a means of mortification it is. Since all the sisters know of your need, they will not be disedified. You will be fulfilling your duty before the Lord, since you are doing this for me. And don't do anything else, for I have experienced the heat there. And it is better for the nuns to be able to attend the community acts than for them all to be sick. What I say to you applies also to any others you see have a need.

3.   I have given praise to our Lord that the election went so well, for they say that when it goes like this the Holy Spirit is intervening.[3] Rejoice in this suffering and don't allow the devil to disturb you with unhappiness over the office. It's funny that you now say you would be delighted to know I am praying for you. It has been a year since not only I but all the monasteries at my request have been doing so, and this is why perhaps everything has gone so well. May it please His Majesty to continue his work.

4.   I already knew that with the arrival of Padre Fray Nicolao[4] everything would be done very well. But a little before your request for him and before he received orders to leave, you were spoiling everything for us. For you were looking out only for your own house, and he was busy with the affairs of the whole order, which depended on him. God has provided in accord with who he is. I would have liked Fray Nicolao to be there and also here until I saw a final conclusion to a matter so important. I would have greatly desired that he come at a time when we could have talked. Now this cannot be, for you know that five days ago Father Vicar[5] sent a patent letter for me to go to Villanueva de la Jara, which is near La Roda, to found a monastery. For almost four years, both the city council from

there and other persons, especially the inquisitor of Cuenca, who is there as public prosecutor,[6] have been pressing us to do so. I was finding many reasons against making the foundation. Padre Fray Antonio de Jesús[7] and the prior of La Roda[8] went there. The promoters of the foundation so insisted that they got what they wanted. The distance is twenty-eight leagues from here.

5.   I would consider it a very fortunate thing if I could go by way of Seville so as to see you and satisfy my desire to argue with you; or, to put it better, to speak with you, for now after the trials you've gone through you must have become more mature. I have to return here before Easter,[9] God willing, for my permission lasts only until the feast of St. Joseph. Tell Father Prior[10] so that if that place is on his way he can stop to see me.

6.   I have written to him by way of Madrid, and I would have written to him, and to you, more often, but since I thought the letters would be lost, I didn't dare. I am delighted that mine were not lost because in one of them I wrote what I thought about the choice of a subprioress, although you know better than I what is fitting for your house. But I tell you it is absurd to have both a prioress and a subprioress with poor health, just as it would be also to have a subprioress who cannot read well or preside over the choir, something contrary to the constitutions.[11] Who is preventing you when you are occupied in some other business from appointing in your place whomever you desire? And should you be very sick I don't think Gabriela[12] would deviate from what you tell her. And if you give authority to her and your approval, she has the virtue not to give a bad example, and so I am glad to see you are inclined toward her. May God ordain what is best.

7.   I was amused by what you said about not believing everything that San Jerónimo[13] says, after I had written the same thing to you so often. And even in a letter addressed to Garciálvarez,[14] which you tore up, I said a great deal lest one give credence to

what she says about her spiritual life. Nonetheless, I say that she is a good soul and as long as she does not go astray, there is no reason to compare her with Beatriz;[15] for she errs through a lack of understanding, not out of malice. Now it can be that I am mistaken. If you do not allow her to confess except with the friars of the order, an end will be put to the matter. And if at times she confesses to Rodrigálvarez,[16] tell him my opinion and always give him my best regards.

8.   I was glad to see by these letters written to me by the sisters their love for you, and I thought the letters were just fine. In a certain sense reading them was recreation for me; and I was delighted with your letter. If only my displeasure with San Francisco[17] would go away. I believe it is because her letter seemed to me to show little humility and obedience. For this reason you should look after her progress—for some of the things from Paterna must be sticking to her—and don't allow her to exaggerate so much.[18] Even though with her circumlocutions she thinks she is not lying, it is far from the demands of perfection to use such a style when she speaks with someone to whom she should speak clearly and by doing so prevent a superior from committing a thousand follies. Tell her this in response to the letter she wrote me and that when she corrects her manner I will be satisfied. I want us to please this great God, for little attention should be paid to me.

9.   Oh, my daughter, if I had the time and head to tell at length all the things that have gone on in this house[19] so that you could gain experience and even ask God pardon for not having kept me informed. I have learned that you witnessed some things that I would dare wager have not taken place in any of the very lax monasteries in all Spain. A good intention could have excused some; for others it was not enough. May you learn a lesson from this and keep close to the constitutions—since you are so fond of them—if you do not want to end up gaining little from the world and losing out with God.

10.   There are not any nuns now who do not realize what danger they were walking in, and they say so, except Beatriz

de Jesús,[20] who so loved the sisters that despite the evidence she never informed me; nor does she say anything to me now about it. She has lost much in my esteem.

11. Since I have come, the one who served as confessor[21] no longer does so, nor do I think he ever will. This is what the town needs, for the whole thing was awful, and certainly he would do well if he were subject to another. May God pardon the one who caused him to harm this house, for he could have benefitted and all the nuns with him. He understands well that there is a reason for what is being done. He comes to see me, and I have been most gracious to him—for that is what is necessary now—and I feel at ease with his simplicity. A lack of age and experience does much harm. Oh, *mi madre*, the world is so malicious that it doesn't find good in anything! If with the experience we have had we are not careful, everything will go from bad to worse. You should now look as carefully at everything as an old woman—since you have received a share in so many trials for love of our Lord—and I will do the same.

12. I have noticed that you have not sent me any carols,[22] for certainly there are quite a few to choose from. I like to see joy in your house, with moderation, for if I said something, it was for certain situations. My Gabriela is to blame for this. Give her my best regards; I would really like to write to her. I am bringing Sant Angel[23] for subprioress, and the prioress will come from Toledo, although I have not decided who this will be.[24] Pray much to the Lord that this foundation will be of service to him. And I entrust Beatriz to you, for she must be pitied. I am happy with the message from Margarita,[25] may she continue in this spirit. Time will smooth things over as they see the love you have for them.

13. I am amazed at what we owe the good Father Prior of Las Cuevas.[26] Give him my warmest regards. Ask all the nuns to pray to the Lord for me, and you do the same, for I am feeling tired and am very old. It is no surprise that Father Prior[27] likes me, for he is very indebted to me. May God preserve him for us; in having him we have a great good and you are very much

obliged to pray for him. May God be with your reverence and watch over you for me, amen.

14.   I am not telling you about the responses of Mother Prioress and Beatriz[28] because I am very tired.

15.   You should know that my brother[29] has written two letters to me here. He tells me to write to you about his need—he thinks it is greater than yours—and that you would be doing him a real favor if you gave him now even a half of what you owe him. I gave the letters to someone here to keep so I could send them to you. Now they cannot find them. You would understand in reading them that I would not be urging you if he himself were not. You should know that he has used up a good part of the rent[30] that you are giving him and that anything you send would be a help to him now. I would have given him something here, but these business matters take up everything.

Your reverence's unworthy servant,

Teresa of Jesus

16.   From the length of this, you will see how much I was desiring to write to you. It is four times the length of those I send to the prioresses up here, and seldom do I write them in my own hand. I was delighted by the good order into which Father Prior put your financial affairs. With regard to what you owe my brother, do not do yourselves harm, even though we are in need. Here all the nuns are very happy, and with such a prioress they have every reason to be. I tell you that she is among the best we have in all our houses, and her health is good, which is an important thing. The house is like a paradise. With regard to the financial loss, I have set up a plan by which they can earn enough to survive. Please God it will help; at least nothing will be lost because of the prioress, for she is a great administrator.

17.   Many greetings to Padre Fray Gregorio,[31] ask why he has forgotten me; and to Padre Soto,[32] whose friendship has been very helpful to you.

Serrano[33] is doing well in his place ... you must pray to God for this house; it was well divided. I wish he would return to stay there, for I consider him virtuous and faithful.

---

1. 1 February; she meant to write Purification.
2. In her *Constitutions* (no. 12), the inner tunics were to be made of fine wool. Teresa, however, always insisted on allowing for exceptions in the kind of cloth because of one's health or the heat.
3. In the elections of 1 January 1980, María de San José was unanimously elected.
4. Nicolás Doria, to whom Teresa had given instructions in preparation for those elections.
5. The vicar general, Angel de Salazar.
6. Agustín de Ervías (see F. 28.8–11).
7. Antonio de Jesús (Heredia).
8. Gabriel de la Asunción (see F. 28.11).
9. Easter was to fall on 3 April that year. She left Malagón on 21 February, and Villanueva de la Jara on 20 March.
10. Nicolás Doria, the prior of Pastrana, who at the time was in Seville.
11. See *Constitutions* no. 35.
12. Leonor de San Gabriel, who had been suggested by Teresa for the office of subprioress (see Ltr. 319.8).
13. Isabel de San Jerónimo, who had some mental weaknesses.
14. The former confessor.
15. Beatriz de la Madre de Dios (Chaves).
16. Rodrigo Alvarez, a Jesuit in Seville.
17. Isabel de San Francisco (see Ltr. 319.14).
18. Isabel had been prioress of the lax community in Paterna. Since she was the community chronicler, Teresa was particularly concerned about her tendency toward exaggerated and inflated language.
19. She is referring to the situation in the house at Malagón (see Ltrs. 316 and 317).
20. Beatriz de Jesús (Cepeda) had been vicaress in Malagón (Ltr. 319.3).
21. Gaspar de Villanueva, whose replacement was the discalced Carmelite, Felipe de la Purificación.
22. None were sent after the Christmas feasts, as was the custom.
23. She is bringing Elvira de San Angelo with her to be subprioress in Villanueva de la Jara.

24. The prioress of Villanueva de la Jara will be María de los Mártires, a nun Teresa brought from Toledo.

25. Beatriz de la Madre de Dios (Chaves) and Margarita de la Concepción, the two who had caused the trouble in the community of Seville (see Ltr. 319).

26. The Carthusian prior Hernando de Pantoja.

27. She seems to be referring to Nicolás Doria.

28. The prioress, Jerónima del Espíritu Santo, and Beatriz de Jesús (Cepeda).

29. Lorenzo de Cepeda.

30. The rent was worth a thousand ducats (see Ltr. 331.9).

31. Gregorio Nacianceno, a discalced friar at the discalced monastery of Los Remedios in Seville.

32. An elderly priest who had retired and lived at Los Remedios.

33. Though not clear in the manuscript, the name is probably Serrano, a faithful messenger of Teresa's (see Ltr. 319.1). This last, torn postscript was added on with the address.

331. To Madre María de San José, Seville
Malagón, 8–9 February 1580

(Autograph: DCN, Valladolid)

Teresa had just received a letter from María de San José with sad news about the serious accident of the Carthusian prior and about the illness of the subprioress in Seville who had just been elected. She is worried about the nuns' projected move and concerned about her brother's financial situation. Doria would be leaving Seville soon, and Gracián would be returning there. She is most grateful to the nuns for their generous contribution toward paying the expenses of the negotiations in Rome.

For Mother Prioress of St. Joseph's in Seville

1.   Jesus. The grace of the Holy Spirit be with your reverence, my daughter. Today, 8 February, I received the last letter that you wrote me, which was the one dated 21 January.

2.   I felt the greatest distress over the mishap of our holy prior;[1] and if he dies from this accident, I'll feel it more than if God were to call him because of age or illness, which I don't think would cause me so much grief. Now I know this is silly, for the more he suffers the better this is for him. But when I recall what I owe him and the good that he has always done for us, I can't get over feeling that a saint will be gone from earth while those who do nothing but offend God live on. May His Majesty give him what is most fitting for his soul, for this is what we ought to ask, we who owe him so much, instead of thinking about what the house will be losing. We are all praying fervently for him. I am also distressed that I don't know where you can write me about his health, to La Roda or Villanueva de la Jara (which is nearby). It will be a miracle if God leaves him here on earth for us.

3.   You perceive it as diffidence on the part of the monasteries that they did not write to you. If they had, it would have been a courtesy we ought to avoid.[2] But you should know that they were very diligent about praying for all of you and felt very sorry. When I told them what the Lord had done to correct everything, they were greatly consoled. But the prayers were so many that I believe you will begin to serve God in that house with an entirely new fervor, for prayer is always efficacious.

4.   I have been sorry about the illness of the new subprioress,[3] for I thought she was as healthy as usual. And this is also what made me want her to be subprioress, that she relieve you of some work. When one feels like that, it is very beneficial in this region (on the advice of good doctors) to drink four or five sips of rose water. It does me much good, and orange blossom water does me much harm; although the scent of orange water is beneficial for the heart, but it's not good to drink it. Give her my best regards. Despite everything, I hope in God she will carry out the office well. Always give her authority and punish those who in your absence do not obey her as they would you. You have to give her authority, and that is very necessary.

5.　　I have always been a bit suspicious of that little Leonor.[4] You do well to proceed with caution—I mean suspicion—that she will pay heed to her relative.[5] The elderly one[6] seems to me to be very balanced. And it is for her that I have felt most sorry. Give her my best regards.

6.　　I have written you a long letter through Serrano,[7] for he told me he was going to leave for Seville soon. He cannot get used to it here. Look after him, for the licentiate[8] has told me that he told him he wants to go to the Indies. This has been weighing on me, for it is a foolish idea. I will never finish thanking him for the fidelity that he showed all of you there in a time of so much need. I also wrote through him to Padre Nicolao,[9] and I don't believe he has left yet. I wish I had the letters here. I have already written you at length about this foundation on which I am going.[10]

7.　　In one of them, I believe, I wrote to Father Prior not to go ahead with buying a house without your first seeing it and seeing it again and again, for the superior will give permission for this at once. Remember what happened there and how poorly those fathers[11] understand what is necessary for us nuns in such situations. All things take time, and how true is the saying, "whoever doesn't look ahead …"[12] Always keep before your eyes what the devil did to destroy that house, and the trials it cost us, so that you don't move without having consulted many and having thought the matter over well. In business matters, I wouldn't trust much the prior who is there.[13] And don't let it ever cross your mind that there is anyone who would be more delighted if all of you were well situated than myself.[14] And always realize that it is more necessary that the house have nice views than that it be in a good place—and an orchard if possible.

8.　　The discalced Franciscan nuns in Valladolid thought that they had done very well by getting a house near the chancery and they moved from their former place. They were left, and still are, very much in debt and are most disturbed, for they feel as though they are in a cave, and they don't know what can be done; they can't make the least sound without being heard. I certainly love you more than you think, that is, tenderly, and so I desire that you do the right thing in all matters, especially in one so serious. The bad thing is that the more I love the less I can bear any mistake. Now I well know that this is foolish and that by making mistakes one gains experience. But if the error is serious, one is left with nothing, and so it is well to proceed cautiously.

9.   I feel very sorry that you have to pay interest, for doing this is a wearisome thing and produces nothing. But since it is Father Prior's[15] opinion, it must be the best you can do. May it please the Lord to provide a solution for you soon; this is very disquieting. I greatly wish my brother[16] could wait. Were he to see that you are in need, I know that even though his is great he would wait. Certainly I have never told him that you received something from the Indies.[17] He has a good deal of interest that he has to pay, and in Valladolid he has sold a part of what you are giving him, which is worth a thousand ducats in Seville,[18] and here one hundred ducats less. So he has gone to live in the small place he bought. He spends a great deal, and since he is accustomed to having more than enough and being the type who won't ask anyone for anything, he is worried. He has written me here twice concerning the matter. I am delighted about what you are doing, for he himself didn't ask you to give any more than a half of what you owe, if possible. Recommend this matter urgently to Father Prior.[19]

10.   You have been generous in what you have given to the order.[20] May God reward you. No house has given so much, save Valladolid, which has given fifty more. And it comes at just the right time, for I didn't know what to do for our friars who are in Rome. From what they say, they deserve great pity. And this is the time now when they are most needed there. May God be praised for everything.

11.   I sent the letters to Padre Gracián.[21] He is writing to Padre Nicolao about it, according to what he wrote me. I was greatly

relieved that we can at least write to him. Since he is going to be down there, my daughter, be careful about what you do. There is in your midst someone who is watching you. Recall the dangers we placed ourselves in because of a carelessness filled with good intentions. And if we have not corrected ourselves after this, I don't know what it would take, since this cost us so dearly. For the love of our Lord I beg you not to act otherwise. Since he is no longer visitator, we don't have to fear what they might give him to eat.[22] There is no need of doing what we did when he was visitator.

12.   I don't know how you can say that I guessed about the corporals that you made, for you yourself wrote to me about it in the letter brought by Serrano. Don't send them to me until I see a need for them. May God watch over you—he who cares for all things—and make you very holy.

13.   Do not oppose or regret Father Prior's leaving, for until what is so important has been concluded, it is not right for us to be looking out for our own benefit. Always keep this in your prayers and me as well, for I now have more need of them so that this foundation will be successful. Consider greetings from the prioress[23] and sisters as given, for writing tires me out.

Today is 9 February

Your reverence's servant,

Teresa of Jesus

If Padre Nicolao has left, tear up the enclosed letter for him. You may read it if you want, but then tear it up.

---

1.   The prior of the Carthusian monastery in Seville, Hernando de Pantoja, had a fall (see Ltr. 332.6). More than 80 years old, his term in the office of prior (since 1567) had ended in January.

2.   María de San José had complained that the Carmels in Castille had not written to the Seville Carmel during the time of their troubles.

3.   Leonor de San Gabriel (see Ltr. 319.8).

4.   Leonor de San Angelo (Chaves).

5. Her relative, a cousin, was Beatriz de la Madre de Dios (Chaves), the nun who had caused so much trouble in the community.

6. She was Beatriz's mother, Juana de la Cruz.

7. Teresa's messenger in Seville, who couldn't adapt to life in Castile.

8. Gaspar de Villanueva, who had been chaplain and confessor for the community in Malagón.

9. Nicolás Doria, the prior in Pastrana, who was on business in Seville.

10. She is preparing her trip for the foundation in Villanueva de la Jara.

11. She is referring to the mistakes the discalced friars made in preparing for her foundation in Seville (see F. 24.15–20;25.1–8).

12. The Spanish saying is: "Whoever doesn't look ahead, gets left behind."

13. The prior of Los Remedios was Gaspar de San Pedro.

14. Teresa says this because she had opposed their buying a new house.

15. Nicolás Doria.

16. Lorenzo de Cepeda.

17. She is alluding to an inheritance of 800 *pesos* that came from the Indies for the community in Seville (see Ltrs. 319.7 and 332.6).

18. See Ltr. 330.15.

19. The prior of Pastrana, Nicolás Doria, who was in Seville and had taken care of the transfer of the money to Lorenzo.

20. The community in Seville had made a contribution to help defray the cost of the two discalced friars in Rome who were negotiating the establishment of a separate province.

21. Jerónimo Gracián was returning to Seville, where at Los Remedios he had been elected prior on 19 February 1580 (cf. MHCT 2: 146–47).

22. When he was visitator she feared they might poison him.

23. The prioress in Malagón, Jerónima del Espíritu Santo.

332. To Don Lorenzo de Cepeda, La Serna (Avila)

Malagón, about 9–10 February 1580

Teresa was in the newly built monastery in Malagón, ready to start out on her trip to Villanueva. She had received letters from Lorenzo, asking, in his need for money, that she request the Carmel of Seville to pay on their loan from him. She had also received letters from the prioress in Seville with some good news about their financial state.

✦ ✦ ✦ ✦

1. Jesus. The grace of the Holy Spirit be with your honor. Although I wrote to you a few times recently, I would do so more often if I had a messenger. Since I don't know whether I will have one in Villanueva, I am writing this.[1]

2. I thought we would be gone by now, although they are not late in coming for us. It bothers me to be traveling during Lent.

3. I was delighted with what the prioress of Seville writes about paying what they owe you.[2] She says that almost four hundred ducats will soon be delivered, as you will see from the small paper enclosed. Since the letters have so far to go, I didn't dare send them all. I received two letters from you in which you directed me to ask her for the money. My letter in which I mentioned this to her must have arrived before I wrote to her again. I already told her that you would be satisfied with even half the amount and that if you knew they were in need, you would endure your own without asking them for anything. I don't know if it wouldn't be better that the money remain down there, for you always said you wanted it for the chapel, and now you won't do anything but spend it all.[3] May God direct things; since you want it for him, may you make a profit on the livestock.[4]

4. As I said in the other letters, I am feeling better than I did in Avila, although not without the usual ailments.

5. Soon Padre Nicolao will be back in those parts; you may write to him, for he will be closer than I. When I know he is in Pastrana, I will arrange that he give you that money. The prioress in Toledo is charged with collecting the money that is there. Now I am writing her that on collecting it she give it to you.[5]

6. They are doing well in Seville. From the elderly woman who died in the Indies,[6] they inherited eight hundred ducats

which they have now received. I don't know any other news except that the prior of Las Cuevas is at death's door from a fall that he had. Pray for him; we owe him much.[7] What he does for the nuns is tremendous. They will be suffering a great loss.

7.   May it please His Majesty that in that solitude[8] you gain a wealth of eternal riches, for eve   rything else is like make-believe money; although with one who uses money as well as you do, it is not bad.

I kiss your hands many times.

Today is ... February

Your honor's unworthy servant,

Teresa of Jesus

1. She left Malagón for Villanueva on 13 February. Lent began on the 17th. They stayed a few days in La Roda (17–19 Feb.). On the 21st they were in Villanueva.
2. This was the old debt contracted by the Carmel in Seville with Lorenzo.
3. Lorenzo had planned to build a chapel for his burial at the Carmel of St. Joseph's in Avila. But Teresa fears that he will spend the money and leave nothing for the chapel.
4. La Serna, where Lorenzo lived, had pastureland, a mountain, and livestock.
5. The three involved in the loan are María de San José (prioress in Seville), Ana de los Angeles (prioress in Toledo), and Nicolás Doria, (prior in Pastrana).
6. No information about this benefactor remains.
7. In addition to all his previous assistance, the Carthusian prior, Hernando de Pantoja, had helped them during all their troubles of the previous year.
8. La Serna, Lorenzo's property.

333. To Padre Jerónimo Gracián
Malagón, 11(?) February 1580

(Autograph: DCF, Larrea [Vizcaya])

In preparation for the foundation in Villanueva, those nuns who were to accompany Teresa arrived in Malagón from Toledo. At this time she heard of certain rumors circulating, which prompted her strongly to defend John of the Cross and his support for Gracián and the negotiations in Rome. The autograph of this letter is in poor condition and not always legible.

✦✦✦✦

1.   Jesus be with your paternity.[1] You should know that today Padre Fray Ambrosio,[2] prior of Almodóvar, has come and is hoping to speak to Fray Gabriel,[3] who will be the one to come for us. Certainly, *mi padre*, he has seemed to me to be an upright and intelligent man. I do not say this because I spoke openly with him about anything small or great; rather I proceeded with great caution in everything, with a yes or a no. But I say I am delighted to know that these factions —[4] if there ever were any—thought to be still in existence, have broken apart. Regarding Fray John of the Cross I can swear that nothing of the sort ever entered his mind, rather he helped the friars in Rome[5] as much as he could, and he would die, if necessary, for you. This is the absolute truth.

2.   This Fray Ambrosio has great zeal for the good of the order, and so I don't think he will do anything he shouldn't. He comes from Seville and has seen what is going on there, and Padre Nicolao had no small thing to put up with from those people …[6]

3.   I found my Isabel[7] getting a little chubby, and her color was something to praise God for. Those who are in Madrid are also well, and your sister Señora Doña Juana,[8] too, as I recently learned.

4. Don't neglect to send me the permission for Antonio Gaytán's daughter.[9]

5. Of course, I am annoyed at Padre Mariano[10] for not sending me the documents you sent for me; may God pardon him.

6. The prioress[11] and all the nuns recommend themselves to your prayers ...

7. May the Lord watch over you, and for your goodness toward us give you what most befits you as well as an abundance of grace in the midst of so much turmoil, amen.

Your paternity's unworthy daughter,

Teresa of Jesus

1. These words, supplied later, are missing in the deteriorating autograph.

2. Ambrosio de San Pedro.

3. Gabriel de la Asunción, Padre Ambrosio's first cousin, who arrived in Malagón on 12 February to accompany Teresa and her founding nuns on the journey to Villanueva de la Jara.

4. These factions resulted from the disagreements among the discalced friars with respect to their future and their future superiors (see Ltrs. 324.6; 325.9).

5. St. John of the Cross supported the trip to Rome by Juan de Jesús and Diego de la Trinidad to carry out the negotiations necessary to establish a separate province for the discalced Carmelites.

6. The manuscript is damaged here and illegible.

7. The young Isabel Gracián, who was residing in Toledo and came with those nuns who were to take part in the new foundation in Villanueva.

8. Juana Gracián, Padre Jeronimo's younger sister, who was attending a school for young girls in Toledo when Teresa came to know her.

9. Mariana de Jesús, Gaytán's daughter, needed a dispensation because of age in order to enter the Carmel in Alba de Tormes. Gracián must have obtained it from Angel de Salazar, vicar general for the discalced Carmelites.

10. Mariano de San Benito.

11. The prioress in Malagón, Jerónima del Espíritu Santo.

334. To Padre Jerónimo Gracián, Madrid
Malagón, 12 February 1580

Teresa is on the eve of her departure for Villanueva de la Jara. News has arrived from Madrid, and she rejoices over Gracián's freedom from all the restrictions that had been laid on him. Two discalced friars have come to accompany her. She would be happy if she could also make a foundation in Madrid.

❧ ❧ ❧ ❧

1.   Jesus. The grace of the Holy Spirit be with your paternity, *mi padre*. Today Padre Fray Antonio and Father Prior have come from La Roda to get us.[1] They have a coach and a wagon, and from the news they are reporting, I think the foundation will turn out well. Pray to our Lord for this. The good Fray Antonio cannot deny his love for me, since despite his old age he now comes here. I don't like having to go so far; I have already written to you about the reason. Padre Fray Antonio looks well and has gained weight. It seems to me that this year's trials are causing our friars to gain weight.

2.   Tell Señor Velasco[2] that I received his letters and would like to respond to them. I don't know if I will have time because I am very busy.

3.   May God reward him for obtaining for us the freedom to be able to communicate with you.[3] Together with all the nuns, I pray much to our Lord for him. I would love to know who got this blessing for us and if between himself and Señor Don Luis Manrique[4] a plan could be worked out for obtaining permission from the archbishop[5] to found a monastery in Madrid. On my return from this foundation, I could make a foundation there very quickly without anyone knowing about it until it was done, for I already have someone who will provide the funds for the house. And if the archbishop wants the house to have an income, you already know that Luis Guillamas's[6] daughters are going to enter soon. They will be receiving 400,000 *maravedis*

each year, which for thirteen nuns is enough. Father Vicar[7] will give me the permission right away. Perhaps those gentlemen will know some friend of the archbishop's who might obtain it for us.

4.   If you think it opportune, do not fail to take up this matter so that we know whether the answer is yes or no. If by chance the foundation can be made, you must let me know at once. Find someone with whom you can send me letters so that I can keep informed about your health. May our Lord grant it to you, as he can and as I beg of him. Today is 12 February.

Your paternity's unworthy servant and daughter,

Teresa of Jesus[8]

I don't think our *Madre* says anything about me. I remain very much alone without you, and feel it more than I would like. In your charity pray for me; I truly need it. May His Majesty watch over your paternity and bring you here to us very soon, as we desire, amen.

---

1.   The prior was Gabriel de la Asunción. Antonio de Jesús (Heredia) was 70 years old at the time.
2.   Juan López de Velasco, a secretary to the king.
3.   The sentence by the nuncio, Sega, was now lifted, and Gracián, free of all restraints, could communicate with the nuns as before.
4.   Chaplain to the king, he had worked to set Gracián free and to help establish a separate province for the discalced Carmelites.
5.   The archbishop of Toledo, Gaspar de Quiroga.
6.   A gentleman living in Avila.
7.   Angel de Salazar.
8.   The following postscript was added by the prioress in Malagón, Jerónima del Espíritu Santo.

335. To Madre María de San José, Seville
Toledo, 3 April 1580

(Autograph: DCN, Valladolid)

Teresa is writing on Easter Sunday and has been seriously ill since Holy Thursday. On arrival in Toledo, she found that Madre Brianda, the former prioress of Malagón, was at the point of death. Her concerns cover a broad field: the danger of war between Portugal and Castile; the election of a new general for the Carmelite order; the negotiations for the establishment of a new province for discalced Carmelites; a new foundation in Palencia that will require a long journey; the purchase of a new house for the community in Seville; and her friend, the prior of the Carthusians, in his illness. Doria has brought her a written account of the troubles that took place in the Seville community as well as his own verbal account.

✢ ✢ ✢ ✢

For Madre María de San José, prioress of the discalced Carmelite nuns.

1.   Jesus. The grace of the Holy Spirit be with your reverence, my daughter. You can well believe that I would be happy to be in a condition to write you a long letter, but my health has been poor these days. It seems I am paying for having been well in Malagón and Villanueva and along the roads.[1] Not for many days or even years, I believe, had my health been so good. It was a great favor from our Lord, so now it doesn't matter that I'm not well.

2.   Since Holy Thursday[2] I have had one of the worst attacks ever of paralysis[3] and heart pains. I've had a fever up until now—which still hasn't left—and I am in such a state of weakness that I accomplished a great deal in managing to stay at the grille with Padre Nicolao,[4] who has been here two days now and whose presence made me happy. At least you were not forgotten. I am amazed at how you have fooled him. I am

helping you in that, for I see that this won't be a bad thing for that house. What is worse is that it seems his illusion is sticking to me. May it please God, my daughter, that you don't do anything to disillusion him, and may the Lord be your guide. I was very happy about the good things you told me concerning those sisters. I would very much like to meet them. Tell them that and give them my regards and ask them to pray for the negotiations going on over Portugal[5] and that Doña Guiomar[6] may have children. It is a pity to see the state the mother and daughter are in because she doesn't have any. Take this very much to heart, for you owe it to her. She is a very good Christian, but this trial is costing them both dearly .

3.   I have received some letters from you, although the one that Father Prior of Pastrana brought is the longest. I am delighted that he has left the affairs of that house in such a good state, and now with Padre Gracián[7] going there you will not lack anything. Make sure, my daughter—there may be someone who will exaggerate what you are doing—that you avoid occasions for criticism. In truth, I believe that he is well aware of this.

4.   I was startled by some of the things Padre Nicolao told me. Today he gave me the reports,[8] which I will read little by little. That soul[9] frightens me. May God provide a remedy. The plan for dealing with her that he gave you seems fine to me. Don't get careless about the other nun either.[10]

5.   He told me how generous you were in contributing toward the cost of the negotiations for the order.[11] God reward you, for I did not know what more to do here. Mostly everything is done. They are expecting the official communication to come any day, for it has arrived there, and the news is very good.[12] All of you thank our Lord. Because Father Prior will write at length, I am not saying anything more about this.

6.   Regarding that house they are selling you, he praised it highly to me, and also for having an orchard and views. In our manner of life, this is an important matter, especially because

of the income you are going to have. That it is so far from Los Remedios[13] presents a difficulty, I think, for the confessor. He doesn't say whether it is far from the city or adjacent to a section of it. Whatever be the case, you should not negotiate the purchase of anything without seeing it first, along with two other nuns from among those you think are more knowledgeable. Any superior will authorize your going out for this. Don't trust any friar, or anyone else; you well know the trick they tried to play on us.[14] I wrote to you about this in another letter; I don't know if it arrived there.

7.   My brother's[15] response to your letter to him is enclosed. I opened it by mistake but did not read any more than the beginning words. As soon as I saw it was not for me, I closed it. Father Prior is leaving with me the documents for withdrawing the money here,[16] but I lack the delegation to do so. Roque de Huerta has it and he has left for your region on official business.[17] Anyway, send it with the document Father Prior asked you to send for Valladolid and address it to the prioress of this house.[18] For if God gives me a little health, I won't be here much beyond the end of this month. They are giving me orders to go to Segovia and from there to Valladolid to found a house in Palencia, which is four leagues from there.[19]

8.   I told them to send you the account[20] of the foundation in Villanueva, and so I am not saying anything more here except that they are doing very well and I believe that our Lord will be greatly served there. From here I brought as prioress a daughter of Beatriz de la Fuente.[21] She seems very good and as suited for the people there as you are for Andalusia. San Angel,[22] from Malagón, is subprioress there in Villanueva. She handles the office very well, and the other two with her are truly saints. Ask our Lord that he may be served by these foundations. Remain with him, for I am in no condition to say more. Although the fever is slight, the pains in the heart and the uterus are severe. Perhaps it won't amount to anything. Pray for me, you and all the nuns. Beatriz de Jesús will tell you about Madre Brianda.[23]

Your reverence's servant,

Teresa of Jesus

9.   Our *Madre* arrived here on the eve of Palm Sunday,[24] I along with her. We found Madre Brianda to be so sick from the blood she has spit up that they wanted to give her extreme unction. Now she is somewhat better, although some days she still spits blood and she has a continual fever. There are days when she gets up. Think what would have happened if they had brought her to Malagón. She—and the community—would have been lost, and the nuns would have undergone a real trial because of the needs of the house.

10.   Our *Madre* has taken away two other nuns now; please God that will be enough. Have the nuns pray for her and for me, for I have great neéd.

11.   Pray for the election of the general,[26] that they will elect someone who will be a good servant of His Majesty. I encountered Padre Gracián here; he is well. Concerning the stove,[27] we want you to know that we spent almost one hundred *reales*, and it was worthless—so much so that we broke it apart. It used up more wood than any benefit that was coming from it.

12.   Send someone to visit the prior of Las Cuevas[28] for me and give him my best regards, for—being in my present condition—I'm unable to write. And see to it that now you take more care to have someone visit him so that it doesn't appear that because he is not in a position to help us, we are forgetting him; it would seem bad ...[25]

---

1. From the middle of February she had traveled to Malagón, La Roda, Villanueva de la Jara, and Toledo, where she arrived on 26 March.
2. On 31 March that year.
3. Cf. L.7.11.
4. Nicolás Doria, who stopped off in Toledo on his way back from Seville to Pastrana where he was prior. The grille was a grating in the parlor separating the enclosed nun from her visitor.
5. She is referring to the conflict over the successor to the king's crown.

6. Guiomar Pardo de Tavera, the daughter of Luisa de la Cerda and wife, after her first husband's death, of Juan de Guzmán, son of the Count of Alba de Liste.

7. Jerónimo Gracián, who is on the way to be prior in Seville after having been elected unanimously on 19 February 1580.

8. These probably contained an account of all the troubles that took place in the community the previous year.

9. Beatriz de la Madre de Dios, who played a role in causing the troubles.

10. Probably Beatriz's accomplice, Margarita de la Concepción.

11. See Ltr. 331.10.

12. The dispatches representing the king and the nuncio had arrived in Rome (see MHCT 2: 108–145). They were awaiting a favorable response from the Holy See, which would be obtained on 6 June 1580.

13. The monastery of the discalced Carmelite friars in Seville.

14. See Ltr. 331.7 and 221.14.

15. Lorenzo de Cepeda.

16. The money the community in Seville still owed Lorenzo, who was now in Toledo.

17. Roque de Huerta was the king's chief forest guard.

18. The prioress in Toledo, Ana de los Angeles.

19. This would not come about until 29 December 1580.

20. This story of the foundation in Villanueva constitutes chapter 28 of her *Foundations*.

21. The prioress of Villanueva de la Jara, María de los Mártires.

22. Elvira de San Angelo.

23. Brianda de San José, the former prioress of Malagón. Numbers 8–12 are written by a secretary, Beatriz de Jesús.

24. 26 March in that year.

25. The rest of the postscript is torn.

26. The vicar general, Giovanni Battista Caffardo, was elected general.

27. The stove was an invention of María de San José's, but it did not prove effective in Castile.

28. Hernando de Pantoja, who in January was hurt in a fall and no longer held the office of prior.

336. To Doña Isabel Osorio, Madrid
Toledo, 8 April 1580

(Autograph: Palace of the Counts of Berberena, Miranda de Ebro)

Isabel was sick, but had not given up on her idea of becoming a Carmelite nun. Teresa promises to meet her secretly in Madrid. Teresa herself has also been sick since Holy Thursday.

❧❧❧❧

1.   Jesus. The grace of the Holy Spirit be with your honor, my lady. I arrived here in Toledo on the eve of Palm Sunday,[1] and although I had traveled thirty leagues, I wasn't tired but felt healthier than usual. After arriving here, my good health has turned bad. I don't think it will amount to anything serious.

2.   I was delighted with the news they gave me here about your improvement. I received your letter in which you tell me that the illness did not suffice to take away your good resolve. May God be praised for everything. I hope in His Majesty that when you are well enough to follow through on your plan, what I have mentioned[2] to you will be accomplished. And if it is not, an alternative will be provided so that your holy desire may surely be realized.

3.   I am certain, if God gives me the health, that before long I will go on from here to Madrid, although I wouldn't want anyone to know about this. I am not sure how we will be able to meet, but I will inform you secretly of where I am staying. Write to me and do not forget to pray to our Lord for me and to give my regards to Padre Valentín,[3] although I don't want you to inform anyone of my plan to go there.

4.   They tell me that a provincial[4] now appointed for this province of the Society will soon be there, if he hasn't already arrived. You should know that he is one of my best friends. He was my confessor for some years. Try to speak with him, for he is a saint, and do me the favor of hand delivering my enclosed

letter to him when he arrives, for I don't know how I would get it to him in any better way. May our Lord guide you in all things, amen.

5.   I found that our Sister Inés de la Encarnación[5] had gotten so chubby that I was surprised, and I was consoled to see what a great servant of God she is. May he guide her. She excels in the obedience and in all the virtues.

> Your unworthy servant,

> Teresa of Jesus

6.   Father Prior[6] has been well. I gave him your message. I owe him much. I ask you to get an answer to the enclosed letter and send it to me in a very safe way, for this is important to me.

Today is 8 April.

---

1.   She arrived from Villanueva de la Jara on 26 March.
2.   The desire for a foundation in Madrid (see Ltr. 314.3).
3.   Valentín López, a Jesuit from Madrid; probably Isabel's confessor.
4.   Baltasar Alvarez, named provincial in Lent of 1580.
5.   Isabel's sister.
6.   Gabriel de la Asunción, who was prior of La Roda, near Villanueva de la Jara.

337. To Don Lorenzo de Cepeda, La Serna (Avila)
Toledo, 10 April 1580

Having returned from Villanueva de la Jara, Teresa took sick in Toledo. Then Pedro de Ahumada, her emotionally unstable brother, finding life with Lorenzo impossible, stopped by on his way to Seville. Teresa seeks help for him from Lorenzo,

manifesting how different her love for each of the brothers was.
Also, she is planning another trip, this one to Segovia.

❖❖❖❖

1.   Jesus. The grace of the Holy Spirit be with your honor. I
tell you that God is allowing this poor man[1] to keep tempting
us to see the extent of our charity. And indeed, my brother, I
show so little charity toward him, that it greatly grieves me. It
is not the kind that I should be showing my brother, nor even
the kind I should show my neighbor. There is every reason for
me to be feeling pity for him in his need, and I feel hardly any.
I make up for this by thinking immediately of what I ought to
do to please God, and with His Majesty in the picture there's
no trial I would not undergo. If it were not for this, I tell you I
would not have tried in the least to prevent his trip. My desire
to see him out of your house was so great that my happiness
far surpassed anything I felt on account of his trial. And so I beg
you for the love of our Lord, to do me the favor of not bringing
him back into your house no matter how much he begs and
how great his need, so that I may be at peace. Indeed, in this
matter of wanting to stay with you, he is crazy, although he may
not be so in other things. I know from learned men that this is
truly possible. And the fault does not lie with La Serna but with
his illness, for he wanted to do the same before there was any
idea of going there. And truly I have this fear that some disaster
will befall him.

2.   He says that you are right in being angry, but that he can't
do anything more. He well understands that he is a drifter, and
he must be exhausted. He says that he was so unhappy at La
Serna that he would have rather died than stay there. Now he
has arranged with a muleteer to go to Seville tomorrow, but
I don't know for what purpose. He is so fragile that one day
of sun along the road will kill him—he was already suffering
from a headache—and in Seville there will be nothing for him
to do but spend money and beg alms for the love of God. I, in
fact, believed that he still had something that was being kept
by Doña Mayor's[2] brother, but he doesn't have anything. It has

seemed to me, and only for the sake of God, that I should make him wait until a reply to this letter comes from you, although he is convinced it won't be of any help. Nonetheless, since he is beginning to realize—finally—what a lost situation he is in, he is going to wait. For goodness' sake answer me right away and send your letter to the prioress,[3] for I am writing to her to forward it to me the first chance she gets.

3.   This unexplainable sadness of yours that you write me about must be caused, I've been thinking, by his departure, for God is very faithful.[4] And if this brother is crazy in this matter, as I believe he is, clearly you would be more obliged by the law of perfection to assist him as you can, not allowing him to go where he will die, and to take the alms you have for others and give them to him as to someone to whom you are more obliged, just as you would be if you were in debt to someone. Otherwise, I don't see that you owe him anything, but much less did Joseph owe his brothers[5] anything.

4.   Believe me that God wants anyone to whom he grants the favors he gives you to do great things for him—and this is a very great thing. But I tell you that with your temperament if he should die along the way, you would never finish lamenting the fact, or God perhaps allowing it to weigh heavily on you. So it is necessary that we consider these things before making an irremediable mistake. If you conduct yourself before God as you ought, you will not be any the poorer for what you give him, for His Majesty will give it back to you in other ways.

5.   You gave him two hundred *reales* for clothing and more for food and for other things that he used while in your house. All of this may seem little, but the cost mounts up to more than you may think. With what you have given him he has enough for his food this year wherever he may choose to go. With another two hundred *reales* that you might give him each year for food added on to what you were giving him for clothing he can live with my sister[6] (who he says invited him) or with Diego de Guzmán.[7] The latter gave him one hundred *reales*, which

he will spend on this trip. Next year when you decide to give him something you must not give it to him all at once, but give it little by little to the one who will be providing his food, for from what I see he will not be staying long in one place. It's a great pity. But in exchange for his not staying in your house I consider it all for the good. Figure that you are giving a part of that money to me as you would if you saw me in need. I will be grateful, considering it to have been given to me, and have a strong desire not to be a burden to you. I tell you that for some time now I have been longing to see him out of your house, for I sometimes felt afflicted by having to see you put up with that torment and by the fears I mentioned.[8]

6.   Since this matter was the purpose of my writing, I have nothing else to add except that I will get the documents from Padre Nicolao,[9] for I believe he is bringing them from Seville and said he will come to see me. I was delighted that Lorencico[10] was so close by. And may God be with him. I will try not to stay here long, for my health isn't as good here as in other places. God willing, I will go to Segovia.[11]

7.   Fray Antonio[12] says that, even if for no other reason, he will go there to see you. Padre Gracián is no longer here. My regards to Don Francisco.[13]

Today is Quasimodo Sunday.[14]

     Your reverence's unworthy servant,

       Teresa of Jesus

---

1.   The reference is to her brother Pedro de Ahumada, a dissatisfied drifter, unable to live compatibly with Lorenzo despite the latter's charity toward him.
2.   Doña Mayor was Juan de Ovalle's sister, a Benedictine nun in Alba.
3.   The prioress in Avila, María de Cristo, who will forward the letter to Toledo.
4.   The words are from 1 Cor 10:13, a text that left a deep impression on Teresa (see L. 23:15).
5.   An allusion to Jacob's sons (see Gen. 42–45).
6.   Juana de Ahumada, living in Alba.

7. The son of Teresa's older half-sister, María de Cepeda. Lorenzo had proposed that Pedro go live with him.

8. In no. 1.

9. Nicolás Doria. He was bringing the documents that authorized payment of the money owed Lorenzo.

10. Lorencico was Lorenzo's youngest son, passing through Seville on his way to the Indies.

11. She will arrive in Segovia on 13 June.

12. Antonio de Jesús (Heredia).

13. Francisco de Cepeda, Lorenzo's son.

14. The first Sunday after Easter.

338. To Lorenzo de Cepeda, La Serna (Avila)
Toledo, 15 April 1580

(Autograph: Pedro Martínez Pinedo, Madrid)

Another letter to Lorenzo expressing her worries about Pedro. She does not want to undertake her planned trip to Segovia until she receives Lorenzo's reply, which she urges him to send at once. Any notion that Pedro might be able to live in a monastery of discalced friars meets with Teresa's outright rejection as totally unworkable.

1.   Jesus be with your honor. Because you will have received my long letter[1] on this subject of Pedro de Ahumada, I now have nothing more to say than beg you to answer at once and give the letter to Mother Prioress,[2] for many people travel here from Avila. The poor man is here spending his money and must be very distressed judging by how thin he has gotten. It would sadden me very much if the answer were not to come before the time I depart, which I think will be soon.[3]

2.   I am better than I was. In sum, it must be all due to my former illnesses, and there's no reason to be surprised. But I am surprised that I am not worse. I think it was good for my

health in Malagón not to have so many letters to answer and so much business.

3.   We have heard again from Rome. The negotiations are going very well, although opposition is not lacking.[4] Pray to God about this and about what must be done for Pedro de Ahumada, that His Majesty may enlighten you as to what is the best action to take.

4.   I already told you that I had been given the four hundred *reales*.[5] He must have been using what Diego de Guzmán gave him, and has spent it all. I tell you that with my nature I agonize over not being able in good conscience to give him anything. I would be very happy to do so just to relieve you of this burden. May the Lord provide a remedy.

5.   It's painful for me that you do not have Mass except on feast days. I keep trying to think of a solution, but I don't find any. Pedro de Ahumada tells me that your house, especially the bedrooms, is much better than the one in Avila, which made me very happy. But it seems to me that having the young plowmen living in the house would cause a lot of turmoil. If you built some little house for them to stay in, you could get rid of a great deal of noise in the house. Why didn't you divide the kitchen as we had agreed? Well, such jabbering! I realize that each one knows his own house better ...[6]

6.   This Serna[7] who is bringing these letters says he will return here within eight days. If you have not already sent your reply, have him bring it to me, for I will not yet be gone. Even if I should have to leave, I would wait.

7.   Regarding what you said about Pedro staying in one of our monasteries, he already mentioned it to me, but that wouldn't work out.[8] They don't take in seculars, nor would he be able to bear eating the meals given him. Even now if the meat in an inn is not tender and well cooked, he can't eat it; he will go along on only a pastry. When I can, I send him some trifle, but this isn't often. I don't know who would be able to put up with him and be so precise in serving him.

8.   This humor[9] is a terrible thing that does harm to oneself and to everyone else. May God give you the good I beg for you and free you from Pedro's returning to your house. All other means of helping him I desire to try so that if he should die, neither you nor I will have any regrets.[10]

9.   My best regards to Don Francisco and to Aranda.[11] May God watch over you and make you very holy, amen. Why don't you tell me how you are getting along in solitude?

Today is 15 April.

> Your unworthy servant,
>
> Teresa of Jesus.

1. Ltr. 337.
2. The prioress of St. Joseph's in Avila, María de Cristo.
3. She set out for Segovia on 7 June.
4. The negotiations in Rome concerned the establishment of a separate province for discalced Carmelites.
5. It doesn't seem that she had mentioned this to Lorenzo. Diego de Guzmán had given Pedro 100 *reales* (see Ltr. 337.5).
6. An incomplete and softened version of the Spanish saying:"a madman knows more about his own house than the wise know about someone else's."
7. This Serna was one of Lorenzo's servants (see Ltr. 172.1,5).
8. This thought was that he might be able to reside in one of the monasteries of discalced Carmelite friars.
9. She is referring to melancholy, the black humor, a term Teresa often used with wider application than is often given it.
10. Her fear of some tragic mishap was expressed in Ltr. 337.1.
11. Lorenzo's son and the housemaid, Francisco de Cepeda and Jerónima de Aranda.

339. To Madre María de Cristo, Avila
Toledo, 16 April 1580

(Autograph: DCN, La Imagen, Alcalá de Henares)

Teresa's brother Lorenzo has been waiting for some years for the repayment of money he lent to the Carmel in Seville.

Nicolás Doria has arrived in Toledo with news that Lorenzo's money will arrive shortly. María de Cristo is being asked to deliver letters to Lorenzo and Padre Angel de Salazar.

❧❧❧❧

1. Jesus be with your reverence. Yesterday I wrote to you and afterward the occasion arose to send some letters to Father Vicar.[1] You being so poor, it isn't right to make you pay so much postage, but this cannot be helped.

2. In your charity, please send this letter to my brother[2] along with the one addressed to him so that he will know that Padre Nicolao,[3] having arrived late today, is now here. I immediately asked him about the money for my brother. He tells me that he will leave me authorization so that the prioress[4] here may withdraw the money from the amount they will be sending and send it to you. He tells me that the one who has the money has assured him that he will give it to him at once. So from what I understand it will be collected soon. The money from Valladolid, it seems, was sent to Seville for some business transactions and will be recovered; if not it will be paid back in some other way; that is certain.

3. Give my regards to María de San Jerónimo[5]—tell me how she is—to Isabel de San Pablo,[6] to Teresa,[7] and all the others; may God make them all saints. May he be with you.

4. In any case try to send me the answers from Father Vicar and my brother, as I have already mentioned to you in other letters. If Father Vicar is gone, let me know where; and the letters for him return to me.

Today is 16 April.

Your reverence's servant,

Teresa of Jesus

---

1. The vicar general is Angel de Salazar.
2. Lorenzo de Cepeda, in Avila.
3. Nicolás Doria, prior of Pastrana.

4. The prioress in the Carmel of Toledo, Ana de los Angeles.
5. Teresa's cousin who was a nun in the Carmel of Avila.
6. The subprioress.
7. Teresa's niece, Lorenzo's daughter.

340. To Padre Jerónimo Gracián, Madrid
Toledo, 5 May 1580

Teresa had suffered a terrible month with influenza in which she thought she would die. She answers several of Gracián's letters dealing with a number of topics: a moral case being disputed in Alcalá, the improvement of her health, the possibility of a foundation in Madrid, the Carmel in which Velasco's sister should enter, news of the business in Rome, her orders to travel again, and Gracian's new commissions.

1.   Jesus. The grace of the Holy Spirit be with your paternity. Yesterday I received your letters. They came after the one about the rector of Alcalá.[1] I discussed this with Señora Doña Luisa [2] and with the licentiate, Serrano. And he answered in the enclosed letter.

2.   Regarding the clash of opinions[3] you mention, I was very happy to learn that your opinion prevailed; for even though the fathers must have enough reasons, it would have been worse not to do what was safest at that time, but to be thinking of points of honor. When honor of the world is lost by one's acting in this way, one begins to understand how important it is to look only to God's honor. It could be they feared that a greater harm might result from a change in approach toward the enmity. The truth is that God provides with his grace when we are determined to do something for him alone. You have nothing to feel distressed about in this case, but it would be good if you presented some reason for excusing those fathers.

I feel more distressed to see you going around in the midst of those contagious fevers.[4]

3.   Blessed be God that you are in good health, for my illness no longer amounts to anything, as I have written to you. Only weakness remains, for I went through a terrible month, which I spent mostly on my feet. Since I am used to dealing with chronic pain, I thought that in spite of feeling quite sick, it was possible to put up with it. Certainly, I thought I was dying, although I didn't completely believe this, nor did whether I die or live matter to me. God grants me this favor, which I consider a great one, for I remember the fear I used to have at other times.

4.   I was delighted to see this letter from Rome; for although the dispatch[5] is not coming as soon as was thought, it seems certain it will come. I don't know what kinds of turmoil its arrival might cause, nor why. It is good that you wait for Father Vicar, Fray Angel,[6] even if for no other reason than to prevent the appearance that you cannot wait to set out on your mission as soon as you receive it; he will take note of everything.

5.   You should know that I wrote to Beas and to Fray John of the Cross that you are going down there[7] and about the commission that you have. Fray Angel wrote to me of how he had given it to you. Although I thought for a while that I should be silent, it seemed to me that since Father Vicar told me about it there was no need to be silent. I would so much like not to lose time, but if our documents[8] are to arrive soon, it will undoubtedly be better to wait so that everything can be carried out with greater freedom, as you say.

6.   Even if you don't come to see me, I considered it a great gift for you to say that if I want you will come. It would be a real joy for me, but I fear the remarks of our brothers and the fatigue it would cause you, for you still have a long way to travel. I must satisfy myself with the thought that you will have to come eventually out of necessity. I would then like some of your time one day to find relief in conferring with you about the things of my soul.

7.   When I get a little more of my strength back, I will try to speak with the archbishop.[9] If he gives me permission for a foundation in Madrid, it will be undoubtedly much better for her to enter there than elsewhere. These nuns become so disappointed when what they want isn't done that they torment me. Since I am waiting to see whether the Madrid foundation is possible, I have not written to the prioress in Segovia,[10] nor have I spoken seriously about their receiving her. I believe that although the prioress doesn't like the idea, all the other nuns would accept her. But I don't have time to go into this because according to what Father Vicar wrote me, I cannot stay here any longer than is necessary for me to be strong enough to travel, and I am becoming scrupulous about not moving on.[11] There are many nuns in Segovia, and now they want to receive another. But since she would be going there only temporarily, it shouldn't matter to them.

8.   If nonetheless you think it worthwhile I will write to the prioress in Segovia. You too should tell her that you would be very pleased if they accepted her, that this is very important. That house has been of little help or almost no help in all our business matters. And when you tell her about all we owe to Velasco,[12] it will have a good effect. Here they just gave five hundred ducats at my request to St. Joseph's in Avila. A tangle of things happened there, which I will tell you about, that was no one's fault; otherwise I would have already dealt with the matter.

9.   Truly, until I speak to the archbishop, I don't know if it would be good to bring this matter up in Segovia. Let me know soon what you want done, for there are many carriers who will come here, if you pay a good portage. To bring her to Segovia without the nuns' knowing about her and wanting her would be unacceptable. And the permission from Padre Fray Angel—which I already have—sets this acceptance down as a condition. I didn't mention to him who she was. I tell you that I desire to accept her much more than you do. I think it would be better to speak with the archbishop in his house, entering

through a church where he says Mass. When I am well enough I will do this and inform you. I have no more to say for now except that may God watch over you and give you what I beg of him. It is 5 May.

Your unworthy servant,

Teresa of Jesus

1. The rector of the discalced house of studies in Alcalá, Elías de San Martín.
2. Luisa de la Cerda.
3. The dispute revolved around the obligation in conscience of someone on his death bed to become reconciled with an offender. The question was complicated by ideas concerning "points of honor," and a budding moral probabilism.
4. An epidemic of influenza, from which Teresa had been suffering, was passing through Castile in those days.
5. The letter was a notice given by Abbot Bernardinus Briceno to Philip II that Gregory XIII had granted permission for the discalced Carmelites to establish a separate province (MHCT 2: 180–81). The dispatch, pontifical brief (Pia consideratione), allowing for the separation, is dated 22 June 1580 (MHCT 2: 192–99).
6. Angel de Salazar, the Carmelite vicar general, had given Gracián some official commissions: prior of Los Remedios in Seville and visitator of the discalced Carmelite friars in Almodóvar del Campo (see MHCT 2:148–51; 187–88).
7. Baeza, where at the time St. John of the Cross was rector.
8. The brief from Rome.
9. The Archbishop of Toledo, Gaspar de Quiroga.
10. The prioress was Isabel de Santo Domingo.
11. Responding to the request of the Bishop of Palencia, Don Alvaro de Mendoza, Angel de Salazar gave Teresa orders to go to Valladolid and Palencia.
12. Juan Vázquez de Velasco, who won favor in Madrid for the discalced Carmelites, and Gracián in particular, was the Carmelite aspirant's brother.

341. To Don Pedro Juan de Casademonte, Medina
Toledo, 6 May 1580

(Original: DCN, Teruel)

Still convalescing, Teresa dictated this letter to her secretary. She expects to be undertaking her trip soon. She also is following closely the events in Rome and the financial backing of the project there.

✦✦✦✦

1.   Jesus. The grace of the Holy Spirit be always with your honor. Having been sick for many days, I put off writing this, although I have a great desire to know how your health is. Glory to God, I am now beginning to get better, although I am weak and my head is in a miserable condition. So, this is not written in my own hand. I beg you to write and tell me about the health of both you and Señora Doña María,[1] whose hands I kiss.

2.   You should know that the one hundred ducats have already been paid in Madrid. It made me very happy, as did also the knowledge that our two Romans[2] are well and the business negotiations moving along nicely.

3.   Let me know if you have heard anything about our friend, Licentiate Padilla.[3]

4.   I don't know where your answer to this might reach me, for I don't think I will be here long. You could send it to Segovia.[4]

5.   May our Lord preserve you with the holiness I desire, amen.

Toledo, 6 May.

Your honor's unworthy servant,

Teresa of Jesus

---

1.   Don Pedro's wife.
2.   The two discalced friars negotiating in Rome for the separate province: Juan de Jesús and Diego de la Trinidad (See Ltr. 293. 1–2).

3. Juan Calvo de Padilla, who had been imprisoned by the Inquisition.
4. Another month passes before she actually gets started on her journey.

342. To Doña María Enríquez de Toledo, Duchess of Alba
Toledo, 6 May 1580

The duke of Alba has gotten out of prison only to be sent away to lead an army against Portugal. While consoling the duchess, who must suffer his absence again, Teresa in turn begs her to intercede in favor of the Jesuits, who are being threatened with expulsion from their new foundation in Pamplona. After a very grave illness with much suffering, she is a little better and looking ahead to another trip which will take her to Madrid, Segovia, and Avila.

❧❧❦❦

1. Jesus. The grace of the Holy Spirit be always with your excellency. I have had a great desire to write to you ever since I learned that you were home. But my health has been so poor that since Holy Thursday[1] a fever had not gone away until only eight days ago, and it was the least of what I suffered. The doctors were saying that I had an abscess on the liver. With bloodlettings and purges God was pleased to leave me in this sea of trials. May it please His Majesty to give them to me alone and not to someone for whom I would feel more pain than by suffering them myself. Here we have learned that the whole business[2] you've been undergoing has come to a happy conclusion.

2. I don't know what to say except that our Lord does not want us to experience joy without some sadness, as I believe you must feel having to be apart from the one whom you love so much.[3] But may our Lord so ordain that you gain greatly in his sight and afterward come to enjoy all consolation together. May it please His Majesty to do for you what I and all these houses of nuns with the greatest care beg of him. So that the outcome

be a happy one, I have instructed them to take this very much to heart in their prayers. And, even though wretched, I keep this intention before me, and this we will do until receiving the news I desire.

3.   I am thinking about the pilgrimages and prayers you will now be occupied with and how it will often seem to you that life in prison was more restful. Oh, God help me, what vanities are those of this world! And how much better it is not to desire rest or anything having to do with it, but to place everything involving ourselves into the hands of God, for he knows better than we do what befits us.

4.   I long to know how your health is and how everything else is going for you, and so I beg you to let me know. Don't worry in the least if the message isn't in your own hand. For since it has been so long since I have seen anything in your handwriting, the messages that Padre Maestro Gracián[4] sends me on your part satisfy me. I am not going to mention where I will be going when I am ready to leave here or anything else, because Fray Antonio de Jesús[5] will be going to Alba soon, and he will give you an account of everything.

5.   Anyway, a kindness you must render me now—for it is important to me that the favor you show me in everything be known—regards the Society of Jesus. They founded a house in Pamplona de Navarra and experienced a very peaceful beginning. Afterward such a great persecution arose against them that the people wanted to expel them from there. They sought the protection of the constable,[6] and he supported them, speaking kindly to them and favoring them in many ways. What I ask you to do for me is write a letter to the constable thanking him for what he has done and directing him to continue helping them in every way he can.

6.   Since—for my sins—I know the affliction that religious go through in seeing themselves persecuted, I have felt great pity for them, and I believe that whoever helps and favors them gains much in the sight of His Majesty. And I would like

you to experience this gain, for I think His Majesty will be so pleased that I would even dare ask the duke to do this if he were here.

7. The people of the city say that the cost of having them will mean less left for themselves. But a gentleman is providing a house and a very good income for them, certainly not leaving them in poverty. And even if they were founded in poverty, the people would be showing very little faith in so great a God if they thought he was not powerful enough to provide food for those who serve him.

8. May His Majesty watch over you and give you so much of his love that during the time of the duke's absence you will be able to endure your loss with calm, for I believe it will be impossible to do so without pain.

9. Along with the one who brings your answer to this, I beg you to send also the letter I am here begging of you. And it must not be so written as to seem to be the usual letter asking for a favor, but it must say that it is your will that this be done.

10. But how importunate I am! Yet after all the suffering that you cause me, and have caused, it will not be hard for you to put up with my boldness.

Today is 8 April, from this house of St. Joseph's in Toledo—I meant to say May.

Your excellency's unworthy subject and servant,

Teresa of Jesus

1. 31 March.
2. The duke was released from his imprisonment in Uceda and sent to lead an army against Portugal.
3. She will be separated from her husband once more.
4. Gracián had spent periods of time with the duke during the imprisonment at Uceda.
5. A family friend of the duke's.
6. Francisco Hurtado de Mendoza, Viceroy of Navarra.

343. To Padre Jerónimo Gracián, Madrid
Toledo, 30 May 1580

Teresa responds to several letters from Gracián. She is preparing for a trip to Segovia. Planning to travel by carriage in the company of the ailing Padre Antonio de Jesús, she hopes Padre Gracián will come with them.

❖❖❖❖

1.   Jesus be with your paternity, *mi padre*. After having sent you a letter yesterday, the feast of the Most Blessed Trinity, I received the one you said you had written to me at the same time as to Padre Nicolao.[1] The others arrived today. It was truly necessary that our friars remain there in the midst of that turmoil.[2] Blessed be the One who so ordains things. So that you won't feel sorry thinking that your letters were lost, I am writing this one, and I regret that Señora Doña Juana[3] has to be paying so much in postage. I recommend myself to her prayers.

2.   I have also received a letter today from the prioress in Segovia[4] who tells me to bring Juana López[5] with me, that all the nuns will be delighted. But I had written to them in such a way that they couldn't have done otherwise. This wasn't necessary as regards the prioress, for she is willing to please you and me. Blessed be God that the need for me to be negotiating these matters, and the others that arose, has come to an end. For I tell you, *mi padre*, much ingenuity was required, for each prioress looks after her own house and then thinks the rest will get by.

3.   It is really necessary that she be provided with a bed, for this can't be avoided, as well as the money for her trousseau. I would have liked to pay for these, but I am extremely poor right now for reasons I will explain when I see you. If you think it would not be good to bring this up now, we will look for another way, although certainly for the moment I don't see any. In what regards the dowry, things will go better if that other foundation is made.[6]

4. For many reasons, I don't think anything would be lost if you came here for Corpus Christi[7] and we were to set out together. Coming in a carriage will not be very tiring. Although Padre Fray Antonio will not let go of the idea of coming with me, his condition is such that we will have much to do for him.[8] Once Corpus Christi has passed there will be nothing else to wait for, except the authorization from the archbishop,[9] which never gets finalized. I was most happy with Beatriz.[10] And what a hurry Padre Nicolao is in to have you go there![11] In my opinion, for the very same reason, this would not be fitting, and now he himself agrees. This would kill you, even if there were no other drawback. Because we will be speaking of this and other things, please God, I'll say no more.

Your paternity's servant,

Teresa of Jesus

<hr>

1. Nicolás Doria.
2. She is alluding to the troubles that took place in the Carmel of Seville.
3. Juana Dantisco, Gracián's mother, was taking care of the correspondence between Teresa and her son and paying the postage (See Ltr. 347.19). Gracián was also short of money.
4. Isabel de Santo Domingo.
5. Juana López de Velasco, who in Carmel received the name Juana de la Madre de Dios (and later received spiritual direction in Segovia from St. John of the Cross) (See Ltr. 340).
6. The hoped-for foundation in Madrid.
7. The feast of the Most Holy Body and Blood of Christ, which was on 2 June that year. Gracián did not come to Toledo, but he did accompany Teresa from Madrid to Segovia. Teresa left Toledo on 7 or 8 June, passed through Madrid, and arrived in Segovia on 13 June.
8. Antonio de Jesús (Heredia) was around seventy and so sick that Teresa was afraid of traveling with him for fear they would suffer delay during the trip (see Ltr. 344.3).
9. Gaspar de Toledo, from whom Teresa was awaiting permission to found a Carmel in Madrid. It was never actually granted during her lifetime.
10. Beatriz de la Madre de Dios, who responded favorably after the past disturbances.
11. To Seville.

344. To Padre Jerónimo Gracián, Madrid

Toledo, 3 June 1580

Teresa is answering Padre Gracián's letter by return mail through a safe messenger, Madre Brianda's brother. Her trip to Madrid has been delayed because Archbishop Quiroga is not giving her permission for a foundation in Madrid, nor even an audience. In the meantime her health has improved as has Padre Antonio's, but Gracián has not come to Toledo to accompany them. Teresa is still trying to have an interview with the archbishop and also with Gracián and Angel de Salazar. In passing, she mentions some news about the Princess of Eboli.

1.   Jesus. The grace of the Holy Spirit be with your paternity, *mi padre*. I don't know what our Lord intends by allowing so many obstacles to my departing and speaking with this angel.[1]

2.   So as to be able to leave, I wrote him today in the form of a request—it was suggested that I do so, and we shall see what the result is. But another snag arose today, which is my fear that we will miss Padre Fray Angel[2] on the journey. He wrote that after the feast days he would come to Madrid. If we finish our business with the archbishop, however, I don't think waiting for him would be reason enough to delay; so we will set out next Tuesday.[3]

3.   Padre Fray Antonio[4] is now much better. He is saying Mass. And so you can be at ease, for I will speak with you there; and if not, we shall see each other in heaven. Padre Fray Antonio was in such a condition that I was afraid to go alone with him, thinking that he might die along the way. And since it would have made me happy for you to come, I tried to bring this about, still failing to realize that when I myself try to get something in this life the opposite happens.[5] Since he was so sick, you had the

occasion for coming to see him—and it would have appeared right. It would be good to write to him and express your happiness over his recovery, for you have been cold toward him.

4.   Padre Fray Hernando del Castillo[6] is here. They said the Princess of Eboli was back in her house in Madrid; now they say she is in Pastrana.[7] I don't know which is true; either of these is very good for her. My health is good, glory to God. Let me know as soon as Padre Fray Angel arrives there. These carriers deliver the letters quicker and more reliably. I have already written you two in which I told you that I had received Padre Nicolao's[8] letter and those that came with it. The one dated the Tuesday before Corpus Christi was given to me today, Friday, the day after this feast.

5.   I am answering you through Madre Brianda's[9] brother; she is doing all right. All the nuns ask for your prayers; I ask for those of Señor Velasco.[10] Since I wrote to him recently, I am not doing so now. I really hope the letter was not lost, for it is important that his sister[11] be there when I pass through.

6.   Padre Nicolao told me that he left eight hundred ducats on deposit in Seville, since the prioress[12] wanted to have them on reserve for any need that would arise regarding the negotiations. I tell you this so that the person who lent you the hundred ducats may be sure of receiving them back soon. It will be enough for me to write to Casademonte,[13] and he will send you the amount at once—I mean if you cannot obtain a loan there. May God direct everything as he sees necessary, and watch over you as I beg of him.

Your paternity's servant,

Teresa of Jesus

7.   Have this letter sent to Padre Nicolao and find out from the Carmel what they know about Padre Vicario; and if possible let me know, although I believe we will be leaving here

on Tuesday or Wednesday—unless something else comes up, for it seems a kind of spell has been cast over us.[14]

---

1. The angel was the grand inquisitor, Gaspar de Quiroga, the Archbishop of Toledo.
2. Angel de Salazar, their vicar general, whom she wanted to meet in Madrid. He was to travel from Salamanca to Valladolid and then Madrid. Teresa's plan was to travel through Madrid to Segovia.
3. Tuesday, 7 June (cf. no. 7).
4. Antonio de Jesús (Heredia).
5. See Ltr. 343.4.
6. Hernando del Castillo, a Dominican from Madrid who was a great friend of Teresa's and had intervened in the case against the Princess of Eboli.
7. Ana de Mendoza, the widow of Ruy Gómez de Silva, became suspect of having had a role to play in the murder of Juan Escobedo, secretary to Don Juan of Austria. She had been confined to the castle of Santorcaz by order of the king and then moved to the family palace at Pastrana. More than once Teresa sent Gracián to Santorcaz and Pastrana to try to comfort her.
8. Nicolás Doria (see Ltr. 343.1,4).
9. Brianda de San José, the former prioress in Malagón, sick in Toledo at the time.
10. Juan López de Velasco, a secretary of the king's.
11. Juana López de Velasco, who was to travel with Teresa to Segovia to enter the Carmel there.
12. The prioress in Seville, María de San José (see Ltr. 331.10–11).
13. Pedro Juan de Casademonte, a merchant from Medina del Campo.
14. She is referring to the strange delays that kept them from setting out on their journey to Madrid and Segovia.

345. To Don Lorenzo de Cepeda, La Serna (Avila)
Segovia, 15 June 1580

(Autograph: DCN, Sanlucar de Barrameda)

Teresa came from Toledo, passed through Madrid, and now had been in Segovia for two days. She is wondering why she has not heard from Lorenzo and is worried about him. She sees the possibility in Segovia of a good marriage for Lorenzo's elder son, Francisco, and is directing her attention to that.

❖ ❖ ❖ ❖

1.   Jesus. May the Holy Spirit be with your honor. I am in Segovia, and very worried, and I will continue to be so until I hear how your health is. For I don't understand why it is that immediately after Pedro de Ahumada left, I received a letter from you and then have heard nothing more from Avila. I am afraid that you might be sick that for this reason the nuns at St. Joseph's are not writing to me.[1]

2.   Padre Fray Antonio, who will be seeing you, is bringing this letter and will give you an account of everything. As a result, and because I am very busy, I am not going to be long and will leave it to him.[2]

3.   The marriage of the gentleman about which you wrote me did not come about, nor were they in favor of it here. The prioress speaks so well of the young lady that I would consider it most fortunate if she were brought into our family. The prioress is a good friend of hers and is having her come to see me. We will try in roundabout ways to have the prioress send out a feeler to see if you could approach her on such a matter. May the Lord bring about whatever will render him the most service, and may he watch over you.[3]

4.   Let me know quickly about your health. I wrote to you from Toledo. I don't know if you received the letter. My best regards to Don Francisco;[4] Padre Gracián who is here sends his also. May God keep you and make you very holy, amen. We arrived here the day before yesterday.

Today is 15 June.

Your honor's servant,

Teresa of Jesus

---

1.   She reveals a kind of foreboding that something is not right. Lorenzo died a few days later. It was her nuns in the Carmel of St. Joseph's in Avila who were not writing to her.

2. See Ltr. 337.7 where she alludes to Padre Antonio's esteem for Lorenzo.
3. The prioress in Segovia was Isabel de Santo Domingo. The possibility of arranging a betrothal between this young Segovian lady and Francisco, Lorenzo's elder son, did not materialize.
4. Lorenzo's son.

346. To Don Lorenzo de Cepeda, La Serna (Avila)

Segovia, 19 June 1580

Teresa responds to a letter from Lorenzo, who misses her presence, and seems saddened by presentiments of his death. Teresa would like to visit him in Avila, but it is not possible. The autograph, no longer extant, was damaged when a copy of it was made.

❊·❊·❊·❊

1.   Jesus be with your honor. They were late in telling me about this messenger …[1] I don't know how you know that you are going to die soon[2] or why you think such foolish thoughts or afflict yourself with what will not come about. Trust in God who is a true friend and will not fail either your children or you. I greatly wish you were in a condition to come here, for I am not able to go there. At least it is very wrong of you not to have visited St. Joseph's in so long a time,[3] for it is close and you wouldn't feel alone. The exercise would do you good. For goodness' sake, don't go on like this, and let me know about your health.

2.   I am feeling much better since I've been here, and the small fevers I had have left me. As regards the matter[4] about which I wrote you, I haven't attended to it and won't be able to do anything until after Padre Fray Angel[5] is gone—and he will be here for eight days.

3.   Mother Prioress, Padre Gracián, and San Bartolomé send their best regards, and give mine to Don Francisco.[6]

Let me know about your health, for goodness' sake, and remain with God, for I have no more time.

Today is 19 June.

Your honor's servant,

Teresa of Jesus

4.   Perhaps it will be necessary to send you a messenger, for in regard to that matter a step forward has been made which doesn't seem bad. Not until Padre Fray Angel is gone can I do anything.[7]

---

1.   The beginning lines were indecipherable in the autograph.

2.   Lorenzo's premonitions of death turned out to be true. He died quite suddenly on 26 June 1580.

3.   The discalced Carmelite nuns in Avila. Since moving to La Serna, Lorenzo was going to Avila to hear Mass only on special feast days. La Serna was about three miles from Avila.

4.   Probably the matter referred to in Ltr. 345.3.

5.   Angel de Salazar, the vicar general for the discalced Carmelites.

6.   The persons referred to here are Isabel de Santo Domingo, Jerónimo Gracián, Anne of St. Batholomew (Ana de San Bartolomé), Teresa's nurse, and Francisco de Cepeda, Lorenzo's son.

7.   Teresa added this postscript, about arranging an engagement for Don Francisco, at the beginning of the letter. For a complement to this letter, read Ltrs. 347.2–7 and 363.

347. To Madre María de San José, Seville
Segovia, 4 July 1580

(Autograph: DCN, Valladolid)

Teresa gives here a detailed account of her dear brother Lorenzo's death to the prioress and community in Seville. She has received letters from Seville and also news of an uprising of Moriscos in that city. The needs of the community in Salamanca as well as Seville and a possible foundation in Portugal are on her mind. She is getting ready for a trip to Palencia to make a new foundation, and plans to stop along the way in Avila and Valladolid.

❧❧❦❦

For Mother Prioress at the Carmel of St. Joseph's in Seville.

1.   Jesus. May the Holy Spirit be with your reverence, my mother. It seems our Lord doesn't want me to go long without having something to suffer.

2.   You should know that our Lord has been pleased to bring to himself his good friend and servant Lorencio de Cepeda.[1] He was struck by such intense hemorrhaging that he suffocated from it in less than six hours. He had received Communion two days before and died fully conscious, entrusting himself to our Lord.

3.   I hope in the divine mercy that he went to enjoy the Lord, for he was at a point in which anything that did not deal with serving our Lord wearied him. For this reason he was happy to stay at his country property[2] which was a league from Avila. He used to say that worldly compliments made him feel uneasy. His prayer was continual because he always walked in the presence of God, and His Majesty granted him so many favors that sometimes I was amazed. He was very inclined toward penance and so he did more than I would have desired him to do. He looked to me for advice in everything; it was strange, the credit he gave to what I told him, and this was because of his great love for me. I am repaying him by rejoicing that he has gone forth from so miserable a life and that he is now safe. And this is not just a way of speaking, but I feel joy when I think of this. I feel sorry for his children,[3] but I think that because of their father God will show them his favor.

4.   I have given you such a full account because I know that his death will cause you and all my sisters there, to grieve, and I want to console you thereby. It is a wonderful thing how much he felt their trials and his love for them. Now it is time to repay

him and recommend him to our Lord, on the condition that if he has no need of your prayers (as I believe he doesn't, for our faith allows me to think this way), they may serve to benefit the souls most in need of them.

5. You should know that a little before he died he wrote a letter to me here at St. Joseph's in Segovia, which is where I now am (eleven leagues from Avila), telling me things that didn't seem to imply anything else than that he knew what little time he had left to live, for it has amazed me.[4]

6. It seems to me, my daughter, that everything passes so quickly that we should be thinking more about how to die than how to live. Please God, since I am left here, I may serve him in some way, for I am four years older than he,[5] and I never manage to die; rather, I've recovered from the illness I had,[6] and only experience the usual ailments, especially headaches.

7. Tell Padre Fray Gregorio[7] to consider this letter to be for him and to remember my brother, for he felt deeply the trials of the order. And tell him that I understand what he must be going through with that task, but that he must be patient, and you too. Each day we are waiting for the dispatch to arrive from Rome,[8] and our father[9] is keeping himself busy since it wouldn't seem right for him not to be here when it arrives. He is well, glory to God. Here he has been visiting this house with Father Vicar, Fray Angel,[10] and he will return with me to Avila the day after tomorrow. I don't know how long I'll have to stay there in order to arrange for what must be given to Teresa.[11] The poor soul has lost a great deal with the death of her father—for he deeply loved her—and the community did also. May God provide a remedy.

8. You should know that the authorization you gave for payment of the four hundred ducats is worthless, for the trust fund in Toledo will not pay so soon, and please God the amount will be paid. I turned the matter over to the nuns there before leaving. Regarding Valladolid, I will write now to Padre Nicolao to send me the documents because when I am finished in Avila, I

think I will receive orders to go there on my way to the founda-tion in Palencia,[12] and I will then see if something can be done. I should even be going there at once from here. But now that they have a broker, he will be in a greater hurry to collect that money. Consider how you might pay what you owe. If a good postulant comes along, it wouldn't hurt to accept her with this in mind and for what you are contributing to the negotiations in Rome.[13]

9.   May God provide a remedy for it all, for I was afraid that the holy prior of Las Cuevas would be missed very much. Nonethe-less, I am happy they are allowing him to rest.[14] Let him know this for me and send him my best wishes and highest regards, and the same to Padre Rodrigo Alvarez[15] and tell him that his letter arrived just at the right moment—all about the good that comes to us through trials—and that if God is already working miracles through him during his life, what will happen after his death.

10.   I would consider it a miracle, in fact, if this poor soul[16] has become as well aware of her fault as you say. What seems to you very good in that she condemns Garciálvarez,[17] seems bad to me, and I wouldn't believe much of what she might tell me about him. I think he is a conscientious man, and I have always believed that it was she who made him lose his head. Nonethe-less, even though everything may not meet our desires, I was delighted with the news. Many prayers here were offered for her; perhaps the Lord has shown her mercy. I was really sorry after I saw in the reports[18] that they had allowed her to receive communion. I tell you, *madre*, it is not right for things like this to go unpunished, and it would have been good not to allow her to be released from the perpetual prison to which it was decided to condemn her.

11.   Your letter took so long to reach me that I think it is too late now to go into the matter in question, for I don't know when this letter of mine will go out. They gave me your letter on the vigil of the feast of St. Peter, and it bore a date in May, the 15th

I believe. I don't know what to say. But to be waiting for Padre Gracián to come is foolish. The best thing to do is to have her admit and take back all of her lies before he comes so that it won't appear that he persuaded her to do this.[19] I am amazed that this did not occur to you.

12.　In case she has spoken calumnies that at some time might do harm, it is necessary that Padre Rodrigo Alvarez consider what must be done and that she retract what she said and sign it. Please God, my daughter, that this will appease God and that this soul may not be lost. May His Majesty console that poor Pablo.[20] He must be a good man, since God gives him so many trials.

13.　Do you think it is some small matter to have a house where you can see those galleys. Here they are envious, for it is a great gift with which to praise our Lord. I tell you that if they didn't have it, they would miss it.[21]

14.　Now they have told me that the Moriscos in that region of Seville are planning to rise up with the city. You were on a good path toward becoming martyrs. Find out whether this is true and have Mother Subprioress[22] write us about it.

15.　I am happy that her health is good, but am sorry that yours is poor. For the love of God take good care of yourself. They tell me that for that urine problem one must gather some dog rose when it is mature, then dry and crush it into powder and take a half real[23] in the morning. Ask a doctor about it. And don't be so long before writing me, for goodness' sake.

16.　My best regards to all the sisters and especially to San Francisco.[24] The sisters here and Mother Prioress[25] send their regards. It must seem nice to be in the midst of those flags and the tumult, if you know how to draw spiritual benefit from all the news you probably hear down there, but you need to walk with much care so as not to be distracted. I long for you all to be very holy. But what would happen if the foundation in Portugal[26] were made! Don Teutonio, the Archbishop of Evora, writes me that the distance from here is no more than forty leagues. Certainly, a foundation in Portugal would make me very happy.

17.   You should know that as long as I live, I desire to do something in God's service. Since I've done so little, I don't want to spend the time as idly as I have done these past years in which I only suffered interiorly with nothing else to show. Beg our Lord to give me the strength to do something in his service. I have already told you to give this letter to Padre Fray Gregorio, that he can consider it as for him, for I certainly love him in the Lord and desire to see him. My brother died the Sunday after the feast of St. John.[27]

18.   Watch for me, in your charity, to see when the fleet arrives. Try hard to get information from those coming from Ciudad de los Reyes[28] whether Diego López de Zúñiga[29] is living or dead. And if he is dead arrange to have testimony of this given before a notary and send it to me taking every cautionary measure. And if possible get two or three to testify; in short, do whatever you can. For if he is dead, we can then buy some houses for the nuns in Salamanca. I have arranged for this from those who will inherit them when he dies. It is the greatest pity in the world what the nuns have to put up with where they are. I don't know how it is that they are not dead. He is a gentleman from Ciudad de los Reyes, I mean Diego López de Zúñiga. And if he is alive you must also inform me of when the fleet will leave so that I can send some messages to him. Consider this matter to be very important, for it must be undertaken with great care. He was seventy-five years old and moreover very sick; he is probably by now in heaven.

19.   You can write me by way of Madrid, sending the letters to Padre Gracián's mother, Doña Juana de Antisco. I will try to write to you again soon. Please God this letter will not be lost.

May His Majesty watch over you and do what I desire for you.

Today is 4 July.

Your reverence's servant,

Teresa of Jesus

1. He died at La Serna (Avila) on 26 June.
2. La Serna.
3. His three children were Teresita (at St. Joseph's in Avila), Francisco (in Spain), and Lorenzo (in Peru).
4. Cf. Ltr. 346.1.
5. Lorenzo was born in 1519.
6. See Ltr. 335.2.
7. Gregorio Nacianceno was at Los Remedios in Seville carrying out the task of vicar for the community of discalced friars there during the absence of Padre Gracián. The latter was elected prior on 19 February, but held back in Castile to wait for the dispatch from Rome.
8. The brief for the establishment of a separate province for the discalced Carmelites was signed by Gregory XIII on 22 June, the news of which had not yet reached Spain.
9. Jerónimo Gracián.
10. Angel de Salazar, vicar general for the discalced Carmelites.
11. The daughter of Don Lorenzo, often referred to as Teresita. "What is to be given to her" was her inheritance.
12. See Ltr. 335.7.
13. The financial help for those carrying on the negotiations in Rome (see note 8).
14. Hernando de Pantoja's term as prior of the Carthusians had ceased.
15. A Jesuit in Seville whose assistance Teresa was seeking so as to bring Beatriz de la Madre de Dios back into community life. See Ltr. 330.7.
16. Beatriz de la Madre de Dios.
17. Garciálvarez, the former confessor, had wrongly supported Beatriz in her machinations.
18. The reports about the events that took place in Seville the previous year (see Ltr. 335.4).
19. Her calumnies were against Gracián.
20. Probably Pablo Matía, the father of Bernarda de San José, a nun who had died very young (1577) in the Carmel of Seville.
21. She is referring to the plan to sell the house in Seville and move to a different location.

22. Leonor de San Gabriel.
23. An ancient means of measuring according to the diameter of a silver real.
24. Isabel de San Francisco.
25. The prioress in Segovia, Isabel de Santo Domingo.
26. See Ltr. 319.11.
27. The feast of the birth of St. John the Baptist.
28. Now Lima, Peru.
29. He was the owner of the houses that Teresa wanted to acquire for the community in Salamanca.

348. To the Discalced Carmelite Nuns, Malagón
Medina, August 1580

Here we have a fragment from a letter Teresa wrote on hearing of the death of her former spiritual director and confessor, the Jesuit Father Baltasar Alvarez.

❖·❖·❖·❖

My daughters, this is one of the chastisements that our Lord brings about on earth; he takes away its saints.

349. To the Widow of Juan Alonso Mejía, Valladolid
Medina, 5 August 1580

(DCN: Monastery of the Incarnation, Avila)

The date and addressee of this letter are probable. Don Juan Alonso was a friend of Teresa's from Valladolid.

❖·❖·❖·❖

1.   Jesus. The grace of the Holy Spirit be with your honor and give you the spiritual and bodily strength to bear the terrible blow that this trial has been. If it hadn't come from a hand so compassionate and just, I wouldn't know how to console you, so great is my own grief. But since I know how truly this sovereign God loves us and that you have understood well the wretchedness and instability of this miserable life, I hope in His Majesty that he will give you more and more light to understand

the favor our Lord grants to those he removes from it once they have come to know him. You can be especially certain, in accord with our faith, that this holy soul is where he will receive the reward that accords with the many trials he endured in this life and bore with so much patience.

2. I have very earnestly begged our Lord for this and asked these sisters to do so as well. And I have asked him to give you consolation and health so that you may again take up the struggle of life in this miserable world. Blessed are those who are already in safety. I don't think this is the time to go on at length, unless with our Lord in begging him to console you, for creatures are of little help in a grief like this, especially as deplorable a creature as myself.

3. May His Majesty show you his power and from here on be your companion in such a way that you will not miss the good one you have lost.

Today is the vigil of the Transfiguration.

Your honor's unworthy subject and servant,

Teresa of Jesus

350. To Madre María de San José, Seville
Medina del Campo, 6 August 1580

(Autograph: DCN, Libourne [France])

Five days previous to this letter the news from Rome arrived that the discalced Carmelites could form a separate province within the order. At the same time a tangle of complex responsibilities arose for Teresa because of Don Lorenzo's will. From Avila she had arrived in Medina del Campo and would be on her way to Valladolid.

❖❖❖❖

For the Mother Prioress of St. Joseph's Carmel in Seville

1. The grace of the Holy Spirit be with your reverence, my daughter. You will have already received my letter in which I

told you how God took to himself my good brother, Lorenzo de Cepeda,[1] and how I was going to Avila to look after Teresa[2] and her brother, who feel very much alone. At present I am in Medina del Campo on my way to Valladolid where I am now being ordered to go. You can write to me often because of the regular mail delivery there. You know how happy I am to receive your letters.

2.   I am bringing my nephew Don Francisco with me because some documents have to be prepared in Valladolid. I tell you that before all of this is settled there will be no lack of trials for him or for me. If I hadn't been told that I am rendering God a great service in that I am protecting my nephews, I would have let the whole thing go since I have little desire to become involved in these matters. My nephew is very virtuous.

3.   You have to help me from there with anything having to do with the Indies, and so I beg you for love of God that, when the fleet arrives, find out if there is any money being brought for my brother—please God he may be enjoying glory—and let me know so that arrangements may be made to collect it. And don't neglect to do so with care, and find out if they are bringing any letters; try to get information about what I mentioned in a previous letter, whether Diego López de Zúñiga who was living in Ciudad de los Reyes[3] is dead.

4.   My brother left the money owed to him by your house for the construction of a chapel at St. Joseph's in Avila,[4] that he might be buried in it. I have already told you that the authorization[5] for payment that you sent makes it so difficult to recover the money that I don't know if anything will be collected. At least the money in Toledo—which I entrusted to the charge of the nuns—will be given, I think, little by little and late, if at all. For the debtor says that I don't know what kind of calculations have to be made, because he has letters from somewhere else, or I don't know what, that testify to a partial payment that was made. And he enjoys such prestige that no one wants to pressure him about anything. As for what is owed to Valladolid, I

will now find out if Padre Nicolao[6] sends me the papers. Since I am executor of the will,[7] I will have to try to collect, although I don't want to. So you should arrange to settle this debt. And for what he has lent and given to the order, it wouldn't be a bad idea to accept a nun without a dowry, if you find a good one.

5. The enclosed letter addressed to the president of the Chamber of Commerce in Seville is from the bishop[8] of the Canary Islands, who is a friend of his. He asks him to take care of holding the money should it arrive from the Indies. See that it is consigned to a trustworthy person and that everything is arranged in the best way possible, my daughter. Do all this for me as a way of celebrating what I now wish to tell you.

6. You should know that five days ago our brother Fray Jerónimo Gracián received a letter from Fray Juan de Jesús[9] in Rome. (Padre Gracián is now here, for he has accompanied me on this trip and been of great help to me in these business matters.) In the letter, Fray Juan tells Padre Gracián that the brief[10] concerning the matter of our negotiations has been given to the king's ambassador in Rome to send to the king and that the brief was being brought in the same mail delivery as his own letter. And so we are certain that it is now in the hands of the king. In his letter Fray Juan gives a generous summary of the brief's content. May God be praised who has shown us so much favor. You can truly give him thanks.

7. Padre Fray Jerónimo told me that he would write to Padre Fray Gregorio.[11] I don't know if he will be able to, because he is preaching today. If the mail service allows him the time, he will not fail to write. Otherwise you may give Fray Gregorio this news and my regards. Please God he is in good health, for I felt sorry about his illness. Write to me briefly if he is now well, for until knowing this I am not going to write to him. I also need to beg him to help you get this information I am asking of you. And tell me what kind of summer you're having, for I am afraid for you when I see how hot it is here, and let me know how Beatriz[12] is doing and all the nuns. Give my best regards to them

and especially to Mother Subprioress.[13] Padre Nicolao[14] is well, glory to God.

8.　My health is reasonably good, along with many worries and trials, but they don't bother me much. May His Majesty be with you and preserve you for me. I feel so fortunate to have you there for these business matters from the Indies, for I think everything will be done well. Write to me also as to whether when some money arrives, if I send you the authorization, you would be able to collect it for me and keep it in your house. Write at length about your health. May God bestow it upon you in the measure that I desire and the need that he sees, amen.

Today is the feast of the Transfiguration.

Your reverence's unworthy servant,

Teresa of Jesus

1.　See Ltr. 347.2.
2.　Teresa, Lorenzo's daughter, is a novice at St. Joseph's in Avila.
3.　Lima, Peru.
4.　In his will Lorenzo declared that he wanted the 430 ducats owed to him by the Carmel in Seville to be used for the construction of a chapel at the Carmel in Avila.
5.　See Ltr. 347.8.
6.　Nicolás Doria.
7.　Lorenzo himself in his will appointed her executor.
8.　Don Fernando de Rueda.
9.　A classmate of Gracián's in Alcalá, Juan de Jesús was one of the friars sent to Rome to promote the cause of the discalced Carmelites.
10.　The brief Pia consideratione of Gregory XIII, 22 June 1580 (see MHCT 2: 191–207).
11.　Gregorio Nacianceno, vicar of the discalced friars (Los Remedios) in Seville during the absence of Gracián.
12.　Beatriz de la Madre de Dios (Chaves).
13.　The subprioress in Seville was Leonor de San Gabriel.
14.　Nicolás Doria, the prior in Pastrana, had recently been in Seville helping the nuns there.

351. To Sister Teresa de Jesús, Avila
Medina, 7 August 1580

Teresa's niece was now a novice at St. Joseph's in Avila. She was grieving over the recent death of her father and wrote to her aunt about some of her interior troubles and problems. Teresa gives her some standard counsel and comfort.

❧❧❧❧

For my dear daughter Sister Teresa de Jesús

1.   Jesus. The grace of the Holy Spirit be with your charity, my daughter. I was delighted with your letter, and that my letters make you happy is a great joy for me, seeing that we cannot be together.

2.   As for the dryness, it seems to me that the Lord is now treating you as one who is strong. He wants to try you in order to know the love you have for him, whether it is present in dryness as well as in spiritual delights. Take it as a very great favor from God. Don't let it cause you any grief, for perfection does not consist in delight but in the virtues. When you least expect, devotion will return.

3.   As for what you say about that sister, try not to think of it, but turn away from the thought. And don't think that when a thought comes into your mind, even if it concerns something very bad, you are immediately at fault, for the thought is nothing. I too would like to see that sister experience the same dryness, for I don't know if she understands herself, and for her own good we could desire this. When some bad thought comes to you, bless yourself, or recite an Our Father, or strike your breast and try to think of something else, and you will instead be meriting because you will be resisting.

4.   I would like to answer Isabel de San Pablo,[1] but there is not time. Give her my best regards—for she already knows how you must be the one dearest to me—and also regards to Romero[2] and María de San Jerónimo.[3] I wish someone would write to

me about her health, since she doesn't do so. Don Francisco[4] is like an angel and doing well. Yesterday he received communion, and his servants did so too. Tomorrow we are going to Valladolid. He will write to you from there, for I haven't told him now about this messenger.

May God watch over you, my daughter, and make you as holy as I beg of him, amen. My regards to all.

Today is the feast of San Alberto.

Teresa of Jesus

1. The subprioress at St. Joseph's in Avila.
2. His identity is unknown.
3. St. Teresa's cousin, who was a Carmelite nun at St. Joseph's.
4. Teresita's oldest brother.

352. To Don Gaspar Daza (?), Avila
Medina or Valladolid, 8 August 1580

The recipient, place, and date of this letter are only probable. On 8 August Teresa left Medina and arrived in Valladolid, where she became gravely ill from the perilous influenza spreading through Spain that year. She is eager to learn more details about the brief that came from Rome allowing the discalced Carmelites to form a separate province. At the time of writing her health is still relatively good.

⟫⟫⟪⟪

1.   Jesus. The grace of the Holy Spirit be always with your honor. Because Father Rector[1] and the prioress[2] will tell you about how we arrived here, I will not enlarge on the matter.

2.   I greatly desire to know how your health is and how your business affairs are going. I have more time here—if I could benefit from it—than anywhere else to pray for you. May it please our Lord that I be good for something, for there is no lack of desire in me that you have good health and much holiness.

I am far better than I was there, although I have the usual ailments, especially the palsy; but without the fever and nausea that I had in Segovia, I am doing well.

3.   When I arrived from Avila, they told me that the documents[3] from Rome had arrived and were in accord with our proposal. I haven't heard anything more. I beg you, since this messenger has to return, to inform me about everything—especially about your health.

4.   The prioress[4] is fine; she begs for your prayers. She carries out her office very well. May our Lord make you a great saint.

Today is the 8th.

Your honor's unworthy servant,

Teresa of Jesus

1. Gonzalo Dávila, the Jesuit rector in Avila.
2. María de Cristo.
3. She is speaking of the brief Pia consideratione (granted by Gregory XIII, 6 June 1580). She learned of it on 1 August through a letter from Juan de Jesús Roca in Rome to Gracián (cf. Ltr. 350.6). The brief reached the king in Badajoz on 15 August.
4. Probably María Bautista, the prioress in Valladolid.

353. To Doña Juana de Ahumada, Alba
Valladolid, 9 August 1580

(Autograph: Doña Gumersinda Gómez Miguel, Madridejos)

In Valladolid Teresa had to carry out her tedious obligations as executor of Lorenzo's will. She also had to get involved in arranging a marriage for Lorenzo's son Francisco. In the midst of these responsibilities, she feels for her sister's sadness over the death of their brother Lorenzo.

❖·❖·❖·❖

1.   Jesus. The grace of the Holy Spirit be with your honor. My grief greatly increased at the thought of what you must be going

through. May God be praised who in so many ways grants us favors. Believe, my sister, that suffering is a great favor. Reflect on how everything passes so quickly, as you have seen, and take heart; consider how the gain will be without end.[1]

2.   Since Juan de Ovalle is the messenger—who will tell you what we spoke about—and because it is almost one o'clock in the morning, I will not be long. If I succeed, Don Francisco[2] will accompany Señor Juan de Ovalle, and if he doesn't go now, I'll try to get him to leave soon. You don't need to recommend that I do all that I possibly can.

3.   It is very hard for me now to have to get involved in arranging a marriage[3] after taking care of so many business matters; although I owe all this to the one who is in glory and to having been told that it is for God's service. Beseech him that we might do what is right. I will inform you of what happens here.

4.   My best regards to my niece and nephew.[4] I entrust them to God, who is the one able to give them what they deserve, for to trust in creatures is of little worth.

5.   May His Majesty be with you and watch over you for me. Give my regards to Mother Prioress[5] and tell her I am well. I have some letters of hers here that I haven't been able to read since I arrived yesterday,[6] for there are so many visitors and business matters to take care of—and so neither am I able to write to her.

Your honor's unworthy servant,

Teresa of Jesus

1. Lorenzo's death still weighs on her and she feels for her grieving sister.
2. Juan de Ovalle, Doña Juana's husband, had come to Valladolid in regard to Lorenzo's will. On his return to Alba he will bring Lorenzo's son Francisco de Cepeda with him.
3. When Lorenzo died, the negotiations concerning a marriage for his son Francisco had been put on hold (cf. Ltr. 345.3).
4. Beatriz and Gonzalo, Doña Juana's children. She then alludes to some failed attempts to obtain a position for Gonzalo.

5. The prioress in Alba de Tormes, Juana del Espíritu Santo.
6. She had arrived from Medina del Campo.

354. To Don Diego Sarmiento de Mendoza
Valladolid, 21 August 1580

Don Diego was the chief governor of Galicia and brother of Don Alvaro de Mendoza. He had written to Teresa and her nuns in Valladolid asking prayers for some specified intentions. Teresa's reply is informal, interwoven with jest and truth. Time is limited because the mail carrier is waiting. While she hastily writes her words, three of the young nuns labor over a reply that might be considered worthy of this distinguished person.

1.   May the Holy Spirit be always with your lordship, amen. I tell you that I cannot understand why these sisters and I delighted and rejoiced with such tender feeling in the favor you showed us with your letter. Although we receive many letters and are accustomed to receiving kindnesses and favors from persons of great merit, they don't move us the way all that comes from you does. It's a mysterious thing we do not understand. And this is a fact I have attentively observed in these sisters and myself.

2.   We have only an hour to respond, and in my opinion we would need many hours, for they are anxious to do what you ask of them, and your godmother[1] has the idea in mind that her words must be efficacious. If their effect were to be in conformity with the affection with which she utters them, I am truly certain that they would be beneficial. But this is a matter for our Lord, and only His Majesty can move hearts. It is a great favor he does us in giving you both good desires and insight into things, for in so great a mind it is impossible that God not bring these two about little by little. I can truthfully say that apart from the business that concerns the bishop,[2] I do not now know anything else that gives my soul more joy than to see

you master of yourself. Truly I have thought that only God can fulfill the desires of so courageous a person. And so His Majesty has done well in allowing that on earth you be overlooked by those who could have begun to satisfy some of those desires. You must pardon me, for I am sounding foolish. But how true it is of the boldest and most miserable people that when you give them a little help they want a great deal more.

3.   Padre Fray Gracián[3] was delighted with your message, for I know of his love for you and that he has the desire to serve you whom he is obligated to—and I believe even more so in your case. He recommends you to the prayers of the good persons with whom he deals. And he does so with such desire to help you that I hope in His Majesty these prayers will be heard. He told me one day that your being very good would not satisfy him but that he wants you to be very holy. My thoughts are lowlier. I would be happy if you were satisfied only with what is necessary for yourself and not extend your charity so much that you are trying to get things for others, and I see that if you took into account only your own repose, you could find it and become occupied in acquiring perpetual goods and serve the one who will keep you with him forever and never tire of bestowing his blessings on you.

4.   We already knew when the feast of the saint you mention occurs. We have all agreed to receive Communion on that day for you and thereby settle our debt. We will celebrate that day with joy and in your honor, doing so as best we can. Through the other favors you have done for me, I have seen that I can ask you for many things if I have the need. But our Lord knows that the greatest favor you can grant me is to be where you cannot give me any of those of which you speak, even if you want to. Nonetheless, when I see myself in need I will turn to you as the lord of this house.[4]

5.   I am hearing about the effort María, Isabel,[5] and your godmother are exerting in writing to you. As for Isabelita (de San Judas), since she is new, she is keeping quiet; I don't know

what she will say. I am determined not to correct a word of theirs, so you must bear up with them since you ordered them to speak. Truly it is no small mortification to read foolishness, nor is it a small proof of your humility to be content with such miserable people! May our Lord make us resemble you so that you don't lose the fruit of this good work by our not knowing how to beg His Majesty to repay you.

Today is Sunday. I don't know if it is 20 August.[6]

Your lordship's unworthy servant and true daughter,

Teresa of Jesus

---

1. The meaning of Teresa's words here are not clear and may have significance only for the recipient.
2. Don Diego's brother, Don Alvaro de Mendoza, formerly bishop of Avila, now bishop of Palencia.
3. Jerónimo Gracián.
4. The foundation of the Carmel of Valladolid was made possible through Don Diego's family.
5. María de San José, Gracián's sister, and Isabel del Sacramento. These nuns mentioned were all young.
6. It was 21 August.

355. To Padre Jerónimo Gracián, Medina del Campo
Valladolid, 4 October 1580

Teresa responds to two of Gracián's letters. After arriving in Valladolid, she was struck down, coming close to death, by the epidemic of influenza spreading through Spain that year. According to Gracián, it left her looking old. For even though she had suffered almost continually from various illnesses, she appeared to be much younger than she was. This letter deals mainly with the family problems that arose after Lorenzo's death, making mention as well of Francisco's plan to enter the discalced Carmelites.

❧❧❦❦

1.   Jesus. The grace of the Holy Spirit be with *mi padre*, amen. Today, the feast of St. Francis, I received two letters from you

in which I learned to my delight that your health is improving. Please God, it will always be good, as I beg of him. I have been very happy about the agreement, for it is a good one. Even if it were for less, litigation is not for us.[1]

2.   I am now well, we can say, and I eat better. The same is true of my weakness, for I am recovering some strength, although I don't dare write this myself. Little by little I will get well. Don't be distressed about my sickness; what you have gone through is enough.

3.   Oh, how it bothered me that Mother Prioress[2] in her letter did not mention anything about Don Luis, and how Señora Doña Juana[3] is already better. Our María de San José[4] is already up and around, her fever is gone, and her joyfulness makes it seem she hadn't suffered anything.

4.   In regard to the letter of Pedro de Ahumada,[5] there's no need to pay any attention to it. I thought it would be even worse. He was very wrong in not sending what they asked of him. Don Francisco[6] will not be protected against him unless he turns over his affairs to me, for I am the one to whom Don Pedro will show some respect. That fortune must have diminished greatly, but it doesn't matter because of the gain in what is essential. Now that I am better, things will not bother me so much, for sickness must greatly weaken the heart, especially for anyone who has a heart like mine. Don't think, though, that I am foundering completely.

5.   Teresita's[7] letter pleased me very much as did also the news that Don Francisco is happy and healthy. May God guide him. If Pedro de Ahumada is making the journey on his old nag, it ought to be left with Don Francisco, and Don Pedro should be sent on with a rented mule. But he is so disagreeable that I don't believe he will consent to the idea. The horse does nothing but add to his expenses. And so Don Francisco should tell him that he will not be given lodging at La Serna;[8] and that will put an end to his comings and goings. He should bear with him as best he can without giving him anything or signing anything for him.

He should tell him that he will always be given what my brother left him—which is carefully set down—and remind him that those at La Serna gave him a hundred *reales* at the request of the prioress.[9] I don't know how he can say that he hasn't been given anything. This melancholy of his is a real trial. And my head is in such a condition that although I am not writing this myself, I am not able to go on as long as I would desire. May God watch over you and make you as holy as I beg of him.

6.   Give my regards to those lords and to Mother Prioress, Inés de Jesús.[10] San Bartolomé[11] asks for your prayers and is much consoled to hear that you are well.

7.   I very much want Don Francisco to be firm with Pedro de Ahumada, asking him why he won't agree with Perálvarez[12] in the management of the property. They stand in the way of each other. Although Pedro de Ahumada says he is doing something, he doesn't do anything. An administrator is needed both for what Francisco de Salcedo left to the nuns and for this property,[13] and then we wouldn't have to worry so much.

8.   In no way should Don Francisco hold back from telling Pedro de Ahumada about his desire to change his state in life[14] (and even tell him more if he can). Things can no longer be concealed, as you mention, for that little page has gone around talking about it. And he will talk more there; he knows well how to exaggerate. The Lord Licentiate Godoy[15] told me here that he had heard it from the former magistrate in Avila and that other persons had told him about it here, and so it is already public knowledge. There is no reason for keeping secret what is going to be done. As soon as it is known for certain, everyone will keep quiet. Given his character, I don't think it will matter to Don Francisco. He wrote me a letter that made me praise God. May God be with you.

9.   I am afraid lest that little mule not be good for you, and I think it would be right for you to buy a new one. If this is true, someone can be found to lend the money. I will send the amount to you as soon as we can collect it. Or sell the old

horse if Pedro will let go of it. My only fear, *mi padre*, is that you will buy something that will throw you to the ground. Since that mule is so little, I don't fear your being thrown off. Nor do I think it would be good for Don Francisco to journey to the monastery on an animal that he is not going to donate when he receives the habit.[16] Consider what is the best thing to do in everything, and stop being timid, for you kill me with that.

Your paternity's unworthy daughter,

Teresa of Jesus

10.   Read to Don Francisco the part here about Pedro de Ahumada. See if the best thing wouldn't be for you to send him to me, for here we can come to some agreement.

---

1.   She is alluding to the complicated negotiations carried out by Gracián in Segovia with respect to the dowry of Inés de Jesús (see MHCT 2: 223).

2.   The prioress in Medina del Campo, Inés de Jesús.

3.   Luis Gracián and his mother Juana Dantisco, both of whom were stricken by the terrible influenza of that year.

4.   Gracián's sister, a nun in Valladolid. In his letter to Gracián the following day, the vicar general, Angel de Salazar wrote: "Our *Madre* is much better, although very weak, and all the sisters, too, it seems, are getting stronger; the people are better and planning festivities and merrymaking" (MHCT 2: 223).

5.   Teresa's difficult brother who has now interfered in the business affairs of his niece and nephew, Teresita and Francisco.

6.   Francisco de Cepeda, Lorenzo's son. Teresa was the executor of the will.

7.   Teresa de Jesús, Lorenzo de Cepeda's daughter, now a novice at St. Joseph's, the Carmel in Avila.

8.   The house and farm of Teresa's recently deceased brother Lorenzo de Cepeda.

9.   The prioress in Avila, María de Cristo.

10. The prioress in Medina del Campo.

11. Ana de San Bartolomé (Blessed Anne of St. Bartholomew).

12. Perálvarez Cimbrón, a relative of Teresa's in Avila. In a codicil to his will, Lorenzo transferred the care of La Serna from Perálvarez, as mentioned in the will, to Diego Guzmán. Now Pedro de Ahumada, to complicate matters, prefers to work with Perálvarez.

13. Both Francisco de Salcedo and Lorenzo de Cepeda left legacies for the Carmel of St. Joseph's in Avila. Teresa desires only one administrator for these benefices.

14. Francisco had decided to enter the discalced Carmelites, and Teresa did not want him to conceal this from Pedro.

15. See Ltr. 359.4.

16. Before he received the habit, Francisco was sent away by the prior in Pastrana, Nicolás Doria (see Ltr. 359.2).

356. To the Discalced Carmelite Nuns at St. Joseph's, Avila
Valladolid, 7 October 1580

This letter is a report by Teresa as executor of Lorenzo's estate. Lorenzo had died on 26 June of that year. His intricately formulated will left Teresa with a tangle of complicated tasks. She had to tie every knot to avoid family squabbles and litigation. To make matters worse, she had become gravely ill from the perilous influenza that swept through Spain in 1580.

1.   Jesus be with your reverences, amen. My health is not good, but even if it were very good, I would have no reason for feeling secure about a life that comes to an end so quickly. As a result, I thought of writing to you this report about what should be done if, please God, Don Francisco[1] makes his profession of vows.

2.   The documents concerning the legacy for your house are definitive. God knows the care and labor it cost me to get them to this point. Blessed be God who has done this; they state matters most firmly. We are keeping them in this house in the

chest with three keys. Because I need them at times, I am not sending them now. With them is my brother's will[2] (may he be in glory) and everything else that was necessary for making it legal. These documents will be delivered to you from here, for it wouldn't be suitable that they be kept anywhere else than in your house, and safely guarded in the chest with three keys.

3.   If Don Francisco should make his profession, you will have to find out what is in his will and give him from the annual income all that he needs to spend, for in his will he can only dispose of this year's income and, I believe, movables.[3]

4.   Then the property has to be divided between Don Lorencio and Teresa de Jesús.[4] Until she makes profession, she can dispose of her part as she wishes. Clearly she will do what you[5] tell her, but it is only right that she remember her aunt Doña Juana[6] who is in such need. Once she has made profession everything goes to the house.[7]

5.   Don Lorenzo's part will be entrusted to the same administrator, who will give a separate account of everything that is spent. As for how the money is to be spent, the prioress and nuns have nothing more to do than abide by what the will says.

6.   First of all the chapel my brother wanted—may he be in glory—must be built. What is left from the four hundred ducats owed by the Seville Carmel[8] should be spent on behalf of Lorenzo for the altarpiece, the grilles, and everything necessary. The prioress[9] has already informed me that she will send at least two hundred ducats soon.

7.   It seems to me the will says—I don't remember well—that in the distribution of Don Lorenzo's revenues, I should in some things do what I think best. I say this because I understand my brother's desire was to construct the vault of the main chapel according to the drawing that was made for this and that you all saw. By my signature here, I affirm that it is my will that in building the chapel for my brother—may he be in glory—the said vault of the main chapel be constructed and an iron grille

made, not the most costly but well fashioned and pleasing to the eye.[10]

8.   If Don Lorenzo is called from this world by God and doesn't have any children, then the main chapel should be built as the will directs. Be careful not to trust the administrator too much, but seek to have the chaplains go frequently to La Serna to observe how well it is producing. For this property should be valuable, and if one is not very careful, it will quickly go to ruin. In conscience you are obliged not to let that happen.

9.   Oh, my daughters, how much weariness and strife these temporal possessions carry along with them! I have always thought this, and now I know it through experience; so much so that in my opinion all the worries that I have had in regard to these foundations in a way have not troubled and tired me out as much as this obligation. I don't know whether my grave illness might have been the cause—certainly it contributed. Pray to God that he might make use of these worries for his service—this was the main reason I put all my heart into the task—and pray much for me to His Majesty, for I never thought I loved you so much. May he direct everything for his greater honor and glory and not let temporal riches take poverty of spirit away from us.

On the 7ᵗʰ day of October in the year 1580.

> Your reverence's servant,

> Teresa of Jesus

Keep this report in the chest with the three keys.

---

1. Lorenzo de Cepeda's older son, Francisco de Cepeda.

2. Lorenzo de Cepeda's will.

3. She is referring to the farm and house at La Serna (Avila) where Lorenzo died. The eldest son had the right of primogeniture, that is, to inherit the entire estate.

4. Don Lorencio, the younger son, and Teresa de Jesús, the daughter and novice in Avila.

5. The prioress at St. Joseph's in Avila, María de Cristo.
6. Teresa's sister, Juana de Ahumada.
7. The Carmel of St. Joseph in Avila.
8. The Carmel in Seville still owed Lorenzo this money which he had lent to them for the purchase of their house.
9. The prioress was María de San José (see Ltr. 332.3).
10. In Lorenzo's will there are a number of directives concerning the church and chapels at St. Joseph's where he wanted to be buried.

357. To Madre María de San José, Seville

Valladolid, 25 October 1580

Letters arrived late from Seville and did not mention any-thing about the fleet or give any news from the Indies, for which Teresa was hoping so that the nuns in Salamanca could buy a house and she could settle her deceased brother's accounts. The establishment of the separate province for the discalced Carmelites was delayed because of the serious illness of Pedro Fernández, the appointed executor. Still weak from the influenza she suffered, Teresa dictates this letter.

❧❧❧❧

For the Prioress of St. Joseph's.

1.   Jesus. The grace of the Holy Spirit be with your reverence, my daughter. I received your letters and the one from Mother Subprioress,[1] and although they were really old ones, I rejoiced to see a letter from you. But my happiness was tempered when I learned of your poor health. A letter you wrote to Padre Nicolao[2]—the first part of October—consoled me very much, because in it you say that you are better. Please God you will go on improving. Don't think those swellings are always caused by dropsy. Here there are nuns who suffer from them and have suffered from them, and some are now better and others are on the way to getting better. At any rate, don't fail to take care of yourself and avoid whatever the doctor says is harmful for

you, even if you do so for no other reason than to make me happy and not add to the trials that I am undergoing up here.

2.   As for me, I have been among the sick since I came to Valladolid.[3] This is why I haven't written you. My head is still so weak that I don't know when I will be able to write in my own hand. But my secretary[4] is so good that I can trust her as much as myself. You should know that I was so sick they didn't think I would live. Now I have been without a fever for some days. I don't know why God leaves me here unless so that during this year I might see his servants die, which is a great torment for me. The death of Padre Soto[5] didn't grieve me too much. But I am distressed over what Padre Gregorio[6] and the others at Los Remedios are suffering. This plague has been all over, and so there is no reason for us to be surprised, but to praise God, for even though there has been great suffering in these monasteries, no discalced nun has died. The good María del Sacramento[7] has been anointed in Alba. Pray very much to God for her, and for me that I might serve God in some way, since he has left me here.

3.   What you told me about the former prior of Las Cuevas[8] grieved me very much. For the love of God don't fail to console him in every way you can and send him many greetings on my part—because of my being so weak I am not writing to him—and for my Padre Rodrigálvarez[9] compose a special message and give it to him on my part. I see that Father Prior in Pastrana loves you all so much that he doesn't fail to write often about the things going on here, which consoles me greatly.

4.   As for what concerns Beatriz,[10] you did the right thing in burning that document, and be sure not to speak about it with her or with anyone. If God is pleased to grant us the favor of seeing this province established,[11] then the decision can be made what should be done about this sister, for as I have often said, it is not good that she go unpunished.

5.   I am surprised that there is no message from the Indies for my brother[12] (may he be in glory). At least there should be

some letters, for I don't think it is possible that no letters have been written to him. Let me know when the fleet is leaving and if you have remembered what I wrote you about from Segovia,[13] that you try to get information through anyone coming from Ciudad de los Reyes[14] as to whether a gentleman from Salamanca, Diego López de Zúñiga, is alive. If he is dead get two witnesses to testify to this, for he is the one who has to sell us the house for the nuns in Salamanca; they don't have another one, and I fear lest the community will have to be disbanded on this account.

6.   Beg and beseech Señor Horacio de Oria[15] to look into this for me and ask him to pray for me and tell him I am careful to do so for him and that I am asking this of him because it is for God's service.

7.   Remember to find me a trustworthy messenger through whom I can write to Ciudad de los Reyes in Perú and to the city of Quito. And don't forget to inform me of when the fleet is leaving early enough in advance. There is a regular mail delivery here, for I continually received many letters from this house when I was down there. Or, inform our Padre Nicolao. I am sending him this letter so as to be sure that you inform him.

8.   My head is so weak that even dictating tires me, for this is not my only letter today. The nausea I experienced was so great that it weakened me more than the fever.

9.   Give my best regards to Mother Subprioress and to all the nuns. I tell you that I have a great desire to see all of you. Everything is possible with God. May His Majesty watch over you as I beg of him, and make you very holy. Let me know if the swelling and the thirst decrease somewhat. All the nuns in this house are praying very much for you. They were amused about the Moriscos.[16] If you don't write to me in your own hand, don't worry about it, for you can trust the subprioress in everything.

On the 25th of October.[17]

Your reverence's servant,

Teresa of Jesus

10.   My best regards to San Francisco[18]—whose letter provided great recreation; and many regards to Sister Juana de la Cruz[19] and the Portuguese nun;[20] and ask all the nuns to pray for Padre Fray Pedro Fernández,[21] for he is nearing the end we owe him very much and will now miss him greatly. I am sorry about my Padre Gregorio; I would like to be able to write to him. Tell him that this is how saints are made, and I say the same to you, my daughter. I can't get used to not writing you in my own hand.[22]

---

1. The subprioress in Seville, Leonor de San Gabriel.
2. Nicolas Doria, the prior in Pastrana.
3. She had arrived in Valladolid on 8 August.
4. Blessed Anne of St. Bartholomew.
5. An elderly priest who had been given lodging at Los Remedios in Seville. Other deceased to whom she alludes are Francisco de Salcedo and María de Jesús, of whom she speaks in her *Life* (35.1–2) and who founded a Carmel in Alcalá de Henares to live the primitive rule.
6. Gregorio Nacianceno, who is serving as vicar at Los Remedios.
7. Teresa's companion for the foundation in Salamanca on the night of All Souls (see F. 19.4–5). At the time of this letter she was the prioress in Alba.
8. The former prior, Hernando de Pantoja.
9. The Jesuit Rodrigo Alvarez for whom she wrote two accounts of her soul (see ST 58 & 59).
10. Beatriz de la Madre de Dios, who had served as superior of the community during the time in which María de San José had been deposed.
11. The brief for the establishment of the new province had arrived, but it had not yet been possible to put it into effect officially.
12. Lorenzo de Cepeda (see Ltr. 350.3).
13. In Ltr. 347.18.
14. Lima (see Ltrs. 347.18; 350.3–4).
15. Nicolás Doria's brother, who was a priest.
16. The nuns in Seville had responded humorously to Teresa's query in Ltr. 347.14 about an uprising of the Moriscos in Seville.

17. The remainder of the letter is in Teresa's own hand.
18. Isabel de San Francisco.
19. The mother of Beatriz de la Madre de Dios.
20. Blanca de Jesús.
21. A Dominican priest and former apostolic visitator for the discalced Carmelites in Castile and now designated by pontifical brief as the executor for the establishment of the new province. He died before being able to carry out these duties.
22. Padre Nicolás Doria added the following note to this letter: "Jesus Mary. The *Madre* sent me this letter still open. I read it and am sending it to your reverence along with another she sent to me, so that you can see what is in it about the business matters. As for what she says about Don Francisco, Lorenzo de Cepeda's son, there is no need to pay attention to it because he has already returned to his mother. Pray for our business affairs and that Fray Pedro Fernández will live, even if it takes a miracle. This is so necessary and the Virgin Mary can do it so easily that I do not fail to trust in her if you who profess to be her daughters beseech her urgently. Since I wrote a long letter to you from Madrid and am now in Pastrana, on the feast of All Saints, I will not enlarge on this. Your reverence's servant Fray Nicolao."

358. To Padre Jerónimo Gracián, Seville
Valladolid, 7–8 November 1580

Teresa is thankful that Padre Gracián writes to her frequently. She is concerned about finding a safe way for sending mail and about Gracián's constant traveling, for he had to go to Segovia, Salamanca, and Seville, and then return to Badajoz and Alcalá. Although the permission for establishing a separate province had arrived from Rome, the appointed executor lay dying, which made it necessary to petition Rome for a substitute. The discalced friars were growing anxious about the coming chapter for the establishment of their new province. Because of damage to the text of this letter, the original cannot be deciphered completely.

❖ ❖ ❖ ❖

1.   … tired as I am, I find rest in writing to your reverence in my own hand.[1]

2.   Velasco[2] sent you one letter, and Padre Nicolao[3] sent another to Salamanca. I opened the latter consisting entirely of suggestions that arrived too late for the matter concerned, so I tore it up. Within it was one from Padre Gregorio[4] in which he told you that he was leaving for Almodóvar to await the convocation of the chapter. He was afraid of leaving his house and going without permission. It made me sad. Tell me what you know about this and if they have found any trace of Fray Bartolomé de Jesús.[5]

3.   Father Vicar, Fray Angel,[6] left here for Madrid about fifteen days ago. He left in a hurry. Since Methuselah[7] is now stirring, I wouldn't want it to be against us. It would be nice to know their intentions as you have known them. I also received the note that came with my letter.

4.   I wrote what precedes this yesterday. Today the mail came and with it definite news that although he is not dead, no hope remains that Padre Fray Pedro Fernández[8] will live ...

5.   I have a great desire to know how your trip to Seville went, especially when I think of the dangerous creeks. For the love of God, write to me through all possible means. They tell me the mail comes up here from down there. I will find out, but until I know for certain, I will not send this except through Señora Doña Juana de Antisco.[9] Try to find out yourself and then write to me by that means. For all this is necessary in order that I get well completely, although I'm feeling well now since I'm writing such a long letter.

6.   You should know that Padre Mariano[10] wrote informing me of the important reason why Padre Macario[11] should be provincial and that I should urge this. What a life! They are great friends. This changeableness frightens me. And I with each passing day become more opposed to this, while he pushes ahead with his usual zeal.

7.   Remain with God, *mi padre*, and answer me about Palencia.[12] May His Majesty grant you what I beg of him and repay you

for your charity in writing to me so often after your departure, which was a good while ago.

Today is 8 November.

Your reverence's daughter,

Teresa of Jesus

8.   Let me know when the fleet will be leaving, for I must write to Don Lorencio.[13] And ask if there is any traveler going to Quito.

---

1.   Because of damage suffered by the text, parts of this letter are missing. Actually, it was a long letter (see Ltr. 359.1).

2.   Juan López de Velasco, the king's secretary.

3.   Nicolás Doria, prior of Pastrana.

4.   Gregorio Nacianceno, prior of the discalced monastery in La Roda, wrote to Doria announcing that he was coming to the chapter without its having been convoked and without permission. Startled by this, Doria wrote to Gracián and enclosed Padre Gregorio's letter. Teresa opened the letter, read it, and then tore it up without sending it on to Gracián. Her comment was: "It made me sad."

5.   Fray Bartolomé had been Gracian's secretary.

6.   Angel de Salazar (see Ltr. 359.3).

7.   The nuncio, Felippo Sega.

8.   He had been appointed executor of the pontifical brief for the establishment of a separate province for the discalced Carmelites. He actually died on 22 November 1580.

9.   Juana Dantisco, Gracian's mother, residing in Madrid, took care of forwarding mail between Teresa and her son (see Ltr. 359.1–2).

10. Ambrosio Mariano de San Benito.

11. Code name for Padre Antonio de Jesús (Heredia).

12. Her next project was a foundation for her nuns in Palencia.

13. Her nephew Lorenzo de Cepeda who was in Perú.

359. To Pdre Jerónimo Gracián, Seville
Valladolid, 20 November 1580

It is night, after Matins, and Teresa is dictating hastily to her secretary. She has received no word from Gracián and is anxious

to know how his trip to Seville went. Her nephew Francisco's visit
after his having left the discalced Carmelite novitiate in Pastrana
produced mixed feelings in her. And she has to begin thinking
again of carrying out what was stipulated in her brother's will
about building a new chapel for St. Joseph's.

✣✣✣✣

1. Jesus. The grace of the Holy Spirit be with your paternity.
This letter is not in my own hand because I wrote a great deal
to Avila today and my head is tired out. Yesterday I wrote to
you through Señora Doña Juana de Antisco,[1] and before that I
wrote you another very long letter. Please God it arrived there
better than yours are arriving here—if you wrote any—for I
worry very much until I know whether you arrived there safely.
I am writing now so that you will know about the mail delivery
between here and there and not fail to use it to write to me. I
am well, glory to God, and the fever has also left Sister María
de San José.[2]

2. What I mentioned in yesterday's letter is the story of Don
Francisco,[3] which has astonished us all. It would seem they
undid him so as to remake him into a different person. I am
not surprised about his behavior toward his relatives, but I am
surprised that God so abandons a creature who was desiring
to serve him. Great are God's judgments. I felt great pity when I
saw him. He is now actively engaged in managing his property
and is attached to it, and he is so afraid of speaking with either
discalced friars or discalced nuns that I don't think he would
want to see any of us, and least of all me. They say that he claims
he is afraid that the desire he had will return.[4] In this is seen the
great temptation to which he must be prey. I beg you to recommend him to God and show him compassion. He is looking to
get married, but not outside Avila. It will be a poor marriage, for
he is not without his regrets. The fact that you and Padre Nicolao[5] abandoned him so soon must have influenced his decision
very much. And that house in Pastrana isn't very enticing, in my
opinion. A great burden has been lifted from me.

3.   The chapel[6] is again on track, for Padre Fray Angel[7] wrote me about it yesterday. It all tires me out very much. He never did go to Madrid,[8] for he is coming now to San Pablo de la Moraleja. He says that the general has sent him the acts of the chapter.[9] Padre Pedro Fernández[10] is not dead; he is doing very poorly. Here most of the sisters are well and want to know about you. And my secretary and Madre Inés de Jesús[11] kiss your hands.

4.   Since I think you will be concerned about what was paid to Godoy,[12] you should know that I gave orders for it to appear to be a loan, and so as matters ended up he owed me more than I did him.

It is after Matins and the eve of Our Lady of the Presentation, a day I will not forget,[13] for that was the day the near riot broke out when you presented the brief to the Carmel there. May God watch over you and make you as holy as I beg of him, amen.

Your paternity's unworthy servant and daughter,

Teresa of Jesus

5.   God willing, this letter will be legible considering the haste with which it was written.[14] Francisco is very disturbed, and I have learned that he suffers from stomachaches, headaches, and a weak heart. God granted me a great favor by his not taking the habit. He mentioned often in Avila that nobody forced him to do anything. I tell you, *mi padre*, that I always feared what I now see. I don't know why, but I have felt relief not to have to be responsible for him, even though he says that with regard to his marriage he will not do anything that I would not want. But I fear he will find little happiness. And so if it were not for the fact that I might appear to be displeased over what he has done, I wouldn't bother with what he is planning.

6.   If you saw the letter that he wrote me from Alcalá and Pastrana you would be amazed by his happiness and the haste with which he wanted me to intervene on his behalf so that they give him the habit. He must have undergone a fierce temptation. But I did not speak to him about this, because he

was very upset and a relative of his was with him. He must feel very embarrassed. May God provide, and may he watch over you. In my opinion he would have been a holy man among holy men. I hope in God for his salvation, for he does have a fear of offending God.

7.   Your companion, San Bartolomé,[15] sends her best regards, and she has a great concern and desire to know how you fared along those roads and without us, for here we do very poorly without you; it seems we have been left in a desert. Sister Casilda de la Concepción[16] sends you her regards.

8.   May our Lord keep you for us and allow us to see you soon, *padre mio*, amen. So as not to tire you, I'll say no more.

Your paternity's unworthy subject, Ana de San Bartolomé.

9.   If you learn anything about the good Fray Bartolomé de Jesús[17], let me know, for this would be very consoling to me.

---

1.   Gracian's mother (see Ltr. 358.5).

2.   Gracian's sister, who was a Carmelite in Valladolid.

3.   Her nephew Francisco de Cepeda, who suddenly left the novitiate in Pastrana without having received the habit.

4.   The desire to become a discalced Carmelite.

5.   Nicolás Doria, prior of Pastrana, was somewhat abrupt in saying goodbye.

6.   The chapel that in accord with Lorenzo's will was to be built for St. Joseph's Carmel in Avila.

7.   Angel de Salazar.

8.   See Ltr. 358.3.

9.   The newly elected general was Giovanni Battista Caffardo. For the acts of the chapter (May 1580) pertaining to the discalced Carmelites, which to put it mildly were unflattering, see MHCT 2:189–191.

10.   The Dominican Pedro Fernández died two days later on 22 November. See Ltr. 358.4.

11.   The secretary was Blessed Anne of St. Bartholomew; Inés de Jesús (Tapia) was to accompany Teresa to make the foundation in Pastrana.

12. Licentiate Godoy.

13. It was on the feast of the Presentation of Our Lady in the Temple that Gracián presented the papers to the Carmelites in Seville that authorized him to make an official visitation. This created such an uproar that Teresa feared for his life.

14. She had dictated what preceded (nos. 1–4) and now, in nos. 5–6, writes in her own hand, and then again probably in no. 9.

15. Blessed Anne of St. Bartholomew, Teresa's secretary. She will sign her name in no. 8.

16. Casilda de Padilla (see F. 10–11).

17. Gracian's former secretary (see Ltr. 358.2).

360. To Madre María de San José, Seville
Valladolid, 21 November 1580

(Autograph: DCN, Valladolid)

Teresa is eager to receive news from Seville. Two subjects from previous letters are still on her mind: the establishment of a separate province for the discalced Carmelites; and the recovery of money belonging to the deceased Lorenzo de Cepeda so as to build the chapel at St. Joseph's in Avila. Though she says she is getting better, she has not really recovered from the serious illness she contracted in the summer (see Ltr. 357). The first part of this letter, nos. 1–3, is dictated to her secretary, Anne of St. Bartholomew.

❧ ❧ ☙ ☙

For Mother Prioress of St. Joseph's in Seville

1.   Jesus. The grace of the Holy Spirit be with your reverence, my daughter, amen. I long to know how your health is. For the love of God, take good care of it, for I worry much over this. Let me know how you feel and how consoled you now are to have our Padre Gracián[1] with you. For it is a comfort to me to think of the relief you will find in having him there for everything. I am better, thanks be to God.

2.   I am getting to feel like myself again, although there is no lack of something to suffer with my continual illnesses and cares, which are never wanting. Pray for me, and write to let me know what I should do about these documents you sent me; they're worth nothing for legally withdrawing money.[2] See what can be done, and try to find some aspirant so as to pay the money needed to build the chapel my brother wanted,[3] for one can no longer fail to begin the construction. I don't have any resources here, for which I am very sorry. I can't do anything more than entrust everything to God that he will provide, as he can.

3.   As for the order's business affairs,[4] there is nothing new to say for now. When there is something, you will hear of it from our Padre Gracián. My best regards to all the sisters. Please God they will enjoy the health I desire for them.

4.   I have already written you[5] that the one in Toledo who owes you the money is taking his time, and he is a judge for the archbishop.[6] I don't know how anything can be collected from him except amicably. If Padre Nicolao,[7] when he goes there, should want to stay a few days and inquire about the matter with him, perhaps something could be worked out. I had thought that something could be done about this once Francisco's[8] plan to enter religious life was carried out. Everything is breaking down. May God work it out as he can and give you the health that I beg of him.

5.   Since there is mail delivery to this city, don't fail to make use of it and write me, and tell our padre to do so, and let Mother Subprioress[9] inform me about how the nuns are getting along with him, and if he is well, and tell her she should write me a long letter about everything so that you don't tire yourself.

6.   For goodness' sake be on guard for there is someone in the house[10] who thinks that what amounts to nothing is a serious matter. And let me know how this poor soul[11] is doing, and how Father Prior of Las Cuevas[12] is. Have our *padre*[13] go to see him and give him my best wishes and also to Padre Rodrigálvarez,[14]

who made me happy with his message. My head doesn't permit me to write to him. Let me know how San Jerónimo[15] is. My regards to her and to Sister San Francisco.[16]

Today is the feast of the Presentation of Our Lady

Your reverence's unworthy servant,

Teresa of Jesus

All of you pray hard for the affairs of the order.

---

1. Jerónimo Gracián, being prior of Los Remedios, had recently arrived in Seville.
2. The money was meant to pay back what the Carmel in Seville owed to Lorenzo de Cepeda (see Ltr. 350.4).
3. The chapel to be built at St. Joseph's in Avila in accord with Lorenzo's will.
4. On account of Pedro Fernández's grave illness, a new executor had to be appointed by Rome for the brief that allowed the discalced Carmelites to form a separate province. In fact, notification of the new appointment, made the previous day (20 November), did not reach the king until January 1581 (see MHCT 2: 232–233; 236).
5. In Ltr. 350.4. Up to this point Teresa dictated; now she continues in her own hand.
6. The archbishop was Gaspar de Quiroga, but the identity of this person is unknown.
7. Nicolás Doria.
8. Allusion to her nephew Francisco's plan to enter the discalced Carmelites in Pastrana.
9. Leonor de San Gabriel.
10. María de San José crossed out the words "in the house."
11. Beatriz de la Madre de Dios, who was the cause of the past disturbances in the Carmel.
12. Hernando de Pantoja, the former prior of Las Cuevas.
13. Gracián.
14. The Jesuit Rodrigo Alvarez.
15. Isabel de San Jerónimo.
16. Isabel de San Francisco.

361. To Madre Ana de la Encarnación, Salamanca
Valladolid, Beginning of December 1580

(Autograph: DCF, Burgos)

The business of purchasing the house in Salamanca was still in a tangle. García Manrique had taken an interest in helping, but the prioress was resisting. He wrote from Valladolid saying that he had complained to Teresa. She read his letter and wrote this note on the second page, sending it on to Salamanca.

❖❖❖❖

1.   Jesus. After having written a letter, which your reverence will receive, Padre García Manrique[1] sent me this one. Do not delay or be afraid to do what he asks for here, but go ahead and do so. When, surprised by your new decision, I wrote the letter, I thought that Pedro de la Banda[2] had asked you for some documents and that Padre García Manrique had not been informed, and that is why I asked you to inform me if there is anything else. But I don't see any drawback to doing what he asks here; neither does Madre Inés de Jesús[3] see any reason for your not doing so at once, nor does the prioress.[4] So I beg you, for goodness' sake, to do so. And even if there is some drawback, it is enough that the agreement has at last been reached. Because it didn't seem so nice to us when they didn't keep their word—the gentleman from Salamanca—we wouldn't want to be imitating them.

2.   Because I have gone on at greater length in the letter I mentioned, I'm saying no more than that may God give you a great love for him.

Your reverence's unworthy servant,

Teresa of Jesus

---

1.   A friend of both Teresa and Doña Ana Enríquez.
2.   The ill-mannered owner of the house in Salamanca.
3.   Teresa's cousin from Medina Del Campo who was destined for the foundation in Palencia.
4.   The prioress in Valladolid, María Bautista.

362. To An Unidentified Person
Valladolid, 10 December 1580

These are three fragments of a badly damaged letter. The subject of the letter revolves around the recent marriage, 8 December 1580, of Teresa's nephew Francisco de Cepeda.

❧❧❧❧

1.   Jesus. The grace of the Holy Spirit be with your honor. I don't know how to answer someone with so much humility as is shown in your letter and so much graciousness as well, for I do not deserve to be so treated. May our Lord answer for me, and His Majesty repay you, for he has been pleased that I be unable to serve you in any of the ways that I would like, which would be such a blessing for me. I don't deserve anything more. May he be blessed for everything.

2.   From the letter accompanying this one, you will see how Don Francisco's choice of a state in life[1] did not depend on any opinion of mine. And by my entrusting the letter to you will be seen my esteem for you. And so I beg you ...[2]

3.   ... And it seemed the same to all of us, especially Don Francisco, who showed himself to be what he is, your servant, and with great happiness to be so, and with little desire for Madrid.[3] And that was the conclusion, and he wanted it very much; and I believe he truly did. And so I am not astonished by any signs that may have been given; I trust in your great prudence that this will not take away one iota of the great value you find in him. Nonetheless, I felt deep regret.

4.   Since Diego de Tapia[4] went to Madrid and saw such a tangled mess and what little attention was paid to it, he was astonished and wrote to me at once about what was going on. When I wrote to Avila by way of the commander, I did so in order to find out what took place and inform those who were not in Madrid. But they were already gone. On the feast of the Immaculate Conception of Our Lady, they gave me some letters ...

5. … it was neither Don Francisco's will nor mine that the matter not be brought to completion, for we are not failing to consider your rank as lord. You can be certain that what I can do, which is to recommend you to our Lord in my poor prayers, I will do from here on, and consider myself your servant.

May His Majesty preserve your illustrious honor with much holiness. Amen.

Today is 10 December …

1. This could refer to Francisco's decision to enter the discalced Carmelites or, more probably, to get married.
2. About fourteen lines are missing here.
3. A probable allusion to the preparations for Don Francisco's marriage in Madrid to Doña Orofrisia de Mendoza y Castilla.
4. Probably a relative of Teresa's.

363. To Don Lorenzo de Cepeda (her nephew), Quito
Valladolid, 27 December 1580

(Partial autograph: DCN, Peñaranda [Salamanca])

Teresa writes this letter, although without haste, shortly before leaving Valladolid for Palencia. She must inform her nephew that a month after he had left in May for America his father died and that his brother Francisco was married on 8 December. Realizing that he must feel quite alone in the vast world of Peru, Teresa sends him news of those he left behind, while subtly urging him to keep from the unruly ways he had taken up when still in Spain.

❧❧❧❧

1. Jesus. The grace of the Holy Spirit be with your honor, my son. You can well believe that the bad news about which I must write you in this letter distresses me greatly. But realizing that you will learn of it from someone else and that no one will be

able to inform you well about the consolation that such a great trial may contain, I have wanted to tell you myself. And if we consider well the miseries of this life, we will rejoice over the joy of those who are already with God.

2.   Two days after the feast of St. John, His Majesty was pleased to bring my good brother Lorencio de Cepeda to himself. A hemorrhage caused a quick death. He had gone to confession and received communion on the feast of St. John. And I believe it was a gift, considering the condition he was in, that he didn't live longer. In regards to his soul, I know well that he was always ready. Eight days before, he had written me a letter in which he spoke of how he had only a short time left to live, although he didn't know the exact date.[1]

3.   He died entrusting himself to God, like a saint. And so, according to our faith we can believe that he remained for little or no time at all in purgatory. Although he was always, as you know, God's servant, he was so in the end in such a way that he wanted nothing to do with anything earthly. And except for persons who spoke only of God, everything else tired him to such an extent that I found it hard to console him. So he went to La Serna to find more solitude, and there he died, or to put it better, began to live. If I were able to write some of the details about his soul, you would understand how obliged you are to God for having given you so good a father and would live in a way that shows you are his son. But a letter doesn't allow for more than what was said, except that you should be consoled and believe that he can do you more good from where he is than by being on earth.

4.   It has made me, more than anyone else, feel very sad. And the same is true of the good Teresita de Jesús, although God gave her such courage that she bore the loss like an angel, and she is like an angel and a very good nun as well and happy to be one. I hope in God that she will be like her father. As for me I have had no lack of worries until seeing Don Francisco settled as he is now, for he was left very much alone since as you know we have few relatives.[2]

5.   He was so sought after in Avila for marriage that I feared he might choose an unsuitable wife. God was pleased that he get married on the feast of the Immaculate Conception to a lady from Madrid who has a mother but no father. The mother wanted this marriage so much that we were amazed, for considering her status she could have done much better. Even though the dowry is small, none of the persons in Avila that we considered could have brought as much even had they wanted to.

6.   The bride's name is Doña Orofrisia. She is not yet fifteen; beautiful and very discreet. I mean to say Doña Orofrisia de Mendoza y de Castilla. Her mother is a first cousin of the Duke of Albuquerque, a niece of the Duke of Infantazgo and related to many other titled lords. In sum, on both her mother's and father's side, they say, the noble background is unsurpassable in Spain. In Avila, she is related to the Marquis de las Navas, the Marquis de Velada, and more closely to the wife of Don Luis, of Mosen Rubí.[3]

7.   They gave him four thousand ducats. He wrote me that he is very happy which is what matters. What pleases me is that Doña Beatriz, her mother, is a woman of such merit and discretion that she will be able to direct them both and make adjustments, they say, so as to keep the spending within moderation. Doña Orofrisia has only one brother, who is older than she, and a sister who is a nun. If her brother doesn't have any children, she will inherit the primogeniture. This is possible.

8.   I don't see any other drawback here except for Don Francisco's lack of means, for the estate is so burdened with debt[4] that if he doesn't soon receive what is owed to him from over there, I don't know how he will be able to live. So, for the love of God, do all you can to get it. Since God is giving them so much honor, they need the means to sustain it.

9.   Up until now Don Francisco has shown himself to be very virtuous, and I hope in God that he will continue to be so, for he is a very good Christian. Please God that I will hear news

like this about you.[5] Now you see, my son, how all things come to an end, but the good or bad we do in this life is eternal and will have no end.

10.　Pedro de Ahumada is well, and also my sister and her children, although they are left in serious need because my brother—may he be in glory—was helping them very much. A short time ago Don Gonzalo, my sister's son, was here.[6] He along with others regard you highly, for you have fooled them into having a good opinion of you. I would have liked to see you become better. Please God you will now do so, and may His Majesty give you the virtue and holiness that I beg of him, amen.

11.　You can send letters to the monastery of the nuns in Seville, for the prioress is the same as the one who was there when I was, and all the conflicts have been resolved very well, glory to God. I am writing this in our monastery in Valladolid. The prioress here[7] kisses your hands, and I the hands of our relatives, those lords and ladies.

Teresa of Jesus

1.　See Teresa's quick response to this letter of Lorenzo's, Ltr. 346.

2.　He, his brother, Francisco, and his sister, Teresita, were Don Lorenzo's only surviving children.

3.　In addition to Francisco's bride, the people referred to are Doña Beatriz de Castilla y Mendoza, Doña Orofrisia's mother; Don Gabriel de la Cueva, the Duke of Alburguerque; Don Inigo López de Mendoza, the Duke of Infantado; Don Pedro Dávila, the Marquis of Las Navas; Don Gómez Dávila, the Marquis of Velada; Don Luis Rubí, the Marquis of Fuentesol, and his wife, Doña Maríana de Alarcón, the Marchioness of Trocifal.

4.　Teresa was familiar with Lorenzo's will and the intricate entanglements of his estate.

5.　While still living in Spain Lorenzo had fathered an illegitimate daughter (See Ltr. 427.4–5).

6.　She is speaking of Pedro and Juana, her siblings, and Gonzalo and Beatriz, Juana's children.

7.　The prioress in Seville was María de San José; the prioress in Vallodid was Maria Bautista.

364. To Madre María de San José, Seville
Valladolid, 28 December 1580

(Autograph and Original: DCN, Valladolid)

This response was prompted by two letters from Madre María and two from the Indies. She is particularly concerned about the business with Diego López de Zúñiga for the nuns in Salamanca and is forwarding the documents that need to be forwarded to him in Lima, Peru. She is getting ready to leave for Palencia and dictated almost the entire letter to Anne of St. Bartholomew.

✦✦✦✦

For Mother Prioress of the Carmel of St. Joseph's in Seville.

1. Jesus, Mary. The grace of the Holy Spirit be with your reverence, my daughter, and I hope that His Majesty has given you as holy a Christmas as I desired for you. I wanted very much for this letter to be in my own hand, but my head and the many things I have to do, since the time to leave for Palencia is at hand, prevent me from writing it myself. Pray for us that the new foundation may be a means to render God much service.

2. I am better, glory to God, and consoled to know that you are as well. For the love of God, take care of yourself and be careful about what you drink, for you know the harm it does you. Two sisters who had those swellings were greatly helped by taking an infusion of rhubarb several mornings in succession. Consult with your doctor, and if he thinks it fitting, take it.

3. I received both your letters. In one you mentioned your happiness in having Padre Gracián[1] present. I am also happy that you have someone with whom you feel at ease and can consult; you have been suffering alone for a long time.

4. In the other letter, you were speaking of the business in the Indies. I was delighted that you have someone there who is dealing with this matter carefully, for there is no other remedy for that house in Salamanca. If nothing comes before the

day on which they will be obliged to leave the house where they are,[2] we will find ourselves in dire straits. So for the love of God make every effort to have this packet delivered, for it contains the contract that was made for the sale of that house. If by chance the ones to whom the envelope is addressed are dead, write to those persons you mention so that they might carry out the negotiations. And if the letters are delivered to the one to whom they are addressed, they could also look into the matter, and perhaps they will do so with more enthusiasm than the addressee would and take care to send us a prompt answer, something very important for us. You must then urge them to do this and add the enclosed copy of the contract to the letters you write. If it is necessary to give one to each of them, make further copies to go with each letter, and you and the sisters pray to God that they arrive there and that this business will be brought to a conclusion.[3]

5.   In what you say about the money for the chapel,[4] don't be distressed if you cannot send it so quickly, for I wrote only in regard to the use for which it is meant.

6.   I also received with yours the letter from the Indies. Be sure also that this letter enclosed for my nephew Don Lorencio[5] is sent to him with care.

7.   Best regards to Mother Subprioress[6] and the sisters, and I am happy that they now are all well. They should know that they were not the worst off, considering what has occurred here and how long the illnesses have lasted. I still have not recovered completely.[7]

8.   The letter addressed to Lorencio mustn't go with the packet, because the one place is far away from the other, but you must find someone who is going to that city, or province, or I don't know what. Be careful, daughter, to carry out these tasks with all due regard. In the packet is enclosed another record of the agreement made regarding the house.[8] You couldn't imagine what those nuns suffer and the trials they have had. Write to Don Lorencio at the address he will mention when he

writes that he should write to you at the house of St. Joseph, for perhaps he doesn't remember, and that my brother left orders[9] that, with the money you owe him, a chapel is to be built at St. Joseph's where he is interred. You mustn't send the money to Don Francisco[10] but to me, for I will have him give a receipt. I fear he might spend the money on something else, especially now that he is married. I wouldn't for anything want to be a cause of worry for you, but try to get some of the postulants who are entering there, as our *padre* tells us, to give the money. I wish you had a larger orchard so that Beatriz could be more occupied. I can't accept those excuses,[11] for she cannot deceive God, and her soul will pay for it. In the presence of all the nuns she gave false testimony and did many other things that they wrote me about; either they are telling the truth or she is.

9.   Give my best regards to Rodrigo Alvarez[12] and to the good prior of Las Cuevas.[13] Oh what pleasure you give me by showing him kindness. Best wishes to the good Serrano[14] and to all my daughters.

May God watch over you for me.

Don't forget to ask about the rhubarb, for it is something that has been tested.

Today is the last day of the Christmas feast.

Your reverence's,

Teresa of Jesus

1.   The prior of Los Remedios in Seville, Jerónimo Gracián.
2.   Since 19 September of that year, the nuns in Salamanca were under obligation to vacate the house of Pedro de la Banda and were feeling the pressure to move.
3.   What they needed was the signature and consent of Diego López de Zúñiga to buy some new houses for the community in Salamanca (see Ltrs. 347.18 and 357.5).
4.   The chapel at St. Joseph's in Avila that Teresa's brother ordered to be built from the money owed to him by the nuns in Seville.
5.   The son of Teresa's brother Lorenzo.
6.   Leonor de San Gabriel.

7. She continues the letter in her own hand.
8. The house in Salamanca.
9. Her brother Lorenzo left these orders in his will.
10. Lorenzo's son Francisco de Cepeda.
11. Beatriz de la Madre de Dios, who was emotionally unstable, made different attempts to explain away her past behavior.
12. A Jesuit who was a spiritual director of hers in Seville.
13. Hernando de Pantoja, the former prior of the Carthusians.
14. One of Teresa's faithful helpers and friends in Seville.

Letters 365–428
(1581)

365. To Padre Juan de Jesús Roca, Pastrana
Palencia, 4 January 1581

(Autograph: DCN, Seville)

Padre Juan de Jesús has returned from Rome after a successful mission and is residing in Pastrana, where Nicolás Doria is prior, looking ahead to the chapter for the discalced Carmelites which will take place in Alcalá. He had written to Teresa asking her to intercede for him with the Archbishop of Toledo, to offer her suggestions in regard to the approaching chapter, and to accept a proposed postulant for the Carmel in Villanueva de la Jara. Teresa first deals with these requests and then goes on to give an account of the foundation in Palencia, news which she intends as well for Doria and the nuns in Villanueva.

❧❧❦❦

For *mi padre maestro*, Juan de Jesús Roca, Pastrana

1.   Jesus. May the Holy Spirit be with your reverence. Every time you tell me that you are well, it makes me very happy.

God be praised who grants us so many favors. I would like to serve you by trying to get the letter you mention from the archbishop,[1] but you should know that I have never spoken either at length or even briefly with his sister, nor do I know her.[2] And you already know what little attention the archbishop paid to my letter when you gave me the task to write him at the time you were planning to go to Rome.[3] I am very averse to insisting if nothing will be gained thereby, especially since we will be asking shortly for his permission to make a foundation in Madrid.[4] I would like to do more than this for you to whom we owe so much, but truly I don't see how.

2.   Regarding what you tell me about the constitutions,[5] Padre Gracián wrote me that they said the same thing to him as they did to you, and he has there with him the remarks of the nuns. The things that need to be noted are so few that the response can be given quickly, but it was necessary to be in contact about them with both of you. What seems fitting to me on the one hand seems full of drawbacks on the other, and so I cannot come to a decision. It is very necessary to have everything set so that on our part there won't be any delay.

3.   Now Señor Casademonte[6] wrote me that he was given orders by someone in authority not to allow Tostado[7] to have anything to do with the discalced Carmelites, which is very good. The care this friend of yours takes to give us any good news and keep us informed about everything is extraordinary. We certainly owe him a great deal.

4.   The dowry which you say that aspirant has seems little to me, for it consists in a property that could perhaps be worth much less when sold, and then paid for late and poorly. So I have decided against her going to Villanueva for they have greater need of money there and have more nuns than I would wish.[8] Padre Fray Gabriel[9] has written me about a relative of his whom it would be more fitting for us to accept even though she doesn't have as much, for we owe him a great deal. When I wrote about that sister, they had not brought me the letter that

speaks of the other aspirant. Don't consider the matter any further, for down there they will find the one who is most suited in their case. If they are going to put a burden on the house, it is better that they take someone from their own town.

5.   We left Valladolid on the feast of the Holy Innocents for this foundation in Palencia.[10] The first Mass was said on the feast of King David (in great secrecy because we thought there might be some opposition). And the good bishop here, Don Alvaro,[11] had arranged everything so well that there was not only no objection but no one in the city who fails to rejoice in the fact, certain that our presence here will draw down God's favor on them. It is the most unusual thing I've ever seen. I would have thought this to be a bad sign if I hadn't remembered the previous opposition of many down there who thought it would not be good for us to come here. And so I was very remiss about coming until the Lord gave me little light and more faith.[12] I think it will be one of the best of the houses that were founded and more fervent, for we bought the house next to a shrine to our Lady in the best section of the city. The people there and in all the surrounding region have the greatest devotion to her. The chapter has allowed us to have a grille looking into the church, something seen as a special favor. Everything is done by the bishop. What this order owes him and the care he shows over its concerns are indescribable. He gives us the bread we need.

6.   Now we are staying in a house that a gentleman had given to Padre Gracián when he was here.[13] Soon, with God's favor, we will move to our own. I tell you that you will rejoice to see the conveniences that are here. God be praised for everything.

7.   The archbishop[14] has already given me permission to make a foundation in Burgos. In finishing this one here, if the Lord be served, a foundation will be made there, for it would be too far to come all the way back here from Madrid, and I also fear that Father Vicar[15] would not give permission for Madrid. And I would like it if our dispatch[16] arrived first. It's

appropriate that we will be there where it gets so cold at the coldest time and where it gets so hot at the hottest time and thus have something to suffer, and afterward be criticized by Padre Nicolao,[17] which really amused me because he has more than enough reasons for doing so.

8.   In your charity give him this letter so that he has news of this foundation and both of you may praise our Lord. I would tell you everything about what is going on here so as to stir your devotion, but I am getting tired. The shrine has two endowed Masses every day and many other Masses that are said there. So many people ordinarily visit it that we have been finding this somewhat difficult.

9.   In your charity, if you find some messenger there for Villanueva[18] send them news about how this foundation was made. Madre Inés de Jesús[19] worked very hard. I am no help now with anything except for the noise that the name Teresa of Jesus makes.

10.   Give my best regards to Madre Inés, and I send them to all those brothers of mine.

Tomorrow is the vigil of Epiphany.

11.   In your charity pray for three canons who took it upon themselves to help us, for one especially, who is a saint named Reinoso,[20] and for the bishop.

12.   All the important people favor us very much, the fact is that the joy of all the people in general is extraordinary. I don't know where it will all end.

Your reverence's servant,

Teresa of Jesus

1.   The Archbishop of Toledo, Gaspar de Quiroga.
2.   The archbishop's sister, María de Quiroga, had a niece who was a nun in the Carmel of Medina del Campo.
3.   Juan de Jesús (Roca) had gone to Rome with Diego de la Trinidad in May 1579.

4. She had already asked permission for a foundation in Madrid in June 1580 and will do so again in 1581 (see Ltr. 397.6), but without success.

5. She was concerned about plans to expand the constitutions in the forthcoming chapter in Alcalá de Henares.

6. Pedro Juan de Casademonte.

7. The Carmelite Jerónimo Tostado opposed the steps taken by Juan de Jesús (Roca) in Rome to obtain permission for a separate province of discalced Carmelites (see MHCT 2:209–210). He was reappointed visitator of the Spanish provinces on 18 November 1581, but before arriving in Spain, he died in Naples on 24 February 1582.

8. See F.28.9.

9. Gabriel de la Asunción, the prior of a monastery near La Roda, which was also close to Villanueva de la Jara.

10. They left Valladolid on 28 December 1580 and celebrated their first Mass in Palencia on 29 December.

11. Don Alvaro de Mendoza.

12. She is alluding to a grace mentioned in F.29.6.

13. The house where they could live temporarily had been offered by Canon Serrano (see F. 29.7).

14. Later, the Archbishop of Burgos, Don Cristóbal Vela, actually resisted the foundation (see F.31).

15. Angel de Salazar.

16. The dispatch contained the appointment of a new apostolic commissary to preside over the chapter that was to take place in Alcalá. The dispatch in fact arrived on that very day.

17. Nicolás Doria, prior of Pastrana.

18. The Carmel in Villanueva de la Jara.

19. Inés de Jesús was the prioress in Palencia.

20. Canon Jerónimo Reinoso. The other two were Martín Alonso de Salinas (see F.29.12) and Prudencio de Armentía (F.29.26).

366. To Madre María de San José, Seville
Palencia, 6 January 1581

(Original and Autograph: DCN, Valladolid)

The two main topics on Teresa's mind here are the correspondence with Perú concerning the purchase of property in Salamanca and the recovery of the money owed by the Seville monastery to her brother, Lorenzo, which was to go toward the building of a chapel at St. Joseph's in Avila.

❧ ❧ ❦ ❦

1.   Jesus, Mary. The grace of the Holy Spirit be with your reverence, my daughter, amen. You show me much charity with your letters. I answered them all before I left Valladolid, sending you also the documentation regarding Salamanca.[1] I think that by the time this letter arrives you will have the documentation. We need all the care that you are taking so that the response will arrive in time. May God who sees our need bring this about, and may he give you the health I desire for you. You don't mention how your health is in this letter of yours. And that is wrong, for you know how worried I am. Please God you are better.

2.   We were delighted with what the elderly ladies are saying about our *padre*,[2] and I praise God for the fruitfulness of his sermons and holiness. His holiness is such that I am not surprised by the effect he has on those souls. Write to me about this, for it makes me very happy to know of these things. May God watch over him, as is our need. And you are right in saying that he must cut down on his preaching, for giving so many sermons could do him harm.

3.   With regard to the two hundred ducats you say you must send me, I would be happy to receive them because we are beginning to carry out the orders my brother[3] left (may he be in glory). But don't send the money to Casademonte[4] or forward it through Padre Nicolao[5]—these words are meant only for you—for he might use it there and I would be left in need here. But send the money to Medina del Campo if the sisters there know some merchant to whom you may send a letter of credit. This is the safest way to send the money and would not cost anything. If this is not possible, then try Valladolid, and if that isn't either, then let me know before you send it so that I may tell you how it should be sent.

4.   I am getting along fairly well, but I am so busy with visits that although I had wanted to write this myself, I wasn't able to.

5.   Enclosed is an account of the events surrounding this foundation, for it makes me praise God to see what is happening and the charity, goodwill, and devotion of this city.[6] May God be given thanks; and have all the sisters thank God for the favor he shows us, and give them my best regards. The sisters here recommend themselves to your prayers, especially the secretary;[7] it consoled her greatly to know that you are well disposed toward praying for her, for she is in great need.

6.   I am writing to our *padre* to let him know the reason why I want this money sent directly to me. I have gotten so tired of relatives after my brother's death that I don't want any arguments with them. I tell you I am distressed over the famine that our *padre* tells me is going on in that region, for I don't know how you are living; and I'm also distressed that you have to send this money now. I would rather have it given to you. May God provide a remedy and give you health, for with good health one can put up with anything; but seeing you with little health and in need, is an affliction for me. I fear that the climate down there is bad for you, and I don't know how you could leave. May God provide the means, for he has certainly heard your prayers for trials.

7.   Tell Sister San Francisco[8] that it never enters my mind now to be displeased with her, but I am so pleased that it grieves me to see her so far away. My best regards to all the sisters and to Mother Subprioress.[9] And remain with God, for this head of mine forces me to be brief. Otherwise I would have to scold you, for what you say to Padre Nicolao made me laugh. On the one hand I see that you need to accept nuns; on the other hand, we have experience here of all the trouble that comes when the numbers are not kept small and of the inconveniences that arise for many reasons. May God bring us someone like the one who died[10]—which would settle matters—and watch over you.

Today is the feast of the Epiphany.

8.   The letters for the Indies I sent with the previous mail. They tell me that Fray García de Toledo,[11] to whom they are addressed, is returning. And so it is necessary that you entrust this packet to someone down there, in the event that Luis de Tapia[12] (for some are addressed also to him) has died.

Your reverence's servant,

Teresa of Jesus

1. It concerned the purchase of the house in Salamanca (see Ltr. 364.4).
2. Jerónimo Gracián.
3. The orders he gave in his will that a chapel be built at the Carmel of St. Joseph's in Avila.
4. Pedro Juan de Casademonte, a merchant friend of St. Teresa's.
5. Nicolás Doria.
6. See F. 29.
7. Blessed Anne of St. Bartholomew was the secretary. The handwriting is hers up to the end of this paragraph. The rest is in Teresa's hand.
8. Isabel de San Francisco.
9. Leonor de San Gabriel.
10. Bernarda de San José.
11. Teresa's great friend, the Dominican Padre García de Toledo, who went to the Indies in 1569 with the Viceroy of Perú, Don Francisco de Toledo.
12. Probably a cousin of Teresa's.

367. To Doña Juana de Ahumada, Alba
Palencia, 13 January 1581.

The Christmas season had stirred thoughts in Teresa of her family. Francisco de Cepeda on 8 December 1580 had married in Madrid without informing his relatives in Alba. Teresa is happy with the way the new foundation in Alba has turned out.

❖❖❖❖

1.   Jesus. The grace of the Holy Spirit be with your honor, my sister. I have had the strongest desire to know how you are and

how your Christmas was. Believe me, many a Christmas has gone by in which I never have had you and your household so much in mind as this year, recommending you all to our Lord and even grieving over your trials. May he be blessed who did not come into this world for any other reason than to suffer. And since I understand that whoever best follows his example in suffering, keeping his commandments, will have the more glory, I feel greatly consoled; although I would prefer to suffer your trials myself and let you have the reward, or be where I could more easily spend time with you. But, since the Lord ordains otherwise, may he be blessed for everything.

2.   On the feast of the Holy Innocents, I set out from Valladolid with my companions in the midst of harsh weather for this city of Palencia. But my health is no worse, although the usual ailments are not lacking. When there is no fever, however, one can put up with them.[1]

3.   Two days after our arrival, I installed the bell at night, and a monastery of the glorious St. Joseph was founded. The happiness of all the people here was so great I was amazed. I think this is partly due to the fact that they see they are thereby pleasing the bishop, for he is much loved here and he favors us.[2] Things are proceeding in such a way that I have hope in God this will be among the best of our houses.

4.   I have no other news of Don Francisco than that his mother-in-law wrote a little while ago saying he had to be bled twice. She is very happy with him, and he with both of them. Pedro de Ahumada must be the least happy, according to what he has written to me.[3] For Don Francisco seems to want to live with his mother-in-law, and it is not possible for Pedro de Ahumada to join them. It's a pity that he cannot be at rest anywhere. He wrote to me that he was now well and that he was going to Avila for the Epiphany to find out how to collect the money from Seville, since they are not giving him anything. The more those in Madrid inform me about this marriage,[4] the more reason I see for us to be happy, especially over all they

say of the discretion and pleasing manner of Doña Orofrisia. May God protect them and give them the grace to serve him, for all earthly consolations pass away quickly.

5.   If you send the letter to Mother Prioress in Alba[5] to forward to Salamanca it will surely arrive here, for there is a regular mail delivery. For goodness' sake don't neglect to write to me; you owe it to me these days, for I have had you all on my mind more than I would like.

6.   Let Señor Juan de Ovalle consider this letter as addressed also to him—I would like to know how he is getting along. Regards to Señora Doña Beatriz. May God watch over you all and make you as holy as I beg of him, amen.

Today is 13 January.

7.   Don't fail to write to Don Francisco,[6] which would be appropriate. He is not to blame for having failed to inform you of his marriage; it came about in such a way that there wasn't time. Madre Inés de Jesús[7] is well and sends her best regards to all of you.

Your honor's servant,

Teresa of Jesus

---

1.   She arrived in Palencia on 28 December 1580 with five nuns, among whom was her nurse, Blessed Anne of St. Bartholomew (see F. 29.10). She was still suffering from the effects of the perilous influenza that spread through Spain the previous year and left her so gravely ill in Toledo and then again in Valladolid.

2.   The bishop is Don Alvaro de Mendoza, who supported her first foundation in Avila (1562) and was at the time the bishop of Palencia (see F. 29.1).

3.   Francisco de Cepeda, Teresa's nephew, after a brief attempt at the discalced Carmelite life in Pastrana, got married to Doña Orofrisia de Mendoza y Castilla in Madrid. His mother-in-law, Doña Beatriz de Castilla y Mendoza was soon to clash with Teresa over money matters. Pedro de Ahumada, Teresa's brother, who until the death of Lorenzo had been dependant on him, was now left to himself.

4.   Don Francisco's marriage took place hastily, and Teresa is seeking to prevent her sister from becoming angry at not having been informed properly.

5. Juana del Espíritu Santo.
6. Francisco de Cepeda.
7. Inés De Jesús was Teresa's cousin, who came with her to Palencia and will remain there as prioress.

368. To M. Ana de la Encarnación, Salamanca
Palencia, January 1581

(Autograph: DCN, Clamart, Seine [France])

Teresa thanks the prioress in Salamanca for the gifts she has sent her and tries to console her in the loss of the two nuns taken from her for the foundation in Palencia. Things are going well in Palencia, but they have not found a house yet for the new foundation.

❧❧❧❧

For Mother Prioress of St. Joseph's, Salamanca

1. Jesus. May the Holy Spirit be with your reverence. I deeply regret having to take nuns from your house who please you,[1] but this can't be helped; and since the one who is displeasing to you[2] is also departing, have patience and pray for them all so that they may do well that which they are being called to do and that your house will not lose the good reputation brought to it by those who are leaving. I hope that will be so, for very good nuns are remaining with you.

2. It seems to me you are still going about with your infirmities. It is a great favor God grants us that you can stay on your feet; be careful, for the love of God. May it please him to let me see you finally out of that house,[3] for I tell you it is a cause of much worry for me. His Majesty must desire that you suffer in every way. May he be praised for everything. And may His Majesty reward you for the limes. I had been so ill the day before that they were a delight to me, and also the veil; the one I was wearing I adapted for use as a larger one,[4] for those you sent were lovely. Nonetheless, do me the charity not to send me

anything unless I ask for it; I prefer that you spend the money on caring for yourself.

3.   In this foundation[5] everything is going so well that I don't know where it will end. Ask our Lord to give us a good house; we don't want the shrine.[6] There are many houses, and they are good ones. Many people are looking after us, and the bishop never stops doing us favors. In your charity pray to God for him and for those who are helping us.

4.   Write a note to Fray Domingo,[7] should I fail to write him, so that he will know about this foundation, although I will try to write. If I don't, give him my best regards.

5.   I was most pleased to see the care you took to provide sisters, something that is not always done, and you did the right thing, especially with regard to Isabel de Jésus,[8] who is so deserving. It seems she is happy.

6.   Because she and the others will tell you about everything else, and since I have other letters to write, I'll say no more than ask our Lord to watch over you for me and give you all the holiness I beg of him, amen. The missals are very nice and you sent so much that I don't know when we will be able to pay for it.

Your reverence's servant,

Teresa of Jesus

Padre Maestro Diaz[9] will give the enclosed letters to my Dominican fathers; you can give them to him.

---

1. Two sisters were taken from the Carmel in Salamanca for the new foundation in Palencia: Isabel de Jesús (Jimena), who went as prioress of the new community, and Beatriz de Jesús (Acevedo y Villalobos), who was appointed subprioress.

2. She is probably referring to Beatriz, who had two siblings in the Carmel of Salamanca: Guiomar del Sacramento and Jerónima del Espíritu Santo.

3. The house belonging to Pedro de la Banda, which they were obliged to vacate.

4. The nuns had two veils, a small one, which they wore throughout the day, and a larger one, which they wore only at specified times.

5. The foundation in Palencia.

6. Later she changed her mind and decided to buy the shrine house (F. 29. 13–29).

7. Domingo Báñez, professor at the University of Salamanca.

8. She had already helped Teresa with the foundation in Segovia.

9. Juan Díaz, who was a dedicated friend of Teresa's and a priest disciple of St. John of Avila.

369. To Doña Juana Dantisco, Madrid

Palencia, January 1581 (?)

A fragment of doubtful date.

Yesterday I received a letter from Valladolid. Our Sister María de San José is very happy and joyful. They write me things about my Isabel de Jesús that make one want to praise God. And you should do so, for you have there two angels who are always praying to His Majesty for you.[1]

1. María de San José and Isabel de Jesús are Doña Juana's Carmelite daughters, the one in Valladolid, and the other in Toledo respectively.

370. To Doña Ana Enriquez, Valladolid?

Palencia, February–April 1581

The date and addressee of this thank-you message are uncertain.

❖❖❖❖

1. Jesus. The grace of the Holy Spirit be with your honor, amen. I want you to know that yesterday the bishop[1] sent us twelve bushels of wheat. Since the alms are being given in your name, it is good that you know about it in case you might see it. I beg you to let me know how you are getting along on such humid days and if you have gone to confession for the feast of

this glorious saint.[2] He is a very great saint, and it is right that you be devoted to him, since you are so kind to the poor.

2.   Señora Doña María[3] has sent me word that she will not be satisfied about the reliquary until you give it to me. She speaks of it as though it were her own. It also seems to me that you have a right to it. Since it is the Lord who will repay you for this favor and all the favors you do for us, he will understand this proceeding and render a fair judgment.

3.   May His Majesty preserve and guide you for many years. Mother Prioress[4] and the sisters here ask for your prayers.

Your honor's unworthy servant,

Teresa of Jesus

1.   The Bishop of Palencia, Alvaro de Mendoza, who at the time was providing the community with bread (see Ltr. 365.5).
2.   She is referring either to St. Joseph (according to Silverio) or (according to Efrén-Steggink) to San Julián de Cuenca, a native of Palencia.
3.   María de Mendoza, the bishop's sister.
4.   The prioress of Palencia, Isabel de Jesús (Jimena) or Inés de Jesús (Tapia).

371. To Padre Jerónimo Gracián, Alcalá
Palencia, 17 February 1581

Gracián is in Alcalá preparing for the chapter at which the discalced Carmelite friars and nuns will become a separate province. He has sent Teresa a letter to be circulated among the nuns asking for suggestions. Teresa answers in a strictly confidential tone, expressing her opinion about candidates for provincial.

❖❖❖

1.   … Macario,[1] for I don't think he knows how to conceal his temptation. I believe it is very important for that house of nuns[2] that Fray Gabriel[3] should remain in La Roda. I have

already written to you about this. He has bought another house for them—they say it is a very good one—in the middle of the town. I am concerned, for I don't think it has any views or land. Would you inquire about Macario as though on your own initiative, and be kind to him, for he is a good man and has admirable qualities. If he is somewhat unpleasant toward you, I think it is because he is jealous and thinks you have more regard for others than for him.

2.   It has also occurred to me that if you should remain as provincial you ought to chose Padre Nicolao[4] as your companion. For it will be very important in these beginnings that you go about together, although I am not going to say this to the commissary. Since Padre Fray Bartolomé[5] is so sick that he has to eat meat, some are already looking askance at him. At least in these beginning stages, Padre Nicolao, I tell you, would be the right one, and he has good advice to give in all matters. After having suffered so much from others you will enjoy not having anything to suffer from him.

3.   Give my best regards to Padre Fray Bartolomé, who I believe must be very tired because of the way you live, never allowing yourself to rest. It is enough to kill you and anyone who accompanies you. I remember well the bad color of your face a year ago during Holy Week. For goodness' sake don't be in such a hurry to preach sermons this Lent, nor should you eat fish difficult to digest, for although you don't pay attention, it then makes you sick and the temptations come.

4.   You should know that there is still talk about the chapel for Sancho de Avila[6] and that there are learned men who think that despite the gift the right of inheritance remains. I really think there will be a lawsuit. I have said that no action should be taken on the matter until we have a provincial. I am mentioning this to you here—even though it may seem out of place—because it will be necessary that you inform whoever will be provincial not to take any action without going there and to be very careful, for it is important for that house.[7] Sancho

Dávila is now giving more, and the nuns are in such need of the chapel that I think it is something that should be done. But the conditions and many other things should be looked into and studied with me.

5.   Here things are getting better every day, thanks be to God. We are considering a very good house, for the one next to the shrine of our Lady[8] was not suitable. And it was expensive, so we did not take it. This other one is in a very good location. I am feeling better than usual, and all the nuns are well. San Bartolomé and Inés de Jesús[9] send their best regards. The latter says that however much you flee from the trial, you must believe that the prayers of the discalced nuns will prove efficacious and place you in the midst of it.[10] May the Lord guide you to what will be of the greatest service to him; the rest matters little, even though painful.

6.   I wanted to be brief, and look at the result. I don't know how to keep things short with you. I spoke a great deal with Mariano[11] about his temptation to vote for Macario, for he wrote to me about it. I don't understand that man, nor do I want to talk about this matter with anyone other than you. So what I have written about this is for you alone; that's very important. And don't neglect to have recourse to Nicolao and to let them know that you don't want the task for yourself. And truly I don't know how in conscience a vote could be given to anyone of those who will be there other than to either of you two.[12]

7.   I have already sent your letter[13] to the monasteries. All of them are elated, and I even more so. I will send you their comments. If you receive messages from other places, accept the suggestions that seem worthwhile to you; otherwise there is no need to act on them.

May God watch over you and make you as holy as I beg of him, amen.

Today is 17 February.

8.   If we should think of anything else regarding these houses,[14] I will inform you. Surely the work of the chapter will not be over so quickly as to make this impossible.

Your Reverence's unworthy servant and daughter,

Teresa of Jesus

1.   The code name for Antonio de Jesús. The first part of the letter is missing. Macario's temptation involved both his desire to be provincial and his jealousy of Gracián.

2.   The Carmel in Villanueva. After the chapter Padre Gabriel was sent back to La Roda.

3.   Gabriel de la Asunción had been the prior at La Roda and promoter of the foundation of Villanueva de la Jara, which was close to La Roda (F. 28.11).

4.   Nicolás Doria. In fact the chapter did elect him as first definitor and Gracián chose him as his companion.

5.   Bartolomé de Jesús had served as Gracián's secretary, but because of his ill health often had to eat meat.

6.   Sancho Dávila (Teresa calls him Sancho de Avila) was a priest from Alba de Tormes who wanted to fund a chapel for the Carmel there. He later became bishop in various places.

7.   The Carmel of Alba de Tormes.

8.   In fact, the Carmel was eventually founded next to the shrine (see F. 29.13–24).

9.   Ana de San Bartolomé and Inés de Jesús, who had accompanied her from Palencia.

10. The nuns were praying that Gracián would be elected provincial.

11. Mariano de San Benito was set on voting for Antonio de Jesús (Heredia).

12. According to Teresa, Gracián and Doria were the only two who could possibly take on the office of provincial. But, in fact, Antonio de Jesús received strong backing from the chapter members and lost by only one vote to Gracián.

13. This was a circular letter sent to the Carmels asking for suggestions in view of the coming chapter. This letter and the responses passed through Teresa's hands.

14. She wisely provides for the possibility of sending still more suggestions to the chapter regarding the nuns.

372. To Padre Jerónimo Gracián, Alcalá (?)
Palencia, mid-February (?) 1581

In preparation for the coming chapter at Alcalá, Teresa gives some suggestions concerning the enclosure. She did not want to add restrictions that would leave the nuns dissatisfied. She shows much confidence in Gracián's judgment. The date is uncertain and the text is probably incomplete.

❖❖❖❖

1.   Jesus be with your reverence, amen. From this letter you will see what is going on in Alba with its foundress.[1] The nuns have begun to fear her, and she has made them take in postulants. They must be in great need. I don't see any way of reasoning with her. You will have to inquire about everything.

2.   Don't forget to leave orders everywhere about veils and to explain which persons the constitutions are referring to. And this should be done so that the constitutions[2] don't seem stricter than they are. I fear more the nuns' loss of the great joy in which our Lord is leading them than those other things. I know what a discontented nun is. As long as they continue on as they have in the past, there is no reason to restrict them to more than to what they promised.

3.   There is no reason why the confessors should see them with faces unveiled, or the friars of any order, and much less our own discalced friars. You could explain how in the case of an uncle who has care of them, if they have no living father, or that of some close relative, they would have a reason for doing so. Or for a duchess or countess or some eminent person; in sum, where there would be no danger but benefit. And without a reason of this sort, the curtain should not be drawn back.[3] If some other occasion should arise over which there is doubt, permission should be asked from the provincial; otherwise it should never be done. But I fear lest the provincial give it easily. It seems that spiritual guidance could be carried on without having to draw back the curtain. You can look into this.

4.   I have a great desire that some postulant will come to Alba bringing enough to pay something of what has been spent on the construction.[4] May God direct things according to need. Here the nuns are doing well, for they have more than they need in everything. I mean exteriorly because for inner happiness these things are of little use; more of that is found in poverty. May His Majesty give us such understanding, and may he make you very holy, amen.

Your reverence's unworthy servant and subject,

Teresa of Jesus

1.   The foundress was Teresa Layz. On the poverty of the community see Ltr. 371.4.
2.   See CN.15.
3.   A dark curtain was hung on the inside of the grille so that visitors could not see the nuns.
4.   She returns to the subject she began with concerning the Carmel in Alba de Tormes.

373. To Don Pedro Juan de Casademonte, Alcalá
Palencia, February 1581

(Autograph: S. Salvador, Ejea [Zaragosa])

Pedro Juan de Casademonte was appointed by the king to be present and collaborate at the chapter in Alcalá. He was probably already in Alcalá. He had offered to send reports of the events to Teresa.

❖❖❖❖

1.   Jesus. The grace of the Holy Spirit be with your honor, and may he give you spiritual and bodily health. We are all praying with concern for this, and there is no reason for you to thank us, because it is our obligation to do so. And we are doing the same for Señora Doña María.[1] I earnestly ask for her prayers, and may our Lord repay you for the good news you are always sending me.

2.   Now I am waiting each day for the news that is lacking and should be here without delay. I am certain there will be no want of diligence on your part to inform us soon. Indeed it makes us praise our Lord that you never tire of doing us acts of favor and charity.

3.   I already wrote you that I received the packet of letters from our Father Provincial, Fray Angel,[2] and that I answered him. Now I am writing to him again. If he is not there, would you have the letters forwarded with special care when a messenger is available. It doesn't matter if you don't receive a reply; there is no reason to ask for one.

4.   I have not been very well, having the usual ailments. Now I am better and am happy to see the joy those Fathers of mine[3] will have. May it please our Lord that I see them content with everything and that the meeting will enable us to render him great service.

5.   I beg you that when you see Señor Juan López de Velasco[4] you tell him that yesterday I received his letter by way of Valladolid and that it would be better if letters were ordinarily addressed here because the postmaster[5] is a friend of mine, and that I will do what you ask. I think I have a good deal to do here now for some days, but even if not, I don't think I will leave—unless obedience orders me otherwise—until I see our affairs completed. May God bring this about, as he can, and may he watch over you and give you the temporal and spiritual rest that I and all the nuns beg of him.

6.   Madre Inés de Jesús[6] asks for your prayers. Pardon the fact that this is not written in her hand. I was happy to have had the time to write myself, and I wish this were always so.

From Palencia in this house of St. Joseph,

     Your honor's servant,

                                        Teresa of Jesus

----

1.   Casademonte's wife.
2.   Angel de Salazar, named vicar general for the discalced Carmelites by the nuncio, Sega.

3. The discalced Carmelite Fathers gathered for the chapter in Alcalá.
4. A secretary of Philip II.
5. Diego de Reinoso in Palencia.
6. When prioress in Medina, Inés de Jesús became a friend of Casademonte's. She accompanied Teresa on the foundation in Palencia.

374. To Padre Jerónimo Gracián, Alcalá
Palencia, February 1581

(Autograph fragment: DCN, Corpus Christi, Alcalá de Henares)

Teresa continues to give her suggestions for the coming chapter in Alcalá. She has eight points to make concerning the nuns' constitutions. As for who might be elected provincial, she also has suggestions and urges Gracián not to withdraw his name. The letter is incomplete and the date uncertain.

1.   I consider it very important that vicars[1] not also be confessors to the nuns, and this should be always so. It is imperative for these houses that the nuns have the friars as confessors, as you say and I myself see. I would support having things remain as they are rather than grant that each confessor be also the vicar. There are so many drawbacks to this, as I will explain to you when I see you. I beg you to trust me in this matter, for when St. Joseph's was founded much attention was given to it.[2] And one of the reasons it seemed to some persons, myself included, that it was good that the monastery be subject to the bishop was to avoid this practice. There are serious disadvantages that result from it, as I have learned. And for me one is enough: I have seen clearly that if the vicar likes some nun, the prioress cannot prevent him from talking to her as much as he wants, for he is the superior. This can result in a thousand woes.

2.   For this reason, and for many others, it is also necessary that they not be subject to the priors. It will happen that someone

who doesn't know much will give orders that are disturbing to all the nuns. There won't be anyone like *mi padre* Gracián, and since we have so much experience, we have to look ahead and remove the risks. The greatest good that can be done for these nuns is that no talking with the confessor take place other than what is necessary for the confession of sins. As for safeguarding the recollection of the monastery, it is enough that the confessor inform the provincial.

3.   I have said all this in case someone else or Father Commissary[3] may think otherwise. But I don't believe this will happen, for in his order the nuns in many places have confessors who are not their vicars. Our entire existence depends on our keeping out these wicked devotees, destroyers of the brides of Christ. It is necessary always to think of the worst that can happen in order to remove this occasion of sin, for the devil enters here without our realizing it. This is what can do us harm and that I always fear – as well as our taking in too large a number of nuns. So I beg you to insist that these two things remain firmly fixed in our constitutions.[4] Do me this favor.

4.   I don't know why you say we should be silent in regard to the friars being our confessors, for you see how bound we are by the constitutions of Padre Fray Pedro Fernández,[5] and I confess that it is necessary that we be so. Nor do I understand why you must not speak about matters concerning us. I tell you that I have so stressed in my letter the benefit we derive from your visitations—and this is true—that you can readily discuss anything you like in order to help us. You really owe this to these nuns, for you cost them many tears. I would prefer that no one speak of these matters but you and Padre Nicolao,[6] for it is not necessary that our constitutions or that which you ordain for us be dealt with in the chapter or that the others be informed of them. Only between ourselves did Padre Fernández[7] (may he be in glory) and I discuss these matters. And even though some of the eight things that I set down at the beginning seem unimportant, you should realize that they are very important.[8]

So, I would not want you to remove any of them. In what regards nuns I can have a say, for I have seen many things

5.   You should know that I wanted to arrange to ask Father Prior and the commissary to appoint masters and *presentados* from those among you who are qualified. This is necessary for some matters and so as not to need to have recourse to the general.[9] But since you say that the commissary has no further authority than to assist at the chapter and draw up constitutions, I let the matter go.

6.   It seems they have not granted all that was asked for. It would have been good if they had and done away for some years with any need for us to have recourse to Rome. It will be necessary that you write at once to the general, giving him an account of what is taking place. The letter should be a humble one, submitting to him as his subjects, which is right. And you should write as well to Fray Angel[10] – for you owe it to him – thanking him for the good things he has done for you and asking him to always consider you his son; and be sure to do this!

7.   Now let us deal with what you say of your wish not to be elected or confirmed; in this regard I am writing to Father Commissary. You should know, *mi padre*, that regarding the desire I have had to see you free, I clearly understand that the love I have for you in the Lord is much more at work than the good of the order. From this proceeds a natural weakness that causes me to suffer greatly in seeing that not all understand how much they owe you and how much you have labored; I cannot bear to hear even a word spoken against you. But in considering what could result from this, I see that the general good carries more weight. If, however, Padre Nicolao were elected and then always accompanied by you, I think both wishes could be satisfied. But I truly believe that for this first time it would be better in all respects for you to hold the office, and so I am telling this to Father Commissary. And if this cannot be, then Padre Nicolao accompanied by you would be best

because of your experience and knowledge of your subjects, both the friars and the nuns. I tell you that it is for his lack of experience that we consider Macario unsuited to the task. I am giving you good reasons for it all, and I tell you that Padre Fray Pedro Fernández thought this as well, although he did desire very much Macario's election for reasons valid at that time. But now—the damage he would do!

8. I also included the name of Padre Fray Juan de Jesús so that it wouldn't seem that I am limiting myself to only two; although I told the truth in saying that Padre Juan de Jesús didn't have the gift of governing – since in my opinion he doesn't – but that if he had one of the other two for his companion he could pass, for he listens to reason and would take counsel. And so I believe that if you went around with him, he would in no way distance himself from what you tell him; thus I believe he would do well. But I am sure he would not receive the votes. May God so direct things that whatever is for his greater honor and glory will come about, which is what I hope for, seeing that he has already done the greater part. It is a great pity ...

---

1. Vicars were superiors who had authority over a community of nuns, delegated by either the ordinary or the provincial. Teresa did not want vicars for her communities (see W.5.6; V.39).

2. See W.5.7.

3. Juan de las Cuevas, the commissary who presided over the chapter in Alcalá.

4. Gracián complied with this request (see the CN, 1581, 6.2; and 2.8–10).

5. She is referring to decisions made by Pedro Fernández at the time when he was the apostolic visitator (see MHCT 1:114–117).

6. Nicolás Doria.

7. She mentions this again in Ltr. 376.4.

8. Teresa must have written to the chapter or to the commissary stressing the effectiveness of Gracian's official visitations of the discalced Carmels of nuns. It is not certain whether these eight points were in that letter or at the beginning of this letter, which is a fragment.

9. Giovanni Battista Rossi. The brief Pia consideratione did not grant the presider at the chapter the powers to confer the degrees of master and *presentado* as Teresa wanted.
10. Angel de Salazar, who had been acting as vicar general of the discalced friars and nuns.

375. To Padre Jerónimo Gracián, Alcalá
Palencia, End of February 1581

These are fragments that could probably have come from different letters.

❧❧❦❦

1.   … Give my best regards to Padre Fray Antonio[1] and tell him that the letter I wrote him did not deserve to go unanswered and that since it seems I am speaking to a deaf-mute, I do not wish to write to him. He must be very happy to send Padre Mariano[2] a share of his benefices. May this provide those fathers with more to eat than usual. I tell you that if a remedy for this state of affairs is not found everywhere, you will see where things will end up. One must not neglect to give orders in this regard, for God will never fail to provide what is necessary. If you give them little, he will give little …

2.   … For the love of God, be sure that the beds are clean as well as the table napkins, no matter how much you spend, for it is a terrible thing if cleanliness is not provided. In fact I would like to see this prescribed in the constitutions, and I don't think doing that would even be enough, since …

3.   Oh, what distress these envelopes that address me as reverend cause me. I would like you to remove this title from all your subjects, seeing that it is not necessary in order to know who the letter is for. There is no reason, in my opinion, that among ourselves we be using words of honor that can be avoided …

4.   … Insist on the use of the veil everywhere, for goodness' sake. Say that the discalced nuns themselves have asked for this, as is true, although there is recollection …

5.   ... Please God, *mi padre*, that these houses will not have the great misfortune of being deprived of your presence, for they need the kind of direction that pays close attention to details and someone who understands everything. May His Majesty watch over them; they are your servants.

1.   Antonio de Jesús (Heredia).
2.   Mariano de San Benito, Padre Antonio's close friend.

376. To Padre Jerónimo Gracián, Alcalá
Palencia, 21 February 1581

Teresa continues writing of her concerns about the coming chapter of separation to take place in Alcalá. She has received and reviewed recommendations from different Carmels and is sending them to Gracián. She adds some other new ones of her own for the commissary, and also shows concern about the life of the discalced friars.

1.   Jesus. May the Holy Spirit be with you, *mi padre*. I received the letter you wrote me from Alcalá and was delighted with all that you told me in it, especially that you are in good health. May God be praised, for he shows me great mercy after so many travels and so much work. I am well.

2.   I have written to you by two different routes and sent my recommendations to give the appearance of being somebody. I had forgotten what I have now mentioned in the enclosed letter to Father Commissary.[1] You may read it. So as not to tire myself by writing it out again I am sending you the letter without sealing it. Seal it with a seal that looks like mine, and give it to him .

3.   The prioress of Segovia has reminded me of the freedom we have to invite preachers from outside the order.[2] I had omit-ted this, thinking that it was already a given. But, *mi padre*, we must not consider those who are living at present, but at a later

time some persons could come along who in being made superiors will oppose such freedom and many other things. So do us the favor to strive that this and what I wrote the other day be clearly understood and established through the commissary's authority. For if this isn't done, one will have to have recourse to Rome. I understand the great importance this has for these nuns and their consolation, and how disconsolate they become in other monasteries when held spiritually bound. Souls that are restrained cannot serve God well, and the devil uses this restraint to tempt them. But when they have some freedom, they often pay no attention to it and make no use of it.

4.   If Father Commissary can amend the constitutions and add to them, I would like to see things removed and added in accordance with what we are now requesting. And no one will do this unless you and Padre Nicolao[3] take it very much to heart. As you say and I believe I wrote in my letter to you, the friars should not have a say in our affairs, nor did Padre Fray Pedro Fernández give them any. Between the two of us we came to an agreement about the decrees he set down, and he didn't do anything without telling me about it. I am grateful to him for this.

5.   If it be possible to make new constitutions or remove and add, remember in regard to the "stockings of rough wool or cloth made from rough tow"[4] that nothing be specified or said more than that they should wear stockings so that the nuns won't be having scruples. And where it says "the toques should be made of fine tow" say "linen." And if you think it appropriate, remove the decree made by Padre Fray Pedro Fernández where he says that they should not eat eggs or have bread for collation.[5] I could never succeed in getting him not to do this. It is enough for the nuns to satisfy the obligation of the church without adding anything, for they become scrupulous and it does them harm. For some don't think they have a need when they do.

6.   They have told us that the general chapter has now ordained many things about the prayers we recite and that we

should have two ferias each week.[6] If possible, put it down that we are not obliged to make so many changes, but that we can continue praying as we do now.

Also remember the many drawbacks to having discalced Carmelite friars living in one of the monasteries of the other Carmelites. If possible, say that when the discalced Carmelites have a place where they can stay in a completely edifying way, they don't have to reside in a monastery of the order.[7]

7.   Our constitutions say that our monasteries should be founded in poverty and not have an income. Since I now see that they are all on the way to having an income, consider if it would not be better to remove this and anything else in the constitutions that might refer to it so that no one on seeing them will think our monasteries have grown lax so quickly.[8] Or, Father Commissary could say that since the council[9] gives permission for an income, we should allow for one.

8.   I would like to have these constitutions put into print, for different renderings of them are going about. There are prioresses who when copying them – and without thinking they are doing anything wrong – add or delete whatever they like. A strict, unmistakable precept should be set down against deleting or adding to the constitutions. In all these little things do what seems best to you, I mean in dealing with what concerns us. Also Padre Nicolao should be involved so that it doesn't seem that you are doing this on your own; and even Padre Juan de Jesús,[10] I believe, will consider kindly what concerns us. I would like to enlarge, but it's almost nightfall and they will be coming to get the letters, and I must still write to some friends.

9.   I was deeply moved by what you promised to be for the discalced Carmelite nuns if elected provincial. At least you will be a true father, and they will certainly be grateful to you. And if you were to live for ever and they were to deal with no one else, there would be no need to be making some of these requests. How anxious they are for you to become provincial.

I don't think anything else will satisfy them. May God watch over you for us. All the nuns ask for your prayers.

Today is 21 February.

> Your paternity's true daughter,
>
> Teresa of Jesus

10. They brought me the enclosed recommendations. When they send me the others, I will forward them. I don't know if they are acceptable, but it was indeed necessary for you to say that they should pass through my hands. May God keep you. Only the recommendation made by your friend Isabel de Santo Domingo[11] was well done, and I am sending it as is.

---

1. Juan de las Cuevas, the presider at the chapter.
2. Isabel de Santo Domingo, who had sent Teresa her recommendations for the chapter (see W. 5.1–2).
3. Nicolás Doria.
4. See CN. 12. In the constitutions revised at the chapter in Alcalá (1581), this request and the following one were granted (see BMC 6:431).
5. Padre Fernández had prescribed that on church fast days and Fridays (except during Easter time) the nuns should not eat eggs or milk products, and that on church fast days they not eat bread at collation (MHCT 1:115–16). This request of Teresa's was not granted.
6. This was a chapter of the Carmelite order celebrated in Rome the previous year.
7. This suggestion by Teresa was accepted (see BMC 6:474).
8. C. 9. Teresa's request in this regard was accepted (see BMC 6: 430).
9. The Council of Trent, session 25, ch. 3.
10. Juan de Jesús (Roca). Gracián, Doria, and Roca were the three names Teresa submitted as possible candidates for provincial (see Ltr. 374. 7–8).
11. The prioress in Segovia (see no. 3).

377. To Padre Jerónimo Gracián, Alcala
Palencia, 27 February 1581

(Autograph: part 1: Ponciano Herero, Querétaro [Mexico]; part 2: DCN: Monteverde, Rome; part 3: DCN: Antignano [Italy])

Teresa has received the last batch of recommendations for the chapter and is sending them on to Padre Gracián, adding some further suggestions of her own for the revision of the constitutions. She is a little fearful that some of her letters have gone astray or, worst of all, that Gracián might be a little careless about where he leaves the letters she has written him, so they be read by someone else.

❖ ❖ ❖ ❖

1.   Jesus be with your reverence, *mi padre*. I realize that you have little time now for reading letters. Please God I will know how to be brief with this.

2.   Here are the recommendations that were lacking.[1] You did well in saying that they should be sent here first along with the nuns' requests, for those from the nuns at St. Joseph's in Avila are such that there would be no longer a difference between them and the nuns at the Incarnation. I am frightened by what the devil is doing, and it is the confessor[2] who is most to blame, despite his being so good. But he has always had it in his head that the nuns should eat meat, and this was one of the requests they made. Imagine that!

3.   It has caused me much distress to see how that house has strayed and it will take a great deal of effort to get it to return to its true state, even though there are very good nuns in it. And to add to this, they are asking Father Provincial, Fray Angel,[3] to allow some nuns who have poor health to keep something in their cells to eat. And they are asking him in such a way that I wouldn't be surprised if he gave it to them. You can guess who encouraged them to ask Fray Angel! This is the way things get started, and little by little everything deteriorates. Such is the reason for the prescription at my request that superiors not be

allowed to give the nuns permission to keep anything in their cells.[4] It is necessary that this prescription have some force to it, even when a nun is sick. In that case the infirmarian can leave something at night for the one who has need. And there should be the greatest charity about this when the sickness calls for it.

4.   I forgot to mention this, but others who have written reminded me: your chapter should decide on the prayers the friars should say for a nun when she dies. We will do the same, for they only recite prayers, and so far, I think, do not say Mass for us. What they do here is offer a sung Mass and an office for the dead recited by the community. I think this comes from the old constitutions,[5] for this is what was done at the Incarnation.

5.   Don't forget this. And also consider whether we have an obligation to observe the *motu proprio* that we not to go into the church, not even to lock the door.[6] This is what should be done when possible, for it is the safest thing to do even if the pope hadn't given the orders. It is better that it be set down now, and where it is not possible because the house is just beginning that it be followed in the future. But I believe it will be followed in all our houses, for they now know that they must not do otherwise. Don't neglect to do this, for goodness' sake. In Toledo they have already locked the door that leads into the church, as well as in Segovia – without even telling me – and these two prioresses[7] are servants of God and cautious. And since I am neither, I want them to keep me attentive. Well, this is done in all enclosed monasteries.

6.   Regarding the request I made that those who set out for a new foundation remain there, unless they hold the office of prioress in their own house: the statement is too short. Do me the favor of adding "or for some other important reason ."[8]

7.   I believe I have already asked you to put the constitutions and all the acts of the apostolic visitators together, which would be good. For since the two make some contradictory statements in certain matters, the nuns who are less educated

get confused. Although you have a lot to do, be careful, for the love of God, to take the time to make things plain and clear. Since I have written to you about this in so many letters, I fear lest you find yourself swamped in words and forget the better part.

8.   Since you have not informed me of having received any of my letters, I have the temptation to think the devil has plotted to prevent the substance of my notes to reach you as well as the letters I wrote to Father Commissary.[9] If this should be so, would you send me a private courier at once, and I will repay you, for it would be terrible if you didn't receive them. I truly believe this is a temptation because the courier here is a good friend of ours,[10] and he recommended that the bundle be delivered with great care.

9.   You should know I have been informed that some of those voting want Padre Macario[11] to be elected. If God does this after so much prayer, it will be for the best; his judgments are his own. One of those who now tell me this was, from what I saw, inclined to vote for Padre Nicolao,[12] and if they change they will vote for him. May God direct it all and watch over you. However badly things might go, what is essential at any rate has been accomplished. May he be praised forever.

10.   I would like it if you wrote down on a separate piece of paper the important points of what I wrote you and burn my letters, for in the midst of all that confusion someone might chance upon one of them, and that would be terrible.

11.   All the sisters here send their best regards, especially my companions.[13]

Tomorrow is the last day of the month. I believe today is the 27th.

We are doing well here, and each day gets better. We have begun negotiations for a house in a very good location. I have been wanting to be free of my duties here so as not to be so far away.

12. See that you do not place any obstacle in the way of the foundation at St. Alexis.[14] For the present, even though it may be a little far away, they will not find so good a site. It pleased me very much when I passed by there, and that woman[15] paid with her tears. I would like this monastery to be the first, and then the one in Salamanca,[16] for they are good places. They shouldn't think they can be choosy before making the foundation, for they don't have any money. Afterward God will provide. In Salamanca, houses are worth their weight in gold. We don't know what to do about finding one for the nuns. Believe me, for goodness' sake, for I have experience. And, as I say, God will bring everything to a good end. Even though you have only a little nook, it is important in a place like that to get started. May His Majesty bring everything to the conclusion necessary for his service, amen.

Your paternity's unworthy subject and servant,

Teresa of Jesus

13. I would very much like to see this matter of St. Alexis attended to at once so that apart from the main reason for doing so you would be close by. But they cannot come until they have arranged to receive a license from the abbot. The bishop is on better terms with him, and his sister will give the guarantee. Tell those fathers for me that they ought to begin the negotiations, for if they spend a lot of time in the beginning looking for a good site, they will end up with nothing.

---

1. The suggestions made by the nuns for the chapter, which will be dealing also with their affairs.
2. Julián de Avila.
3. Angel de Salazar.
4. This was forbidden in the constitutions, nos. 10 & 26.
5. See the constitutions of the Incarnation (BMC 9:484–85) and Teresa's own (no. 33).
6. De sacris virginibus of Gregory XIII (30 Dec. 1572). Enclosed nuns were not allowed to enter the public church or chapel of the monastery to lock or unlock the door of the church. This prescription was included in the constitutions of Alcalá, 1581(ch. 3, no. 3).

7. Ana de los Angeles (prioress in Toledo) and Isabel de Santo Domingo (prioress in Segovia).
8. See CN (1581), ch. 2, no.7.
9. Juan de las Cuevas.
10. The chief courier in Palencia, Diego de Reinoso.
11. Antonio de Jesús (Heredia).
12. Nicolás Doria.
13. Ana de San Bartolomé and Inés de Jesús.
14. See Ltr. 303.3. Gracián brought this foundation about right after the chapter.
15. The hermitess who took care of the shrine.
16. A foundation for the discalced friars in Salamanca was also in the planning stage.

378. To Doña Ana Enríquez, Valladolid
Palencia, 4 March 1581

While Teresa was busy with the foundation in Palencia, the chapter for the separation of the discalced Carmelites into a separate province was taking place in Alcalá. The very day this letter was written, Padre Jerónimo Gracián was elected provincial. Doña Ana had congratulated Teresa on the news about the chapter and sent her a statue for the new foundation in Palencia. Teresa is planning to go to Burgos.

1.　Jesus. May the Holy Spirit be with your honor. If I had written you as was my desire, I would not have waited for the favor of your letter before writing to you – I would have written several letters by now. But I have had so many to write these days and so much business to tend to, along with the setting up of a province and my poor health, that I don't know how I kept my head.

2.　Mother Prioress,[1] María Bautista, has written me of your joy over the favor God has shown us in regard to our becoming a separate province. And it wasn't necessary for her to do so. I already know that even if this favor didn't concern those who are such servants of yours, it would be enough that it have to do with the service of God for you to be happy, since you belong to his house and kingdom. I tell you this favor has brought me great relief, for it seems we will have peace from here on, which is a wonderful thing. And those who have begun this journey will not be impeded by having superiors so different from them, but they will have their own superiors who will understand what they must do. May he be blessed forever.

3. I don't know when I will be able to see that you have something that brings you happiness. It seems to me that God wants to hold everything back so that your happiness will be greater in that eternity that will have no end. And your poor health is not the least of your trials. Now, since the good weather is coming, perhaps you will feel some improvement. May the Lord bring this about as he can. Once that pain in my side left me, I have felt better, but I don't know how long this will last.

4. Here, things are going very well, and with each day one understands better how right it was to make this foundation here. The people are charitable and straightforward, without duplicity, which I like very much. And the bishop[2] (God watch over him) is just right for us; it is unusual the way he favors us. I ask you to remember him at times in your prayers to our Lord.

5. You have honored us greatly with the statue you donated, which stands alone on the main altar, and it is so well-done and large that there is no need for others.

6. We brought a very good prioress here,[3] and nuns that, in my opinion, are also very good. So, the house seems as though it was founded a good time ago. Nonetheless, regarding matters of the soul, I feel alone, for there is no one here that I know from the Society. Truly, I feel alone everywhere, because before, even when our saint[4] was far away, it seems he was a companion to me, because he still communicated with me through letters. Well, we are in exile, and it is good that we feel this life to be one.

7.   What do you think of how honorably Fray Domingo Bañez[5] managed to receive his chair? May it please God to watch over him, for there aren't many left like him. There will be no lack of work with this, for it is a very costly honor.

8.   I beg you to give Señora Doña María[6] my best regards. I long to see her in good health, but my prayers are of no value except to add to people's trials. You can see for yourself whether this is not true.

9.   I beg you to tell Padre García Manrique,[7] if he is there, that I would like very much to have him here, and not to forget me in his prayers.

10.   We never succeed in buying this house, and I certainly desire to do so, for if God be served, I would like to go to Burgos,[8] since the good weather is coming, so as to return quickly and have more time to stay with you .

11.   May His Majesty work this out, as he can, and give you much spiritual consolation during this holy time, since you are so far it seems from having any temporal consolation. I kiss the hands of Señor Don Luis.[9] I beg God to make him very holy.

From this house of St. Joseph's. Today is 4 March.

Your unworthy servant and subject,

Teresa of Jesus

---

1.   The prioress in Valladolid.
2.   The bishop of Palencia, Alvaro de Mendoza.
3.   A prioress for Palencia, Isabel de Jesús (Jimena), brought from Salamanca.
4.   The Jesuit, Baltasar Alvarez, who had been Doña Ana's confessor and guide as well as Teresa's. He had died 25 July 1580.
5.   She is referring to Báñez's success in the tight competition for the chair of Prime at the university of Salamanca on 20 February 1581.
6.   María de Mendoza.
7.   A go-between for Teresa in the purchase of the house in Salamanca.
8.   Before Burgos, she will go to Soria to make a foundation there.
9.   Luis Fernández de Córdoba, Doña Ana's husband.

379. To Agustín Ahumada, Perú (?)
Toward Spring 1581

This is all that remains of the correspondence between Teresa and her youngest brother. We know through Lorenzo de Cepeda that she sent him a number of messages. This text comes from Jerónimo de San José's Historia del Carmen Descalzo *(Madrid: Francisco Martínez, 1637). The message so frightened Agustín that he returned to Spain.*

❖❖❖❖

My brother, do not accept the position, for our Lord has made it known to me that should you accept it and die in it, you will be condemned.

380. To Padre Jerónimo Gracián
Palencia, 12 March 1581

(Autograph: DCN, Corpus Christi, Alcalá de Henares)

Though Teresa requested that this letter be torn up, only the first part is missing. Gracián had been provincial of the discalced Carmelites since 4 March, and Teresa brings up some matters needing his attention. She also asks him to visit and encourage her nephew in Madrid, who hastened into marriage shortly after leaving the novitiate of the discalced Carmelites. She wonders how the chapter might have affected Padre Antonio de Jesús, who was a close contender for provincial.

❖❖❖❖

1.   … not to displease the prioress[1] because her nuns are very much in accord, and she wouldn't want to introduce a note of discord. In Medina there are many melancholic nuns. But her presence would be disturbing anywhere; and I am not surprised. Although, in the end, the nuns are supposed to help one another, it doesn't seem appropriate for a foundation

just beginning. I was thinking of bringing her to Burgos, not as foundress but as a penitent,[2] for if God wills that a foundation be made there, I plan to leave Inés de Jesús as prioress.[3] She would much prefer to go there than to Madrid, although she dislikes being prioress anywhere. And the subprioress[4] in Valladolid can go as subprioress. This will be pleasing to them both. And, after all, these two know her and will proceed prudently, but Inés de Jesús will find it very difficult. For love of God, think of what might be the best solution, for it is necessary to prescribe a remedy at once before she's lost. She hasn't left her cell, nor would it be good if she did.

2.   Because I believe you will have many things to do, I don't think it would be wise for me to go on at length, and for the same reason I have not allowed Mother Prioress[5] to write to you. Carry on as though you have received that letter. She sends her best regards, and I send mine to Padre Mariano[6] and all the others.

3.   If you go to Madrid I would like you to do me the favor of going to see Don Francisco and his wife[7] since he would not dare, being so timid, go to see you. He has written to me of how happy he is for having done what he did. You could encourage him in the service of God and not let it seem that because he gave up on being a friar you are disgusted with him. Because of poor management on his part, I think he is going to suffer a great loss, and I tell you that the marriage is not a good one. I would love to withdraw from all of them, but the mother-in-law[8] has befriended me and is asking me things I am obliged to answer, which is very wearisome to me. But he was running the risk of total ruin because she learned that he was receiving an income of two thousand ducats. I told her the truth so that they will be careful about what they are spending. Padre Fray Angel[9] went to see them at once without my asking him, and so it will seem, as I say, ill-will on your part not to pay him a visit. May our Lord watch over you.

4.   See that you do not fail to write me—you know what a comfort your letters are for me—and at length; tell me how Macario[10] has been, and tear this letter up.

5.   We have not yet managed to buy the house; we are in the process of doing so. I have brought two lay sisters[11] without any other authorization than my patent letters—for this is what I usually did so as not to have to ask someone who would be presiding for so short a time. I praise God greatly that he[12] is as good as you say and has done everything so well.

Today is 12 March.

> Your reverence's servant, daughter, and subject—and how willingly!

> Teresa of Jesus

6.   I am doing well, except for the usual ailments. I cannot find Juliana's letter. It is all about her not wanting to return to the Incarnation, for she thinks it would amount to regressing. If she wrote, it is because she thought the prioress and I wanted her to return. There is no need to pay any attention to what she says.

---

1.   She is probably referring to the prioress in Valladolid, Maria Bautista.

2.   Perhaps she is referring to Juliana de la Magdalena, the daughter of Nicolás Gutiérrez (see F. 19.2). Juliana came from the Incarnation in Avila and lived in the discalced Carmels of Valladolid, Segovia, Pamplona, and again Valladolid.

3.   Inés de Jesús remained in Palencia as prioress. Tomasina Bautista became the prioress for Burgos.

4.   Dorotea de la Cruz became the subprioress in Palencia.

5.   The prioress of Palencia (Isabel de Jesús Jimena).

6.   Ambrosio Mariano de San Benito and the members of the chapter, for the meeting will continue until 17 March.

7.   Her nephew Francisco de Cepeda and Orofrisia de Mendoza, who were recently married.

8.   Francisco's mother-in-law, Beatriz de Castilla y Mendoza.

9.   Angel de Salazar.

10. Code name for Antonio de Jesús (Heredia), who came close to being elected provincial.
11. Juana de San Lorenzo and Jerónima de la Visitación.
12. The apostolic commissary, Juan de las Cuevas, whose presidency terminated at the conclusion of the chapter at Alcalá.

381. To Madre María Bautista, Valladolid
Palencia, March 1581?

This fragment is of an uncertain date. The estimated date has been moved from July 1577 to March 1581 as more likely in view of the reference to Ana Enríquez.

❖ ❖ ❖ ❖

For my daughter, María Bautista, Valladolid.

1.   … I am very sorry and feel greatly distressed in seeing that the devil is striving in every way he can to do us harm. May our Lord set things right and give you good health, which is what matters.

2.   I was sorry about the illness of María de la Cruz.[1] God must want you to be a saint since he gives you the cross in so many ways. Those who suffer the illness she thinks she has never have a fever or that nausea, but appear to be strong and in good health.

3.   The confessor did her great harm by not understanding her; I saw that. Inform the chaplain about this for me and give him my best. And do not allow Estefanía[2] those times of solitude and fasting, if you don't want to end up with another similar case.

4.   Doña Ana Enríquez[3] has just written me, and I have felt very sorry about her trials. Well, this is the path on which those who want to enjoy him must walk, for it is the one he took. May he be with you and watch over you for me, amen.

---

1. María de la Cruz was one of the first nuns at St. Joseph's in Avila. Sickly and scrupulous, she went to the foundation in Valladolid in 1568.

2. Estafanía de los Apóstoles, a lay sister in Valladolid who had a bent toward excessive penances.

3. The daughter of the marquises of Alcañices.

382. To Don Jerónimo Reinoso, Palencia
Palencia, Middle of March 1581

(Autograph: DCN, Calahorra [Logroño])

Jerónimo Reinoso was a canon in Palencia who was a great help to Teresa when she made her foundation in that city (F. 29.9–27). He served as both her confessor and aid in choosing and purchasing a suitable house. At a time when all were leaning toward the purchase of Tamayo's house, she sent him this message early in the morning thanking him for his services from the day before and telling him not to buy Tamayo's house but the little one next to it, or at least rent it. Shortly afterward, during Mass, the Lord told her to buy another house, the one previously rejected, near the shrine of Our Lady of the Street (F. 29.18).

❧ ❧ ❦ ❦

1. Jesus. The grace of the Holy Spirit be with your honor. I beg you to tell the one who delivers this letter how you fared last night and if you are very tired. I returned not tired but very happy, and the more I think about the house, the more convinced I am that the other one did not suit us because for our purposes only the courtyard was usable. And if the other little house is sold to us,[1] the nuns will be able to live there well for many years; indeed, very well. I beg you then to try to get this little house. And if it is not for sale, see if they will rent it to us for a few years, since it would be needed by the woman who serves us.

2. You could tell Tamayo[2] that to buy just his house you would have to pay more for it and that we wouldn't be able to pay for the two together except over a period of time. If you agree, it is better that he not know that he displeased us but

that he think that at some time in the future we will be able to buy his house. One of the sisters made the witty remark that in Holy Week the two will become friends again and that thus the purchase must be concluded at once.

3.   The prioress[3] and sisters kiss your hands for having found them so good a house. They are very happy and are right because everything is very suited to our needs. And it is a great thing for them to see that they will be able to expand by buying more land. It would be great if after Easter[4] we could begin to tear down walls. May the Lord bring this about and watch over your honor as all the nuns beg of him.

Your honor's unworthy servant,

Teresa of Jesus

1.   See F. 29.15.
2.   Sebastián Tamayo was a canon in Palencia whose house Teresa was thinking of buying (see F.29.14).
3.   The prioress in Palencia, Isabel de Jesús (Jimena) who had come from Salamanca.
4.   Easter fell on 26 March that year. They didn't move into their new house until the end of May.

383. To Don Alonso Velázquez, Burgo de Osma
     Palencia, 21 March 1581

At the complicated moment in which Teresa had to disentangle herself from the purchase of one house so as to buy another one which she had previously rejected, a letter arrived from the bishop of Osma requesting her to make a foundation in Soria. Before doing so, she would have to bring to a conclusion the foundation she was working on and postpone the Burgos plan.

❖ ❖ ❖ ❖

1.   Jesus. The grace of the Holy Spirit be with your lordship. Although I have desired to write you a long letter, I have not

been fortunate enough to find the time, even though the gentleman who brought your letter and came one day to see me did not fail to remind me. You favor me in every way. I have written you by a different route and believe you will by now have received the letter. At present there is nothing new except a further complication[1] about a house which makes me fear I will have to stay here this summer.

2.   Regarding the matter you wrote me about, even though it seems good for all of us, I don't know if I want to see you in the midst of the trials that accompany these things, which are terrible.[2] Entrust it all to the Lord; His Majesty will guide you.

3.   I am well; and it seems our affairs[3] are going well. Please God, you will be well always. I am being so pressed to hurry that I cannot say more.

Today is Tuesday of Holy Week.

Your unworthy servant and subject,

Teresa of Jesus

1.   Teresa had decided against buying the houses near Our Lady of the Street and to buy others when an interior voice told her to purchase the former.

2.   The matter concerned a foundation in Soria, which it seems was the subject of the letter written to her by Velázquez.

3.   She is referring to the good results of the chapter that was held in March in Alcalá. She followed the proceedings with great interest from Palencia (see F. 29. 30–33.).

384. To Padre Jerónimo Gracián

Palencia, 23–24 March 1581

It is Holy Thursday and Teresa had received the previous day information from Gracián about the chapter in Alcalá. She would like to have the new constitutions for the nuns printed and asks Padre Gracián, now provincial, if he could transfer Fray John of the Cross back to Castile. She describes her recent

*hesitations over the purchase of a house in Palencia and tells
of the nuns' joy at having Gracián as their new provincial.*

❖·❖·❖·❖

1.   Jesus be with your paternity and reward you for the
consolation you have given me with the information you sent,
especially for letting me see the printed brief.[1] All that was lacking for everything to be complete was to have the constitutions[2]
printed as well. God will provide, for I am well aware that the
work must have been difficult for you. It could not have been
easy to put all this in order. May he be blessed who gives you
so much talent for everything. This whole affair seems like a
dream. For even though we would have had to think hard about
what to do, we wouldn't have succeeded in doing anything as
well as God has. May he be always praised for everything.

2.   I still have hardly read anything, for I do not understand
what is in Latin and have to wait both for a translator and until
Holy Week is over. Yesterday, the Wednesday of Tenebrae,
they gave me the things you sent. So as to have a head capable
of assisting at these services, and since we are few, I did not
dare push myself to do any more than read the letters. I would
like to know where you are thinking of going after your stay in
Madrid, for I will always need to know where you are in case
something arises.

3.   You should know that I have been looking for a house here,
and still am, and nothing is found except very expensive ones,
with a lot of defects. So, I think we will take the houses that are
close to Our Lady despite the disadvantages. If the chapter[3] gives
some large corrals that are there, which with time we will have
the means to buy, we can prepare a good vegetable garden. The
church is built and endowed with two chaplancies. The price
has been reduced four hundred ducats, and I believe they will
reduce it further. I tell you that I am amazed by the virtue shown
in this place. The people give much in alms, and since it will only
be necessary that the nuns have enough to eat – the expenses
for the upkeep of the church being many – I think it will be one

of the best houses you have. By removing some upper galleries, they say the cloister will be brighter. As for rooms, there are more than necessary. May God be served there, and may he watch over you. This is not a day for me to go on at length, since it is Good Friday.

4.   I forgot to ask you for something, as an Easter treat; please God you will do it. You should know that up until now in consoling Fray John of the Cross[4] for the suffering he endures living in Andalusia (for he cannot bear those people), I told him that as soon as God let us become a separate province I would see to it that he got back up here. Now he asks me to keep my word – he is afraid they will elect him in Baeza. He wrote asking me to beg you not to confirm it. If this is something you can do, there is every reason to console him because he is tired of suffering. Certainly, *mi padre*, my desire is that there be only a few houses in Andalusia, for I think they will be harmful to those up here.

5.   The prioress at San Alejo,[5] they say, is mad with joy. Her dances and the things she does, they tell me, are charming, and all the discalced nuns here never end their rejoicing at having such a father.[6] Their joy is complete. May God give us such joy in that place where it never ends, and may he give you a very happy Easter. Wish the same to those gentlemen for me, and they will have a happy one if you are there.

6.   All the nuns send their best regards, especially my companions.[7] The rest I will leave for my letter to Padre Nicolao. Oh, how delighted I am that you have such a good companion![8] I would like to know what happened to Padre Fray Bartolomé.[9] He would make a good prior for a foundation.

Your reverence's daughter and subject,

Teresa of Jesus

---

1.   The brief Pia consideratione of Gregory XIII, which authorized the discalced Carmelites to form a separate province (MHCT 2:191–99).

2. The constitutions for the discalced Carmelite nuns had been amplified at the chapter in Alcalá.
3. The cathedral chapter (see F.29.13).
4. St. John of the Cross had been a member of the chapter at Alcalá and was elected third definitor for the new province. On 14 June he would finish two years as rector in Baeza. But despite Teresa's plea, he was soon elected prior of the community in Granada.
5. The hermitess mentioned in Ltr. 377.12.
6. She is referring to their joy at having Padre Gracián as their provincial.
7. Ana de San Bartolomé and Inés de Jesús (see Ltr. 377.11).
8. Doria was elected first definitor and Gracián appointed him to be his companion (see Ltr. 374.7).
9. Bartolomé de Jesús had been Gracian's secretary.

385. To Madre María de San José
Palencia, End of March 1581

This fragment from a letter was recounted by María de San José. The context is the chapter of Alcalá in which the discalced Carmelites became a separate province and Padre Gracián was elected provincial.

Now, my daughter, I can say what holy Simeon[1] said, since I have seen in the order of the Blessed Virgin our Lady what I was desiring to see. So I ask and beg you not to pray or ask for me to live but that I may go to rest, for I am no longer of any usefulness.

1. What Simeon said in Lk 2:29.

386. To Antonio Gaytán, Alba
Palencia, 28 March 1581

(Autograph fragment: DCN, Salamanca)

Letters have arrived from the prioress in Alba and from Antonio Gaytán. The latter, who had just entered upon his second marriage, informed Teresa about the calumnies against her niece, Beatriz, that were spreading through Alba, and he complains that she is distancing herself from him and his cares. According to the prioress, Gaytán was not fulfilling his obligations to his little daughter, Mariana, who was living in the Carmel of Alba.

❧❧❦❦

1. Jesus. The grace of the Holy Spirit be with your honor. I have received a letter from you and would have written you more often if I had paid heed to my desires. But the workload and business matters these past years were such that I had a hard time attending to everything. Glory to God who has brought us out of it all successfully.

2. As Mother Prioress[1] will tell you, I praise God because you are so happy with the state in life that he has given you.[2] May it please him that, since there are saints in that state just as there are in others, you will become one if you do not lose the opportunity through your own fault.

3. Any complaint that I might have against you in those other matters is that you did not let me know as soon as you yourself knew.[3] Perhaps we would have been able to avoid any negligence and prevent all the evil the devil brought about by making one believe that the evil was really there. And even if everything that woman imagined were true, being who she is, one would have had to behave differently and not engage in such unrestrained defamation. When God does the judging we will understand what we cannot judge here below without offending him greatly, for where such great friendship existed,[4] and for so long a time, there was no reason, unless through malice, for such a heavy condemnation.

4. My sister's[5] demeanor with everyone is so gentle that it doesn't seem she could be harsh with anyone, for she is gentle by nature. Nor have I ever seen in her daughter[6] any rudeness of the kind that would make it necessary for my sister to be harsh, but only a great deal of calm. Truly, I have not seen them often, but I have shared a great part of the pain for the offenses

that must have been committed before God by the one who so perverted the truth. My sister swears up and down that it is a calumny, and I believe it because my sister is not a liar, nor would anyone in that place have any reason to treat her badly. But her poverty is the reason they all hold her in so little esteem. God allows it that she might suffer in every way, for truly she is a martyr in this life. May God give her patience.

5.   I tell you that if it were up to me, since it's a matter of calumny, I would remove the occasion. But I could at least help them through prayer, if my prayers were of any value. I am so wretched, however, that they do no more good than what you see. Nor was it any good for me to be your servant so that you would, as I said, tell me about this at once. When you say that I am no longer the way I used to be, I don't know what you can base this on, for nothing that concerns you fails to concern me, and I do with words what I cannot do with works – speak of your merits – and this is all true. You are the one who has drifted from me, in such a manner that it surprises me. The truth is, I don't deserve any more.

6.   Mother Prioress has written me that you said you had agreed with me on the dowry for that little angel[7] they have in their house. If this is so, I don't remember anything more than that you told me that everything you had you wanted for her and that you could give her seven hundred ducats free of entailments. And I remember this because with the desire I had to serve you, I was delighted that the dowry would be so good that Father Visitator (who was then Padre Gracián)[8] would want to give the permission. So I wrote to him, urging him as much as I could, for apart from Casilda and Teresita and Padre Gracián's little sister,[9] no child has been received in these houses, nor would I consent to this. I no longer have the power in all the houses that I used to have, for the decisions are made by a community vote. According to the constitutions[10] that have been drawn up, the habit cannot be given to anyone under twelve, nor can one make profession until the age of sixteen. So now the matter cannot even be considered.

7.   Would you try to pay something on the cost for her food, for since you have other expenses, you cannot give whenever you want. They tell me that it is for I don't know how long that you haven't given them anything, and so they think that this is the way it will be with the dowry. Certainly if it were up to me I wouldn't bother you about this. May God give you the peace I desire, amen.

From St. Joseph's in Palencia on the last day of the Easter feast.

> Your honor's unworthy servant,
>
> Teresa of Jesus

1.   The prioress in Alba de Tormes, Juana del Espíritu Santo.
2.   She is alluding to his second marriage.
3.   "Those other matters" dealt with the calumnies uttered by a woman who, consumed with jealousy, spread a story that her husband was having relations with Beatriz Ovalle, the daughter of Teresa's sister Juana.
4.   Friendship between Teresa's brother-in-law Juan de Ovalle and the husband of the woman who was spreading the calumny.
5.   Juana de Ahumada.
6.   Her daughter, Beatriz de Ovalle.
7.   Gaytan's daughter, Mariana, who from the time she was a child lived in the Carmel in Alba. She didn't make her profession until 1585.
8.   Jerónimo Gracián was now provincial (see Ltrs. 205 & 333.4).
9.   Casilda de Padilla, Teresita de Ahumada, and Isabel Gracián were the other three children received by way of exception into the Carmels of Valladolid, Toledo, and Avila.
10.   The constitutions that were expanded that month in the chapter at Alcalá set the required age for admission at 17 years, not 16 (CN 1581, ch.2 no.1).

387. To Don Jerónimo Reinoso, Burgos
Palencia, Middle of April 1581

(Autograph fragment: DCN, Tlacopac [Mexico])

This is a postscript to a letter that has been lost. Canon Reinoso was assisting Teresa in the preparations for a foundation in Burgos. The nuns were planning to move to a house previously occupied by the Jesuits.

✦ ✦ ✦ ✦

1.   After I wrote that letter,[1] I spoke with Canon Salinas. He and Canon Rodríguez[2] think that in order to take possession of the foundation, there would be no house more suitable than the one belonging to the Jesuits[3] and that even by acquiring another house near it the nuns could for many reasons perhaps stay there. And they say that Señora Catalina de Tolosa[4] and you are trying very hard for this because it doesn't matter to those lords, for if it did Padre Maestro Ripalda[5] wouldn't offer it to me. It is very important for us to be granted this favor, even if we have to rent the house, for since you have been living in it for so long, it is not the fault of those fathers. They can think you gave it to us, if the nuns get established; although if we say that we plan to stay there only for a short time no one can complain. They say that once we are there the people in the area will get to know us better.

2.   Well what is very important is that both of you in your charity do all you can. If those fathers mind, then I wouldn't want it.

3.   If this becomes impossible, they say a house will be looked for in the San Juan quarter[6] ... or at the gate of Santa Gadea. Anyway, it should be where there are people, for it could happen, they say, that after several years it still might not be known that a monastery is there.

4.   It also seems that unless the nuns are living in that house where the Most Blessed Sacrament[7] had been reserved, they should not have it reserved at once, and so a platform need not be made, for perhaps when they have their own house, a monstrance can be made. May the Lord direct all for his greater service.

---

1.   This letter has been lost.
2.   Martín Alonso de Salinas and Juan Rodríguez are canons in Palencia, friends of both Teresa and Reinoso.

3. The house belonging to the Jesuits was probably one of the first houses occupied by the Jesuits in Burgos, in a central part of the city.
4. Doña Catalina de Tolosa was helpful and welcoming to both the Jesuits and Teresa.
5. It was Ripalda's idea that Teresa make a foundation in Burgos.
6. Teresa had doubts here about the name of the place and crossed out half a line that followed. The San Juan quarter was actually outside the walls of the city.
7. Before the foundation was officially made, which would have allowed the nuns to have Mass and reserve the Blessed Sacrament, they stayed temporarily in a house provided by Catalina de Tolosa. This house had been previously used by the Jesuits who had kept the Blessed Sacrament reserved in a chapel there (see F. 31.21–26).

388. To Don Jerónimo Reinoso, Burgos
Palencia, 24 April 1581

It being a propitious time for a foundation in Burgos, the archbishop of this city gave reasons for hope to Canon Reinoso (F.31.5–6), who went from Palencia to Burgos for Teresa on a mission to see him about the foundation of one of her Carmels there. She responds quickly now to the news he sent back to her.

❖❖❖❖

1.   Jesus. The grace of the Holy Spirit be with your honor. I received your letter and spoke with Canon Salinas[1] about the house you say belongs to Don Luis Osorio.[2] And he says that it is located in a place where there is a lot of noise from the street and surrounded on all sides by vulgar people. If you have leased it, I have nothing more to say, and all we can do, as you state, is move in there. But if you have not, wait and don't take it until you see whether we can find another house in a neighborhood more suited to our way of life, especially if the houses of Francisco de Burgos or Agustín de Torquemada on the Calle de la Puebla, or others like them, are available; that would be great.

2. Because I am writing this in the speak room in the presence of Canon Salinas, I'll say no more than that the St. Joseph[3] will not be made now until we see what will happen here. These sisters will finish this letter.

Today is the vigil of St. Mark.

Your honor's servant,

Teresa of Jesus

I kiss the hands of Señora Catalina de Tolosa[4].

---

1. Martín Alonso Salinas, a canon in Palencia and collaborator of Teresa's for the foundations in Palencia and Burgos (see F. 29.12 & 31.18).
2. Luis Osorio was from one of the most noble families in Burgos who had a house at the Plaza Mayor and another at the Mercado Mayor. The latter is the one referred to by Teresa.
3. A statue of Saint Joseph.
4. She was the benefactor for the foundation in Burgos and later became a discalced Carmelite nun herself (see F.31).

389. To Sister Ana de San Agustín, Villanueva de la Jara
Palencia, 22 May 1581

It was a little over a year since Teresa made the foundation in Villanueva de la Jara. From Malagón she had brought Sister Ana de San Agustín with her, who was a young, recently professed nun. Teresa wrote this affectionate letter to her with perhaps the secret intention that the letter end up in Padre Gabriel's hands. Teresa wanted him to take an interest in the nearby Carmel of Villanueva de la Jara. Despite her esteem for him, he resisted Teresa. "He is a father for whom I have great affection, although he has little for me" (Ltr.130.4).

✤✤❖❖

To Sister Ana de San Agustín

1. May Jesus be with your charity and may he watch over you, amen; and make you as holy as I desire. I am delighted

that you tell me you are praying for me. Padre Fray Gabriel[1] also writes the same. Please God, you will not forget to do so, for I don't know if you love me as much as I do you, for I don't know whether or not you have deceived me and Padre Fray Gabriel. Be careful about what you are doing.

2.   May God pardon you, for I tell you that your letters make me so happy that I can't believe it. Don't fail to write to me always and give me an account of your soul in great detail, and tell me how you are getting along with Padre Fray Gabriel, for I think it was for you that our Lord brought him back there. This was a strong desire of mine,[2] and I wanted him to be prior again so that you would be more certain of having him there; although I believe he will stay there now, with the help of God, and will do much good for you in many ways. Whoever loves all of you the way he does will not fail to find the occasion for showing it. I will do what I can so that they do not remove him from there. I certainly love him very much and would greatly regret his being transferred.

3.   When you see him, tell him that San Bartolomé[3] sends her best regards and that she was very happy that he remembered her. She asks him to pray for her out of charity and says that she will do so for him, although her prayers are poor and miserable. She asks the same of you, and don't neglect to do so, since you owe it to her, for you are good friends. Remain with God, and may His Majesty make you very holy.

From Palencia. It is the day after the feast of the Holy Trinity.

Your charity's servant,

Teresa of Jesus

1. Gabriel de la Asunción was prior at La Roda, near Villanueva de la Jara. At the chapter of Alcalá (1581), he was elected a definitor alongside St. John of the Cross.
2. On 17 February, Teresa suggested to Gracián the wisdom of making Padre Gabriel prior of La Roda once again (see Ltr. 371), for his presence was very important to the nuns in Villanueva de la Jara.

3. Ana de San Bartolomé (Blessed Anne of St. Bartholomew), Teresa's nurse and secretary at this time.

390. To Padre Gracián, Salamanca
Palencia, 23 (?) May 1581

(Autograph: DCN, Corpus Christi, Alcalá de Henares)

Gracián was on his way to Valladolid for a foundation of discalced friars there. He had stopped off in Palencia to visit Teresa briefly. She had wanted him to be present for the inauguration of the new Carmel in Palencia and to accompany her on the long trip to Soria for a foundation there. But Gracián appointed Doria in his stead, which saddened Teresa.

❖ ❖ ❖ ❖

1. Jesus. May the Holy Spirit be with your reverence, *mi padre*. Now do you see how short-lasting my happiness was? I was desiring to make this trip,[1] and I believe I would have regretted to see it end, as happened at other times when I was in the company that I now thought would be mine. May God be praised, for already I seem to be growing tired. I tell you, *mi padre*, that, in the end, the flesh is weak and so has become sadder than I would want, for the sadness was great. Your departure could have been excused if you had stayed at least until seeing us move into our house,[2] for eight days more or less didn't matter. There has been much loneliness here, and please God that he who was responsible for taking you away will act in a manner better than I fear he might. God deliver me from such urgency. And then he talks about us!

2. Truthfully, I have nothing good to say now, for I have little inclination to do so. The only comfort would be freedom from the fear that I could have, and have had, that they might touch me in what is my holy of holies.[3] For I assure you the temptation I go through in this regard is a strong one. And in exchange for this not happening, I would suffer everything to come raining down on me – and it is a raining a lot now, so afflicted have I

felt. Everything becomes very displeasing, for after all the soul suffers from not being with the one who governs and comforts it. May God be served through it all, and if this be so, there is no reason to complain however painful it may be.

3.   You should know that when you were here I put off discussing something with you until your return – which would have given me more time to pray over the matter. It concerned something that Padre Juan Diaz[4] urgently recommended to me. And I felt very sorry afterward when I learned that you are not returning, because he came here for no other reason. He has about decided to change his state and enter either our order or the Jesuits. He says that after being here for some days he is leaning more toward this order and wants to know your opinion and mine and asks that we pray for him.

4.   What I feel about this and what I told him is that it would be very good for him if he were to persevere. If he didn't it will be harmful, bringing discredit to the publications with which he is engaged. And so I say this now, although I am a little less fearful of it, because he serves our Lord very much and in the end will have to overcome many things; but he will end up well if he settles down in one order. He says that he will give the monastery where he enters all that he has from Maestro Avila.[5] In my opinion, if it is like the little that was given to me to read, the sermons would be of great benefit to people who are not as knowledgeable as you are. He is a man who is edifying no matter where he is. We should think carefully about this. I will speak of it with Padre Nicolao.[6] I have mentioned it here to you so that if he has not yet spoken to you about it, you will do me the charity of letting him know that I spoke of the matter with you. He would have reason to complain about me if I hadn't. And will you pray about this. Since you know him better than I do, you will understand what the appropriate answer for him would be, and let me know if you find a means of doing so, since even this will present another difficulty.

5.   Enclosed is a letter to me by the Bishop of Osma,[7] and a paper that I wrote; I didn't have time for more.

6.   In my opinion, your reverence did not have to go to Alba without Padre Nicolao.[8] He would have seen clearly into those intrigues and calculations about the alms left by the benefi- ciary.[9] You did me a great favor by sending him (for no one could be better).[10] You couldn't have sent some young lad, but it had to be someone who speaks and presents himself well. Oh, *mi padre*, praise be to God who made you so charming in the presence of those with whom you deal that no one seems to fill this void, for everything wearies poor Lorencia.[11] She asks for your prayers. She says that there is no quiet or rest for her soul except in God and with anyone who understands her as you do. The rest is a cross for her beyond exaggeration.

7.   San Bartolomé[12] has been left very sad. She sends you her best regards. Give us your blessing and pray much for us to His Majesty.

May he watch over and guide you, amen.

8.   You should know that there they also have a strange fear of the prioress[13] and the custom of never saying anything about anything to the major superior. Regarding the students who serve them,[14] you need to be careful. May God keep you.

Your reverence's unworthy servant and daughter,

Teresa of Jesus

1. The long trip to Soria which began on 29 May and for which Teresa had expected the companionship of Gracián, a great friend of the Bishop of Burgo de Osma, who was sponsoring the foundation in nearby Soria. Instead, it was Doria who accompanied them on their journey (see MHCT 2:286–87).
2. In Palencia (see F. 29.29).
3. The "holy of holies" was Gracián. Teresa was fearful of the gossip that could start up against him by those who claimed that instead of attending to provincial matters he was spending too much of his time assisting Teresa.
4. Padre Juan Díaz was a disciple and relative of St. John of Avila, had inherited the latter's manuscripts, and supported the foundation of the discalced Carmelite friars in Almodóvar del Campo (see MHCT 1:186).

5. St. John of Avila.
6. Nicolás Doria, who was in Palencia at the time.
7. Alonso Velázquez, the Bishop of Osma, was the spiritual director for whom Teresa wrote the last account of the state of her soul (see ST 65).
8. Nicolás Doria was in Palencia at the time.
9. The beneficiary was probably Sancho Dávila (see Ltr. 371.4).
10. Nicolás Doria was an expert in financial matters.
11. A code name for Teresa herself.
12. Blessed Anne of Saint Bartholomew.
13. The prioress in Salamanca, Ana de la Encarnación (Tapia).
14. These were student priests who had offered their service to the community.

391. To Padre Jerónimo Gracián, Salamanca
Palencia, 25 May 1581

(Autograph: Monasterio de Las Huelgas, Burgos)

On the feast of Corpus Christi, the day before the solemn transfer to the new house, Teresa had some important visitors: the Bishop of Palencia, Alvaro de Mendoza, Nicolás Doria, and Juan de Jesús Roca. A number of friends from Palencia also came for a visit, and those sent by the Bishop of Osma arrived to accompany her group to Soria. But Teresa keenly felt the absence of Gracián.

✣✣✣✣

1. Jesus. The grace of the Holy Spirit be with your paternity, *mi padre*. I am tired and it is very late at night, so I will say no more than that the bishop[1] came yesterday; and today arrangements were made for the procession, which was no small thing. It will take place in the afternoon with all the solemnity possible. We will go from here to San Lazaro.[2] The canons will not celebrate the feast[3] tomorrow except to take the Blessed Sacrament from there. I believe we will enter St. Clare's[4] which

is along the way. Everything would be nice if *mi padre* were here. So, I don't know what to say.

2.   They also came from Soria this morning for us. But I think they will have to wait until Monday.[5] I am well. The bishop was here all afternoon, showing such eagerness to help this order that it is something to praise God for. May His Majesty be with your reverence.

3.   Give my regards to Padre Juan Díaz.[6] All the sisters here send you their best. Padre Nicolao[7] is well, and I the same. He preached a good sermon for us today.

4.   I was delighted with Fray Juan de Jesús.[8] The more I observe his love for you, the more I like him. Do not show him any dislike, for a good friend nowadays should be highly esteemed.

Your reverence's servant and daughter,

Teresa of Jesus

Sister Isabel de Jesús[9] is bringing this; in your charity show her much kindness.

---

1.   The Bishop of Palencia, Alvaro de Mendoza. The procession and inauguration took place on 26 May.
2.   San Lázaro was the parish church from which the Blessed Sacrament was brought in procession to the Carmel.
3.   It was one of the festive days within the octave of Corpus Christi.
4.   A monastery of Poor Clare nuns.
5.   The following Monday, 29 May, the party of travelers set off for Soria.
6.   The disciple of St. John of Avila (see Ltr. 390.3).
7.   Nicolás Doria.
8.   Juan de Jesús (Roca), who had been a classmate of Gracián's at Alcalá.
9.   Isabel de Jesús (Jimena) was returning to Salamanca where she will become prioress. She had been prioress in Palencia until 3 May.

392. Addressee Unknown

Palencia, 25–27 (?) May 1581

This letter could be addressed to one of the Duke of Alba's servants, who may have delivered some important papers to Teresa from the duke. Through him she now sends greetings to the duke, who was in Lisbon.

❖❖❖❖

Jesus. The grace of the Holy Spirit be with your honor. I received the papers and will do what you command. May our Lord repay you for the care you have shown. With my poor prayers, I will do what you ask, and so I beg you to keep me in yours, and do me the favor of telling his excellency, the duke,[1] that my departure, God willing, will take place Monday.[2] I am beseeching his excellency to see if he can render me some service, for he has so many things to do that I don't ask him for anything more, for which I kiss his hands. May our Lord guide him always.

Your honor's unworthy servant,

Teresa of Jesus

1. Probably, the Duke of Alba, Fernando Alvarez de Toledo.
2. She is probably referring to the departure from Palencia to Soria, which took place on Monday, 29 May.

393. To a nun

Teresa answers a nun who wanted to transfer to one of her Carmels. Neither the nun nor the place where she lived are known to us. The date would have to come after March 1581, the time of the chapter in Alcalá. These fragments come to us through Francisco Ribera's early biography of Teresa.

❖❖❖❖

1. As for the main request that your honor makes, I cannot be of help in any way, and this because of our constitutions.[1] The regulation, sought by me, is that no nun from another order

is to be accepted into one of these houses. So many wanted, and want, to enter these houses that even though some were a consolation for us, there are many drawbacks to opening the door to this practice. So I have nothing more to say about this, for the desire I have to please you can do or serve for nothing more than afflict me.

2.   Before beginning to found these monasteries, I lived for twenty-five years in one where there were 180 nuns.[2] And because I am in a hurry, I will only say that for anyone who loves God all those things will be a cross for her and of benefit to her soul, and they will not harm it if you keep in mind the advice that you and God alone are in that house, and as long as you do not have an office that obliges you to observe things, don't pay any attention to them, but strive to acquire the virtue that you see in each one, love her for that, benefit from it, and forget about the faults you see in her.

3.   The benefit to me was such that even though there were so many nuns it mattered no more than if there were none; they were only an advantage for me. After all, my lady, we can love this great God everywhere. May he be blessed, for there is no one who can prevent us from doing this.

1.   The new constitutions from the chapter in Alcalá forbade the provincial to receive nuns from another order or from the mitigated rule of the Carmelite order.

2.   She is referring to the Carmelite monastery of the Incarnation in Avila.

394. To Don Gaspar de Quiroga, Toledo
Soria, 16 June 1581

(Autograph: Cathedral, Cadiz)

Teresa here seeks a license from the archbishop to found a Carmel in Madrid, which he had previously agreed to but never carried through on. Perhaps he delayed giving it because of his niece, Doña Elena, a widow and mother of four children who wanted to become a discalced Carmelite nun. He preferred that she give her attention to caring for her children, some of whom were still minors.

✦ ✦ ✦ ✦

1.   Jesus. The grace of the Holy Spirit be always with your most illustrious lordship. I have been waiting for an answer to a letter of mine that must have been delivered to you during Holy Week or a little after[1] that, according to what I was told. In it I asked you to grant me the favor of a license to found a monastery in Madrid, which you had previously told me would please you.[2] But you did not give me the license at the time because of a certain obstacle, which our Lord has now removed. I don't know whether you remember and how you told me that once the barrier were gone you would grant me this favor. Considering this to be certain, I have been preparing some things for this foundation, since it will be easier to find a less expensive house before his majesty comes to Madrid.[3]

2.   At present I am in Soria where a monastery has been founded. The bishop[4] of this place invited me to come to found it, and it has been established very well for the glory of God. I would not want to leave this town until you grant me this favor,[5] for otherwise I would have to travel many leagues out of my way. And as I told you, there are some persons[6] in that city waiting and suffering from the delay. Since you always help those who seek to serve our Lord – and from what I understand he will be served by this work which will be most beneficial for this order – I beg you not to delay any longer the bestowal of this favor, if it would please you to do so.

3.   My lady, Doña Elena,[7] continues steadfast in her purpose. But until the license comes from you, this is of little use. She is so holy and detached from everything that they tell me she would like to enter the monastery in Madrid, with the hope truly of seeing you some day. I am not surprised.

4.   I too always have this desire to see you, and I take special care each day to pray to our Lord for you and to have the nuns in these monasteries do the same .

5.   May it please him to hear us and preserve you for very many years with the increase of holiness that I beg of him, amen.

Written in Soria in this house of the Carmel of the Holy Trinity on 16 June.

> Your most illustrious lordship's unworthy subject and servant,

> Teresa of Jesus

---

1.   Between 19 and 29 March of that year. The letter has been lost. She had written again on 3 June (see Ltr. 344.2), a letter that was also lost.

2.   This conversation probably took place a good time before, back in the summer of 1577.

3.   The king was in Portugal at the time.

4.   The bishop was Alonso Velázquez (see F. 30).

5.   She actually left Soria on 16 August. Before doing so she had received a reply from the archbishop (see Ltr. 407.1).

6.   There were some aspirants to Carmel waiting in Madrid to enter there.

7.   Doña Elena, the cardinal's niece, was a widow and mother of four sons and two daughters. She wanted to become a discalced Carmelite nun and in October of that year entered the Carmel of Medina, where her younger daughter was a nun. Her daughter later became her prioress.

395. To Madre María de San José, Seville
Soria, 16 June 1581

This is only a fragment. It shows Teresa's solicitude for the health of the prioress in Seville as the community approaches the heat of an Andalusian summer.

❧❧❦❦

For Mother Prioress of the Carmel of St. Joseph, Seville

1.   For goodness' sake do not rely much on that extra weight and take care of yourself. I recommend that Madre Juana de la Cruz[1] watch that you do this, and Mother Subprioress,[2] and San Francisco;[3] and they should let me know if you don't.

2.   Father Provincial[4] has now given me again the authorization to do certain things. By that authority I command you to do what is necessary for the good of your health and whatever my dear Juana de la Cruz tells you to do, and both of you should report to me on how you are doing. Otherwise, for your penance I will not write to you.

3.   For the time being we don't want your penances but that you do not give them to others with your illnesses and that you be obedient to me and not kill me. Truthfully I tell you I would not feel the loss of any prioress as much as I would losing you. I don't know how it is that I love you so much.

---

1.   Madre Juana is in fact a lay sister, the mother of Beatriz de la Madre de Dios.
2.   Leonor de San Gabriel.
3.   Isabel de San Francisco.
4.   The provincial was Jerónimo Gracián.

396. To Padre Jerónimo Gracián, Salamanca
Soria, 27 June 1581

(Autograph fragment: La Seo, Zaragoza)

Teresa had been in Soria since the beginning of June, and all was going well. She is looking ahead, then, to her next tasks.

❧❧❦❦

1.   … If it is necessary for me to go now to Avila[1] and let the other project go, it would be let go forever, it seems. But it

occurs to me that if I am prioress and Fray Gregorio[2] is there, I could be absent for a few months. I would greatly prefer having you nearby when this has to be decided. Please God this letter will go quickly, for you can answer me by way of Avila – Padre Nicolao[3] told me he would have a messenger sent – and also by way of Palencia and Valladolid, for although the letters are slow in arriving, they write to me. Don't set aside one way for the other.

2.   Please God you are well, for such bad lodging in this heat is a hard thing. I have envied your being near the river, though.[4] It has always seemed to me that it would be a good place, at least so as to take possession of the foundation. Here it gets very hot at times, especially now as I am writing this. But the mornings and evenings are nice. All the nuns are well.

3.   The prioress[5] is carrying out her duties very well. As for this lady,[6] she is extremely good. May God carry the work forward, for it seems that this foundation is a success, and may he watch over you for us, amen.

Today is 27 June.[7]

---

1. The first part of the autograph is damaged. Teresa remained in Soria until the middle of August and arrived in Avila on 6 September (see F. 30.12–14).
2. Gregorio Nacianceno could be the confessor and she the prioress.
3. Nicolás Doria.
4. Gracián had founded a house of studies for the discalced Carmelites in Salamanca in what was formerly a hospital (San Lazaro) near the river Tormes.
5. Catalina de Cristo, prioress in Soria.
6. The benefactress for the foundation in Soria, Beatriz de Beamonte y Navarra (see F. 30.3–4, 8–9). She later entered the Carmel in Pamplona.
7. The text continues, but is illegible.

397. To Dionisio Ruiz de la Peña, Toledo
Soria, 30 June 1581

Dionisio Ruiz de la Peña was the personal secretary and confessor of the Archbishop of Toledo, Gaspar de Quiroga. Three business matters brought Teresa into communication with Cardinal Quiroga: The inquisition's examination of The Book of Her Life, *which passed through his hands; a foundation of discalced Carmelite nuns in Madrid; and the more thorny problem of his widowed niece's desire to become a discalced Carmelite nun even though she had children who were still minors.*

❖❖❖❖

To the most illustrious Señor Licentiate Peña, confessor of the most illustrious Cardinal Archbishop of Toledo, my lord.

1. Jesus. The grace of the Holy Spirit be with your honor. The day after I sent a private messenger who had brought a letter for me from Señora Doña Luisa,[1] they brought me your letter. I was very sorry because I would have wanted to answer at once and since there is no ordinary mail delivery[2] in this place, I don't know when this letter will go out. I would have wanted it to go quickly so that you would be aware of how little I am at fault, or rather not at all, This is so true that out of respect for the relationship[3] of that person about whom you wrote to me with his illustrious lordship, I did not tell the latter about the efforts I made in this case to impede her entrance into one of these houses. If Padre Baltasar Alvarez,[4] who was provincial of the Jesuits in this province, were alive, he would be a good witness to how I begged him to prevent such a thing, since this lady had more respect for him than for anyone else, and he promised to do so.

2. For some years now I have been standing in her way, and I don't think this is because his illustrious lordship is opposed to her entering, but out of fear that what happened in the case of another lady who entered one of our monasteries, leaving daughters behind, might happen to us. This was done

without my approval, for I was far away from that city when she entered.[5] I tell you that ten years of unrest and great trials have gone by (for she entered that long ago), and she is a good servant of God. But since the order of charity,[6] which is obligatory, is not being observed, I think God allows her and her daughters to pay for such a failure, and the nuns as well. And I have mentioned it so much in these monasteries that I am certain the prioress[7] in Medina becomes upset every time she thinks of what might happen. Consider how although this is true, the devil has found a way in which they can accuse me of the opposite.

3.   Our Lord often finds a way of granting me joy in suffering calumnies, which have not been rare for me in this life, but this one in a way has caused me distress. For if I owed his lordship gratitude for nothing else than his having allowed me to kiss his hands there,[8] that would be enough, but how much more do I owe him for so many favors; and in the case of some he does not know that I am aware of them. And knowing what his will is in this regard, I couldn't give my consent now to such a thing, unless I were out of my mind. It is true that sometimes, since this lady cries so much when I tell her many things so as to dissuade her, I may at times have given her some reasons for hope while trying to cheer her up, and perhaps she thought I was in favor of this, although I don't especially remember such a thing.

4.   I certainly love her honor very much, and am indebted to her, and so – leaving aside what concerns us – if for my sins what I am speaking of should happen, I strongly desire that she succeed in everything. Yesterday I was told by the prioress of this house[9] (who is from the monastery in Medina, for she is the one with whom this lady frequently communicated) that she had been told by her that the vow she had made to enter contained the condition that she would do so when she could and that if she were told it would be for the greater service of God that she not enter, she would renounce her desire. It seems to me that since she still has children to care for and

her daughter-in-law is so young, she is not yet able to enter. If you think it appropriate, tell his lordship about this so that he will understand how the vow was made. Some learned men with whom she speaks disturb her, and the little they say to someone who is so holy is enough to do that.

5.   If your letter had come before the one Señora Doña Luisa wrote me, in which she tells me that his lordship has been freed from any illusion about my being at fault in this matter, it would have pained me very much. Blessed be God who so favors me that without my understanding how his lordship has come to know the truth. Never in all my life would I have dreamed of excusing myself since I didn't think I was at fault. I kiss your honor's hands for having informed me of this. I consider it a special favor and consider myself newly obliged to serve you always more with my poor prayers, although up until now I have not failed to do so.

6.   As regards the license for a foundation in Madrid, I have begged this of his most illustrious lordship because I think our Lord would be served thereby and because the discalced friars and nuns have urged me, for they say that it would be very useful for everyone to have a house there. But since his illustrious lordship stands in the place of God, I would feel no disturbance if he doesn't think it would be good to grant the permission. I would believe that accepting his denial would be of greater service to God, for I would not be refusing any trials; and I tell you there are many in every foundation.

7.   What would be a great trial for me would be the thought that his illustrious lordship is displeased with me on account of calumnies uttered against me, for I love him tenderly in the Lord. And even if this doesn't matter to him, it is a consolation to me that he know the truth, for being loved doesn't matter to our Lord either, yet he is happy with this love alone. Truly, if love is present, it then shows itself in works and in not departing from his will. Through these works I cannot serve his illustrious lordship in any better way than by refusing to oppose him as

much as I can. Be certain of this, and do not forget me in your holy sacrifices, as we have agreed.

8.   Since you will learn of my travel plans from the mother prioress[10] there, I will not mention them. I have better health here than usual, glory to God. It is a great comfort to me to know that his illustrious lordship is in good health. May God give you health, and the holiness I beg of him for you, amen.

From this monastery of the Holy Trinity in Soria, the end of June.

Your honor's unworthy servant,

Teresa of Jesus

---

1.   Luisa de la Cerda, a friend of Cardinal Quiroga's.
2.   When there was no ordinary (or official) mail delivery, one had to contract a personal messenger.
3.   She is alluding to Doña Elena de Quiroga, who was the cardinal's niece and who wanted to enter the Carmel in Medina where her daughter was already a professed nun.
4.   Baltasar Alvarez, Teresa's former spiritual director at the Incarnation, later lived in Medina del Campo and was director of Doña Elena. He died 25 July 1580.
5.   She is referring to the Flemish woman, Ana Wasteels, who was widowed at age 31 with two daughters and entered St. Joseph's in Avila, taking the name Ana de San Pedro.
6.   She has in mind the theological doctrine that the first ones to whom our love should be directed are children and parents.
7.   Alberta Bautista.
8.   She is alluding to an interview that she had with Quiroga in Toledo (see Ltr. 394.2).
9.   The prioress of the house in Soria, who had previously lived in Medina and known Elena de Quiroga.
10.   The prioress in Toledo, Ana de los Angeles.

398. To Don Sancho Dávila, Salamanca
Soria, End of June 1581 (?)

(Autograph: DCN, Badajoz)

Don Sancho Dávila (1546–1624), from the family of the Marquises of Velada, was professor of theology and Rector Magnifico of the University of Salamanca. He and his devout mother, Juana Enríquez de Toledo, were good friends of Teresa's.

❦❦❦❦

1.   Jesus. The grace of the Holy Spirit be always with your honor, amen. I tell you that you are a real source of mortification. Do you think that because I am far away I have stopped both knowing what you are doing and feeling displeased about it? No, certainly not; rather it distresses me even more. For I am aware of the great consolation that those sisters[1] receive from the kindness you show them and how consoled they are when they can go to confession to you. And so the prioress[2] in writing to me is very distressed, and she is right.

2.   For even though Father Provincial[3] is there now and consoles them, not everyone will always be pleased to confess with just one. Nor should you worry about your happy spirit. I regret that I wasn't there at a time when I could have enjoyed your kind ways; I urgently entrust myself to your prayers. If Father Provincial approves, it is enough that I be a relative of yours for me to give you my highest approval, how much more so because of your other qualities.

3.   Since I hear about you from the prioress, and you hear about me, and on account of my many duties – it was restful for me there compared to what goes on here – I do not write more often. But I will not forget you in my poor prayers, so I beg you to remember me in yours ...[4]

---

1.   The Carmelite nuns in Salamanca.
2.   The prioress in Salamanca, Ana de la Encarnación.

3. The provincial of the discalced Carmelites, Jerónimo Gracián.
4. The text has suffered damage.

399. To Dionisio Ruiz, Toledo
Soria, 8 July 1581

She continues on the topic brought up in Ltr. 397 concerning the desires of the cardinal's niece to become a discalced Carmelite nun. Consulting a Dominican theologian in Soria, Teresa found that he agreed with her in her opposition, but that another important theologian had supported Doña Elena.

1.   Jesus. The grace of the Holy Spirit be with your honor. Not long ago I answered your letter, and since that letter will have to go from here by such roundabout ways, perhaps this one will arrive sooner. Not daring myself to write to the cardinal[1] so often, although I would be glad to do so, I wanted to write to beg you to tell him that after I wrote to his illustrious lordship, I spent some time with the prior at the house of Santo Domingo in this city, who is Fray Diego de Alderete.[2] We spoke a long while about the matter concerning Señora Doña Elena.[3] I told him that when I had finished my visit with her there a short time ago she was more scrupulous than ever about realizing her desire.[4]

2.   He had no more desire than I – and I can't stress enough that I am opposed – that she carry out her wishes. Listening to the reasons that I presented to him about the dissipation that could result, of a kind that really frightens me, he concluded that it would be much better for her to remain at home. He pointed out that since we do not want to receive her, she is freed from her vow; the vow was to enter this order and she is not obliged to anything more than to request this. That fact was a great consolation to me because I hadn't known about this.

3.   He lives in this city where for eight years he has enjoyed the fame of being a very holy and learned man, and so he seemed to me. The penance he does is great. I had never met him, and so it consoled me greatly to come to know him. It is his opinion in this case that since I am so determined – and that whole house as well – not to receive her, we could inform her that she could never be accepted, and that should appease her. For if this drags on with many words, as has happened up until now, she will always go about disquieted. And truly it does not contribute anything to the service of God for her to abandon her children, as Father Prior agreed. But he told me that he had learned that she had received the approval of a theologian so renowned that he did not dare contradict him. His lordship can now be at ease about this matter.

4.   I have given notice that even if his lordship grants the permission, she should not be received, and I will inform the provincial.[5] You could tell his lordship whatever in this letter you think will not tire him, and kiss his hands for me. May God keep your honor for many years and give you as much of his love as I desire and beseech of him.

From Soria, 8 July.

      Your honor's unworthy servant,

                    Teresa of Jesus

---

1. Gaspar de Quiroga, archbishop of Toledo, whose confessor was Dionisio Ruiz.
2. A Dominican friar, who was the son of Francisco Fernández de Alderete and Doña María de Quiroga, sister of Cardinal Quiroga.
3. Doña Elena de Quiroga. The matter concerned her desire to become a discalced Carmelite nun, even though she still had children needing her care.
4. The vow Doña Elena had made to become a discalced Carmelite nun.
5. The provincial of the discalced Carmelites, Jerónimo Gracián.

400. To Don Jerónimo Reinoso, Palencia
Soria, 8 July 1581

(Autograph: Carmelitas Terciarias, Sorrento [Italy])

Teresa was in Soria, deeply involved in the construction of the house. Among those who had accompanied her on the trip from Palencia were Pedro Ribera, the procurator of the cathedral. She needed him for the return trip, which she wouldn't be able to make until August. But Ribera had used up all the time that was granted to him, and so Teresa wrote to her friends in Palencia to seek an extension for him.

❖❖❖❖

To the illustrious Señor Canon Reinoso, my lord. Palencia.

1.   Jesus. The grace of the Holy Spirit be with your honor. A short time ago I wrote by way of Burgos to you and to Canon Señor Salinas.[1] God deliver me from the roundabout ways that are necessary both to send a letter and to receive news about your honors. Please God you are well. I am fine and so are the sisters, and everything is going well for us.

2.   Now I am writing quickly because they told me about a messenger that was going to Madrid. I am sending my letters by this way and am writing to the administrator[2] asking him to have the chapter give Ribera,[3] the procurator, permission for a stipend of twenty days in August – if possible thirty would be better. I assure you that I can't find anyone in this city who could accompany me, and by that time the adaptations on the house will be finished. For today we used the covered passageway[4] to go to the church, although the choir still remains to be constructed, and we are now using a chapel that has been lent for our use. But there is little left to do. I figure it will take eight or ten days for the trip. I don't know yet which way our Lord will want us to go.[5] Ask the Lord to direct things for his greater service and insist as much as possible, together with Canon Salinas, on obtaining the license, for it is something very

necessary. Don't think there is anyone here who will take up our cause as there is in that place.

I kiss his honor's hands, and I beg him to take this as addressed to him, for it isn't possible that I write any more.

3.   With such a small piece of paper and so little time it wouldn't be possible to mention all that we owe to the procurator and the ways he finds to help us. Well, it's like Palencia. What can you do? May our Lord make you as holy as I beg of him, amen.

4.   Give my best regards to Señor Suero de Vega[6] and to Señora Doña Elvira;[7] and to Señor Canon Santa Cruz.[8]

From Soria, 8 July.

Your honor's unworthy servant and daughter,

Teresa of Jesus

1.   Martin Alonso de Salinas, a canon in Palencia and a friend of Reinoso's.
2.   The administrator of the cathedral in Palencia, Prudencio Armentia (see F. 29.26).
3.   Pedro Ribera, the procurator for the cathedral in Palencia (see F. 30.12).
4.   See F. 30.8.
5.   She will leave on 16 August by way of Segovia and Villacastín for Avila.
6.   Suero de Vega, one of Teresa's benefactors in Palencia, son of the Viceroy of Navarra and Sicily.
7.   Elvira Manrique, wife of Suero de Vega, daughter of the Count of Osorno.
8.   Juan Rodríguez Santa Cruz, a priest from Palencia.

401. To Don Jerónimo Reinoso, Palencia
Soria, 13 June, 1581

In Soria Teresa was preparing to return to Avila rather than go on to make a foundation in Burgos. Reinoso had gone to Burgos to prepare the ground for her, but she here writes to him explaining that she is not convinced of the bishop's firm support.

❧ ❧ ❦ ❦

1.   Jesus. The grace of the Holy Spirit be with your honor. Your letter consoled me greatly. May our Lord reward you. It didn't strike me as long. I would like to go on at length in this one, but so many letters have arrived together. Messengers so rarely come around here that I think it is better to be where you have ordinary mail delivery. Well, when God desires one to suffer, it doesn't do any good to flee.

2.   In the letter I am writing to Catalina de Tolosa,[1] I am telling the prioress, Inés de Jesús,[2] to show it to you so that you learn the public reasons for the change in itinerary – although I plan to tell you and Mother Prioress the other reasons as well – for you say you would like to know the reasons for my change of plan,[3] and you are right. If it were a matter of deep concern to the order, as was our becoming a separate province, one could surmount all difficulties, however numerous; but because I do not have time I will not expand. And if the journey lasted a day longer, but no more, it could be tolerated. But to go so many leagues on an adventure is something for which I see no reason whatsoever, for this order is not so fallen or in need of such a foundation.[4]

3.   Since I have been here, they have written me from two other cities where I am also refusing to go. One is Ciudad Rodrigo, and the other is Orduña.

4.   To assume now what the archbishop[5] will do is not wise in my judgment. For without wanting to be suspicious, we have seen clear reasons for being so. In what Canon Juan Alfonso[6] writes me, the archbishop says that he always remembers the tumult that arose in Avila at the time of the first monastery. Despite the great good that came about as a result, he says that because of his experience he is obliged to prevent anything like this from happening again. What can be hoped for from this?

Seeing that he fears what may never happen, it is clear that he will not give the permission when the devil stirs up some uproar; and I will appear frivolous for having gotten involved in it.

5.   He also said to a member of the Society of Jesus that the consent of the city was wanting and that without it, or without an income, he would in no way give permission. Two persons have already told me that he has a very hesitant nature. If this is so we would be bringing him more trouble and, in the end, obtain nothing, as has been the case so far. But for something that is not an offense against God, after all that the Bishop of Palencia[7] did in this regard, one should be ready to take every risk.

6.   I have my reasons, *mi padre*, for what I say. If this is something to strive for, if we have to negotiate the matter with the city,[8] it will be better to do so from afar and slowly. Since it is something that cannot be done in eight days or perhaps even a month, a miserable foundress would have to stay in the house of a secular, which would be the occasion for much talk. I consider it better to travel many leagues and then return here than to go through all the inconveniences that can arise. If God wants it, it will come about more gently, and he will succeed despite the devil, but it won't come by force.

7.   Since it seems to me that I have done all that I could about this, I tell you truthfully that not even in its first stirrings did I feel any grief; rather I rejoiced – I don't know why. Only when I read the letters of that blessed Catalina de Tolosa, who tried so hard, does it seem that I wanted to make her happy.

8.   The designs of the Lord we do not understand, and it could be more fitting for me to go elsewhere now. So much resistance on the part of the archbishop contains some mystery, for I certainly think he desires the foundation. I haven't said anything about this to the bishop here,[9] for he is so busy that he hasn't been able to see me these days. Nor do I think it necessary, for I feel so much repugnance toward telling him about

these things. Rather I was surprised there were some who still thought it would be good to make the foundation, after what happened to the Bishop of Palencia. I am not going to speak of these things, but only of those about which I'm certain, such as the winter cold and the harm it would do to my health if we went at the beginning of winter. To the archbishop I am saying that I do not want to expose him to all this disturbance until the matter is negotiated with the city, and I thank him for the favor he shows me. May the Lord do what is most for his service.

9.   The procurator didn't think it suitable for certain reasons to entrust our response with the same messenger, so we waited for this other one who is certainly going to Valladolid. Write to me truthfully what you think of these reasons that I have given. If they carry but little weight, I have many others. And it is my deep conviction that if I were to speak with you, you would agree.

10.   I am very sorry about all the work you have to go through for those alms, but since it is all for the poor, I don't think you mind it. Apart from what you send, God will awaken other people to give, and little by little he will arrange everything. I didn't want you to neglect the collections in the villages, although some preacher from the order should have gone to preach. For that reason, it could be that not so much will be collected this year.

11.   May our Lord repay you for the advice you gave about the rent for this house. Before Padre Nicolao[10] left, he drew up the contracts, and he did so well that while one thought of an income at only fourteen per thousand, as would have been possible, twenty were obtained; the act is already recorded. Padre Nicolao also brought the document to be registered in the name of the monastery.

12.   Thank that little saint, the procurator, for what he is doing, for he will be very pleased if I mention this to you. He is a soul who I don't think is well known; so much humility cannot be present without much richness. May you give me permission to finish more willingly than I would you.

13.   One thing I beg is that in all openness you let me know what you think of the prioress and how she acts and if there is need to give her some advice and how you get along with her, for she never finishes telling me what she owes you.

May our Lord watch over you and be pleased to permit me to see you again. I am well.

Today is 13 July.

> Your honor's unworthy servant and daughter, even though the title bothers you,

> Teresa of Jesus

14.   I kiss the hands of Señor Don Francisco and anyone else's you wish me to, and my regards to San Miguel, in your charity. It matters little if they delay in changing the door of the sacristy. That they close the church early, I praise our Lord. I would like to see the grate put up. I hope in him that in this house of our Lady, she and her son will now be served with greater purity. More grates will be needed, and they could be brought from Burgos if necessary. And perhaps, if the little chapel of our Lady is built, the smallest grate will be needed there. I will try to find the means to pay for them if they are not available there. Every day I become more attached to that house; I don't know why.

---

1.   The devout woman promoting a Teresian foundation in Burgos.
2.   The prioress of Palencia.
3.   She decided to return to Avila rather than go to Burgos.
4.   The foundation in Burgos.
5.   The Archbishop of Burgos, Don Cristóbal Vela.
6.   The canon from Palencia sent by Don Alvaro de Mendoza to Burgos to prepare for a foundation there (see F. 31.5).
7.   Don Alvaro de Mendoza.
8.   If it is something that has to be negotiated with the city authorities.
9.   Alonso Velázquez, the Bishop of Burgo de Osma.
10.   Nicolás Doria, who accompanied her on this foundation.

402. To Padre Jerónimo Gracián. Valladolid
Soria, 14 July 1581

The context of the foundation in Soria was a peaceful one. But there were many projects pending, in Avila, Madrid, Burgos, Toledo, and Alba. A major concern was the Carmelite vocation of the widow Doña Elena and the opposition of her uncle, Cardinal Quiroga of Toledo. Future plans included a foundation in Madrid and one in Burgos. Teresa desired to maintain a good relationship with the Carmelite general and to have the text of the nuns' new constitutions put into print. There were some difficult nuns at St. Joseph's in Avila.

❖❖❖❖

To our Father Provincial of the discalced Carmelites, Valladolid

1.   Jesus. The Holy Spirit be with your reverence, *mi padre*. I received a letter of yours dated the feast of St. John and afterward the one that came with Padre Nicolao's.[1] One very long one that you said you wrote me never arrived here. But even though these were short, the happiness they brought me in informing me of your good health was not small, for I was worried. May he, as he can, give you health.

2.   I have written you some letters. I wouldn't want the one to get lost where I begged you not to give permission to Doña Elena[2] to become a nun. Now they tell me this messenger for Valladolid, where according to what you say I think you will be, is a very safe one. Since you will be there so close to San Alejo,[3] I thought of sending you these letters from Toledo so that you may see how upset the archbishop[4] is over it, and I do not want us in any way to have him for an enemy. And apart from this, never is there talk about her entering that I do not feel great resistance. For where mother and daughter[5] and other relatives are present, along with what is known about this woman, I fear there will be much disquiet and that she won't be very happy. And so even before I spoke to the archbishop, I had asked Padre

Baltasar Alvarez[6] to prevent it, and he promised to do so, for he agreed with me, and he knew her very well. See how it can seem that I persuaded her. I have written to the cardinal that I will inform you,[7] and not to worry, for she will not be received, and that I would be very distressed if her entrance were not prevented.

3.   You realize how secret the contents of this letter must be. In any case, tear it up so that no one thinks that it is because of him that we are not accepting her, but that it is because it would not be opportune either for her or for her children, as is true. We already have a lot of experience with these widows.

4.   Before I forget, I am afraid that these constitutions[8] are never going to get printed. For goodness' sake do not neglect to do this; see how important it is. By now we could have had a large volume of history published.

5.   Now let's take up Burgos.[9] I am enclosing the response, and I am surprised by those who think I can just get up and go there. In my answer to the bishop,[10] I told him that because of my illnesses you ordered me not to go to Burgos at a time in which I would have to be there in winter – you once wrote this to me. This I did so as not to put in doubt the archbishop's[11] intentions and cause hostilities between him and the Bishop of Palencia, something to be avoided. After writing to the Bishop of Palencia, I wrote to the Archbishop of Burgos that because I thought I would be a bother to him if the city did not grant the license[12] – since I thought they would pay little attention to me – I would let the project go until the city authorized it. The hour for this foundation must not have arrived. I think that Fray Baltasar's[13] hour arrived first; so goes the world.

6.   A foundation in Madrid is what would now be fitting, and I believe that when the archbishop sees that what he wants is being done, he will authorize it quickly. The bishop[14] here, who is going there in September, tells me that he will give his support. I will be finished here, with God's help, in the middle of August. After the feast of Our Lady, if it appears all right to

you, I will be able to go to Avila – for it doesn't seem to me that those sisters spoke clearly with Padre Nicolao – for here I have nothing to do. But if there is no big need, it would give me great consolation not to have to remain as prioress,[15] for I am no longer fit for the task. It requires more energy than I have and makes me feel scrupulous.

7.   If Padre Fray Gregorio Nacianceno remains there, as I wrote to you, the prioress will suffice[16] since there is no one else there. And although I say "will suffice," I think I am lying because I don't think there is anyone who can handle the internal affairs of the house. You will see what is best there. The concern I have for that house enables me to give little importance to whatever labor I would have to undergo so as to overcome its difficulties, and the fact that I will be waiting there for the Lord to open the way to a foundation in Madrid will be of some help. But one's human nature will not fail to feel in that place the absence of my brother and friends,[17] and what is worse the presence of the ones who have remained.

8.   As for the trip to Rome, I now see that it is very necessary, although there is nothing to fear in going to give obedience to the general.[18] And because of the risk of the journey and our need, I would like to see friars sent who would not be missed so much if anything were to happen. You would certainly miss Padre Nicolao a great deal, although he would be the one who could best smooth everything over. I think that if from time to time you give to the general signs of our obedience and respectfulness there will be no problem. This is very necessary so that he understand that you are his subjects and that you all realize that you have a superior. Things must not be as in the past, nor the expenses,[19] for this would be a burden for all the houses.

9.   I forgot to mention the joy the agreement about the chapel[20] brought me, for it is very well done. Glory to God, some benefit came from delaying.

With that daughter of the Flemish woman,[21] I fear that you will have work for a whole lifetime, as you do with her mother; and please God she won't be worse. Believe me I fear an unhappy nun more than many devils. God pardon the one who took her back. Do not give permission for her profession until I come there, if God desires. I am writing Padre Nicolao to let me know if they have equipment there for travel, for I don't see much here. May God dispose everything for his greater service.

10.   Please God you have been able to do something in that matter concerning Beatriz.[22] For some days I have been afflicted over it. I have written a number of letters to her and her mother telling them terrible things that should have been enough for them to make some amends. For although they were without fault, I set before them the dangers that before God and the world they could have gotten into. In my opinion, though, they are not exempt, and the parents are more to blame because they allow her to give them orders. It's a lost cause, and I believe that if they do not remove the occasion completely, things will go from bad to worse, if such is possible, for they are bad enough now. As for honor, it is already lost, and I am passing over the matter even though it troubles me to do so. I wouldn't want souls to be lost, but I see them, parents and children, so lacking in good sense that I don't find any remedy. May God provide one and give you the grace to bring things to an appropriate conclusion. I see no other remedy than to put her in a monastery, but I don't know how considering their financial situation. It would be a solution if she could remain as a student.[23]

11.   I beg you to write and let me know what you did and what you decide about my going to Avila. Given the scarcity of messengers and the brevity of your letters, you need to write in time.

May God preserve you with the holiness I beg of him, amen, amen.

Today is 14 July

12.   The bishop is leaving here[24] within ten days for the synod. The foundress[25] asks me to give you her best regards; consider

them received along with those from all the others, for I am tired – although well.

Your reverence's unworthy servant and subject – how gladly I say this,

Teresa of Jesus

If Padre Nicolao is not there, read the letter that is enclosed for him.

---

1. Nicolás Doria, who accompanied her to Soria and was now on his return, either in Avila or Valladolid.
2. Elena de Quiroga, niece of the Cardinal Archbishop of Toledo, Gaspar de Quiroga, who wants to be a discalced Carmelite nun against the desires of her uncle.
3. A monastery of friars on the outskirts of Valladolid.
4. The Archbishop of Toledo, Gaspar de Quiroga.
5. Doña Elena, a widow, wants to enter the Carmel of Medina where her daughter, Jerónima de la Encarnación, is a nun.
6. Her former Jesuit confessor (F. 28.14–16).
7. See her letter to the Cardinal's secretary, Ltr. 399.4.
8. The constitutions prepared for the nuns at the chapter of the discalced Carmelite friars in Alcalá. Gracián had them published this same year.
9. She is referring to a plan for a foundation of discalced Carmelite nuns in Burgos.
10. The Bishop of Palencia, Alvaro de Mendoza, who interceded in favor of the foundation (see F. 31.3).
11. The Archbishop of Burgos, Cristóbal Vela, had promised to give permission for the foundation, but doesn't seem disposed to carry through on his promise.
12. She had to obtain a license from the city of Burgos first.
13. A troubled Carmelite who had transferred to the discalced friars, and disliked Gracián, was working to make a foundation in Madrid.
14. Alonso Velázquez, Bishop of Osma.
15. Prioress of St. Joseph's in Avila, a monastery that was having serious difficulties. In fact she had to accept the charge as soon as she arrived back (10 September).
16. The prioress in Avila was María de Cristo. Teresa had proposed Padre Gregorio Nacianceno for confessor to her discalced nuns in Avila.

17. An allusion to the recent deaths of Francisco de Salcedo and Lorenzo de Cepeda.

18. The general of the Carmelite Order, Giovanni Battista Caffardo.

19. She is referring to both the conflicts the discalced friars had with the central government of the order and the expense of their trips to Rome to negotiate their becoming a separate province.

20. She is alluding either to the chapel in Alba (see Ltr. 371.4) or the one for St. Joseph's in Avila willed by her brother, Lorenzo de Cepeda.

21. The Flemish woman was Ana Wasteels (Ana de San Pedro), a nun at St. Joseph's in Avila; her daughter, Ana de los Angeles, after spending a year with the Bernardan sisters in Avila, also entered St. Joseph's.

22. Her niece Beatriz de Ovalle had been the victim of a calumny at that time.

23. As one living in a convent school, receiving an education.

24. The Bishop of Osma, Alonso Velázqez.

25. The foundress, or benefactor, for the new Carmel in Soria, Beatriz de Beamonte.

403. To Padre Jerónimo Gracián, Salamanca

Soria, 7 August 1581

(Autograph: DCN, Consuegra [Toledo])

Things were going well in Andalusia. The new foundation in Soria was moving along peacefully. But Gracián was meeting with financial difficulties in Salamanca. The autograph is incomplete.

1. I am delighted that things in Andalusia have gone so well, although it will still be necessary that you make the visitations there this winter when the pestilence is completely gone. I am delighted to know that according to what Casademonte[1] writes me it is already gone.

2. You wouldn't believe how much I desire to send you a lot of money, because you have so little, and truly everyone should come to the help of that house[2] because it will be so beneficial

for the order. I have been devising different schemes; I don't know what I'll come up with. I don't think it will be much.

3.   It's very hot here. Be careful not to get absorbed in overseeing the work, because the sun is now beginning to burn ...

4.   Today is the feast of our Father St. Albert.[3] A Dominican friar preached and spoke a great deal about him.

Your reverence's servant and subject,

Teresa of Jesus

1.   Pedro Juan de Casademonte, a merchant friend of Teresa's.

2.   A foundation for discalced Carmelite friars in Salamanca, which was greatly desired by both Teresa and Gracián because of the University that was in Salamanca.

3.   A Carmelite priest living in Sicily in the 13th century who was remembered for his purity and prayer, preaching and miracles.

404. To Doña Juana de Ahumada, Alba

Segovia, 26 August 1581

(Autograph: DCF, Burgo de Osma)

The difficult journey from Soria to Segovia (see F. 30.12–13) lasted from 16–23 August. Teresa was eager to see both her sister Juana and her daughter Beatriz, and one of the reasons for this was the gross calumny that a jealous woman was spreading against Beatriz, then about 21 years old, accusing her of an illicit relationship with her husband (see Ltr. 409.7).

1.   Jesus. The grace of the Holy Spirit be with your honor. I arrived here in Segovia on the eve of St. Bartholomew[1] feeling well, glory to God, although very tired because the road was bad. So I will stay here six or seven days to rest, and then, if the Lord be served, I will leave for Avila.

2.   Since I am coming from such a distance, it wouldn't amount to much for Señor Juan de Ovalle to grant me the

favor of giving you and your daughter permission to come to see me, even though there may be some obstacles to this and he would have to stay and watch the house. He could come to see me on another day. Beg him to let you come and let him take this letter as being addressed also to him. Since this messenger has to leave at once, I am not writing him directly. I greatly desire that he grant me this favor, for you can come and stay with Pedro de Ahumada, and I will pay the round-trip traveling expense for the animals. Perhaps I will have to go far away again, and in no manner would I want to do so without seeing you.[2]

3. Because I trust you won't do otherwise, I'll be waiting for you to come some time before the feast of our Lady.[3]

4. My best regards to Señor Don Gonzalo and to Señora Doña Beatriz. May God watch over you all and make you as holy as I beg of him, amen.

Today is 26 August.

Your honor's unworthy servant,

Teresa of Jesus

5. Because I hope in God that we will see each other soon, I'll say no more. Give my best regards to Señora Doña Mayor[4] and to whomever else you think it opportune to do so.

---

1. 23 August.
2. Teresa had in mind a trip to Madrid to make a foundation there (see Ltr. 420.1–2). On 10 September she was elected prioress of St. Joseph's in Avila and remained there until 2 January 1582, when she left to make a foundation in Burgos.
3. The feast of the Birth of the Virgin Mary (8 September). It doesn't seem that Juana and her daughter arrived in Avila until after 15 December. There they spent their last Christmas with Teresa.
4. Gonzalo and Beatriz were Juana's children, and Doña Mayor de Ovalle, Juan de Ovalle's sister, was a Benedictine nun in Alba.

405. To Madre María de San José, Seville
Villacastín, 5 September 1581

(Autograph: Augustinian nuns, Villadiego [Burgos])

On the journey from Soria to Avila they had to stop in Segovia for six or seven days because of bad roads. Then they had another delay in Villacastín because of the difficulties in travel.

❖❖❖❖

For Mother Prioress of the discalced Carmelite nuns, behind San Francisco in Seville.

1. Jesus be with you, my daughter. I arrived last night, 4 September, in this town of Villacastín, really tired of traveling, for I am coming from the foundation in Soria on my way to Avila, with more than forty leagues to go. We got into many troubles and dangers. Despite everything, I am well, glory to God, and that new monastery is going well also. May God be pleased to make use of all the suffering, for that makes it worthwhile.

2. When he saw that everything was ready for my departure, Padre Acacio García came to the inn here to see me – for Sister San Francisco[1] knows him well – and said that he had a reliable messenger. I am now writing these lines so that my daughters will have news of me.

3. I am very happy to learn that the pestilence is gone and that you are all well. The Lord shows his love for you. Our Father[2] is also well; he is in Salamanca. Padre Nicolao[3] is awaiting me in Avila, for he is going to Rome (which I am very sorry about) to get better confirmation of our affairs, for the king has desired this. He has been sick with typhus fever, but now is well. Pray fervently for him, for everyone owes this to him.

4. My daughter: the two hundred ducats have not reached me. They tell me that Señor Horacio de Oria[4] has them. If that is so, they are in good hands. I have already told you to send them to me by way of Medina.[5] I would now like to begin the

chapel for my brother –[6] God give him glory – for this is on my conscience.[7] Would you give orders that they be sent to me, for otherwise I cannot take them into account.

5.   May our Lord watch over you and all the nuns for me, and make you all as holy as I beg of him, amen, amen and allow me to see you.

Your reverence's servant,

Teresa of Jesus

1.   Isabel de San Francisco, born in Villacastín.
2.   Jerónimo Gracián.
3.   Nicolás Doria, who had accompanied her to Soria for the foundation there and from where he then went to Salamanca.
4.   Nicolás Doria's brother, a canon in Toledo.
5.   See Ltr. 366.3.
6.   Lorenzo de Cepeda.
7.   Teresa had been appointed executor of Lorenzo's will.

406. To Don Jerónimo Reinoso, Palencia
Avila, 9 September 1581

Teresa arrived back in Avila unwell after a long and difficult journey. On the very following day the prioress of St. Joseph's, María de Cristo, renounced her office, and Teresa was elected prioress.

1.   Jesus. The grace of the Holy Spirit be with your honor. I am now in Avila, *mi padre*, where I would most willingly be your daughter again if you were here, for I feel very much alone in this city where I find no one who can console me in my present situation. May God provide a remedy. The more I go on, the less I find in this life that can provide consolation.

2.   I was not well when I arrived here, but had a slight fever caused by a certain circumstance. Now I am well, and it seems the body is relieved for not having to go on another trip so soon. For I tell you, these trips are very tiring, although I can't say that

about the one from here to Soria. That trip was recreation for me, it being a smooth journey, often with a view of rivers that provided pleasant company. Our good procurator[1] will have told you about this experience.

3.   It's a strange thing that not one of those who desire to do me a favor escapes without a good deal of trouble, but God gives them the charity to enjoy it, as he has done with you. See that you do not fail to write me a letter when you have a messenger, even though you may find it tiring to do so, for I tell you there is very little in which to find rest, and many trials.

4.   I am delighted that Dionisia[2] has entered. I beg you to tell the chief mail carrier[3] and give him my regards, and don't forget to pray for me. Since I arrived only a short time ago, there is no lack of visitors and so little opportunity to relax by writing to you.

5.   I kiss Don Francisco's[4] hands. May our Lord watch over you with an increase in holiness, as I beg of him, amen.

Today is 9 September.

Your honor's unworthy servant and daughter,

Teresa of Jesus

---

1.   Pedro Ribera, who accompanied Teresa on the long journey from Soria to Avila.
2.   Dionisia de la Madre de Dios entered the Carmel of Palencia and made her profession the following year.
3.   Diego Reinoso, Jerónimo's brother, was the chief mail carrier.
4.   Francisco Reinoso, Jerónimo's brother.

407. To Dionisio Ruiz, Toledo
Avila, 13 September 1581

Only about a week after she arrived in Avila, tired and in poor health, Teresa gave up on the plan for a foundation in Burgos. She longs to make one in Madrid, but Cardinal Quiroga is not in any hurry. Meanwhile his niece, after her children are settled in life, wants to become a discalced Carmelite nun. Teresa lends her strong support.

❖❖❖❖

1.   Jesus. The grace of the Holy Spirit be with your honor, and may His Majesty repay you for the kindness you showed me with your letter and the consolation it brought. I received it while in Soria. Now I am in Avila where Father Provincial[1] sent me to stay until, our Lord be pleased, the cardinal gives us permission to make a foundation in Madrid.[2] It would be a very long time for me to have to wait until his illustrious lordship goes to Madrid, for since he has to convoke the bishops in Toledo,[3] I think Lent will go by first. So I am trusting that he will do me this favor beforehand, if for no other reason than to prevent me from having to spend the winter in such severe weather as one finds here in Avila, for it usually does me much harm. I beg you not to forget to remind him from time to time. In the letter he wrote to me in Soria,[4] he did not expand on the matter.

2.   Now I am writing him about this affair concerning Señora Doña Elena,[5] which causes me much grief, and I am sending him a letter that she wrote me, for from what she says, if we do not receive her in this order, she wants to go to the Franciscans. I am very disturbed, for she will never be happy there from what I understand of her spirit, which is more suited to our order. And, after all, her own daughter[6] is here and she is near her children.

3.   I beg you to pray for this and try to get his illustrious lordship to answer me, for she is most distressed, and since I love her so much, I feel very sad about it and don't know what to do for her.[7]

4.   This is meant for you alone. May our Lord watch over you with the increase of holiness that I beg of him for you.

Written in St. Joseph's on 13 September.

Your honor's unworthy servant,

Teresa of Jesus

1. Jerónimo Gracián.
2. Madrid was at the time under the jurisdiction of the Archbishop of Toledo, Gaspar de Quiroga.
3. Quiroga convoked a provincial synod in Toledo to open on 8 September. It dragged on until September of the following year, 1582.
4. See Ltr. 397.
5. Doña Elena de Quiroga in Medina, the cardinal's niece.
6. Jerónima de la Encarnación, a discalced Carmelite nun in Medina. One son was married and living in Medina; the other two were priests, appointed canons in the cathedral of Toledo.
7. In the end Doña Elena entered the Carmel in Medina on 14 October of that year, and her uncle was very pleased.

408. To Padre Jerónimo Gracián, Salamanca
Avila, 17 September 1581

(Autograph: DCN, Corpus Christi, Alcalá de Henares)

Teresa received the jarring news that Casilda de Padilla had left the Carmel in Valladolid to enter the Franciscan community of Santa Gadea, where she would become abbess. Teresa had written glowingly of her and her vocation at a young age in The Book of her Foundations, *chaps. 10–11. But Teresa quickly regained her composure and expresses compassion for the "poor girl" under so much pressure from her wealthy family.*

1.   Jesus be with your reverence, *mi padre.* I have also written you by way of Toledo. Today they brought me this letter from Valladolid with news[1] that at first really astounded me. But then I reflected that God's ways are great and that after all he loves this order and will draw some good from what happened or prevent some evil of which we are not aware. For love of our Lord, don't be distressed.

2.   I feel very sorry for the poor girl.[2] She is the worse off, for it is nonsense to think that the one who went about with such joy[3] is now unhappy. His Majesty must not want us to be receiving honor through the lords of the earth but through those who are little and poor, as were the apostles. So there is no need to pay any attention to the matter. And since they also got the other daughter to leave Santa Catalina de Sena[4] along with her, nothing will be lost here; I mean as far as the worldly criticism goes, for with respect to God, as I say, perhaps it is better that we keep our eyes on him alone. May she go with God.

3.   May he deliver me from these all-powerful lords with their strange reversals! Even though that poor little thing did not understand, I don't think it would be good for us if she were to return to the order. If there is something bad, it is the harm that things like this can do us when we are still in our beginning stages. That her unhappiness was as great as is that of the sister who is here[5] does not surprise me. But I would consider it impossible for her to have hidden her unhappiness for so long a time if it were so.

4.   This intrigue must have begun when the subprioress of Palencia[6] began to disagree with the prioress in Valladolid.[7] The confessor was a Jesuit father, a very good friend of María de Acuña's, and I learned that he counseled the sisters not to vote for anyone but the prioress, because the subprioress was at odds with Doña María de Acuña. And since Doña Casilda had not renounced her inheritance and Doña María wanted it for a school, everything would have perhaps worked together toward that end; although if they had seen that Casilda was happy, I don't think they would have done it. God deliver us from all this conniving.

5.   Despite everything, I don't think it would be fitting for us to change in our attitude toward members of the Society. For many reasons this would not be good for us to do, and one of the reasons is that most of the nuns who come here do so through them, and if aspirants were to think they ought not

consult with the Jesuit fathers, they wouldn't be coming to us anymore. But it will be a great thing to have our own fathers, because we can then detach ourselves little by little from the others. May God give you light, for since this messenger has to leave now, I'll say no more.

6.   Your crucifix was left here and I don't know how to send it so that it won't break. Take another one from the nuns in Toledo, and we will send them this one from here. I feel sorry for what that poor prioress is going through and for our María de San José.[8] You should write to her. I am certainly very sorry to see you go so far away now; I don't know what has happened to me. May God accompany you with blessings, and give my regards to Padre Nicolao.[9] All the nuns here send their regards to you and him.

Today is 17 September.

Your reverence's subject and daughter,

Teresa of Jesus

7.   Doña María de Acuña wrote to the prioress begging her many times for pardon and stating that she wasn't able to do more and that the prioress should figure out what she owes the community for their having provided food for her daughter. She is thinking of keeping the inheritance, and for this reason they must allege a reason why the profession was made before time. Since they had a brief from the pope,[10] I don't know how she can say this. I pity poor Casilda, because her love for the order was so great. I don't know what demon got into her. May God be with her.

---

1.   News of the sudden departure of Casilda de Padilla from the Carmel in Valladolid.
2.   Casilda de Padilla.
3.   Casilda was overjoyed when permission for her to make profession came from Rome (see Ltr. 145.2). In 1580, the previous year, Teresa had lived with her in the Carmel of Valladolid for almost five months (August–December).

4. The other daughter, María de Acuña y Manrique, had been a Dominican nun at Santa Catalina's.
5. A probable allusion to Ana de los Angeles (Wasteels).
6. Dorotea de la Cruz (Ponce de León), who was formerly subprioress in Valladolid.
7. María Bautista.
8. Gracián's sister, a Carmelite nun in Valladolid and a close friend of Casilda's.
9. Nicolás Doria.
10. A brief had been obtained from Rome so that Casilda could make her profession before the required age (see Ltrs. 145.2; and 164).

409. To Sancho Dávila, Alba
Avila, 9 October 1581

(Autograph: DCN, Ocaña [Toledo])

Don Sancho was from Avila, a priest, theologian, and professor at Salamanca. In a letter to Teresa he sought her guidance over some problems with his interior life. He had written a biography of his own mother, who had died two years before in the odor of sanctity. After giving him some guidance, Teresa seeks his help for a problem that was causing her much pain. Some calumnies were being spoken against her niece (Beatriz), and nobody seemed to be doing anything about it. After Teresa's death, Beatriz became a discalced Carmelite nun serving the order well in a number of responsible positions.

To the very illustrious Señor Don Sancho Dávila, in Alba.

1. Jesus. The grace of the Holy Spirit be with your honor always. It was a great favor and gift for me to have a letter from you. Yet, since I had been hoping for a visit from you one of these days and I now see that I won't be able to have that joy, the happiness your letter brought me is somewhat diluted. I have praised our Lord and have considered what you hold to be a loss a great favor from him, for no benefit could come

to a soul, or health, from such extreme suffering. So you can thank His Majesty, for in taking it away he did not take from her the possibility of serving our Lord, which is what is most important. You do not feel within you that great determination not to offend him, but when the occasion arises to serve him and to reject what could be for you an occasion to displease him you find you are strong – that is the authentic sign of a true desire, in my opinion. And that you are happy to receive the most Blessed Sacrament each day and feel sorry when you do not is the sign of a close friendship, and not as common as you think. Always consider the favors you receive from his hand as given for the purpose of growing in his love, and stop going about looking for all the little subtleties of your miseries, for these show themselves to everyone *en masse*, very much so, especially with me.

2.   In regard to being distracted during the recitation of the divine office, although I am perhaps much at fault, I like to think it is due to a weakness of the head. And you should think the same, for the Lord knows well that when we pray we would like to pray very well. Today I confessed this to Padre Maestro Fray Domingo,[1] and he told me not to pay attention to it, and I beg of you the same, for I consider it an incurable evil.

3.   Your trouble with your teeth makes me feel very sorry, for I have had much experience with how painful that can be. If one is infected, it usually seems that they all are – I mean that all hurt. I have not found a better remedy than having it pulled, although that doesn't help if the pain is caused by neuralgia. May God take away the pain as I will beg of him.

4.   You did very well to write the life of so holy a person.[2] I would be a good witness to the truth of her holiness. I kiss your hands for what you do for me in allowing me to see it.

5.   I am getting along better. Compared to last year, I can say that I am well, although not much time goes by that I am not suffering something; and since I see that as long as one lives, suffering is what is best, I bear it willingly.

6.   I would like to know if the marquis[3] is there, and to receive some news about Señora Doña Juana de Toledo, his daughter, and about how the marquess is.[4] I beg you to tell them that even though I have gone far away, I do not forget to remember them to our Lord in my poor prayers. I don't do much for your honor since you are my father and lord.

7.   I kiss your hands for assuring me that you will be so for me if I need to ask you for help; and I want to do so. Because I am so confident that you will help me, if you see that it is fitting, I want to tell you alone of a great sorrow that I have been bearing for almost a year. It could be that you might be able to provide some remedy. I truly believe that you will know – for they tell me that, for my sins, it is something public – about the great jealousy of Don Gonzalo's[5] wife. They have told her, and she takes it to be true, that her husband is involved in a wicked friendship with Doña Beatriz,[6] my sister's daughter. And she says and asserts this so publicly that the majority of the people believe her. And so, with respect to the young girl's honor, it must now be so lost that there is no point for me to even consider it, but I am concerned about the many offenses committed against God. I am extremely sorry that a relative of mine should be the occasion for this, and so I have arranged with her parents to have her move away from there, for some learned men have told me the parents have an obligation to do this. And even if they didn't, it seems to me it would be wise to flee as from a wild animal the tongue of a woman inflamed with jealousy. Others tell the family that doing so would make a lie appear to be true, and that they shouldn't move. They tell me that the husband and wife are separated. I see that there is already talk about it by the wife's sister here in Avila, and many calumnies are being spread by those doing the talking. And the talk has extended even to Salamanca. The evil is spreading and neither from one side nor from the other is any remedy being applied. Her parents pay no attention to the things I tell them – which are not a few –[7] but say I am being deceived.

8.   I beg you to write me and let me know what I should do so that these offenses against God may stop, for as I say, it would be hard now to salvage her honor in the people's opinion. I had thought of a means, but I would find it hard to put into effect. If you have any dealings with that Don Gonzalo, perhaps you could convince him to leave that place for maybe a year or a half year until his wife returns to normal, since he has a good residence elsewhere and sees the harm that is being done to this girl because of him. And in the meanwhile perhaps the Lord will so arrange that by the time he returns the girl will no longer be there. For without this, the way things are going – and what there is now is already bad – I fear some great evil will arise.

9.   I beg you, if you see any way in which you can help me, to take this trial from me. May our Lord do so as he can, and may he give you the holiness that I beg of him for you, amen.

Today is 9 October.

Your honor's unworthy servant and daughter,

Teresa of Jesus

10.   I beg you to give greetings for me to Don Fadrique and to my lady Doña María,[8] for my head is in no condition to write to them, and pardon me out of love for God.

---

1.   The Dominican, Padre Domingo Báñez.
2.   Sancho Dávila had written a biography of his mother, Doña Juana Enríquez de Toledo, the daughter of the counts of Alba de Liste and wife of the son of the marquises of Velada (also known as Sancho Dávila). She was a highly esteemed friend of Teresa's.
3.   The Marquis of Velada, Gómez Dávila, Don Sancho's brother.
4.   The Marquess of Velada, Ana de Toledo y Monroy. The daughter was Juana de Toledo.
5.   Don Gonzalo is someone who appears often in Teresa's last letters to her sister Juana de Ahumada. His wife became extremely jealous of him and Teresa's niece.
6.   Beatriz de Ovalle.
7.   See Teresa's insistence in her letters to her sister and brother-in-law: Ltrs. 404; 414; 420; and 439.

8. Fadrique de Toledo, (the Duke of Alba's son) and his wife María de Toledo y Colonna.

410. To Padre Jerónimo Gracián, Salamanca
Avila, 26 October 1581

Teresa had been prioress in Avila for a month and a half, but had not heard from Gracián. A number of problems have arisen for which she needs his counsel or intervention. She no longer suffers from interior fears of being deluded as she formerly did and feels much less need of spiritual guidance from others beyond her confessor.

1.   Jesus. The grace of the Holy Spirit be with your reverence. Apart from the loneliness it makes me feel to have had no word of you for so long a time, it's painful for me not to know where you are. If something were to arise in which I would need your advice, this would cause problems, but even apart from that, such ignorance is hard for me to bear. Please God you are well. I am well and have become a grand prioress,[1] as if I didn't have anything else to attend to. The notebooks are now done, and all the nuns are happy with them.

2.   You should know that I told Ana de San Pedro's[2] daughter that she should not consider herself a tacitly professed nun. She saw that I was determined that she should not make profession except in the mitigated rule, but that afterward she could stay here, for this was the agreement her mother and I came to; and that she would give a dowry here and another one at the Incarnation. The one who insisted most that she was not suited for here was her mother. The daughter felt this very much and says that she is willing for them to test her as many years as they want and that she will accept the confessors that they give her and that after that, if they want to send her away, she will leave willingly. Well, we have seen a turnabout that has amazed us all, although it hasn't been going on for long, not more than fifteen days.

3.   All her trials of soul have disappeared and she goes about most joyfully. She is clearly happy and in good health. If this continues, one couldn't in conscience refuse her profession. I inquired of her and of her confessors and I am told that these anxieties were not normal for her, that she hadn't had them for more than a year and a half. Here they had given me to believe that she had always felt them, but I had never been here when she did. It seems also that she is more open. In your charity pray for her. Sometimes I have wondered if it isn't the devil who is making her wise, without all those anxieties, so as to deceive us and leave us afterward tormented by both her and her mother, although the mother is conducting herself well now. Her mother liked the idea about the Incarnation, and so did I.

4.   The daughter would like to nullify the contract and give more to this monastery, and she asked me to allow her to speak to Doctor Castro;[3] yet she didn't tell me why, but he told me. And he looked at the contract and says that it is very tightly drawn up. She asked for his opinion, and he didn't want to give it, but he told her that he was a friend both of the Theatines[4] and of this house also and that he was on good terms with both, that she should ask someone else. I told him that there was no need to get into this, for we would not take her for the sake of her fortune but only if she were suited for the life here; nor would we send her away for such a reason if she were doing well. The truth is that I spoke with reserve.

5.   Tell me who this man is and if he can be trusted, for his intelligence, charm, and manner of speech please me very much. I don't know whether that may be due to the fact that he is so close to you. He has come here a few times. One of the days, during the octave of All Saints, he will preach to us. He doesn't want to hear the confessions of anyone. But it seems to me that he would like to hear my confession, and what I suspect – since in general he is adverse to hearing confessions – is that his desire comes from his curiosity. They say that he is very much opposed to revelations, that he even says he doesn't

believe those given to St. Bridget. He didn't say this to me but has said it to María de Cristo.[5] If this occasion had arisen previously, I would have tried at once to discuss my soul with him, for I used to be drawn toward those who I knew had such opinions, thinking that they would be the ones who would free me from illusion if I were being deceived –[6] more so than others. Since I no longer have those fears, I don't feel this desire so much, but only a little. If I didn't have a confessor and it seemed all right to you, I would go to him. But I no longer seek guidance much from anyone, except my former confessors, since I am at peace.

6.   I am enclosing a letter from Villanueva, for I felt distressed and sorry for that prioress who has to suffer so many trials on account of the subprioress.[7] The situation is almost the same as at Malagón. The disturbance that these nuns with such humors bring to the peace of all the others is a terrible one, and thus I have such fear of allowing them to make profession. I so wish you would go to that house. And if the foundation is made in Granada,[8] it wouldn't be a bad idea to bring her there with one or two lay sisters, for under the guidance of Anne of Jesus and in a larger house, they would get along better, and there would be friars in that place to hear their confessions. Despite everything, I think the house in Villanueva will continue making progress, for there are good souls in the community. And even if they accept two postulants who are relatives of the parish priest, as he desires, things will work out very well if they are given what they should be given.[9]

7.   Nicolao[10] desires very much that you go to Seville, and the reason is for what his brother[11] tells him, and it must be of some importance. I have already written him of how well the nuns there are doing, for I received a letter from the prioress.[12] I already wrote him that it wasn't possible for you to leave Salamanca.

8.   Here I ruled that when someone is sick the nuns should not visit her together, but one at a time, unless the sickness is

of a kind that requires some other procedure. There are many drawbacks to having a number of nuns congregating together, for we are few in number, and this can sometimes lead to gossiping. If you think it would be good, make this a rule there too; and if not, let me know.

9.　　Oh, *mi padre*, how difficult Julián[13] is being! He is incapable of refusing to allow Mariana[14] to see him every time she wants, but he even asks her to come and see him. With him everything is holy; but God deliver us from confessors who are up in years. It would be a good thing if this practice were uprooted. What would happen if we were not dealing with such good souls? After having written this letter, I went through certain things here with one of the sisters that displeased me very much, which is why I mentioned this, for I had not thought of speaking about it. The remedy will be to take the two away from here if the foundation is made in Madrid.[15] Although it is holy, I cannot put up with it. May God make you what I beg of him and watch over you for us.

Today is the vigil of St. Vincent; tomorrow the vigil of the two apostles.

　　　　Your reverence's unworthy servant and subject,

　　　　　　　Teresa of Jesus

10.　　According to what the prioress of Toledo[16] writes me, the one who is bringing this letter will ask me tomorrow to petition you to give him the habit. This I am doing now. Give orders wherever you are that the prayers for the deceased be said for María Magdalena,[17] whom the good Lord took, as you will see from the enclosed letter – and inform all the monasteries.

1.　See Ltr. 402.6, where she asked not to have to continue being prioress.

2.　Ana de San Pedro (Wasteels), the Flemish nun; her daughter received the name Ana de los Angeles.

3.　Pedro de Castro y Nero, future bishop of Lugo and of Segovia, had been a classmate of Gracián's in Alcalá.

4. The Jesuits (called Theatines), in Avila, to whom the Wasteels had left a portion of their inheritance.
5. María de Cristo had been prioress of the monastery in Avila until 10 September of that year.
6. See ST 58.
7. The prioress of Villanueva de la Jara was María de los Mártires, and the subprioress, Elvira de San Angelo, who suffered from the emotional illnesses of scrupulosity and melancholy.
8. The Carmel in Granada was founded in January, 1582, by Anne of Jesus with the help of St. John of the Cross.
9. The parish priest of Villanueva de la Jara was Agustín Ervías, "a learned man of great virtue" (F. 28.8).
10. Nicolás Doria.
11. Horacio de Oria (see Ltr. 405.4).
12. The prioress of Seville, María de San José.
13. Julián de Avila, the chaplain at the Carmel of St. Joseph in Avila.
14. Mariana de Jesús, a Carmelite nun in Avila.
15. A foundation of a Carmel in Madrid was a strong desire of Teresa's and in the planning stage.
16. Ana de los Angeles (Gómez).
17. María Magdalena Tejada, a professed nun at the Incarnation in Avila, who then became a discalced Carmelite nun in Malagón, where she died.

411. To Don Gaspar de Quiroga, Toledo
Avila, 30 October 1581

(Autograph: Señores de Huarte Garrán, Valladolid)

Cardinal Quiroga had opposed his niece's desire to become a discalced Carmelite nun and erroneously blamed Teresa for encouraging her. Surprisingly, he later changed his mind and begged Teresa to give his niece the habit. Teresa here responds happily and respectfully to the cardinal's two letters.

1. Jesus. The grace of the Holy Spirit be always with your most illustrious lordship. I received two letters from you, a favor that was for me a great consolation. I kiss your hands many

times. I have already obeyed the orders you gave me in them to give the habit to our dear sister Elena de Jesús.[1] As you will see from the enclosed letter, I hope in the Lord that she will bring much glory to our Lord and good to this holy order of his glorious Mother and that she will serve you more through her prayers; the more she grows in holiness, the more pleasing they will be to God.

2.   I give great thanks to His Majesty in learning that you are in good health. May he be pleased that this continue for many years, a petition that all of these subjects of yours make to him. I have confidence that through these prayers he will grant us this favor, for I know that these are good souls praying for you. Since I am so wretched, I have little trust in my own prayers, although I keep you truly present, especially each day when I am in his presence.

3.   Our Father Provincial[2] went to give the habit to your nephew and wrote to me of the great happiness this brought him.

From this house of St. Joseph's in Avila, 30 October.

Your most illustrious lordship's subject and servant.

Teresa of Jesus

---

1. She had received the habit on 14 October 1581, in the Carmel of Medina del Campo.
2. Jerónimo Gracián.

412. To Madre María de San José, Seville
Avila, 8 November 1581

(Autograph: DCN, Valladolid)

This long letter was written with an interval of fifteen days between its two parts. The first part (nos. 1–16) answers a letter from María de San José, which dealt with her heart ailments, the illness of the subprioress, the happiness in the community, minor doubts about the constitutions, and some delicate matters about the money left in Lorenzo's will. In the second part Teresa responds to Padre Rodrigo Alvarez's request to read her Interior Castle. *She is also entangled in both a difficult financial situation at St. Joseph's in Avila and complications that have arisen over her brother's will.*

✤·✤·✤·✤

For Mother Prioress at St. Joseph's, discalced Carmelite nuns, Seville.

1.   Jesus. May the Holy Spirit be with your reverence, my daughter. Your letter consoled me greatly, which is nothing new, for inasmuch as other letters weary me yours bring me relief. I tell you that if you indeed love me, I am grateful that you tell me and enjoy your doing so. How true it is that our human nature wants to be repaid. This could not be wrong, since our Lord also wants this, although there is no comparison between what we give His Majesty and all the love he deserves; but let us become like him however we can.

2.   I wrote you a really long letter[1] from Soria. I don't know whether Padre Nicolao[2] sent it to you. I ever have the fear that you didn't receive it. Many prayers were offered here for all of you. I am not surprised that you are well and at rest, but that you are not already saints. For since you had so many needs, the nuns have always offered many prayers for you here. Repay us for them now that you are without trials, since we have many trials, especially in this house of St. Joseph's in Avila, where they have made me prioress now out of sheer hunger.[3] Think of it, at my age and with all I have to do, how this can be borne!

3.   You should know that a gentleman[4] here left these nuns I don't know how much that doesn't pay for a quarter of what they need and which they won't be able to use for another year. And now almost all the alms that were being given them have ceased coming in, and they are so weighed down with debt that I don't know how it will all end. Pray for this and for

me, for one's human nature grows tired, especially of this being prioress with so much chaos all together. If God is served by this, nothing done is enough.

4.   It weighs on me that you resemble me in anything, for everything with me is going from bad to worse, especially in bodily ills. When they spoke to me about the condition of your heart, I didn't become very distressed, for even if the pain is hard to bear when intense it will soak up other pains, and in the end the condition is not dangerous. Since they told me they were afraid of dropsy, I considered the heart problem a good thing. You should know that they don't like to apply many remedies together, but calming the bodily humors is indispensable.

5.   Enclosed is a prescription for pills that are approved by many doctors, and a doctor who is highly regarded prescribed them for me. I think they will be very beneficial for you, even though you take one only every fifteen days. They have helped me very much, and so I am far better; although never completely well, because I still experience the vomitings and my other ailments. But the pills have done me great good and don't cause any other disturbance. Don't fail to try them.

6.   I had already known about the improvement of my Gabriela,[5] and I had also known about her serious illness, for our *padre*[6] was here when he received your note. I was very sorry about it and so was Teresa,[7] for she loves you all very much. She sends her regards to you and to all the sisters. If you saw her you would give praise to God for her understanding of the way of perfection and virtue. In your charity ask God to guide her onward, for the way the world is going one cannot trust in anything. We pray very hard for her. May God be praised for everything, for he left her here. Pray much for her, for me, and for all the nuns. Tell Sister San Francisco[8] that I was delighted with her letter and inform her that Acacio García[9] died, and that she should pray for him.

7.   I was extremely delighted to know that my good Padre García[10] has returned. God reward you for such good news,

for even though they had told me, I couldn't bring myself to believe it however much I desired it to be true. Be very gracious to him for me; be aware that he becomes a founder of this order when you consider all the help he gave me. So with him you shouldn't be using the veil that hides your faces. For all the others you should, in particular and in general, and, with the discalced friars first of all, for this is what is done in all the houses.

8.   They haven't brought anything from the Indies, for when they wanted to send it, they learned that my brother[11] had died – may he be in glory – and it is necessary for them to have a letter from Don Francisco[12] in order that the money be sent. Lorencio[13] is married and very well situated. They say that he has more than six thousand ducats in income. It is no surprise that he didn't write to you since he only just heard about his father's death. Oh, if he knew about the trials of his brother and what I have to go through with all these relatives! And so I run away from having any dealings with them. Since I told this to Padre Nicolao, he wanted me to agree, while I was in Palencia, to send the amount and that later the sum would be given to me here. I told him that in no way would I do that. So, I wrote you not to send me the money through Madrid; I had feared what did happen, and it didn't seem right to me, for I am a friend of openness.[14]

9.   Now he has written me again saying that he will send one hundred ducats and that I should collect the other hundred from someone who will not be able to pay it very soon. I wrote to him showing that I was very annoyed with you and saying that you both should have come to an agreement – that had actually passed through my mind. Despite my advice, you did what you did. What you deserve is to have to pay the amount twice, which is what you will have to do if the money isn't sent to me. But Horacio[15] is wrong, for if you gave him the money to send to me, it is not sufficient for his brother to allow him to keep it as a reimbursement without your authorization.

10.   Padre Nicolao says that from an alms of 1500 ducats Horacio is obliged to give your house 1,000. From that amount you can take something for what you still must pay. I have written to him to share a little of it with this house,[16] for it is certainly in extreme need. If the occasion arises beseech him a little on our behalf – for his brother[17] is also doing so – and arrange with him to withdraw 200 ducats. I am tired of speaking about it to Padre Nicolao, and I'll say no more about it to him. The chapel[18] is going to be started; and if while I am here nothing is done, at least it will have been started. I don't know how or when this will be, for I hope, please God, to go from here to Madrid[19] for a foundation there.

11.   You should know that the will speaks of 430 ducats,[20] it seems to me. I also vaguely remember your saying this, that he had given you thirty ducats. Since he had already made out the will when he went down there, and there is no further declaration, I don't know whether or not the thirty ducats has to be subtracted. Would you find out about this. So as not to tire myself, I am not going to read the will again to see if these thirty ducats are supposed to be in addition to the other amount. You will know down there. Believe me that if they were mine or in my power, I would much prefer not to have to bother with the matter. If you saw the state of ruin into which his property is falling! It's a pity, for this lad[21] was above all made for God. And although I want to withdraw from it all, they tell me that I am obliged in conscience. So, losing so good a brother was nothing in comparison to the trials those who remained have caused me. I don't know how it will end up.

12.   As for Padre Nicolao, he thought that the money should be given at once so as to pay his brother right away, but what has displeased me is his stubbornness in my regard and that you both in the end acted against my wishes. Certainly, even were I to desire it, I don't know which house could afford to give me that money, even though some might owe it to me. If the expenses of the province are shared and some houses are paying their quota,[22] other houses are not able to pay; and

some others have already given much. It would be better for his brother to wait than for us to fail to build the chapel, a task my brother left to me. And if I die, that would be the end of the matter, considering the need in which his son[23] finds himself. It could be that the money would be spent for something else; in fact, from what I see, that would be certain.

13. Don't fail to write to me about how your spiritual life is going, for that will bring me joy; in view of what you have gone through, it couldn't be going any other way than well. And send me the poems too. I delight in having something to make my sisters happy, for they need this. Let me know if Mother Sub-prioress has recovered completely. Since God has left her with us, may he be forever blessed.

14. Compline and recreation are observed as usual. I have asked learned men and have mentioned the drawbacks and also that the rule says that silence should be kept until the prayer beginning with the word pretiosa of Prime and no longer, and that here we keep it all day long.[24] This did not seem bad to our *padre*.

15. The entrance from the sacristy into the church should be bricked up. One should never go out that way – not even to close the street-door – for according to the *motu proprio*[25] one thereby incurs excommunication. Where it is possible, the woman helping us remains inside and closes the door from there. Here where we do not have a woman helping us, we made a lock by which the door can be opened from both the outside and the inside. And a helper from the outside closes it and opens it in the morning. We keep the other key so that if something happens we can get out. The trouble is that the church cannot be kept very clean, but this can't be helped.

16. There should be a turn for the chapel and a good sacristan. Because of the excommunication imposed by the pope concerning both this and the entrance, nothing else can be done. And it was sufficient that it was prescribed by the constitutions,[26] for the danger of not having such a rule about this

has already been discovered. To habitually transgress one of these prescriptions is a mortal sin.

17.   I wrote this letter over fifteen days ago, I believe. Now I received another from you and from my Father Rodrigo Alvarez,[27] toward whom I am greatly obligated because of the good he has brought about in that house. I would like to answer his letter, but I don't know how because some of the things about which he asks me cannot be put in a letter. But if I were to see him – who is one who knows my soul – I wouldn't hold back about anything; on the contrary, I would be very happy because I don't have anyone here with whom I can discuss this matter, which would be a consolation for me. If God brings Padre Fray Garcia here, I will have great consolation. Oh, how annoyed it made me that you didn't mention anything about him in your letter. He must have come to Madrid, for that is what I was told, and for that reason I am not writing to him although I have a great desire to do so and to see him. You would be amazed if you knew all that I owe him.

18.   To return to what I was saying, since our *padre* told me that he had left a book there in my handwriting[28] (which you certainly wouldn't be disposed to go through), would you read it to Padre Alvarez[29] when he goes there – the part about the last dwelling place. Do so under the seal of confession, which is what he in his great prudence asks for. Only the two of you should hear it. Tell him that the person referred to[30] reached that point and experiences that peace that is described there and continues living a life of great calm and that very learned men say that this is all right. If the reading cannot be done there, by no means should you give it to him, because of what could happen. I will not answer until he sends me his opinion about what is written in that book. Give him my regards.

1.   She is probably alluding to Ltr. 395, of which only a fragment remains.

2.   Nicolás Doria, who had accompanied Teresa to the foundation in Soria.

3.   The community of St. Joseph's in Avila was in dire financial straits.

4. Probably Francisco de Salcedo.

5. Leonor de San Gabriel.

6. Jerónimo Gracián.

7. Teresa's niece, a novice then at St. Joseph's in Avila, who formerly, at the age of nine, lived with the nuns in Seville (1575–76).

8. Isabel de San Francisco.

9. A priest whom she met in Villacastín (see Ltr. 405.2).

10. García de Toledo (see Ltr.366.8).

11. Lorenzo de Cepeda.

12. Francisco de Cepeda, Teresa's nephew.

13. Lorenzo de Cepeda, Teresa's younger nephew, who had returned to America.

14. In previous letters (366.3–6; 405.4), Teresa gave careful instructions about sending money owed to the deceased Lorenzo de Cepeda. Despite her warnings, the ducats ended up in the hands of Canon Horacio Doria who kept them as repayment for what he had loaned the discalced Carmelite friars.

15. Horacio Doria, brother of Nicolás Doria.

16. St. Joseph's in Avila.

17. Nicolás Doria.

18. The chapel that Lorenzo de Cepeda left orders to have built at St. Joseph's in Avila with the 200 ducats.

19. As things turned out she went not to Madrid but to Burgos.

20. Lorenzo wanted the 430 ducats to go for the chapel (see Ltr. 350.4).

21. Lorenzo's son, Francisco de Cepeda.

22. Since the 200 ducats were being held by Horacio in view of the 200 ducats he had advanced to the discalced friars for their trip to Rome on behalf of the nuns, he should now rather collect the sum from the discalced Carmelite nuns.

23. Francisco de Cepeda.

24. Teresa had introduced into her constitutions an hour of recreation (when silence was dispensed with) after Compline, whereas the rule prescribed a greater silence from Compline until the end of Prime of the next day. They kept a less strict silence all day long. The prayer *pretiosa* was a part of the office of Prime. In the present revision of the breviary, one finds a morning prayer and a night prayer similar to these.

25. She is alluding to *De Sacris Virginibus* of Gregory XIII (30 December 1572).

26. She is referring to a prescription in the constitutions redacted in Alcalá (1581), chapter 3.
27. A Jesuit in Seville.
28. The autograph of *The Interior Castle*.
29. Rodrigo Alvarez.
30. Teresa herself, who wrote *The Interior Castle*.

413. To Don Martín Alonso de Salinas, Palencia
Avila, 13 November 1581

Teresa received a letter from Palencia, where Canon Salinas and his friends were negotiating for a Teresian foundation in Burgos. Encouraging their efforts, she gives them some instructions. In Avila they are having much snow, but her health is better than usual.

1. Jesus. The grace of the Holy Spirit be with your honor. As a way of resting from other tiresome business, it would be good for you to write to me at times; for certainly when I see a letter from you, it is for me great grace and comfort, even though it renews in me the feeling of solitude at seeing you so far away and me so alone in this place. May God be praised for everything. I give him many thanks that your health is good and that those gentlemen, your brothers, arrived in good health.

2. Since you are now in Burgos, it wouldn't seem right to me – provided you agree – if you failed in any way to make every effort toward a foundation there, since God is now inspiring Señora Doña Catalina[1] to sponsor this. Perhaps there is some mystery involved.[2] She has written me. And now I am answering her and writing also to the person to whom she asked me to write. I am beseeching you here to write the letter that Mother Prioress[3] asked you to write and other letters that you judge appropriate, for perhaps fear is holding us back. Doña Catalina says that after we began discussing this foundation, the city gave permission for the foundation of other monasteries.[4]

I don't know why they have to make such a fuss over thirteen women – for the number is very small – unless because this is most troublesome to the devil. What you say seems to me a drawback, but there will be other ones to follow. If this is the devil's work, it will prove useless if God wants the foundation.

3.   May His Majesty direct everything to his service and preserve you in the holiness that I beg of him for you every day, miserable though I am.

4.   Since I have so many letters to write, I cannot be as long as I would like. My health is better than usual, and I don't feel that the cold is doing me any harm, although there is a lot of snow.

From this house of St. Joseph's in Avila, 13 November.

Your honor's unworthy servant,

Teresa of Jesus

5.   I beg you to do me the favor of giving my best regards to Señor Suero de Vega[5] and to Señora Doña Elvira and assure them that I always take care to pray for them and those angels of theirs.

---

1. Catalina de Tolosa.
2. She is referring to the strange resistance of the archbishop.
3. The prioress in Palencia, Inés de Jesús (Tapia).
4. Others trying to make foundations were the Basilians, the Minims of St. Francis de Paula, and the Carmelite friars (see F. 31.13).
5. A gentleman from Palencia who was a friend and benefactor of Teresa's. His wife, Doña Elvira Manrique, was the daughter of the Count of Osorno.

414. To Don Juan de Ovalle, Alba

Avila, 14 November 1581

Teresa continues on the topic of Beatriz de Ovalle. Passivity on the part of the parents while their daughter was being calumniated grieves Teresa, who wants at all costs to save the reputation of her young niece. Suggesting different solutions, she presses the parents to leave Alba now that winter is coming. At the same time she is hoping that financial help will come for them from her nephew in America.

✦·✦·✧·✧

1.   Jesus. The grace of the Holy Spirit be with your honor. You can well believe that I am not at ease and will not be as long as I know you are in Alba. And so I want to know what is being done about this and that you are not neglecting to take action, because the occasion for trouble has by no means gone away.[1] For the love of our Lord, do not be negligent. Winter has begun so early that it won't be a bad idea to go where you will have a more pleasant climate, as is your custom.[2] The devil – believe me – is not sleeping, as I have been informed. This is true, and so I am very much afraid that it will be impossible to set matters straight if we wait. And for us to be silent about her[3] will not be taken in a good light.

2.   And certainly, setting aside all these very important considerations – that cannot be exaggerated – the means that is being suggested is a fitting solution to your daughter's situation; she can't be living with her parents forever.[4] If by chance Gonzalo Yáñez does not offer his house, you cannot avoid going to Galinduste and then coming here from there as was the agreement. In one way or another, for the love of God, stop killing me.[5] Best regards to my sister. My health is reasonably good.

3.   You should know that letters have arrived from the Indies, but no money; at the moment in which they were going to send some, they learned of my brother's death (may he be in glory) and need certain documents in order to send it.[6]

4.   Agustín de Ahumada says that he will return here in a year, not rich but with hope of favor from the king. They say the king will honor him because he has served much, and that he will be favored by the viceroy who has returned.[7]

5.   Don Lorencio married the daughter of a judge who managed to get the natives to pay Lorencio what the king had awarded him.[8] They have done so in such a way that it is said that he receives around seven thousand ducats in income. His wife is a woman of graceful manners, and they say that he is a very discreet and good man. In the letter from his brother, he sends his best regards to you both and to Señora Doña Beatriz as well.

6.   He says that he is not sending you anything now because he has had many expenses, that he will send it with another fleet when Agustín[9] returns. Please God it will be something, for however small, it will be a help. I will insist on this very much when I write to him. It wouldn't be a bad idea for you to write and congratulate him and send me the letter.

7.   My best regards to Señor Don Gonzalo, and tell him to remember what he promised me; and my greetings to Señora Doña Beatriz. I don't know when she will repay me for all my prayers to God for her.[10]

May His Majesty be with your honors and make you as holy as I beg of him, amen.

Today is 14 November.

Your honor's servant,

Teresa of Jesus

---

1.   Beatriz de Ovalle was being calumniated by the wife of a friend of the Ovalles (see Ltr. 409.7–8).

2.   Juan de Ovalle usually wintered in Galinduste.

3.   About the calumniator.

4.   Beatriz was 21 years old. Gonzalo Yáñez was Juan de Ovalle's cousin and owner of the house in which they were living in Alba.

5.   She is alluding to the deadly distress she is in because of Beatriz's situation, which is only being exacerbated by the parents' passivity.

6.   The money was owed to Lorenzo de Cepeda, who died 26 June 1580. Now authorization for sending the money was required from his son Francisco before it could be sent (see Ltr. 412.8).

7. He was counting on help from the viceroy of Peru, Francisco Alvarez de Toledo, who had recently returned to Madrid. Actually Agustín did not manage to return to Spain during Teresa's lifetime.

8. Don Lorencio is Teresa's nephew. In America he married María de Hinojosa, daughter of a judge, Pedro de Hinojosa.

9. Agustín de Ahumada.

10. Gonzalo and Beatriz were the Ovalles' children.

415. To Don Pedro de Castro y Nero, Alba
Avila, 19 November 1581

(Autograph: Cathedral, Córdoba)

Doctor Castro y Nero was a friend of Gracián's and had been a classmate of his at the University of Alcalá. A professor at Salamanca, a canon in Avila, he later became bishop of Lugo (1599) and then of Segovia (1603). Teresa had given him a copy of her Life *to read, and in a note she had just received from him, he reveals the powerful impact the book had on him. She responds with much feeling and begs him to come to see her the following day.*

✤✤✤✤

To my lord, Doctor Castro.

1.   Jesus be with your honor. The favor that your honor showed me by your letter so moved me that I first gave thanks to our Lord with a Te Deum laudamus, for it seemed I was receiving it from the very hands of the one from whom I have received so many other favors. Now I kiss your hands an infinite number of times, and I would like to do so through deeds rather than with words. How great the mercy of God, that through my wickedness you should benefit; and with reason, for I am not in hell, which for a long time I have deserved. So, this book is entitled *On the Mercies of God*.[1]

2.   May he be always praised, for I had never hoped for less than what he has now accorded me. Nonetheless, every severe word was disturbing to me. I would rather not say more

on paper, and so I beg you to come to see me tomorrow, the eve of the Presentation, that I might present to you a soul often undone, so that you might bring about all that you understand as fitting for her in order that she please God. I hope in His Majesty for the grace to obey you all my life, for I don't think your absence will let me feel free, nor do I want to, for I have seen changes come about by reason of this desire. It would be impossible for a great good not to come to me through this obedience – provided you do not abandon me, and I don't think you will. As a pledge of this obedience, I am thinking of keeping this note,[2] although I have another more important one.

3.   What I beg of you is that for love of our Lord you always keep what I am in mind so as not to pay attention to the favors granted me by God unless for the sake of considering me even worse than you thought, since I make such poor use of them; clearly the more I receive from him the more indebted to him I am. Repay this Lord of mine, since His Majesty desires to punish me only with favors – which is no small punishment for anyone with self-knowledge.

4.   When you finish these papers, I will give you others.[3] On seeing them it will be impossible for you to keep from abhorring someone who should be other than what I am. I think you will like them. May our Lord give you his joy as I beg of him for you.

5.   You have not lost any of my esteem by the style of your letters. I ought to be praising you for its elegance. Everything is useful to God when the desire to serve him is at the root. May he be blessed for everything, amen. Not for a long time have I had as much happiness as I have had this night. I kiss your hands many times for the title you give me, which is a very lofty one for me.[4]

---

1. The Book of her Life. After having examined this work by Teresa, the Inquisition decided to keep it out of circulation. Teresa was here using a manuscript copy of it that had been in the possession of the Duke and Duchess of Alba.

2. The note that Dr. Castro had sent her.

3. These papers probably refer to her Life. The "others" could refer to The Interior Castle or to some of the Spiritual Testimonies.

4. The letter has no signature.

416. To Don Pedro Castro y Nero, Avila
Avila, end of November 1581

Don Pedro had sent a note to Teresa. He was bothered because of an insistent request that he preach at the profession of Ana de los Angeles. To top it off, the novice's mother, also a nun at St. Joseph's in Avila, through her son-in-law was putting further pressure on him to preach. With this note, Teresa softens the request, and in the end Don Pedro did preach the sermon.

✦ ✦ ✦ ✦

1.   Jesus be with your honor. My capacity for insight is too small for me to have ever imagined yesterday evening that you would say "no" as you did today. You were much more able to sense and dispel the distress of that poor little soul,[1] for she certainly had to go through a painful day, and that wasn't the only one, for she has gone through many. I don't have anything more to say to her mother,[2] but only have to do what you command, for that is what it means to be a subject. And even if it were not what it means, it is so repugnant to my nature to ask someone to do something burdensome that I would act the same way.

2.   Now they tell me that Ana de San Pedro has asked Don Alonso[3] to be sure to go and beseech this of you. That was before your note arrived, for I would never in any way have agreed to this after the note. The sermon can be omitted if Father Provincial[4] doesn't come. Clearly, a sermon should not be requested of someone who would not be pleased to comply, but to her parents it will seem a greater loss than spoiling the

partridges,[5] and I don't know what they will do. May our Lord make you as holy as I beg of him.

3.   I hope this letter reaches you before Don Alonso arrives, for not in the slightest way would I want you to think I am doing anything against your will; what is more, I get very annoyed with this meddling.

> Your honor's daughter and servant,

> Teresa of Jesus

---

1. Ana de los Angeles, who will make her profession after many difficulties on 11 November 1581.
2. Ana de San Pedro (Wasteels), who was a nun at St. Joseph's in Avila.
3. Alonso Sedeño, Ana de San Pedro's son-in-law.
4. Jerónimo Gracián. He did not arrive in Avila in time for the profession on the 28th.
5. The good meal that would be prepared for the preacher.

417. To Don Pedro Castro y Nero, Avila
Avila, 28 November 1581

Teresa is writing at night. She had spent a blessed afternoon with St. John of the Cross, who had traveled from Andalusia hoping he could convince Teresa to travel herself to Granada to found the Carmel there. That morning Pedro Castro had surrendered to the nuns' desires and preached a solemn sermon for the profession of Ana de los Angeles. Teresa now thanks and praises him.

❖ ❖ ❖ ❖

1.   Jesus be with your honor and may His Majesty repay you for the joy and help you have given me today. I also have a desire and if you do not do what you can to fulfill it, I will think it would have been better for me not to have known you, so much will my suffering be. And my trial is this: it doesn't make me happy for you to go to heaven, for you have much to do

in God's church. I begged God urgently today not to allow so good a mind to be occupied in anything else.

2.   These sisters kiss your hands. You have brought them much consolation. Let me know if you got tired and how you are; but not by mail, for as happy as I would be to receive a letter from you, I wouldn't want to tire you any more than I think necessary, and that is already a lot. I am very happy this evening because of a visit with a father of our order,[1] even though I neglected to send a message to the marchioness,[2] for he is passing through Escalona.

The letter for Alba is going in a very safe way.[3] And I am your honor's daughter and servant,

Teresa of Jesus

1.   This was St. John of the Cross, who had traveled from Andalusia to arrange with Teresa for a foundation of her nuns in Granada and to bring her with him on the foundation, if possible.
2.   The Marchioness of Villena, Doña Juana Lucas de Toledo.
3.   The letter will be delivered by Padre Ambrosio de San Pedro, prior of Almodóvar, who will meet Padre Gracián in Salamanca.

418. To Madre María de San José, Seville
Avila, 28 November 1581

(Original and autograph: Poor Clares of Astorga)

One of the nuns at St. Joseph's made her profession on this day, and Teresa is now tired after the celebration. St. John of the Cross is in Avila planning with Teresa for a foundation of nuns in Granada, and Teresa begs María de San José to offer two nuns for the new foundation. Busy with many matters, Teresa dictates this letter to Blessed Anne of St. Bartholomew.

❧ ❧ ❦ ❦

1.   Jesus watch over your reverence for me. I wrote you a long letter today, and so I will not enlarge on this one because of my many other occupations; we had a profession[1] today and I am really tired.

2.   For the foundation in Granada I have given the order that they take two nuns from there, and I am trusting that you won't give the worst.[2] So I ask this of you please, for you well know how important it is that they be very virtuous and competent. In this way you will have more room so that you can accept some new nuns and repay me sooner, for it pains me to have to leave for Burgos without any work having been begun on my brother's chapel.[3] And they tell me I am obliged in conscience to have this built. I tell you this so that you will realize that I cannot wait much longer to get the work started.

3.   So, do what you can to send me the money, and pray for me, because after Christmas I am going to make that foundation in Burgos – and that region is very cold at this time. If it were close to where you are and I knew I would get to see you, the trip wouldn't bother me at all. But our Lord will arrange that we meet again some day.

4.   My health is reasonably good, thanks be to God, for through your prayers and those of all the nuns, the Lord is helping me bear the trials. Teresa[4] sends regards to you and all the sisters.

May His Majesty keep you for me and make you as holy as he can, amen.

From this house in Avila, November twenty-eighth.[5]

Many regards to all the sisters.

    Your reverence's servant,

Teresa of Jesus

---

1.   The profession was made by Ana de los Angeles (Wasteels).
2.   The two nuns given for the foundation in Granada were María de Jesús and María de San Pablo.
3.   Her brother left orders in his will that, with money he was owed, a chapel should be built at the Carmel of St. Joseph's in Avila.
4.   Teresa's niece, Teresita.
5.   The remaining words are in Teresa's hand.

419. To Doña María Enríquez, Duchess, Alba
Avila, 28 November 1581

The duchess had a copy of Teresa's Book of Her Life. *On hearing about this, Teresa asked to see it. Sending it to her, the duchess asked that it be returned to her at once. Teresa now asks to keep it longer, for she had given the book to her learned friend Don Pedro Castro y Nero to read. In the morning of this day Ana de los Angeles (Wasteels) made her profession, and in the afternoon, Teresa had a long visit with St. John of the Cross, who was planning a foundation of the nuns in Granada.*

❖·❖·❖·❖

1.   Jesus. The grace of the Holy Spirit be with your excellency. So great was the favor you did me in sending the book[1] that I wouldn't know how to exaggerate it. I kiss your hands many times, and will keep my word as you request. But not knowing whether the book will be safe during your long journey away from home, I would like to keep it, if you wouldn't mind, until you return to Alba. If you want it returned, let the prioress[2] know that you don't want to grant what I have requested (I should say begged for), and she can inform me. If she doesn't say anything, I will take this to mean that you are granting me this favor.

2.   May it please our Lord to keep you in the good health that I and all of your subjects beg of him. I have much to offer His Majesty, for he knows what I feel in seeing you go away without my having the chance to kiss your hands. May he be forever blessed who wishes me to have so little happiness on earth. His will be done in everything, for I well see that I don't deserve more.

3.   In a way, if I had been there I would have been able to bear better what I suffered in hearing of your trials, for I would have been able to kiss your hands …[3]

4.   God give you the health that I beg of him for you each day, and may he keep you for me many years – at least for more

than he does me. News about your cold kept me from enjoying completely the favor you granted me by your letter. I beg you never to do so again on my account, for it would have been enough for me to have your secretary write a few words. So I beg you to let me know from time to time how you and Don Fadrique[4] are faring.

5.   May the Lord be pleased to grant good health to his lordship and her ladyship the duchess,[5] for although they may have forgotten me, I don't fail to do what I am obliged to do in my poor prayers, and also for the one I know you love dearly.[6]

6.   Father Provincial[7] has been sending me hopeful news about the success of the negotiations there, which has been most consoling for me; and also about the favor you showed him in requesting him to accompany you. I don't think it's wrong that I am envious of him. He desires very much to comply with your wishes from what he writes to me. I would like to beg you for now that out love of our Lord you not so order him, for he is at present busy having the constitutions[8] printed, and this is something for which we have the greatest need, and the monasteries are waiting for them.

May the Lord be with your excellency.

Your excellency's unworthy servant and subject,

Teresa of Jesus

---

1.   The Book of Her Life, the autograph of which was in the hands of the Inquisition. She is referring here to a copy that had been made by Bartolomé de Medina, O.P., at the request of the duchess.
2.   The prioress in Alba, Juana del Espíritu Santo.
3.   The text has suffered damage here.
4.   Don Fadrique de Toledo, the duchess's son.
5.   Doña María de Toledo y Colonna, Don Fadrique's wife.
6.   Her husband, the Duke of Alba, Don Fernando Alvarez de Toledo.
7.   Provincial of the discalced Carmelite friars, Jerónimo Gracián, who was in Salamanca working toward the foundation of a house of studies for his friars.

8. These were the constitutions for the discalced Carmelite nuns composed during the chapter at Alcalá (1581) and edited by Gracián in Salamanca (1581).

420. To Don Juan de Ovalle, Alba
Avila, 29 November 1581

Fifteen days had gone by and nothing had been done yet to defend Beatriz against calumny. Teresa does not want to leave Avila for the new foundation in Burgos without a visit from her sister and a settlement to Beatriz's situation. She proposes a plan and sends it with her own messenger so as to be sure of an immediate reply from her brother-in-law..

(Autograph: DCN, Vélez-Málaga)

✤✤✦✦

To the illustrious Lord Juan de Ovalle, my lord, for your hands or those of my sister. Alba

1. Jesus. May the Holy Spirit be with your honor, amen. Recently I wrote you, and I have a great desire to know what is being done about everything.[1] Today I received a letter in which they tell me the city of Burgos has granted the license for me to make a foundation there, for I already have permission from the bishop. I think I will go there to make a foundation before Madrid. I regret going there without seeing my sister first because it could be that I will be going from there to Madrid.[2]

2. I was thinking that if Doña Beatriz has the desire to be a nun, it would be a good idea if I brought her with me, first giving her the habit here. She will enjoy getting to know the monasteries, and afterward I can bring her to Madrid. She will be a foundress before making profession and hardly realizing it will be outside herself with joy and be able to return to Alba.[3] Our Lord knows how much I desire for her to be at peace and for you and my sister to be greatly consoled at seeing her with the habit. Think this over well and pray about it, for I am

doing so urgently. May it please His Majesty to guide the matter to what brings him most glory, amen. And may he watch over you.

3.   Let my sister consider this to be for her, too. Best regards to my niece and nephew and also to Teresa and the two of you. The messenger is a private one, for he is going to Salamanca to our Father Provincial to get the license for a certain resignation. I am having him pass through there on his way and on his return. Answer me and give the letter to Mother Prioress,[4] but don't say anything to anyone for now about this Burgos matter.

Today is 29 November.

Your honor's unworthy servant,

Teresa of Jesus

4.   Turn the page. If you do that it won't be necessary for you to leave there.[5] The fact that I am going so far away is sufficient reason for my sister to come to see me; afterward I can say that I want to bring my niece with me and no one here will have anything to object to.

5.   If this seems alright with you, I will let you know once we set the time for my departure.[6] Even if they come beforehand, nothing will be lost. I never received any news about Señora Doña Mayor's[7] health, which I would like; nor have I found anyone with whom to send these toques. Since they weigh so much, no one wants to take them. Give her my regards and let me know how she is. I am doing fairly well.

---

1.   She has in mind the calumnies (see Ltr. 414). Catalina de Tolosa was promoting a foundation for the discalced Carmelite nuns in Burgos (see F. 31). The day of Teresa's departure for Burgos will be 2 January 1582.

2.   Regarding her desire to see her sister Juana, see Ltrs. 404 and 414. Teresa never did get to make the foundation of nuns in Madrid.

3.   Actually Beatriz did not become a Carmelite nun until after Teresa's death. Teresa decided to take Teresita with her to the foundation in Burgos.

4. See Ltr. 421. Her sister is Juana de Ahumada; her nephew and niece are Gonzalo and Beatriz (Ovalle); Teresa is her brother Lorenzo de Cepeda's daughter, a novice at St. Joseph's in Avila.; the prioress in Alba is Juana del Espíritu Santo.
5. She is alluding to the plan set forth in no. 2. This idea would take care of the objection raised by the Ovalles that to move to Alba would be like admitting the accusation.
6. They will arrive in Avila a little after 15 December (see Ltr. 427.8).
7. Doña Mayor was Juan de Ovalle's sister, a Benedictine nun.

421. To Padre Jerónimo Gracián, Salamanca

Avila, 29 November 1581

Teresa had gone to bed at 2 A.M. and risen with the community at 6. She is tired and she misses those who went with St. John of the Cross to make a foundation in Granada. She had not approved of one of Gracián's choices for Granada. She is also trying to decide which niece to bring to Burgos with her, Teresa (de Cepeda) or Beatriz (de Ovalle), and who to appoint as vicaress at St. Joseph's in her absence. Antonio Ruiz has given her money to send to Gracián – which she is tempted to keep – but St. John of the Cross was unable to give her anything for him.

❧·❧·❦·❦

1.   Jesus be with your reverence. Today the nuns left,[1] which was painful for me and leaves me feeling very lonely. The nuns don't feel this way, especially María de Cristo who is the one who wanted to go most. The plan had already been made public, but the other nun[2] was not suited for this, as you will agree. Nonetheless, I felt very scrupulous since you were the one who told me to send her. Doctor Castro[3] freed me of my scruples.

2.   Fray John of the Cross was longing to send you some money and did a good deal of calculating to see if he could give something from what he brought with him for the journey, but he wasn't able to. I think he will get something to send to you.

3.   Antonio Ruiz[4] came here three or four days ago and was determined to go with me. He greatly desired to see you, and he is writing to you. He gave me two coins to send you that should be worth about four *escudos*. Of course, I will not send them to you until I have a safe messenger.[5] I am doing all I can not to keep them for myself. The way things are going, it won't be long before I'm tempted to steal them.

4.   Inés de Jesús[6] sent me this enclosed letter with others of hers, but the departure will be too soon if it takes place after Christmas. I have already written her that you have to go down there and that they will have to wait. This blessed prioress has to act in such a way because she sees these ladies[7] so filled with ardor. So don't promise to preach there after Advent, for you will have many occasions to do so here. Doctor Castro wants you to come and spend Christmas at his house, and I too; but few of my desires are fulfilled.

5.   Now I believe we cannot fail to bring Teresica,[8] for it seemed a good thing to the learned man I consulted, and she is taking my departure so hard – especially after that of the other sisters – that I think it will be necessary. She is going about a little sad and if some temptation were to assail her while in this state, I don't know what she would do. So it seemed to me well to give her some hope, even though I feel reluctant to do so. Glory to God who wants everything to rain down on me.

6.   I am trying hard to see who to leave here in my place,[9] and how well known the desire of Ana de San Pedro[10] was to go. I cannot bear to think of leaving her in charge. It's a terrible thing, because otherwise I think she would do well. Mariana would do well, for she has many talents for the task, if Julián[11] were not in the middle, although he is remaining quite apart for now and not interfering in anything. May God give you light; and when you are here, we will speak about everything.

7.   The veil was given yesterday. Mother and daughter are as though mad with joy.[12] It has all tired me very much and I didn't get to bed until two. Those I have designated[13] were the three

from here, three from Beas with Anne of Jesus, who goes as prioress, another two from Seville, and two lay sisters from Villanueva who are very good. But the prioress[14] wrote me that it was fitting to send them because they have five lay sisters and it is right to want to help that house in Granada about which so many good things are said. This will not satisfy Anne of Jesus,[15] who likes to direct everything. If it seems all right to you, hold to your decision, for no other better nuns will be found. If not, do as you think best, and remain with God, for I didn't get to bed until two o'clock and then rose early; my head is in bad shape. The rest is going reasonably well.

8.   The drawback that now comes to mind is what to do about Teresa if Beatriz[16] needs to be taken with us, for in no way could the two of them come. That would prove a burden, although Teresa would bring me some relief, for she prays well. So, I won't say anything. But Beatriz must be careful not to be a burden. And in my opinion, it would not be fitting for you to come with Tomasina.[17]

Your reverence's unworthy servant and subject,

Teresa of Jesus

1.   Two of the three from Avila who were chosen for the foundation in Granada: María de Cristo and Antonia del Espíritu Santo.

2.   The identity of the other nun is unknown. It seems she was chosen by Gracián but excluded by Teresa. St. John of the Cross then chose a replacement for her in Toledo, Beatriz de Jesús.

3.   Pedro de Castro y Nero (See Ltr. 410.4).

4.   Antonio Ruiz from Malagón.

5.   See Ltr. 423.1.

6.   The prioress in Palencia, Inés de Jesús.

7.   The ladies in Burgos who were pressing for the foundation there.

8.   *Teresica* was one of the names Teresa used for her niece, Teresa de Jesús (Teresita), who was a novice at St. Joseph's in Avila and who would accompany Teresa and the other nuns for the foundation in Burgos.

9.   She is wondering who to leave in her place as prioress at St. Joseph's in Avila.

10. Ana de San Pedro Wasteels, the Flemish nun.

11. Julián de Avila, the confessor and chaplain of the community (See Ltr. 410.).

12. Ana de San Pedro and Ana de los Angeles (both Wasteels). The daughter (Ana de los Angeles) had made profession the previous day.

13. Those designated to go to make the foundation in Granada.

14. The prioress of Villanueva de la Jara: María de los Mártires.

15. See the changes Anne of Jesus makes to these plans of Teresa's in Ltr. 451.

16. These are Teresa's two nieces.

17. Tomasina Bautista (Perea), from the Carmel in Alba, destined for the foundation in Burgos.

422. To Padre Jerónimo Gracián, Salamanca

Avila, end of November 1581

Because of her poor health and for fear of the cold weather, Teresa was beginning to have doubts about going personally to Burgos, when the Lord spoke to her and urged her to go (see F. 31.11–12). In this fragment, which is all that remains of the letter, Teresa seems to be clarifying for Gracián that the Lord did not say she must leave at once. Joseph was her code name for Christ.

It doesn't seem to me that I ever heard Joseph say that I should go immediately to Burgos. He didn't say anything about leaving sooner or later, but only that I should not entrust the task to someone else, as I was thinking of doing.

423. To Padre Jerónimo Gracián, Salamanca

Avila, 1 December 1581

Teresa entrusts the money given by Antonio Ruiz for Gracián to a discalced friar on his way to Salamanca where

Gracián was entangled in establishing a foundation for discalced friars.

✦ ✦ ✦ ✦

1.   Jesus. Padre Fray Ambrosio is bringing the eight *escudos* that Antonio Ruiz[1] gave me to send to you. I obtained two with the help of good reasons; I couldn't get any more. It seems I am learning how to be a beggar – something really new for me – and I don't feel the least bit embarrassed. It's true that since the money belongs to the order, I don't get troubled. May our Lord make you very holy, as I beg of him, amen.

2.   Give my best regards to Mother Prioress.[2] If those fathers[3] are so cold in the house they are buying, what must the nuns[4] be undergoing? Their faith will save them, for I certainly have little faith as regards that house.

It is the first of December.

3.   Let me know how your feet are. You must be having really cold weather if you are now getting chill blains, for nothing else causes them. I am doing fairly well, although tired.

4.   All the nuns recommend themselves to your prayers, especially Teresa, who is very happy with her diurnal;[5] and the other nuns are happy with their books.

Your reverence's servant, subject, and daughter,

Teresa of Jesus

For our Father Fray Jerónimo Gracián de la Madre de Dios, provincial of the discalced Carmelites, *mi padre*, Salamanca.

---

1. Ambrosio de San Pedro, prior of Almodóvar del Campo brought the money to Salamanca (see Ltr. 417.2). Antonio Ruiz was Teresa's good friend from Malagón (see Ltr. 421.3).
2. The prioress in Salamanca, Ana de la Encarnación (Tapia).
3. The discalced friars recently established in Salamanca.
4. The condition of the nuns' monastery was worse than that of the friars.
5. Gracián had sent Teresa's niece, Teresita, a book of choral prayers.

424. To Padre Jerónimo Gracián, Salamanca
Avila, 4 December 1581

Teresa is writing this at midnight. Her two concerns are the complications over the purchase of a house for the Carmel in Salamanca, and the machinations of Francisco de Cepeda's mother-in-law, who has her eyes on Teresita's inheritance. Teresa is awaiting Gracián, who will come to accompany her on the trip to Burgos.

❖❖❖❖

1.   … left without one or the other, as you say. Renting it will not do, because they are forced to buy a house as soon as possible, be it good or bad.[1] And I don't know why it is that I cannot feel disappointed that they couldn't come to an agreement over the Monroy house, for it seems to me they would die if they stayed there. Not all the monasteries are in places where the nuns would have wanted to be, but only where they could be. Anyway, you will see what is best. I don't know how you can say that you will come with my sister,[2] or how you could find time for that.

2.   This enclosed letter written to me by Francisco's mother-in-law[3] came two days ago, and it annoyed me very much to see such bad motives. The learned men from around here say that the will can not be annulled without one's sinning mortally.[4] I believe I will find it necessary not to allow this child[5] to be separated from me; and so they will be unable to do anything about this, nor would we permit it. That she be left to go free is what I fear. She is now sick with a bad cold and a fever. I very much recommend her as well as all the nuns to your prayers.

3.   Remain with God, for it just struck twelve o'clock. Either inform them[6] about what has to be done so that they can make the trip, or let me know.

Anne of St. Bartholomew[7] does not stop writing; she helps me very much. She kisses your reverence's hands.

You should know that I don't have anyone to go with me to Burgos, so don't think of abandoning me.

Today is 4 December.

1. The text is damaged. She is referring to the efforts of the community in Salamanca to acquire a house (see Ltr. 423.2; F. 19.11).
2. Juana de Ovalle, from whom Teresa is expecting a visit in Avila (see Ltr. 420.3–4).
3. Francisco de Cepeda's mother-in-law is Beatriz de Castilla. She wants money from Lorenzo's will to go to Francisco at the expense of Teresita.
4. Teresa is the executrix of the will.
5. Teresita, who could be cheated out of her inheritance.
6. Her sister Juana and niece Beatriz in Alba.
7. Blessed Anne of St. Bartholomew, who was serving at the time as Teresa's nurse and secretary.

425. To Doña Beatriz de Castilla y Mendoza, Madrid
Avila, 4 December 1581

(Autograph: DCN, San José, Guadalajara)

Doña Beatriz, Francisco's mother-in-law, was interested in contesting Don Lorenzo's will and was trying to gain influence with Teresita, whom the complicated will favored. Teresa wanted to be faithful to her brother's wishes regarding both Teresita and the chapel to be built at St. Joseph's in Avila as a place for his burial.

❊❊❊❊

1.   Jesus. May the grace of the Holy Spirit be with your honor always. It seems to me that in begging you not to write to me, I was referring to the business about the will. To refuse the favor of receiving letters from you would be foolish of me,[1] for I well understand what a great favor you do me by writing. But it pains me deeply when the purpose concerns things that in conscience I cannot do. And some others that, as I understand it from what they tell me, would not be right for Don Francisco[2]

to do either. But since you are being told otherwise, you cannot help being suspicious of my good will, which is very painful to me; and so I have a strong desire to see all these things brought to a conclusion. May the Lord work everything out in conformity with what most accords with his service, for this is the very thing you would like. I never had any other desire, not even its first stirring. I have always wanted what would bring you peace and have seen the many things that Señora Doña Orofrisia[3] deserves.

2.   As for what you say about my having written you that our Lord would give you sons, I repeat it and hope in His Majesty that you will have them. I have never paid much attention to the aims of Pedro de Ahumada,[4] and this is also true now. I am so tired of becoming involved in what turns out to be nothing that if I were not obliged in conscience, I would abandon everything, and I had decided in fact to do so. But Perálvarez[5] told me that a decision like that would displease you because it would affect St. Joseph's.[6]

3.   Since for my sins they have now made me prioress there,[7] I see that you are right; and also that it is necessary, as far as the house goes, to value its rights so that a conclusion can be reached sooner than what I was told by some learned men. Even though my brother's children (may he be in glory) did not think the will was valid, it remains valid because it cannot be known who opened it;[8] many lawsuits would result. You are right in demanding that everything be clarified, for it is a terrible thing and a huge expense to go about consulting lawyers.

4.   May our Lord take care of this matter, as he can, and preserve you many years to the benefit of your children, amen.

Your honor's unworthy servant and subject,

Teresa of Jesus

5.   Sister Teresa of Jesus kisses your hands. I hope in God that before long we will both kiss them. She and I send our best regards to Señor Don Francisco.[9]

---

1.   See Ltr. 424.2.
2.   Francisco de Cepeda, Teresa's nephew, is being manipulated by his mother-in-law, Doña Beatriz.
3.   Francisco's wife, daughter of Doña Beatriz.
4.   Teresa's troublesome brother (see Ltrs. 355 & 367.4).
5.   Perálvarez is Pedro Alvarez Cimbrón, who in Lorenzo's will was appointed administrator.
6.   Lorenzo's daughter Teresita resided at St. Joseph's in Avila.
7.   She was made prioress on 10 September 1581.
8.   The will was contested because it was opened; but it clearly stated that, even if found opened, it should be honored.
9.   Teresa de Jesús (Teresita) and Francisco are Lorenzo's two children.

426. To Padre Jerónimo Gracián, Salamanca
Avila, Beginning of December 1581

(Autograph: DCF, Larrea [Vizcaya])

Teresa is answering a letter of Gracián's late at night so that the messenger may bring her answer back on his return. Gracián is going to come to Avila to accompany her on the journey for the foundation in Burgos, and Teresita is eagerly awaiting him. Her sister Juana and niece Beatriz might come with Gracián from Alba. Also sending him letters for the Duchess of Alba and her sister Juana, she in turn will send messages for him to Madrid.

1.   Jesus be with your reverence, my father. I greatly rejoiced both to receive your letter, which they gave me tonight along with the rest of the scapulars, and to observe how determined you are that I see you soon. Please God you will have a good trip, *mi padre*. If something still needs to be done on the constitutions, leave instructions. And for goodness' sake, if you have to preach the last day of Christmas, don't leave until the following day so that you won't get sick, for I don't know where you get the energy.

Blessed be he who gives it to you. I am amused at how rich you have become.[1] May God make you so with eternal riches.

2.   Now I don't understand some forms of sanctity. I'm referring to the one who doesn't write to you. And the other one, who says he does everything following his own opinion, has tested my patience. O Jesus, how rarely does one find perfection in this life![2] Such great foolishness! Because this messenger is going to be leaving, I will not enlarge on the matter, and I am in the process of finishing a letter to the Marchioness of Villena[3] whose personal messenger is waiting.

3.   I believe it would be good if you sent me a personal messenger, provided my sister[4] is not in Alba. If you think, have someone go fetch her. But if that young girl[5] has to return the way she came, I have no desire that she come here, nor do I know why she should, except to tire me out. As for her staying at the Incarnation, that's a joke, for I don't think that it would suit her, and the expense is terrible. God be with them who give me such a life.

4.   Teresa[6] is well, and I think we can be sure about her, for she has made her intentions clearly known, as you will learn. I am reasonably well.

5.   The duchess[7] has written to me again through a chaplain. I answered her briefly and said that I had written her at length through you. I am saying this so that you will send her the letter. If you haven't done so because I mention that you cannot accompany her,[8] it doesn't matter.

6.   Have this enclosed letter sent to my sister, if you think it opportune. Perhaps on her return God will help Beatriz to be better disposed, if she has not decided to leave. If she were always to stay in the country,[9] I wouldn't mind. But once summer comes, they will return to Alba – and it will begin again.

7.   The day after tomorrow a departure for Madrid is scheduled. I will be sending your messages. The scapulars are really edifying, they inspire devotion. Don Francisco sent to ask his

sister[10] for one. It distresses me. I remind you again that if it is necessary for you to send me any messages when those people come here that you do so. Remain with God, for it is late at night.

8.   You should know that we have arranged a little place for you to stay; but I don't think Dr. Castro[11] will agree to it. I get along very well with him. I gave him the part of that book[12] that I had here. He never stops talking about the benefit he derived from the other book. As for me, it is enough that he is your friend for me to like everything about him. I think that for a confessor to understand me and not go about with fears, there is nothing better than for him to read one of these writings; it spares me a lot of grief.

May God keep you and give you the rest that I ask him to, amen, amen.

> Your reverence's servant and subject,
>
> Teresa of Jesus

9.   I am not writing[13] to your reverence because the thought of your coming makes me so happy that it doesn't allow me to do anything else than thank you very much and kiss your hands for the great care you show for my health and comfort. I am well, in the hope of seeing you soon and the happiness the diurnal[14] brings me. May it please God to repay you in the manner I beg of him.

10.   I find Teresa's[15] message a delight. Now I believe there is no greater remedy than love. May God grant it to us with His Majesty.

---

1.   She is probably referring in a joking manner to the eight *escudos* that Antonio Ruiz has sent him (see Ltrs. 421.3 & 423.1).

2.   She is probably referring to two of the friars under Gracian's authority. The first mentioned could be Antonio de Jesús Heredia; and the second, Nicolás Doria.

3.   Juana Lucas de Toledo.

4.   Her sister, Juana de Ahumada, to whom she is sending a letter (see no. 6).

5. Juana's daughter, Beatriz de Ovalle.
6. Teresa's niece, Teresita de Cepeda (see Ltr. 424.2).
7. The Duchess of Alba, María Enríquez de Toledo.
8. The duchess wanted Gracián to accompany her on a journey, a plan which Teresa opposed (see Ltr. 419.6).
9. The Ovalle family were spending the winter in Galunduste. Teresa felt sure that the calumnies against Beatriz would begin again if she returned to Alba when winter was over.
10. Francisco de Cepeda and his sister, Teresita.
11. Pedro de Castro y Nero, a friend of Gracian's living in Avila who would be trying to get Gracián to stay at his house.
12. This was probably a part of her *Interior Castle*; the other book was Teresa's *Life*, which Castro had recently read (see Ltr. 415.1, 4).
13. This note (no. 9) was added by Teresita, Lorenzo's daughter.
14. See Ltr. 423.4.
15. Teresita.

427. To Don Lorenzo de Cepeda (son), Quito
Avila, 15 December 1581

(Original: DCN, Quito)

A year after Teresa sent a previous letter to her nephew Lorenzo, an answer from him arrived. She also received a letter from her brother Agustín de Ahumada. But a letter from an old friend of her brother Lorenzo brought more news. This nephew Lorenzo had been fortunate in America with respect to his father's estate and in the marriage he contracted there at the age of nineteen. Living in Avila not far from the Carmel was the little girl whom Lorenzo had sired outside wedlock before going to America. Teresa was waiting for her sister Juana, who was going to care for the little girl, to arrive in Avila, and reminds her nephew of his responsibilities to be generous and provide for the child's education. This letter was dictated by Teresa to Ana de San Pedro.

❧❧❦❦

1.   Jesus. The grace of the Holy Spirit be with your honor, my son. I received your letter. In addition to the great joy it brought

me with the news of the good fortune our Lord has bestowed on you, it stirred up again the pain I feel over the sorrow you recently had, and so rightly.[1] Because at the time of the death of my brother (may he be in glory) I wrote you at great length, I do not want to stir up your pain again. I have had much grief at seeing how differently things have turned out from the way I would have wanted them to; although as I have written you, I am greatly relieved to see Don Francisco[2] as well settled as you are. Setting aside the fact that his wife is tied on all sides to the most illustrious families in Spain, she has so many good personal qualities that they would be enough. Write to her with all the courtesy you can and do something for her that will please her, for she deserves it. I tell you that even though Don Francisco has a good-sized fortune, he married well. But with the restrictions set down by his father (may he be in glory), the provisions made for Teresa,[3] and the payment of debts, so little remained that if God doesn't provide, I don't know how he will live.

2.   May he be praised forever who has so favored you, for he has given you a wife with whom you can live in great peace. This is most fortunate, for it brings me great joy to think that you have a wife like this. I kiss the hands of Doña María[4] many times. In me she has someone who will pray for her, and many other nuns along with me. We would very much like to enjoy her presence here, but if this would require her to undergo the trials that are here, I would rather see her at rest there than suffering here.

3.   I find my consolation in Sister Teresa de Jesús. She is now a woman and always growing in virtue. You can truly accept her counsels, for I had to smile when I read the letter she wrote you. God truly speaks in her, and she does well what she says. He is guiding her, for she is edifying to us all. She is very perceptive, and I think she will be able to deal with everything. Don't neglect to write her, for she is indeed alone. Knowing how much her father loved her and the kindnesses he showed her, I feel pity to see that nobody remembers to

pay any attention to her. Don Francisco loves her very much, but he can't do anything more.

4.   Diego Juárez[5] went on at greater length than you and my brother[6] in telling us about the qualities of Señora Doña María[7] and the other good things that have gone favorably for you, for you write very short letters for someone who is so far away. It is a great favor from God's mercy that you have met with such good fortune and married so soon, for considering how you started out so early in life to go astray you could have been for us a cause of great worry.[8] Herein I see how much I love you, for even though what you did was very distressing to me because of its being an offense against God, when I see how much this little girl resembles you, I can't help but welcome and love her. As little as she is, it's wonderful to see how much she resembles Teresa in the practice of patience.

5.   May God make her his servant, for she is not at fault, and so don't be negligent in taking care to see that she is brought up well. That will not be the case if when she grows older she remains where she is. It will be better if she is brought up by her aunt[9] until you can see what God may be wanting to do with her. You could send a sum of money here from time to time – since our Lord has given it to you – to be deposited, and the interest could be used for her support. When she is twelve years old, the Lord will ordain what may be done for her, but it is very important that she be taught the way of virtue, for that is the revenue for what she will become. Certainly she deserves it, for she is pleasing to everyone and, being so little, she wouldn't want to leave here.[10]

6.   It wouldn't have been necessary for you to send anything if it were not for the fact that this house is now in great need. Francisco de Salcedo[11] has died – may he enjoy glory – and has left a legacy, but it is not sufficient to pay for the food, not even enough for supper. After that, almost all the alms stopped coming in. Although things should get better with the passing of time, up until now nothing has been brought to us, and so

there is much suffering. A dowry for Teresa will be a great help, if God allows her to make profession. She has a strong desire to do so.

7.   At times my health is better than usual. After your departure God founded a monastery in Palencia, one in Soria, and another in Granada, and after Christmas I am going to make a foundation in Burgos.[12] I am thinking of returning here quickly, if God be so served.

8.   Now I am awaiting my sister and her daughter.[13] Her need is so great that you would feel much pity for her. I already feel great pity for Doña Beatriz, for although she wants to be a nun, she doesn't have the means. It would be a great act of charity if, when you can, you would send them something, for however little it might amount to, it will be a lot. I am the one who doesn't need money, but I ask God to let me do his will in everything and make you all great saints, for everything else comes to a quick end.

9.   All the nuns in this house send you their best regards, especially Madre San Jerónimo,[14] and we continue to pray for you. Look, my son, that since you have the name of so good a father you have the works as well.

10.   When this arrives, according to what he writes to me, my brother Agustín de Ahumada,[15] will be on his way. May it please God to grant him a good voyage. If he has not departed, would you send him this letter, for I don't have the head today for much writing. I tell you that if he doesn't have enough for his food, he will suffer a great trial, for he won't find anyone to provide his food; and I will suffer a great trial, too, because I won't be able to help him. The viceroy has already arrived, and Padre García is well, although I have not seen him.[16] It is a hard thing to undertake so dangerous a journey at such an advanced age for the sake of a fortune, when we shouldn't be attending to anything else than preparing for heaven. May God grant it to us and may he make you as holy as I beg of him, amen, amen.

11.   I kiss repeatedly the hands of all those lords and ladies, and I say no more but refer to the letter by Teresa de Jesús. If you do what she advises, I will be satisfied.

From this house of St. Joseph's in Avila, 15 December, in the year 1581.

> Your honor's servant,

> Teresa of Jesus

---

1.   The good fortune was Don Lorenzo's recent marriage with Doña María de Hinojosa. The pain was due to the death of his father about which Teresa informed Lorenzo in her previous letter.

2.   Francisco is Lorenzo's brother. With regard to his wife, see Ltr. 363. 5–8.

3.   This is the sister of the two brothers, and the youngest in the family, sometimes referred to as Teresita, but in this letter as Teresa de Jesús. She is a novice at St. Joseph's in Avila and 15 years old at the time.

4.   María de Hinojosa, Lorenzo's wife.

5.   He is probably one of those in charge of the deceased Lorenzo's estate in Peru.

6.   Agustín de Ahumada, who had also written to Teresa.

7.   Doña María de Hinojosa.

8.   She is referring to Lorenzo's having begotten a child earlier out of wedlock.

9.   Juana de Ahumada, Teresa's sister.

10.   The monastery of St. Joseph's in Avila.

11.   He had died 12 September 1580.

12.   Palencia in 1580; Soria and Granada in 1581.

13.   Juana and Beatriz de Ovalle from Alba.

14.   María de San Jerónimo, a nun at St. Joseph's.

15.   He never carried through with his plan.

16.   The viceroy was Francisco Alvarez de Toledo, and his adviser was the Dominican García de Toledo, a great friend of St. Teresa's.

428. To the prioress and discalced Carmelites of Soria
Avila, 28 December 1581

(Autograph: DCN, Pamplona)

Teresa was the prioress in Avila. She was preparing for the new foundation in Burgos. The nuns in Soria had written and sent her financial help. Although swamped with correspondence and business matters for the new foundation, Teresa writes to express her grattitude.

❖❖❖❖

1.   Jesus. The grace of the Holy Spirit be with your reverence and with all of the nuns, my daughters. Believe me truly that I would like to write to each one of you individually, but there is such a barrage of correspondence and business matters pouring down on me that it is even difficult to be able to write these lines to all of you together. This is especially so because we have approached the eve of our departure. Pray that our Lord will be served by everything, especially by this foundation in Burgos.

2.   I am greatly consoled to know through your letters, and even more so through your words and deeds, of the great affection you have for me. I truly believe, though, that you still fall short of repaying me what you owe me for my affection, even though you have been very generous in the help you have given me. Since the need was great, I have prized your help very much. Our Lord will reward you. It truly seems you serve him, since you have enough to be able to do such a good deed for these poor nuns.[1] All of them are grateful to you for it and will pray to our Lord for you. Since I do this continually, I have nothing to add.

3.   I am delighted that everything is going so well for you, especially since there have been some occasions for your being criticized without your having been at fault; that is a lovely thing, for you have had little to endure on this foundation by which you could merit. Concerning our Padre Vallejo,[2] I say

no more than ask our Lord always to repay him for the great services he renders His Majesty, along with increasing trials. And since he is doing such a great work for that house, I am not surprised that the Lord wants to give him the means for gaining more and more merit.

4.   Look, my daughters, it is right that, when this saint[3] enters, Mother Prioress[4] and all the nuns help her with kindness and love, for where there is so much virtue it is not necessary to be strict about anything, for it will suffice for her to see what the nuns are doing and to have so good a father; I believe you will be able to see this for yourselves.

5.   That Mother Subprioress[5] is better was a great joy for me. If she always needs to eat meat, it doesn't matter that she does so even in Lent, for one does not break the rule when a necessity is present; nor should one be strict in this matter. I ask our Lord to give me virtues, especially humility and love for the others, which is what is important. May it please His Majesty that I see you all growing in these, and ask of him the same for me.

The vigil of the feast of King David. Today is the day on which we arrived for the foundation in Palencia.

6.   Best regards to my little ones[6] – for I am delighted that they are well and so pleasant – and to the doctors.[7] The improvement in Madre María de Cristo's[8] condition makes me very happy, as well as the fact that you have added such beautiful things in such a short time.

Your servant,

Teresa of Jesus

---

1. The nuns at St. Joseph's in Avila, who were in need of alms and financial help.
2. Diego Vallejo, a canon in the collegiate church of Soria and confessor to the Carmelite nuns.
3. Leonor Ayanz y Beamonte had obtained an annulment of her marriage and was planning to enter the Carmel in Soria. She took the name Leonor de la Misericordia.

4. The prioress of Soria, Catalina de Cristo (Balmaseda).

5. The subprioress in Soria, Beatriz de Jesús (Villalobos).

6. These are the two novices who received the habit at the hands of Teresa in Soria: Isabel de la Madre de Dios (16 years old); and María de la Trinidad (Gante y Beamonte, 14 years old).

7. She is probably referring to Cebrián de Cuenca, Juan de la Castilla, and Diego Vallejo.

8. María de Cristo (Pinedo) had come with Teresa for the foundation in Soria.

Letters 429–468
(1582)

429. To Dionisio Ruiz de la Peña, Toledo

Medina, 8 January 1582

On this winter journey to Burgos to make a foundation there, Teresa and her companions stopped in Medina del Campo. The foundation in Madrid had not been made but was still pending. She wants very much to be remembered to Cardinal Quiroga in Toledo. The natural aversion she feels toward the long journey to Burgos is not completely hidden.

➤➤◆◆

1. Jesus. The grace of the Holy Spirit be always with your honor. I arrived here in Medina del Campo a day before the eve of the Epiphany, and I did not want to go further without telling you of where I am going – in case you want to give me some orders – and ask you to kiss the hands of his illustrious lordship[1] for me and tell him I have found that our Sister Elena de Jesús[2] is well and that the others are too.[3] So great is her happiness that it made me give praise to our Lord. She has even grown heavier. All are so extremely pleased with her that it seems her

509

vocation is truly from our Lord. May he be always praised. They kiss the hands of his illustrious lordship many times, and I and the other nuns take special care to ask our Lord to preserve him for many years.

2.   It's a great consolation for me to learn the good news about his lordship. May it please His Divine Majesty to always give him an increase of holiness. Sister Elena de Jesús is so much at ease and fulfills her duties as a religious so well that she seems to have been one for many years. May God guide her and his lordship's other relatives, for certainly souls like these are to be esteemed.

3.   In no way had I planned on leaving Avila until making the foundation in Madrid. Our Lord has been pleased that some persons in Burgos have had so great a desire that one of these monasteries be founded there that they have obtained permission from both the archbishop[4] and the city. So I am going there with some sisters to bring this about. The project requires obedience from me, and our Lord wants it to cost me more; because when I was as close to Burgos as Palencia, he wasn't pleased that a foundation then be made, but afterward when I was in Avila. For it is no small trial now to make such a long trip.

4.   I beg you to ask His Majesty that this foundation will be for his glory and honor, for if this is so, the more suffering there is the better. And don't fail to let me know how the health of his lordship is and how yours is. Certainly the more monasteries he has, the more subjects he will have to pray to the Lord our God for him. May it please His Majesty to watch over him as is our need.

5.   We are leaving for Burgos tomorrow. May God give you as much of his love as I and these sisters beg of him.

Do not forget me in your holy sacrifices, for the love of our Lord, and do me the favor when you see Doña Luisa de la Cerda to tell her that I am well, for I don't have time to say more.

Today is 8 January.

Your honor's unworthy servant,

Teresa of Jesus

1. The Cardinal Archbishop of Toledo, Gaspar de Quiroga.
2. The cardinal's niece, who had been living in the Carmel for only about three months.
3. The cardinal's other relatives in the Carmel of Medina are Jerónima de la Encarnación, Ana de la Trinidad, and María Evangelista (the daughter, niece, and cousin of Doña Elena respectively).
4. The Archbishop of Burgos, Don Cristóbal Vela. The permission was not a written one but only oral.

430. To Doña Catalina de Tolosa, Burgos
Palencia, 16 January 1582

(Autograph: Pilar, Zaragoza)

Teresa, who was 67 years old, was on her way from Avila to Burgos. The winter was severe, the roads muddy, and travel slow. She had spent four days in Valladolid and would spend another five in Palencia regaining her strength. Sick with palsy and a serious cold as she writes this, she has been on her way since 2 January.

❖❖❖❖

1.   Jesus. The grace of the Holy Spirit be with your honor. On our arrival in Valladolid, I arranged for the Mother Prioress[1] there to inform you. I remained there four days because I was not well, for on top of a bad cold, I had a slight attack of palsy. Nonetheless, after improving a little, I departed because I feared making your honor wait, as well as those lords – whose hands I kiss many times. I beg their honors and you as well not to blame me for the delay. If you all knew what the roads were like, you would blame me more for coming. I am also now in pretty bad condition, but I hope in the Lord that this will not

prevent me from setting out again shortly if the weather gets a little better. They say that the trip from here to Burgos is an arduous one, and so I don't know if Father Provincial[2] will want to depart until he sees that I am better, even though he is eager to continue the journey. He kisses your hands and has a great desire to meet you. He is very much obliged to pray for you because of all that you do for the order.

2.   If it is necessary for you to send us a message, make use of a special messenger, and we will pay the cost here. In matters like this, the cost should not matter much. It could be that if the weather gets better, as it is today, we will leave Friday morning and that a letter sent by ordinary mail will not arrive on time. In case you haven't sent anything or we have already departed, here is how we plan to go.

3.   Father Provincial does not want us to fail to see the crucifix[3] in that city, and so they say that before we enter, it is necessary to go there and that from there, or a little before, notify you and go to your house in as hidden a way as possible, and if necessary to wait until nightfall. Then Father Provincial will go to receive the bishop's[4] blessing so that on the next day the first mass may be said. You should know that until this is done, it is better that no one knows. This is what I have been almost always doing. Every time I think of how God has done everything, I am amazed and see that it is all the fruit of prayer. May he be ever praised and pleased to watch over you, for he has surely reserved a great reward for you because of your work.

4.   I don't think I accomplished a small feat by bringing Asunción[5] with me, considering the resistance to this. She is happy to come, in my opinion. Her sister[6] is well. I have already told you that we will bring her back soon. The prioress[7] here kisses your hands and so too do the nuns accompanying me. We include the five who will remain there and myself and two companions. In sum, there are eight of us[8] traveling. Don't bother about beds, for we can adapt in any arrangement until we get settled. I find that these angels are pleasant and joyful.

5. May God watch over them and give you many years; don't be distressed over my sickness, for I am often like this, and it usually goes away quickly.

Today is the vigil of St. Anthony.

Your honor's unworthy servant,

Teresa of Jesus

---

1. María Bautista (Ocampo).
2. Jerónimo Gracián, who had been accompanying Teresa since the departure from Avila.
3. A famous crucifix in Burgos that at the time was venerated in the church of the Augustinians; and now, in the cathedral (see F. 31.18).
4. Cristóbal Vela. This Gracián did in fact do (see F. 31.21).
5. Catalina de la Asunción, a daughter of Catalina de Tolosa, who made her profession in Valladolid (22 Aug. 1579). The prioress, María Bautista, opposed this plan.
6. Casilda de San Angelo, also Catalina's daughter, remained home at the Carmel in Valladolid.
7. The prioress in Palencia, Inés de Jesús (Tapia).
8. They were: Tomasina Bautista, Inés de la Cruz, Catalina de Jesús, Catalina de la Asunción, and María Bautista; Teresa's two companions were Anne of St. Bartholomew and her niece Teresita.

431. To Don Diego Vallejo, Soria
Burgos, 4 February 1582

(Autograph damaged: Poor Clares, Gelsa [Zaragoza])

This damaged autograph is addressed to a canon of the collegiate church in Soria who is confessor to the Carmelite nuns there.

❖·❖·❖·❖

To my illustrious lord and father Canon Vallejo, my lord.

1. ... Because Padre Fray Pedro de la Purificación,[1] who is delivering this, will give you a long report about everything

and since I am not well, I will not say any more than beg you again that in one way or another you arrange matters so that they don't fail to bring the documents, for there is no danger of anything being lost. With the proof that there is an income, we can conclude our business. May the Lord bring this about since it is for his glory, and may he preserve you for many years so that you may always support and favor us.

2.   It is very important that you let Señora Doña Beatriz[2] know how much she gains before our Lord and how she loses nothing.

Today is 4 February

3.   My letters and those from our padre[3] that are addressed to Señora Doña Beatriz are left open. Read them (you, Mother Prioress,[4] and Subprioress), and then seal them in order to give them to her. And take great care to keep the secret, for you see how important this is to us …

1.   Gracián's companion for the foundation in Burgos.
2.   Doña Beatriz de Beamonte y Navarra, the founding benefactress for the Carmel in Soria.
3.   Jerónimo Gracián, the provincial.
4.   Catalina de Cristo (Balmaseda).

432. To Madre María de San José, Seville
Burgos, 6 February 1582

(Original [Anne of St. Bartholomew]: DCN, Valladolid)

Teresa has not heard from Madre María de San José in a long time and sends her this exceptional messenger, Pedro de Tolosa, to bring back to Burgos the money that the Seville Carmel still owes her. In Burgos Teresa has met with opposition from the archbishop and is still sick from the journey with a serious sore throat. She dictates the letter to Anne of St. Bartholomew.

❖❖❖❖

For Mother Prioress, María de San José, the discalced Carmelite nuns, in back of San Francisco, Seville.

1.   Jesus be with your reverence, my daughter, and watch over you for me, amen. I am writing this from Burgos where I now am. It's been twelve days since I arrived, and nothing has been done regarding the foundation. For there has been some opposition. Things are going somewhat the way they went down there.[1] I am beginning to see how much God will be served in this monastery, how all that is happening will be for the best, bringing it about that the discalced nuns will become better known. Since this city is a kingdom, there would perhaps be no remembrance of us if we entered in silence. But this noise and opposition will do no harm, for there are already some women moved to join us even though the foundation has not yet been made. You and the sisters pray to God for this foundation.

2.   The one who will bring you this letter is a brother of the lady[2] who is allowing us to stay in her house and through whose intervention we have come to this city. We owe her very much. She has four daughters who are nuns in our houses, and two others who I think will do the same. I say this so that you will be very gracious to him, if he goes there. His name is Pedro de Tolosa.

3.   By means of him you can answer me, and you can even send me the money.[3] And for goodness' sake do all you can and send the entire amount, for I am obliged by contract to pay it this year. Don't send it to me the way you did the other money,[4] or I will become angry with you. For by sending it in the way I mentioned, through Pedro de Tolosa, the money will come safely. It will suffice for you to give it to him, and he will deliver it here. If you can in some way show him some kindness, for goodness' sake do so. We won't be losing anything, and we owe it to his sister.

4.   Our Father Provincial[5] has been here and has been very efficient in all that has to be done. He is in good health. May God watch over him as is our need. I also have Teresita[6] with me, for they told me that her relatives wanted her to leave the

monastery, so I didn't dare have her stay behind. She is virtuous in a very pleasant way. She sends her regards to you and to all the sisters. Give them my best and ask them not to fail to pray for me. The sisters I brought here send there regards. They are very good nuns and bear the trials with a wonderful spirit.

5.   Traveling along the way, we got into serious dangers because the weather was so harsh that the attempt to cross the rivers and torrents was bold. As for myself, the trip must have done me harm, for ever since Valladolid, I have had a bad sore throat (and continue to have one). Although they have tried different remedies, it doesn't go away. Now I am better, but I can't eat anything that has to be chewed. Don't be upset, for with the help of God and all your prayers it will soon go away. Such is the reason this letter is not in my own hand. The sister[7] who is writing it asks you in your charity to pray for her.[8]

May he watch over you for me and make you holy, amen.

Your reverence's unworthy servant,

Teresa of Jesus

6.   See that your answer is a long one. You can do so through the person who is giving you this, for it is a long time since I have seen a letter from you. My regards to Mother Subrioress[9] and to all the nuns.

---

1. This is a veiled allusion to the archbishop in Burgos who, like the archbishop in Seville, did not at first welcome Teresa and her nuns.
2. Catalina de Tolosa (see F. 31).
3. The ducats that the community in Seville owed to Teresa's deceased brother Lorenzo.
4. The 200 ducats that ended up in the hands of Horacio Doria.
5. Jerónimo Gracián.
6. Teresita, a novice in Avila, was being pursued by her brother Francisco's mother-in-law so that Francisco might have a larger inheritance.
7. Anne of St. Bartholomew.

8. What follows is in Teresa's hand.
9. Leonor de San Gabriel.

433. To Don Martín Alonso de Salinas, Palencia
Burgos, 1 March 1582

(Autograph: University of Mundelein Library, Mundelein, Illinois[1])

The nuns had moved from Catalina de Tolosa's house into the hospital of the Conception (see F. 31.27). Although Gracián has left in order to preach Lenten sermons in Valladolid, they are still trying to find a house, and the archbishop will not authorize a foundation until they have one. While Teresa was writing this letter, the price on the house they were hoping for was raised, making it impossible for them to acquire it. The autograph of this letter had been lost and only recently was found.

1. Jesus. The grace of the Holy Spirit be with your honor. We are getting along well in the hospital, glory to God. I am reminded here of all the merit you gain in yours.[2] It is a great thing to take part in a work like this. Blessed be God who so takes care of the poor. This is indeed consoling to me.

2. The archbishop[3] has sent someone to see me and ask if I need anything. For my consolation he said that finally out of regard for the Bishop of Palencia,[4] for me, and for all those who have been praying for this foundation he will give his authorization – as soon as we have a house – for it is out of the question that we go back to where we came from,[5] which makes one suspect that someone asked him to send us back.

3. These fathers[6] are defending themselves vigorously and are complaining about me because I wrote to the lord canon,[7] something they say they would never have done. I don't know who could have told them, although it matters little to me. Now, as soon as we left the house of Catalina de Tolosa, they went to see her. And they sent me word that I shouldn't tire myself in

trying to get them to come to see us, for unless their general[8] in Rome gives them orders to do so, they will not come to see us until we have a monastery. They don't want to give the impression that their order and ours is all one order – look at that for an idea! – and that half of Palencia is in revolt because of what I wrote. I have recounted this so that Lord Canon Reinoso will know about it and to beg both of you not to try to help me in this regard. They know what they are doing. The day will appear when others will come with a different attitude.

4.   The fact is that if we want to make a foundation, we must have a house. And so we are waiting for these sisters to make the renunciation,[9] for until they do so Catalina de Tolosa can do nothing although she would like to. Even while we are here, she showers us with favors and takes wonderful care of us. Now we are conferring about a house for which it is said they are asking two thousand ducats; and that's a gift, for it is very well built, so much so that the sisters will not have to do anything to it for many years. It is however in a bad area. It belongs to Fulano de Mena.[10] But we are not wanted in a place that is very central. There are so few places, that even though the house has some small defects, we desire it very much.

5.   I had finished writing this when they sent to tell me that if we didn't have the two thousand ducats we would have to pay nine thousand *maravedis* in rent – and would be required to put down six hundred ducats to be redeemed – which has discouraged us. If we had the means, it would be wonderful, for we would never have to spend anything on it for many years, and a beautiful church is ready. Tell me what you think and how you are. Since I am used to receiving frequent letters from you, I am not resigned to doing less. Let Canon Reinoso take this as addressed to him too. May our Lord watch over your honor for me, as I beg of him, amen.

Today is the first of February.[11]

Your honor's unworthy servant,

Teresa of Jesus

1. This letter was originally published in Antonio de San José's *Epistolario* in 1771. At that time the autograph was in the Carmelite monastery of friars in Duruelo. In 1862, when Don Vicente de La Fuente published his edition of the letters, he said it was in the possession of Señor Don Mauricio Carlos de Onís, in Madrid. This was the last record of it, and its whereabouts was unknown until it recently came to light in the Cardinal Mundelein collection. Cardinal Mundelein had several autograph collectors on his payroll, one of whom was a man from New York named Thomas F. Madigan, who had some fame himself in the autograph world, having written a book about autographs. In this book he mentions Cardinal Mundelein's collection, which he helped build, as being one of the finest collections of autographs of saints outside the Vatican. The amount on the original bill of sale for the Teresa letter, which was one of the most expensive autographs Mundelein bought, is $1,250.00. In researching the correspondence between Madigan and Cardinal Mundelein, all that could be discovered was that Madigan had found the Teresa letter in Europe. He must have found the letter in 1927 and sent it to Cardinal Mundelein in December of 1927. I am grateful to Rev. Michael Fuller for this information.

2. He was the administrator of the hospital of San Antonio in Palencia.

3. The Archbishop of Burgos, Cristóbal Vela.

4. Don Alvaro de Mendoza.

5. On first arriving in Burgos they stayed in the house of Catalina de Tolosa, who had two discalced Carmelite daughters living in Palencia.

6. The Jesuits in Burgos (see Ltr. 450.2-3).

7. Canon Jerónimo Reinoso, Salinas's friend.

8. The general of the Jesuits at the time was Claudio Acquaviva.

9. The renunciation by Catalina de Tolosa's two Carmelite daughters in Palencia of their share of the estate.

10. In the end they did not buy from him, but instead bought a house belonging to Manuel Franco and Angela Mansino.

11. A mistake of Teresa's; it was the first of March and they had been living in the hospital since 23 February.

434. To Sisters María de San José and Isabel de la Trinidad, Palencia.

Burgos, first days in March 1582

(Autograph: DCN, Yepes [Toledo])

Two of Catalina de Tolosa's daughters are Carmelite nuns in Palencia and have renounced their inheritance so that Teresa could use the money to buy a house in Burgos for the foundation she was trying to make there. This letter is one of gratitude to the two nuns. The date is approximate.

✦ ✦ ✦ ✦

To my beloved daughters, Sister María de San José and Sister Isabel de la Trinidad, Carmelites.

1.　Jesus. May the Holy Spirit be with you, my daughters. I received your letter and the document[1]. As often as you write me, it will be a consolation for me. It would also be one for me to respond if I didn't have so many things to do, and because of these duties I cannot answer every time.

2.　I am delighted that you are now foundresses,[2] for I tell you that certainly if you had not helped in this need, I don't know where I could have found the means to buy a house. Although Señora Catalina de Tolosa[3] desired to buy one, she couldn't do any more than she was already doing. So it was ordained by God that you would be able to do this. Since the archbishop[4] did not want to give the license unless we had our own house and since we didn't have the deposit needed to buy one, see what a troublesome situation we would have been in. With your help, even though the money is not all given at once but just a little, we can buy a good house, with God's help.

3.　Praise him very much, my daughters, for you are the source of so great a work; not everyone deserves this grace that he has given to mother and daughters.[5] Don't feel sad about what we have suffered here, for this shows how disturbed the devil is and will serve to bring more prestige to this house. I hope in God that when we have our own house, the archbishop will give the license. Never be disturbed, my daughter, that we suffer, for so much is gained by this.

4.   You should know that Elenita de Jesús[6] will make a great nun. She is with us and we are very happy with her. Teresa[7] is better. She sends her best regards and so does Madre Tomasina[8] and all the nuns, and they thank you very much for what you have done, and will pray to God for you.

May His Majesty watch over you for me, amen; and may he make you holy.

Your charity's,

Teresa of Jesus

---

1.   The document in which they both renounce their portion of the paternal and maternal estate.
2.   She calls them foundresses in an affectionate and respectful way because of the financial help they contributed.
3.   Catalina de Tolosa is the mother of these two nuns.
4.   The Archbishop of Burgos, Cristóbal Vela.
5.   She is referring to Doña Catalina and her two daughters, to whom this letter is being written.
6.   Catalina de Tolosa's youngest daughter, who is already living the Carmelite life with Teresa and her nuns at the hospital of the Conception.
7.   Teresa's niece, her brother Lorenzo de Cepeda's daughter.
8.   Tomasina Bautista, who will become the prioress of the community in Burgos.

435. To María de San José, Seville
Burgos, 17 March 1582

A fragment in which Teresa highly praises the prioress in Seville.

⤛⤜⤛⤜

For Mother Prioress at St. Joseph's in Seville

I was amused by the authority you show with your bell, and if it gets one hopping, as you say, you are right. I hope in God that your house will advance far, for they have suffered much. You say everything so well that if my opinion were followed, they would elect you foundress after my death. And even if I were living I would be eagerly in favor, for you know much more than I do – and are better; that is the truth. I have the advantage over you through having a little experience. But not much attention should be paid to me any more, for you would be startled to see how old I am and how incapable of anything, etc.

436. To Padre Ambrosio Mariano, Lisbon
Burgos, 18 March 1582

This was the decisive day in the history of the foundation of the Carmel in Burgos when the purchase of a house took place. With this letter Teresa now seeks a letter of support from the Duchess of Alba that they might have Mass in their own house without having to go out each day for Mass. It is a permission the archbishop has been refusing to grant.

1.   May the Holy Spirit be with your reverence, *mi padre*. A short time has passed since I wrote you, and our Father Provincial[1] will have already given you an account of what has taken place here with the archbishop[2] and how he said that we must buy a house. Give glory to God, for we have now bought one,[3] and a very good one. We would like to leave this hospital[4] because we are very crowded and would like to see where this whole affair is going to end up.

2.   The archbishop said that the house is a good one and that he is pleased with it. But the suspicion of everyone is that he is not about to do anything more than he has done up until now. And so I would like to have authorization from the nuncio[5] to have Mass at home. With this we could endure the long delay. And so I am writing a letter to the duchess[6] to enclose with this one that she might write us a letter of support. Would you read it and send it to her, in charity, sealing it first. Be sure you arrange

to receive an answer and send it to Padre Nicolao[7] or to Juan López[8] in Madrid, and put in writing what must be done so that the authorization will be received quickly. Realize that you are doing us the greatest charity, for although the house is near a church, it is hard for us to have to go out to hear Mass.[9]

3.   If you think that by your asking the duke[10] in my name, he would respond positively, the authorization might perhaps come more quickly – and I figure it would be something easy to get. As I said in the letter to the duchess, the house has a chapel, which was not used for anything except the celebration of Mass. But also, the Society[11] had lived in the house where we were wanting to make the foundation and the Blessed Sacrament had been reserved there for fourteen years. The archbishop, however, never allowed us to have Mass there. If you had heard all the nice words about what he desired, you would have thought there was nothing else to do but ask. It doesn't seem it depended on him, for certainly the devil very much regretted our making this foundation. So there is no reason to think the archbishop will give the authorization once we have our own house. We could have to wait a long time before he becomes tired enough to give it to us.

4.   I would very much like to know if you gave my letters to those gentlemen and if anything was done. Whatever the case, nothing is lost by trying. In your charity, don't forget to do me this favor.

5.   Padre Fray Antonio's[12] manner of proceeding was so painful to me that I decided to write the enclosed letter. If you think he will not resent it too much, seal it and the others as well and send them to him, for I don't know any other way of sending them.

6.   Greetings to Licentiate Padilla[13] and to Padre Fray Antonio de la Madre de Dios.[14] These sisters send greetings to you.

May God watch over you and make you as holy as I beg of him.

From Burgos, 18 March.

Your reverence's servant,

Teresa of Jesus

1. Jerónimo Gracián, who had been with Teresa in Burgos until recently.
2. The Archbishop of Burgos, Cristóbal Vela (see F. 31.31).
3. They bought it on the vigil of the feast of St. Joseph (see F. 31.36).
4. The hospital of the Conception, where they had lived in crowded conditions since 23 February (see F. 31.28,32).
5. Luis Taverna.
6. The Duchess of Alba, María Enríquez de Toledo.
7. Nicolás Doria, who is the first councilor to the provincial.
8. Juan López de Velasco, one of the king's secretaries in Madrid.
9. First in the church of San Lucas and afterward in that of the Augustinian nuns.
10. The Duke of Alba, Fernando Alvarez de Toledo, probably in Lisbon at the time with the king.
11. The house of Doña Catalina de Tolosa where Teresa first resided on arriving in Burgos (see F. 32.24).
12. Antonio de Jesús Heredia.
13. Juan Calvo de Padilla.
14. Antonio de la Madre de Dios, nicknamed "the preacher," was in Lisbon with the first group of discalced Carmelite missionaries. Having set sail for missionary work in the Congo, they all tragically perished in a shipwreck.

437. To Madre Inés de Jesús, Palencia

Burgos, 26 March 1582

Finally, after about three months of resistance from others, on 18 March Teresa was able to buy a house and move the community into it. But the archbishop of the city continued to make impossible demands, so Teresa here asks the prioress in Palencia to beseech her friend Don Alvaro de Mendoza, the bishop there, to intervene. All that remains of this letter is its French translation.

❧❧❦❦

1.   Jesus be with your reverence and watch over you for me. You should know that we have now moved into the house and are hurrying to adapt it to our needs. May it be His Majesty's will that everything end well and that we obtain the license[1] to remain there, and that the other stipulations[2] not oblige us to abandon it.

2.   Now they are angry with me for having taken possession.[3] I have written again to the bishop[4] to ask him to write a letter of supplication. We will see if it has any effect. You could also, if you think it would help, ask him to do us this favor so that he will write as soon as possible. I don't think I will be able to write to him with this mail, for it is already very late. In any case, I have decided to write to the bishop, as I have said, about the matter I pointed out to you in this letter.

3.   As for my health, I am now beginning to feel better, although not completely. I am happy about our house, for it is a very cheerful one. Praise God for having brought this about.

4.   I am not writing to Medina[5] because it is already late. Give them my greetings and tell them that I will write on another day. My regards to Mother Subprioress[6] and all the other nuns. Those in this house are doing well, and Teresa[7] goes from good to better, glory to the Lord. She sends her regards to you and to all the nuns, and she always prays to God for you that he will be always with you.

Today is 26 March.

5.   I kiss the hands of all those lords[8] and of Canon Reinoso; tell him that I had begun to write to him, but then I didn't have the time.

Teresa of Jesus

---

1.   Teresa has a license from the city (see F. 31.13), but not from the archbishop (see F. 31.41)

2. The stipulations were made by both the owners (see F. 31.37) and the archbishop (see F. 31.41).

3. See F. 31.22.

4. She wrote to the Bishop of Palencia, Alvaro de Mendoza (see F. 31.43-44).

5. She is not writing to the Carmel in Medina.

6. The subprioress in Palencia, Dorotea de la Cruz.

7. Teresita de Cepeda (see Ltr. 432.4).

8. They are her good friends who collaborated for the foundation in Palencia: Alonso de Salinas, Suero de Vega, Prudencio Armentia, and above all, Jerónimo Reinoso.

438. To Padre Nicolás Doria, Pastrana (?)
Burgos, end of March 1582

Nicolás Doria was the first counselor at the side of Gracián, the provincial. Both were elected at the chapter in Alcalá a year before. In September of the previous year Doria had been chosen to go to Rome for business with the Carmelite general regarding the new province of discalced Carmelites (see Ltr. 405.3). Recently, Gracián had appointed Doria prior in Pastrana. Now Doria has written Teresa a letter filled with humble sentiments about his inability to govern. Teresa here responds.

1.   Jesus be with your reverence, *mi padre*. It's a trial to have to be in such far away places and without your reverence,[1] which displeases me very much. May God give you health. There must have been a great need in that house[2] if our *padre*[3] agreed to allow you to be separated from him. The humility of your letter made me very happy, even though I don't plan on doing what you say so that you learn to suffer. Look, *mi padre*, all beginnings are difficult, and so this one of yours will be so for now.

2.   Regarding what you say about the disadvantages of learning, it would be truly unfortunate if in so short a time this defect were already noticeable. It would be better to have no learning

than to show this so soon. You shouldn't think that the business of governing lies in always knowing your faults, for it is necessary so as to carry out your office to forget yourself often and recall that you stand in the place of God. He will give you what you lack, for this is what he does with everyone since no one is perfect. So don't be shy and fail to write to our *padre* about the way things appear to you.

3.   A short time ago, I sent another packet of letters to you through Señora Doña Juana.[4]

May God watch over you and make you as holy as I beg of him, amen.

> Your reverence's servant,

> Teresa of Jesus

1.   A grateful allusion to the journey she made with Doria from Palencia to Soria in May 1581.
2.   The house in Pastrana where Doria had been made prior.
3.   Jerónimo Gracián, the provincial. Besides being first counselor, Doria was Gracian's traveling companion, from whom he was separated when made prior in Pastrana.
4.   Doña Juana Dantisco, Gracián's mother.

439. To Doña Beatriz de Ovalle, Avila

Burgos, beginning of April

This is either a note or a fragment from a longer letter. Beatriz has finally left Alba and gone to Avila to stay with Perálvarez Cimbrón.

❖❖❖❖

One sees clearly how different your cares are from mine, and you should know that the reason I didn't send anything is that I couldn't. I was consoled and gave thanks to God that things are going so well for you in the house of Señor Perálvarez, your uncle.[1] Give him my many regards, because I am very grateful for the favor that he and his wife have shown you. I don't have time to write to them now. I'll do so on another day by mail. It's a great favor from God that you have been freed from the pestilence of that woman.[2]

1. Beatriz could not stay at the Incarnation (see Ltr. 426.3,6), but found lodging with Pedro Alvarez Cimbrón, a great friend of Teresa's.
2. The vicious calumniator in Alba (see Ltrs. 414.1-2; 420.2).

440. To Don Diego de Montoya, Rome
Burgos, beginning of April 1582

Diego de Montoya was an agent for the Inquisition and in Rome on business for Philip II to the Holy See regarding reform. Don Diego had also collaborated with Teresa so that the discalced Carmelites could become a separate province of the order.

1.　Jesus. The grace of the Holy Spirit be with your honor. Since you left Spain, I have been so busy and in such poor health that I can be excused for not having written before. But I did not fail to share in your joy over the brother-in-law given you by the Lord. Señora Doña María[1] wrote to me about it and also begged me to pray to God for some business matters of yours since it doesn't seem that you are lacking trials. May he be praised for everything.

2.　These sisters and I have prayed for this intention and would like to know if the tempest has passed. I always have and will have care about such request for prayers, however wretched I am, since I am obliged to have it. I don't consider it bad that in the midst of so much prosperity from God you experience some adversity, since this is the path along which he has led all his chosen ones. Now it seems we are at peace here, as you will learn from Padre Nicolao de Jesús María[2] since he is the one bringing this. And since you will also learn from him everything that I could say here, I won't go on with any more. May our Lord watch over you and help you progress in his service.

Your honor's unworthy servant,

Teresa of Jesus

3.   I hadn't heard anything about the good Bishop of the Canaries until a little before he embarked. He was well.[3]

---

1.   Doña María de Montoya, mother of Don Diego.
2.   Nicolás Doria, who is going to Rome to render obedience to the general of the order in the name of the discalced Carmelites.
3.   Teresa is referring to Fernando Rueda, a canonist to whom she often presented her canonical problems and who (in 1580) succeeded the Archbishop of Burgos, Cristóbal Vela, as Bishop of the Canary Islands.

441. To Don Alvaro de Mendoza, Palencia
Burgos, 13 April 1582

Since the tenacious resistance to the Carmelite foundation by the Archbishop of Burgos continued, Teresa asked the Bishop of Palencia to intervene. This he did in a scathing letter that Teresa did not dare give to the archbishop. Instead she pleaded with Don Alvaro to write another more delicate letter. Not without a struggle, he complied with Teresa's wish, and the outcome was a happy one. She here expresses her overflowing gratitude.

✦·✦·✦·✦

1.   Jesus. The grace of the Holy Spirit be with your most illustrious lordship. The archbishop[1] was so delighted with your letter that he immediately began to hurry along this project, without anyone's asking him, so that it will be finished before Easter. And he wants to say the first Mass and bless the church. For this reason we will have to wait, I believe, until the final day of the Easter celebration,[2] since the other days are taken. The

necessary formalities required by the provisor are already being taken care of; almost nothing is lacking. They are all quite new for me. The priests of the first parish were convoked to see if they had any problem with it. They said that on the contrary they would do all they could for us. It can all now be considered as finished, and so I sent thanks to the archbishop. May God be praised, for it seemed to be an impossible struggle to everyone; although not to me, for I always considered the foundation to be as much as made – and so I am the one who has suffered the least.

2.   All the nuns kiss your hands many times because you have freed them from so great a trial. Their joy and the praises they give to God would be a delight for you to behold. May he be ever praised who gave you so much charity that it was enough to bring you to write the letter to the archbishop.[3] Since the devil saw the benefit that was to come from it, he put up more opposition. But it was all to little avail because our most powerful God will do what he wants.

3.   I hope the Lord has given you the health necessary to deal with the great amount of work you have had these days, for I have had this intention very much in mind, and all of us have been praying hard for you. Even though a synod means a lot of work, you do very well to have one, for the Lord will give you the energy for everything. It is of great benefit to the Sisters[4] to have you there, but envious ones[5] are not lacking. And I rejoice in the happy Easter you will have.

4.   May our Lord give you happy Easters for many years with as much health, which is something necessary for this whole order, amen.

Today is Good Friday.

The last day of the Easter feast, the first Mass will be said, with God's help. And if the archbishop is able, perhaps before.

Your most illustrious lordship's unworthy servant and subject,

Teresa of Jesus

1. The Archbishop of Burgos, Cristóbal Vela, to whom Don Alvaro had written two consecutive letters: the first was an unsealed letter, which if given to him by Teresa would have ruined everything; the second was more carefully written and the one to which Teresa refers here (see F. 31.43-44).

2. This would be the Tuesday of Easter week.

3. She is alluding to the sacrifice he made by writing another more diplomatic letter.

4. The Sisters in the Carmel of Palencia.

5. Their gain was a loss for the Sisters in Avila, where Don Alvaro had formerly served as bishop.

442. To Don Fadrique Alvarez de Toledo, Alba

Burgos, 18 April 1582

In this letter Teresa congratulates the Duke and Duchess of Alba over the news that the duchess is expecting a child. Teresa writes on the very day in which the long nightmare surrounding the foundation in Burgos ended, with the archbishop granting the license.

1.   Jesus. The grace of the Holy Spirit be with your most illustrious lordship. I shared so much in your joy that I have wanted to let you know about it, for certainly my happiness has been great. May it please our Lord to make it complete by helping my lady the duchess at the time when she gives birth, and may he preserve you in good health for many years.[1]

2.   I kiss the hands of her excellency many times, and I beg her not to fear but to have much confidence, for our Lord who has begun to grant us a favor will bring everything to completion. The Sisters and I will take very special care to beg His Majesty for this intention.

3.   The trials and poor health I have had since I last wrote and the fact that I have received news about your health through other means were the reasons for my seeming to be neglectful. Yet truly I have not been neglectful of you in my poor prayers but very mindful – whatever be their worth – and will be so always. And I have keenly felt your illnesses. Please God they have gone away, and may he watch over you for many years.

From Burgos, 18 April,

> Your most illustrious lordship's unworthy servant,

> Teresa of Jesus

1.   The duchess is Don Fadrique's wife, María de Toledo y Colonna, who was expecting a child as Teresa makes known in the next number. She gave birth to a son on 19 September.

443. To Madre Ana de los Angeles, Toledo
Burgos, 23 April 1582

> (Autograph fragment and original: DCN, Zaragoza)

Ana de los Angeles entered the monastery of the Incarnation in Avila at the age of seven and then transferred to the discalced monastery of St. Joseph's in Avila when it was founded in 1562. There Teresa appointed her subprioress. She was prioress first in Malagón (1568-69) and then in Toledo for many years (1569-85). Teresa has received the license for the foundation in Burgos, and now her eyes are on Madrid, for which she needs permission from Cardinal Quiroga. Both Ana de Los Angeles and Luisa de la Cerda could be helpful intermediaries.

❧❧❦❦

1.   … it seems the arrival of the king has been delayed,[1] and I beg you to give the cardinal an account for me of how well this foundation has been made,[2] even though the archbishop[3] held off from giving the permission. In sum, settle the matter there according to what you think. If Señora Doña Luisa[4] is not

there, write to her for me, for I don't have time to do so now. I felt her trials deeply.

2.   May God give you the quiet rest that I desire for you. To be sure, you are an old friend who cannot bear to see me with sufferings; you indeed owe me this.

Today is the feast of St. George. Your reverence's servant,

Teresa of Jesus

My best regards to Madre Brianda de San José ...[5]

---

1.   King Philip II was in Portugal and did not get back to Spain until 1583.
2.   Teresa wants her to give an account to Cardinal Quiroga of her foundation of discalced Carmelite nuns in Burgos.
3.   The Archbishop of Burgos, Cristóbal Vela, gave the license only after much resistance on his part.
4.   Doña Luisa de la Cerda.
5.   The former prioress in Malagón, now ill and living in Toledo.

444. To Sister Leonor de la Misericordia, Soria
Burgos, 6 May 1582

(Autograph: Sres. Méndez Parada, Ayala, Madrid)

Leonor Ayanz y Beamonte received the habit in Soria four months previous to this letter. She came to know Teresa at the time the foundation was made while she was still living with her husband, Don Francés, in a marriage that was annulled a little later.

For Sister Leonor de la Misericordia, Soria.

1.   Jesus. The grace of the Holy Spirit be with your charity, my daughter. Although it is night and the clock will be striking one while I am writing this, I did not want to miss sending you this letter. I have been wanting to find a mail carrier for Soria and have written for one, but I don't know what happened to my

letters, and they don't take much care there about writing to me. Now the one who is bringing this to you[1] is someone who will be able to give you an account of what is going on here. And I would like you to give an account of what is going on with you to this father of your soul in all openness and let yourself find consolation in his words, for he knows how to bring relief in every way. I am delighted that you will get to know him.

2.   Because the lad[2] he is bringing with him must return, let me know, for goodness' sake, how you are, whether you are happy and about everything else -- I pray much for you -- and tell me what Señor Don Francés[3] has done, for they have told me that he still hasn't decided against marrying, which has surprised me very much; I want him to succeed in serving our Lord.

3.   Señora Doña María de Beamonte[4] has been sick for some days. Write to her and to Doña Juana.[5] Thank her for the favor they have done us. And remain with God, for the head can do no more. Give Padre Vallejo[6] a warm greeting for me and ask him to tell our *padre* about anything that might need correction in that house.

        Your reverence's servant,

        Teresa of Jesus

4.   You can speak to our *padre* about Pamplona.[7] The Lord will guide everything if it is to be for his service. But if we would have to build from the beginning, I don't think it would be suitable.

---

1.   The provincial, Jerónimo Gracián, who is on his way to Soria to see his father, Diego Gracián, off to Rome.

2.   The young man who is accompanying Padre Gracián on the trip from Burgos to Soria.

3.   Don Francés Beamonte y Navarra, who had been Sister Leonor's husband in a marriage that was annulled the previous year. Teresa is referring to the fact that when the marriage was annulled he also made a vow of chastity, but he is now starting to change his mind. He got married to Doña Juana de Beamonte y Navarra in 1585.

4. María de Beamonte, Sister Leonor's aunt.
5. Doña Juana is probably another aunt, sister of Doña María.
6. Diego Vallejo, a canon of the collegiate church in Soria and confessor of the discalced Carmelite nuns there.
7. A plan for the foundation of a Carmel in Pamplona, which in fact Sister Leonor together with Catalina de Cristo made the following year.

445. To Don Pedro Manso, Burgos
   Burgos, 7 May 1582

Doctor Manso, a friend and classmate of Gracián's at the University of Alcalá was later president of the Council of Castile and Bishop of Calahorra. At this time he was a canon at the cathedral in Burgos. He supported Teresa at the time of the foundation and gave lodging to Gracián in his own house. This letter notified him of Gracián's need to leave quickly for Soria without the time to say goodby.

➵➵➵➵

1.   Jesus. The grace of the Holy Spirit be with your honor. Our Father Provincial[1] asked me to tell you that he received a letter from his father[2] who was going to Rome and said that on his way he would stop to speak with him in Soria. So Father Provincial could not delay and had to leave this morning. He would very much have liked to see you, but he was so busy yesterday that he couldn't. I beg you to pray for him. We are left very much alone. For this reason I beg you to remember that from now on you have daughters and that I am so wretched that you must not forget me. Mother Prioress[3] and all the nuns kiss your hands.

2.   They say the reception of the habit[4] will take place on Friday. His excellency will give it. May God give us himself so that we don't feel these absences and may he watch over you with a great increase in sanctity. Before you speak with any of the clergy about staying here, you need to speak to me. But if you do come across someone, don't let the opportunity pass.

Your honor's unworthy subject and servant,

Teresa of Jesus

1. Provincial of the discalced Carmelites, Jerónimo Gracián.
2. Don Diego Gracián de Alderete, secretary of Philip II.
3. The prioress of Burgos, Tomasina Bautista.
4. On 11 May, Doña Beatriz de Arceo y Cuevasrubias received the habit from the hands of the archbishop, Cristóbal Vela.

446. To Don Pedro Juan de Casademonte, Madrid
Burgos, 14 May 1582

In Burgos, Teresa had taken steps toward a foundation in Madrid. She had been sick with an unpleasant illness and was still not over it.

❖❖❖❖

1.   Jesus. The grace of the Holy Spirit be with your honor. Three days ago I received your letter and was truly delighted to know that you are well. May our Lord give you the health I beg of him. You don't need to urge me to do what I am obliged to do for you. Concerning the poor health of Señora Doña María,[1] I have nothing to say, for I know that our Lord seeks to give something good to you and to her with such a continuous trial. Although I have had some trials here, for I have had an unpleasant illness from which I am still not freed, your trial has pained me more.

2.   I indeed believe that you rejoice in all the good things that happen to this order; our Lord will reward you as he can. But if you saw the trials that were suffered in this project, the good outcome would make you even happier. Blessed be God who has done this. I kiss the hands of Señora Doña María.

3.   I desire a foundation in that place[2] very much, and I am making every effort I can. When our Lord is pleased, things will work out. Until then, there isn't much I can do. The enclosed

letters were sent to me from Granada for you. May our Lord watch over you for many years.

From this house of St. Joseph in Burgos, 14 May.

       Your honor's servant,

                   Teresa of Jesus[3]

---

1. Don Pedro's wife.
2. Madrid.
3. On the reverse side of the autograph, Casademonte wrote: "1582, from Burgos, from Madre Teresa de Jesús, 17 May, received on 23 of the same, 1582."

447. To Padre Jerónimo Gracián, Soria (?)

Burgos, 14 May 1582

A recently discovered letter that is substantially authentic.

1. Jesus be with your reverence. Because the messenger is in such a hurry that he finds it difficult to wait for this, I am only going to say that I was annoyed that you would go to the extreme of accepting another blood sister in a community where there are already two.[1] I don't see that it is yet time to transfer one who is already there.

2. You should not in any way give your consent for those two sisters to write to Don Luis what their father[2] says, nor even a word that could be taken for a request; rather you should tell them that in no way will she be received there since there are already two others. And tell them they should ask him not to talk about this, for it will make them very unhappy. And see that nothing different is done. When the next messenger comes I will write again.

3. Tell him that when a monastery is founded in Madrid, you will try to do something, but that for now the charity that was extended to the two is sufficient.

Today is 14 May, for I have no time to write more.

I was delighted to see a letter with your handwriting.

Your Reverence's

Teresa of Jesus

1. María de la Trinidad (de Gante y Beaumont) and Ana de los Angeles.
2. Juan de Gante.

448. To Roque de Huerta, Madrid
Burgos, 14 May 1582

A fragment from a note entrusting the delivery of several letters to Roque.

1.   Jesus be with your honor. Not knowing where Casademonte[1] is living, I cannot avoid giving you some work …

Our *padre*[2] was here last week. He is doing well and was on his way to Soria. From there he has to make some more rounds, which is disturbing to me since much time will pass without our having any news of him …

1. Pedro Juan de Casademonte, a merchant from Medina and friend of Teresa's.
2. Jerónimo Gracián, who went to Soria to see his father who was on his way to Rome, sent by the king.

449. To Sister Leonor de la Misericordia, Soria
Burgos, 15(?) May 1582

(Autograph: Marqués de Guendulain, Pamplona)

Teresa with this letter answered two letters of Sister Leonor, who had sought counsel concerning some of her spiritual experiences. Teresa analyzes what is happening to the novice and gives her some practical advice. She tries to offer her a little

further encouragement by telling her what a good impression
she had made on Padre Gracián in his recent visit to Soria.

✣✣✣✣

For my dear daughter Sister Leonor de la Misericordia.

1. Jesus. May the Holy Spirit be with your honor, my daughter. Oh, how I wish I had no other letters to write than this answer both to your letter that came through the Jesuits and to the latest one. Believe me, daughter, that every time I see a letter from you, it brings me special delight. So I don't want the devil to tempt you to neglect writing to me.

2. Regarding the temptation that makes you think you are not making progress, you will gain in a wonderful way – time will provide the testimony. God is leading you as though you were someone he already has within his palace, who he knows will never leave and to whom he desires to give more and more by which you can merit. Up until now it could be that you received those little feelings of tenderness because God in wanting to detach you from everything found this necessary.

3. I remember a saint[1] I knew in Avila, for certainly it was clear that she lived the life of a saint. She had given everything she had to God, but kept a mantle to wear, and afterward she gave that away. Then God granted her a period of great interior trial and dryness. Afterward she complained very much to him and said: "Is this the way you are, Lord? After leaving me with nothing, then you yourself also leave me?" So, my daughter, this is the way His Majesty is, for he repays great services with trials; and there can be no greater pay because those trials make the love of God increase in us.

4. I praise you, for interiorly you are advancing in the practice of virtue. Leave your soul to God; it is his spouse. He will be responsible for it and lead it to the place that most suits it. Also, the novelty of the life and practices seems to drive away that peace, but afterward it will return. Don't be at all distressed by this. Prize being able to help God carry the cross and don't

be clinging to delights, for it is the trait of mercenary soldiers to want their daily pay at once. Serve without charge, as the grandees do the king. The king of heaven be with you.

5.   Regarding my departure, I am answering Señora Doña Beatriz[2] and will mention the important things.

This Doña Josef[3] of hers is a good soul, certainly, and very much suited for us. But she is so beneficial to that house that I don't know whether it would be right to get her to leave it. So I resist this as much as I can, and I am afraid of stirring up enmities. If the Lord so desires, it will come about.

My regards to those lords, those brothers of yours whom I know.

May God watch over you and make you what I desire.

Your reverence's servant,

Teresa of Jesus

6.   I forgot to mention how happy our *padre*[4] was with you (he couldn't finish praising you), and to ask Mother Prioress[5] why they don't move the refectory downstairs, where with wooden platforms things would work out all right. It would involve much work for those who serve the food to have to carry up wood, and water, and all the rest, whereas this other arrangement would seem to be easier to manage.

---

1.   She is thinking of María Díaz to whom she refers in her *Life* (27.17).
2.   Beatriz de Beamonte, the founding benefactress of the Carmel in Soria and aunt of Sister Leonor (see F. 30.2-3).
3.   She is alluding to a nun in Leonor's family who wants to transfer from her own order to the discalced Carmelites, to which Teresa is opposed.
4.   The provincial, Jerónimo Gracián (see Ltr. 444.1).
5.   The prioress in Soria, Catalina de Cristo (Balmaseda).

450. To Don Jerónimo Reinoso, Palencia
Burgos, 20 May 1582

(Autograph: Cathedral, Palencia)

The foundation in Burgos had been in existence now a fortnight, but the Jesuits in the city were continuing to oppose it. While Teresa was staying with her nuns in the house of Catalina de Tolosa, they wouldn't come near (see Ltr. 433.3). Their "despicable interests" were pecuniary, since Catalina de Tolosa, who had previously been a benefactor of the Jesuits, was now a benefactor of Teresa's nuns.

❧❧❧❧

To the illustrious Canon Reinoso, Palencia.

1. Jesus. The grace of the Holy Spirit be with your honor. Whenever I see a letter from you, I feel consoled. And it pains me that I cannot give myself frequently the comfort that comes from writing to you. I know that you realize this, and nonetheless it bothers me not to be able to do more.

2. Through my letter to Father Rector Juan del Aguila,[1] which is enclosed and which Mother Prioress[2] will show you, you will learn something of what is going on with the Society, for it truly seems that a manifest enmity is beginning to take shape. And the devil bases it on accusations of things for which they ought to thank me. Truly serious calumnies are being spread, some of which they themselves are responsible for. It all ends up with these despicable interests that they say I wanted and strove after, and it's a relief that they didn't add "thought about." And since I believe that they wouldn't tell a lie, I see clearly that the devil must have a hand in this muddle.

3. Now they told Catalina de Tolosa[3] that they didn't want her to have anything to do with the discalced nuns lest she be contaminated by our manner of prayer. To the devil it must be very important to promote quarrels between us since he has become so active. They also told her that their general[4] was

coming here, that he had already disembarked. I recall that he is a friend of Señor Don Francisco.[5] If he could undo these machinations and establish silence by learning the truth, it would be a great service to God. That people so serious should be engaged in such childishness is a pity. Would you look into this and in conformity with what you think apply a remedy.

4.   Those papers[6] must be really tiring you. I beg you to send them to me, as soon as you find a very safe means, and pray for me to our Lord. May His Majesty watch over you, as I beg of him, amen.

Today is 20 May. I kiss the hands of both Señor Don Francisco and those ladies,[7] your aunts.

> Your honor's unworthy servant,
>
> Teresa of Jesus

1. The Jesuit rector of the Society's college in Valladolid. He had been Teresa's confessor.
2. The prioress of Palencia, Inés de Jesús.
3. A noblewoman in Burgos who was supporting Teresa's foundation there.
4. The General of the Society of Jesus, Claudio Acquaviva. His arrival in Spain was pure rumor.
5. Don Francisco Reinoso, Don Jerónimo's uncle and future Bishop of Córdoba. He had spent several years in Rome and there came to know Claudio Acquaviva.
6. She may be alluding to her *Spiritual Testimonies*.
7. These are Don Jeronimo's uncle and aunts: Don Francisco Reinoso and Doñas María and Leonor Reinoso, three very good friends of Teresa's.

451. To Madre Ana de Jesús, Granada
Burgos, 30 May 1582

(Autograph, incomplete: DCN, Seville)

This has been called "the terrible letter." At the end of November, St. John of the Cross had gone to Avila to ask Teresa

to return to Andalusia and make a foundation in Granada. Al-
though unsuccessful in his attempt to get Teresa to come and
make the foundation in Granada, he did return to Andalusia
with two nuns from Avila and also one from either Toledo or
Malagón. Teresa in the meanwhile had obtained two nuns from
Seville and had convinced Anne of Jesus to be the foundress
in Granada in her place. Finally, two lay Sisters were brought
from Villanueva de la Jara. But then Anne of Jesus brought three
more nuns from Beas, who had not been a part of Teresa's
plan. To make room for these three, the two lay Sisters were
sent back by Anne to Villanueva. Neither Gracián nor Teresa
were being informed of all that was taking place. Teresa also
feared that being so many, the nuns were an imposition on
their generous hosts.

❧❧❦❦

1.   Jesus. May the Holy Spirit be with your reverence. I was
amused by the loud complaining of all of you about our Father
Provincial[1] and your neglect to keep him informed after the first
letter in which you told him that you had made the foundation.
And you all acted in the same way with me.

2.   Father Provincial was here on the day of the Cross,[2] and
he didn't know anything more than what I told him, which
came through a letter that the prioress in Seville[3] sent me,
in which she said that you bought a house for 12,000 ducats.
Where there was so much prosperity, it is not surprising that
the patent letters were strictly worded. But down there you're
so crafty at not obeying that this latest fact pained me in no
small way because of the bad impression it will make in the
whole order and also because of the custom that may result
by which prioresses will feel independent and will also think
up excuses. And since you esteem your hosts[4] so highly, it has
been a great indiscretion to stay there with so many nuns. You
sent back those poor nuns[5] as soon as they arrived, making
them retrace so many leagues – I don't know how you had
the heart to do this. Those who came from Beas could have

returned there and others with them. It was terribly impolite to stay in that house with so many – especially knowing that you were a bother; and inconsiderate to bring so many from Beas knowing that you did not have your own house. Certainly I am amazed at the patience of your hosts. Mistakes were made from the beginning, and since you have no other solution than the one you mention, it will be good for you to try it before you end up with greater scandal, seeing that you hold that it would be scandalous to allow one more sister to enter the community. For so large a city this seems a trifle to me.

3.   I laughed to myself over the fear you wished to create in us that the archbishop[6] will suppress the monastery. He no longer has anything to do with it, I don't know why you give him such a large role to play. He would die before succeeding. And if the monastery should continue, as is now the case, by introducing into the order principles that show little obedience, it would be much better if it didn't last. Our worth will not come from having many monasteries but in having nuns in them who are saints.

4.   I don't know when these letters that have now come for our *padre* can be given to him. I fear that he won't be here for another month and a half, and then I don't know where I can be certain in sending them. He went to Soria from here and from there to many places on visitations. Nothing is known for certain where he will be or when we will have news of him. As I figure it, he will be in Villanueva when the poor nuns[7] arrive. It's very painful for me to think of what he will have to go through when they arrive, and the gossip. The place is so small that nothing is secret, and much harm will be done at the sight of such foolishness. They could have been sent to Beas until informing him. They didn't even have a license to return there for he had already officially made them conventuals in Granada, and they were returning right under his eyes. There must have been some way in which the matter could have been remedied, so the fault is all yours for not having mentioned the number of nuns you were bringing from Beas and whether you included

any lay Sister. You paid no more heed to our *padre* than you would have if he hadn't received the office of superior.

5.　From what he has told me and considering what he has to do, it will be impossible for him to go there before winter. Please God, Father Vicar Provincial[8] will be able to do it, for they just gave me some letters from Seville, and the prioress writes me that he is struck down by the plague that's afflicting them there – although it's being kept secret – and Fray Bartolomé de Jesús[9] also, which saddened me very much. If you haven't learned of this, pray for them; losing them would mean a great loss for the order. On the envelope of the letter someone wrote that Father Vicar is better, although not out of danger. The nuns are very tired and understandably, since they are martyrs in that house and undergo many more trials than you – although they don't complain as much. Where the nuns are healthy and there is food to eat, being a little crowded won't kill them, especially where they have the support of many sermons. I don't know what the complaining is about, for everything doesn't have to be in perfect shape.

6.　Madre Beatriz de Jesús[10] tells Father Provincial that they are waiting for Father Vicar to send the nuns from Beas and Seville back to their houses. The nuns in Seville do not agree with this idea. Besides, Seville is very far and in no way would this be proper. If the need is so great, our *padre* will see to the matter. Regarding those from Beas, it would be indeed the right thing to do. If it were not for my fear of contributing to an offense against God through disobedience, I would send you an explicit order, for in all that regards the discalced nuns I stand in the place of our Father Provincial.

7.　In virtue of this authority I tell you and order you that as soon as it can be arranged you send back the nuns that came there from Beas with the exception of Mother Prioress, Anne of Jesus. And this should be done even if you have moved into your own house; at least if you have not a good income that will free you from the straits you're now in. For no reason is it good to have so many nuns living together at the beginning of a foundation, whereas this may be appropriate in other situations.

8.   I have prayed to our Lord over this matter during these days – for I didn't want to answer the letters at once – and I find that by your doing things this way, His Majesty will be served, and the more you suffer from this the more you will serve him. For any kind of attachment, even to the superior, is very foreign to the spirit of discalced nuns, nor would they ever grow spiritually in this way. God wants his brides to be free, attached only to him; and I don't want them to begin acting in this house as they did in Beas. I never forget the letter they wrote me from there when you left office,[11] for a calced nun would not even have written it. This is how cliques begin and many other unfortunate things, although they may not be recognized at the beginning. And for this time, don't follow any opinion but mine, for heaven's sake. For once things are settled and the sisters more detached, they can return if it is fitting.

9.   I truly don't know who they are who went, for you kept it really secret from me and from our *padre*, nor did I think you would take so many nuns from there, but I imagine they are very attached to you. Oh, true spirit of obedience, how when seeing someone in the place of God no repugnance is felt toward loving her! For the sake of God I beg you to take care to inspire souls to be brides of the Crucified, that they crucify themselves by renouncing their own will and the pursuit of childish trifles. Look, this is the beginning in a new kingdom,[12] and you and the other nuns are more obliged to behave as valiant men and not as worthless little women.

10.   What is this, madre mía, that you are paying attention to whether Father Provincial calls you presider, or prioress, or Anne of Jesus?[13] It is clear that if you were not in charge, he wouldn't have reason to give you a title above the others, for they have also been prioresses.[14] You have given him so little news of what is taking place that he doesn't know whether

elections have been held or not. Certainly, I am ashamed that in so short a time the discalced nuns are paying attention to these trivialities, and after paying attention to them, making them the topic of their conversations, and that Madre María de Cristo[15] makes such an issue out of it. Either through trials you have all become silly or the devil has introduced hellish notions into this order. And after this she praises you as being very courageous as though acting differently would mean you were not. God desires my discalced nuns to be very humble, obedient, and submissive, for all these other kinds of courage mark the beginning of many imperfections without these virtues.

11. Now I recall that in one of your previous letters you wrote that one of the nuns had relatives there who would be helpful if brought with you from Beas. If this is so, I leave it to the prioress to make the decision, but not the others.

12. I truly believe that you will have many sufferings in the beginning. Do not be surprised, for a work as great as this cannot be done without them since, as they say, the recompense will be great. Please God that the imperfections with which I am doing this do not deserve more punishment than reward, for I always have this fear. I am writing to the prioress of Beas[16] to help with the expenses of the journey. You are so short of means there! I assure you that if Avila were closer, I would be very happy to take back my sisters. That could happen with the passing of time and the help of the Lord. So you can say that once the foundation is made and there is no longer a need there, because nuns will be entering from that area, they may return to the houses from which they came.

13. A little while ago I wrote at length to you and to those madres, and to Padre Fray John,[17] and gave you an account of what has been taking place here, and so it seems that I need to write nothing further than what is in that letter, which was meant for everyone. Please God, things being as they are, you will not be offended as when our padre called you "presider."

Until we had an election here, when our padre came, this is the term we used, and not "prioress," and it's all the same.

14.   Each time I forget to mention this. They told me that in Beas even after the chapter,[18] the nuns were leaving the enclosure to clean the church. I don't know how they can do that since not even the provincial can give permission for this. The prohibition comes from the pope's motu proprio,[19] with severe threats of excommunication, not to speak of the strict prescription of our constitutions. At the beginning this was difficult for us; now we are delighted with it. The Sisters in Avila[20] know well that they cannot even go out to lock the door that opens onto the street. I don't know why you were not informed of this. You should take care of this matter, for goodness' sake. God will provide someone to clean the church and there is a solution to everything …[21]

15.   Every time I think of the crowded conditions in which you have placed your noble hosts, I cannot help but feel bad. I already wrote the other day that you should get a house even if it is not very good or suitable, for you will not be as crowded as you are now, and even if you are it is better that you suffer than to make those who have been so good to you suffer. I am now writing to Señora Doña Ana,[22] and I would like to have words to thank her for the good she has done us. She will not lose anything with our Lord, which is what matters.

16.   If you want something from our padre, remember that you have not written to him. For, as I say, it will be late before I can send him letters. I will try. From Villanueva he will be going to Daimiel to receive that monastery, and to Malagón and Toledo; then to Salamanca and Alba, for the elections of I don't know how many prioresses. He told me that he didn't plan to be in Toledo until August. It distresses me to see him have to do so much traveling in places where the weather is so hot. All of you pray for him and try as much as you can to get your own house …[23]

17.   The Sisters could stay there until you have notified the provincial and he decides what the best thing to do might be,

for you haven't kept him abreast of anything or written him to tell him the reason you are not taking those nuns.

May God give us light – for without that, there is little one can be sure of – and watch over your reverence, amen.

Today is the thirtieth of May.

Your reverence's servant,

Teresa of Jesus

18. I am writing to Mother Prioress in Beas about the departure of those nuns and that this should be done with as much secrecy as possible. When it comes to be known, it won't matter. Let Mother Subprioress,[24] her two companions, and Padre Fray John of the Cross read this letter addressed to you, for I don't have the head to be writing more.

---

1. Jerónimo Gracián.
2. May 3.
3. María de San José.
4. Doña Ana de Peñalosa and Don Luis de Mercado, St. John of the Cross's very good friends, who provided lodging for the nuns while they looked for a place in Granada where they could live.
5. The two lay Sisters who came from Villanueva de la Jara.
6. The Archbishop of Granada, Juan Méndez de Salvatierra.
7. The two nuns who were sent back from Granada to Villanueva de la Jara.
8. The Vicar Provincial for the discalced Carmelites in Andalusia, Diego de la Trinidad, who during this time died of the plague in Seville.
9. A discalced Carmelite friar in Seville who had been a secretary for Gracián at one time.
10. One of the founding nuns in Granada who had come from either Toledo or Malagón.
11. She gave up her office as prioress in Beas so as to prepare for the foundation in Granada.
12. In the kingdom of Granada.

13. She is referring to the patent letter in which Gracián appointed her to make the foundation in Granada.
14. María de Cristo and Beatriz de Jesús had been prioresses of their communities.
15. María de Cristo had come from St. Joseph's in Avila.
16. Catalina de Jesús Sandoval y Godínez.
17. St. John of the Cross.
18. After the chapter of Alcalá in 1581.
19. She is alluding to the pontifical decrees on enclosure issued after the Council of Trent: Circa pastoralis officii of Pius V (1 Jan. 1566); Decori et honestati of Pius V (2 Feb. 1570); and De sacris virginibus of Gregory XIII (30 Dec. 1572).
20. Two nuns came from St. Joseph's in Avila: María de Cristo and Antonia del Espíritu Santo.
21. The text is damaged here and a line is missing.
22. She had turned over a large part of her house to the nuns for their temporary quarters.
23. Again something is missing in the text.
24. María de Cristo; her two companions from Castile were Antonia del Espíritu Santo and Beatriz de Jesús.

452. To the Discalced Carmelite Nuns in Toledo
Burgos, June (?) 1582

This fragment is contained in a letter by Blessed Mary of Jesus to Teresa's niece, Beatriz de Jesús in Madrid: "And the last letter that she wrote to us from Burgos was one of gratitude. While she was very sick in that place, we sent her 200 ducats of silver to help her, and she wrote saying …" Teresa's words that are quoted in that letter follow in this text.

God reward you, my daughters, for having shown me so much charity. And who other than you should have done this and helped me in a time of so much need? I tell you that God will never fail you, and may he bless you for me.

453. To Dionisio Ruiz de la Peña, Madrid
Burgos, 4 June 1582

Now that the Carmel in Burgos had been established, the time had come to turn to the plan for a foundation in Madrid. The cardinal was residing there, but the king had not yet arrived with all the flurry of his court. Teresa had written to the cardinal, but had received no answer. Though her health had been very poor, she still had the desire to make a foundation in Madrid.

❖ ❖ ❖ ❖

1.   Jesus. The grace of the Holy Spirit be with your honor and may he give you on this feast[1] a great plenitude of his love, as I beg of him. May he repay you for what you give me with your letters, which is very great; and which is so with the most recent one. It would make me very happy, since you are in Madrid, if God were to ordain the establishment of that foundation[2] because I would also then be able to communicate with you more and be near his most illustrious lordship.[3] I was delighted that you did not stay long enough in Toledo for the heat to arrive, and I praise our Lord for the good health he gives his lordship. May God be pleased to preserve him for many years; when founding a house, we begin to pray for such an intention.

2.   The foundation here has now been completed, glory to God. I have always had poor health in this place. Nonetheless, I wouldn't want to leave except to go to Madrid. This is what I wrote to his lordship. And afterward, please God, I want to do no more traveling, for I am very old and tired.

3.   Here some are saying that the king already wants to go there;[4] others say he will not go there so soon. Regarding the foundation, it seems it would be more fitting that it be already made when he arrives, if the cardinal were to give his consent. I trust that His Majesty will enlighten him about the best thing to do and that he might want to grant me a favor. Yet I would not want to be a bother. But, since his illustrious lordship has

so many things to do, and I know this to be for the service of our Lord, I would not want it to be neglected because of a lack of effort on my part. And so I am reminding him, feeling very certain that God will give him the light to do what is best and at the best time.

May His Majesty watch over you, as I beg of him, amen.

From this house of St. Joseph in Burgos, on the second day of this feast of the Holy Spirit.

> Your honor's unworthy servant,
>
> Teresa of Jesus

---

1. The third day of Pentecost.
2. A foundation in Madrid.
3. Cardinal Gaspar de Quiroga. Dionisio Ruiz de la Peña was a secretary to the cardinal.
4. He was in Portugal at the time.

454. To Padre Jerónimo Gracián, La Roda
Burgos, 29 June 1582

> (Autograph [torn]: Sanlucar la Mayor [Seville])

Gracián had departed from Burgos in February. The archbishop had now ended his resistance and accepted the new Carmel there. But Teresa's bad throat, aggravated by the cold weather, continued to be painful. She suggests a transfer for Fray Felipe in Malagón and Ana de los Angeles in Toledo, both of whom could be helped by one. The nuns in Salamanca were experiencing logistical difficulties in their present monastery. Teresa gives her own suggestions to Gracián about these matters.

❖❖❖❖

For Our Father Provincial

1.   Jesus. The grace of the Holy Spirit be with your reverence, *mi padre*. I still do not have an answer to the letters I sent you

with a private messenger, and I desire a response very much so as to know how your health is. It has been somewhat comforting to me that so far we have had continually cold weather here. I hope that it will not be as hot down there as usual. May God do what he sees as necessary. I hold that it is taxing for you to be traveling about in this weather, so it would be a relief for us to have more frequent news of you. I have a strong desire that you not delay there and that the thought not even enter your mind to go to Seville, whatever may be the need, for they are definitely undergoing a pestilence down there.

2.   For the love of our Lord, do not give in to the temptation to go and ruin us all, at least me. Although God gives you health, the danger you place your health in is enough to take mine away up here ... [1]

Finding the money to pay the expenses will be no small task, for she[2] wants everything to be perfect and her brother will not give anything for now. Behold the nice seasoning to go with the poverty in which we are all walking! If you find anyone in Malagón who will lend us five hundred ducats – I mean to say, if the prioress should have them – I would accept them gladly, since that is not much for so many nuns. The main thing is that here, *mi padre*, I don't think they will ever be in need. For now, there will be some struggle.

3.   As for finding someone to say Mass for us, we haven't succeeded. It will be necessary for now – and all our friends think so – to have a friar come. Since you had the same idea in your letter, we were all very happy. I don't find anyone like Fray Felipe,[3] for I know that he is very distressed there and doesn't do anything but send me letters. As a result he cannot be kept there much longer in so unhappy a state. If he comes here, we will have a confessor, and he will be better off than down there ...

4.   You should know, *mi padre*, that the prioress in Toledo[4] writes me that she is very ill, and indeed it is for me a matter of conscience because of what she endures there, for truly

the climate is killing her. I have thought, if you agree, that even though they elected her there – for if they hadn't it would be strange – you could bring her to Avila. That way two things could be done: first, test her health; second, she could leave a president there of her own choice, and one could see how that one does without being a prioress.[5] It would be a difficult burden for Avila if she is so sick, but also if she is well it would be very beneficial. And accepting her is something they owe her, for every year since St. Joseph's was founded eight hundred ducats are given for her. There are many difficulties in this regard, but she has worked hard within the order, and I couldn't bear just leaving her to die.

5.   You will see there what is best; and realize that she has been tempted to think that you don't like her, and the letter that you wrote her about not touching the money made her think that you consider her to be a spendthrift. I have already written to her about your aim for them, which is that they have an income and little by little build a chapel.

6.   These nuns can be a burden for you, *mi padre*; but you are indeed indebted to them, for they have deeply felt your trials, especially in Toledo…

7.   … if it isn't acquired by the fixed date, we are left without knowing what to do about the monastery,[6] and the danger is great that they will spend what they have for buying one. In sum I have written to them not to turn away Cristóbal Juárez[7] until you get there, for you will see from everything what is best to do. The walls[8] are almost finished. Only one is made of clay; the others are of lime and stone.

8.   May God watch over you for me. I wouldn't want to ever end this. My throat feels as usual, and no worse. Otherwise, I am fine and everything is going well, glory to God. Don't let this sadden you, for because of what I owe His Majesty and the favors he grants me each day, it is good to suffer something.

9.   I beg you to give heed to this matter about the friar. And if you can't send the one mentioned, send another you

might think good for this office, for these souls are very good and tranquil.

Today is 25 June. Yesterday was the feast of St. John. The friends are well.

Your reverence's servant and subject,

Teresa of Jesus

1. The autograph has deteriorated, so the text is not always clear.
2. Doña Catalina de Tolosa, the founding benefactress of the Carmel in Burgos. Her brother is Pedro de Tolosa.
3. Felipe de la Purificación, brought by Teresa to Malagón to be confessor there.
4. Ana de los Angeles, who came from the monastery of the Incarnation in Avila.
5. Teresa herself continued being prioress there even though absent.
6. She is alluding to the Carmel in Salamanca.
7. A gentleman from Salamanca (ordained a priest in 1582), who gave his house to the discalced Carmelite nuns when they abandoned the house of Pedro de la Banda (22 June 1582).
8. For the Carmel in Burgos.

455. To Madre María de San José, Seville
Burgos, 6 July 1582

(Original [Ana de San Bartolomé]: DCN, Valladolid)

Finally a few lines with some precise information arrived from Madre María de San José in Seville, where a serious pestilence was threatening the lives of the inhabitants. Teresa was not too well, but was planning a journey back to Avila.

For Mother Prioress of the Carmel of St. Joseph. The discalced Carmelite nuns behind San Francisco. Postage, one half real.

1. Jesus. The grace of the Holy Spirit be with your reverence, amen, amen. Yesterday I received a letter from you which,

although there were only a few lines, brought me the greatest delight, for I was very afflicted over what they told me about so many people dying.[1] I am praying urgently to God for you, as they are doing in all these houses, for I sent to ask them for their prayers. I feel anxious at every moment to think of you amid so many trials.

2.   I already knew of the death of Padre Fray Diego,[2] and I praised God that Padre Fray Bartolomé[3] remains, for I was very grieved that he might die, for this would have been a great loss to you. May God be praised for all that he does.

3.   I would have liked to have been told of this letter so that my answer could have been in my own hand, but I was informed only now when the letter carrier is ready to leave and my head is very tired, for I have been writing the whole afternoon. But even if they aren't in my own hand, I didn't want to neglect sending these few lines.

4.   I haven't mentioned how amused I was by your complaints regarding the Mother Prioress in Granada,[4] and rightly so. For she should rather be thankful for what you did in sending the nuns in so dignified a manner – and not riding some donkeys, for God and the whole world to see. Even had you sent them by litter, I wouldn't have been upset if nothing else was available. May God preserve you, my daughter, for you did very well.[5] And don't worry about it if someone thinks otherwise. They are only quibbling. She must have been displeased because in the making of that foundation things weren't done according to their plan. But I think everything will be all right. Even if there is some trial, the outcome isn't worse for that reason.

5.   This house is in very good condition, well established and paid for, and the nuns for many years will have no need to work to support themselves. So I think I will soon start on my way back to Avila.[6] Pray to God for me. My throat continues as usual, as do my other infirmities.

6.   Greetings to Padre Fray Bartolomé and to all the Sisters. Those who are here send you their regards. Pray for Teresa,[7]

who is a little saint and has a great desire be a professed nun. May God guide her and preserve you and make you very holy.

From this house of St. Joseph's in Burgos, 6 July.[8]

Your reverence's servant,

Teresa of Jesus

1. Because of the pestilence that was afflicting the region.
2. Diego de la Trinidad, who had been the vicar provincial, died from the pestilence in Seville.
3. Bartolomé de Jesús, who was a good friend of Gracián's.
4. The mother foundress of the Carmel in Granada, Anne of Jesus.
5. María de San José wrote in the margin: "Our Holy Mother says this because of the criticism that two nuns were sent by coach from Seville to Granada for the foundation there. Here one sees the opinion of our mother."
6. She left Burgos on 26 July, but never did reach Avila.
7. Her niece Teresita made her profession on 5 November, less than a month after Teresa's death.
8. Only the remainder is in Teresa's hand.

456. To Sister Leonor de la Misericordia, Soria
Burgos, 7 July 1582

Teresa received news that Sister Leonor was sick and writes to urge her to care for herself. Teresa herself had not been well, and cannot travel. Nonetheless she had her heart set on making a foundation in Madrid.

1. Jesus be with your charity, my daughter, and may he watch over you and give you the health I desire for you, for it has greatly grieved me that you are not well. Do me the charity of pampering yourself. And what they tell me in these parts about what the Sisters are doing with you delights me very much, for if they didn't behave this way, they would be acting badly. You should be as happy with the comforts as you are without

them, for obedience will consider whether you need them or not, and in fact that's what it's doing. Please God, my daughter, that the illness will not get worse. Let me know, when you have a messenger, if you are better, for I am worried.

2.   What I said to you in the other letter,[1] I would like to say often, if I could see you. But this won't take place so soon, for the cardinal[2] has written me promising to give me the permission when the king[3] returns, and they are already saying that he is coming. But however soon, it won't be until September or later. Don't be sad about this, for I would be as happy to see you as you me. Since this cannot happen now, God will arrange it in another way.[4] I am in such poor health that I am in no condition to travel either down there or anywhere else, although I am better than I was some days ago. May God be praised.

3.   I took some pills, and so I didn't write this letter myself, for I don't dare.

May God give you an abundance of grace, my daughter, and do not forget me in your prayers.

It is 6 July.

    Your charity's servant,

Teresa of Jesus

---

1. See Ltr. 449.
2. The Cardinal Archbishop of Toledo, Gaspar de Quiroga.
3. Philip II, who was in Portugal at the time. Actually he did not leave Lisbon for Madrid until after Teresa's death, 11 February 1583.
4. They never did get to see each other again. On 15 September, Teresa wrote to the prioress in Soria, "Oh, how I would like to come for her profession" (Ltr. 468).

457. To Madre María de San José, Seville
Burgos, 14 July 1582

(Original [Anne of St. Bartholomew] & Autograph: DCN, Valladolid)

Because of a scarcity of news, Teresa is still worried about the pestilence in Seville. But two more optimistic letters have arrived: from Madre María de San José and from Pedro de Tolosa. She is preparing a journey for the end of the month, despite her illnesses.

❧❧❧❧

For Mother Prioress of the Carmel of St. Joseph, the discalced nuns behind San Francisco. Seville. Postage, one half *real*.

1.   Jesus. May the Holy Spirit be with your reverence, my daughter, and protect you for me from all those tribulations and dangers of death.

2.   Your letter was a great consolation in that you tell me the nuns are not sick – not even a headache. It doesn't surprise me that they are well considering the prayers that are offered for them in every house; they even ought to be saints after so many supplications. I at least am ever concerned about all of you and will never forget you. Believe me you must not be ready, since you are not dying along with so many others being removed by God from that city. May the Lord watch over them for me, and over you in particular, for certainly your dying would grieve me terribly. The death of Father Vicar[1] grieved me, and it would have been worse had it been Padre Fray Bartolomé[2] because of how much your house would have missed him. May God be praised for all things, because in every way we are obliged to Padre Bartolomé.

3.   I read a letter from Pedro de Tolosa – which his sister gave me –[3] where he says that the situation in that city is improving, which was better news than in your letter. I also told his sister to give him my thanks for what he does for your house. Pray much for him and for his sister, Catalina de Tolosa – our

whole order ought to do this – for after God this house owes its existence to her, and I think God will be served very much in it. When he comes there, give him my best regards. And pray for me. My health continues as usual.

4.   I plan, God willing, to leave at the end of this month for Palencia. Our *padre*[4] left word there that I should spend a month in that house. Then I must go for the profession of Teresa,[5] for she has finished her year of novitiate and desires to make her profession. Pray for her, you and all the nuns, with great care at this time that God will give her his grace. Consider how she needs it; for although she's lovely, she's only a child after all.[6]

5.   I already sent your letter to Padre Fray Pedro de la Purificación,[7] for he is in Alcalá as vice-rector. Our *padre* left him there when he passed through. And I think he misses him very much. Now, they told me, he is in Daimiel and will be in Malagón, and that he is well, thanks be to God.

6.   Many regards to all the sisters and give those who have had relatives who died my condolences and assurance of prayers. Regards in particular to Mother Subprioress,[8] San Jerónimo, and San Francisco. Tell them I would be delighted to write to them if I could, but my health is of no assistance to me, and that is why this is not written in my own hand. I am no worse, however, than usual, but my head is tired and I don't dare push myself with these letters, for there are others required by courtesy that cannot be avoided.

May God be blessed and give you his grace, amen.

It is the fourteenth of July.

7.   I received a letter from good Padre Nicolao,[9] which made me happy. He is already in Genoa and feeling fine, for the trip by sea went very well. And he has received news that our most reverend Father General[10] will be there within ten days. Padre Nicolao will discuss all the business matters with him there, and then return without going any further. This made me very happy. Pray for him and for his mother, who has died. He urges

us very much to do this, and in your house there you truly owe it to him.

8. For goodness' sake don't fail to write me about how things are going for you. You already see how worried I am, they will forward me your letters from here. May the Lord be pleased to grant me the favor of keeping you in good health and watching over you especially. All the nuns here are well, are happy with how things are going, and send their regards.

Your reverence's servant,

Teresa of Jesus

Give my best to Fray Bartolomé.

---

1. The vicar provincial of the discalced Carmelites in Andalusia, Diego de la Trinidad, who died from the pestilence (see Ltr. 455.2).
2. Bartolomé de Jesús, who had been Padre Gracián's secretary.
3. Doña Catalina de Tolosa. Pedro de Tolosa had been the carrier of the previous letter.
4. Jerónimo Gracián.
5. Teresita, Teresa's niece.
6. The passage beginning with "Consider" was added in Teresa's own hand. Teresita was 16 years old at the time.
7. He had accompanied Padre Gracián and Teresa on the trip to Burgos.
8. The subprioress of Seville, Leonor de San Gabriel. The other two were Isabel de San Jerónimo and Isabel de San Francisco.
9. Nicolás Doria went to Italy to meet the general in the name of the new province.
10. The general of the order at the time was Giovanni Battista Caffardo.

458. To Madre Tomasina Bautista, Burgos

Palencia, 3 August 1582

(Original, damaged: DCN, Burgos)

Teresa here responds to a letter from the prioress in Burgos about some matters of house management there. The joyful news she reports concerns Doria's cordial meeting with the general in Genoa, Italy.

❖·❖·❖·❖

To Madre Tomasina Bautista, Burgos.

1.   Jesus be with your reverence, *mi madre*, and make you a saint. I so delighted in your letter that it would seem I hadn't seen you only a few days ago.[1] May God give you health and preserve you for me, also Sister Beatriz de Jesús,[2] whose illness weighed on me very much. I am already praying for her. Tell her this and give her my regards.

2.   As for the parlor: when Catalina de Tolosa[3] goes away, close the part that was opened at the time of the flood.[4] And if Catalina de Tolosa remains there, leave it as it is, but do not allow anyone else to have access to it. And as I say, if afterward she should desire to return, there would be little that would have to be removed, just a partition wall. And you could give her a room if she so desires. But a window should be so positioned that the garden cannot be viewed through it. For they have already seen us enough.

3.   My throat is better, for I haven't felt so well in days. Since I can eat without any pain hardly, and today there is a full moon, I think it's important. My room is very cool and nice, and the whole house seems nicer than I thought it would. Everything is so neat that it couldn't appear bad.

4.   Teresa[5] sends you her regards. She doesn't seem so gracious as she did when in Burgos. All the sisters are well, as is also Mother Prioress.[6] They send you their regards, and I send mine to Mother Subprioress[7] and to all the sisters, and to Catalina de Tolosa, to Beatriz and Lesmitos,[8] to Doña Catalina and her mother,[9] and all the friends. St. Bartholomew sends her best to you and to all the sisters, and to your young ones.[10] As for giving my greetings to friends, you may do it for me always, even if I don't mention it to you. I give you the permission to represent me.

5.   I have observed how they do the washing here, using no more than two sisters and thought that you could do this there if María[11] enters, and this would be cheaper for you. Consider this carefully, for I am not suggesting it unless it would be more beneficial. The water there is very good. Isabel[12] could also serve to help María with the wash.

6.   I received a letter from Padre Fray Nicolás[13] and he tells of how the general came after ten days as he had said in the other letter.[14] He got along very well with the general and was most willingly and graciously granted what he went for. This is evident by the fact that the general made him his procurator for the entire province of discalced friars and nuns in such a way that everything going to the general must pass through his hands and be submitted to his counsel.

7.   Padre Fray Nicolás's brothers[15] got on very well with the general, and so he departed truly satisfied. Since the calced friars saw that Padre Fray Nicolás stayed in their house,[16] they thought that he wanted to become a calced friar and they told him that if he stayed in that house they would make him prior, an office he can't bear the thought of![17] It could be that he is already back in this country, for he says that he wants to leave at once if he can find room on a ship. Pray much for him and give thanks for the great favor His Majesty has granted us in being in such good graces of the general. Organize a procession and give thanks to the Lord, for now nothing remains for us to do than to be very holy and use these favors for the service of God. May he be with you and give you his grace.

It is the third of August.

8.   So that I can be courteous with friends, you will have to forgive this handwriting which belongs to someone else. Since I am not writing to my doctor,[18] he will think that it wasn't possible for me to do so. Kiss his hands for me and tell him the news that makes me so happy, and for goodness' sake may all the nuns be so, since God has granted us so many favors.

May he watch over you, my friend, and make you a saint.

Your reverence's

Teresa of Jesus

1. She had left Burgos only eight days before.
2. Beatriz de Jesús (Arceo), the widow of Benero from the court of Philip II. She had taken the habit in Burgos 15 May.
3. Teresa's great friend and benefactor in Burgos, who herself later entered the Carmel in Palencia.
4. The Arlanzón river overflowed its banks and flooded the Carmel in Burgos shortly after it was founded.
5. Teresa's niece, Teresita.
6. The prioress in Palencia.
7. The subprioress in Burgos, Catalina de Jesús, a directee of St. John of the Cross.
8. Beatriz and Lesmitos are Catalina de Tolosa's daughters. They later became discalced Carmelite nuns.
9. Catalina Manrique, sister of the magistrate of Burgos, and her mother, Doña María.
10. Blessed Anne of St. Bartholomew is Teresa's secretary, and the two young ones are probably the two little daughters of Catalina de Tolosa: Beatriz and Elena.
11. María de la Concepción, who made her profession on 2 April 1585.
12. Isabel de Santa Ana, who made her profession on 1 April 1585.
13. Nicolás Doria (see Ltr. 457.7). The general was Giovanni Battista Caffardo.
14. The other letter was received in Burgos before 14 July (see Ltr. 457.7).
15. Doria being Genoese was able to visit with his renowned family while there and introduce the general to them.
16. The monastery of the Carmelite friars in Genoa.
17. He disliked being superior (see Ltr. 438).
18. Doctor Pedro Manso was a canon in Burgos and had served as Teresa's confessor there (see F. 31.24). The text beginning with no. 8 is in Teresa's hand.

459. To Doña Catalina de Tolosa, Burgos
Palencia, 3 August 1582

Only a photocopy of the damaged original is known to exist.

Although there is mention of the difficulties that Doña Catalina and the Carmelites were having with the Jesuits, the impairment done to the text makes it difficult to read the details of what is being said. Understandably, Teresa shows special interest in Catalina's children.

1.   Jesus. May the Holy Spirit be with your honor. I looked at the address and I am grateful that in responding you removed the title "illustrious." I tell you that the nuns and I were very pleased with *mi Lesmes*.[1] May God watch over him and make him a saint. Those two little angels[2] bring me joy. I have asked Maruca to help me pray. She is the portress and does everything well. They both want to see you, just as I do too.

2.   May the Lord hear our prayer and repay you for the favor you showed me with your letter, for I was afraid about the condition of your health. I am already desiring to see another letter with news that Beatriz[3] is improving. May God bring this about. The letters I brought still haven't been delivered because I am waiting …

What they did wasn't a sufficient reason for giving up all communication with them, even if during a novena that you had in the house, you didn't see any of them present. I mentioned what a bad impression that made in the city. I am taking great care to deliver the letters as soon as possible.[4] Please God no one will send them elsewhere. Tell this to Isabel de Trazanos[5] and give her my regards.

3.   You should know that the abbess of Santa Dorotea[6] gave me two ducats without knowing …

Remain with God, for I have much to do … My throat is better. I don't know how long this will last.

Today is Friday.

Your honor's servant,

Teresa of Jesus

---

1. Doña Catalina's son, still a small child, who later became a discalced Carmelite.
2. Doña Catalina's two daughters, nuns in the Carmel of Palencia: María de San José (Maruca) and Isabel de la Trinidad. Or, she could be referring to Catalina's two smallest children: Lesmes and Beatriz.
3. Beatriz de Jesús (Arceo), who was sick in the Carmel in Burgos.
4. She is alluding to letters entrusted to her by Catalina to be delivered in Palencia. A damaged passage follows and several lines are then intentionally effaced in the autograph.
5. The identity of this person is unknown.
6. The canonesses regular of St. Augustine in Burgos.

460. To Doña Teresa de Láyz, in Alba
Palencia, 6 August 1582

Doña Teresa de Layz is the founding benefactress of the Carmel in Alba (see F. 20). She was demanding and meticulous, so that the nuns began to fear her (see Ltr. 372.1). Now she has written to Teresa urging the return of Tomasina Bautista, who was at the time prioress in Burgos. Teresa answers in the negative, but promises to go there personally to investigate matters (see Ltr. 390.6). In writing this letter, Teresa intends it to be read also by the nuns' chaplain.

✢ ✢ ✢ ✢

1. Jesus. The grace of the Holy Spirit be with your honor. I received your letter, but in regard to what you said I can do very little. When I speak about it with Madre Tomasina Bautista,[1] such a change comes over her that from the soles of her feet to the top of her head, she says, she feels upset at the thought of returning to that house. And the reasons she gives why this would disturb the tranquility of her soul are such that no superior would order her to do so. She is now experiencing great peace, living in a very nice house, much to her liking. If you

truly love her, you will rejoice over this and not want someone to come to be with you who doesn't want to. May God pardon her, for I desire your happiness so much that I wish it were possible for me to give everything you ask for. For love of God do not be afflicted, for there are many nuns in the order who can make up for the absence of Madre Tomasina.

2.   If you are distressed by the thought that Madre Juana del Espíritu Santo[2] will remain as prioress, you need not be, for she has already written me that not for anything in the world would she accept that office again. I don't know what to say about those nuns. I fear that no prioress will last there, for they all take flight. I beg you to consider that this is your house and that God cannot be served where there is disquiet. So, it is very important that you concern yourself with them, for if they are what they should be, what can any prioress do to them? These attachments and childish ways are far from the behavior one expects from discalced nuns, and such conduct does not exist in the other houses. I can more or less figure out which ones are agitating the others, and if God gives me the health, and it is possible, I will try to go there to investigate these machinations. For it is painful for me to learn through a certain source that friars from another order were told of things that should have been kept private and that became the subject of talk even among seculars outside that city. Truly, through their childishness and imperfections, these nuns have done a great wrong to the order, for people will naturally conclude that all the other nuns are like them.

3.   I beg you to tell them this and try to promote peace, for soon our *padre*[3] will be going there. Do me this favor, for whoever is elected must be your servant. I tell you that if I had known some of the things they now tell me, I would have corrected them before. I will now have to do everything possible to provide a remedy.

4.   I ask you to show this letter to Padre Pedro Sánchez,[4] and to give him my respects, so that he will reprehend the culpable

and not let them receive Communion so frequently. They shouldn't think that it is some small matter to upset the peace of a monastery or talk to outsiders about things so harmful to those whom the world esteems as good nuns. Ah, my lady, how differently things go where the true spirit reigns!

May God give you this spirit and preserve you for us many years with the holiness I desire.

Today is the feast of the Transfiguration.

Your honor's unworthy servant,

Teresa of Jesus

---

1. Tomasina Bautista was Teresa de Láyz's niece. At this time she was the prioress in Burgos, but had been in Alba and had served as prioress and novice mistress.
2. She was the prioress in Alba at the time.
3. Jerónimo Gracián.
4. The nuns' chaplain and confessor in Alba. He wrote an encouraging answer to this letter (see Ltr. 467).

461. To Madre Tomasina Bautista, Burgos
Palencia, 9 August 1582

New friendly letters arrived from Burgos. Teresa's response regards the serious illness of one of the Sisters there and the poverty of that house there. In Palencia the heat was terrible. She is agreeable to prolonging her journey back to Avila by way of Alba and Salamanca.

✣ ✣ ✥ ✥

1.   Jesus. The Holy Spirit be with your reverence, my daughter. I tell you I felt very sorry about the illness of that sister.[1] For, apart from the fact that she is very good, I greatly regret the trial it means for you at this time. Always keep me informed about your health, and be careful about getting too close to her. You can truly cater to and care for her and still follow this counsel. I have already written to you of how necessary it is to

have charity for the sick. I know you will have it, but I always give this advice to everyone.

2.   Concerning what you say about begging for alms, it disturbed me very much, and I don't know why you are asking me what I want you to do, for I told you so many times when I was there that it wasn't appropriate for us to make known our lack of income,[2] how much less to beg. And even the constitutions say, I think, that only in great need may we beg.[3] You are not in great need, for Señora Catalina de Tolosa told me that little by little she will give you the children's share of the estate. If it were known that you had no income, it would be different. Don't say anything, and God deliver you from begging at this time. You won't gain anything, and what on the one hand you do gain, on the other you will lose in many ways. Rather, speak to those lords for me and tell them about this.

3.   I have already written,[4] telling you to give them my regards always. I subscribe in advance to all these good wishes that you extend for me, and so it is not a lie.

4.   It's terribly hot here, although this morning it was a little cooler, and I was glad for the sick Sister, for it must also be cooler there. Tell the licentiate Aguiar[5] that even though he enters the monastery every day, he must know how painful it is for me not to see him, for he made me very happy with his letter. But I think he will be happy not to find an occasion to make me write again so soon, and the same goes for Doctor Manso,[6] for it is true, and I always send him my regards and ask him to write and let me know how his health is, and the same with Padre Maestro Mata.[7] They greatly envy a confessor like that here.

5.   You should know that the cleric in Arévalo was not the one we thought, and it is he himself who said he would go. I spoke with him yesterday, and we were in agreement.

6.   Tell the subprioress and Beatriz, and my little roly-poly,[8] that I was delighted with their letters, but they know they must pardon me from answering when there is no particular reason

for doing so; tell the same to Pedro's daughter, and give her my regards. Remain with God, my daughter, and may His Majesty preserve you in the holiness I beg from him for you, amen, amen.

It is Vespers of San Lorenzo.

7.　　Our *padre*[9] has written me from Almodóvar. He is well, but it is necessary to pray he not go to Andalusia, for he would be willing to do so. He tells me that he would like me to go to Alba and Salamanca before going to Avila, and I have written to Alba and perhaps I will stay there this winter if possible.

　　Without any doubt your servant,

Teresa of Jesus

1. Beatriz de Jesús (Arceo), whose illness (see Ltr. 458.1), it seems, was contagious.
2. The people in Burgos thought the monastery, founded in poverty, had been founded with an income (see F. 31.48).
3. Begging was expressly forbidden in the first constitutions, no. 9; and also in the later constitutions (from Alcalá), chap. 7, no. 2.
4. Ltr. 458.4.
5. Antonio Aguiar, a physician in Burgos, friend of Gracián's. He cared for Teresa while she was in Burgos.
6. Pedro Manso, a canon at the cathedral in Burgos and friend of Gracián's.
7. A Dominican from the monastery of San Pablo in Burgos, and confessor for the discalced nuns.
8. Those mentioned are: Catalina de Jesús (subprioress), Beatriz de Jesús (the sick Sister), and Catalina de Tolosa's daughter, who received the habit in Burgos when still very young.
9. The provincial, Jerónimo Gracián. He is not going to Andalusia because of the epidemic there.

462. To Don Sancho Dávila, Alba
Palencia, 12 August 1582

Teresa came from Burgos to Palencia on her way through Valladolid and Medina, not yet knowing for sure whether she would have to go to Alba. If she did go she would have the opportunity to speak with Don Sancho. She thanks him for his many favors.

✢✢✢✢

1. Jesus. The grace of the Holy Spirit be always with your honor. If I had known that you were in this area, I would have answered your letter before, for I longed to tell you what great consolation it gave me. May the Divine Majesty repay you with the spiritual blessings that I always beg of him.

2. During the time of the foundation in Burgos, there were so many trials, so little health, and so many things to do that not much time remained for this joy. Glory to God that the work is over and done well.

3. I would very much like to go there where you are, for it would give me great happiness to speak with you in person about some things, which can't be done through letters. There aren't many instances where our Lord allows me to do my own will. May the will of His Divine Majesty be done, which is what matters.

4. I would very much like to see the biography of my lady the marchioness.[1] My lady the abbess,[2] your sister, must have received my letter late, but I don't think she sent me the account so that she could read it herself. You are very right in wanting so holy a life to be remembered. Please God you will include all that you have to say, for I fear you will cut it short.

5. Oh lord, how much I suffered to get the parents of my niece[3] to leave her in Avila until my return from Burgos! Since they saw how persistent I was about it, I succeeded.

6. May God preserve you, for you take such care to favor them in everything; I hope that you will be their support. May God watch over you for many years with the holiness I always beg of him, amen.

From Palencia, 12 August 1582,

Your honor's unworthy servant and subject,

Teresa of Jesus

1. The marchioness was the deceased mother of Don Sancho Dávila, of whom he had written a biography.
2. Don Sancho's sister was Doña Teresa de Toledo, a Bernardine nun at Santa Ana in Avila. The abbess it seems was someone else.
3. Beatriz de Ovalle (see Ltr. 409).

463. To Madre Ana de los Angeles, Toledo
Valladolid, 26 August 1582

(Original [Anne of St. Bartholomew] & autograph: DCN, Cuerva)

The prioress in Toledo wrote to Teresa seeking counsel about the purchase of some new houses in Toledo. Teresa answered very quickly because the former bishop of Avila, Don Alvaro de Mendoza, was passing through on his way to the Council of Toledo and would bring the letter. She is disappointed that Gracián has gone to Andalusia despite her objections.

1.   May Jesus give your reverence his grace. I received your letter in Palencia but not in time for me to answer. I am doing so now, although in a great hurry because the bishop[1] who is going to bring this wants to leave. For charity's sake, if he should go there, see to it that everyone treats him very graciously and that you have someone visit him frequently, for we owe him everything.

2.   As for what regards the house, what Diego Ortiz[2] desires to do and the plan he presented seems fine to me. If he buys that house, what follows will be very good, and that condition that is necessary in order have the house pertains more to him than to us. Don't worry at all about his trouble, for he's always troubled. Do all you can to gain time.

3.   With regard to Madre Brianda de San José's[3] sister, she is not able to be either a nun or a lay Sister, not because she

doesn't have good intelligence, or good judgment, or serenity, which she clearly seems to have, but because she can't do anything more than what she is doing, for she is very weak. And according to what she says nothing impedes her from giving herself to God and praying as much as she wants. Her life is set up just right for this. If she has some trials, she will have them elsewhere – and even greater ones.

4.   As for my going there now, I don't know how this could come about, for the trials I have here are frightening, and the business matters are killing me. But God can do everything. Pray to His Majesty for these intentions.

5.   Give my best regards to everyone. Because I am in a hurry, I will not enlarge on this; the same reason goes for why this is not in my own hand.[4]

Today is 26 August.

6.   At the end of this month, please God, I will be in Avila.[5] This trip by Father Provincial[6] at this time pained me very much. May God be with him. I have already sent a personal courier to Padre Antonio de Jesús with the patent letters. If he accepts and desires to go there, everything will turn out well.

7.   As I say, I am very happy with the plan, but you don't tell me how you are going to help Diego Ortiz buy the house. But any help will be worthwhile, if in moderation, and so leave the church free. It is an extremely better plan than the previous one, so you can begin discussing it immediately. And even if one proceeds slowly, building the church little by little with the income, Father Provincial will be pleased, for he takes very much to heart the good of that house. This will be seen later. In sum, I don't think we should neglect buying the house so as to build the church. That can be taken care of afterward. But first you have to see whether what is going to be given will be sufficient.

8.   Keep me informed about all the details. I will be here until after the feast of our Lady in September,[7] and then for the rest

of the month in Medina. You can write to me at either of these two places.

Regards to everyone, for I am in a great hurry.

Your reverence's servant

Teresa of Jesus

---

1. Alvaro de Mendoza, Bishop of Palencia. He was on his way to the Council of Toledo, which lasted from 8 September until 12 March 1583.

2. Diego Ortiz was not easy to deal with (see F. 15.4). The plan never did work out.

3. The former prioress in Malagón who was then in Toledo on account of her illness. She had a sister, a Carmelite (María del Espíritu Santo), who accompanied Teresa to Burgos for the foundation there. Now she is referring to another sister who wants to enter the Carmel in Toledo.

4. The letter was dictated to Blessed Anne of St. Bartholomew up to this point.

5. On 9 August she had still planned to go by way of Alba-Salamanca-Avila (see Ltr. 461.7).

6. Gracián had decided to go to Andalusia despite Teresa's objections.

7. The feast of the Birth of the Blessed Virgin Mary, 8 September.

464. To Madre Tomasina Bautista, Burgos

Valladolid, 27 August 1582

(Original [Anne of St. Bartholomew] & autograph: DCN, Peñaranda}

This is the last letter to Burgos. Many persons are mentioned: Catalina, a novice with vocation difficulties; the rector of the Jesuit community; Doña Catalina de Tolosa; Doctor Aguiar, the physician who cared for Teresa; Dr. Manso; Gracián; the subprioress; two lay Sisters; the sick nuns; the novices; and all nuns and friends in Burgos in general. In Valladolid she had many trials, a veiled allusion to the cool reception she received there by the prioress María Bautista (Ocampo). Her health had improved a little.

❧❧❦❦

1.   May Jesus give your reverence his grace, watch over you for me, and strengthen you for the many trials he sends you. I tell you, my mother, you are being treated as one who is strong. May God be praised for everything. I am reasonably well, better than usual. I don't believe I'll be here many days.[1] As soon as a messenger whom I am awaiting arrives, I will depart. Pray for me; it weighs on me very much to move farther away from your house and from you.

2.   Don't be distressed about Catalina de la Madre de Dios.[2] It's a temptation and will pass away. Don't let her write to anybody. If she wants to write to me or to Ana,[3] all right; but not to anyone else. If for her consolation you let her write, do not send the letters. I am delighted that the rector[4] has gone there. Be very gracious with him and go to confession sometimes to him, and ask them[5] to give the nuns some sermons.

3.   Regarding Catalina de Tolosa,[6] don't be surprised, for she is so burdened that first of all you need to console her, and even though she says this today, she won't do it tomorrow. Anyway, I am very much obliged to the licentiate.[7] May God watch over him.

4.   Why don't you tell the nuns the news about our *padre*?[8] Mother Subprioress[9] tells me she desires to know where he is. My regards to her and to all the nuns. I am sorry about María's[10] illness. Blessed be God that you have help from the other Sister.[11] Let me know how she does.

5.   I don't know if I will be able to write to the licentiate; since I love him so much, I will consider it recreation to write to him if I have time. Give him my best wishes and also tell the doctor[12] I am loaded down with things to do of a thousand kinds and to pray for me. I tell you that although you free me from the distress of having to know that the nuns are sick, there is

no lack of other reasons for being distressed. When I have time I'll write you about some. Note that I don't think that I'll stay here beyond the feast of our Lady,[13] and that the books should reach the prioress in Palencia[14] in time for her to send them to me.

6. May God watch over you for me. I don't have time for more except to ask that you always be careful not to burden the novices with many tasks until you understand what their spirits are capable of. I say this for Catalina's sake who was so overburdened that I am not surprised she was thinking she could no longer bear it. And you need to be compassionate in your speech. You think all the nuns should have your spirit, and you are very much mistaken. And believe that even though you may have an advantage over me in virtue, I have more experience. As a result, some of the things I pointed out, I would not want you to forget. May God watch over you for me; since these things are mentioned as though to my own soul, I would want you to realize that they are not said without reason.

I've already mentioned that I give you the power to extend regards for me to all my friends.[15]

Today is 27 August.

> Your reverence's servant,

> Teresa of Jesus

1. She left for Valladolid on 15 September (see no. 5).
2. A novice who had doubts about her vocation (see no. 6). She never did make profession.
3. Bl. Anne of St. Bartholomew, Teresa's secretary.
4. The rector of the Jesuit community in Burgos, Gaspar Sánchez, who had been keeping his distance from Teresa and her nuns.
5. The Jesuits.
6. The founding benefactor of the Carmel in Burgos.
7. The physician, Antonio Aguiar.
8. The provincial, Jerónimo Gracián.
9. Catalina de Jesús.

10. María de la Concepción.

11. Isabel de Santa Ana, a lay Sister recently admitted as a novice in the Carmel of Burgos.

12. Pedro Manso, a member of the cathedral clergy in Burgos.

13. Feast of the Birth of the Blessed Virgin Mary, 8 September.

14. Inés de Jesús (Tapia).

15. In Ltrs. 458 & 461.

465. To Padre Jerónimo Gracián, Seville
Valladolid, 1 September 1582

(Autograph, incomplete: DCN, Brussels)

During the summer Teresa traveled from Burgos (26 July) to Palencia and Valladolid (20 August) intending to go on to Medina and Avila, which she never reached. Still suffering from her sore throat and with her head in "wretched" condition, she attended to responsibilities as foundress. Gracián had left her alone with many problems in Castile and had gone to Andalusia, which disturbed her. She wrote to Cristóbal Suárez, Padre Antonio, the rector of the discalced friars in Salamanca, the Carmelite nuns in Alba, and those in Salamanca. This letter presents Teresa as thoroughly engaged in a variety of practical matters needing her attention.

❧ ❧ ❦ ❦

1. Jesus. The grace of the Holy Spirit be with your reverence. It is not sufficient for you to write me often in order to take away the pain, although it brought me great relief to know that you are well and the region healthy.[1] Please God, this will continue. I have received all your letters, I think.

2. The reasons for your decision to go didn't seem to me to be sufficient. A means could have been found here for giving orders about studies and not hearing the confessions of beatas. In that way those monasteries could have gotten along for two months and you could have put the houses here in good order. I don't know why, but I so felt your absence, at such a time, that

I lost the desire to write to you. As a result I didn't do so until now when I cannot avoid it. It is the day of the full moon, for I had a night that was truly wretched, and so too is the condition of my head. Up to now I had been doing better. Tomorrow I think, when the full moon is past, this indisposition will pass. The throat is better, but the trouble doesn't go away.

3.   Here I had to put up with a great deal from Don Francisco's mother-in-law,[2] whose behavior is odd and who is determined to initiate a lawsuit against the validity of Lorenzo's will, and although she has no right to anything, many people favor her and some say that she does have a right. And I have been advised that if Don Francisco is to avoid total ruin, and we the expense, that an agreement be reached. This would be detrimental to St. Joseph's.[3] But I hope in God that, since what St. Joseph's has coming to them is assured, the community will receive the entire inheritance. I was eaten up with sadness over this – and still am – although Teresa has carried on well. Oh, how she suffered from your not coming. Up until now we have kept it secret. On the one hand I rejoice because she is coming to understand what little reason there is for trust except in God; and even in my case, it didn't do me any harm.

4.   Enclosed is a letter from Padre Fray Antonio de Jesús,[4] which he wrote to me. I am surprised that he has turned to being my friend again – truthfully, I have always considered him to be one. Since we are communicating again everything will go well. Even if this were not so, in no way could someone else be appointed for the elections. I don't know how it is that you didn't realize this, or that now is not the time to found a house in Rome. You don't have nearly enough men for the houses you have here, and Nicolao[5] misses you very much, for I think it is impossible for him to tend to so many things by himself. Fray Juan de las Cuevas[6] told me this, for I spoke with him at times. He has a strong desire that you succeed in everything. And he wishes you well to such an extent that I feel obliged to him. And he even told me that you were going against the chapter ordinances,[7] which prescribed that in not having one's own

associate another one be chosen – I don't know if he said in the opinion of the priors – and that he considered it impossible for you to do everything alone, that Moses took I don't know how many to assist him.[8] I told him that there were not any capable, that not even enough could be found to fill the office of prior. He answered that this was essential.

5.   After I arrived here, they told me to note that you do not like to take talented persons with you. Now I see the reason, how they are needed elsewhere. But since the chapter[9] is approaching, I wouldn't want to see them placing the blame on you. Consider this for the love of God and how you are going about preaching in Andalusia. I never like seeing you spend much time down there. Since you wrote me one day of the trials some underwent, God spares me the pain of seeing you undergo the same; and as you say, the devil does not sleep. At least believe that as long as you are in that region, I will be ill at ease.

6.   I don't know for what purpose you have to stay so long in Seville, for they told me you will not be returning until the time of the chapter – which greatly increased my pain, even more than if you had gone back to Granada. May the Lord direct things for his greater service. There is dire need of a vicar there. If Fray Antonio[10] does well here, you could consider entrusting him with the task. Don't think of becoming an Andalusian; you don't have the temperament for living among them. With regard to preaching, I beg you again that even though you do not preach much, you be very careful about what you say.

7.   Do not be disturbed about what happened here concerning that friar. The matter was not as serious as it seemed, and God provided a very good remedy. Nothing about it became known. The prioress[11] is writing to you about how sick the discalced friars are, which is why the patent letter was not given to Fray Juan de Jesús,[12] for it would be inhumane for him to leave them since he is the only one who is well, and he takes care of everything. I stopped by that house in coming here and

everything seemed to be in very good order. They enjoy a good reputation in that place.

8.   Concerning the matter in Salamanca, there is much to say.[13] I tell you that it was the cause of some rough times for me, and please God a solution has been found. On account of this profession of Teresa[14] it wasn't possible for me to go there,[15] because it wasn't possible to bring her with me and less so to leave her behind. And more time would be needed to go there and then to Alba and return to Avila. Fortunately, though, Pedro de la Banda and Manrique[16] happened to be here. I rented the house for another year; so the prioress[17] can be at peace, and please God this will prove beneficial.

9.   I tell you that she is charming. She is so much a woman that she has begun negotiations no more nor less than if she already had the license from you. And to the rector she says that everything she does is for my order (although she doesn't know about this purchase, nor does she want to, as you know) and for me because the rector[18] is doing it at your orders. It's a devil's tangle, and I don't know what her reason is, for she will not lie. But the great longing she has for that miserable house is twisting her mind.

10.   Yesterday Fray Diego[19] came from Salamanca (the one who was here with you at the time of the visitation), and he told me that the rector at San Lázaro got involved in that matter against his will for love of me. He even went so far as to say that every time he dealt with the matter he had to go to confession afterward, since it seemed to be so contrary to God's will. But the prioress was so insistent that he couldn't do anything else, and all Salamanca was criticizing the purchase. And Doctor Solís[20] had told her that she couldn't in conscience own it, for it wasn't safe. And that rush in my opinion caused them to resort to cunning so that I wouldn't know, and with the enclosed letter you will see how with the tax included the price came to six thousand ducats. Everyone is saying that it wasn't worth twenty-five hundred ducats and are asking how poor nuns can waste

so much money. And what is worse, they don't have it. But in my opinion this is a trick of the devil to destroy the monastery, and so for now what they are trying to do is gain time in order to undo everything little by little.

11.   I wrote to Cristóbal Juárez begging him not to do anything more about this until I come, which would be at the end of October. And Manrique wrote the same to the scholastic, who is his good friend. I told Cristóbal Juárez that I wanted to see how he would be paid (for they told me that he was the guarantor) and that I didn't want him to suffer any loss, letting him know that there was nothing with which to pay him. He didn't answer me. Through Padre Fray Antonio de Jesús[21] I am writing him again to try to prevent this. God has allowed that money be loaned to them, otherwise they would have already given it away along with that of Antonio de la Fuente.[22] But just now I received another letter in which the prioress tells me that Cristóbal Juárez has sought the thousand ducats while waiting for Antonio de la Fuente to give them to him, and I am afraid they have deposited them already. Pray to God for this matter that every effort possible will be made.

12.   Another serious drawback is that for them to move into the house of Cristóbal Juárez,[23] the students[24] would have to move to the new house of San Lázaro, which would kill them. I wrote to the rector not to give his consent and that I would be keeping my eye on the matter.

13.   As for the eight hundred ducats they owe the nuns,[25] don't worry, for Don Francisco[26] says that he will pay them within a year. And the best part of all is that they don't have the money now to give. Have no fears, for I will get it. But it is more important that the students have good accommodations than for the nuns to have so large a house. Where will they find the money now to pay the interest? This whole business leaves me stupefied. If you gave them permission, why do they turn to me after the fact? If you didn't give it to them, how is it that they give away money (they gave five hundred ducats to the daughter

of Monroy's[27] brother-in-law)? And how is it they consider the matter to have reached such a stage that the prioress can write and say that it cannot be undone? May God provide a remedy, for I am certain that he will. Don't be disturbed, for we will do everything possible.

14.   For love of God be careful about what you do down there. Don't believe the nuns, for I tell you that if they want something they will make you believe a thousand things. And it is better for them to find a little house like poor nuns and enter with humility (for afterward they can find something better) than to be left with many debts. If at times your absence makes me happy, it is to see you free of these problems, for I would much rather go through them alone.

15.   In Alba, my letter (in which I told them how annoyed I was and that I was going there) had its good effect. It will be worthwhile for me to do so. With God's favor we will be in Avila at the end of the month. Believe me, it was not fitting to continue bringing this child[28] from place to place. Oh, *mi padre*, how oppressed I have felt these days. When I learned that you are well, it went away. Please God, you will get even better.

16.   My regards to Mother Prioress[29] and to all the Sisters. I am not writing to them because through this letter they will learn about me. I am happy that they are well. I urge them not to bother you, but to care for you. My regards to Padre Fray John of the Cross.[30] St. Bartholomew[31] sends hers to you. May our Lord watch over you, as I beg of him and free you from dangers, amen.

        Your servant and subject,

                                Teresa of Jesus

1.   She had already begged him not even to think about going to Seville because of the pestilence (see Ltr. 454.1-2).

2.   Beatriz de Castilla y Mendoza, Francisco de Cepeda's mother-in-law, was trying to have Lorenzo de Cepeda's last will and testament annulled to the detriment of Teresita and the Carmel of St. Joseph's in Avila.

3. Teresita was a member of the community of St. Joseph's in Avila and hoped to make her profession there in the hands of Padre Gracián.

4. Antonio de Jesús Heredia had been annoyed with Teresa over a number of little things. Now he was acting as vicar for the discalced Carmelites in Castile in place of Gracián (see Ltr. 375.1). Moreover it was fitting that Gracián delegate him to preside at the elections of the superiors in each monastery.

5. Nicolás Doria had gone to Italy to negotiate with the general of the order in the name of the discalced Carmelites. He had set aside for the moment any idea of making a foundation in Rome.

6. A Dominican who presided at the chapter for the discalced Carmelites at Alcalá where Gracián was elected provincial.

7. The chapter ordinances of Alcalá (1581) obliged the provincial to choose for himself another associate in case the one chosen in the chapter were to die or become sick.

8. Ex 18. 25-26.

9. It was opened in Almodóvar on 1 May 1583 according to the constitutions which prescribed that it be celebrated every two years.

10. Antonio de Jesús Heredia, vicar provincial in Castile during Gracián's absence in Andalusia.

11. The prioress of Valladolid, María Bautista, wrote to Gracián about how sick the discalced friars in Valladolid were because of the unhealthy conditions of the property.

12. The superior of the discalced friars in Valladolid could not be transferred because he was the only one in the community who was not sick and so very much needed there.

13. She is alluding to the purchase of the house for the Carmel in Salamanca (Ltr. 454.7).

14. Teresita who was to make her profession in Avila at the end of these travels with Teresa.

15. Salamanca.

16. Pedro de la Banda, the unsatisfiable owner of the house in Salamanca; and Pedro García Manrique, a religious who had already mediated in the process of purchasing the house.

17. Ana de la Encarnación, prioress of Salamanca.

18. Agustín de los Reyes, rector of the college for discalced Carmelites in Salamanca.

19. A lay brother Carmelite in Salamanca.

20. Perhaps Cristóbal Juárez de Solís, a recently ordained priest (see Ltr. 454.7).

21. The vicar provincial.
22. Near Salamanca.
23. See Ltr. 454.7.
24. The discalced Carmelite students in Salamanca. In fact on 22 June 1583 the nuns moved to Cristóbal Juárez's house and on 16 August to the Hospital del Rosario until moving definitively in 1614.
25. The discalced Carmelite friars in Salamanca owed this to the nuns in that city.
26. Don Francisco de Fonseca, a friend of Teresa's.
27. Alonso de Monroy (see Ltr. 424.1).
28. Her niece Teresita, who had been with her even though still a novice from Avila.
29. The prioress in Seville, María de San José.
30. St. John of the Cross at the time was prior in Granada.
31. Blessed Anne of St. Bartholomew.

466. To Madre Ana de los Angeles, Toledo
Valladolid, 2 September 1582

(Original [Ana de San Bartolomé]: DCN, Cuerva [Toledo])

This letter, with Juan de las Cuevas as its carrier, repeats much of what was said in Letter 463 just in case Don Alvaro de Mendoza, with many obligations and other things on his mind, forgot to deliver the previous one.

1.   May Jesus give your reverence his grace. I received your letter in Palencia at a time when it wasn't possible for me to answer because I was about to continue on my journey.[1] I'm writing from here, and I don't think they will give you the letter I sent to the bishop[2] when he was about to leave so that he could have it delivered to you. (He had so much luggage[3] it wouldn't be surprising if he forgot.) So I will repeat here what I said there. First of all, I ask you to send someone to see the bishop, and do so frequently as long as he is there. And if he

should come to the monastery, you must all be most gracious toward him, for we owe him everything.

2. As for what regards the house, what Diego Ortiz[4] desires to do and the plan he presented seems fine to me. If he buys that house, what follows will be very good, and that condition that is necessary in order to have the house pertains more to him than to us. Don't worry at all about his trouble, for he's always troubled. Do all you can to gain time.

3. With regard to Madre Brianda de San José's sister,[5] she is not able to be either a nun or a lay Sister, not because she doesn't have good intelligence, or good judgment, or serenity, which she clearly seems to have, but because she can't do anything more than what she is doing, for she is very weak. And according to what she says, nothing impedes her from giving herself to God and praying as much as she wants. Her life is set up just right for this. If she has some trials; she will have them elsewhere – and even greater ones.

4. As for my going there now – I don't know how this could come about, for the trials I have here are frightening and the business matters are killing me. But God can do everything. Many regards to everyone. Because I'm in a hurry, I won't enlarge on this.

Valladolid, 2 September.

5. I feel reasonably well, and I think I will depart on Monday after our Lady's feast.[6] I won't stay in Medina long, so that I can arrive on time in Avila. But I don't think I will be able to remain there long because I will have to go to Salamanca. They are tangled up in the purchase of a house.[7] It is very necessary that I go to them. May God provide a solution and watch over you for me, amen.

Teresa[8] and St. Bartholomew[9] send you their best regards.

Your reverence's servant,

Teresa of Jesus

The carrier of this letter is Padre Fray Juan de las Cuevas,[10] who tells me he is going there. Be very gracious to him.

---

1. She departed from Palencia on 20 August.
2. The Bishop of Palencia, Alvaro de Mendoza.
3. Don Alvaro and his retinue were attending the Council of Toledo and needed a great deal of luggage.
4. He served as a mediator between Teresa and the founding benefactors of the Carmel in Toledo.
5. See Ltr. 463.3.
6. That Monday was 10 September.
7. See Ltr. 465.8-9.
8. Her niece Teresita.
9. Blessed Anne of St. Bartholomew, her secretary.
10. The Dominican who had presided at the chapter of the discalced Carmelite friars in 1581 in Alcalá and was now going to attend the Council of Toledo.

467. To Don Pedro Sánchez, Alba
Valladolid, 5 September 1582

(Original [Bl. Anne of St. Bartholomew]: DCN, Burgos)

The relations between the Carmelite community in Alba and its founding benefactress, Teresa de Layz, were tense and difficult. She wanted the prioress in Burgos to be transferred back to Alba as prioress, which Teresa had to refuse. Referring the matter to the community's chaplain and confessor, Teresa received a kind response from him favoring the nuns in Alba.

For *mi padre*, confessor of the Carmelite nuns. He is *mi padre*. Alba.

1.   Jesus. The grace of the Holy Spirit be always with your honor, *mi padre*. Your letter consoled me greatly. May God watch over you, for with respect to what you are doing, the house will not suffer any loss. You offer many excuses for them,

and it doesn't seem bad to me that in everything you carry out your office as father. You are much indebted to the Sisters, who tell me so many things about you. After all, they are good souls, and even though the devil finds ways to disturb them, God does not cease to guide them.[1] May his name be blessed, for at all times he shows mercy toward his creatures.

2.   You have shown me great favor by removing the burden which that house was for me. Since you are their confessor, what you say is more satisfying than everything else. Please God, I will go there soon, and we can have a long talk. Pray for me. I don't have much time and many business matters have arisen here.

3.   Give my regards to Señora Teresa de Layz,[2] for I don't think I will have a chance to write to her. You can tell her that I was delighted to receive her letter and that, God willing, all will be well. May God give you his grace.

Valladolid, the fifth of September,

Teresa of Jesus

---

1.   Alusion to the difficulties between the community in Alba and the founding benefactress, Teresa Layz. See Ltr. 460.

2.   See F. 20.

468. To Madre Catalina de Cristo, Soria

Valladolid-Medina, 15-17 September 1582

Here Teresa answers various letters from the prioress in Soria who had presented her with a number of questions concerning: the location of the kitchen and refectory; the good conduct of the novices; dealings with the Jesuits; the transfer of a nun to the Carmel in Palencia; and a doubt over possibly delaying profession for the novices. Teresa was about to continue her travels and was very busy. She began the letter in Valladolid and finished it in Medina.

❖❖❖❖

1.   Jesus be with your reverence, my daughter, and watch over you for me. I received your letters and much happiness along with them. In what regards the kitchen and refectory,[1] I would be delighted if you did so, but you who are there can make the best decision as to the arrangement. Work things out as you wish.

2.   I am glad that Roque de Huerta's daughter[2] is pleasant. As regards the profession of the Sister[3] you mentioned, I think it is good that it be delayed until when you say, for she's young and it doesn't matter. Don't be surprised if she experiences some setbacks, for at her age these don't amount to much. They happen, but afterward these persons are usually more mortified than others.

3.   Tell Sister Leonor de la Misericordia[4] that I would like to do for her what she asks and even more. Would that I could attend her profession. I would do so gladly and it would please me much more than a lot of other things I have to do here …[5] may God bring this about, if it be for his service.

4.   Regarding the foundation,[6] I will not decide to make it unless there is some income, for I see already so little devotion there that we need to proceed in such a way. And the place is so far from all our other houses that a foundation ought not be made if the community is not provided for. Here one community helps another when it sees there is need. It is good to begin in this way and that you come to know and find devoted people. If the work is desired by God, he will move these persons to do more than is being done at present.

5.   I will be only a short time in Avila because I cannot neglect going to Salamanca,[7] and you can write to me there. But if the foundation is made in Madrid[8] – and I am hoping for this – I would prefer to go there since it is closer to us here. Pray for this intention.

6.   Regarding that nun about whom you write, if she should want to go to Palencia, I would be delighted, for they need someone in that house. I am writing to Madre Inés de Jesús[9] so that you and she can come to an agreement about it. As for the Theatines,[10] I am happy you are doing what you can with them, for this is necessary, and the good or the bad, and the graciousness we show them ...

7.   Tell Señora Doña Beatriz[11] for me all the things you think would be suitable. I would so like to write to her, but we are about to leave, and I have so many matters to attend to that I don't know where I'm at. May God be served by it all, amen.

8.   Do not think that when I mentioned delaying the profession I was giving preference to one novice over the other,[12] for these are worldly considerations that offend me very much, and I wouldn't want you to be looking at things like that. But it is because she is young that I am glad for a delay and so that she may practice more mortification. And if some other interpretation for this delay were made, I would give orders to have the profession at once. For it is good for the humility we profess to be evident in our deeds. I had given precedence to the other knowing that in her humility Sister Leonor de la Misericordia doesn't pay any attention to these worldly points of honor. And this being so, I am truly happy that this child is waiting a little longer before her profession.

9.   I can not enlarge any more, for we are about to leave for Medina. I'm feeling as usual. My companions send you their regards. It wasn't long ago that Anne wrote you the news from here. My best regards to all the Sisters. May God make them saints, and you along with them.

Valladolid, the fifteenth of September.

Your reverence's servant,

Teresa of Jesus

10.   We are now in Medina and so busy that I cannot say more than that the trip went well. The deferring of Isabel's profes-

sion must be done with discretion so that it is not thought that anyone is of higher status, for that is not the main purpose of the delay.

1. Teresa had suggested they move the kitchen and refectory to the ground floor to save the cook extra work (see Ltr. 449.6).
2. María de la Purificación, 16 years old, to whom Teresa gave the habit before leaving Soria.
3. Isabel de la Madre de Dios (Medrano), 17 years old.
4. Before entering the monastery, her name was Leonor de Ayanz y Beamonte (see Ltrs. 444;449;456).
5. Here the text has suffered damage, also in no. 6.
6. She is alluding to a plan for a possible foundation in Pamplon(see Ltr. 444.4).
7. She changed her itinerary on the following day by order of Padre Antonio de Jesús (Heredia), who was waiting for her in Medina and wanted her to go at once to Alba.
8. She was never able to realize her plan for a foundation in Madrid.
9. The prioress in Palencia.
10. The Jesuits.
11. Beatriz de Beamonte, the founding benefactress of the Carmel in Soria.
12. Isabel was 17 years old and Leonor de la Misericordia (born in 1551) entered the Carmel of Soria after having her marriage to Don Francés de Beamonte annulled.

Biographical Sketches

Biographical Sketches

Aguiar, Antonio. The doctor from Burgos who treated Teresa during her stay there, January to July 1582. Licensed by the University of Alcalá, he was a friend of Gracián's, and in getting to know Teresa, he became a great admirer of hers. In June of 1582 he acquired the powers to buy a house in Teresa's name. They had to proceed with great caution and Doctor Aguiar was a true help to Teresa, whom she lauds in her *Foundations*: "Doctor Aguiar is a very intelligent man and saw clearly that if our desire were made public we would either have to pay much more for the house or not buy it … . Such was the outcry in the city that we saw clearly how right the good Doctor Aguiar was to keep the whole matter secret … Indeed we can say that, after God, it was he who gave us the house. Good intelligence is a great help in everything. And since he has so much, God moved him and brought this work to completion through him" (31.32-39). And in one of her last letters she writes in reference to Doctor Aguiar: "Since I love him so much, I will consider it recreation to write to him" (Ltr. 464.5).

Albornoz, Juan de. The husband of Inés Nieto, who was a secretary of the Duke of Alba and accompanied him to Flanders and to Portugal. Juan de Albornoz appears in Teresa's correspondence in her letters to his wife. Teresa wrote to him about her nephew Gonzalo de Ovalle being a page in the service of the Duke of Alba. From Seville he sent Teresa a beautiful image of Our Lady, and he offered financial help to some of the Carmelite vocations (Ltr. 78).

Alvarez Cimbrón, Pedro (Perálvarez). A relative of Teresa's who, though not rich, lived comfortably. In Avila he welcomed family members of Teresa and became a good friend of Lorenzo's when he returned from America, stirring some jealousy in Juan de Ovalle (Ltr. 115.3). To Teresa's great relief (Ltr. 439), in 1582, he welcomed into his house a niece of hers, Beatriz de Ahumada, during a painful experience of calumny. In Lorenzo de Cepeda's will, Perálvarez was named as tutor of his sons. He was also helpful to Teresa in subsequent family entanglements (Ltr. 355.7; 425.2).

Alvarez, Rodrigo. Born in Lebrija (Seville) in 1523, he entered the Society of Jesus when already a priest and over 40 years old. Before his entry into the Society he underwent imprisonment by the Inquisition in Seville, but was then set free. He later became a qualifier for this same Inquisition. His encounter with Teresa took place in Seville (1575-1576) when she was accused to the Inquisition. Together with two other Jesuits, Jorge Alvarez and Enrique Enríquez, they examined Teresa's case. Badly disposed to her in the beginning, after she wrote two accounts for him (ST 58 & 59), he became a strong supporter of Teresa's. But she does not advise consulting him in the case of two sisters in the community with psychological problems: "By no means speak to Rodrigo about it" (Ltr. 132.6). Yet at another turbulent time in the Carmel she advises: "In case she has spoken calumnies that at some time might do harm, it is necessary that Padre Rodrigo Alvarez consider what must be done and that she retract what she said and sign it" (Ltr. 347.12). The last page of the autograph of the *Interior Castle* contains a warm approval from the theological viewpoint by Rodrigo Alvarez. He was one of the first theologians to value the Teresian writings without reserve.

Ana de los Angeles (Ordóñez / Goméz). Born in Avila in 1535, she entered the monastery of the Incarnation when only seven and there came to know Teresa, living with her there for about twenty years. According to Gracián, she was one of only three who profited from what Teresa in the course of many years said to them (L. 13.9). In 1562, she transferred to Teresa's new community at St. Joseph's, where Teresa made her subprioress. But not until 1572 did she formally renounce the mitigated rule, although she had lived the life of a discalced nun. She accompanied Teresa on the foundations made in Medina (1567), Malagón (1568), and Toledo (1569). She became prioress in Malagón in 1568, and in Toledo in 1569 to 1585, despite the precarious condition of her health at the time. "I don't think there is another who would be better for that house," Teresa states in a letter to Gracián (Ltr. 92.1). In 1585 she left Toledo to make a foundation in Cuerva. She was prioress there a number of times before her death in 1605. Three letters of Teresa to Ana de los Angeles have survived.

Ana de San Agustín (Pedruja). Born in Valladolid in 1555, she got to know Teresa there and decided to become a Carmelite. She entered the Carmel in Malagón and made profession there in 1577. In February of 1580, she journeyed with Teresa on the foundation in Villanueva de la Jara. Teresa refers to her in one of her letters, in which she speaks of the foundation in Villanueva:

"San Angel, from Malagón, is subprioress there in Villanueva. She handles the office very well, and the other two with her are truly saints" (Ltr. 335.8). These other two were Ana de San Agustín and Constanza de la Cruz. Ana became prioress of Villanueva de la Jara in 1596. In 1600 she founded the Carmel in Valera, where she became prioress. She returned as prioress to Villanueva de la Jara in 1616. She was greatly loved by Teresa: "I tell you that your letters make me so happy that I can't believe it. Don't fail to write to me always and give me an account of your soul in great detail" (Ltr. 389.2). Ana received many mystical graces. Under orders from her provincial, she dictated her autobiography, which was dated and signed by her 12 August 1609 and is conserved in the Carmel of Villanueva de la Jara. She died in the odor of sanctity in 1624. Alonso de San Jerónimo wrote a biography of her entitled: *Vida, virtudes, y milagros de la prodigiosa virgin y madre Ana de San Agustín.*

Anne of St. Bartholomew, Blessed. Born in Almendral (Toledo) in 1549, Anne entered the Carmel of St. Joseph's in Avila in 1570 at age 21 as a lay sister, and made profession in 1572. In 1574 she accompanied Teresa for the first time on her trip to Valladolid and Medina del Campo. After an illness that impeded her from traveling with Teresa during the years the years 1575-1577, she began accompanying Teresa again in 1577. From that time on she dedicated herself to the tasks of Teresa's nurse and secretary, taking dictation for numerous letters and assisting Teresa with her many health problems. Above all she was at her side in her last illness from Burgos to Alba de Tormes in 1582. Between 1578 and 1580 the two visited Medina, Valladolid, Salamanca, Avila, Toledo, Malagón, La Roda, Villanueva de la Jara, Toledo, Madrid, Segovia, and then returned to Avila. Sister Anne at Teresa's side shared in the foundations of Villanueva de la Jara, Palencia, Soria and Burgos. Teresa died in the arms of Blessed Anne in Alba de Tormes. Later in 1595 she went with María de San Jerónimo on the foundation in Ocaña. In 1604, she traveled from Avila to Paris, France with the group of sisters who founded the Teresian Carmel in Paris in that year. In the following year she received the black veil of a choir sister so that she could be named the prioress of the Carmel in Pontoise of which she was the foundress in 1605. In September of that same year, she was brought back to Paris as prioress. In 1608 she founded the Carmel of Tours. The difficulties that arose between the Spanish Carmelite nuns and Pierre de Bérulle led Anne after much struggle to accept the invitation of Isabel Clara Eugenia to leave France and come to the Spanish Netherlands. After a brief stay in Mons she arrived in Antwerp and founded the Carmel there in 1612, in which she became prioress. She died there in 1626.

Anne was the most fruitful writer among the disciples of Teresa, although she published nothing during her lifetime. Among the numerous writings, her *Autobiography, Conferences, Meditations, and Defense of the Teresian Inheritance* stand out. And the number of her letters so far discovered has reached 665 in the recent edition of her works by Julián Urkiza. She repeatedly wrote or dictated her recollections of Teresa and her spirit. She also left various writings on the origins of the Teresian Carmel in Spain and France and a series of festive poems. While she was still alive, her prioress María de San Jerónimo, Teresita, and Francisca de Jesús wrote about her. But most of all Gracián wrote in 1613 an important work on her life, published for the first time in 1933. A few years after her death, Padre Crisóstomo Enríquez published a large volume entitled *The Story of the Life, Virtues, and Miracles of the Venerable Mother Anne of St. Bartholomew Inseparable Companion of the Holy Mother Teresa of Jesus* (1632). Anne had the good fortune of living to see the beatification (1614) and canonization of St. Teresa (1622). She herself was beatified in 1917.

Casademonte, Pedro Juan de. A merchant in Medina with business in Valladolid and Madrid. He became a friend of Teresa's through Inés de Jesús and rendered her many services, transporting money, letters, or other messages. He collaborated in sending the two discalced Carmelites on their journey disguised to Rome (Ltrs. 293.1; 312.2). Teresa had recourse to him with her mail when she could not make use of the services of Roque de Huerta. Given the charge by Philip II, he helped with the financing and organization of the chapter of the discalced friars in Alcalá (1581). When Teresa was in Burgos, she sought to know through him any news about the foundation in Madrid and she sent him a packet of letters that arrived for him from Granada (446.1,3). Casademonte obtained the full confidence and gratitude of Teresa "for the goodwill you have shown toward this order and your good deeds, which certainly cause me to praise God" (Ltr 293.4). Teresa was equally a friend of Doña María, the wife of Casademonte. In Teresa's correspondence five letters to Casademonte have survived.

Castilla y Mendoza, Beatriz de. A widow residing in Madrid, she became the mother-in-law of Francisco de Cepeda, Lorenzo's son, and wanted more money from Lorenzo's will for Francisco. Teresa wrote to Gracián: "This enclosed letter written to me by Francisco's mother-in-law came two days ago, and it annoyed me very much to see such bad motives. The learned men from around here say that the will can not be annulled without one's sinning mortally" (Ltr.424.2). Though Teresa left the door open for further dialogue, an unfavorable encounter with the mother-in-law took place in Valladolid on Teresa's last journey from Burgos to Alba. The mother-in-law even managed to turn the prioress María Bautista against Teresa. Teresa speaks of this in a letter to Gracián: "Here I had to put up with a great deal from Don Francisco's mother-in-law, whose behavior is odd and who is determined to initiate a lawsuit against the validity of Lorenzo's will" (Ltr. 465.3).

Castro y Nero, Pedro. Born in Ampudia (Palencia) in 1541, he was a companion in studies with Jerónimo Gracián in Alcalá and explained philosophy at the University of Salamanca. He later became a canon of the cathedral in Avila, where he first came to know Teresa. Teresa had given him a copy of her *Life* to read, and in a note she had received from him, he revealed the powerful impact the book had on him. She responds with much feeling and begs him to come to see her the following day: "How great the mercy of God, that through my wickedness you should benefit ... . I'd rather not say more on paper, and so I beg you to come to see me tomorrow, the eve of the Presentation, that I might present to you a soul often undone, so that you might bring about all that you understand as fitting for her in order that she please God" (Ltr. 415.1-2). Shortly after this she writes again: "It doesn't make me happy for you to go to heaven, for you have much to do in God's church. I begged God urgently today not to allow so good a mind to be occupied in anything else" (Ltr. 417.1). He was later made Bishop of Lugo and then of Segovia, where he died in 1611.

Catalina de Cristo (Valmaseda). The venerable Catalina de Cristo was born in Madrigal de las Altas Torres in 1543. She entered the Carmel in Medina del Campo in 1571 and made her profession in 1573. In 1579 she had the opportunity of living in that Carmel with Teresa herself, who then took her with her to the foundation in Palencia in 1581, and from there to Soria where Teresa left her as prioress. The last letter we have of Teresa's is to Catalina de Cristo in which Teresa answered many questions that she had put to her. Teresa's esteem for Catalina is obvious in some words of hers to Gracián: "Catalina de Cristo knows how to love God very much and is a very great saint and has a very lofty spirit, and doesn't need to know anything else in order to govern. She will be as good a prioress as any." In 1583, Madre Catalina left Soria for Pamplona and founded a Carmel in that city. Before leaving Soria, however, by orders of Gracián, Catalina dictated her autobiography to Leonor de la Misericordia, and the latter later wrote a biography of Catalina. Leonor also accompanied her to Pamplona and Barcelona. Catalina was the prioress in Barcelona until 1592, when she became seriously ill. She died in 1594. Ten years later her remains were transferred back to the Carmel in Pamplona, where today they are still venerated.

Catalina de Jesús. Born in Valderas (León) she entered the Carmel of Valladolid where she made profession in 1572. In 1580 she went with Teresa on the foundation in Palencia. There she received a letter from St. John of the Cross sent from Baeza by way of Teresa, since he didn't know where she was. She again accompanied Teresa on the foundation in Burgos, 1582, and was one of the "five who will remain there" (Ltr. 430.4). She was elected subprioress (Ltr. 461.6). When Teresa was begging money from her Carmels to cover the cost of the expenses of the friars who went to Rome, she concludes a letter to Valladolid with these words: "In any case, let Sister Catalina de Jesús read this letter to everyone — I would be very much saddened if anything were omitted — and the other enclosed letters from Rome as well" (Ltr. 295.11).

Catalina de Jesús (Godínez). Born in 1540; after the death of her parents, Catalina, along with her sister María de Jesús, began negotiating for a foundation of one of Teresa's Carmels in Beas. After a serious illness, she went personally to Madrid in 1573, but following three months of efforts without obtaining anything, she wrote to Teresa about all that happened. Teresa then wrote to the king and with his favor the license was granted. And then Teresa agreed to come and make the foundation. The erection of the Carmel in Beas (Jaén) took place in 1575, and the two sisters, Catalina and María, received the habit from Teresa herself on the very day the foundation was made. She made her profession in 1576 and succeeded Anne of Jesus as prioress in 1582 and was reelected in 1584. She received spiritual direction from St. John of the Cross from the time he met the two in Beas in 1578. Teresa wrote of her in 1574: "The truth is they are saying wonderful things about the holiness and humility of one of the two ladies who are sponsoring the foundation; they are both good" (Ltr. 73.5). Gracián said of her that she was one of the holiest sisters the order had. She died in Beas in 1586 while prioress. St. John of the Cross transcribed personally Catalina's autobiographical account.

Cepeda, Luis. The son of Teresa's first cousin Francisco de Cepeda, he lived in Torrijos and more than once provided Teresa with lodging in his house. In a letter to her sister María, Teresa sought some correspondence (Ltr. 93.2) from Luis, especially since his father had just died (Ltr. 143.6). When Teresa broke her arm he regaled her with gifts for which she cordially thanked him.

Cuevas, Juan de las. A Dominican who was highly esteemed by Teresa because of the excellent manner in which he presided at the chapter of Alcalá. He was born in Coca (Segovia) in 1524 and made profession at San Esteban (Salamanca) in 1551. He did his studies at San Gregorio in Valladolid and had been superior in a number of houses before Talavera. It was in Talavera that he was superior when he received his appointment to preside at the chapter of Alcalá. This was because Pedro Fernández, the apostolic visitator of the Carmelites in Castile, was then in his last illness. Cuevas presided at the chapter and promulgated the new constitutions for the discalced Carmelite friars and nuns. After the chapter, he continued proposing how the decisions of Alcalá might be taken up in Rome. In his order,

Cuevas was next elected provincial. From 1587 to 1596 he was an advisor to Archduke Alberto in Portugal, and in 1596, he was made Bishop of Avila. He died in 1599, and his remains lie in the cathedral of that city. In one of her last letters Teresa writes: "The carrier of this letter is Padre Fray Juan de las Cuevas. Be very gracious to him, for he tells me he is going there."

Dávila, Gonzalo. A distinguished Jesuit, born in 1536 in Avila, rector of various colleges, and in 1578 rector of San Gil in Avila. It was then that he came into communication with Teresa. He had recourse to her to get Padre Mariano to come to the college on an engineering project (Ltrs. 247.4 and 258.7). This was the same year in which the provincial, Juan Suárez, was accusing Teresa of creating Gaspar Salazar's vocational difficulties. Later Padre Dávila wrote asking for spiritual advice, to which Teresa answers: "I have never desired so eagerly to tear up a letter from you. I tell you that you know well how to mortify me and make me understand what I am, for it seems to you that I think that by myself I am able to teach. God deliver me! I wouldn't even want to think of such a thing" (Ltr. 249.1). After Teresa's death, he became provincial of Toledo, then Castile, and then visitator of Aragón. He died in 1606.

Dávila y Toledo, Sancho. A priest and theologian friend of Teresa's. He studied in Salamanca, taught there and was at various times rector there. In a letter to Teresa he sought her guidance over some problems with his interior life . After giving him guidance, Teresa sought his help for a problem that caused her much pain. Some calumnies were being spoken against her niece Beatriz; and greatly distressed about it, she sought his assistance (Ltr. 409. 1-3; 7-8). He had written a biography of his own mother, who had died two years before in the odor of sanctity, and which Teresa had expressed a desire to read (Ltr. 462.4). He died in 1625.

Díaz, Juan. A priest friend and advisor to Teresa. A relative and disciple of St. John of Avila, he got to know Teresa before her journey to Andalusia in 1575. Teresa consulted him regarding certain matters in her task as foundress: a house in Toledo (Ltr. 114.5); a certain vocation (Ltr. 122.6); the foundation for discalced friars in Salamanca (Ltr. 135.12); affairs in Madrid (176.6); and to mediate in a lawsuit against the nuns in Caravaca (Ltr. 181.10). In the Spring of 1581, he came to Teresa with questions of his own, whether to enter the Jesuits or her own discalced Carmelite friars. The substance of Teresa's answer to him is expressed in a letter to Gracián, who was also considering the request: "What I feel about this and what I told him is that it would be very good for him if he were to persevere. If he didn't it would be harmful" (Ltr. 390.4). Juan Díaz prepared the first edition of the writings of St. John of Avila and promoted the cause of his beatification. After Teresa's death, Gracián continued to have good relations with Juan Díaz.

Doria, Horacio. The brother of Padre Nicolás Doria, a canon in Toledo, and administrator of the Hospital de la Santa Cruz. He had dealings with Teresa in Toledo, and there lent her 200 ducats, which after a time caused a certain tension between the two. To begin to respond to one of the demands in the will of Lorenzo de Cepeda, Teresa sought to recover 430 ducats that she had lent to the Carmel in Seville. She gave María de San José strict instructions about how the 200 ducats should be sent to her, but María did not pay heed and sent the money to Nicolás Doria, who in turn gave it to his brother. Teresa was not happy, and expresses this in a letter to María: "Despite my advice, you did what you did. What you deserve is to have to pay the amount twice, which is what you will have to do if the money isn't sent to me. But Horacio is wrong, for if you gave him the money to send to me, it is not sufficient for his brother to allow him to keep it as a reimbursement without your authorization" (Ltr. 412.8).

Elena de Jesús (Quiroga). A native of Medina del Campo who at the death of her husband was the mother of seven children. She came to know Teresa at the time of the foundation in Medina del Campo in 1567. In 1575 her youngest daughter entered the Carmel in Medina. From this time on, Elena began to feel desires to enter a Teresian Carmel. But her uncle, the future Cardinal Quiroga, tenaciously opposed it. Although blamed by the archbishop, Teresa, wanting to remain in his good graces, in no way supported the vocation of Elena, even writing to Baltasar Alvarez and Gracián to impede her (Ltrs. 397; 399; 402). But finally the archbishop gave in to the persistent demands of Elena, and in 1581 she entered the Carmel of Medina, where her daughter was. Some years later, acceding to the desires of Cardinal Quiroga, both mother and daughter transferred to the Carmel in Toledo, where he was archbishop and where they each at different times became prioress. She was unjustly deposed from her office as prioress and returned to her original Carmel of Medina del Campo. She died there in 1596. Although Teresa refers to her in her letters, none of the letters that Teresa wrote to her has come down to us.

Enríquez, Ana. A friend of Teresa's and collaborator with her on several foundations. She knew many of Teresa's friends: María de Mendoza and the bishop, Don Alvaro (Ltrs. 370; 378.4); Dona Guiomar, Baltasar Alvarez, and Domingo Báñez (Ltrs. 77; 378.6). Together with Doña Guiomar they had planned a foundation in Zamora (Ltr. 77.5). She sent a statue for the foundation in Palencia for which Teresa thanks her: "You have honored us greatly with the statue you donated, which stands alone on the main altar, and it is so well done and large that there is no need for others" (Ltr. 378.5). There are actually four letters of Teresa to Ana in the correspondence that has come down to us (Ltrs. 77, 101, 370, 378).

Estefanía de los Apostoles. She entered the Carmel of Valladolid as a lay sister and received the habit from the hands of Don Alvaro de Mendoza in 1572, making her profession the following year. She played a part in the dramatic episodes surrounding the vocation of Casilda de Padilla (F. 11). Despite their different social backgrounds, Estefanía and Casilda became close during the novitiate. Teresa's opinion of Estefanía was very high: "And although Estefanía certainly is a saint in my opinion ... Estefanía's simplicity in everything except what pertains to God amazes me, for I perceive through her words the wisdom she has in regard to the Truth" (Ltr. 77.2-3). Later, while writing on her foundations, Teresa asks the prioress in Valladolid to send a report on Estefanía: "And when you are up to it, prepare a report on Estefanía like the one you sent to Avila, for that was very well done" (Ltr.143.6). But as time went on Estefanía began to go to extremes in her penitential life, and Teresa warns the prioress: "And do not allow Estefanía those times of solitude and fasting, if you don't want to end up with another similar case" (Ltr. 381.3). Nonetheless the fame for sanctity and the simplicity of Estefanía became known even by Philip II, who held her in great esteem. She died in Valladolid in 1617.

Felipe de la Purificación. Born in Malpartida, he made his profession in Mancera de Abajo in 1576. Teresa took him to Malagón with her as confessor, despite opposition. He fulfilled the task well (Ltr. 318.16), so that Teresa could write of him: "Padre Fray Felipe fits perfectly. He has gone to the other extreme, not engaging in talk outside of confession. He is a very good man." During the troublesome days before the foundation in Burgos, Teresa called for him to come as chaplain and confessor for the nuns, a good indication of the confidence she had in him. A number of years later he became a subject of St. John of the Cross in the monastery of Los Mártires in Granada.

Gabriel de la Asunción. Born in Pastrana in 1544, he made profession there as a discalced Carmelite in 1570. He became rector of the college of St. Cyril in Alcalá and from there went on to be prior at La Roda (1576-1580). There he became spiritual director of the extraordinary penitent Catalina de Cardona. Teresa wrote of him: "He is a father for whom I have a great affection, although he has little for me" (Ltr. 130.4). A number of years later she reconfirms this feeling of hers toward him: "I certainly love him very much and would greatly regret his being transferred" (Ltr. 389.2). Becoming very interested in the foundation at Villanueva de la Jara, he personally accompanied Teresa and her companions from Malagón on that foundation (F. 28.18). After Teresa's death he was elected prior in Almodóvar in 1583, but that year made a foundation in Fuensanta and died there in the following year, 1584.

Germán de San Matías. Born in Logroño, he made his profession in Pastrana in 1573 and was transferred to Avila beside St. John of the Cross at the Incarnation. The two were deposed from their charge there by the prior of the Carmelites of the Observance, but quickly restored by the nuncio Ormaneto (Ltr. 102.16). They were taken away again on 1 December 1577. Teresa writes: "The prior here took Fray Germán to San Pablo de la Moraleja. And when he returned he told the nuns that were on his side that he left that traitor in good hands" (Ltr. 221.7). The nuns said that blood was coming from Fray German's mouth as he was taken away. Teresa writes of the two friars at the Incarnation: "The two are excellent religious and have edified the entire city during their five years there. Because of their presence the house has remained in the state it was when I left it" (226.10). Having avoided prison, Fray Germán was transferred to the monastery in Mancera where he became prior in 1579, only to die after a few months. When informed of his death, Teresa writes: "May God have Fray Germán with him in heaven; he had good qualities, but he did not have the talent to understand better the nature of perfection" (Ltr. 316.6). It was Fray Germán who opposed her bringing Fray Pedro de La Purificación to Malagón as confessor there. Teresa writes: "Since Father Vicar finally did what I wanted, Fray Germán was so displeased that he told someone who went to see him that he was sick in bed because of me. But in my opinion I would have been doing nothing had I arrived without a confessor, and there wasn't any other" (226.10).

Godoy, the Licentiate. A faithful friend of Teresa's despite difficulties experienced with his daughter. Teresa refers to him as the "licentiate" or the "licentiate Godoy." He was a lawyer in Valladolid. In 1578, a daughter of his entered the Carmel in Alba de Tormes, not without reservations on Teresa's part. The daughter was not well balanced and quickly became unhappy. Teresa writes in a letter to Gracián about her case: "So as not to trouble you, I have never wanted to mention how difficult to bear is the licentiate Godoy's daughter in Alba. I have done as much as I can so that everything be tried, but nothing works. Since she lacks intelligence, she doesn't reason things through. She must be most unhappy, for she will burst out in loud cries. She claims this is due to a heart ailment; I don't think so" (Ltr. 302.6). Teresa finally succeeded in convincing Godoy that his daughter wasn't suited for Carmel. But Godoy continued being a good friend and collaborator of Teresa's.

Huerta, Roque de. Teresa's friend and collaborator from Madrid, starting in 1577, Huerta was the chief forest guard in the nation, but he fulfilled other charges as well in the court in Madrid. It was through Jerónimo Gracián that Teresa came to know him and become his friend. In the beginning he was the means by which Teresa was able to send letters to Gracián. But he went on to serve Gracián, the discalced Carmelites, and Teresa, not only in delivering mail, but in many other confidential or delicate matters. He kept Teresa informed of decisions made by the nuncio Filippo Sega and, for example, sent her a copy of the royal ordinance favoring Gracián and his visitations (Ltr. 256.2). Teresa in her turn kept him informed, positively and negatively, of how matters were proceeding with the discalced Carmelites. She sent him a long letter about the unfortunate second chapter at Almodóvar (Ltr. 273). This letter shows how much Roque had won Teresa's total confidence. In 1581, his daughter María, a young girl of only 15 years, entered the Carmel of Soria and took the name María de la Purificación. Teresa gave her the habit on the eve of her departure for Soria. Teresa alludes to both father and daughter in her last letter, a few days before her death: "I am glad that Roque de Huerta's daughter is pleasant." Roque de Huerta has left us 16 letters from Teresa, more than we have from any other of her secular friends.

Isabel de Jesús (Jimena). A native of Segovia, she asked for the habit at the end of 1570. Teresa was fully satisfied with the information provided about her by the Jesuit, Juan de León, and allowed her to choose her Carmel, but stated as well that she would like to see her enter where she herself was living so that she could get to know her better. Isabel did choose to enter Salamanca where Teresa was living at the time and brought a large dowry of 3,000 ducats with her. While a novice she sang for Teresa at Easter in 1571 the little song *Veante mis ojos dulce Jesus bueno*, which caused Teresa to go into ecstasy (ST 12; IC. VI.11.8). Whenever Teresa went to Salamanca she would ask her to sing the song for her. Isabel made her profession in 1573, and in 1574 went to Segovia as subprioress. She returned to Salamanca and from there went on the foundation with Teresa to Palencia as prioress. She later returned to Salamanca and was prioress there from 1586 to1589. She made the oldest copy of the *Way of Perfection*. It was reviewed by Teresa herself and signed in 1573. She died in Salamanca in 1614.

Isabel de San Francisco (de Vega). A Carmelite highly esteemed by Teresa, she was born in Villacastín (Segovia) around 1547. She entered the Carmel of Toledo where she made profession in 1574. Accompanying Teresa on her foundation in Beas, she then went with her also on the foundation in Seville. She thus was close to Teresa over a period of about twenty months in the houses of Toledo, Beas, Malagón, and Seville. She also kept up a lively correspondence with Teresa, keeping her informed as house chronicler. Teresa admonishes: "But if Sister San Francisco is going to be the historian, she should not exaggerate but state very simply what has taken place"(Ltr. 294.16). At times Teresa seemed annoyed by some of Isabel's letters (Ltr. 319.14); at other times they provided great recreation (Ltr. 357.10). Teresa, finally, decided that if María de San José were not prioress in Seville, then Isabel could take over (Ltr. 290.3). In fact, Isabel did become the prioress when María de San José ended her term as prioress in 1585. In 1590, through the initiative of Gracián, she went as foundress to Sanlucar la Mayor and later as foundress of the Portuguese Carmel in Cascais in 1599. But since this foundation never worked out, she passed on to the Carmel in Lisbon in 1603, where she lived for twenty-two more years and served as prioress twice. She died in Lisbon in 1622.

Isabel de San Pablo (de la Peña). One of the first nuns pro-
fessed at St. Joseph's in Avila, she was born in Torrijos in 1547.
She was a daughter of Teresa's cousin and entered the Incar-
nation in Avila as did her sisters María and Beatriz de Ocampo.
Still a novice while Teresa was preparing the foundation of St.
Joseph's, she expressed her desire to join the new community.
This she did in fact and her dowry passed to the new Carmel.
She made her profession at St. Joseph's in 1564 at the age of
seventeen, promising her obedience to the Bishop of Avila,
Don Alvaro de Mendoza. Hers is the first profession to appear
in the book of professions. In 1569 she went with Teresa for
the foundation in Toledo and from there went to Pastrana as
subprioress in that same year. In 1574, she was back in Avila
and went with Teresa and St. John of the Cross on the foundation in Segovia. She was one of the nuns who was closest to
Teresa and acted as her secretary. At times she added a postscript of her own, as in Ltr. 237.9, where she asks for a painting
of St. Paul, but that it must be beautiful so that she "will enjoy
looking at it." When Teresa broke her arm in 1578, she wrote
confidentially to Isabel's brother Luis, thanking him for some
gifts he sent: "Although you do this for me, Sister Isabel de San
Pablo is so tempted to love me that she is happier than I about
it. It is a great consolation for me to be in her company, which
seems like that of an angel." She fell seriously ill at the end of
1581 and died shortly after in February of 1582 at the young
age of thirty-five.

Juana de la Cruz. A mother from Seville whose daughter, Beatriz de la Madre de Dios, entered the Carmel of Seville as soon
as it was founded. Teresa writes of them in her *Foundations*:
"a few days after she entered the monastery, her father died.
Her mother took the habit in the same monastery and gave all
she possessed in alms. Both mother and daughter experience
the greatest happiness, edifying all the nuns and serving Him
who granted them so wonderful a favor"(F. 26.15). Actually,
Juana entered the community as a lay sister and brought with
her all her possessions, making her profession in 1577. She

suffered through the eccentric behavior of her daughter when the latter was appointed as vicaress ("the miserable vicaress" Teresa called her in Ltr. 289.2) by the nuncio Sega and caused much disturbance in the community. During this time Teresa was greatly interested in knowing about her mother. And in writing about Juana and the trouble she caused, Teresa adds: "Don't say a word to her mother, for I feel very sorry for her. How is it that no one says anything to me about how she bore all these things and what she said — I've wanted to know this — and whether she knew about her daughter's schemes?"(Ltr. 294.10).

Juana del Espíritu Santo. Born in Avila in 1541, she was a professed religious at the Incarnation where she knew Teresa. One of those who left the Incarnation for the foundation in Toledo, she had been present a number of times when Teresa experienced her ecstasies and was truly astonished. She was also present at Teresa's death, which, according to her, took place at nine in the evening on the feast of St. Francis. She was present as well at the various exhumations of Teresa and smelled the fragrance that at times surrounds the death of a saint. While her sister Catalina returned to the Incarnation, she chose to become a permanent member of Teresa's communities. In Toledo she was subprioress of the community. In 1571 she transferred to Alba and became prioress of the community there. She was the prioress in Alba when Teresa was there on her last journey. She received and assisted her lovingly. However, when Teresa died the prioress was Inés de Jesús (Pecellín) who was much less loving to the dying patient. Because of the interference of the foundress Teresa Layz, Juana was eagerly waiting to finish her term of office (Ltr. 460.2). It was she who received notification of the transfer of the incorrupt body of Teresa to Avila in 1584 and in the process of Beatification testified to the return of the body to Alba in 1587.

Layz, Teresa de. The foundress of the Carmel of Alba de Tormes. Teresa gave a sketch of her life in chapter 20 of her *Foundations*. She was born in Tordilloa (Salamanca) and married to Francisco Velázquez who was employed by the Duke and Duchess of Alba. With her meddling in the life of the community, she began to strike fear in the community members. Teresa wrote to Padre Gracián about the matter and told him to look into everything (Ltr. 372.1). In preparing for her foundation a little after this in Burgos, Teresa took with her as prioress Tomasina Bautista, the niece of Teresa Layz. The latter was insisting on having Tomasina as prioress for the Carmel in Alba. Teresa's answer is classic: "I received your letter, but in regard to what you said I can do very little. When I speak about it with Madre Tomasina Bautista, such a change comes over her that from the soles of her feet to the top of her head, she says, she feels upset at the thought of returning to that house. And the reasons she gives why this would disturb the tranquility of her soul are such that no superior would order her to do so. She is now experiencing great peace, living in a very nice house, much to her liking. If you truly love her, you will rejoice over this and not want someone to come to be with you who doesn't want to. May God pardon her, for I desire your happiness so much that I wish it were possible for me to give everything you ask for. For love of God do not be afflicted, for there are many nuns in the order who can make up for the absence of Madre Tomasina"(Ltr. 460.1). This problem, though, remained a thorny one for Teresa at the end of her life. After Teresa's death in Alba, Teresa Layz thought of herself not only as in charge of the house but of the mortal remains of Teresa as well, and she had them buried in such a way that they could not be easily dug up.

Leonor de la Misericordia (Ayanz y Beamonte). Born in the castle of Guenduláin in 1551 of Navarran parents, she received an excellent education. She had a rare talent for writing and painting, and knew Latin in addition to the other works of women of the time. She also had singular gifts for governing. Her communications with Teresa began with the foundation in Soria in 1581. Leonor was staying temporarily in the palace of the foundress, Beatriz de Beamonte. Although she was married in 1569 to her cousin Don Francés de Beamonte y Navarra, they both agreed on the dissolution of the marriage in 1581. She took the habit of the discalced Carmelites in 1582, and made her profession the following year in the Carmel of Soria. It was here that she learned of Teresa's death. A little before Teresa left Burgos, Leonor received her last letter from her. In 1583 she accompanied Catalina de Cristo on the foundation in Pamplona, which Teresa had already planned. In 1588 she again accompanied Catalina de Cristo, this time for the foundation in Barcelona. Here in 1594, she assisted at Madre Catalina's death, and later wrote her biography. She brought the remains back to Pamplona in 1604, and there died herself in 1620. Three letters written by Teresa in the last year of her life (Ltrs. 444, 449, and 456) show Teresa's affection for her.

Manso de Zúñiga, Pedro. Teresa's collaborator in the foundation of Burgos. He did his studies in Alcalá where he was a companion and good friend of Jerónimo Gracián. On the occasion of the foundation of the Carmel in Burgos, where he was a canon, he gave Gracián lodging in his own house and also mediated with the archbishop, Cristóbal Vela, who was opposed to the foundation. It was he who celebrated the first Mass for the Burgos foundation (F. 31.45). He was named Bishop of Calahorra in 1594. He arranged for a foundation of nuns in 1598, and for one for the friars in 1603. He died in 1612. Only one letter of Teresa's to him (Ltr. 445) has come down to us.

Margarita de la Concepción. Born in Seville in 1556, she entered the Carmel there as a lay Sister and made her profession in 1577. Young and easily moved, she was deceived by María del Corro, the postulant who denounced the community to the Inquisition. But she did not leave the monastery with María del Corro. She also became involved in the disturbance stirred up by Garciálvarez and Beatriz de la Madre de Dios, which led to the deposing of the prioress, María de San José. But Teresa was most concerned about her human and spiritual rehabilitation (Ltr. 294). María de San José brought her along on the foundation in Lisbon and left a kind remembrance of her in her *Libro de Recreaciones*. She died at the age of 91.

María de Cristo. A nun at St. Joseph's in Avila, professed there in 1568, she was the first prioress to be elected after the transfer of the Carmel to the jurisdiction of the order in 1577. She renounced her office in 1581 and in her place Teresa was elected. Before that Teresa had written to Gracián: "the prioress will suffice since there is no one else there. And although I say 'will suffice,' I think I am lying because I don't think there is anyone who can handle the internal affairs of the house" (Ltr. 402.7). She was sent on the foundation for Granada in 1581, traveling to it with St. John of the Cross. She was subprioress in Granada, and in 1585 was made prioress in Málaga, where she died in 1590. Only one letter to María de Cristo from Teresa has come down to us (Ltr. 339), but she is mentioned negatively in the "terrible" letter to Anne of Jesus (Ltr. 451.10). She died in Málaga in 1591.

María de Jesús (Sandoval). One of the two foundresses of the Carmel in the town of Beas. Born of noble and wealthy parents, the two sisters were able to bring Teresa to Beas to make the foundation there, and María received the habit from the hands of Teresa herself in 1575. She made profession the following year. In 1578 she began to receive spiritual direction from St. John of the Cross. Teresa wrote of the two sisters: "The truth is they are saying wonderful things about the holiness and humility of one of the two ladies who are sponsoring the foundation; they are both good" (Ltr. 73.5). Teresa and María must have corresponded rather frequently but only one letter has come down to us: "Do not be brief in writing to me or surprised if I do not answer at once. Be assured that I am delighted with your letters and that I do not forget to recommend you to our Lord." In 1585, María transferred to the monastery in Málaga with the charge of subprioress, and in 1589 to that of Córdoba as prioress, where she died in 1604.

María de San Jerónimo (1541-1602). The daughter of a cousin of Teresa's, she entered the Carmel of St. Jospeh's in Avila in 1563 and made her profession in 1565. She brought with her a good dowry which supplied for the chaplaincy of

Julián de Avila. As a novice she formed a part of the group of young, fervent enthusiasts described by Teresa in chapter 1 of her *Foundations*. When Teresa left to make the foundation in Medina, María remained behind as vicar at San José. When Teresa returned from Andalusia in 1577, María took part as subprioress in the transmission of the obedience of the community from the bishop of Avila, Don Alvaro de Mendoza to that of the order. When Teresa was elected prioress of St. Joseph's in 1581, she had for subprioress María de San Jerónimo. And when Teresa died in Alba the following year, María de San Jerónimo was elected prioress and reelected in 1585. She received the remains of Teresa at St. Joseph's in Avila from Alba in 1585, but they remained there little more than nine months before their final return to Alba. In 1591 she transferred to the Carmel in Madrid where she took over as prioress in the difficult situation of the deposition from office of the prioress, María del Nacimiento. Happily finishing the term there, she returned to St. Joseph's in 1594 as prioress. But the following year she made a foundation as prioress in Ocaña. At the end of the triennium she returned to Avila and was elected prioress there in 1598. In these different displacements, she took Blessed Anne of St. Bartholomew with her. Blessed Anne was also at her side when she died after a most painful illness in 1602 at the age of 61.

María de San José (Gracián). A sister of Jerónimo Gracián, born in Madrid in 1563. She was accepted in the Carmel of Valladolid when she was only 15 years old. She accompanied her mother, Juana Dantisco, and visited Teresa with her mother at St. Joseph's there. She made her profession in Valladolid in 1579. In letters to Gracián, Teresa wrote of her: "Sister María de San José is loved by everyone; she is a little saint" (Ltr. 303.4); or again, "Sister María de San José is ... an angel" (Ltr. 307.4). She was transferred to the Carmel in Madrid and then Consuegra where she was prioress twice. She continued to correspond with Gracián even after his expulsion from the order and became the trustee of his papers. She died in Consuegra in 1611 at the age of 48.

Mejía, Juan Alonso. An inhabitant of Valladolid and collaborator with Teresa. She wrote a letter of sympathy to his widow on the occasion of his death in 1580.

Mendoza, Diego Sarmiento. The Count of Ribadavia, governor of Galicia, and brother of Don Alvaro de Mendoza, whose wife was Leonor de Castro y Portugal, the Countess of Lemus. He was a good friend of Teresa's and the nuns in Valladolid. He was also a friend of Gracián's family. In August of 1580 he wrote to the Carmelite nuns in Valladolid for prayers for certain intentions and expected a quick reply. "We have only an hour to respond" (Ltr. 354.2). The only response that has come down to us is Teresa's, a very warm letter, but also a carefully worded one: "Through the other favors you have done for me, I have seen that I can ask you for many things if I have the need... Nonetheless, when I see myself in need I will turn to you as the lord of this house" (Ltr. 354.4).

Mendoza y Castilla, Orofrisia de. At a very young age, she married Teresa's nephew Francisco de Cepeda. "She is not yet fifteen," writes Teresa (Ltr. 363.3). Her mother Beatriz was instrumental in seeking to nullify Lorenzo de Cepeda's will in order to gain the riches that were left to Teresita and the Carmel of St. Joseph's in Avila. In his want, Francisco set out again for America (1591), leaving Orofrisia alone in Madrid. In order to meet the demands of debtors, she sold the property of La Serna in 1593 at a loss, and lived her final years in solitude and poverty. She maintained a good relationship with her husband's cousin, Beatriz de Jesús (Ovalle), prioress of the Carmel in Madrid. Despite Teresa's conflicts with Francisco's mother-in-law, Beatriz, she always had a high regard for Orofrisia: "The more those in Madrid inform me about this marriage, the more reason I see for us to be happy, especially over all they say of the discretion and pleasing manner of Doña Orofrisia" (Ltr. 367.4). Or again in a letter to her nephew Lorenzo: "Setting aside the fact that his wife is tied on all sides to the most illustrious families in Spain, she has so many good personal qualities that they would be enough"(Ltr. 427.1).

Montoya, Diego López de. A canon from Avila residing in Rome, representing the king before the Holy See. His mother, living in Avila, was a good friend of Teresa's. The latter sent a number of letters to Montoya in Rome explaining the difficulties of the discalced Carmelites in Spain at the time. When, in a disguised manner, Padre Juan de Jesús Roca was able to journey to Rome, she sent Montoya a packet of letters of recommendation in which was contained even a letter from the king (Ltr. 290.4). To Montoya, Teresa had to give a sum of money to pay for the Roman expenses. But yet she is grateful to him and writes: "Apart from this I now have to raise two hundred ducats that I promised Montoya, the canonist, for he has given us life; and please God that amount will be enough and bring all this to an end" (Ltr. 295.5). Montoya had to travel to Spain to bring the cardinal's hat to Archbishop Quiroga (Ltr. 440), but now the negotiations in Rome could be carried out by Juan de Jesus María: "Fray Juan de Jesús has arrived in Rome. The negotiations here are going well. Montoya, the canonist who was carrying on our business for us in Rome, passed by on his way with the cardinal's hat for the Archbishop of Toledo. He won't be needed any more" (Ltr. 309.8). The only letter of Teresa's to Montoya that has come down to us is Ltr. 440.

Nieto, Inés. A good friend of Teresa's, she was the wife of Juan de Albornoz, secretary to the Duke of Alba, living at times in Madrid and at other times in Alba. An exchange of correspondence and favors took place between Teresa and Doña Inés. Doña Inés had recommended to Teresa a friend of hers, Isabel de Córdoba, for the Carmel in Valladolid (Ltr. 78.2). Teresa also wrote to console Inés at the imprisonment of her husband and at the death of her friend the Marchioness of Velada. In her turn Teresa asks Inés to intercede to have her nephew Gonzalo de Ovalle removed from the list of pages in the service of the duchess of Alba, and also thanks her for a statue of our Lady: "The more I look at the statue, the more beautiful it seems" (Ltr. 94).

Ortiz, Diego. An inhabitant of Toledo and one of the founders of the Carmel there, very demanding and punctilious. Teresa records: "I immediately began to take up the business matters with Alonso Alvarez and a son-in-law of his, named Diego Ortiz. The latter, although very good, and a theologian, was more unyielding in his opinion than Alonso Alvarez. He did not readily soften his demands. They began to ask for many conditions that I didn't think I could easily agree to" (F. 15.4). Ortiz continued to make all kinds of demands for the foundation. In 1571 he wrote Teresa a letter whose difficult tone we can guess from Teresa's response: "You show me so much kindness and charity through your letters that even were your last letter more severe, I would have felt well repaid and obliged once more to serve you" (Ltr. 33.1). A few years later he wrote through Gracián to ask Teresa for help with a business matter he had in Madrid (Ltr. 97). He also sent her images of Our Lady and St. Joseph for the foundation in Andalusia (Ltr. 165). In a postscript to the manuscript of Madrid of the *Way of Perfection* Teresa writes: "This was approved and seen by Padre Fray García de Toledo and by Doctor Ortiz, an inhabitant of Toledo." At the time of his death in 1611, he had read Teresa's writings and her biography by Ribera.

Osorio, Inés and Isabel. These two sisters from Madrid were begging Teresa for permission to enter Carmel, but Teresa wanted them to wait because of the troubles in the order at the time (1578) and because of her hopes for the foundation of a Carmel in Madrid (Ltr. 265). Inés (de la Encarnación), chose not to wait and entered the Carmel in Toledo. There she lived at times with Teresa, who once wrote to her sister: "Certainly she is an angel. She rejoiced to be with me." Inés died in Toledo in 1635. Isabel, on the other hand, Teresa kept urging to wait for the foundation in Madrid (Ltr. 313; 314). But then Isabel became sick herself, although she persisted in her desire to be a Carmelite (Ltr. 336.2). Teresa died before a Carmel in Madrid was ever founded. Of the letters that have come down to us, one is addressed to the two sisters together, and three to Isabel.

Peñalosa, Ana de. Doña Ana de Mercado y Peñalosa was from Segovia. Becoming a widow in 1579, she retired to live with her brother, Luis de Mercado, in Granada. They both welcomed in their home Anne of Jesus with her companions on the foundation in Granada. She was a directee of St. John of the Cross for whom he wrote *The Living Flame of Love*. When John died in Ubeda, it was she who arranged to have his remains transferred back to Segovia in 1593. Teresa refers to her and to her brother in Ltr. 451.2.

Quiroga, Gaspar de. Born in Madrigal (Avila) in 1512, he did his studies at Valladolid and Salamanca, where he received his doctorate in law. He had many ecclesiastical charges in his life and eventually became the Archbishop of Toledo in 1577, and was created cardinal the following year. Teresa entered into communication with Quiroga when Jerónima Quiroga entered the Carmel of Medina. But what really brought him into contact with Teresa was the denunciation to the Inquisition of *The Book of her Life*, which he read with much personal interest. But the book was nonetheless kept in the hands of the Inquisition as long as Teresa lived, even though Gracián did dare to try to retrieve it.

A problem Teresa encountered with him was over the vocation of his niece to Carmel. Although Teresa opposed the vocation, the archbishop seemed to blame her for the whole thing. But actually Teresa had no intention of accepting the niece until the archbishop gave his permission. A final matter for the archbishop was the foundation of a Carmel in Madrid, a diocese of his. But he delayed his permission and did not want the Carmel to be founded in poverty. After Teresa's numerous attempts at a foundation, the archbishop finally agreed to it once the king returned to Spain. Teresa writes of this permission in one of her letters: "the cardinal has written me promising to give me the permission when the king returns, and they are already saying that he is coming" (Ltr. 456.2). But the wait was too long, for the king did not return until 1583, after Teresa's death. The cardinal died in Madrid in 1594. Despite her difficulties with the cardinal, Teresa always had a veneration and love for him. She writes in a letter to Ruiz de la Peña: "What would be a great trial for me would be the thought that his illustrious lordship is displeased with me on account of calumnies uttered against me, for I love him tenderly in the Lord" (Ltr. 397.7).

Reinoso, Jerónimo. A canon of the cathedral in Palencia and friend and servant of Teresa's. "He is very discreet, holy, and shows good judgment in everything, even though he is young" (F. 29.21), Teresa wrote of him. He had done his studies at Salamanca. Besides being a canon in Palencia, he was also the provider for the hospital of San Antolín. Serving as one of Teresa's confessors, six letters of hers to him have come down to us. Of special interest is the last one dealing with some of the problems with the foundation of the Carmel in Burgos (Ltr. 452). Reinoso died in Palencia in 1600.

Ribera, Francisco de. Born in Villacastín (Segovia), he did his studies at the University of Salamanca where he graduated as bachelor of arts and doctor of theology. After finishing his studies, he withdrew to his little town and studied Greek and Hebrew and the Bible. He next decided to enter the Society of Jesus. After his novitiate, he was assigned to teach the minor prophets, but he wrote on many other biblical topics besides his great work on the minor prophets. He knew Teresa, heard her confessions, and was a great admirer of hers. Right after her death, he set two goals for himself: to write her biography and publish her writings. On finishing her biography, he encountered difficulties with the Jesuit general, Padre Aquaviva, who thought it was inappropriate for a scripture scholar like Ribera to be writing the life of a nun, all the more because at the time the Society had become an object of illuminist suspicions. After many letters back and forth between Ribera and the general, Ribera finally received permission to publish his biography of Teresa. It was first published in 1590 with the title *The Life of Mother Teresa of Jesus, Foundress of the Discalced Carmelite Nuns and Friars*. Containing 563 pages of text, it spread Teresa's fame throughout Europe and was translated into all the major

European languages. Ribera was less fortunate in his second proposal because Fray Luis de León published her writings before him. Nevertheless through his critical work with the autographs, he is counted among the first Teresian editors. In his biography of Teresa he asserts more than once that he is quoting from the original and not from a printed edition. He died in Salamanca in 1591.

Ripalda, Jerónimo Martínez de. A friend, confessor and collaborator of Teresa's, he was born in 1536 and entered the Society of Jesus at the young age of 15. He became a distinguished professor of the humanities, philosophy, and theology and was successively rector in Villagarcía, Salamanca, Burgos, and Valladolid. In listing her confessors in her report given to the Inquisitor of Seville, Teresa mentions Ripalda as being "very unfavorable to her until she talked with him" (ST. 58.3). When he was in Valladolid, he directed vocations to the Carmel there, and also when in Burgos. He urged Teresa to make a foundation in Burgos, and also encouraged her to make the foundation in Palencia (F. 29.4). When he was rector at Salamanca, he ordered Teresa to write the *Book of her Foundations* (F. Pro. 2). Ripalda died in Toledo in 1618.

Ruiz, Antonio. A good merchant friend of Teresa's, who met her when she founded in Malagón. He accompanied her in her journey to Seville and also on her return from Seville to Toledo, in which the following incident took place: "Oh, *mi padre*, what a terrible thing happened to me! ... a large salamander or lizard got in between my tunic and bare arm ... but my brother got hold of it at once and when he threw it away, it hit Antonio Ruiz right in the mouth. The latter was most helpful along the way" (108.9). The Carmelite nuns in Seville continued to owe him money, and Teresa urges them at different times to pay him back: "Try at least to get those 300 ducats that you are obliged to pay this year, for I assure you it bothers my conscience that you do not give poor Antonio Ruiz his money. He needs this for food for himself and for his livestock in Malagón" (Ltr. 146.2; 148.8). Teresa entrusted him confidentially with certain charges in regard to the construction of a monastery in Malagón. She writes: "Since Antonio Ruiz is there, the nuns have nothing to worry about" (Ltr. 124.11).

Ruiz de la Peña, Dionisio. A priest, confessor, and personal secretary to the Archbishop of Toledo. Teresa turned to him to mediate with the archbishop in certain matters. Two in particular were of concern to her: the foundation in Madrid and the vocation of Elena, the archbishop's niece. Concerning the latter she writes: "I don't know when this letter will go out. I would have wanted it to go quickly so that you would be aware of how little I am at fault, or rather not at all. This is so true that out of respect for the relationship of that person about whom you wrote to me with his illustrious lordship, I did not tell the latter about the efforts I made in this case to impede her entrance into one of these houses. If Padre Baltasar Alvarez, who was provincial of the Jesuits in this province, were alive, he would be a good witness to how I begged him to prevent such a thing, since this lady had more respect for him than for anyone else, and he promised to do so" (Ltr. 397.1) . As for the first she writes also to Dionisio: "As regards the license for a foundation in Madrid, I have begged this of his most illustrious lordship because I think our Lord would be served thereby" (Ltr. 397.6).

Salinas, Martín Alonso de. A canon from Palencia and administrator of the Hospital of San Antolín. A very learned and charitable man, Teresa describes him in her *Foundations*. He came to know Teresa through her friend Jerónimo Reinoso. They both collaborated with her in the foundation in Palencia and supported the foundation in Burgos: "It had been decided that the foundation be made immediately, and I had brought my letters from Canon Salinas for his relatives and friends strongly urging them to favor this foundation. (Canon Salinas, the one I mentioned in discussing the foundation in Palencia, comes from this city and from an important family. He worked just as hard for this foundation as for that of Palencia)" (F. 31.18).

She wrote to him from Avila recommending the foundation in Burgos (Ltr. 413), and again later from the Hospital de la Concepción in Burgos telling him that the foundation had still not been made because they were without a house and without the license to found. That Teresa frequently sought his advice is obvious from remarks in one of her letters to him: "Tell me what you think and how you are. Since I am used to receiving frequent letters from you, I am not resigned to doing less"(Ltr. 433.5).

Sánchez, Pedro. A priest and confessor to the Carmelite nuns in Alba. Teresa appealed to him in regard to the interference in the life of the nuns by the foundress Teresa Layz. He answered her with a kind and peaceful letter. Teresa's reply is one of great happiness with the confessor and how he is dealing with the nuns (Ltr. 467).

Soto y Salazar, Francisco de. Born in Bonilla, a town in the province of Avila, he attended the University of Salamanca and afterward was named inquisitor in Córdoba, and then in Seville, and Toledo. In 1575 he became Bishop of Salamanca. He died in 1578. A relative of Teresa's, he blessed the marriage of Teresa's younger sister, Juana, with Juan de Ovalle. Teresa had recourse to him in the discernment of her mystical graces. In an account she wrote of her spirtual life for the inquisitor of Seville, she mentions having consulted Francisco Soto: "It was about thirteen years ago, a little more or less, that the Bishop of Salamanca went there, for he was the inquisitor, I believe, in Toledo and had been here. For the sake of greater assurance she arranged to speak with him and gave him an account of everything. He told her this whole matter was something that didn't belong to his office because all that she saw and understood strengthened her ever more in the Catholic faith"(ST 58.6). At one point he asked her to beg God to let him know if it would be in the Lord's service for him to accept a bishopric. Teresa received a good answer from God of which she speaks in the closing chapter of her *Life*. He is not to be confused with another Padre Soto, a priest friend of Teresa's whom she mentions a few times in her *Letters*, but of whom we have no particular information.

Suárez, Juan. A Jesuit born in Cuenca and, in the time of Teresa, provincial of Castile. He knew Teresa and was probably her confessor in Valladolid. But he had a heavy manner and was hard to deal with. When as provincial he heard rumors that Gaspar Salazar, Teresa's friend, wanted to leave the Jesuits and join the discalced Carmelites, Suárez supposed that Teresa herself was the instigator and wrote a strong letter accusing her in different ways. Teresa's firm answer was that "I have never wanted this, still less urged him to take such a step" (Ltr. 228.2), but Suarez didn't seem convinced. When he founded the Jesuits in Pamplona, a persecution arose against the foundation. Teresa wrote to the Duke and Duchess of Alba asking their intervention on behalf of the Jesuits (Ltr. 342. 5-7), demonstrating her love for them and that she bore no resentment against Suárez.

Tolosa, Catalina de. Teresa introduces Catalina in this way: "There lived in this city of Burgos a holy widow named Catalina de Tolosa ... I could go on at length telling about her virtues, her penance as well as her prayer, her generous almsgiving and charity, her good intelligence and courage" (F. 31.8). Born in 1538, she had nine children, one of whom had died before Teresa first met the family. When the small caravan of Carmelites arrived in Burgos to make the foundation there, they first got installed in the home of Catalina de Tolosa, who had been desiring the foundation of a Carmel in Burgos. Teresa ended up attracting to Carmel Catalina's daughters and two sons. Eventually the mother herself entered the Carmel of Palencia at age 49. In the Carmel she became a subject of her own daughter, Isabel of the Trinity, who was prioress of the community, and of her son, Sebastián, who was provincial of Castile at the time. She herself also became prioress of the community. She died in 1608. Again, Teresa wrote of her: "But Catalina de Tolosa did everything so well, because she was so generous and showed so much good will, that she provided us all in a room where we were secluded with food for a month, as though she were mother of each one" (F. 31.24). Of the many letters between Teresa and Catalina, only two have come down to us (Ltrs. 430; 459).

Tomasina Bautista (Perea). Born in Medina del Campo, she was a niece of Teresa Layz. She took the habit in Medina in 1568 and made profession the following year. In 1570 she went on the foundation to Salamanca, and in 1571 to Alba de Tormes. In 1581, she left Alba to accompany Teresa on the foundation in Burgos and was left there as prioress. Hardly had she got settled in Burgos than urgent requests for her return to Alba came from Teresa Layz, but Teresa paid no heed (Ltr. 460). After Teresa left Burgos she wrote Tomasina three letters with cordial recommendations about the sick; the poverty of the house; relations with the foundress, Catalina de Tolosa; with the doctor; and with the Jesuits. In one of these letters, Teresa remarks: "And believe that even though you may have an advantage over me in virtue, I have more experience. As a result, some of the things I pointed out, I would not want you to forget" (Ltr. 464.6). Tomasina died in Burgos in 1603.

Vallejo, Diego. A canon of San Pedro in Soria and confessor of the Carmelite nuns there. Teresa recommends that he tell Gracián about anything that needed correction in the house: "Give Padre Vallejo a warm greeting for me and ask him to tell our *padre* about anything that might need correction in that house" (Ltr. 444.3). Teresa once sent a packet of letters that remained opened for him to distribute after reading them himself and then sealing them. Among them was one for himself (Ltr. 431).

Velasco, Juan López de. A friend and collaborator with Teresa, born in Vinuesa (Soria), who was a secretary of Philip II. In 1587, he testified: "I knew Mother Teresa of Jesus for seven years. In passing through this city of Madrid to a certain foundation, she stayed in the house of this witness." He had a sister who entered the Carmel in Segovia, but not without much effort by Teresa, for there was hesitation because of her limited intelligence. She took the name Juana de la Madre de Dios. He was one of those who delivered letters for Teresa and she esteemed him highly: "I believe that to him, to Padre Maestro Fray Pedro Fernández, and to Don Luis we owe all the favor now being shown to us"(Ltr. 316.12).

Velázquez, Alonso (bishop). Born in 1533, he did his studies at San Ildefonso in Alcalá, where he graduated in 1552 as a master of arts and theology. Teresa got to know him when he was teacher and preacher at the cathedral in Toledo and took him as her confessor: "While I was occupied with the foundation in Palencia ... they brought me a letter from the Bishop of Osma, named Doctor Velázquez. While he was canon and professor at the cathedral in Toledo ...I entreated him urgently to guide my soul and hear my confession ... I spoke to him about my soul with complete openness as I usually do. This did me so much good that from then on my fears began to lessen" (F. 30.1; ST. 60). He counseled and helped Teresa with the foundations of Villanueva de la Jara and Soria and on numerous other occasions including the project of founding in Madrid. It was for him that Teresa wrote the final account of her soul (ST. 65). She always looked up to him as "a very learned and virtuous man" (F. 28.10). He was transferred to the archdiocese of Santiago de Compostela. Afflicted with illnesses, he retired to Talavera de la Reina where he died in 1587.

Villanueva, Gaspar de. A priest and chaplain for the discalced Carmelite nuns in Malagón. He also became the confessor of the community. Teresa was not happy with the way he was interfering in the running of the house and had Gracián intervene and substitute Padre Francisco de la Concepción. Villanueva accepted with an edifying humility. In fact Teresa later changed her mind and wrote of him: "This poor licentiate seems to me to be a great servant of God, and I believe it is he who is less at fault ... He is in complete accord with all that I tell you should be done here, and he is so humble and sorry for any fault he might have had for what happened that I was very edified (Ltr. 316.3).

Special thanks go to Tomás Alvarez for his fourth edition of the Letters of St. Teresa. *I have used his numbering of the letters and made ample use of his textual explanatory notes. Thanks must also go to Mrs. Tina Mendoza for her careful comparison of my translation with the Spanish text of St. Teresa's letters. I profited greatly from her many valued suggestions. I also want to thank Dr. Carol Lisi for her watchful editorial work in the preparation of this volume. Without her observant eye this book would have many more defects.*

Sources for the Biographical Sketches

Alvarez, Tomás. *Diccionario de Santa Teresa: Doctrina y Historia*. Burgos: Monte Carmelo, 2002.

Efrén de la Madre de Dios y Steggink, Otger. *Tiempo y Vida de Santa Teresa*, Segunda Edición Revisada y Aumentado. Madrid: BAC, 1977.

Peers, E. Allison. *Handbook to the Life and Times of St. Teresa and St. John of the Cross*. London, England: Burns Oates, 1954.

Salvador de la Virgen del Carmen. *Teresa de Jesús*. 2 vols. Vitoria: Diputación Foral De Alava, Consejo de Cultura, 1964–68.

Silverio de Santa Teresa. *Historia del Carmen Descalzo en España, Portugal y América*. 15 vols. Burgos: Monte Carmelo, 1935–49.

—*Obras de Santa Teresa de Jesús*. 9 vols. Burgos: Monte Carmelo, 1915–24.

Index

Index

A letter in bold type indicates that the letter itself is addressed to the person after whose name it appears.

631